Malaysia

0 — 200 km
0 — 200 miles

N

PHILIPPINES

Sulu Sea

Kota K...

Kuala Penyu

SABAH

Lahad Datu

Pulau Labuan

Beaufort

Keni...

Kuamut

Bandar Seri Begawan

Tenom

Pandawan

BRUNEI DARUSSALAM

Tawas

Trusan

Pensiangan

Semporna

Limbang

Long...

Kelabakan

Tawau

Miri

Gunung Mulu National Park

Pulau Sebatik

Sibuti
Niah

Marudi

Ulu-Ulu

Suai

Long

GUNUNG MULU NATIONAL PARK

inau

Pulau Bunyu

Bintulu

Tubau

Lio Matoh

Ambalat

Tarakan

Sabuh

Mantadau

Celebes Sea

Igan

Oya

Mukah

Bailing

SARAWAK

Tanjungselor

Dalat

Sibu

Sariket

Sarawak

Nanga Maru

Saratok

Kanowit

Tanjungredeb

KUCHING

Kuching

Kapit

Rajang

Sematan

Simunjan

Betang

Domaring

Biawat

Sri Aman

Mahesi

Sepinang

KUCHING ENVIRONS

Lubok Antu

B o r n e o

Muarawahau

Bengkayang

Balaikarangan

Putussibau

Sangkulirang

D0792723

Malaysian States

0 — 200 km
0 — 200 miles

N

PHILIPPINES

S I A

Labuan

Sabah

BRUNEI DARUSSALAM

Sarawak

I N D O N E S I A

INSIGHT ⊙ GUIDES

MALAYSIA

www.insightguides.com/Malaysia

⊙ Walking Eye App

Your Insight Guide now includes a free app and eBook, dedicated to your chosen destination, all included for the same great price as before. They are available to download from the free Walking Eye container app in the App Store and Google Play. Simply download the Walking Eye container app to access the eBook and app dedicated to your purchased book. The app features an up-to-date A to Z of travel tips, information on events, activities and destination highlights, as well as hotel, restaurant and bar listings. See below for more information and how to download.

MULTIPLE DESTINATIONS AVAILABLE

Now that you've bought this book you can download the accompanying destination app and eBook for free. Inside the Walking Eye container app, you'll also find a whole range of other Insight Guides destination apps and eBooks, all available for purchase.

DEDICATED SEARCH OPTIONS

Use the different sections to browse the places of interest by category or region, or simply use the 'Around me' function to find places of interest nearby. You can then save your selected restaurants, bars and activities to your Favourites or share them with friends using email, Twitter and Facebook.

FREQUENTLY UPDATED LISTINGS

Restaurants, bars and hotels change all the time. To ensure you get the most out of your guide, the app features all of our favourites, as well as the latest openings, and is updated regularly. Simply update your app when you receive a notification to access the most current listings available.

Shopping in Oman still revolves around the traditional souks that can be found in every town in the country – most famously at Mutrah in Muscat, Salalah and Nizwa, which serve as showcases of traditional Omani craftsmanship and produce ranging from antique khanjars and Bedu jewellery to halwa, rose-water and frankincense. Muscat also boasts a number of modern malls, although these are rare elsewhere in the country.

TRAVEL TIPS & DESTINATION OVERVIEWS

The app also includes a complete A to Z of handy travel tips on everything from visa regulations to local etiquette. Plus, you'll find destination overviews on shopping, sport, the arts, local events, health, activities and more.

HOW TO DOWNLOAD THE WALKING EYE

Available on purchase of this guide only.

1. Visit our website: www.insightguides.com/walkingeye
2. Download the Walking Eye container app to your smartphone (this will give you access to both the destination app and the eBook)
3. Select the scanning module in the Walking Eye container app
4. Scan the QR code on this page – you will be asked to enter a verification word from the book as proof of purchase
5. Download your free destination app* and eBook for travel information on the go

* Other destination apps and eBooks are available for purchase separately or are free with the purchase of the Insight Guide book

Contents

THE BEST OF MALAYSIA: TOP ATTRACTIONS

A selection of Malaysia's top sights, from natural splendours and diverse wildlife to stunning heritage houses and mouth-watering multi-ethnic cuisine.

△ **Mount Kinabalu.** The hike to the summit of one of the highest mountains in Southeast Asia to watch the sunrise is indescribable and well worth the sore legs on the way down. See page 320.

◁ **Kinabatangan river.** Sabah's jewel is one of the best places in Southeast Asia to see wildlife, including proboscis monkeys and Borneo pygmy elephants, orang-utans, crocodiles, oriental darters and hornbills. See page 334.

△ **SkyBridge, Langkawi.** Walk along this gravity-defying curved bridge that is suspended from a single pylon over a 100-metre (328ft) drop to the forest floor below. See page 203.

△ **Pulau Sipadan.** Sabah's most famous island and Malaysia's only oceanic isle, Sipadan is deservedly rated one of the world's top dive sites. See page 338.

△ **Melaka and George Town.** Two World Heritage Sites and historic Straits of Malacca cities, with distinctive multicultural roots and colonial architecture. See pages 211 and 181.

◁ **Sepilok Orang-utan Rehabilitation Sanctuary.** See Borneo's adorable young apes feed and learn to live in the rainforests of Sabah at the largest orangutan sanctuary in the world. See page 332.

◁ **Gunung Mulu National Park.** Sarawak's vast cave system boasts amazing formations and millions of bats that spiral over a lush rainforest. See page 300.

△ **Cameron Highlands.** Enjoy mountain hikes, sip tea and eat scones overlooking tea plantations dotted with vegetable and strawberry farms and Tudor-style buildings. See page 157.

▽ **Street food.** The nation's most loved way to eat is as diverse as it is delicious thanks to the country's multi-ethnicity. Find street food in coffee shops, five-foot-ways, open-air car parks and down dingy alleyways. See page 94.

▷ **Kuala Lumpur.** The nation's capital is a city of architectural contrasts – from colonial buildings to the world's tallest twin towers. See page 125.

THE BEST OF MALAYSIA: EDITOR'S CHOICE

Views from the top, museums, heritage sights, markets, natural attractions and unique experiences... here, at a glance, are our top recommendations for making the most of your visit.

A night view of Kuala Lumpur.

TOP VIEWS

Observation Deck at KL Tower, Kuala Lumpur. On a clear day, you will get stunning 360-degree views of the capital city, including the spectacular Petronas Twin Towers. See page 135.

Machinchang Mountain, Langkawi. Take a 15-minute ride on

Langkawi's cable car.

the world's steepest cable car to the top station for 360-degree views of the island and the Andaman Sea. See page 203.

Mount Kinabalu's Via Ferrata, Sabah. If you are fearless and fit, follow the Low's Peak Circuit for spectacular views from the mountain's north side. See page 321.

Danum Valley Canopy Walkway, Sabah. Climb up 26 metres (85ft) to the walkway's highest point for views of the forest canopy in one of Sabah's key conservation areas. See page 340.

Penang Hill, Penang. Board the zippy train to the top for spectacular views of George Town and the Straits of Malacca. See page 163.

BEST MUSEUMS AND HERITAGE SIGHTS

Sarawak Museum (Old Wing), Kuching. Houses the wildlife specimens collected all over Borneo by Alfred Russell Wallace, the co-founder of the theory of evolution. See page 282.

Agnes Keith House, Sandakan. Formerly the home of an American writer and prisoner-of-war, this poignant museum describes her life in Sandakan. See page 332.

Lembah Bujang Archaeological Museum. See the remains of Kedah's millennium-old *candi* (temples) and artefacts indicating early Buddhist and Hindu influences. See page 196.

Orang Asli Museum, Gombak. This museum in an Orang Asli settlement in Gombak provides an insight into the lives of some of the country's indigenous people. See page 163.

Gua Tambun, Perak. See the largest prehistoric rock art in the peninsula, numbering over 600 motifs on an exposed cliff face in Perak. See page 167.

Kellie's Castle Batu Gajah, Perak. It would have been a spectacular Mughal- and Moorish-styled house had it not been for the untimely death of its Scottish owner. See page 169.

Suffolk House, Penang. With its colonnaded first floor and flat roof, this is a fine example of Anglo-Indian architecture and Penang's first "Great House". See page 188.

BEST OUTDOOR DESTINATIONS

Maliau Basin Conservation Area, Sabah. Trek into Sabah's "Lost World"; surrounded by sheer cliffs; this biodiversity haven is home to many exciting flora and fauna, including some new species. See page 341.

Wreck diving Pulau Tioman, Pahang. If you are a technical diver, it is worthwhile exploring the World War II shipwrecks here at depths of at least 227 metres (745ft). See page 244.

Gua Tempurung, Perak. Go adventure caving and explore one of the peninsula's most beautiful caves, which continues to be formed by an underground river. See page 168.

Kilim Karst Geoforest Park, Langkawi, Kedah. Kayak through narrow water channels and between mangrove tree roots right up to sleeping snakes while exploring this amazing ecosystem.

See page 205.

Desaru Beach, Johor. Come and ride the 1.2-metre (4ft) high waves during the monsoon season or learn how to surf from the locals. See page 232.

Fraser's Hill International Bird Race, Pahang. Of the over 250 bird species, see how many you can identify within 24 hours. See page 161.

Whitewater rafting the Kiulu and Padas Rivers, Sabah. Adventure thrill seekers join whitewater-rafting trips down Sabah's treacherous rivers, all in the name of fun. See pages 318 and 326.

Ginseng Falls at Maliau Basin – Sabah's "Lost World".

BEST NATURAL ATTRACTIONS

Taman Negara, Pahang. Go on jungle trails, observe nocturnal wildlife from animal hides or even ascend the mighty Mount Tahan. See page 267.

Endau-Rompin National Park, Johor/Pahang. Challenging trails and beautiful cascades can be experienced alongside unique plant life (including 71 palm species) and animals. See page 234.

Bako-Buntal Bay, Sarawak. Considered the "Kinabatangan of Sarawak", you can watch resident dolphins, estuarine crocodiles, proboscis monkeys and

thousands of migratory birds here. See page 286.

Sungai Pulai, Johor. One of three RAMSAR sites in Johor, it has the country's largest sea-grass bed, important food for endangered seahorses and sea cows. See page 229.

Kinabalu Park, Sabah. From hot springs to rare orchids, Rafflesia flowers to pitcher plants, this huge park around Mount Kinabalu has everything. See page 321.

Turtle Islands Marine Park, Sabah. Between July and September, watch excitedly as green and hawksbill turtles clamber ashore Pulau Selingan to lay their eggs. See page 333.

Kampung Ulu Geroh, Perak. Tour the rainforest with the Orang Asli as they (hopefully) introduce to you the world's largest flower and the magnificent Rajah Brooke's Birdwing (butterfly). See page 168.

BEST MARKETS

Central Market, Kuala Lumpur. Formerly a wet market, this Art Deco building now houses Malaysian and Southeast Asian souvenirs, from ikat fabrics to Kelantanese silverware. See page 126.

Petaling Street Bazaar, Kuala Lumpur. Bustling night market offers copies of everything – handbags, watches, T-shirts and more. The

food here is excellent. See page 130.

Central Market, Kota Bharu, Kelantan. This fresh-produce market makes for an unforgettable experience with its colours, smells and noise. Get a panoramic view from upstairs. See page 258.

Chowrasta Market, Penang. This wet market also has a dry section offering Penang

specialities and preserved fruit in a wild array of colours. See page 187.

Jalan Satok Sunday Market, Kuching, Sarawak. Dayaks from the surrounding countryside sell an assortment of jungle produce, wild boar and monkeys alongside fruit, vegetable and orchids. See page 284.

Tamu Besar, Kota

Belud, Sabah. This is the bigger version of the regular Sunday market and also features colourful Bajau horsemen and buffalo racing. See page 318.

Gaya Street Fair, Kota Kinabalu, Sabah. Sunday morning market with food, clothing, orchids, trinkets and treasures, as well as local families on outings. See page 315.

Devotees making their way to Batu Caves for Thaipusam.

Ipoh Old Town chick blinds.

A fisherman painting his bangau boat at Bachok beach.

Boys playing in the shadow of the KLCC skyline.

A VIBRANT BLEND

One of Southeast Asia's most progressive countries, Malaysia provides enrapturing experiences aplenty with its rich mix of cultures, cuisines and landscapes.

A Kadazan dancer at Hamin Do Kakadazan house.

Diversity colours Malaysia, from its multi-ethnic, polyglot people and mouth-watering culinary concoctions to its truly startling variety of plants and animals. For centuries, Malaysia has been open to, and absorbed influences from, peoples from all over the world.

The country has been part of Buddhist and Hindu empires, as well as hosted a Muslim one, while some areas spent time as Portuguese and Dutch colonies, before the British put most of the units together that make up today's Malaysia. Because of its location on seminal shipping routes, the country has been key in international trade since prehistoric times, and today it is one of the world's top 30 trading nations.

Malaysia comprises the peninsula that sits at the bottom of the Asian continent and the states of Sabah and Sarawak on Borneo island, across the South China Sea. Over two-thirds of Malaysians live on the peninsula, and are generally categorised as Malays, Chinese, Indians and indigenous people – within which are many more groups.

About half the country is home to various tropical forest ecosystems, with the more outstanding pristine biodiversity being in Borneo. A fifth of the land comprises plantations of oil palm and rubber, and these, together with manufactured goods and oil and gas, have powered Malaysia to newly industrialised country status. The aim is to reach developed nation status by 2020, ambitions viscerally manifested in modern cities, particularly the cosmopolitan capital Kuala Lumpur.

Muslim women in Kuala Lumpur.

Tourism is a significant income earner, and so infrastructure and tourist products are generally plentiful and well developed. Therefore, a Malaysian holiday could comprise everything from dancing to house music at a ritzy Kuala Lumpur nightclub, to photographing Malay *kampung* on the coast or visiting tribes once known for their headhunting. And, there's adventure too, everything from climbing to the clouds on Mount Kinabalu to scuba diving at world-famous Sipadan island.

Go off the beaten track to discover idyllic beaches, elaborate festivals and hidden corners of UNESCO sites. The diversity is endless, stunning and memorable.

Mist over the mountains and rainforest in Kinabalu Park, Sabah.

THE NATURAL WORLD

From lush and ancient rainforests to the teeming coral reefs that fringe its shores, Malaysia has some of the most important – and fragile – ecosystems on earth.

Lying a mere 140km (81 miles) north of the equator, Malaysia's hot, sunny and rainy climate makes it the perfect home for tropical rainforests, the most biologically diverse ecosystems on earth. Malaysia is in fact one of only 12 mega-diversity areas in the world, according to the United Nations National Biodiversity Index. Not only is it home to a staggering number of different flora and fauna species, many of these are endemic and found nowhere else in the world, even in other rainforests.

What's more, in addition to the wildlife that Malaysia is famed for, in particular the orangutans, an unknown number of species – perhaps equal to or even greater than what is known – has yet to be identified. They live in structured and complex communities, with fascinating interdependencies. These living things are also precious history books of evolution, with ancient roots. In the centre of Peninsular Malaysia, for example, the forest is estimated to be 130 million years old.

While rainforests are found throughout the country, there is a key difference in the ecosystems of the two geographical parts of Malaysia. The peninsula is conjoined to the Asian continent, which means that the species here are linked to and have been influenced by those on the mainland. The Bornean part of the country, however, is on an island. This means that while there are links to the Asian mainland, its species have had the chance to evolve separately and more quickly.

Nonetheless, both parts of the country have marvellous examples of different forest types, as well as unique sites where rare flora and fauna thrive. With the pressures of a growing population, globalisation and climate change, tourism

An orang-utan at Lok Kawi Wildlife Park.

DIPTEROCARPS

About four-fifths of forested land in Malaysia comprise dipterocarp forests, so named for the large trees found there, which belong to the *Dipterocarpaceae* family. These trees can grow up to 80 metres (260ft) tall and include many species that have proved valuable to the timber trade thanks to the trunks being hard and durable. Dipterocarps derive their name from their fruits, which have two-winged seeds. Borneo has the greatest number of dipterocarp species, while the oldest one recorded in Malaysia is on the peninsula: a *cengal (Neobalanocarpus heimii)* in Terengganu's Pasir Raja Forest Reserve, estimated at 1,300 years old.

has become a key means and effective argument to conserve these ecosystems.

Geological foundation

The story of the forests begins with that of the land. Over 500 million years ago, what is now Malaysia was part of the prehistoric super-continent called Gondwanaland, which encompassed all the parts of the world that now belong to the southern hemisphere.

Today, evidence of this exists in Langkawi, in the sandstone of the Machinchang mountains, the oldest rock in the country. As sea levels rose and fell and the landforms and landscapes changed, Langkawi's rocks became repositories of this amazing history. Forests began to take root, and creatures inhabited these forests. Today, Machinchang is one of several geologically important areas in Langkawi that are protected and open to tourists. These are special conservation areas within permanent forest reserves and are collectively known as the Langkawi Geopark (see page 201), which has also received international recognition as a Unesco Global Geopark.

At Machinchang, stunning mountain views encompass features such as a series of hogback

In the foothills of Mount Kinabalu.

RAFFLESIA

The *Rafflesia* is the largest flower in the world, measuring up to 1 metre (3.5ft) in diameter when in full bloom. *Rafflesia* can be found in a few sites in Malaysia, including the Main Range and Malaysian Borneo. A parasite, the plant embeds itself on the roots of a woody climber, *Tetrastigma* sp. The flower takes many months to develop, but the magnificent open bloom lasts only for a few days before it starts to decay and smell like rotting meat. Popular as traditional medicine, *Rafflesia* are now protected, and education and tourist dollars are used to encourage villagers to manage conservation sites on their lands.

ridges – steeply tilted ridges – while close-ups reveal giant cube-shaped rocks and impressive layering of rock, both the result of erosion. Mixed dipterocarp forest abounds in the foothills, giving way to stunted vegetation similar to heath forests at the top. The forests here are scantily researched but are considered among the oldest in the country. The Forestry Department of Peninsular Malaysia is keen to protect them and has even coined a special label for them, calling them "geoforests". Nonetheless, stronger, more comprehensive legislation is needed to back the need for this protection. It is also hoped that better tourist interpretation would lead to support and understanding for geological conservation as a whole in this richly endowed environment.

Highlands

Mountains and hills cover much of Malaysia. The mountain range of the Banjaran Titiwangsa, or Main Range, cuts through the length of peninsular Malaysia like a backbone. It rarely dips below 1,000 metres (3,300ft) above sea level, with its highest summit being Mount Tahan (Gunung Tahan), which stands at 2,200 metres (6,600ft) high. Meanwhile, the highlands in Borneo are slightly taller, peaking along the Indonesian border in Sarawak, while in Sabah they cover the entire state. Sabah is also where the highest mountain in Southeast Asia can be found: Mount Kinabalu (Gunung Kinabalu) (see page 320), standing at 4,093 metres (13,430ft).

The main forests in the highlands are the hill dipterocarp forests and these are the most intact of all forests in the country, thanks to the steep slopes and rugged country being unsuitable for logging, settlements or agriculture. Indeed, Malaysia has legislation banning logging from slopes steeper than 30 degrees.

Hill dipterocarp forests resemble their lowland cousins but are less diverse. They are distinguised by species such as *seraya* (*Shorea curtisii*), noticeable from afar by their silvery crowns. There are also relatively fewer animals and insects, but these include birds and tree specialists such as monkeys and squirrels. In higher altitudes, oak-laurel and montane forests are found. The higher the elevation, the shorter and more sparse the vegetation; trees can be stunted and gnarled, while moss and ferns dominate.

The finest example of a highland forest, arguably, is in the Kinabalu National Park (see page 321), which protects the mountain after which it is named. Far-ranging research confirms it as one of the world's most important centres of plant diversity, with a high level of endemism. The park is particularly famous for its rhododendrons, orchids and pitcher plants. Mammals here include wild cats, gibbons and two species of shrew that are found only on the mountain.

Lowlands

The most extensive lowland forests in Malaysia are lowland dipterocarp forests. These are characterised by a rich diversity of fauna and flora. Typically divided into levels, the understorey comprises saplings, palms and rattans; the main canopy, small and large trees often overgrown with epiphytes and climbers; and the emergent level, the tallest trees, which poke out of the canopy.

Malaysian lowlands are where the large mammals roam, iconic creatures such as the Asian elephant (*Elephas maximus*) and the Malayan tiger (*Panthera tigris jacksonii*), which is found only in the peninsula, as well as the Bornean orang-utan (*Pongo pygmaeus*) in Sabah and Sarawak. Considering their size, these animals are incredibly difficult to see in the dense rainforest. Visitors always have better luck spotting reptiles, amphibians, birds,

Rajah Brooke's Birdwing is the national butterfly.

ORANG-UTANS

The world has just two species of Orang-utans found respectively in Borneo and Sumatra. In Borneo, with less than 50,000 left in the wild, they are endangered and as such, protected. Asia's great apes, orang-utans are the largest tree-living animals in existence, and live in low-lying peat swamp forests but are difficult to spot in the wild. The best places to see them are at the Semonggoh Wildlife Centre outside Kuching, Sarawak and the Sepilok Orang-utan Rehabilitation Centre (see page 332) near Sandakan, Sabah. Both centres rehabilitate orphans to reintroduce them into the wild.

the smaller primates, squirrels and the millions of insects, all of whom boast equally fascinating diversity.

Unfortunately, these lowland forests have largely lost the fight against human pressures and exist only in small pockets or in protected areas. In the peninsula, the largest protected tract is Taman Negara in Pahang, where lowland forest makes up 10 percent of the park area. The dipterocarps here grow to an immense size, complete with buttress roots as tall as houses. Outdoing even the dipterocarps are legumes such as the *tualang* (*Koompasia*

A jungle trail in the Cameron Highlands.

excelsa), an emergent that is often "decorated" with massive beehives. At least 200 species of mammal live in the park, including the most iconic Malaysian ones, as well as eight species of hornbills, among the 250 bird species recorded.

In Borneo, mixed dipterocarp forest (comprising both lowland and hill forest types) covers about 40 percent of Sarawak's Gunung Mulu National Park (see page 300). The park is one of the world's richest sites for palms and has magnificent trees such as the *belian* or Bornean ironwood (*Eusideroxylon zageri*). In addition to its gigantic insects, Mulu is also home to numerous primates, the endangered Sunda pangolin (*Manis javanica*) and squirrels galore, including those unique to the region.

The beautiful Rajah Brooke's Birdwing, with its emerald markings on jet-black wings, is Malaysia's national butterfly.

Mulu is better known, however, for its cave ecosystems. The exteriors of these caves have limestone flora that is extremely diverse and one of the best preserved in Southeast Asia. This includes the endemic palm *Salacca rupicola*. The caves are home to 12 species of bats, two of which live only in the park.

Wetlands

Malaysia's lowlands were formed by either rivers or coastal processes, depositing sediment to form plains. The country has numerous rivers that begin in the highlands and form large and sometimes complex networks as they flow to the sea. Large river systems include the Rajang in Sarawak, the Kinabatangan in Sabah and the Pahang in the peninsula.

As the rivers make their way down, they cut into the rock and form waterfalls. Some are magnificent and the more easily accessible of these are popular recreational spots. Southeast Asia's tallest waterfall is actually in the peninsula: the Stong Waterfall in Kelantan, which flows down seven tiers from a height of 300 metres (900ft).

Many large rivers are also dammed to produce hydroelectric power, which meets 10 percent of the country's energy needs. Some of these artificial lakes are also popular holiday sites, for example, Terengganu's Kenyir dam and Sarawak's Batang Ai dam. Because the rivers are dammed in the middle or upper courses, the surrounding forests, generally of the hill dipterocarp variety, are kept intact.

Naturally occurring lakes are rare in Malaysia and are constantly being threatened by pollution and development. The largest freshwater lake system in the peninsula is Lake Bera in Pahang. This is a seasonal riverine lake system which empties into the Pahang river. The lake system includes swamps with reeds and grasslands and supports different lake and swamp flora and fauna, which include over 300 species of algae, as well as all the amphibians and reptiles recorded in Malaysian tropical swamps. Tasik Bera is protected as a wildlife reserve under the Wildlife Department and certified as a RAMSAR Wetland of International Importance.

Gravely at threat, however, is the peat swamp forest, a coastal forest characterised by permanent waterlogging of the soil, which makes the water brackish. While less diverse than its freshwater cousin, it supports large mammals such as the Malayan tiger, Asian elephant and the Bornean peatswamp specialist, the proboscis monkey *(Nasalis larvatus)*.

Coastal

Mangrove forest is a special wetland that exists only on the coasts. Growing in the zone between land and sea, mangroves undergo a

A crab in the mudflats on Pulau Langkawi.

in Sabah, although the largest protected area is in Matang, Perak, which is a world-example of sustainable forest management.

The Malaysian Nature Society manages Kuala Selangor Nature Park (see page 145), where mangroves cover a third of the 320-hectare (800-acre) park and are its most important ecosystem. Besides the *Rhizophora* species, the forest there has large numbers of *Bruguiera* species, another key mangrove tree. Silvered leaf monkeys *(Presbytis cristata)* and long-tailed macaques *(Macaca facicularis)* abound in the trees, while the mudflats teem with mudskippers and

Mangrove forest in Langkawi.

daily regiment of being flooded by salt water followed by a drying-out period. Mangrove ecosystems are usually transacted by numerous rivers and comprise mudflats and shallow seas.

Because of the harshness of the environment, mangrove forests are only a habitat to hardy species that are most recognisable from their otherworldly aerial roots and waxy leaves. Among these are two trees that typify the ecosystem: *bakau minyak (Rhizophora apiculata)* and *bakau kurap (Rhizophora mucronata)*. These trees are the reason why mangroves are called *hutan bakau* in Malay.

Malaysia has the third-largest area of mangroves in the Asia-Pacific region after Indonesia and Australia the most extensive is found

INDIGENOUS PEOPLES

Principally living in forest-based communities, Malaysia's indigenous peoples have rich knowledge about the country's forests. Their knowledge is key to understanding species and therefore crucial to conservation. Tied up with this is a rich heritage of beliefs and folklore related to the forest, one that is largely contained within each community and passed down orally.

These traditional lifestyles are being eroded as forests are depleted and communities move on, whether voluntarily or otherwise. What is at stake is the loss of the best interpreters of biodiversity and custodians of the forest.

fiddler crabs. But it is the birds that are its main attraction. In general, birds are most active at dawn and before sunset, but at low tide the mudflats teem with waders and other birds.

Marine

Off the coasts of Malaysia lie hectares of coral reefs, home to the most diverse and colourful marine species in the world. With its shallow and relatively calm waters as well as bountiful sunshine year round, Malaysia has the perfect ingredients for the growth of these rainforests of the sea.

problems such as pollution, sedimentation and unsustainable tourism.

Nonetheless, non-governmental organisations are working with government departments, locals and tour operators on conservation awareness and education. Besides harbouring life, the reefs protect Malaysia's shorelines, sustain fisheries and support livelihoods, and are important tourism destinations.

The most famous of these reef ecosystems is Pulau Sipadan (see page 338) in Sabah. One of the world's top scuba-diving destinations, this oceanic island has a drop-off that plunges

Snorkelling among the fish off Langkawi.

Like their land cousins, these reefs are a complex, highly diverse and beautiful ecosystem, about which only a little is scientifically known.

The healthiest and most extensive reefs are found off the islands on the east coast of the peninsula and off Borneo. Different laws have been passed to protect these reefs. Sarawak has one marine park and Sabah four, which are protected by the respective state laws. A "federal" law protects over 40 island reef ecosystems in the peninsula and Labuan, specifically, two nautical miles of ocean from land. The islands themselves, however, are generally not protected, except for several forest reserves. This gives rise to land-based

hundreds of metres into the ocean. It is home to hundreds of coral species and over 3,000 species of fish, including thousand-fish-strong schools of bigeye trevally *(Caranx sexfasciatus)* and barracuda *(Sphyraena* sp.*)*. Its sea turtle population is also large, specifically green sea turtles *(Chelonia mydas)* and hawksbill sea turtles *(Eretmochelys imbricata)*, both of which are endangered.

Malaysia's natural wonders and wealth of diversity do not attract all the global attention they deserve. However, its important environments are worthy of superlatives, as well as the world records it sets. The challenge for Malaysia today is to keep these splendid ecosystems conserved and to manage them properly.

Environmental issues

Tackling environmental issues is a balancing act that requires a change of mindset and will at all levels of Malaysian society.

Whether Malaysia can conserve its unique natural heritage will depend on its ability to balance sustainability with economic development and a fast-growing population. The number of Malaysians almost tripled between 1970 and 2010 and the population is expected to double again by 2030. Over two-thirds of Malaysians live in urban areas, where the jobs are. Pressures from population growth and urbanisation are greater in the peninsula, where just 40 percent of the country's land mass has 80 percent of its population.

As Malaysia continues to industrialise and urbanise, controlling water and air pollution as well as waste remains challenging. In 2008, Malaysia was ranked in the top 25 percentile of per capita carbon dioxide-emitting countries based on UN statistics. In the years associated with the El Niño climate pattern, a haze enveloped the country, caused largely by smoke from the burning of forests in neighbouring Indonesia. Forests in Borneo are susceptible to fires in this period too.

Deforestation

Meanwhile, competition for land use had reduced forest cover to about 60 percent of the land mass by 2011. Large-scale deforestation began under British colonial rule, as land was cleared by the early 1900s for tin mining and rubber plantations. Post-independence, the country's developmental thrust saw more forest give way to first agriculture and land development schemes, then industrial development and urbanisation. Today, oil palm cultivation is the main reason for the loss of lowland forests, particularly in Borneo.

Moreover, of the remaining forest areas, just under half are permanently reserved for logging but WWF Malaysia estimates that only about 15 percent of forests are properly legislated as protected areas. Meanwhile, illegal logging continues to denude the remaining forests; Transparency International found that this was linked to corruption, from the bestowing of logging concessions to the breaking of regulations. Additionally, the trafficking of protected and threatened wildlife is rampant.

Eco-awareness

The plethora of laws related to environmental issues and government agencies managing them in Malaysia makes tackling them complicated. This is compounded by state governments having a substantial say in issues related to land, particularly in Sabah and Sarawak. At public level, environmental awareness is also generally low. Meanwhile, inadequate resources are available to increase the scientific knowledge to support conservation. To date, the economic *raison d'être* for conservation is tourism, but "ecotourism" is often poorly understood and has led to more degradation of sensitive areas.

Deforestation to make way for palm oil in Sandakan province.

Nonetheless, consciousness is growing and attitudes changing at all levels. Malaysians have, over the years, suffered the effects of various environmental problems. While farmers and fishermen have lost their livelihoods, the state is having to spend millions in efforts like flood mitigation and keeping water sources clean. Meanwhile, globalised trade demands more environmentally friendly production of goods and services. Dwindling natural resources and higher prices are forcing policies to become greener. Environmental activism is on the rise. Importantly, local communities are beginning to demand transparency and participation in governmental decision-making. On paper, sustainable development already exists in Malaysia's legislation and policies; making it happen is the next step.

Snapshots on a longhouse wall.

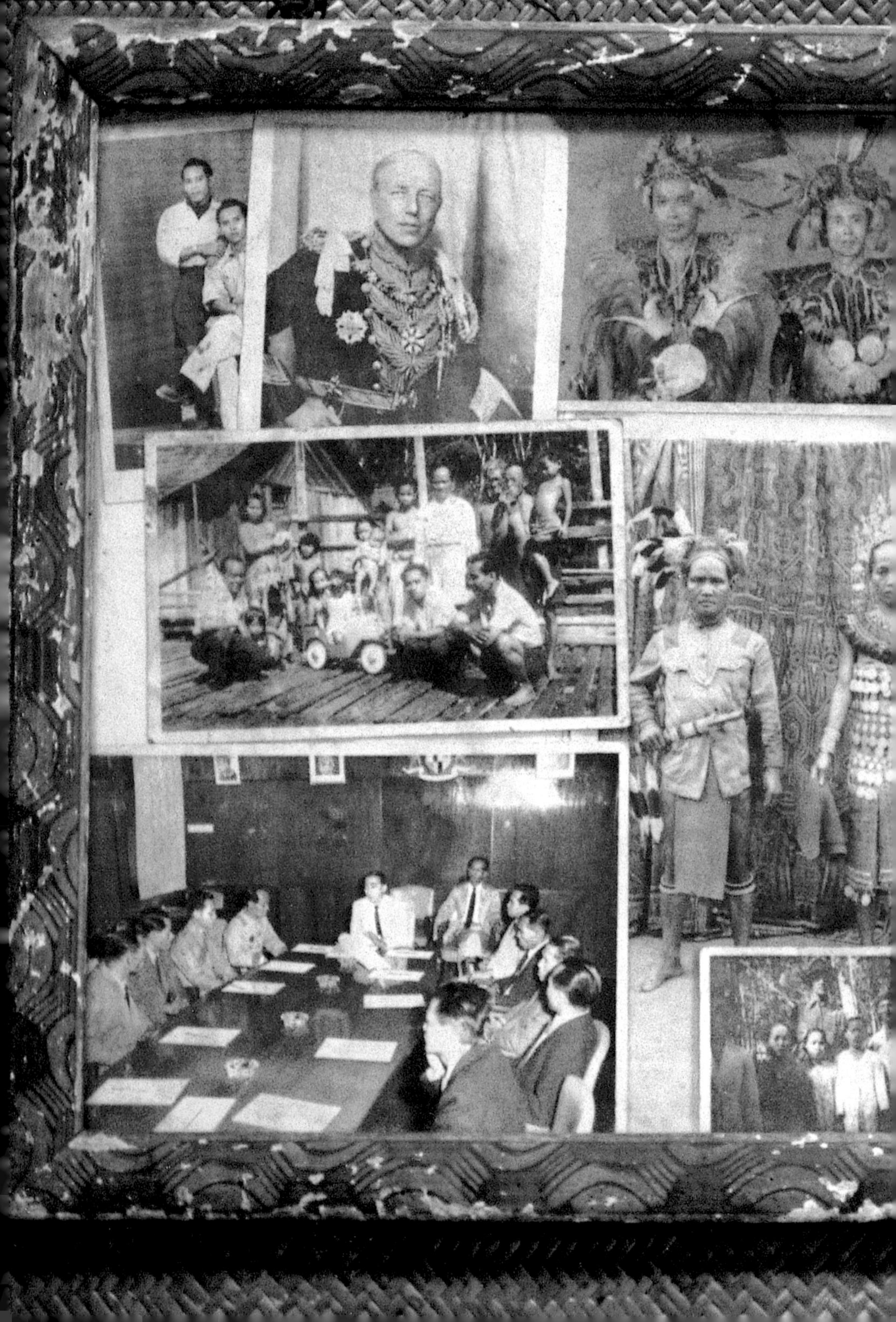

DECISIVE DATES

Prehistory

c.1.8 million BC
Handaxe dates to oldest human habitation in Lenggong Valley, Perak.

c.74000 BC
Handtools indicate use by the possible ancestors of the oldest people in Malaysia, the Negritos.

c.10000–2500 BC
Austronesians, the ancestors of Bornean natives and Malays, settle in the region.

c.2500 BC
Earliest signs of trade.

Early kingdoms

AD 200–700
Rise of Buddhist-Hindu trading kingdoms in Kedah and Sarawak.

AD 700–1200
Peninsula comes under the Indian empires of Srivijaya and Cola; Borneo comes under the kingdom of Po'ni.

c.1400
Founding of Malacca by Parameswara.

A detail from A Famosa fort in Melaka.

1411
Parameswara converts to Islam; establishes Malacca sultanate.

1459–77
Malacca's golden age; the empire expands and Islam spreads through the empire.

1500s
Borneo comes under the Bruneian empire.

1511
Malacca falls to the Portuguese.

1528
The sons of Malacca's deposed sultan establish the sultanates of Johor and Perak.

1641
The Dutch take over Malacca from the Portuguese; Malacca sidelined for Batavia.

1658
Brunei cedes north and east Sabah to Sulu.

c.1780s
Bugis take over Johor sultanate and set up Selangor sultanate.

1786
The British occupy Penang, the first step towards colonisation.

British Malaya

1824
Anglo-Dutch Treaty carves up Malay area, setting the boundaries of Peninsular Malaysia and Indonesia.

1826
Singapore, Malacca and Penang become Straits Settlements under British control.

1840s
Tin rush attracts an influx of Chinese tin miners.

1841
James Brooke established as rajah of Sarawak.

1863
Sarawak expanded, British recognise Brooke's independence from Brunei.

1874
Pangkor Engagement is start of British intervention in Perak, Selangor and Negeri Sembilan.

1881
British North Borneo Chartered Company established.

1884
Start of Indian labour influx.

1891
The Dutch and British settle border disputes; modern-day Kalimantan and Sabah/ Sarawak borders determined.

1895–1905
North Borneo expanded to encompass today's Sabah.

1896
Federated Malay States created, comprising Perak, Selangor, Pahang and Negeri Sembilan.

1909
Treaty of Bangkok transfers four northern Malay states from Thai sovereignty to British.

1914
Johor brought under British control; the entire peninsula now under British rule.

The making of Malaysia

1941–5
Japanese Occupation.

1945
British reoccupy Malaysia. Anti-colonial movements build.

1946
Malayan Union scheme introduced but is opposed; formation of United Malay National Organisation (UMNO); Sarawak and British North Borneo become Crown colonies.

1947
First multi-ethnic political movement organises strikes.

1948
Federation of Malaya founded.

1948–60
Communist insurgency – The Emergency.

1953
Alliance coalition comprising UMNO, Malayan Chinese Association (MCA) and Malayan Indian Congress (MIC) formed.

1955
First general elections; landslide win for the Alliance.

1957
Malaya becomes independent; Tunku Abdul Rahman is the first prime minister.

1963
Creation of Malaysia, formed of Malaya, Singapore, North Borneo (Sabah) and Sarawak.

1963–6
"Confrontation" with Indonesia.

1965
Singapore leaves Malaysia.

1969
May 13 incident which sees civil unrest after general elections.

1970
New Economic Policy (NEP) intended to redistribute wealth; affirmative rights for *bumiputra*.

1973
The Alliance coalition is reorganised as the 10-party Barisan Nasional (BN).

The Mahathir era

1981
Prime minister Tun Dr Mahathir Mohamad takes office.

1983–4
Government strips power from the sultans and muzzles media; companies created to marry government and big business.

1987
"Operation Lalang" sees detention of many prominent government opposition figures.

1988
Tiger economy years; GDP grows at 9 percent per annum.

1990s
Large-scale industrialisation and mega-projects such as the building of Putrajaya.

1997
Petronas Twin Towers complete. The Asian economic crisis hits.

1998
Kuala Lumpur is first Asian city to host Commonwealth Games. Deputy prime minister Anwar Ibrahim arrested on charges of corruption and sodomy.

2003
Mahathir retires as Malaysia's longest-serving prime minister.

Mohd Najib Abdul Razak.

2004
BN wins landslide in elections; Anwar released from prison.

Political tsunami

2008
BN loses two-thirds of its parliamentary majority; Anwar-led Pakatan Rakyat opposition takes over five states.

2009
Mohd Najib Abdul Razak becomes prime minister but is dogged by controversy. Anwar on trial again for sodomy.

2012
Largest-ever street demonstration demanding electoral reform.

2013
Coalition retains government with weakened majority.

2014
Two tragedies hit Malaysian Airlines: in March, flight MH370 disappears with 239 people on board; and in July, flight MH17, carrying nearly 300 people, is shot down over the Ukraine.

2015
Anwar's sentence to five years in jail is upheld in highest court.

An ancient megalith at Negeri Sembilan.

BEGINNINGS

Trade came early to Malaysia and shaped it in many ways over the following millennia. The country's location on the ancient east-west seafaring route was seminal in the development of maritime trade and empires.

The beginnings of human settlement in Malaysia go back almost 2 million years. Clues to what had come to pass in the days before writing have been unearthed through the archaeological record: cave drawings, skeletons, burial sites, pottery shards, megaliths, Buddhist temples and abandoned forts. Later, ancient Indian, Chinese, Arab and even Greek texts and maps would reveal descriptions, details and impressions. These were written and drawn variously by traders, envoys, monks and scholars. While much remains to be uncovered, what is certain is that Malaysia has long been an important centre of global migration and trade, with a key role in powering the global economy and the discovery of lands and routes.

Prehistoric Malaysia

Archaeological discoveries since the 1980s have revealed Malaysia to be an important prehistoric site, with a long record of human habitation. The centre of this is the Lenggong Valley in Perak, where endlessly rich offerings have revealed evidence of habitation ranging from as far back as 1.83 million years until 10,000 years ago. It is relatively unusual to have a single location host archaeological evidence covering such a long period of time, namely the Palaeolithic, Neolithic and Metal ages.

The valley was also part of the ancient migratory route from Africa to Australia around 74,000 years ago, something demonstrated by the rare, undisturbed Kota Tampan stone-tool workshop. Kota Tampan is now a reference site for the Palaeolithic (Stone Age) period of Southeast Asia. The evidence indicates that the people who used the tools were Mesolithic (Middle Stone Age) hunters and shifting cultivators. They lived in rock shelters and caves in

Neolithic burial site at Niah Caves, Sarawak.

THE AUSTRONESIANS

Austronesians are the ancestors of today's natives of Sabah and Sarawak as well as the Peninsular Malays. One theory of origin, based largely on linguistic evidence, suggests that Austronesians migrated to the archipelago from Taiwan 3,000–4,000 years ago after an increase in population; they later spread to mainland Southeast Asia and the Pacific. Another theory, using mitochondrial DNA studies, suggests that the movement was from south to north, and happened even earlier, 10,000 years ago. The inhabitants of the archipelago dispersed throughout the region after massive floods caused by climate change drowned their lands.

the limestone hills of the peninsula and used stone implements for cutting and grinding, as well as for hunting wild animals. Based on linguistic evidence, these people may have been the ancestors of the Negrito indigenous people or of their successors, the Senoi.

The earliest evidence of human life in Borneo is provided by a *homo sapiens* skull discovered in Sarawak's Niah Caves. Codenamed the "Deep Skull", it is believed to date from the late Pleistocene period. One, somewhat contentious, estimate puts it at 40,000 years old. The skull suggests that the people who lived here

The Neolithic period saw the use of more sophisticated stone and earthenware technology, as well as the planting of grains such as rice. One of the most important and largest sites for pottery production in this time was Bukit Tengkorak, in southeast Sabah near Semporna. This site also proved a trading connection between Southeast Asia and the Pacific. Over 2,000 years later, it was trade again that saw civilisation in the peninsula propelled into the Metal Age, this time of a maritime nature. Bronze drums and bells found here were similar to those from the Bronze Age in

View of the dolmen Batu Ritong, on the edge of Pa Lungan village.

were hunter-gatherers, who were later displaced by migrants named Austronesians. Austronesians were largely agriculturalists except for the Punan/Penan who were hunter-gatherers, and who had probably moved inland from the coasts when the agriculturalists arrived.

The Neolithic period

Around 2500 BC, the Palaeolithic inhabitants of the Malay Peninsula began to be exposed through trade to older civilisations in Thailand. This very rapidly sparked the advent of the Neolithic period. In Sabah, the Neolithic period came through connections with Taiwan and the Philippines, whereas in Sarawak the influences came from the latter but also the peninsula.

North Vietnam and which were widely traded in Southeast Asia. Meanwhile, beads suggest trade with Burma and the Indian subcontinent, while other products indicate that links were also established with China.

The peninsula was particularly ideally suited for trade. Its location interrupted direct sailing on the main sea route between east and west and the area experienced alternating monsoons – southwesterly followed by northeasterly. These factors made it the natural meeting point for Indian and Chinese traders to exchange their wares. They also came to buy the produce of the region itself, such as gold – the Malay Peninsula was known to early geographers as "the Golden Chersonese"

– as well as aromatic woods and the much-treasured spices.

The first of these Indian and Chinese trading voyages are believed to have taken place in prehistoric times. By the beginning of the Christian era, the trade routes were already well established. Convenient ports of call soon sprung up, which would later become the nuclei for other minor states.

Early kingdoms

The earliest kingdoms established were Buddhist. In the peninsula, Kedah was the most

Over in Borneo, the greatest seaport in this period was Santubong in Sarawak. Excavations suggest that traders used Santubong as part of a network linking Southeast Asia with West Asia and China during the time of the Tang and Song dynasties (618–1279). From the 10th century, this trading centre was also a producer of iron, possibly employing methods that are still used by the indigenous Orang Ulu people today.

Throughout all of this, the local people themselves journeyed across the seas, reaching north-eastern India and the Arab Peninsula. They also

Melaka was once a bustling trading port.

important of these due to its strategic location at the northern entrance to the Straits of Malacca. Chinese records established that Kedah's Bujang Valley was already in contact with India in the 2nd century and became a key and powerful commercial centre for Indian traders in this part of the world.

By the 7th century, the kingdom of Chi tu was also already established in Kelantan on the east coast of the peninsula. It was part of, or affiliated with, the ancient Indian empire of Wat Funan in Vietnam. Chi tu had a political relationship with China, and it is from Chinese documentation that evidence of this kingdom was gleaned, all physical traces of it having vanished.

travelled to China, mostly in the form of tribute missions.

The Indian period

Between the 7th and 13th centuries, Kedah, the Straits of Malacca and the Borneon coasts came under the control of Indian empires, whose regional bases were in Sumatra. So deep was the impact of these kingdoms on local society that the 1,500 years of Malaysian history between the arrival of the first Indians and the coming of Islam is called the Indian period.

The Buddhist Srivijaya kingdom reigned for four centuries and the Hindu Cola empire for one, and these civilisations left behind numerous *candi* religious edifices at Bujang Valley and

Santubong, as well as religious figurines and votive tablets.

During this period, Buddhism, Hinduism and South Indian culture and language became widespread. Locals added to their pantheon of existing deities, multiple Hindu gods as well as giants and demi-gods. These appear in Malay folklore, superstition and literature. Many Malay words are derived from Sanskrit and Tamil, and some Malay social customs, especially wedding rites, reflect Hindu customs. Kingship was affected as well. Local rulers were known as *raja*, taken from the Sanskrit term

A Malacca tree.

devaraja, meaning "god-king"; the royal head of the state of Perlis is still called the *raja*.

The rise of Malacca

At the dawn of the 15th century, the first home-grown maritime power came into being: Malacca (now Melaka). The history of Malacca is documented in the *Sejarah Melayu (Malay Annals)*, written in the early 1600s. Part historical fact and part legend, the text traces the transformation of a small coastal village into this famous trading empire.

According to the *Malay Annals*, it all began on the island of Tumasek (now Singapore) at the tip of the Malay Peninsula, which at the time was ruled by a Palembang prince with

> During the Malacca period, the term Melayu (Malay) for the locals was synonymous with being Malaccan, distinguishable from the rest of the Malay archipelago. When Malacca became Muslim, the definition expanded to include Islam.

the Hindu title of Parameswara. When Javanese forces attacked Tumasek, Parameswara and his followers were compelled to flee northwards to the peninsula.

One day, when Parameswara was out hunting near the coast, one of his hounds was kicked by a white mousedeer. The king, always appreciative of valour, was said to have exclaimed, "This is a good place! Even the mousedeer are full of fight!" Taking a cue from this good omen, Parameswara decided to build a settlement on the site. As he happened to be standing near a *melaka* tree, he decided that the settlement should bear its name.

Parameswara and his followers cleared the land around it, planted rice and orchards and exploited the rich tin deposits inland. News of the settlement's wealth spread, which soon began to attract passing traders.

Chinese protection

At this time, the Ming emperor of China was sending out large fleets of ships to expand trade with Southeast Asia and beyond. In 1409, one of his most famous admirals, Cheng Ho, called at Malacca. He recognised Parameswara as its legitimate ruler, and at Parameswara's request, placed the new port under China's protection. In 1411, Cheng Ho took Parameswara back with him to China – a trip which confirmed Parameswara's status as a sovereign ruler owing fealty to China alone. These moves were very important for Malacca's survival, for the new port-state was under constant threat of Siamese attack.

Malacca's harbour soon became crowded with ships of all kinds, the streets of the city alive with merchants from all parts of Asia. Its bazaar was crammed with exotic goods: silks, brocades and porcelain from China; cloth, glassware and jewels from India; jade and diamonds from Burma; pepper, sandalwood, ebony and rice from the Spice Islands (Moluccas) of the Indonesian archipelago; and tin, gold and other produce from Malacca's own hinterland.

An important reason for Malacca's success was its ability to ensure the safety of the traders who called there. As with Srivijaya and the previous maritime empires, Malacca's rulers commanded the allegiance of the Orang Laut, or sea gypsies, who managed to curb the pirate menace in the Straits of Malacca.

The arrival of Islam

A big change swept through the region when Parameswara adopted Islam and established the Malacca sultanate. Muslims first arrived in Southeast Asia in the 11th century in the form

Islam throughout the region. By 1413, Malacca had become a fully-fledged Muslim sultanate. Islam became established throughout Malacca's empire, which, by the end of the 15th century, included all the states of the Malay Peninsula and those on the east coast of Sumatra.

Wealthy Muslim traders were drawn to conduct business there, and Malacca also became a well-known centre of Islamic scholarship. As Islam became part of the daily life of local Malays, it gradually had a great impact on the values and outlook of ordinary people. At the same time, however, the Malays managed to

A Dutch-built bridge over the Melaka river.

Muslim traders brought Arabic script to Malacca – the Malay version is called Jawi – which replaced the ancient Indian script Malaccans had used before.

of Arab traders, and it is believed that Islam took hold in the region in Acheh in Indonesia. The Kedah sultanate dates back to this time, when the local king renounced Hinduism in favour of Islam, which was introduced to Kedah by Acheh Muslims.

A century later, Chinese Muslims had settled in Southeast Asia, and yet another century later, it was Indian Muslims who started spreading

retain or merge much of their pre-Islamic customs with the new religion.

The spread of Islam happened at the peak of Malacca's glory between 1459 and 1477 during the reign of the sixth sultan, Mansor Shah. The empire's expansion in this period is largely attributed to the great soldier-statesman Tun Perak, who was chief minister or *bendahara*, and who advised four Malacca sultans altogether. Among other things, Tun Perak built a formidable fighting force. He also honoured brave warriors with the title of *Hang*, or captain, including the bearers of such famous names in Malacca's history as Hang Tuah and Hang Jebat.

Mansor Shah himself forged alliances with conquered states through marriages of his family and ministers. He alone married daughters of important merchants to secure trade relations. However, good economic policies and incentives were what kept trade flourishing, and Malacca would be the meeting place for such diverse people as the Gujarati, Chinese, Japanese, Javanese, Bengalis, Persians and Arabs.

Malacca's golden era

Malacca's population at the zenith of its might was 40,000, and Malay was used as the *lingua franca* in this cosmopolitan milieu. The city was located at the mouth of a river and was divided

The Portuguese first arrived in Melaka in 1509.

into two halves. The sultan's palace and the Malay *kampung* were south of the river, while on the north bank the houses and stores of the merchants provided the international bustle of the city. The two halves were linked by a bridge, on which, like the bridges of many medieval European cities, a number of merchants built their shops.

The palace was the centre of life. Peasants, traders and noblemen had the right to present their petitions to the sultan in his *balai*, or audience hall. The sultan would sit on a raised platform, surrounded by richly embroidered cushions and flanked by his ministers, two or three steps below him.

As sultan, the ruler's power was absolute, but government was according to well-defined

laws, which were administered by a hierarchy comprising a *bendahara* (chief minister), a *temenggung* (chief of police) and a *laksamana* (admiral). Below them were the various titled nobles. The royalty, common people and traders abided by this system.

Importantly for the traders, *shahbandars* or harbourmasters were appointed, each representing a particular community of traders. He watched over the daily affairs as well as settling disagreements among the sailors and merchants in his group.

The biggest crime, though, was *derhaka* or disloyalty to the sultan. This concept is well illustrated by the famous tale of Hang Tuah and Hang Jebat, two of the sultan's most famous warriors, who were also good friends. In an act of treachery intended to please a capricious sultan, Hang Tuah murdered his old friend Hang Jebat. The killer was regarded at the time to have acted correctly; loyalty to the ruler, right or wrong, came above all else.

The Portuguese invasion

The spices that came through Malacca from the Spice Islands were the most lucrative commodity in the trade between Europe and Asia. Since the 11th century, Arab traders had been monopolising this trade. Their European counterpart was Venice, which, in turn, had the monopoly on spice distribution in the continent. In the 15th century, the Portuguese decided to break these monopolies. At the same time, they wanted to continue their crusade against Islam, for they had just liberated their own homeland from the Muslims. Besides diverting the trade route to a new one around Africa's Cape of Good Hope, a relationship with Malacca was key, for, as the Portuguese apothecary and writer Tomé Pires put it, "Whoever is Lord in Malacca has his hand on the throat of Venice."

The Portuguese finally arrived in Sultan Mahmud's Malacca in 1509. They sought permission to establish a trading post, but were rebuffed; what's more, 20 of their number were taken prisoners, giving the Portuguese a good excuse to return in force. This took place two years later, when a large Portuguese fleet, led by Alfonso de Albuquerque, the architect of Portuguese expansion in the Indian Ocean, attacked Malacca. The Portuguese concentrated their onslaught on the bridge over the river, where the Malaccan defenders put up a courageous resistance. Even

Sultan Mahmud and his son were in the thick of battle, riding on caparisoned elephants.

On 24 August 1511, Malacca fell and the sultan and his followers fled into the countryside. Most of the Muslim traders also took flight, and the Chinese government and their traders, incensed, boycotted the port. Malacca had lost its independence, and under a string of foreign rulers, never regained its days of glory.

Portuguese Malacca

De Albuquerque set up a Portuguese administration and built a fort, calling it A Famosa ("The Famous"). Within its formidable walls, a medieval Portuguese-style city developed, with a town hall, offices and homes for the Portuguese civil servants, while locals and other workers lived outside the walls of the town.

The Portuguese set about restoring Malacca to its former status as the leading emporium in the region, while also going directly to the Spice Islands and setting up bases there. They also tried to make Malacca a great centre for Catholic missionary work among the local population. St Francis Xavier, the well-known Catholic missionary, stayed in Malacca three times whilst spreading the Christian gospel.

But the Portuguese did not succeed in either aim. They attempted to acquire a monopoly of the spice trade by requiring all ships using the straits to obtain passes from them and by imposing arbitrary duties at the port of Malacca. Such actions aroused strong anti-Portuguese feelings, and they found themselves fending off attacks from neighbours on all sides. In many cases, A Famosa proved to be the only saving factor. As for the attempts to proselytise, Catholicism did not appeal to the local population – least of all to the Muslims.

Meanwhile, following his flight from Malacca, Sultan Mahmud settled in Bintang in the Riau archipelago. He made two unsuccessful attacks on Malacca, and died in 1528. His elder son established himself in Perak and started the sultanate there, while his younger son started a new sultanate in Johor. Both joined forces to harass Malacca periodically. At the same time, Johor started to develop as a rival entrepôt.

Meanwhile, in north Sumatra, Aceh had a growing monopoly over pepper and became an important local power. It launched attacks on its main rivals in the area – Malacca and Johor.

This three-cornered contest for control over the trade of the Straits of Malacca dragged on throughout most of the 16th century.

Dutch rule

Developments in Europe led to the arrival of the Dutch and the English in Southeast Asian waters. In 1594, the port of Lisbon, now the spice mart of Europe, was closed to Dutch and English merchants, compelling them to go directly to the source of the spices as Portugal earlier had. The Dutch trading companies combined to form the United East India Company

Alfonso de Albuquerque led the Portuguese conquest of Melaka in 1511.

> The A Famosa fort, built by de Albuquerque in the early 1500s, was so solidly constructed that no enemy managed to breach its walls for over 130 years.

(VOC) in 1602. The VOC's interests were primarily focused on the Spice Islands. However, they considered control of Malacca necessary to complete their own monopoly over the spice and local trade of the region.

In 1640, they joined forces with Johor and Aceh to overthrow the Portuguese. After blockading the port of Malacca and bombarding A Famosa, the Dutch encircled the town. As the siege continued, the Portuguese garrison and the people trapped in the fort began to starve and were forced to eat whatever came into sight – rats, dogs, cats and snakes. The acute hunger was aggravated by diseases such as malaria, typhoid and cholera. Finally, in 1641, after a seven-month siege, the Dutch forces stormed A Famosa and fought on to victory.

The Dutch were much more powerful and efficient than the Portuguese and were able to establish a more effective monopoly over the trade of the region, particularly in spices, which

The A Famosa fort in Melaka still stands today.

they rigidly enforced. Since they made Batavia (now Jakarta) their headquarters, Malacca declined in importance as a trading centre. However, it proved useful as a base from which to control the local trade (such as tin and pepper) of the Straits of Malacca.

The Dutch capture of Malacca put paid to the triangular contest for control of the straits with the Acehnese and Johoreans, because the trade of both Aceh and Johore suffered as a result of the Dutch monopoly. Johore was further weakened by a disastrous war with Jambi, one of its former vassals in Sumatra in the 1670s, and at the end of the century, the last of its rulers directly descended from the sultans of Malacca was assassinated.

The pattern of a triangular contest to control the trade of the Straits of Malacca was repeated during the 18th century, but the players were newcomers – the Bugis, traditional seafarers and mercenary warriors from Celebes; the Minangkabau, based on the Sumatran state of Siak; and the Dutch themselves in Malacca.

By the 1780s the Dutch had come out on top, but by this time Bugis "underkings" were in effective control of the Johor sultanate and had established an independent sultanate of their own in Selangor. The Minangkabau settlers in the hinterland of Malacca had also established an independent state in the form of a federation called Negeri Sembilan (The Nine States). Of the rest of the peninsular states, Perak, Terengganu and Pahang still owed allegiance to the sultans of Johor but in practice ran their own affairs. In the north, Kelantan and Kedah had fallen within the orbit of the Siamese.

Such was the state of affairs when the British appeared on the scene in the form of Francis Light and founded a settlement on Penang Island in 1786.

Borneo under the Bruneians

Meanwhile, by the 13th century, a kingdom called Po'ni in northwestern Borneo was in control of much of the island. One theory is that the kingdom was established by a royal family from the kingdom of Funan. A hundred years later, Po'ni's powers had declined, but it was then that the Bruneian empire took seed when a local king converted to Islam.

Two centuries later, Brunei had conquered almost all of Borneo as well as parts of the Philippines. It was also a thriving centre of trade connecting China, Malacca and India. As with the earlier Sivijaya and Malacca kingdoms, the Brunei Sultan had at his call an army of pirates who were loyal to him, in his case, seafarers who were servicing the South China Sea and the coastal areas of Borneo. While Sabah came completely under the control of the sultan, Sarawak was a province that was loosely governed.

The Bruneian empire started ceding territories in 1658, when north and east Sabah was given to the Sulu sultanate as compensation for help in settling the Brunei Civil War. Nonetheless, peace did not last, and more wars, piracy and Spanish colonisation of the Philippine territories followed until the British arrived in the 19th century.

salan
LA DI
SALAN

SIAM

Cornaui
Along
Clai
Pulo Cara
GOLFO DI SIAM
Pulo Panjag
Pulo Ubi

I. Ligor
Lagor
Bondelon
Wanting
Singor
Cabo Patane
P. Coffin
Iuaro
S.P. Rou
Pinaca

Pendaon
P. Boulon
Keidah
Queda
Vechio
Patane
F. Secco
F. Kalantan
Pulo Ridang

STRETTO DI MALACCA

P. Iado
P. Pisang
Torano
P. Serga
Bazuas
Soengei
Boroas
Salom
Poncian
Bahan
Kedaor
F. Bossot
F. Dongon
Pulo Capes

Lago di Diamanti
delli Olandesi
P. Sambila
Soengri
Pao
F. Palang
Pontigoran
P. Barbala

I. del
Aqua
P. Iara
Peira
Solongor F.
Pulo Pracelar
Tingaran
P. Verella

Gori
Parri
Casang
Brama
Porto Besar
P. Ara
C. Rachardo
MALACCA
Pahang
P. Timon
P. Pisang
P. Laor
P. Tingi

Col. di Loque
Col. di S. Anna
Behaci I.
Utir I.
P. Medang
I. Pedrus
I. Naos
C. Romania

Col. di
Tempesta
Cincel
Boere
Pita
Bancalis
Siasqua
C. Pantou
Strello di Sincaporea
Bintan

Cincon
Batahan
Sickerban
Carimon
Saban
Domines

P. Boby
P. Baton
Camper

Passaman
Acui
Priaman
Catatengg
Padang
Tellekan
Andragiri
Olandesi
Lingen
Gelgote
Sojo
Fratelli
Equina

Manacabo
Saleda
Iamby
Speriamo
Baros
Telombuan
ISOLA BANC

Petten I.
Pietra di Guvin
I. Cocos
I. Willems
Endrapour
Remtapou
Mathovuecho
Lomabira
Bantal
Salear
Palambam

Nasson I.
Mosquiten I.
I. Tartaruga
I. Cocos
3 Monti
Lamang
Cattoin
Ipce
Pencolen

I. Bassa
Fort
Martebourg
Monte Sillebar
Sillebar
met Recif
Sanjon Tiande
Pongon
Pisang I.

ISOLE

Engano I.

James Brooke, the first "White Rajah" of Sarawak.

BRITISH MALAYA

Malaya's location on vital trade routes attracted a powerful Britain eager to control the wealth. Imperialism transformed the local landscape indelibly.

The British first arrived in Southeast Asia in the early 17th century. But finding their trading opportunities stymied by their more powerful Dutch trading rivals, the British had concentrated their efforts on India.

The English East India Company (EIC) had, by parliamentary charter, been granted monopoly rights over all British trade with India and beyond. In the 200 years since its first unsuccessful forays into the region, the EIC had developed a very profitable trade with China, exchanging Bengal opium for Chinese tea. A base along the way would protect the trade and serve as collecting centre for straits produce.

By this time, Malays and indigenous people on both sides of the straits had had centuries of participating in international trade and had put in place effective and profitable systems and networks of collecting produce and distributing it. At the same time, disputes and skirmishes over succession among the rulers

The Francis Light monument in Penang.

The Straits Settlements were the responsibility of the British government in India until 1867; from then on they came under direct control from London.

was a persistent pattern in the region. The victor would often be the one who made the most alliances with powerful local chiefs, as well as the Portuguese, Dutch and Siamese.

However, the 19th century was a period of rapid change, technological advances and Western powers who saw the world as theirs to exploit. The locals were no match for imperialism.

The Straits Settlements

The first step in the formation of Britain's Straits Settlements occurred in 1785 when Sultan Abdullah of Kedah allowed the EIC to establish a base on the island of Penang. The sultan saw this as his chance to obtain protection against Siam, his northern enemy, and was prepared to grant trading rights to the British in exchange.

Captain Francis Light, who had negotiated the agreement on behalf of the EIC, landed in Penang in 1786 and raised the Union flag on the sparsely populated, jungle-smothered island. But it soon became obvious that the EIC had no intention of keeping to their part of the deal. The angry sultan assembled his ships to recapture Penang, but Light attacked first and destroyed the fleet. The resulting treaty guaranteed the sultan $6,000 a year in return for Penang. This type of dealing was to recur through the years.

Penang was declared a free port, attracting merchant vessels from all over the east–west trade route. The population grew rapidly and Light followed the Malay and Dutch practice of appointing several *kapitan* – local community leaders. Penang prospered, but proved a little too far up the Straits of Melaka to be a focal point of regional trade.

The second of the British settlements in the straits was Singapore, occupied when the EIC's representative, Stamford Raffles, founded a trading post there in 1819. As with Light, he took advantage of a succession dispute to the Johor throne, supporting the claim of Tengku Hussain against his rival in Riau who was actually in power but was unwilling to recognise the British. The British gained full possession of Singapore by treaty between the parties in 1824 and Singapore became a regional bastion of free trade.

The last of the three British settlements in the straits was Melaka itself. In 1824, under the terms of the Anglo-Dutch Treaty of that year, which settled conflicting British and Dutch interests

George Town, Penang, c.1876.

COMPETING COLONIALISTS

Besides the Siamese, the British constantly had to fight off interest in the peninsula and Borneo from competing colonial powers. These included the Dutch in the Dutch East Indies (now Indonesia) and southwest Borneo; the French on Cochinchina (southern Vietnam) and Cambodia; the Spanish on the Philippines and north Borneo; and the Germans on the Pacific. In 1824, the seminal Anglo-Dutch Treaty divided the Malay world into two: the Malay Peninsula came under Britain, and the Dutch East Indies the Netherlands. A later agreement in 1891 between the two powers settled border disputes in Borneo.

in the region, the British acquired Melaka in exchange for their Sumatran settlement of Bencoolen (southwest Sumatra).

In 1826 Penang, Singapore and Melaka came together under one administration based in Singapore, and given the collective name of the Straits Settlements. With its free port status and strategic position, Singapore became the new emporium and, after the opening of the Suez Canal in 1869, became one of the greatest ports in the world.

Intervention in other states

Strictly speaking, the British were concerned only with trade and had an official policy of non-intervention in other affairs. But there were murmurs of dissatisfaction from the merchants

Debt slavery – mortgaging yourself to your creditors in return for financial help – was common practice in 19th-century Malaya. In bad times, it was the only way a peasant could raise finances.

of the Straits Settlements. The Malay Peninsula had always been rich in tin, its ore mined and traded for centuries. In the mid-19th century, with the rise of the canning industry, demand for the metal shot up. Straits Settlement mer-

also threatened to overflow into the Straits Settlements. Moreover, British officials feared that if they did not intervene in these states, investors would seek assistance from a rival imperialist power, such as France or Germany.

In 1874, the British signed the Pangkor Engagement with Raja Abdullah, the new sultan of Perak, which settled a dispute over the throne of Perak and imposed a British "resident" on the new sultan whose advice had to "be asked and acted upon on all questions other than those touching Malay religion and custom". A similar agreement was soon made with Selangor, and

British officials pose for the camera.

chants with money invested in the new mines of Selangor, Perak and Negeri Sembilan now campaigned for British intervention in these states to safeguard their interests.

For the tin rush brought with it widespread unrest. Malay chiefs blessed with rich tin deposits in their domains became rich and powerful magnates whom the sultans could no longer control. Conflicting ambitions led to disputes and civil war. Chinese from southern China flocked to the peninsula to work the mines, encouraged by the British. They, too, were divided among rival secret societies that constantly fought.

These uncertainties threatened investments and caused a drop in tin exports just as world demand began to exceed supply. The troubles

after that, with Sungai Ujong, the largest of the Negeri Sembilan states.

The residential system

The success of the residential system very much depended on how each resident exercised his power.

The first resident in Perak was intolerant and tactless, with little regard for local customs and impatient for change. His proposed reforms of taxation and the banning of debt slavery threatened to undermine the social fabric of the state. The reforms were naturally opposed by the Perak chiefs and by the sultan himself. A year later, the resident was killed.

His eventual successor, Hugh Low, took a

different approach and laid the foundations for the effective working of the residential system. One of his innovations was the setting up of a state council. Its members included the resident, the sultan, major chiefs and one or two Chinese leaders who discussed the government's policies. The council provided a useful sounding board for public opinion, even if the resident was the real policymaker. The format of the Perak State Council was adopted by the other states in the residential system. Low also succeeded in ending debt slavery in Perak, but by gradual means which avoided hardship.

In 1896, Selangor, Perak, Negeri Sembilan and Pahang were brought together as the Federated Malay states (FMS), with its capital at Kuala Lumpur. A British resident-general was appointed with jurisdiction over the four states. The purpose of this move was to ensure uniformity in administration, promote faster economic development, and to help the richer members assist the poorer ones, especially Pahang.

The rulers agreed to the federation thinking that they would exercise more control over the residents and regain their lost authority. Unfortunately, this did not happen. Instead, the resident-

Hugh Low, who laid the foundations of the Residential System.

Sultan Abdullah of Perak.

The Federated Malay states

In Selangor, things went a little more smoothly. Likewise, in Sungai Ujong, where the progress brought about by the residential system led to the formation of the Negeri Sembilan Federation in 1895.

Meanwhile, exaggerated reports of great mineral wealth in Pahang awakened British interest in the state. In 1887, Pahang's ruler, Sultan Ahmad, was forced to accept a British resident. But the Pahang chiefs resented the new regime because of their loss of power and income. In 1891, a number of them rebelled against the British presence, led by Dato' Bahaman of Semantan (Temerloh). Though the British were far too strong to be defeated, the rebellion took four years to quell.

general now exercised real power, which he used without reference to the residents or the rulers. In effect, "federation" centralised power in the hands of British officials.

The Unfederated Malay states

Meanwhile, Kelantan, Terengganu, Kedah and Perlis in the north of the Malay Peninsula recognised the general overlordship of Siam. However, Thai power over these states was vague and fluctuating. In 1909, the British made a treaty with Siam so that these states now became British protectorates under British advisers with similar status to the British residents in the FMS.

This change was made without consulting the Malay rulers concerned, which caused a lot of resentment, as these states had run their own affairs quite satisfactorily. In Kedah, a treaty defining the role of the British adviser was not signed until 1923 because of the hard bargaining to win Malay acceptance of the British presence. In Kelantan (1916) and Trengganu (1928), there were popular anti-British uprisings which were put down by force. Finally, in the south, Johor – the most progressive of all the Malay states – was pressured into accepting a British adviser in 1914. British control was complete, and the Malay Peninsula was divided into three separate parts – the Straits Settlements, Federated Malay States (FMS) and the Unfederated Malay States.

The Malay Peninsula had just undergone rapid change. Meanwhile, the Borneo states were themselves undergoing developments.

Sarawak's white rajah period

In 1839, Sarawak was a province of Brunei confined to the area around Kuching. However, Brunei's power was already in decline and real authority lay in the hands of Malay and Arab chiefs who controlled river trade, and Iban chiefs who were constantly warring with each other. The Raja Muda of Brunei, who was in charge, was struggling with all this when an Indian-born Englishman working for the EIC, James Brooke, arrived in Kuching to deliver a message from the Singapore governor. On returning a year later, Brooke decided to help the Raja Muda. The rebellion was crushed and Brooke induced the Brunei Sultan to award him control of the province. In 1841, Brooke, aged 38, was installed as rajah of Sarawak, a "white rajah" rule that was to last a century.

With the help of local chiefs, Brooke set out to establish law and order. This meant overcoming resistance from Iban and Malay chiefs using a combination of British firepower – comprising warships and forts – and diplomacy, through the use of existing laws and incorporating the local chiefs in government, who remained authorities in their own regions. In this way, more territories were brought under Sarawak's control, at the same time that Brunei ceded land for payments.

Brooke was always short of money, but he refused to allow in the Straits Settlements merchants; he was concerned about maintaining the indigenous way of life, as well as his own authority. Nonetheless, the economy was linked to and sustained by that of British Malaya in the peninsula. In 1857, a Chinese revolt nearly overthrew

Brooke, but it was quickly suppressed. In 1863, Britain officially recognised Brooke's independence from Brunei.

Brooke's nephew, Charles Brooke, became the second rajah. A better administrator than his uncle, he brought Sarawak out of debt, reduced headhunting, expanded trade and brought greater prosperity. He also expanded into Bruneian territory, not always through scrupulous means.

The North Borneo Company

Meanwhile, by the late 19th century, North Borneo (present-day Sabah) was becoming important

Frank Swettenham, the resident of Selangor.

for trade between China and Australia. In 1877, North Borneo was acquired from the sultans of Brunei and Sulu by Overbeck, the Austrian consul-general in Hong Kong, Alfred and Edward Dent, prominent Hong Kong businessmen, and William Treacher, acting governor of Labuan.

In 1881, Overbeck was bought out by the Dents who formed the British North Borneo Company under a royal charter and Treacher became North Borneo's first governor. In 1888, the Brookes, the Company and Brunei were granted protectorate status by Britain for security against outside attack.

The North Borneo Company, like the Brookes in Sarawak, faced considerable opposition to the imposition of its rule. The most serious resistance came from Mat Salleh, a Sulu chief, who rose up in revolt in 1895. The introduction of new taxes had created general discontent, and Mat Salleh gathered many supporters. In 1900, Mat Salleh was killed, but the rebellion was not quelled until five years later.

In competition with Charles Brook, the company started acquiring territory until in 1901 it included most of what is today's Sabah. However, it was not jungle produce, but timber, tobacco and later, rubber, that set its economy on a firm footing.

demand for Malayan tin on the world market. By 1904, the peninsula was producing more than half the world's tin supply.

Besides the political repercussions on the Malay States, this also led to a huge influx of Chinese immigrants. Most came as indentured labour, and those who survived the tough work conditions thrived, using the cooperative *kongsi* concept for business organisation and having access to credit. Virtually all were members of secret societies, representing different clans, and these clans fought among themselves as well as getting involved as allies in the civil wars among

Sarawak's Ibans with their perahu, or small boats, were no match for the British warships.

Other than the elimination of headhunting, most of the region did not benefit from British presence. North Borneo's hugely diverse and divided ethnic groups were not consulted in governance and therefore did not support the colonial government.

Tin, rubber and migrants

Throughout the colonial period, tin and rubber were the main exports. It was these that engendered the development and great social changes in the region.

Tin rose in importance in the mid-19th century because of the invention of the tin can, the rise of the canning industry and other new uses for tin plate. This created an ever-increasing

Malay rulers. However, as the British took control of the Chinese, the societies eventually gave way to peaceful mutual aid associations.

Meanwhile, the rubber tree arrived in Malaya as a foreign plant but grew to become the mainstay of its economy. Rubber seeds were transported from Brazil to London's Kew Gardens for experimentation as an Asian crop in the 1870s. Some of the seeds were sent to Malaya, where they were planted in Singapore and elsewhere. The millions of rubber trees in Malaysia today all stem from these original seedlings.

The birth of the motor-car industry and the consequent demand for rubber tyres triggered the rush to farm the plant. Many fortunes were made in the great rubber boom which followed.

And while the industry went through gluts and slumps, it remained the mainstay of the Malaysian economy right up to the 1970s. Due to a decrease in Chinese migration because of the fall in tin prices, large numbers of Indian indentured labour were brought in to work the rubber estates. Mostly Tamils ethnically, they were brought in based on the experience of European planters who had previously worked in South India. The British government also found this labour supply useful for public works and construction and infrastructure development. The plantation workers, in particular, worked in appalling conditions,

> "The White Man's Burden" was a poem by Rudyard Kipling that justified imperialism, exhorting white men to colonise and rule other nations for the benefit of the "new-caught, sullen peoples, half devil and half child".

segregated from the rest of society and with no opportunities outside the sector.

Revenue from tin and rubber was used to build up the country's infrastructure and social amenities. Attention was focused on the tin mines and rubber estates at the expense of the less profitable areas. Development and social change were noticeably slower in Sabah and Sarawak, although rubber was still very important to both their economies. As the tin and rubber industries boomed, Malaysia's plural society developed.

The impact of British rule

British rule changed the local landscape in fundamental ways. Administration started to become centralised, new centres of power came into being and technology and systems were set up. The cooperation of the Malay ruling elite was vital to the success of colonial rule, and so Britain richly rewarded the sultans and protected them from succession challenges, while large numbers of the nobility were incorporated into the bureaucracy.

A huge task for the British was managing labour, particularly the mix of locals and the large numbers of new migrants. Social reconstruction became key.

The colonialists subscribed to the Victorian racial ideology whereby Europeans sorted themselves and others into groups based on physical appearance and attributed "natural"

characteristics to these groups. Groups were categorised and assigned roles. Therefore, despite their vastly different backgrounds, origins and belief systems, the British clumsily classified migrant Javanese, Minangkabau, Achehnese and some indigenous *orang asli* with Malays; workers from different dialect groups, rivalling clans and provinces in China as Chinese; and Tamils, Ceylonese, and other minorities from the subcontinent, as Indians.

Along with this categorising was the establishing of racialised economics. The British considered all Malays resistant to wage labour and

Tapping latex, the raw material of rubber.

therefore fit only to work their own paddy fields. All Chinese were considered industrious and so were "suitable" for mines and shops. Indians were adjudged drunkards and abject, and were hence confined to their role as cheap labour in plantations. The groups were governed accordingly and separately by Europeans, the "superior race", not only to ensure the maximisation of profit but to meet their obligation of "the white man's burden".

In reality, these administrative divisions were challenged by all groups, and some long-standing inter-community trade and other networks and associations persisted. However, as these categories started hardening, they took on a political meaning.

THE MAKING OF MALAYSIA

The Japanese Occupation precipitated the end of the British empire, and decolonisation unfolded in a period of counter-insurgency and massive social upheaval.

Until 1941, British rule in Malaya focused on fine-tuning the environment to maximise profits. Legal, administrative and financial systems were put in place and communications and transport networks established. Tin and rubber continued to be the economic mainstays and in 1924, oil palm, a new crop which, like rubber, was imported, began to be planted on a large scale. In North Borneo, it was timber that started topping exports and Sandakan became one of the world's key timber ports. Likewise in Sarawak, although the Brookes' priority was geared more to preserving the indigenous people's way of life.

Ethnic unbalance

Migrant labour continued to be imported whenever needed, not only from China and India, but the Netherlands Dutch Indies (now Indonesia). Large-scale migration laid the foundation for future issues which included the position of the Malays and other indigenous peoples vis-à-vis that of the Chinese and Indians, who were beginning to regard Malaya as their permanent home.

British policy was to stick to the principle that Malaya was the land of the Malays and that Sabah and Sarawak were also the lands of their indigenous peoples. This was acceptable when there were no pressures. But rising nationalism, the threat of international communism and the impact of the Great Depression of 1929–33 increasingly rocked the balance. The Chinese in Malaya and Borneo were increasingly politicised by mainland China's Communist Party and the Kuomintang but increasingly wanted a political stake in Malaya. They also started "squatting" as seasonal agriculturalists in the rural areas traditionally farmed by Malays.

A Japanese Occupation newspaper reports on Japan's successful invasion, 1943.

Economically, the British made sure business laid in the hands of the Chinese, and as political masters, all ethnic groups answered to them, not to the Malay rulers or chiefs. What's more, by 1931, there were actually more Chinese than Malays in the region.

Malay attitudes started to be radicalised by the need to protect Malay interests. One elite group comprised English-educated civil servants who came from royal families, continuing the tradition of noble leadership. Another consisted of Malay-educated intellectuals, especially teachers and journalists, who came from the peasantry. This latter group was the precursor of the radical left movement and formed the first national political organisation in British Malaya in 1938, the Kesatuan Melayu Muda ("Young Malays Union"), led by the anti-colonial Ibrahim Yaacob. Their goal was to unite all Malays, regardless of origin, and create a Greater Indonesia.

The Japanese Occupation

But what finally ended for ever the supremacy of British rule was the sudden extension of World War II – raging in Europe since 1939 – to Southeast Asia. The writing on the wall was obvious in 1937, when Japan invaded China,

The Japanese-issued currency was referred to as duit pisang (banana money), after the 10-dollar banknotes, which had motifs of banana trees. Hyper-inflation made it almost valueless; the British aided this by producing counterfeited notes.

British warships in the first week of the invasion, and the British were instantly crippled.

The Japanese Occupation caused great hardship among the peoples of Malaya. The Japa-

Japanese leaders surrender their swords in 1945.

committing horrific war crimes. But Chinese resistance was fierce, and the growing Japanese need for strategic raw materials such as oil and rubber made Southeast Asia the target, especially the British and Dutch possessions where these materials abounded but the Japanese were denied them by the Western powers.

In December 1941, Japan launched her attack on Western colonial powers in the region. Within nine weeks, Japanese forces had overrun the whole of Malaya. Among the many reasons advanced for Britain's humiliating failure to defend Malaya – poor strategies, untrained troops, guns pointing in the wrong direction, etc – the most telling was British weakness in the air. Japanese airpower sank two capital

nese arrived with persuasive propaganda about a "Co-prosperity Sphere" and "Asia for Asians". But they ruled with an iron fist to control the resentment of a population suffering from shortages of food and essential goods, high inflation and low incomes.

Japanese brutality

The Japanese were especially brutal towards the Chinese, many of whom were hostile towards them because of strong loyalties to China. Tens of thousands of Chinese in Malaysia were executed or imprisoned. Europeans (except for those whose nationalities were neutral or Japanese allies in the war) ended up living under atrocious conditions in detention camps. Tens of thousands of prisoners of war were sent to work on the notorious "Death Railway" – constructed to provide a rail link between Thailand and Burma. Conditions there were even worse, and many died.

Unsurprisingly, Chinese made up the bulk of the resistance, with the main components of the Malayan Peoples' Anti-Japanese Army (MPAJA) being the Malayan Communist Party (MCP) and radical Malay groups. These guerrillas lived in the jungles and were aided by civilian organisations.

Meanwhile, the Japanese reinforced the ethnic division between the Chinese and Malays. Malays were used in troops that fought the mainly Chinese resistance groups. The Japanese also encouraged Malay nationalism among elites who had already begun organising themselves two decades earlier. In July 1945, the Japanese allowed a political movement to be formed under Ibrahim Yaakob and one of Malay nationalism's greatest ideologues, Dr Burhanuddin Al-Helmy, to work towards independence and political union with Indonesia. However, this barely had time to take root.

Post-war

The Japanese Occupation ended a month after the dropping of atomic bombs on the Japanese cities of Hiroshima and Nagasaki. British and Australian forces landed in Malaya and Borneo – in fact the liberation of Borneo had already begun – and re-established British authority.

In the chaotic period before full order was established, however, the MPAJA retaliated on Japanese "collaborators", a retribution that took on ethnic tones because the former were mostly Chinese and the latter, mostly Malays. The result heightened Malay nationalism. But nationalism across all groups had grown because, even though the Japanese did not fulfil their plans for an Asia for Asians, the period of "white supremacy" was psychologically over.

The war in Europe had bankrupted Britain, and the British needed to focus on rebuilding their own country; Britain had moreover signed the Atlantic Charter restoring self-government to all nations. First though, the British wanted to make sure they created a viable nation-state. The first step was to form the different constituents of the Malay Peninsula, minus Singapore, into a single state to be called the Malayan Union. The union would have a central government headed by a (British) governor and

the rulers of the former Malay States simply remaining as heads of Islam.

At the same time, to punish the Malays for their perceived support of the Japanese, Malays were no longer to be privileged above others; instead, a common citizenship was to be created, including long-term Chinese and Indian residents as well as the Malays. In short, Malay sovereignty was to be transferred to the British Crown, turning Malaya into a colony and destroying Malay political pre-eminence. After considerable pressure, all the Malay rulers accepted the scheme.

A communist caricature.

BRITISH BORNEO

Sarawak and North Borneo became crown colonies in 1946. The cost of post-war reconstruction was beyond the resources of the Brooke government and the British North Borneo Company. The change was accepted without protest in North Borneo, but in Sarawak there was serious opposition, particularly from the Malays who feared they would lose their privileged position without the Brookes. The climax of this opposition came in 1949 when the new British governor was assassinated in Sibu. This action was too extreme for most Malays, and the movement gradually lost momentum and faded away.

Federation of Malaya

However, this proposal was strongly opposed by everyone; the Malays, in particular, felt that they were being sold down the river. In March 1946, representatives of 41 Malay associations met in Kuala Lumpur to form a national movement to oppose it. This led to the birth of the United Malay National Organisation (UMNO), an elite organisation led by Dato' Onn Jaafar, the Chief Minister of Johor. UMNO demanded the repeal of the union and drummed up so much opposition that two years later, the Union was replaced by the Federation of

A British jungle patrol to flush out communists.

Malaya, which preserved the sovereignty of the rulers and restored the rights of states. Citizenship terms for other communities were also more restricted.

Ironically, despite stating that they were fostering political action among the different ethnic groups, the British opted to side with the conservative UMNO rather than the multiethnic left movement that had opposed the Malayan Union. The movement was led by the All-Malaya Council of Joint Action, a coalition of political and civic groups, and PUTERA, comprising Malay left-wing parties.

The movement attempted to elevate Malayan party politics above rival racial interests and had developed the more inclusive People's

> The grimness of the 1950s was brightened by the dramas and comedies of P. Ramlee, filmmaker and composer, who depicted the Malay everyman in those challenging times. He drew from the cinematic traditions of India, Hollywood, Hong Kong and Japan.

Constitution in opposition to the conservative Federation Constitution, which the British had secretly developed with UMNO and the rulers post-Malayan Union. The movement also organised a successful nationwide *hartal* (strike) in 1947, which crippled the country for one day. The Federation Constitution was passed nonetheless.

Social unrest

After the war, the British started colonising the hitherto lawless hinterlands of the mines and plantations, for food production. This was badly administered, however, causing widespread unrest and discontent among all communities in the rural areas. Chinese triads and guerrillas acted as protectors and terrorists among Chinese settlers and the radical Malay left started tapping the unease and disaffection in Malay *kampung* because of weak leadership.

Meanwhile, their role during the Japanese Occupation fuelled the aim of the Malayan Communist Party (MCP) to expel the British and set up a communist republic in Malaya once the war was over. The MCP adopted a moderate stance and consolidated organisation and unity through the trade union movement, which comprised Chinese and Indians. A series of strikes among dockworkers, tin miners and rubber plantation labourers demanding better living conditions alarmed the colonial authorities, and laws were passed to bring the trade unions under stricter control.

However, the rural unrest also started affecting the MCP's hold on unions at the same time that it was undergoing internal strife. In 1948 the MCP abandoned its non-violent strategy in favour of armed insurrection. Under its new leader, Chin Peng, the MCP was reorganised and all its activities moved underground. After a spate of attacks on European miners and planters, the government proclaimed a national state of emergency in June that year.

The Emergency

"The Emergency" became the official name for the communist insurrection which lasted 12 years. The Emergency was also used to squash violently the multi-ethnic left movement: thousands were arrested or banished and organisations banned. From their secret jungle bases, the communists caused widespread terror. But they also had a lot of support in terms of food, intelligence and recruits from the rural Chinese squatters, not always through the use of fear. This made clamping down on guerrilla activity difficult, along with the lack of coordination between the various security forces.

However, the tide began to turn with the appointment of General Sir Harold Briggs as Director of Operations in 1949. Briggs, a veteran of the World War II Burma campaign against the Japanese, set up war executive committees which coordinated military and civil operations, and created 500 protected new villages to re-house rural squatters in less remote areas. As anticipated, the insurgents attacked the new settlements, but the security forces, now fighting on their own ground, were too strong for them. These forces were soon able to concentrate on jungle operations to destroy the communists and their camps.

In 1953, areas from which the communists had been eliminated were declared "white areas". Food restrictions and curfews in them were relaxed, inducing fuller local cooperation with the government. A year later, a large number of the communist guerrillas had been eliminated. Many more surrendered later, and the few remaining guerrillas retreated deep into the jungle. The state of emergency officially ended on 31 July 1960.

Independence

A condition that the British set for independence was the putting into place of multi-racial politics. Counter-insurgency was used to create unity among ethnic groups through a common cause of fighting communism. Platforms were built for inter-community bargaining, particularly over citizenship and the position of Malay rulers.

By this time, UMNO had a new leader, Tunku Abdul Rahman, a Kedah prince who had read law at the University of Cambridge. The Malayan Chinese Association (MCA) had been formed by business elites in urban areas

trying to regain authority in the hinterlands, which they had lost after the Japanese occupation. The Malayan Indian Congress (MIC) had emerged as a political voice for the Indian community, although in reality it had no support from the lower-class labourers.

Nonetheless, the British agreed to elections for the Federal Legislative Council for the first time in 1955 when the three communal parties formed a political coalition called the Alliance. When the Alliance won 80 percent of the votes cast, Tunku Abdul Rahman became Malaya's first chief minister.

Tunku Abdul Rahman gives the Merdeka salute, declaring Independence in 1957.

The 1957 independence or merdeka celebrations were held in a purpose-built KL stadium. Stadium Merdeka symbolised humility, by being built into the ground, equality by being circular and unity as a common venue for Malaysians to gather.

A commission of Commonwealth legal experts was appointed to draw up a constitution. The draft document, based on a memorandum submitted by the Alliance, was flawed but finally accepted by the Malay rulers, and the British and Malayan governments.

Malaya became a constitutional monarchy, with the king selected from among the nine Malay rulers every five years. Parliament consisted of a fully elected lower house and a senate of nominated members. Executive power lay mainly in the hands of the lower house. Each state had its own fully elected state assembly. Malaya became an independent state at midnight on 30 August 1957.

The formation of Malaysia

Nonetheless, the Cold War was still ongoing. To keep communism at bay, and for economic

Tun Razak (with cane) succeeded Tengku Abdul Rahman as PM.

purposes, in 1961, Tunku proposed the formation of Malaysia, a wider federation which would include the then left-leaning and mostly Chinese Singapore. To ensure the Malay ethnic balance would be maintained, he also proposed the inclusion of North Borneo, Sarawak and Brunei, coining the term *bumiputra*, literally, sons of the soil, to cover Malays and indigenous people.

In Singapore, opinion was sharply divided over the merits of the plan; Brunei decided in the end to stay away. A commission of Malayan and British members investigated the reaction of the inhabitants of Sabah and Sarawak and found that the majority of people

there were in favour of the plan. Therefore, the British and Malayan governments set 31 August 1963 as the date on which Malaysia would be established.

But Indonesia condemned the whole scheme as a neo-colonialist plot, and in January 1963 announced a policy of "Confrontation" against Malaysia. Meanwhile, the Philippines also opposed the creation of Malaysia, claiming that North Borneo belonged to them. Confrontation took the form of armed Indonesian incursions across the borders of Sarawak and North Borneo. Indonesia and the Philippines both repudiated a United Nations survey which confirmed that the Borneo territories wanted to be a part of Malaysia.

Territorial disputes

When the Federation of Malaysia was officially inaugurated on 16 September 1963, Indonesia and the Philippines severed diplomatic ties with Malaysia; Indonesia intensified its attacks along the borders of Sarawak and North Borneo (now renamed Sabah) and Indonesian troops made landings in Peninsular Malaysia to carry out acts of sabotage. But they were quickly foiled by the security forces.

In 1966, Sukarno was ousted from power and the new Indonesian regime wanted to end confrontation – negotiations settled the conflict. The Philippines also dropped its claim on Sabah and recognised Malaysia.

Meanwhile, political differences had surfaced between Malaysia and Singapore. On 9 August 1965, Singapore left the Federation and became an independent state.

When Malaysia was formed, its population stood at 10.4 million – Malays forming 47 percent, Chinese 34 percent, Indians 9 percent, Dayaks 4 percent, Kadazans 2 percent, other indigenous groups 3 percent and foreign immigrants 2 percent. Turning this medley of peoples into one nation was not an easy feat. UMNO decided that the basis for a Malaysian identity would be the Malay language and culture. Other ethnic groups wanted an identity that was multilingual and multi-ethnic. Language and education became lightning rods for discontent.

The May 13 incident

The tension erupted in 1969 when the Alliance lost many seats to largely Chinese-based opposition parties, including the Democratic Action

Party (DAP). Motivated by political firebrands, civil unrest broke out on 13th May between the Malays and Chinese. Although it was confined mainly to the capital, Kuala Lumpur, and quelled in four days, the "May 13 incident" represented a watershed in Malaysian politics.

Emergency was declared again; all administration came under a civilian-military committee which suspended the constitution for 21 months, legislated the Sedition Act making it illegal to debate on the rights of Malays, the Sultans and Islam; and established a Department of National Unity to formulate a national ideology and social programmes. The controversial New Economic Policy (NEP) was put into place to address economic inequality and to eradicate poverty by growing the economic pie. A key element of the policy was affirmative action rights for *bumiputra*.

Tunku Abdul Rahman was forced to resign, and his successor, Tun Abdul Razak, consolidated political power by reorganising the Alliance into the Barisan Nasional (BN) or National Front in 1973, incorporating every political party, except the DAP and some smaller parties. In the next year's general elections, the BN won a landslide majority, and again in 1978.

Economic policy

The NEP aimed to address unequal distribution of wealth among the ethnic groups. At independence, although the nation's new constitution had given the Malays considerable political power, their participation in the country's trade and commerce was minimal, weighing in, for example, at only 2 percent of corporate equity. The Chinese, on the other hand, practically ran the economy, holding prominent positions as bankers, brokers and businessmen.

The NEP involved setting up corporations and share-ownership schemes to elicit greater Malay participation in the economy. Racial quotas, scholarships and subsidies were introduced to raise the Malay stake in the economy to 30 percent in 20 years. However, the plan was to achieve this by increasing the size of the pie, and not at the expense of the non-Malays. Therefore, everybody would benefit.

The NEP was inevitably deemed unfair by many critics, particularly the non-Malays, who felt that the Malays already had too many privileges and that "positive" discrimination on the basis of race and not merit would seriously undermine the economic, political and cultural position of non-Malays.

Economic transformation

However, the 1970s were boom-time for Malaysia economically and there was seemingly enough for everyone. When the country became independent in 1957, the economy was almost completely dependent on exports of commodities, whose prices fluctuated tremendously. In the early 1970s, the government launched an ambitious crusade to transform Malaysia from its agro-mining foundation to

An elderly Chinese woman comforts children in a refugee centre after the "May 13 incident".

a mixed economy with a strong manufacturing sector. By the end of the decade, substantial progress had been made. Light industries had been formed and were now saturating the local market. The country was poised to make an industrial leap to becoming an exporter of manufactured goods and in concentrating on heavier industry. The 1970s also witnessed the harvesting of newly found offshore oil and natural gas reserves in the South China Sea, giving a spectacular boost to the economy.

Still to come, though, were the 'Tiger economy' years, a period that began in the late 1980s during the leadership of prime minister Tun Dr Mahathir Mohamad.

Malaysian Prime Minister Najib
Razak.

CONTEMPORARY MALAYSIA

Following 30 years of major economic development, Malaysia is prosperous and forward-looking, although recent years have brought a fair amount of political tumult.

The appointment of Tun Dr Mahathir Mohamad as Malaysia's fourth prime minister in 1981 marked the start of a new era in the nation's politics. It was an era that lasted over two decades until his retirement in 2003 – one of the longest terms of political leadership in Southeast Asia.

The Mahathir era marked a break with the past. Unlike his three predecessors, Mahathir was not only a commoner, but also the first Malaysian prime minister to have received all of his education locally and not in Britain. He was also much younger on taking office, a member of the post-World War II generation of students who fought for independence from the British.

Right from the start, Mahathir was a stormy petrel in UMNO politics. He was expelled from the party in 1969 for criticising what he saw as then Prime Minister Tunku Abdul Rahman's failure to protect Malay political interests. As soon as he took office in 1981 Mahathir prioritised shaking the Malaysian, and more particularly the Malay, mindset out of its colonial

Students graduating from Universiti Teknologi MARA (UiTM) in Selangor.

> The zeitgeist of the anything-is-possible Mahathir era was the catchphrase Malaysia Boleh! (Malaysia can do it!). Record breaking was key, and ranged from the world's tallest building to Malaysia's longest satay.

mould, to make Malaysians more self-reliant and to raise their self-esteem. He also wanted to establish Malaysia as a power to be reckoned with.

Looking east

To achieve these aims Mahathir resorted to shock tactics. One of them was to jolt Malaysians out of their reverential attitude towards all things Western, and particularly British. In 1982 came his "Buy British Last" campaign. This was in retaliation for several moves by the British government that disadvantaged Malaysia in commercial and educational arenas. He also urged Malaysians to adopt a "Look East" policy, and singled out Japan as a role model of hard work and efficiency that Malaysia should emulate.

Mahathir also commissioned numerous civil engineering projects, building highways, airports, skyscrapers and an entire new administrative centre. These high-profile schemes also served collectively to demonstrate Malaysian ability in the spirit of *Malaysia Boleh!* (Malaysia can do it!).

In the same vein, he encouraged Malaysians to make their mark in the world arena by going for world-class exploits. By the turn of the 21st century, Malaysians had climbed Mount Everest, taken part in international safaris and even sailed solo around the world, charting a new course on the way. The successful hosting of the Commonwealth Games in Kuala Lumpur in 1998, the first Asian country to do so, seems to have marked the apogee of Mahathir's efforts to put Malaysia on the international map.

The Opening Ceremony at the Commonwealth Games in 1998.

Mahathir also projected himself as a world leader, a champion of the Third World and a cheerleader for the countries of the undeveloped "South" in their attempts to secure better deals from the wealthy industrialised "North". Mahathir's strident criticism of Western values and policies was good for Malaysian pride throughout his leadership, although critics slammed some of it as anti-Semitic and racist.

Mahathiresque economics

Nevertheless, the most important of Mahathir's initiatives lay in economic policy and affairs. After riding out the global recession in the early 1980s that had hit commodity exports, the Barisan Nasional (BN) ruling coalition decided to increase spending on infrastructure and heavy industries through foreign borrowing. Public enterprises were privatised to divest expenditure – 150 in total, including power and water utilities, telecommunications companies and the national airline.

At the same time, closer collaboration between the public and private sectors was forged to accelerate industrial development, and the financial sector was modernised. This whole enterprise had its catchy slogan, "Malaysia Inc." – ie the entire nation as a commercial enterprise involving everybody.

Exports recovered in the mid-1980s, and Malaysia started enjoying the beginning of the decade-long tiger economy years, when foreign capital poured in, business boomed, unemployment fell, the property market expanded and the stock market soared. Migrant labour poured into the country from the surrounding region.

By the early 1990s, locally manufactured products had become the country's largest export earner. Malaysia had also become one of the fastest-growing economies in Asia, with one of the highest GDPs in the region. Providence also played its part, not least the discovery of substantial natural gas and oil reserves off Malaysian shores.

A benevolent dictator?

Malaysia's tiger economy progress found philosophic expression in Vision 2020 (*Wawasan 2020*), a statement setting out the targets that the nation should achieve by 2020. Though primarily economic – ie to reach developed nation status by that year – the "vision" also included creating a common and unified "*bangsa* Malaysia" (*bangsa* being Malay for "race"); this identity was to replace the various communal identities – Chinese, Indian, Malay and so on.

However, these plans were placed in serious jeopardy by the Asian financial crisis of 1997. Over the next 18 months, the stock market index fell by 80 percent, precipitating a political crisis on top of economic problems.

The political crisis centred on the sudden dismissal in 1998 of Mahathir's successor, Anwar Ibrahim, and his subsequent arrest, trial and imprisonment on charges of corruption and homosexuality. The vicious manner in which this was carried out on the deputy prime minister and the perceived unfairness of the court proceedings evoked *Reformasi* (Reformation), a protest movement on a scale not witnessed since independence. More than anything else, these events put in high relief the most prominent political trend manifest during the Mahathir era – the steady growth of authoritarian government.

Mahathir's long tenure was due to his shrewd politics, but a deep-rooted desire for security and stability and a fear of communal unrest

and qualifications. The prerogatives of the monarchy were reduced and the legislature robbed of much of its authority. In 1987, the Emergency era Internal Security Act was used to arrest over 100 opposition leaders and social activists in "Operation Lalang" (Weeding Operation). Following this came the muzzling of the media through legal instruments.

After this, Mahathir was challenged in his leadership for the first time in 12 years and UMNO was divided. Mahathir won, but his opponents went to court claiming fraud. Although he won there too, a year later he

A crowd watches PM Abdullah Ahmad Badawi delivering his opening speech at the general assembly of the ruling UMNO in Kuala Lumpur, 23 September 2004.

and disorder formed the glue binding many Malaysians to the BN. The good times during the tiger economy period also boosted Malaysians' support for the coalition. Still, election time was always tainted by allegations of electoral fraud, including gerrymandering, vote-buying and the use of government resources in electioneering. Nonetheless, the BN romped home in every general election with a two-thirds majority mandate that enabled them to change the constitution at will.

As a result, during the Mahathir era, the constitution was amended almost beyond recognition; the fundamental rights which it originally enshrined strangled by various escape clauses

prompted another constitutional crisis, which subordinated the judiciary to the executive.

Meanwhile, the Malaysia Inc. concept had turned the system of *bumiputra* patronage to one of cronyism; the biggest benefactors of the New Economic Policy (NEP) became politically connected Malays, the so-called *Umnoputra*.

Against this background and with the Asian financial crisis ending the decade-long run of good times, the Anwar affair provided the impetus for political change. Anwar set up his own political party, Parti Keadilan Rakyat (Justice Party) and formed a loose coalition with political opposition stalwarts the Democratic Action Party (DAP) and the Islamist Parti

Islam Se-Malaysia (PAS) to challenge the ruling party in 1999.

Although one more state came under the opposition – Terengganu, which was won by PAS – and the BN lost half of the Malay vote, the opposition fared badly as the BN continued to be supported by the non-Malay voters.

"Political tsunami"

A year later, the economy had recovered and Mahathir made a shock announcement that he would retire, naming his deputy Tun Abdullah Haji Ahmad Badawi as successor.

Pakatan Rakyat supporters march in 2008.

The people responded to the hope promised by a new leadership, particularly Abdullah's moderate and consensus-seeking style, by voting overwhelmingly for the BN in the 2004 elections.

However, Abdullah failed to stem the tide of systemic corruption and abuse of power. Religion became a lightning rod, with the mishandling of high-profile religious conversion cases and the destruction of Hindu temples. Two street demonstrations drew unexpectedly large support, respectively by Indian rights group Hindraf, demonstrating over the plight of Indians, and non-governmental organisation coalition Bersih, asking for electoral reform. These were seminal in voicing

> *"ABU", or "Anything but UMNO/BN", summed up the 2008 elections, when a disillusioned electorate voted for other parties regardless of candidate. The campaign was popularised by activist Hishamuddin Rais; "ABU" appeared as graffiti everywhere.*

out and fanning dissatisfaction, particularly when the government responded brutally to the demonstrations.

The arrogance of a BN that had lost touch with the popular sentiment of anger and frustration was punished severely in the 8 March 2008 general elections, an event known as the "political tsunami". Although the BN won government, the shocking losses included veteran big-ticket names, five states, including the economic powerhouse of Selangor, and half the popular vote. For the first time since 1969, the BN was denied the two-thirds parliamentary majority allowing them to amend the Malaysian constitution at will.

Even more cataclysmic was the continued loss of the traditionally secure Malay support, now no longer merely a pro-Anwar protest, but one against the BN abuse of the NEP in favouring the *Umnoputra*.

The March 2008 elections also marked the return of Anwar Ibrahim, who although barred from running for elections because of his previous conviction, kept the broad opposition pact going. A month later, the opposition factions formalised their alliance by calling themselves the Pakatan Rakyat.

THE PAKATAN RAKYAT

The two component parties of the Pakatan Rakyat, along with Anwar's Parti Keadilan Rakyat, are old political hands. PAS had its beginnings in 1947 in anti-colonial action; its founding principle is the formation of an Islamist state. However, it has relinquished this goal within the Pakatan and the party is now led by moderates. The DAP is an offshoot of a Singapore political party and has a Chinese core constituency although its aims are social democracy regardless of ethnicity. Their last big win was in the 1969 elections, which were followed by the May 13 incident. It is presently trying to woo more non-Chinese members.

Post-2008

The immediate effects of the political tsunami of the 2008 elections were manifold. One was the realisation that the electorate had the power to change government after 50 years of BN rule. The spectre of May 13 was laid to rest to some degree when the handover of power was peaceful despite threats of violence from various quarters. This marked the beginning of a period of transition.

The BN launched a multi-million ringgit propaganda campaign called "1 Malaysia" to convince Malaysians that unity was a priority for the government. Far more pervasive than previous campaigns, it featured in state programmes, policies and organisations, while a theme song and a salute was even devised. Nevertheless, the BN continued to align strategies along communal lines, sending out contradictory messages. To appeal to non-Malay voters, funds were funnelled to the sensitive areas of education and temples. Carefully worded promises were made to re-examine the New Economic Policy (NEP).

Yet concurrently, to win back the Malay vote, the vitriol on race was ratcheted up to "remind" the Malay electorate of their supremacy (*ketuanan Melayu*) and accept that UMNO, as part of the BN, was the only party that could defend that. Tools used included government media such as the Malay-language daily, *Utusan Malaysia*, and constant pronouncements by the supremacist group Perkasa, formed with the backing of Mahathir.

In recent years, a climate of tension and crisis has been perpetuated as old bogeymen such as communism have been rolled out. Religious issues have become flashpoints, with Malaysian Christians particularly upset by the banning of the use of the word "Allah", Arabic for God, by non-Muslims, which has been a presence in Malay-language Bibles produced in Indonesia since before independence. This move by UMNO has also been part of its competition with PAS to appeal to more conservative Muslims.

In 2008, Anwar Ibrahim was charged again with sodomy. A year later, a political putsch saw the opposition state of Perak back in the

Riot police.

CHANGING TECH

In 1996, the ambitious Multimedia Supercorridor aimed to transform the country into a "knowledge society". While it fell short of its goals, Malaysia's infrastructure, services and communities have been digitised, opening up new possibilities and empowering its citizens.

A 2010 survey found that 41 percent of Malaysians were internet users; about 70 percent used social media and the most active were 20–24-year-olds. Today, the proliferation of online news and blogs circumvents stifling media laws, and was one reason for the 2008 "political tsunami". In the aftermath, politicians took to Twitter with a vengeance. Community mobilisation and grassroots activism have never been more effective.

At the same time, singer-songwriters are reaching stardom through platforms such as YouTube, and the local blogosphere is rife with opinions and images of Malaysians' favourite pastime – eating. The advent of affordable digital video equipment made Malaysia's independent filmmakers the toast of international film festivals in the noughties. These movies continue to cross state-directed boundaries, addressing social and civil conflicts, including the taboo subject of sexuality.

However, the majority of engaged and globalised Malaysians live in cities and the digital divide threatens to widen the socio-economic gap with their rural compatriots.

hands of the BN through defections from the Pakatan.

2013 parliamentary elections

In May 2013, following the dissolution of parliament, Malaysia held general elections. The result was the worst-ever for the ruling BN. Despite winning the popular vote and gaining some seats, the PR coalition led by Anwar Ibrahim failed to win the majority of seats needed to form a federal government. Najib Razak of BN became the Prime Minister once again. While the BN coalition secured

A palm oil plantation.

a simple majority, it failed to regain the two-thirds parliamentary majority it lost for the first time in 2008. Thousands of Malaysian opposition supporters rallied against alleged fraud in the election, defying police who said the protest was illegal. It was the largest street demonstration in Malaysia's history to date.

While support for the ruling coalition from the country's majority ethnic Malays remained solid, the Chinese – who make up a quarter of Malaysians – continued to desert BN, accelerating a trend seen in 2008. Ethnic Chinese had turned to the opposition, attracted by its pledge to tackle corruption and end race-based policies favouring ethnic Malays in business, education and housing.

Economic goals

As the deadline for Vision 2020 approaches, the current administration, headed by BN's Najib Razak since 2009, has put into place an Economic Transformation Programme to improve services in seven focused areas and double per capita income. Using management criteria such as key performance indices, some success has been achieved. *Bumiputra* quotas have also been gingerly lifted from several sectors of the economy.

Malaysia's trade-driven economy is generally in good shape, with China its largest trading partner followed by Singapore and Japan. Globally, Malaysia is the second-largest exporter of palm oil, one of the largest exporters of semiconductor devices and a pioneer and leader in Islamic banking. It has profited from higher energy prices as an exporter of oil and gas, and has 20 companies in the 2013 Forbes 2000 list of the world's biggest public companies. Unemployment remains low, at about 3 percent in 2014 .

Yet Malaysia's ranking in the Transparency International corruption perceptions index has been slipping yearly, with the country landing at number 50 among over 170 countries ranked in 2014. High-level "grand corruption" also remains a major concern, and the police and political parties are considered the most corrupt institutions.

State of the opposition

The results of the governance of opposition-held states have been mixed in the face of governments being formed largely of first-time lawmakers and all states struggling to dismantle entrenched systems and mindsets. Penang has been the most successful economically, and all state governments have attempted to be more transparent in their dealings. Nevertheless, the Pakatan parties have faced some of the same problems as the BN in trying to manage the old patriarchal warhorses, who have not always proved open to different ways of running a political party. Anwar himself has sometimes been perceived as a millstone around the neck of his party.

For 16 years he has dominated Malaysian opposition, and for almost as long he has been fighting the same judicial battle against charges he has always said were politically motivated. He is the first opposition leader to pose a serious challenge to the governing party's hold on power, using his own charisma and negotiating skills to bring three very different parties into

Malaysia Airlines was hit by two tragedies in 2014. Flight 370 went missing in March; 17 months later, debris washed up on Réunion. In July, Flight 17 crashed in eastern Ukraine, likely shot down over the conflict zone there. 537 people are thought to have died overall.

a coalition which managed to win the popular vote, although not a majority of seats.

In March 2015, Malaysia's top court upheld opposition leader Anwar's conviction for sodomy after rejecting his appeal. Anwar must now serve a five-year jail sentence and a five-year ban from office. It will be hard for him to bounce back again, and hard for the opposition Pakatan coalition to hold together without him. But it will be as hard for the government to reverse its flagging popularity after the verdict many Malaysians see as a manoeuvre to remove the man who was seen as its principal threat.

The future

Things have changed for Malaysians as the possibilities of a different sort of people power and multi-ethnic politics have become more evident. Increasing numbers of citizens are becoming politicised and taking to civil disobedience as a way to get their voices heard. The 2011 Bersih 2.0 rally lobbying for clean elections saw unprecedented support from Malaysians, and indeed, the Bersih lobby has become increasingly powerful. It was also active during the 2013 parliamentary elections, alleging some irregularities in the vote.

The immediate goal for the future is to bring in a two-party system that works. Whatever the outcome of future elections, it is a long road towards the dismantling of institutions, habits and attitudes which impede democratisation. Issues will remain, such as reconciling Islam with secularism in a multi-ethnic society. However, Malaysia's near-term economic outlook remains good, despite some risks. The economy has diversified from commodities and the government has managed to broaden their revenue base. Unemployment continues to be low and so does inflation.

Nwar Irahim (centre) with supporters of the "Bersih" (Clean) electoral reform coalition at a rally in Kuala Lumpur.

POLITICS IN BORNEO

Politics in Sabah and Sarawak has always had little relevance to peninsular Malaysia, and vice versa. However, Sabah's and Sarawak's support for the BN in the federal parliament has been vital. Without it, the BN stands to lose its parliamentary majority. As a result, the BN government's policy towards these states' political parties has been highly flexible, subject to their unquestionable loyalty.

Kuala Lumpur has never tolerated any chief minister in either state showing signs of independence. Hence, the ousting of Kalong Ningkan, Sarawak's first chief minister, in 1966; the eclipse of Dato Mustapha Harun, Sabah's first head of state, in 1976; and the downfall of Pairin Kitingan, the chief minister of Sabah, in 1992.

In Sarawak, the ruling coalition – led by the Parti Pesaka Bumiputera Bersatu Sarawak (PBB) – has been in power for over a quarter of a century. Its staunch loyalty meant that the BN has had no need to establish a presence in the state.

However, the strong opposition to federal influences in Sabah resulted in UMNO making a base there in 1992. With Kuala Lumpur's financial backing and carefully redrawn constituency boundaries, UMNO and its local allies have ruled the roost ever since.

A cross-section of society on Tanah Rata's main street.

A boy in Tanjung Aru village, Sabah.

PEOPLE

From skin tones to language and festivals, the diversity of Malaysians is the result of populations brought by the ancient trade network joining indigenous peoples and followed by generations of intermixing.

The most striking characteristic of Malaysians is their diversity: of ethnicity, speech, cultural observances, religion and food. It is a heady mix, manifested obviously in tourist-targeted cultural showcases but more subtly in daily life, from the babel of languages to dress and rituals.

These different people make up Malaysia's over 30 million people, four-fifths of whom live in the peninsula, although Borneo is more than twice its size. This diversity has been a long time in the making, dating back to the first century, when the Malay archipelago was part of a trade network spanning the Indian Ocean and China. From then began what historians call a slow filtering in of different peoples, a continuous process that has resulted in a society which has shared the same land and experienced hybridisation and heterogeneity for hundreds of years.

Today, while the core ethnic values of each group are largely followed – particularly when

At the Sunday market in Kota Kinabalu.

Malays are officially categorised in the grouping of bumiputra, literally "sons of the soil", together with indigenous people, Thai and Portuguese Malaysians.

it comes to religion and marriage – borrowings and adaptations from one group to the next continue to be widespread and creative. Sometimes embraced, sometimes decried, these borrowings are unavoidable in Malaysia because cultural boundaries are so porous. Therefore, the categorisation of people into "ethnic groups" is really only a starting point for understanding Malaysians.

State-led categorising along ethnic lines for divide-and-rule purposes – courtesy of British colonialists – is wielded by politicians for political reasons, and is most obvious in institutional life. In fact, political and institutional racialisation hits at the heart of a society which derives strength and enrichment from its pluralism.

Indigenous people

The first people to populate the Malay Peninsula and Borneo were the indigenous people, the first group having settled in the peninsula 25,000 years ago. They comprise a large variety of ethnic groups, 18 in the peninsula and 68 in Borneo. Unfortunately, the majority face the same struggles as indigenous people the world over. These include land rights and identity and, especially in the peninsula, institutional integration into mainstream society.

Peninsular Malaysia's indigenous people are called *Orang Asli*, which in Malay means "original people". They make up less than 0.4 percent of the population and are so marginalised that many urban Malaysians have never encountered them. Most *Orang Asli* live on the fringes of, or in, urban areas in permanent settlements; only a fraction retain their fully traditional lifestyles. Likewise, many are no longer animists but have converted to Christianity or Islam.

indigenous to Southeast Asia.

In the south are the agrarian Aboriginal Malays, who arrived about 3,000 years ago and work in plantations or as fisherfolk. Some intermarried the islanders in today's Indonesia and Borneo, hence their resemblance to the Malays. Their languages are old forms of Malay.

Bornean natives

The indigenous people of Borneo are even more diverse. Referred to as "natives", they actually form the majority of the people here, and have strong political representation. Even fewer

An Orang Asli woman in the Cameron Highlands.

A fashionable young Malay in Kota Kinabalu.

Orang Asli are divided into three main groups. The Negritos are the oldest group, and are linked to the Vietnamese Palaeolithic Age people. Originally nomads, today they live in the peninsula's northeast and northwest. They still live largely forest-based lives, selling forest produce for cash.

The Senoi are Mongoloids who settled in the peninsula several thousand years after the Negritos. Traditionally cultivators, they are the largest group today and the most integrated into mainstream society, working in plantations and in the urban centres which their villages fringe. They live primarily in the middle of the peninsula. Both the Negritos and Senoi speak languages that belong to the Mon-Khmer language family, the language family that is

of the natives are animists compared to the Orang Asli, most having converted to Christianity and some to Islam.

About 60 percent of Sabahans are indigenous, and among them, speak half the indigenous languages found in Malaysia. Of the 39 groups, the largest is the Kadazandusun, who live in northwestern and central Sabah, mainly in urban areas. Mount Kinabalu is their spiritual resting place and their biggest festival is the Kaamatan (Harvest Festival).

The Murut, the "hill people" of northeastern Sabah, were purportedly the last group to give up headhunting. Meanwhile, the coastal dwellers are the Bajau and Malayic families, traditionally skilful fishermen and boatmen.

Sarawak is home to 29 ethnic groups, the largest of which is the Iban, who originated from Kalimantan and are also known as Dayaks. Traditionally longhouse dwellers and rice-planters, the Gawai Harvest Festival is their most important cultural celebration. Making up 30 percent of Sarawak's population, they are mostly urbanised, as are the next largest group, the Bidayuh, who live in the greater Kuching area.

The interior dwellers are the Orang Ulu, the most skilful handicraft-makers and artists in the land. The Melanau are coastal folk, famed as sago planters and fishing folk; they have a stronghold on politics in Sarawak. The Lun Bawang and Kelabit are highland dwellers, while the Penan are the arguably Borneo's most famous ethnic group, thanks to international media attention on the logging of their forest homes.

Malays

Malays and other *bumiputra* make up about 60 percent of Malaysia's population. They are the majority ethnic group in the peninsula, dominating populations in Terengganu, Kelantan and Putrajaya.

Malays or the *Melayu* people arrived in the region 3,000–5,000 years ago from southern China and Taiwan. Through the years, they intermarried and assimilated with other Chinese, Indians, Arabs and Thais, and make up today's Malays, Indonesians and Filipinos.

In Malaysia, Malay culture shows strong Javanese, Sumatran, Siamese and especially Indian influence. Linguistically, Malay is Austronesian, but people will recognise vocabulary that is Arabic, Sanskrit, Tamil, Portuguese, Dutch, Chinese and English.

Malays were largely Hindus before they were converted to Islam in the 15th century. They also led largely rural, agrarian lifestyles before responding in the 1960s to Malaysia's move towards industrialisation by moving to urban areas.

Today, over half live in towns and cities. They are a dominant presence in government, the civil service and key sectors of the economy. The Malay-only UMNO political party has led government since independence, as part of the BN. In daily life, Malay customs are observed, most noticeably to outsiders in the clothing that Malay women wear. Islam is key, and the most obvious manifestation of this is the crowding of mosques on Fridays for prayers.

Indians

About 7 percent of the population is of Indian descent. Most of them live in the peninsula, with the largest groups in the Klang Valley, Perak and Negeri Sembilan. The majority are Tamil, with a sprinkling of Malayalis, Punjabis, Telugus, Sikhs and Sri Lankans. Largely Hindu, other religions practised include Christianity, Sikhism and Buddhism. Indian Muslims are classified as Malay or bumiputra.

Indian traders arrived in northern Kedah in the first century, leaving a lasting influence on Malay culture, language and even notions of

Indian men in Kuala Lumpur.

kingship. However, most of today's Malaysian Indians are descendants of 19th-century British-imported indentured workers from South Asia for plantations and, to a lesser degree, the civil service. Indians make up the largest number of professionals per capita, especially doctors and lawyers. Many also run their own businesses.

Indian culture is a rich and colourful part of Malaysian life: clothing such as *kurtha* tops and the *salwar-khameez* trouser suit are popular, Hindi movies have a huge fan base, Hindu temples and celebrations such as Thaipusam and Deepavali enrich the collective consciousness, while nothing beats ethnic divide-bridging like banana-leaf curries and *teh tarik* (Indian tea).

Chinese

Chinese make up 24 percent of the country's population, living mainly in urban areas throughout the country. In Kuala Lumpur and Penang, they make up over 40 percent of the population.

Like the Indians, the Chinese have had a long history in the Malay archipelago through maritime trade that began in the 5th century. However, most of today's Malaysian Chinese are descendants of indentured labour imported by the British in the 19th and 20th centuries. Originally from South China, they worked the tin mines in the peninsula and eventually

Baba-Nonyas. Aspects of their culture are manifest in language (infused with Malay and Thai words) dress (particularly the Malay-influenced sarong *kebaya*), food (strong curries and spicy salads) and architecture (largely Chinese with colonial influences).

Other communities

There are small communities of Malaysians of mixed Asian and European ancestry, mainly Portuguese, Dutch and English. Eurasian communities were established in Melaka during the Portuguese colonial period in the 16th

Old Chinese men playing mah-jong in Penang.

set up businesses and plantations. By the time independence came around, they controlled the economy.

Affirmative action policies favouring *bumiputra* have seen their share of the economic pie eroded, but they still make up the majority of the middle- and upper-income classes.

Comprising three main dialect groups, Cantonese, Hokkien and Hakka, the Chinese are mainly Taoist/Buddhists or Christian, and their main festival is the Chinese New Year, a 15-day familial, religious and gormandising celebration.

The 15th-century Chinese migrants who settled in the Malay Peninsula's ports, adopted Malay customs and/or married locals, came to be known as Peranakan, "local-born" or

and 17th centuries. The community there still speaks a distinct form of Portuguese called Kristang. Another sizeable Eurasian community is in Penang, formed by 18th-century Thai-Portuguese migrants. While a minority, Eurasians played a key role in education and the establishing of Catholicism.

There are many more smaller groups of different peoples, and Malaysia's ethnic composition continues to become giddily more complex with the presence of new migrant labour on which the country has been heavily dependent since the 1970s. Migrant labour, both legal and illegal, makes up at least 10 percent of the population, a whopping 2.8 million people. The largest groups come from Indonesia, Bangladesh,

Nepal, India and Myanmar (Burma). In Sabah, Indonesians and Filipinos are believed to make up at least a quarter of the population.

The race card

Malaysians do live in harmony, but unfortunately politics is racialised, as the ruling coalition comprises race-based political groups. For tourists, the state projects a perfect-harmony utopia, encapsulated by Tourism Malaysia's tagline, *Malaysia Truly Asia*. But when the state's power is threatened, it projects the scenario of a society on the brink of tribal blood-shedding, particularly by invoking the "May 13 Incident" (see page 54).

Affirmative action policies for *bumiputra* have led to political and institutional racialisation, leading to resentment among non-Malays towards Malays. However, the policies have also been criticised among others for lulling Malays into complacency and encouraging them to be dependent on state handouts. In addition, the uneven implementation of policies has caused resentment among the *bumiputra*, by, among others, favouring Malays above other *bumiputra* and favouring politically linked *bumiputra* above others.

This dissatisfaction was among other impulses that led Malaysians to vote in a historic number of opposition lawmakers in the 2008 and 2013 general elections. This has, in turn, politicised a segment of Malaysians, particularly the younger generation, and Malaysians are beginning to look beyond race at the possibility of a more equal society.

At street level, though, Malaysians enjoy living in a multi-ethnic society. Influential pollster the Merdeka Centre found that in 2011, 82 percent of people polled thought so. However, they still stereotyped: Chinese were greedy, Indians untrustworthy and Malays lazy. Nonetheless, stereotyping occurred within the respective groups themselves and in addition, respondents did not really understand their own cultures. Moreover, there was clear recognition that racialised politics were responsible for a racialised society. Levels of trust between communities had also dropped a little since the previous poll in 2006. Another study done by the Merdeka Centre in 2012 revealed that

A blend of different cultures meeting at Kota Kinabalu night market.

IT'S ENGLISH, LAH

Listening to Malaysians speak English can be confusing. You could get East Coast American, Received Pronunciation or staccato unintelligibility – sometimes from the same person, and in the same conversation. For English as it is spoken in Malaysia is as multicultural as the Malaysians themselves.

English was introduced in the 19th century under British rule. Then as now, Malay (Bahasa Malaysia) was the lingua franca and English linked to social status and education. Standard British English is taught in schools. Increasingly though, English is the language of commerce, science and communication and, particularly in Kuala Lumpur, it is an emergent lingua franca, serving to level out ethnic differences.

In daily communication, though, the localisation of the language by a people who live and interact across multiple languages has sprouted colourful varieties. Malaysian English has an unfair reputation as being ungrammatical, sing-song, even pidgin – outsiders even call it Manglish. In reality, these varieties have their own systematic and coherent grammar, vocabulary and pronunciation, which are understandable by all users.

What cannot be denied is that Malaysians love their "Englishes" and have fun with them, not only in conversation but also in local English-language media, literature and theatre.

public confidence in state of ethnic relations had declined.

Still, having bought into the model of achieving developed nation status, Malaysians tend to be more concerned about jobs and the economy, rather than racial and unity issues. In fact, affluence and the pursuit of material gains tend to level out differences.

Economic status

Fifty years of a developmental approach has pushed Malaysia into the rank of high human development, according to the United Nations

Young Malays hit the beach in Penang.

LOCAL FASHIONS

The ubiquitous T-shirt and jeans aside, urban Malaysians' fashion style is varied and colourful; traditional dress appears alongside office wear, designer labels and street fashion. The Malay *baju kurung* and Indian *kurtha* are worn to work by women across ethnic lines. Indian women wear saris and Muslim women wear the *tudung*, the headscarf, in a variety of ways, The Chinese tend to wear traditional outfits only during festive periods and weddings and Muslim and Hindu men wear traditional outfits when they go to pray. For the middle class, designer brands are important, including some local designers who have a strong following.

Human Development Index. In Southeast Asia, Malaysia is ranked highest after Singapore. Adult literacy is above 90 percent, life expectancy above 70 years old and unemployment a low 3 percent (2014).

In 2011, the Gross Domestic Product (GDP) per capita was US$12,700, which was a third that of the US and the UK. In 2014, it dropped down to US$10,804. Malaysia's economic aim is to achieve a GDP of a "developed nation" by 2020, which means almost doubling the GDP in less than a decade.

In tandem with that developmental outlook, Malaysians throughout the country prefer to live in urban rather than rural areas. Drawn by jobs and big-city living, 20 percent of Malaysians live in the Klang Valley alone.

KL-ites have a GDP that is double the national average; likewise the employment to population ratio is twice that of other metropolitan areas. About 80 percent of the total employment is in the service sector. Globally, it is considered a very important world city that links major economic regions and states into the world economy. In terms of being a global service centre in accountancy, advertising, banking and law – criteria used to measure "world city-ness" by the UK-based Globalization and World Cities Study Group and Network – Kuala Lumpur was, in 2012, in the same grouping as Chicago and Brussels and higher than Melbourne, Munich and Washington.

Urban-rural divide

Even as urbanisation and industrialisation continue, Malaysians' ties with their home towns and villages remain strong. This is manifested in the mass exodus called *balik kampung* – literally "going home" – whereby during major festival periods such as Hari Raya Puasa and Chinese New Year, big cities like Kuala Lumpur, Kuching and Kota Kinabalu empty out.

More and more, though, the town or city where the children live is becoming the *kampung*, as older parents relocate too. While there are concerns about eroding family values, the family unit is still important to Malaysians, and extended families are common.

And so the divide between urban and rural – and therefore the rich and the poor – grows. The middle-class, smartphone-toting youngster in Kuala Lumpur was raised by a maid, holidays in Sydney and aspires towards a Harvard education. In contrast, the Kelabit teenager in Bario, Sarawak, skips school, occasionally helps his farmer father in the rice-fields and eats his dinner by the light of a kerosene lamp. The world each lives in might as well be Mars for the other.

East–West divide

Herein lies the other divide among Malaysians, that between the mainland and island parts of the country. Referring to each other respectively as *"Orang Semenanjung"* (people from the peninsula) and "East Malaysians", the societies are so different as to appear as if they belong to two separate countries.

Sabah and Sarawak are economically less developed than the peninsula and incomes are lower. The ethnic mix is also very different, comprising mainly indigenous peoples, most of whom are Christians. In addition, there is less state-led racialisation in the Bornean states.

Peninsular Malaysians tend to consider the East Malaysians either backward or exotic; other than those who are based there as civil servants or for business, Peninsular Malaysians would consider Borneo a tourist destination in the ilk of Thailand or Indonesia. Meanwhile, East Malaysians are drawn to the peninsula for jobs and higher incomes. Some also resent the *Orang Semenanjung*, particularly those in administrative positions in their states, because of Kuala Lumpur's colonial mentality towards the states.

The majority from either side have never crossed the South China Sea to visit the other part of the country.

Affluence

Income and rural–urban gaps notwithstanding, as Malaysians become more affluent, society is changing. Like other new moneyed communities, Malaysians have the infrastructure but lack the maintenance mentality and high service standards; they follow the latest trends but civic consciousness and social graces are still catching up. The good life has come easily and so the approach to life is laid-back, rather than edgy and competitive.

Even as they embrace the latest technology and trends from Silicon Valley or Bollywood, mediums, Malay healers (*bomohs*) and fortune tellers are consulted. Striking the lottery (the "4D" or *empat ekor*) is an obsession – in fact,

traffic jams double when there is a road accident because of a combination of the *kaypoh* factor (nosiness), and the scribbling down of what might be the lucky number to that RM1 million jackpot.

Even in Kuala Lumpur, people are relatively less sophisticated and hard-edged compared to their economically high-flying neighbours in Hong Kong and Singapore. In general, visitors will find Malaysians warm, friendly and curious to the point of nosiness, happy to help and have a chat about strangers' backgrounds and cultures.

A Kelantan worker in a rice paddy field.

WOMEN IN MALAYSIA

Customs and traditions influence women's roles in society even though their individual rights are protected by civil law. Childcare and the household are still considered the domain of women, even if they hold full-time jobs, though this is gradually changing among urban, educated families. Regarding family matters, women abide by a combination of civil, customary and Islamic Sharia laws. Polygamy is illegal for non-Muslims, but Muslim men may marry up to four wives. About half of local women have jobs; most are low-paying but Malaysia has one of Asia's highest number of women in senior management, higher than the US and the UK.

RELIGION

Malaysians' belief systems are as diverse as their makeup, their collective landscape characterised by devoutness, tolerance and a fascinating hybridity.

For anyone wanting a crash course in comparative religion, Malaysia is the place to come. From Islam to the latest revivalist movement, Malaysia is home to all the world's major beliefs and a host of minor ones besides. Religion is found everywhere – in mosques, temples and churches, in the perpetual round of religious festivals, in diverse rites of passage, and in a multitude of everyday sights and sounds.

Every Malay is a Muslim, but there are also sizeable numbers of Indians, Melanaus (in Sarawak) and Bajaus (in Sabah) who are Muslims, as well as small but significant groups of Chinese, Kadazandusun, Murut and other converts. Buddhism is allied to the Chinese, while most Chinese who are not Buddhists are Confucians or Taoists. Hinduism is observed largely by Indians. Christianity is practised by a range of Indians, Chinese and indigenous communities of Sabah and Sarawak such as the Ibans, Bidayuhs, Orang Ulu, Kadazandusuns and

A monk in Chinatown, Kuala Lumpur.

> One advantage of living in a land with many different creeds is a proliferation of public holidays. All the major religious festivals are national holidays, as are several minor ones at state level.

Muruts. Folk religion also holds sway among a diminishing minority in these Bornean states; likewise, in the interior of the peninsula, only small numbers of the indigenous Orang Asli hold on to their animistic beliefs.

Religious tolerance

This great variety of faiths within the compass of a small nation is hardly surprising, given the rich ethnic mix that Malaysia enjoys. What is more surprising is that the followers of these different creeds – some of whom are at daggers with one another elsewhere – live here in relative peace and harmony.

Although Islam is the official religion and Muslims account for over half the total population, the constitution guarantees the free pursuit of all other beliefs. Due to long and deep historical interactions and continued daily interaction, there is a lively awareness among people at large of the destructive and antisocial consequences of religious intolerance. However, this tolerance is to some degree being eroded by politically motivated and state-initiated policies and actions (see feature box, page 81).

What might be surprising to visitors is the devoutness of the adherents of all faiths, considering the Westernisation and globalisation of much of Malaysian society, particularly in cities. Religion is a living force in Malaysia. At prayer times mosques and temples are packed and the large congregations in churches must be the envy of any parish priest in the West. Hindu and Chinese devotees perform penance in their thousands while participants in religious parades and processions runs to the tens of thousands. Religious devotions are observed with equal zeal at home.

festival is celebrated with prayer, food and the visiting of family and friends. Many Muslims also save for years to perform the *hajj* or pilgrimage to Mecca, during the Dhu al-Hijjah month. The end of this season is observed with the Hari Raya Haji or Aidiladha festival, when animals are sacrificed and the meat distributed.

Muslims are subject to secular laws for secular affairs, while domestic religious issues (such as property rights, marriage and apostasy) remain under the jurisdiction of the Islamic *syariah* courts.

The constitutional enshrinement of Islam as

Women wearing the hijab in Masjid India Bazaar, Kuala Lumpur.

Of course, not all Malaysians take religion so seriously. But religious faith is real and palpable, and forms an important element in determining public values to a degree rarely found in modern Western society.

Islam

The ubiquity of mosques and the *azan*, the call to prayer, are indication of the primacy of Islam in Malaysia. Muslim women generally wear the *tudung* (head covering), the congregational Friday prayer in mosques is well attended by men and the eating of halal food strictly observed.

During the Muslim month of Ramadan, Muslims fast from dawn to dusk. At the end of the fasting period, the Hari Raya Puasa or Aidilfitri

the official religion of Malaysia has meant that the state has been heavily involved in determining the kind of Islam practised. Malaysians follow the Sunni branch of Islam and the Shafi'i school of jurisprudence. Shia and other Islamic denominations are outlawed.

The administration of Islam

Officially, each of the nine Malay rulers is the religious as well as political head of his state, while in states not headed by Malay royalty – such as Sabah and Sarawak – the king of Malaysia fills the gap.

However, the state also established and sanctions a hierarchy of Islamic authority that makes pronouncements on how Muslims should live their lives. For example, Islamic laws designate the consumption of alcohol and the non-observance of fasting during Ramadan as crimes for Muslims. These crimes are prosecuted in the *syariah* court. A common criticism of these laws is that they turn the personal obligations of Muslims to their religion into crimes against the state. Proponents of the laws say they are essential to keep the moral fabric of Muslims intact.

Despite its obvious pre-eminence today, Islam was a late arrival in the Malay archipelago, long preceded by Hinduism, Buddhism and animism. Folk beliefs drew from one or more of

a quarter of the Malaysian population. The line between Chinese philosophy and religion being tenuous, many ethnic Chinese, including Buddhists, incorporate aspects of Chinese folk religions in their belief system. Hence the ubiquitous household altars, little shrines along the roadside, giant joss sticks smouldering at temple thresholds, and little prayer slips and red paper banners serving a multiplicity of purposes – keeping evil spirits at bay, seeking a cure for an illness and paying respect to the dearly departed.

Chinese Buddhists have been long estab-

Making an offering at Tua Pek Kong Temple in Kuching.

Kwan Yin statue at Kek Lok Si Temple.

these, as well as other influences, and are still held to varying degrees. For example, there still exists the worship of *keramat*, the gravesites of distinguished, often spiritually pious Muslims, frequently of Arab descent. The sites that go back centuries are a fascinating window into syncretist practices over time. Today, many *keramat* have been destroyed as this worship is considered anti-Islamic, but it is still carried out quietly, and place names such as "Datuk Keramat" indicate where the important sites were; the honorific "*datuk*" is added as respect.

Buddhism and Chinese religions

Next to Islam in Malaysia, in terms of numbers, comes Buddhism, which is professed by

lished in Malaysia, being synonymous with Chinese settlement in the country. Their earliest contact probably goes back to the Sri Vijayan empire during the 9th century, when its capital, Palembang in Sumatra, was a great centre for Buddhist studies. But Chinese Buddhism only achieved a permanent presence when the Chinese began to establish themselves as a community in Melaka. Most Chinese Buddhists today are the descendants of the droves of Chinese immigrants who arrived during the 19th century and the first half of the 20th.

Buddhists fall into one of two main schools, the Mahayana and Theravada (Hinayana). The Mahayana (Great Path) School is the Buddhism of the Chinese, while Theravada (Little Path) Buddhists consist of Malaysian Thais and smaller Burmese and Sinhalese groups.

The main difference between the two seems to be one of sophistication. The Theravada School is much simpler, more abstract and claims to be much closer to the original teachings and way of life of the Buddha. The Mahayana School, having absorbed other influences in the lands where it flourishes (such as in China itself) acknowledges a number of deities. The Mahayana School also has far more complicated rituals and observances.

in roadside shrines, is the *na duk gong*, whose name derives from the Malay "*datuk*" honorific and "*gong*", meaning "deity". Sporting a Malay *songkok* headdress and carrying a *keris* short sword, this deity is believed to be a derivation of either, or both, the *datuk keramat* and the *penunggu* (guardian spirit), once venerated by Malays until Islamisation.

Other deities peculiar to Malaysia are those of real people, such as Yap Ah Loy, the 19th-century Chinese leader who developed Kuala Lumpur. He had built the Sin Sze Si Ya temple to honour two fallen comrades, and when he

Offerings at the Tree Temple in George Town.

Buddhist worship

Buddhists worship at home and in temples, the majority of which are Chinese. However, many Thai and Burmese temples are found in the peninsula's north. Sinhalese temples make up a small but important percentage; the Maha Vihara in Kuala Lumpur is a key temple in Malaysia, and a centre for Wesak Day celebrations, which honours the birth, enlightenment and death of the Buddha. In recent years, Tibetan Buddhism has started attracting followers.

Malaysian Buddhists acknowledge different deities. The most widely worshipped of these is the goddess of mercy, Guan Yin, considered the pinnacle of mercy and compassion. Interestingly, another popular deity, seen particularly

SIKHISM

The Sikh presence in Malaysia stems from when the British recruited members of this community to form the core of the country's police force. Devout Sikhs commit to a daily recitation of passages from the Sikh holy book, the *Gurū Granth Sāhib*, both at home and in *gurdwaras*, the Sikh places of worship. *Gurdwaras* are particularly active on weekday evenings and on weekends. The Sikh faith also involves participating in the communal meal cooked at the community kitchen, which are open to visitors. The biggest public festivity is Vaisakhi, the religious New Year celebration, a colourful event with singing, *bangra* dancing and eating.

died, was himself deified there. Besides Wesak, temple celebrations include the Chinese New Year and the "birthdays" of deities.

Hinduism

Hinduism in Malaysia goes back to the 1st century, when it arrived with the first Indian traders to Malaysian shores. This Hindu period, which lasted for 1,500 years before it was replaced by Islam, has left its traces in Malay language and literature, in Malay art forms such as the shadow play (*wayang kulit*) and in such traditions as the *bersanding* ceremony, when the bridal couple sit in state during a Malay wedding.

Today's Hindus now number around two million, and are the descendants of mostly Tamil immigrants from South India, who came to work as contract labourers over the last 200 years. With them came a sprinkling of English-educated clerks, apothecaries, shopkeepers and merchants who laid the foundations of a modern Indian middle-class.

Hindu temples in Malaysia are managed by local committees, following closely the traditions of their place of origin in India. Temples in the plantations were quite simple structures, and when plantations made way for built areas, they ended up standing in sometimes incongruous locations in the middle of housing or commercial estates, testament to the history of that area. Temples in the towns are more sophisticated affairs, supported by wealthier members of the community.

Hindu worship

Many Hindus follow the Shaivite tradition, where Shiva is worshipped, the oldest of the four major sects of Hinduism. A common representation of Shiva in temples is the *lingam*, a cylinder on a circular base, which symbolises the union of mind and body.

However, many different Hindu deities are worshipped, and among the most widely venerated in Malaysia is Ganesha, the elephant god and the remover of obstacles. Another important deity is Murugan, a manifestation of virtue and valour and dispenser of favours. The celebration of Murugan at Thaipusam is arguably Malaysia's most colourful and emotional festival, particularly at the key sites of the Batu Caves temple in Kuala Lumpur and the Waterfall temple in Penang.

Ipoh has a lesser-known Murugan temple where a stalagmite in a limestone cave is worshipped as having taken the form of Murugan's *vel* or divine lance. The Gunung Ciruh temple is one of several cave temples in Ipoh where Hindu and Buddhist temples have been established.

Daily worship is a smaller affair. At home, prayers are performed at dawn at a small altar, whereas temple prayers or *puja* involve symbolic offerings to the deities and are usually performed in the mornings and evenings.

Another important Hindu festival is Deepavali, which occurs towards the end of the year.

Worshippers on their way to Batu Caves for Thaipusam.

Known as the "festival of lights", oil lamps are lit to celebrate the triumph of good over evil. A ritual cleansing oil bath is taken in the morning before visiting the temple, and the entrances of houses are decorated with "kolam", floral designs on the floor, to welcome Lakshmi, the goddess of wealth.

Christianity

There are 2.7 million Christians in Malaysia, 70 percent of whom are in Sabah and Sarawak. The three main Christian divisions are all present, but Orthodox Christians constitute only a handful. Roman Catholics form the largest group, about a third of the whole. The Protestants are represented by Anglicans, Methodists and Presbyterians, largely American-dominated, and smaller groups among which the Baptists and Charismatic churches are the most prominent. Christian proselytisation became widespread in the 19th century at the start of the British colonial era. Official British policy was not to interfere with the locals' beliefs, but Church missions and schools were established throughout the colony and Chinese and Tamil Christian migrants brought in. In Sarawak, a missionary presence was established to provide education and to aid the suppression of head-hunting; this presence soon spread to Sabah.

A Malaysian couple posing for wedding photos.

Christian missionary activity got a second wind after World War II. Local involvement and lay leadership were intensified, and the Bornean states saw mass conversion of the indigenous people by the local Sidang Injil Borneo, today the largest Protestant Church in the country.

Christian celebrations

The church is central to the religious lives of Malaysian Christians. Most Christians are regular weekly churchgoers. Depending on their parish, services can be held in different languages, including Malay, Tamil, Mandarin, Iban, Kadazan and other indigenous languages. Rites of passage and major celebrations such as Easter and Christmas see large, well-attended masses.

Despite that, like everywhere in the world, Christmas is commercialised. Shopping is a large part of the celebration, with stores decked out in cotton wool and Christmas trees while seasonal foods such as turkey – even halal turkey – and fruitcake appear on restaurant menus.

Visually the most spectacular Christian event is the July candlelight procession at the historic St Anne's church in Bukit Mertajam, Penang. This Catholic festival honours the saint who was the mother of Mary and attracts crowds of 100,000 over the 10 days.

A local peculiarity is a several-week-long fast and prayer leading up to the Malaysian independence day on 31 August. The intercessional event has been for the likes of promoting religious harmony and freedom, the recovery of the economy from recession and smooth general elections.

SPIRITS IN THE WORLD

The spiritual is very much part of Malaysian society: Animism is found in Hinduism, Buddhism and Chinese religions and indigenous belief systems revolve around a close and complex relationship between the natural and supernatural worlds. Maintaining harmony with the spirits is key, for imbalance is thought to result in misfortune such as illness. Hence, offerings are made in ceremonies led by spiritual leaders and healers.

The conversion of indigenous people to Christianity and Islam has seen many communities abandon traditional beliefs, though some still retain some practices. Several Orang Asli communities in the peninsula's interior still perform ceremonies, including the Senoi (*sewang terang* and *sewang gelap*) and the Mah Meri (*Ari'Muyang*). In Borneo, harvest festivals are the last few being celebrated traditionally and include the *Gawai Dayak* in Sarawak and the *Kaamatan* in Sabah.

Malay cosmology includes *makhluk ghaib* ("unseen beings") such as *jin* (genies) and *penunggu* (guardian spirits). Despite Islamic authorities' best efforts to quell these beliefs, they are widespread, as indicated by the flourishing practices of *bomoh* (witch doctors). Among all communities, trees are widely believed to be hosts for spirits. Big trees are especially venerated. It is not uncommon to see altars, statues of gods and food offerings among their roots.

Islam in politics

An ever-increasing Islamic conservatism and impact on civil liberties is the result of an ongoing battle by political parties to "out-Islamise" each other.

Growing Islamic conservatism and primacy in Malaysia are rooted not in Arabisation (as popularly perceived) but politics. Since the 1990s, the competition for the Malay-Muslim vote has seen a reinforcing of the Islamic bureaucracy.

Proponents of Islamic politics in Malaysia have stood for many things from the Islamisation of law and banking to the intensification of missionary activities. In contemporary Malaysia, Islam's role in politics has its roots in the 1950s, when Islam was mobilised to articulate anti-colonial statements. The identification of Islam as an ideology of Malay nationalism also rejected the secular, nationalist rhetoric that was the basis for the formation of the United Malays National Organisation (UMNO), which claimed to represent all Malays.

This ideal of an Islamist state was the founding principle for the Pan-Malaysian Islamic Party (PAS). While PAS was – and continues to be – ambiguous about the inclusion of non-Muslims within this ideal, it introduced a new form of party political identification among Malays. This put in place a rivalry between UMNO and PAS that still colours politics. PAS has led the state of Kelantan since independence, imposing strict regulations on its largely Muslim population regarding alcohol consumption, dress codes and entertainment. However, the rights of non-Muslims have been respected.

Increasing Islamism

Meanwhile, under UMNO leadership, the nation began to experience the rise of authoritarian politics and the beginnings of moral policing to secure political power. Right-wing student "Islamist activism" of the 1970s was followed a decade later by the Islamisation of the government machinery under prime minister Mahathir Mohamad. In the 1990s, Mahathir extended the state's role in policing values, beliefs and private lives, ranging from the banning of American rock performers to entering homes to apprehend Muslim adulterers. Non-Muslims were also told they had no right to comment on matters Islamic. All this gave cause for alarm for both Muslims and non-Muslims.

A turning point for Malaysians came in 1998 with the summary dismissal of Anwar Ibrahim, the then deputy prime minister. This led to the beginnings of a reformist opposition politics, within which Islam and specifically PAS has had a significant role to play. An outcome of this has been intensified competition between UMNO and PAS for the Malay vote, leading to the enforcing of an ever more conservative form of public Islam to prove their credentials.

The next turning point was the 2008 and then

A Muslim man in Sungai Petani.

2013 elections which saw PAS gain more political ground as part of the Pakatan Rakyat, supported not only by Muslims but voters of other faiths as well. What's more, Anwar's multi-ethnic Parti Keadilan Rakyat attracted sizeable Malay support too. Since then, increasingly questionable tactics and vitriol have been employed by state apparatchiks including state-owned media and state-supported hate group Perkasa, to ratchet up tensions between ethnic groups.

Nonetheless, the field is now open for a notable experiment in a democratic politics shared by parties representing diverse cultural and religious perspectives. It is within this environment that different proponents of Islamic politics now have to work.

*Old and new buildings contrast on
Kalan Hang Kasturi, KL.*

ARCHITECTURE

From traditional homes to the splendour of
postmodern skyscrapers, Malaysia's buildings reflect
both its colourful past and its hopes for the future.

Malaysia's vernacular and modern architecture documents not only the history of the land, but also the essence
of its various peoples. The country's architectural evolution has been guided by historical
markers, the colours of which are strong even
today: the first settlers from mainland Asia;
Indian and Arab traders from the West; the
era of the wealthy sultans; the European influence; imported Chinese and Indian cultures;
the elation of independence; and contemporary globalisation.

Contemporary architecture

Most visitors' architectural journey begins at
the ultra-modern Kuala Lumpur International
Airport, characterised by conical columns-
cum-air-conditioning vents; inspired "forest-
canopy" effect lighting; and the surprisingly
effective "forests" within the building. As the
autobahn-standard highway approaches the
capital, Kuala Lumpur rears into view with as
much drama as surprise.

The highway links directly with the Kuala
Lumpur City Centre (KLCC), the heart of the
commercial and financial district known as the
Golden Triangle. Here, postmodern skyscrapers in various stages of completion compete to
catch the eye. None, however, can match the
statuesque Petronas Twin Towers, the country's
tallest buildings and one-time world record-
holder (see pages 133 and 87). The towers
brought Kuala Lumpur an instant cachet.

This sentiment was evident even earlier,
when the heady years after independence in
1957 saw a real search for styles that could
proclaim independent statehood and reflect
local identity. Architects worked to reinter-
pret the International Style, then in vogue, by

The Istana Kenangan in Kuala Kangsar.

incorporating local materials as well as coming
up with design elements that were suitable for
the climate.

Monumental national symbols were constructed, including the Parliament House, with
its pineapple skin cladding; the Masjid Negara
(National Mosque), with its folded-plate roof
form in the shape of an umbrella; and the
Muzium Negara (National Museum), a beautiful and powerful interpretation of traditional
Malay architecture. Today, throughout both
Kuala Lumpur as well as other cities, eagle-eyed
visitors will spot many high-rises with pitched
roofs: a contemporary vernacular that captures
domestic Malaysian sensibilities and couples
them with modern design.

Colonial styles

Contemporary architecture is a development from colonial architecture, which is essentially a hybrid, and which had formed and influenced the identity of Malaysia's urban landscapes. When the British constructed their administrative core in Kuala Lumpur, no one had seen the style or scale of the neo-Saracenic public buildings; they were even deemed too far ahead of their time. Combining 19th-century Indian Muslim style and Victorian Gothic and classicism, these gracious buildings feature arches and columns galore as well as minarets and domes aplenty.

A detail of Melaka's Stadthuys.

This style came to be repeated elsewhere in British colonial centres; outstanding examples include Penang's Kapitan Keling Mosque, Ipoh's Railway Station and Kuala Kangsar's Ubudiah Mosque.

Even before the British, the Dutch had made Melaka their regional trade hub. They left an architectural legacy that is outstanding. Central to this legacy are the former administrative building, the Stadthuys (town hall) and Christ Church, the oldest Protestant church in the country. Together, they represent probably the most complete examples of 17th-century colonial Dutch architecture in the region.

Across the South China Sea in Kuching, more straightforward early 20th-century European buildings remain from the Brooke era. These include the Astana, an English country home, which was the official residence; the Court House, which draws on classical architecture but with a tropical twist; and the Sarawak Museum, a copy of a Normandy town hall in France.

Straits Eclectic style

European style has featured in local urban architecture since the 15th century. The favoured building type in the Straits Settlements (from Penang down to Singapore) was the "shophouse", a double-storey unit with a lower-level business floor and a veranda to keep pedestrians sheltered from the sun or rain, while upstairs the family maintained a residence.

This style, known as the Straits Eclectic style, evolved from buildings favoured in mainland China, but European as well as Malay, Indian and Arab flavourings have created the lively and

CONSERVING MALAYSIA

The conservation of built heritage in Malaysia is an uphill battle against the general proclivity towards development, modernisation and renewal. The movement in Malaysia is driven by NGOs, including the Badan Warisan Malaysia (Heritage of Malaysia Trust) and the Penang Heritage Trust. There are also associations in Perak and Sarawak, as well as smaller groups associated with specific sites. Besides advocacy, these groups hold talks, publish and organise heritage tours. Major achievements of this movement have included helping to pass the National Heritage Act 2005 and the joint listing of George Town and Melaka as Unesco World Heritage Sites in 2007.

Individuals' conservation efforts have won local and international recognition; Penangites have been leaders in this. Pioneer conservation architect Laurence Loh is the man behind the restorations of the Straits Eclectic Cheong Fatt Tze Mansion in his hometown, as well as Stadium Merdeka in Kuala Lumpur, where Malaysia's independence was declared. Social historian and prolific author Khoo Salma Nasution advocates conservation through publications, networks and activities, working in both Penang and Perak, as well as regionally. Janet Pillai uses theatre and other arts forms in non-formal community programmes in arts and heritage education and cultural sustainability.

colourful variations on every street facade. These shophouses have also evolved over time, going from transitional to neoclassical and Art Deco before adopting a modern form. Shophouses have since matured into the most ubiquitous commercial architectural form in Malaysia.

Among other things, it is for their exceptional range of shophouses and townhouses from different eras that George Town and Melaka are jointly inscribed as a UNESCO World Heritage Site. The most complete surviving historic city centres on the Straits of Malacca, the cities are also feted for their religious buildings and ethnic enclaves, which are testament to 500 years of history.

For example, George Town's "kongsi" enclave of Chinese clanhouses, which includes the fantastically elaborate Khoo Kongsi, typifies the complex relationships between origins, dialects and family. Meanwhile, in Melaka is the oldest Catholic church in the country, St Peter's, a blend of Portuguese and Dutch styles; it was erected during Dutch occupation of Melaka after a period of Catholic persecution.

Religious structures

Contemporary mosques differ quite a lot from the first ones built in the Malay Peninsula. The oldest standing mosques date back to the 18th century and include the wooden Masjid Kampung Laut in Kelantan and the Masjid Terengkera in Melaka. They sport what is dubbed the "Southeast Asian mosque style", which is based on tiered, pyramidical Chinese pagodas. Contemporary mosques have been drawing more from Persian influences.

Chinese temples stay true to their southern Chinese roots but with dialectical differentiation; the tallest temples are generally Cantonese and the more ornate ones Hokkien. Red is prominent, symbolising the sun as well as joy and prosperity, while decorative elements derive largely from nature. Local elements are often incorporated; a quirky example is a pair of Sikh guards standing at the entrance of the Khoo Kongsi clanhouse.

Indian temples also keep to traditional shapes found in India. The range of structures varies greatly though, as the religious practices are diverse. "Orphan" temples are everywhere, shrines located especially amongst the roots of trees. Plantation temples have low brick walls and zinc roofs. The most elaborate structures

are the Chettiar temples, characterised by their large decorative multi-tiered *gopuram* (entrance towers); these temples are dedicated to the deity Murugan.

The architecture of old churches follows Western church traditions. Therefore, there are the likes of the Dutch Protestant Christ Church in Melaka with the characteristic Dutch gables; the Anglican St George's Church in Penang, reminiscent of a Greek temple; and the twin-spired St John's Cathedral in Kuala Lumpur, laid out like a neo-Gothic cathedral. Restrictions on the building of new churches have seen contempo-

Malay kampung vernacular architecture.

rary ones undistinguished from any shophouse or factory lot in which they are housed.

Vernacular architecture

Once out of the urban centres in the peninsula, the *kampung* (villages) are characterised by vernacular architecture that is representative of the ethnic Malay lifestyle. The basic elements are a single-level wooden structure, raised off the ground, with wooden or bamboo walls and a steeply sloping thatched roof; these have evolved to incorporate decorative influences from Indonesia and Thailand (in the south and north of the peninsula, respectively).

There are four acknowledged styles of Malay house – Perak, Melaka, Kedah and East Coast.

The styles are primarily differentiated by roof shapes, geometric patterning of the wall panels, fenestration and layout.

A Chinese version of these houses can still be spotted in very small towns in the Malay Peninsula. These were built for and adapted by the 19th-century Chinese labourers, the main difference being that their houses were not raised on stilts.

Over in the states of Sabah and Sarawak, the longhouse (see page 296) and water villages are typical indigenous structures. The basic construction of the longhouse follows the lines of a *kampung* house, but is extended to provide

Kuala Kangsar's Ubudiah Mosque.

dwellings for many families – and sometimes an entire village. While the layout remains simple, including a "street" formed either between facing rows of living units or on their perimeter, the social organisation is highly complex; where, when and how units are allocated are based on hierarchy, and define cultural rituals of welcoming visitors, marriage, childbearing and security.

Water villages built on stilts are common along riverbanks and seafronts. Each hut usually houses one family and is linked to other huts by plank walkways; jetties are a feature, where boats are anchored on the sides. Transport around the village is usually by sampan or motorboat. The most extensive water villages are those of the Bajau Laut on the east coast of Sabah.

Tourist showcases the Sarawak Cultural Village (see page 284) outside Kuching and the Sabah State Museum and Heritage Village (see page 315) in Kota Kinabalu actually do have fine examples of indigenous architecture. The former brings together, in one sumptuous setting, six different dwellings from all over the state, built by builders from the specific indigenous groups. Likewise, the latter has 10 well-constructed traditional houses set in the museum gardens.

The future

In the light of contemporary attempts at seeking a distinct Malaysian architectural identity, an all too common current approach is to slap a suitably Islamic motif on a pre-packaged curtain wall system. This is one accusation that is constantly levelled at the entire city of Putrajaya.

Nonetheless, a move in the right direction, and perhaps propelled by the need to keep costs down, is sustainable buildings, whereby environmental responsibility and good resource management are adopted throughout a building's life cycle. In the 1970s itself, eco-architecture was being pioneered by Ken Yeang. Today, Yeang is a world leader in green architecture. Among other things, he invented the "bioclimatic skyscraper", a prime example of which is the award-winning Mesiniage building in Subang Jaya, Selangor.

The green movement was boosted in 2009, with the development of the industry-driven Green Building Index (GBI) by the Malaysian Institute of Architects (PAM) and the Association of Consulting Engineers Malaysia (ACEM). Besides resource efficiency, the idea is to have buildings harmonise with the local climate, traditions, culture and the surrounding environment.

THE MALAY KAMPUNG HOUSE

Set on stilts, the Malay *kampung* house has a climate-friendly design with a veranda, a sleeping area, main living room and a kitchen at the back. There are several practicalities to the design: the raised floor protects against floods, fauna, and heat gain from the ground by circulating air beneath the structure; the steep roofs shed water quickly and their deep eaves shade windows – while the high interior disperses warm air effectively. Windows are shuttered and set at a low height to allow occupants to look out when seated. Today, many thatched roofs have given way to zinc sheeting, and wooden walls to brick.

Capital towers

As land in Malaysia's big cities becomes more expensive, skyscrapers are taking over the skyline. Kuala Lumpur leads the way.

High-rise buildings started to be part of Malaysia's skyline in the 1970s. Among the country's postmodern skyscrapers, the 88-storey Petronas Twin Towers remain a symbol of Kuala Lumpur's – and the country's – aspirations and economic might. Still one of the world's top 10 tallest buildings at 452 metres (1,480ft) tall, the buildings recall pagoda architecture with their tiers, while the cross-sectional form of the buildings is based on Islamic geometric principles.

Architecturally, the towers are practically faultless: the Argentine architect Cesar Pelli delivered a Gotham-esque vision shinily clad in about 85,000 sq metres (280,000 sq ft) of imported European stainless steel. Scores of imported consultants laboured for just under – a remarkably short – four years to deliver the Kuala Lumpur skyline an attention-grabbing silhouette.

When first commissioned, the towers were the subject of much contention. Many quibbled on points of political motives, white elephants, Other People's Money and general irrelevance. Nonetheless, there is no denying the extraordinary power of such monumental architecture. The spirit of the Twin Towers was historic and "millennial"; the fact that they were built in Malaysia at all was a harbinger of the power of globalisation and how projects of any nature and size would be developed in years to come the world over. The buildings were built on the world's deepest foundations, going down 120 metres (75ft). The blistering construction schedule saw two daily 12-hour shifts utilising over 2,000 workers at any given time. The double-level skybridge on the 42nd level is one of the highest in the world at 170 metres (560ft) and took four weeks to lift into place. Its "double-deck" lifts run at speeds of 5 metres (16ft) per second – it takes only a minute to go from the basement to the top.

With the topping of two 75-metre (246ft) stainless-steel spikes, the towers were proclaimed the world's tallest buildings in 1998, a record broken after six years by Taiwan's Taipei 101 tower. Still, Malaysia can stake its claim to the world's tallest *twin* buildings.

New heights

The Twin Towers are focal point of the Kuala Lumpur City Centre (KLCC), and it is at this prestigious address and its vicinity that the city's skyscrapers are concentrated. Big names have been mustered for the more outstanding of these, such as Norman Foster, who is behind the Troika – luxury apartments with dramatic pre-cast cladding; as well as Ole Scheeren, whose Aurora Tower will be a wonder of elevated tower blocks floating above

The iconic towers.

multilevel zones of open horizontal slabs when it is completed in 2015.

Outside of the KLCC, the other skyscraper city within the city is the KL Sentral, where the furious pace of building is revealing the likes of the 348 Sentral, which features a concertinaed glass-clad tower. The project was designed by one of the top architects in Malaysia, Hijjas Kasturi, who is also behind two iconic towers that have become city landmarks: Menara Maybank, with its interlocked blocks, and Menara Telekom, inspired by the bamboo shoot.

Outside of Kuala Lumpur, the firm has tied up with the innovative Italian Studio Nicoletti Associati on the breathtaking Putrajaya Waterfront Development, which conjures up gigantic whimsical sailboats.

Barbecuing fish at a waterfront food market stall in Kota Kinabalu.

CUISINE

Malaysia's deliciously diverse menu is a playground for the taste buds, and in this country it is the humbler outlets that are the real gems.

Malaysia has been blessed with hot, sunny weather, steady rainfall and rich soils: perfect for the cultivation of rice paddies, vegetables, fruits and spices. Meanwhile, mangroves and coral reefs make for precious nurseries for fish and other bounties of the river and seas. These gifts of nature, and the ethnic complexity of Malaysia's population, combine to provide the country with flavours to thrill the palate.

This hedonistic encounter extends not only to tastes, aromas, colours and textures, but also to the vast spectrum of dining experiences available in Malaysia. Eating establishments range from dusty roadside stalls and noisy Chinese *kopitiam* (coffee shops), to smart air-conditioned restaurants and Western-style fast-food joints. The choices are infinite.

What's more, because Malaysians love their food so much, no one ever goes hungry, as there will be a hawker stall or eatery that will be open any time of the day or night.

Delicious satay in Kota Kinabalu.

Malay fare

For centuries, Malays lived in *kampung* (villages) close to rivers and coasts, enjoying the natural abundance of food. Traditional meals consisted of rice, fish, vegetables and chilli sauces (*sambal*), while fresh herbs and coconut milk added fragrance and richness. However, until the 20th century, travel across the jungle-covered country was limited and regional styles of cooking prevailed. The northern peninsular states of Kedah, Kelantan, Perlis and Terengganu, for instance, have incorporated sour tamarind (*asam*), limes and fiery chillies in their cuisine because of the influence of neighbouring Thailand. One of the best-known northern dishes is *nasi ulam*, a dish consisting of rice, finely sliced raw herbs and vegetables, a spicy chilli-coconut

SATAY

Satay is possibly the world's most popular Malay food, but whatever else you've tasted in your own country, nothing can prepare you for the real thing. Marinated bite-sized pieces of beef, mutton or chicken (and pork if sold by Chinese) are barbecued over a charcoal fire on thin bamboo skewers. The sizzling satay is served with thick, spicy peanut gravy; raw onion and cucumber; and *ketupat* – compressed squares of rice. For the adventurous, there are even satay variations of tripe, intestines or crispy chicken skin. The most famous satay is that of Haji Samuri in Kajang, Selangor, whose recipe has spread throughout the town.

sauce, grilled fish and other cooked side dishes.

Indonesian and Arab influences are evident in other states. In Johor in the south, Javanese, Bugis and Arab styles were assimilated into Malay cooking over the past few centuries. In the central state of Negeri Sembilan, Minangkabau settlers from west Sumatra brought with them their rich, spicy dishes cooked in coconut milk. A perfect example is *rendang* – a semi-dry coconut-based curry which needs hours of gentle simmering, melding beef with fresh herbs like lemongrass, turmeric and ginger, and spices such as coriander, nutmeg and cloves. The result is pure ambrosia.

Despite differing regional styles, Malay food is, in general, heavily seasoned. Chillies are an everyday pick-me-up, either in dishes or as a blended *sambal* side-dish. The key to almost any Malay dish, however, is the *rempah* – a pounded paste of onions, garlic, chillies, fresh turmeric and galangal (*langkuas*). The rempah is stir-fried in hot oil in a *kuali* (wok) and patiently stirred to prevent sticking and to release its tantalising aromas. A subtle seafood flavour is often added in the form of dried shrimps, dried anchovies (*ikan bilis*) or a pungent shrimp paste (*belacan*).

Eating breakfast in KL's Petaling Street.

LOCAL EATING HABITS

The traditional way of eating, still practised in the average Malay, Indian and indigenous home, is with your fingers. It may look simple, but it is a skill to be mastered. Using only the tips of the fingers on the right hand (the left hand is considered unclean and never used), pick, tear, and scoop; locals do it with complete deftness. Chinese on the other hand, use chopsticks.

However, many Malaysians use a spoon in the right hand, which is brought to the mouth, and a fork in the left, used mainly for manoeuvring food onto the spoon.

Depending on what time they start work, breakfast can be from as early as 6am, and can be a simple bread meal, if not *nasi lemak* or a hot soupy noodle dish. Lunch is generally from noon–2pm and dinner from 7–9pm. The most common meal across all ethnic groups is rice with several dishes. Malaysians believe no meal is really filling without rice. At a communal table, individuals have their own plate of rice and the dishes are placed in the middle and shared.

Many Malaysians indulge in afternoon tea and supper, particularly on weekends, and buffet breakfasts and lunches are very popular. Weekends are also when Malaysians eat out, and they will not hesitate to drive far, dine at dingy places or experiment to sample the best fare.

Rice and noodles

Mouth-watering as they may sound, Malay recipes are lost without the simple, indispensable staple: rice (*nasi*). Rice dishes take many forms: *nasi minyak* (flavoured with spices like cardamom and cinnamon), nasi tomato (with tomatoes for a hint of sourness), *nasi goreng* (stir-fried with meat, eggs and chillies), and entire meals consisting of rice and side dishes: *nasi padang* (of Indonesian influence) and *nasi dagang* and *nasi ulam* (in Kelantan and Terengganu). Another popular rice dish is *nasi lemak*. The name means "creamy rice" – a savoury rice gently steamed in coconut milk until every drop of the liquid richness has been absorbed. The rice is then served with a fiery *sambal*, cucumber for coolness, small crispy fried fish, and a fried egg or omelette.

When you tire of rice, try noodles. Chinese immigrants introduced noodles to Malay cuisine and they are now an indispensable part of Malay cuisine: *mee* (a spaghetti-like yellow wheat noodle), kway teow (flat strips of smooth rice noodle) and *mee hoon* (thin rice vermicelli) – all can either be stir-fried (*goreng*), served in a light soup, or in speciality dishes such as *mee siam* (*mee hoon* in a red, spicy and sour soup), and *mee rebus* (*mee* in a thick, brown, spicy gravy).

Chinese-style noodle preparations, meanwhile, are equally mind-boggling, as is evident in hawker centres and Chinese *kopitiam*. Among the more popular fare, *wantan mee* are thin, fresh egg noodles either served in a broth or tossed in a chilli and oil-and-soy-sauce dressing, and topped with roast pork slices and prawn and pork dumplings.

Another popular noodle dish is *Ipoh kway teow*. As the name suggests, this soupy dish gained fame in the town of Ipoh, Perak. Smooth, translucent strips of rice noodles are served in a prawn and pork broth and garnished with bean sprouts, shredded chicken and prawns. Ipoh boasts the most delicate *kway teow* and fattest bean sprouts, supposedly because of the soft water which flows down from the surrounding limestone hills.

Char *kway teow* is another classic Chinese noodle dish: stir-fried flat rice noodles, garlic, prawns, cockles, bean sprouts, eggs, chilli paste and lashings of thick, dark soy sauce for a hint of sweetness. The Penang variety is particularly famous.

Chinese fare

Chinese immigrants also brought with them the cooking styles of their mainland regions; Cantonese, Hokkien, Teochew, Hakka and Hainanese predominate. However, the styles here have absorbed many local ingredients such as spices and chilli.

Cantonese eateries are the most common in the country, and the style generally employs a quick stir-fry method as well as boiled soups. Staples include the steamed spare ribs in black bean sauce, *char siu* (barbecued pork) and stir-fried leafy vegetables in oyster sauce. The best-known Cantonese breakfast is *dim sum*, whose selection range from dumplings to steamed buns and radish cakes.

Kueh teow with seafood in Kota Kinabalu.

SYMBOLIC FOOD

The Chinese believe that parts of an animal strengthen the corresponding part in the human body. So, eating pig's-brain soup will increase concentration, braised beef tendons will boost tired legs, and so on. Symbolic meaning also comes from the names of foods, particularly during the Chinese New Year. For example, a kind of seaweed called *fatt choy*, phonetically identical to the Chinese characters meaning "to prosper", is often stewed with dried oysters (*hou si*), which sounds like "good business". Other must-haves during this period are prawns and dried beancurd, both symbolising happiness, and noodles for long life.

Malaysia's other ethnically complex cuisine is Eurasian food. Typically multicultural, Malay herbs enliven Chinese cuts of meat, further enhanced by Indian mustard seeds and chillies.

Teochew fare is simple, and the best known is the teochew porridge, rice broth with various salted and preserved meats and vegetables. However, the richer fare includes the sensuously smoky braised goose and the creamy yam custard dessert.

Nasi lemak.

Hakka fare derives its fame from its *yeung tau fu*, a lovely assortment of beancurd and vegetables stuffed with fish paste. This has a following among Malays too, and can be found in some Malay food centres. Other famous Hakka dishes are the salt-baked chicken and pork belly with mustard greens in thick soy sauce.

Most typical of the Hainanese style is the Hainanese chicken rice, a hawker speciality, where whole chickens are simmered in chicken stock so that each slice is moist and tender. The chicken is served with delicious rice cooked in chicken stock and served with a chilli garlic condiment. The Hainanese were once employed by British colonialists as cooks. They slipped Chinese seasonings such as soy sauce and oyster

sauce into sedate English food, resulting in tastier roasts as well as famous chicken and pork chops slathered with peas, onions and a gravy seasoned with garlic and soy sauce.

Indian fare

Although Indians make up only about 10 percent of the population, Indian stalls and restaurants proliferate. The majority of Indians are Tamils from the South Indian state of Tamil Nadu, whose food is hot and spicy and served with rice. But there are also North Indian restaurants, dishing up milder fare such as tandooris with delicious breads like *naan* and *poori*. In addition, there are eateries run by Indian Muslims, with their *nasi kandar* fare, literally, "rice that is carried on a pole", which is how this food used to be hawked about.

Eating at one of the many South Indian "banana leaf curry" restaurants, you will experience one of the heartiest and most colourful culinary spreads around. The banana leaf itself is not eaten, but acts as a natural, disposable green plate from which spicy dry *varuvel* mutton, fried fish, chicken curry, red curried crabs and a variety of spiced vegetables and pickles are eaten. Vegetarian options are always available.

The meal is often accompanied by fresh yoghurt to cool the palate, and cups of thin, spicy soup (*rasam*) to aid digestion. The meal is strongly seasoned with the dried spices used by Indians for thousands of years: chillies, cardamom, cloves, cumin, fenugreek, cinnamon, fennel and mustard seeds, to name just a few of the aromatics used. Fresh lime juice is almost always available to top it all off.

Mamak food

Nasi kandar meals are known by their popular nomenclature "*mamak*", which means "uncle" in Tamil. The food is usually served in *thali*, round metal trays, with the accompanying dishes served in small bowls. The food tends to be spicier than the Indian varieties, and spices used in Malay cooking are added. Specialities include the local concoction of fish head curry, beef curry in black sauce, tiger prawn masala curry and boiled okra or brinjal. When served, curries are mixed to suit individual tastebeds. The best *nasi kandar* remains in the peninsula's northern states.

Malaysians would stand firm on the claim that India's greatest culinary contribution to Malaysia is the multi-layered, feather-light *roti canai* (flattened bread), which does battle with the Malay *nasi lemak* as Malaysians' favourite breakfast. When visiting Indian hawker stalls, don't forget to try Indian *mee goreng* (fried yellow noodles), which are similar to the Malay version, but with slightly different spices, and Indian *rojak*, deep-fried fritters and vegetables served with a sweet, hot sauce.

Nonya cuisine

Nonya or Peranakan food is a bi-cultural cuisine unique to Malaysia and its island neighbour, Singapore. It is the food of the Peranakan, or Straits-born Chinese, whose women, called Nonya, concocted these unique, delectable dishes.

Nonya food subtly merges typical Chinese ingredients such as pork, soy sauce and preserved soya beans with Malay spices, *rempah* ingredients and the ever-present coconut milk and/or tamarind juice. Some favourites are *babi asam* (a tamarind-based pork curry) and pork satay, with pineapple-enhanced peanut sauce.

Duck, traditionally not consumed by Malays, is popular in Nonya kitchens, where it is braised whole, or made into a curry or sour soup (*itek sio*). Chicken is also commonly used, transformed into varied dishes such as chicken *kapitan* (chicken in spicy coconut milk) and *enchee kabin* (fried chicken with a tangy dip).

Much like Malay cuisine, Nonya food evolved differently in different parts of the peninsula. *Laksa*, a classic Nonya dish, comes in two varieties: Melakan cooks favour *laksa lemak* (also called curry laksa) which consists of noodles, prawns and other toppings bathed in a *lemak* (rich) spicy coconut soup. Then there is *asam laksa*, a famous speciality of Penang Nonyas. This variety, with distinct Thai influences, comprises noodles in a clear, fish-based soup, topped with raw cucumber and onion rings, pineapple chunks and mint sprigs.

Food from the jungle

Traditional Bornean food is hard to find outside the longhouses and remote villages. Rice is the staple, although some tribes still adhere to diets based on boiled sago palm and tapioca root. Raw meats and fish are preserved by smoking or curing in salt. Jungle vegetables like bamboo shoots and fern tips are regular accompaniments, as are lashings of lime and chilli.

Nowadays, what is typical food in Sabah and Sarawak is in fact a Chinese- and Malay-influenced

cuisine. From the Chinese immigrants this century, Borneo food has adopted ingredients like soy sauce, and cooking methods such as stir-frying; from the Malays, chillies, dried shrimp and prawn paste (*belacan*). Using these ingredients, vegetables, jungle animals such as wild boar and seafood from the coast and rivers are deliciously braised and stir-fried.

Flavours from around the world

As if this diversity were not enough, Malaysia is home to plenty of international restaurants as well, particularly in Kuala Lumpur and Penang;

The Nonya dish laksa.

the capital's scene can be upmarket and sophisticated. Quality European cuisine is readily available, particularly Italian and Spanish; likewise Asian cuisine, namely Japanese, Korean, Thai and Vietnamese. Arab restaurants have sprung up to cater to Middle Eastern tourists, and there are excellent options for tajines, grills and humus.

Locally, with centuries of experience in fusing foods, variations of cuisine combinations continue to be popular. There has been a nostalgic wave towards things traditional, manifested most obviously in the contemporary *kopitiam* chains that have overtaken the country. At the same time, organic, vegetarian and vegan cafés are gaining traction, as are outlets offering speciality wines and coffees.

HAWKER FOOD AND OUTDOOR EATS

The best of Malaysia's food isn't served at fancy restaurants but at stalls set up by the roadside, in hawker centres, or in street-side coffee shops.

Patronised by every level of society, hawker stalls are found all over Malaysia, from urban sites beside busy highways to idyllic seaside locations. Feeding and slaking the thirst of the nation is a round-the-clock affair: Malaysians, as a rule, live to eat and not the other way around. With such low prices, who can be bothered to cook? And as most hawkers specialise in only a few dishes, they have perfected their culinary skills to a degree where most people would prefer to eat out than in. Basic tables and stools are provided on-site. Hawkers will often ask if you want to *makan* – "eat there", or *bungkus* – "take away".

Where to eat

Each city has its own famous outdoor eating centre. In Kuala Lumpur (KL), head for Chinatown's famed Jalan Alor for Chinese and other specialities. For Malay food, don't miss the Pasar Minggu in Kampung Bahru. After dark in Penang, Gurney Drive offers an array of multi-ethnic treats by the sea. Melaka's best-known hawker scene for dinner and supper is at the old Newton Hawker Centre.

Locals and tourists alike head to the Kuching Open Air Food Court, which is open all day and night. In Miri, the Bandong Hawker Centre has 60 stalls offering Malay and Chinese food. Kota Kinabalu's open-air hawker street next to KK Plaza comes alive in the evening.

Kuala Lumpur's Jalan Masjid India area is a popular hunting ground for roti canai, as well as for the variety of sweet and savoury snacks known as kuih that proliferate during Ramadan.

Nasi lemak is Malaysia's favourite breakfast, and consists of rice cooked in coconut milk, served with egg, cucumber, anchovies and a spicy sambal sauce.

A wide range of food on skewers at Gurney Drive's food stand 4 in Penang.

Grilling satay, the unofficial "national" dish, over a charcoal brazier at a stall in Chinatown in KL.

ROTI CANAI BREAKFAST

Walk through any Malaysian town at breakfast, and the most crowded eateries will usually be those serving *roti canai*. Its English description, an unleavened pancake served with dhal, just doesn't do it justice. It is deliciously light, flaky and crisp, the perfect vehicle to soak up spicy sauces and curries.

Most cooks show off their skills at the front of their shops; it takes years of practice to swing out the dough until it is paper thin. The theatrical flourishes when tossing the *roti* may appear excessive, but are needed to keep the pancake as light and flaky as possible.

A speciality of Indian-Muslim and now Malay cooks, the origins of *roti canai* probably lie in the Indian subcontinent, and like many Malaysian favourites, it has evolved over generations into a strictly localised dish. Variations include *roti telur* (with egg), *roti sardin* (canned tomato sardines) and as a dessert, *roti pisang* (bananas). This is also the food of choice for late night/early morning supper.

Other popular Indian breads are *putu mayam* (string hoppers), derived from the Keralan variety, the steamed Tamil lentil-and-rice *idli* and the unleavened *poori*.

Stocking up at a roti canai stall in Penang. The best way to eat the dish is with your hands, tearing off flaky portions and dipping them into dhal or your alternative chosen accompaniment.

Jalan Alor's Chinese hawker stalls in Kuala Lumpur are hugely popular with locals.

Sata is a traditional Terengganu dish consisting of spiced fish and coconut roasted in banana leaves.

ARTS AND CRAFTS

The artistic heritage of Malaysia ranges from intricate indigenous craft born of centuries-old tradition, to contemporary art that is gaining global attention.

From prehistoric cave murals to cutting-edge contemporary oil painting, the story of Malaysian art spans over 2,000 years of creativity; traditional crafts, which still survive on the Malay Peninsula's east coast and in the longhouses of Sarawak and Sabah, could well have been around for even longer. Located at the heart of Southeast Asia, at the meeting of the ancient trade routes, Malaysian culture has always been heavily influenced by multiple influences; its arts and crafts a reflection of this cross-cultural interweaving.

Prehistoric art

Over two millennia ago, unknown artists painted abstract designs, human figures and animals on the walls of a cave near Ipoh, Perak. Meanwhile, across the South China Sea in Sarawak, artisans in the Niah Caves were also painting over 100 depictions of human figures and boats, in murals over 50 metres (165ft) long. Cave paintings are rare in Malaysia, and for many years scholars wondered who these artisans were, and what the drawings meant. Later discoveries of con-temporary Orang Asli cave drawings in Perak, in Sarawak and in Sabah suggest that the prehis-toric artists were probably the ancestors of the more recent Orang Asli cave painters, and that the murals depicted the cultural and religious aspects of the original prehistoric painters' lives.

Malaysian crafts date back to the earliest human settlement. A Palaeolithic workshop for making crude stone chopping tools, excavated at Kota Tampan, Perak, dates to 38,000 years ago, while sophisticated flaked stone tools from Sabah's Tingkayu region can be traced back some 28,000 years.

Around 2,000 BC, during the Neolithic era, pottery and polished stone tools appeared.

A carved head in the Sarawak Museum in Kuching.

Wooden paddles and anvil stones were prob-ably used to produce some of the pottery, including sophisticated three-colour urns from the Niah Caves. This production method is still used today by Sarawak's Iban peoples.

In the remote highlands of Bario in Sarawak, and in the lowland wetlands near Santubong, there are some unusual rock carvings where figures and spiral designs have been engraved into boulders. The only stone carvings in Penin-sular Malaysia are a group of carved megalithic stones at Pengkalan Kempas in Negeri Sembi-lan. This group of three stones, of unknown origin and age, are one of Malaysia's greatest archaeological mysteries, as they depict Hindu-type phallic symbols along with the Islamic script for Allah (God). Scholars are divided as to whether the carvings were done at the same time, or whether the Allah inscription was done later to sanctify a pagan site. Stone foundations of buildings and temples found in Kedah's Bujang Valley apparently supported a wooden infrastructure which has long since perished.

Woodcarving

Woodcarving is a popular craft in Sarawak, where the Kajang people still carve wooden burial poles, or *klirieng*, to house jars containing ashes of deceased chiefs. The oldest surviving pole is

An artisan carving at the Cultural Village in Sarawak.

Traditionally, a woodcarver would enter the forest to select his own timber and chant incantations to appease forest spirits.

200 years old, but the tradition is believed to date back many centuries more. The Iban of Sarawak carve spectacular hornbill sculptures, while the upriver Kenyah carve mythical dog-god ancestors. Kuching's Main Bazaar is a centre for the craft from the interior. In the peninsula, ancient woodcarving traditions survive with two indigenous Orang Asli groups. The Mah Meri of Pulau Carey, Selangor, are famed for their marvellous spirit masks and sculptures (see page 143). The

Jah Hut of Pahang sculpt small ceremonial carvings to "trap" the manifold spirits that cause an illness; their tradition is sadly dying.

Malay woodcarvings have a small market decorating the foyers of banks, businesses and government offices, as well as tourist resorts. Some of the finest antique Malay woodcarvings can be seen on the panelling, pillars, windows and doors of the nation's oldest royal palaces, such as what is now the Sri Menanti Museum in Negeri Sembilan, which were all built of wood. Che Long of Terengganu was a celebrated master carver, and during four decades of his century-long life he was the principal builder for the Raja of Besut. Examples of his work still exist in many buildings in Besut, with beautifully carved panels of floral patterns and verses from the Koran.

Metalwork and jewellery

From the first century AD, Indian and Chinese travellers told of legendary Malay kingdoms like Langkasuka and Chi Tu (Red Earth Land). They would describe ancient courts where rulers wore fabulous gold jewellery and dressed in "rose-coloured cloth" – possibly the first-known reference to Malay hand-woven *songket*. It is hard to separate reality from fiction in these fabled accounts, but by the time of the Melakan sultanate in the 14th century, artisans and craftspeople were an integral part of the royal court. Many lived and worked in the villages beside the palace. Sultans, chiefs, nobles and their wives and families were the moneyed class, and silversmiths and goldsmiths, silk-weavers and woodcarvers depended on royal patronage for their existence.

However, when the courts became more westernised, rulers started buying imported jewellery, clothing and artefacts. The habit of betel-nut chewing went out of fashion, for instance, rendering obsolete the silver items used in its preparation, and forcing many artisans to hang up their tools. Similarly, many traditional arts and crafts are in danger of extinction.

Fortunately, silversmiths still thrive in Kota Bharu, despite having vanished elsewhere. These days, jewellery and functional pieces like fruit bowls, tea-sets and spoons are popular, and although past fashions called for different artefacts, the designs and techniques employed are the same. In Islam, it is taboo to use anthropomorphic figures, and many of the patterns are therefore inspired by flowers, branches and even clouds.

Early silverware is often of exceptional crafts-manship, like the earliest surviving example – a royal Johorean betel-set from the early 18th century. Probably the most fascinating of all the old pieces are leaf-shaped modesty discs which until the 19th century were the only clothing worn by little Malay girls.

In the 1800s, the Straits Chinese of Melaka and Penang, also known as Peranakan – whose ancestors were early Chinese traders who inter-married with local women – borrowed heavily from Malay silver and gold traditions to create their own craft, which is distinguishable from

> Batik derives from the Malay word tik, meaning "to drip". It is thought that batik replaced tattooing as a mark of status in Malay culture.

traditional Malay work by its designs, which often feature birds and flowers.

Today, gold is the most favoured metal for jewellery as it is used in ceremonies and as gifts connected with rites of passage across ethnic groups. Traditional designs are popular, with most pieces still handcrafted, but international designs are gaining a following. Contemporary sterling silver jewellery is beginning to find a foothold too.

Woven fabrics

Silk brocades, known as *kain songket*, have always been the favoured textiles for royal occa-sions, and these elegant woven cloths are still the preferred wear, not only for courtly occa-sions but as traditional bridal wear, when both the bride and groom are dressed in sumptu-ous brocade outfits. At a Kelantanese weaver's showroom, a pale mauve colour is still sold only to royalty, and there are certain designs which are even now the prerogative of the tra-ditional ruler.

The very best weavers worked for the pal-ace, like the grandmother of one of Tereng-ganu's top weavers, who was picked from two thousand local artisans of her day to become the sultan's head weaver. Like most other time-honoured crafts, *songket* weaving is practised in Terengganu and Kelantan and the techniques and looms used are the same as in the old days.

Woven on a simple four-posted loom, the brocade consists of a coloured silk back-ground with a floating weft of gold and silver threads. A distinctive part of every length is the *kepala*, a centre panel with a particularly elaborate pattern. The names of the designs echo the Malay affinity with nature and the countryside: one is known as "bamboo shoots", another "the tail feathers of a cock". Traditionally, nobles would design their own *songket* patterns. Under the patronage of the Sul2tanah of Terengganu, *songket* weaving is being revived in through training, employ-

Traditional textiles at the Cultural Village in Sarawak.

ment and financial aid. Products are sold under the Royal Terengganu Songket brand.

Related to the *kain songket* is *tekat*, an ancient craft of gold embroidery on rich, dark velvet. This luxurious material is popular among Malays for home furnishings, wall hangings, cushions and even bedroom slippers.

From Sarawak hails *ikat*, a unique woven fab-ric with a tie-dyed warp. The Iban *pua kumbu* ("grand blanket") is the most revered of these textiles, serving many ritual purposes: newly born babies are wrapped in them to ward off evil influences and in the past, trophy heads from headhunting expeditions were draped with these cloths. Weaving is still a highly respected skill in the Iban community, and the best weavers, usually those living in long-houses, are said to be granted visions by deities in dreams, which they transform into remarkable pieces of art.

Batik

Batik is often used to symbolise Malaysia. The national airline uses it for its uniforms, while batik shirts are *de rigueur* as men's formal attire and are even compulsory dress at the nation's only casino. It is also worn as sarongs and used for the fashionable and traditional women's dress known as *baju kurung*. But batik-making

Batik masks sold as souvenirs on Jonkers Street in Melaka.

is not a traditional Malay craft: it was introduced from Indonesia in the 1930s. However, although it is of recent origin, there is no denying that batik-making is now the nation's most popular craft.

Using a wax-resistant technique, the patterns are stamped onto lengths of cloth using a printing block made from zinc strips bent into the desired shaped, and dipped in molten wax. However, the biggest success story is of hand-painted batiks, where the designs are drawn on the cloth using a *canting*, a "pen" filled with liquid wax, with the dyes then painted on with brushes. This latter method means that more colours can be used than with the vat-dyeing method, and the freehand designs are only

limited by the artisan's imagination. While the majority of craftspeople are based on the east coast of the peninsula, batik workshops are now found all over Malaysia.

It was also in Malaysia that batik was pioneered in fine art in the 1950s. Chuah Thean Teng used traditional batik technique to produce vibrant works featuring expressionistic figures. Half a century later, Fatimah Chik has continued this tradition but with an abstract bend, and garnering attention such as with her award-winning Muslim prayer mat executed in batik.

Pottery and other crafts

Beside the Perak river, opposite the royal town of Kuala Kangsar, is the village of Sayong, renowned throughout Malaysia for the manufacture of *Labu Sayong*. Literally "Sayong Pumpkins", these gourd-shaped pottery water vessels keep liquids cool in even the hottest weather. The women of Sayong are the potters and have been for more generations than they can remember. The pots are made in moulds from local clay and then finished on the wheel, where they are incised with freehand designs. After drying in the sun they are fired in small brick kilns. Both terracotta and black-coloured wares are made, with the latter obtaining their distinct colour from being buried in rice husks while they are still hot from the kiln.

The indigenous peoples are renowned for their skill in weaving baskets, mats and hats. The Orang Ulu of Sarawak weave fine black and white baskets from split rattan. To find the best materials they often have to walk a day's journey deep into the forest, then they dry, split and finally colour the rattan with dye made of forest leaves.

Making mats from *nipah* palm or *pandanus* leaves requires equal skill. Throughout the country, woven mats are an essential part of daily life, used on the floor in *kampung* houses, on beds, on the beach, in mosques, for drying food under the sun and anywhere else that a convenient, light covering might be needed. Weaving begins at the centre of the mat and moves outwards, using dyes to produce simple criss-cross patterns. More professional weavers (mostly women) fashion hexagonal boxes of nipah palm leaves. Orang Asli weavers are highly skilled, and communities such as the Mah Meri in Selangor have formed collectives to keep the heritage going. In Sabah and Sarawak, floral and even pictorial stories are part of the woven mat's design.

Contemporary art

When the British colonial era introduced industrially made goods, it was inevitable that traditional arts and crafts would go into decline. At this same time, however, new arts were being introduced like oil painting and watercolours. At first, Malaysian artists emulated western styles, but particularly after independence artists created their own brand of abstract art.

Since then, the landscape has been marked by a diversification of artists and directions, for example, the mainstreaming of new forms such as video, the entry of controversy-courting performance art and underground movements. The scene is also increasingly sophisticated and commodified, through a growth in art criticism and public outreach as well as a proliferation of art auctions and commercial galleries. Looking ahead, Malaysian artisans and artists are continuing to use and yet go beyond cultural, ethnic and religious precepts to create and inspire.

Contemporary art at the Central Market, KL.

Three of the arguably best known of this group are Latiff Mohidin, who uses indigenous motifs and the environment as inspiration, Syed Ahmad Jamal, who champions abstract expressionism, and Ibrahim Hussein, whose linear printing-cum-collages express complexities of form and dimensions.

The economic boom of the late 1980s and 1990s saw not only newly innovative and prolific artists but public institutions, collectors and patronage. Seminal works include Rafiee Ghani's colourful "roomscapes", Wong Hoy Cheong's epic series on immigration, Ahmad Zakii Anuar's smoke-blurred portraits and Lee Joo For's bonding of eastern and western visual language.

WONG HOY CHEONG

The powerful art of Wong Hoy Cheong is deeply rooted in the socio-politico-historical context. Penang-born and internationally acclaimed, Wong examines identity, questions official narratives and critiques ideology. He researches painstakingly to produce work ranging from charcoal drawings to installations; the hallmarks of his art are both fine detail and elaborate schemes. Wong is hugely influential and as a teacher is leaving an impact on scores of younger artists. His achievements include a Rockefeller Foundation Bellagio Creative Arts Fellowship and exhibitions at numerous Biennales including the 50th Venice Biennale.

Trekking to the giant caves of Mulu National Park, Sarawak.

ADVENTURE SPORTS

Forest-clad mountains, giant caves, roaring rivers and deep oceans make Malaysia an attractive and challenging destination for the thrill seeker.

Root-covered trails, thick vegetation and thundering waterfalls are part of the excitement of trekking or biking in the rugged interior of Malaysia's tropical rainforests. The highland forests are also the source of swift, bubbling headwaters that run into massive river systems, offering superb rafting and kayaking. Some of these streams seep through the porous limestone massifs, forming huge cave systems waiting to be explored and mapped. Their tiny entrances are often masked by thick foliage – which is also why few cliff faces are available for rock-climbing. Those that are suitable, however, are excellent.

Outdoor pursuits

Malaysia's rainforests offer all manner of challenges to both body and mind; centuries before yuppies started tackling them with their high-tech gear, these challenges were, for the indigenous people, part of daily life.

Adventure sports are relatively new in Malaysia, having soared in popularity only since 2005. Interestingly, this trend was boosted by aggressive promotions by gyms and the advent of budget airlines. Younger Malaysians would have been exposed to some of these sports in universities, either locally or overseas.

However, an increase in affluence and interest in travel are seeing more Malaysians donning lycra or trail hikers, particularly those over 40. Trekking, mountain-biking and scuba-diving are the activities of choice. Interest in the more technical sports such as caving and mountaineering tends to be driven by the more affluent and overseas-educated Malaysians as well as expatriates.

Other than for scuba-diving, however, the

Hikers climbing Mount Kinabalu, Malaysia's highest mountain.

infrastructure is nascent, expertise is scarce and sites undeveloped. Because of the lack of standards and governing bodies, safety can be a concern. The remoteness of locations where adventure sports are enjoyed, and lack of good hospitals means that the onus for safety lies with the operator and the participant. The quality of equipment also varies, although a large variety is available; the exception would be cycling, as specialist bike shops tend to be run by enthusiasts. Insurance is available locally but only minimal coverage is provided; as world-over, getting good insurance coverage for these sports is a problem. Participants should therefore ensure they are as well informed and prepared as possible, even for something as "harmless" as a jungle trek.

There are also clubs, mostly based in Kuala Lumpur, but all the big cities have interest groups. Among the more active are mountain-biking, mountaineering, rock-climbing, as well as jungle-trekking. Multi-sport expedition racing has some following, with former international racer Chan Yuen-Li organising short adventure races under the Eco-X label.

Probably the greatest difficulty faced by rainforest-based adventure sports proponents

best jungle guides, it provides a chance to learn about remarkable and fast-disappearing ways of life.

The most challenging jungle-trekking is to be found in the country's mountainous interiors. In the peninsula, these concentrate in the backbone of Banjaran Titiwangsa (Main Range); in Sabah, the Crocker Range; and in Sarawak, the northern Mulu area. Countless routes can be taken, whether in the Livingstonian quest for waterfalls, or to scale a mountain, or simply to experience the many ecosystems that make up the rainforest.

Rock-climbing in Langkawi.

in Malaysia is the humidity, which can reach close to 100 percent in the forest. Dehydration is another problem because of the heat. Luckily there is always an icy-cold river close at hand. In some areas, fortification is necessary against the threat of tropical diseases such as malaria.

Jungle-trekking

Trekking is often a wet experience on muddy trails and across numerous rivers, sometimes by boulder-hopping. However, hot-footing it with a backpack is the best way to experience the amazing jungle and encounter the extremely elusive tropical wildlife. And because the Orang Asli and natives make the

Hundreds of kilometres of trails wind through protected areas, mainly serving conservation objectives. Other trails have been trammelled for generations by the indigenous people who still travel on foot to their remote villages. In wilder country, it is the animal trails along the steep ridges that form some kind of pathway through the thorny rattan- and liana-strewn undergrowth.

Mountain hikes

Many of the longer trails involve ascending to mountain tops, such as the seven-day hike to Mount Tahan (2,200 metres/7,000ft) in Taman Negara, and the four-day ascent to Mount Mulu (2,400 metres/7,900ft). The popular overnight trails up the country's highest peak, Mount Kinabalu (4,100 metres/13,400ft) are relatively civilised, if stamina-sapping.

Far tougher is the adrenalin-pumping and astoundingly beautiful *via ferrata* route to the peak, a mountain route equipped with rungs, cables and bridges enabling access usually limited to mountaineers. Afficionados of the activity shouldn't miss out, as this route is the world's highest *via ferrata*.

Exciting country lies in the largely unvisited northern tracts of Banjaran Titiwangsa in the peninsula's Belum area, steep hilly ter-

Rock-climbing

Rock-climbing has long been popular among tiny pockets of enthusiasts. Sport-climbing, which is more accessible than traditional climbing, has a largish following thanks to the proliferation of artificial climbing walls throughout the country.

Most of Peninsular Malaysia's rock-climbing surfaces are limestone, characterised by steep overhanging rock and often stalactites, which make routes tough (at least 6A French grade; climbing grades range from 3 to 9A). The cliffs are also high, usually 100 metres

Gua Ikan ("Fish Cave") in Kelantan is known as one of Malaysia's most fascinating caves for naturalists.

rain full of hidden waterfalls, and in Sabah's Maliau Basin, termed East Malaysia's last frontier for its less-known landscapes. More accessible peaks include Cameron Highlands' Mount Berembun and Mount Brinchang, which afford views of highland forests, vegetable farms and tea plantations.

In Sarawak, Mount Santubong, the magnificent backdrop for the Sarawak Cultural Village, is a popular climb. Tour groups do organise trips but interest groups probably know the terrain best, including the socially conscious Waterfall Survivors, who have bases in Selangor and Kota Kinabalu, and the Penang-based Anak Hutan and Penang Adventurer's Club.

> Malaysia makes for challenging climbs. Rock faces are always steep, cliffs are often high, and dense vegetation makes some faces almost impossible to scale.

(300ft), so paths have to be established from the ground up.

The most frequently visited rock-climbing spots around the capital are Batu Caves (170 routes) and Bukit Takun (30 routes) near Templer's Park. The former is easy to access and has moderately challenging routes. Takun is a more traditional rock face, which involves a bit of a clamber through thick undergrowth to reach.

However, both offer several interesting routes. The highest grade of climb locally is 7C.

Other popular climbs are Bukit Keteri in Perlis, Gua Musang in Kelantan and the tough Fairy Cave in Sarawak. Pulau Tioman offers bouldering and slab wall climbing as well as the spectacular 270-metre (886ft) high Dragon's Horns.

Cave adventures

Superlatives abound when it comes to the caving haven of Mulu – largest, longest, most decorated. Mulu's giant caves offer superb adventure and technical caving opportuni-

of the Gunung Mulu National Park is the Gunung Buda National Park, home to the deepest vertical drop in Southeast Asia (140 metres/460ft), accessible through challenging ropework amid thundering waterfalls.

In the peninsula, caves that are open as showcaves and for adventure caving include the Dark Cave in Selangor and Gua Tempurung in Perak. Other limestone wonders such as the Perlis Wang Kelian State Park and Perak's Kinta Valley are best accessed through organisations such as the Kuala Lumpur-based Malaysian Nature Society's caving group.

Heading out on a dive boat in Langkawi.

ties. Most of the area's 360km (225 miles) of surveyed passages are wet, with large and sudden water-level fluctuations, depending on rain; dry floors are often thick with guano. There are spectacular traverses, squeezes and stretches of tough ropework and plenty of clambering around massive stalagmites and crossing narrow bridges of fretted rock. No one knows how much more of Mulu remains to be discovered, and joint Malaysian-foreign caving groups come in on surveying expeditions virtually every year.

Nearby are Mount Api, with the second-largest chamber in Malaysia; and the neighbouring Mount Benarat, some to the second-longest cave system in Mulu. North

THE RIGHT OPERATOR

Even if you are recommended an adventure sports operator, ask in detail about the organisation's technical, professional and safety standards. Registered companies ("Sdn. Bhd.") tend to be safer bets than freelancers, as are specialists in adventure sports rather than general tour operators. Ask to see guides' up-to-date certification and if taking instruction, check out the syllabus beforehand. While most operators require participants to sign indemnity forms, this does not necessarily mean that the company is not liable should there be an accident – which is why registered outfits are preferable.

Mountain-biking

While old timber trails in the interior sometimes give hikers access to undisturbed forest, they are more popular with mountain-bikers. The sport is boosted through the efforts of professional riders organising groups, races and rides. Clubs such as the Pedalholics Cycling Club and the Kuala Lumpur Mountain Bike Hash organise short- and long-distance rides, while informal groups comprising friends spend weekends exploring oil palm and rubber plantations, as well as secondary forest near towns. These provide everything

in it is growing and instruction is available. "Cowboy" operators abound, so check if the outfit is licensed by the Department of Civil Aviation (DCA) Malaysia, whether the instructor has certification and that a logbook is maintained.

A pilot's licence is required for winged aircraft and a student licence requires 30 hours of flight training. Microlight or ultralight aircraft flying is based in Melaka. The planes are allowed to fly at a maximum height of 150 metres (500ft), with a 5km (3-mile) radius from the point of take-off. A good introduction is

Parasailing over Batu Feringghi beach.

from fairly simple trails to challenging hilly terrain, and the vegetation makes for much cooler riding than on the road.

Wider and flatter jungle trails can actually also make good, if tough, riding – with their root-covered paths, numerous river crossings and breathtaking views. The Headhunters' Trail in Mulu, Sarawak, is one such trail, while another good trail is the dirt road on the border of Taman Negara which leads from Jerantut to the Kuala Tahan *kampung*, opposite the park headquarters.

Aerial sports

Recreational flying is almost prohibitively expensive to take up in Malaysia, but interest

the 10-minute joyride, where licensed pilots fly visitors over the city of Melaka. A simpler aircraft is the powered paraglider or paramotor, basically paragliders driven by a two-stroke engine worn like a backpack. Instruction is available in Klang, Selangor, and tandem rides on trikes (three-wheeled frames) are a good way to try out the sport.

The most accessible and affordable aerial sport is paragliding, and two centres for this are Jugra Hill in Selangor, which takes in great views of the sea, and the hills of Kota Kinabalu in Sabah, where tandem paragliding is also offered.

Meanwhile, interest is growing in skyjumping, which is available in Kuala Lumpur (with

> Highland rivers can swell to Grade 5 rapids after a downpour. Don't be mislead by local meanings – in some areas, "dry season" means that it only rains in the afternoon instead of all day.

Whitewater action

Malaysia's many rivers offer good whitewater experiences. One of the top sites is the spectacular Padas Gorge in Sabah. Tour operators usually offer rafting experiences on 8- to 10-seater inflatable rafts with river guides. Kiulu River, closer to Kota Kinabalu, offers a softer adventure.

Generally, whitewater tour operators are well organised, experienced and provide safety equipment, a briefing, sometimes insurance, and lunch. Nonetheless, safety is the most overlooked aspect of this sport, and it is

actual jumps in Taiping, Perak) and Segamat, Johor. A 2.5-day static-line course includes ground training, and static jumps must be completed before freefalling is allowed. Tandem skyjumping with an instructor is also

Whitewater rafting at Sungai Kampar in Perak.

available, while experienced jumpers can opt for fun-jumping. Minimum numbers might apply.

Only certified, experienced skydivers are allowed to participate in the extreme BASE jumping, or fixed object jumping. An informal group gathers most Saturdays at Batu Caves. However, the sport's largest event is the annual KL Tower (Menara Kuala Lumpur) International BASE Jump, established in 1999 and today a four-day event which draws tens of participants for day and night jumps; a set minimum length of experience and number of jumps previously completed is required. A newer BASE jumping event is now being held in Sibu, Sarawak.

important to check that tour companies have emergency procedures in place.

North of Kuala Lumpur, Sungai Selangor, Sungai Sungkai and Sungai Kampar are centres for nice-and-easy kayaking and rafting, with up to Grade 3 rapids. The routes are set in rustic, rural landscapes of secondary forest, lush plantations and Malay and indigenous Orang Asli villages. Experienced kayakers will find thrills on offer in other stretches of Sungai Selangor as well as the tougher multi-day Sungai Singor route in the Belum forest reserve.

Riverboarding is the newest whitewater sport to take hold in Malaysia and centres on Perak and Selangor.

Scuba-diving

Malaysia's coral islands offer a multitude of stunning possibilities for scuba-diving, and with local tourism boards promoting sites heavily – particularly Terengganu and Sabah – tourists are flocking to them as snorkellers; most will also try their hand at diving.

Almost every diveable Malaysian destination has operators offering tours, full equipment rental and dive instruction in padi, naui, ssi and/or sdi. Most resort-based facilities accept walk-in trade, but scheduled dive trips are offered by operators in Kuala Lumpur,

photographers for its exotic life unique to the silt, while hammerhead and manta ray enthusiasts head for Layang Layang, situated in the South China Sea.

Malaysia's reefs and marine life are among the world's richest and most diverse. Each dive destination, and sometimes dive spot, is characterised by endemics, from odd macro life in Kapalai to pelagics in Tenggol, coral-wreathed wrecks in Labuan, to the huge diversity of marine life in Redang.

Other sea sports, while popular, do not enjoy such enthusiastic patronage. You'll

A cycling group in KL.

Kuala Terengganu, Mersing, Tawau, Labuan and Kota Kinabalu.

While there are internationally rated dive centres, at the other end of the scale are operators who are not registered with dive agencies, or are lax about medical and safety equipment such as buoyancy compressors. The Malaysian Scuba-Diving Association is working with government agencies to set local standards, ensure enforcement of marine park rules and promote the sport.

The most developed facilities and services are in Sabah, off whose coast is the region's premier dive destination, Sipadan. Close to Sipadan is the muck-diving haven at Mabul, which is popular with underwater

> *Underwater photography is becoming popular, with some operators renting out underwater cameras too. For experienced divers, a few operations offer nitrox and technical diving as well.*

find wind-surfing at beach resorts, while sailing has a small, mainly expatriate following among members of yacht clubs. The peninsula's east coast, are sea sport centres, particularly in Pahang and Johor. The range of activities is quite wide, including beach and shore-break surfing during the monsoon period of November to February.

Tanjung Aru water village in Sabah.

Traversing the FRIM canopy walkway in Selangor.

Bukit Bintang in Kuala Lumpur.

An Orang Asli house in the Cameron Highlands.

INTRODUCTION

A detailed guide to the entire country, with principal sites clearly cross-referenced by number to the maps.

A dragon wall carving at Kuek Seng Onn Chinese Temple in Kuching.

Malaysia is a land of surprising contradictions: picturesque fishing villages and opulent hotels share the same sandy beach, cosy colonial resorts nestle on hillsides that host spirit-worshipping tribal ceremonies, while secondary forests are penetrated by the strains of karaoke. Throw in the cultural pastiche that is the Malaysian people and the result is an irresistible combination of charm and adventure that is still just a glimpse of the "real" Malaysia.

Situated right in the middle of Southeast Asia, Malaysia is about the size of Japan and has a population of over 30 million. The country's infrastructure is well set up for tourism and consequently, it is fairly easy and safe to travel anywhere in the country.

Peninsular Malaysia juts out from the southernmost part of the Asian continent. In the northwestern peninsula, tin-mining plains are punctuated by sheer limestone hills and caves that are home to both prehistoric civilisations and modern temples, as well as the region's first geological park in the Langkawi archipelago. Malaysia is also culturally well endowed. Penang's George Town and Melaka in the southern peninsula are recognised as historical trading ports and inscribed as World Heritage Sites. Between these two places lies the dynamic capital city of Kuala Lumpur, which offers a captivating blend of influences. Meanwhile,

Fishing boats in Marang harbour.

natural riches are never too far away. While the country's oldest national park in the interior harbours the endangered tiger, Malay craftsmen build finely decorated fishing boats by hand on the east coast, where endangered turtles come ashore to lay their eggs.

About 640km (400 miles) of ocean – the South China Sea – separates the peninsula from the East Malaysian states of Sabah and Sarawak on the island of Borneo. While Sarawak tempts visitors to stay at longhouses and experience wildlife watching at many of her sanctuaries, it is Sabah that offers premium and world-class diving, wildlife safaris and Mount Kinabalu, Borneo's highest peak.

Malaysia is a land of contrasts, and it is this that offers visitors such a gamut of experiences and the possibility of endless adventure and exploration.

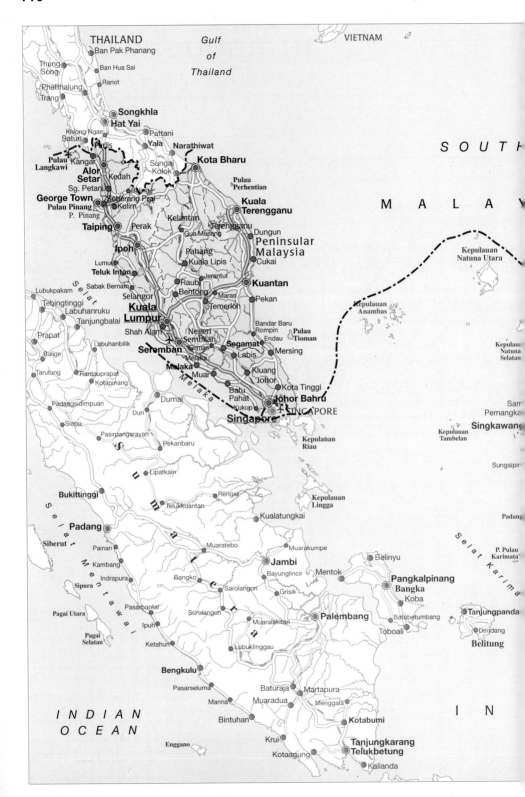

PHILIPPINES

Sulu Sea

HINA SEA

I A

Pulau Banggi

Kudat

Kota Maruda
Kota Belud
Pitas
Simpangan
G. Kinabalu
Lingkabau
4095
Tuaran
Ranau
Klagan
Sandakan

Kota Kinabalu

Kuala Penyu
Tambunan

Pulau Labuan
Beaufort
Keningau
Kinabatangan
Lahad
Datu
Tungku

Bandar Seri Begawan
Tenom
Kuamut

BRUNEI DARUSSALAM
Lawas
Sabah
Pandawan
Pulau Timbun Mata

Miri
Trusan
Pensiangan
Kelabakan
Tawau
Semporna

Sibuti
Marudi
Limbang
Long Pa Sia
Pulau Sebatik

Niah
Gunung Mulu National Park
Ulu-Ulu

Suai
Long Lama
Mensalong

Bario
Malinau
Pulau Bunyu

Bintulu
Ambalat

Tubau
Lio Matoh
Mantadau
Tarakan

Igan
Oya
Sebauh
Celebes Sea

Dalat
Balingian
Belaga
Tanjungselor

Mukah

Nanga Merit

Sibu
Kanowit
Sarawak
Tanjungredeb

Sematan
Saratok
Kapit
Rajang
Domaring

Lundu
Kuching
Sepinang

Bau
Simunjan
Betong
Mahesi

Serian
Sri Aman
Muarawahau

Lubok Antu
Putussibau
Sangkulirang

ngkayang
Balaikarangan

Pahauman
Nangahsurak
B o r n e o

Sanggau
Sintang
Melak

tianak

Nangahpinoh
Samarinda

Kotabaru
Muarateweh
Benagin

Sukadana

au
Nangatayap
Balikpapan
ya

Ketapang
Patangis

Kuala
aguan
Palangkaraya
Amuntai

Sukaraja
Mehakit
Mamuju

Kendawangan
Sampit
Sulawesi

Pangkalanbun
Rantau
Kotabaru

Banjarmasin
Martapura
Pulau Sebuku
Majene

Kualapembuang
Pagatan

Tg Puting
Pelaihari
Kintap
Pulau Laut

Tg Selatan

N E S I A

JAVA SEA

Malaysia

N

0   200 km

0   200 miles

Selat Makassar

Crowded Petaling Street in KL's Chinatown.

KUALA LUMPUR AND ENVIRONS

The economic powerhouse of Malaysia juggles relentless renewal with its distinctly colonial identity, making for a fascinating example of Asian dynamism.

The blue-tiled dome at Shah Alam's Blue Mosque in Selangor.

Located halfway down the west coast of Peninsular Malaysia, Kuala Lumpur sits on the confluence of the rivers Klang and Gombak, 35km (22 miles) from the coast. A metropolis covering an area of 230 sq km (90 sq miles), the city anchors the conurbation known as the Klang Valley, the wealthiest and most industrialised part of the country.

Kuala Lumpur is the capital of Malaysia and the seat of Parliament, as well as its financial and commercial centre: the judicial and executive branches of the federal government are hosted by Putrajaya, south of Kuala Lumpur. The state of Selangor, out of which these two federal territories were carved, is an industrial hub, has a high standard of living and is the country's most populated state.

International brands have made their mark in KL, as seen at this crossing in Bukit Bintang.

The Klang Valley spearheads the country's economic growth and is the centre of everything: business, trade, finance, politics, arts, fashion. You feel it in the air, the mad pace of life, in the traffic-choked streets, the crowded malls, and the incessant beat of house music in the clubs. In its bid for global recognition, the constant drive is to "develop", which translates to construction and the rejuvenation of old parts, particularly in Kuala Lumpur.

Therefore, while tourists like to head to the pockets of colonialism and old Asia, they cannot escape the thrust of modernity. They try to frame a picture of the old Mughal-style mosque with their camera, but it is impossible to exclude the metallic light rail tracks in the background. Even in a traditional wet market, a chicken-seller on a stool is consulting his stockbroker on his smartphone.

Nonetheless, a growing appreciation for sustainability, green spaces, quality of life and built conservation is also shaping the Klang Valley. There are lively neighbourhoods that go back to Kuala Lumpur's early days. Residents in suburbs fight to preserve their patch of forest reserve. And at weekends, families picnic in a park or head to a fishing village to sample seafood. Through all this, multifarious cultures, traditions and religions imbue Kuala Lumpur and its surrounds with a complex, multi-layered persona.

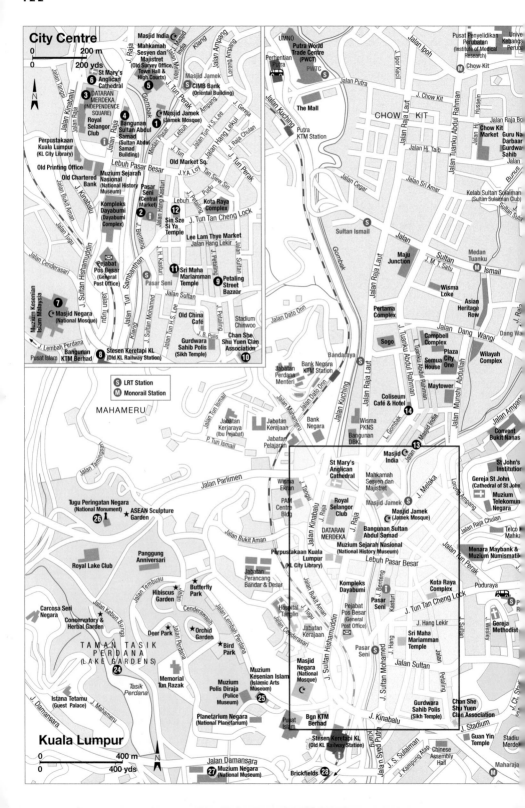

City Centre

0   200 m
0   200 yds

Masjid India
Mahkamah Sesyen dan Majistret (Old Survey Office, Town Hall & High Courts)

6 St Mary's Anglican Cathedral
3 DATARAN MERDEKA (INDEPENDENCE SQUARE)
5
Masjid Jamek
CIMB Bank (Oriental Building)

4 Royal Selangor Club
Bangunan Sultan Abdul Samad (Sultan Abdul Samad Building)
1 Masjid Jamek (Jamek Mosque)

Perpustakaan Kuala Lumpur (KL City Library)
Old Market Sq.

Old Printing Office
Old Chartered Bank
Muzium Sejarah Nasional (National History Museum)
2 Pasar Seni (Central Market)
Kota Raya Complex

Kompleks Dayabumi (Dayabumi Complex)
12
Sin Sze Si Ya Temple
Lee Lam Thye Market

7 Muzium Kesenian Islam Malaysia
11 Sri Maha Mariamman Temple
9 Petaling Street Bazaar
Pejabat Pos Besar (General Post Office)

Masjid Negara (National Mosque)
Old China Café
Stadium Chinwoo
Chan She Shu Yuen Association **10**

Bangunan KTM Berhad
8 Stesen Keretapi KL (Old KL Railway Station)
Gurdwara Sahib Polis (Sikh Temple)

S LRT Station
M Monorail Station

Kuala Lumpur

0   400 m
0   400 yds

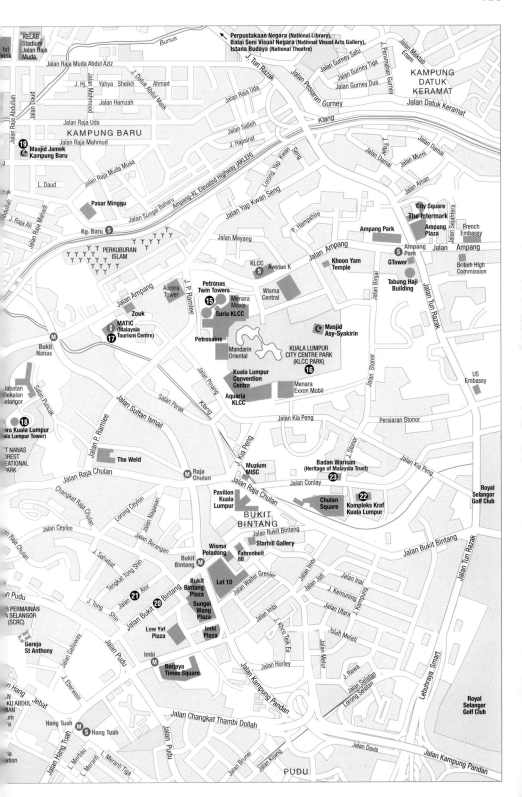

The KLCC skyline from Kampung Baru.

KUALA LUMPUR

Glimpses of old KL can still be seen, but the soaring towers, enthusiasm for global trends and cosmopolitanism of this capital city set the aspirational tone for the rest of the country.

With its constant facelifts and ever-rising skyline, Kuala Lumpur – or KL, as it is popularly known – embodies the aspirations of a nation working hard to carve its niche in an era of globalisation. KL is where you will find the latest and best of everything in Malaysia, from architecture to infrastructure and fashion to food. It also sets the tone for the rest of the country.

Yet among the increased density and overlapping highways, pockets of traditional neighbourhoods and lifestyles are holding on fast. Trendy thirtysomethings trade pleasantries with traditionally garbed shopkeepers. *Feng shui* and Islamic values blend in global deal-making, just as a fortune teller is consulted in the face of leading-edge technology. With its variety of sights, food and shops, cosmopolitan Kuala Lumpur has something for every visitor.

Mining settlement

Miners and traders first came upriver to where the Klang and Gombak rivers converge in search of tin. The Gombak estuary was the highest point upstream that the miners could land their supplies for prospecting tin in Ampang, a few kilometres further inland. They named the settlement Kuala Lumpur, which means "muddy estuary" in Malay. By the 1860s, the landing place had become a flourishing village.

Fierce rivalries over mining claims and water rights led to gang clashes and bitter feuds. Finally, the predominantly Chinese settlement was put under the leadership of Yap Ah Loy, the *kapitan cina* (Chinese headman). The *kapitan* warred against crime, built a prison and quelled revolts. Under his supervision, KL grew into a thriving township.

Then Frank Swettenham, the British resident of Selangor, moved his administration to KL. Brick buildings were introduced and, street by street, the wooden shanties were pulled

Main Attractions

Sultan Abdul Samad Building
National Mosque
Petaling Street
Sin Sze Si Ya Temple
Petronas Twin Towers
KL Tower
Rumah Penghulu Abu Saman
Islamic Arts Museum
Brickfields

A busy hawker stall in Petaling Street.

down. In 1886, the country's first railway line connected KL to the coastal town of Klang.

As the state capital of Selangor, KL was the centre of administration and trade. In 1946, it was established as the headquarters of the Federation of Malaya, with its development intensifying after independence in 1957. But KL truly came of age in 1974, when it became a unit of its own called Wilayah Persekutuan (Federal Territory). Today, it is the seat of the Parliament of Malaysia as well as its financial and commercial centre. The executive and judicial branches of the federal government moved to Putrajaya in 1999.

Historic heart

KL's central attractions are close enough to cover on foot. To reach the sights that are a little further away, trains are the best option during the traffic-choked peak hours. Where there are no rail connections, hop into a taxi. Alternatively, many city tours cover the main sights in KL as well as its surroundings, including a hop-on hop-off option (www.myhoponhopoff.com).

A good starting point is in the historic centre at **Jamek Mosque** ❶ (Masjid Jamek; Sat–Thu 8.30am–12.30pm, 2.30–4.15pm, 5.30–6.30pm and Fri 9am–10.30pm, 2.30–4.15pm, 5.30–6.30pm; free), standing proudly at the confluence of the Gombak and Klang rivers, where the first miners landed. This elegant structure, which was adapted from a Mughal mosque in northern India by architect A.B. Hubback and built in 1909, is an oasis of serenity once you enter the palm tree-filled grounds through the *sahn* (walled courtyard). Visitors must be properly attired.

Close to the river confluence, bordered by Lebuh Pasar Besar and Medan Pasar, is the Old Market Square or **Medan Pasar Lama**, the business and social centre for the early settlers. The original demarcations of the square have disappeared due to urban renewal. Look out for a clock tower; this was built to mark the coronation of England's King George VI in 1937.

Around the market square are double- and triple-storey shophouses, ubiquitous in the city's historic parts. These are typical in many parts of Southeast Asia where immigrants from southern China settled. They extend 30–60 metres (100–200ft) to the back, with the ground level used for business, while upstairs was where the proprietor's family lived. The newer three-storey shophouses, built in 1906–7, incorporate classical decorative details like fluted pilasters and ornate window frames and fanlights.

The original market on Medan Pasar was moved south to the place now occupied by **Central Market** ❷ (Pasar Seni; tel: 03-2031 0399; daily 10am–10pm) on Jalan Hang Kasturi. A former fruit-and-vegetable market, this Art Deco showpiece is one of the city's most popular tourist stops, with souvenir shops purveying everything from batik scarves and regional handicraft to portraits done on the spot. Along the side of Central Market is Kasturi Walk, a pedestrian mall

Couples at Independence Square at dusk.

adorned with an outsized *wau* (kite), with more souvenir stalls and where occasional cultural performances are held. Behind is the Annexe Gallery, a venue for cutting-edge and eclectic art exhibitions, performances and talks.

Colonial centre

To the west of the river confluence is the colonial core, distinguished architecturally by domes, minarets and large arches of the neo-Saracenic style. This 19th-century style was developed by British architects in India and combines features of Islamic architecture with Gothic elements.

At the heart is the **Independence Square ❸** (Dataran Merdeka). Originally called the Padang (Malay for "field"), this parade ground was renamed to commemorate Malaysia's independence. It was here, at midnight on 30 August 1957, that Britain's Union flag was lowered and the flag of the newly independent Malaya was flown for the first time on 31 August.

Today, Independence Square is an occasional venue for the National Day parade. It is also a popular one for events such as the vibrant Colours of Malaysia, which showcases a cultural parade and booths for tour packages and tourism products. Whenever there are events on the square, the adjacent road, Jalan Raja, is closed to traffic and is abuzz with people enjoying the breeze and the bright lights. Casting a 95-metre (310ft) high shadow on the green is a giant flagpole.

Sultan Abdul Samad complex

To one side of the green is a group of colonial-era buildings collectively known as the Sultan Abdul Samad complex, which now houses government offices. Arguably the most imposing of these is the long structure with the clock tower, the **Sultan Abdul Samad Building ❹** (Bangunan Sultan Abdul Samad). This former colonial administrative centre was built between 1894 and 1897, and was the first of the neo-Saracenic buildings introduced by the chief architect, A.C. Norman. Particularly pretty when it is lit up at night, the building is constructed of red bricks, with

Jamek Mosque.

The Sultan Abdul Samad Building.

A 95-metre (310ft) flagpole marks the spot where, on 31 August 1957, the Union flag was lowered and the Malaysian flag hoisted, marking independence day.

A candy stall in Petaling Street.

three Mughal-inspired domes covered in copper, surrounded on all sides by wide and shady verandas. The architectural style was something new in the Federated Malay States then. It went on to be reproduced in a number of buildings, including the **Old Federated Malay States Survey Office**, the **Town Hall** and the **High Court** ❺ north of the Sultan Abdul Samad Building, as well as the **General Post Office** south of it.

Opposite this complex across Independence Square is the mock-Tudor-style **Royal Selangor Club**, built in 1884. Formerly nicknamed the Spotted Dog, a derisive allusion to the club's emblem of a running leopard, it is the oldest membership club in Malaysia and the nexus of late 19th-century European social life in KL. Today, lawyers and businessmen prop up the long bar where the British once sat over their *stengah* (literally "half", meaning half a peck of liquor).

To the north of the square is the neo-Gothic **St Mary's Anglican Cathedral** ❻ (tel: 03-2692 8672; daily, but best time for visitors is Tue–Fri 9am–3pm; free). An earlier structure, consecrated in 1887, was destroyed by fire, and the current building was constructed in 1922 on the site of the Royal Selangor Club's former horse stables. The church has some interesting features, including stained-glass windows honouring colonial planters and depicting crops such as rubber and oil palm, which were once the agricultural mainstays of the economy.

At the southern end of Independence Square, the former **Chartered Bank of India, Australia and China** continues the neo-Saracenic architectural tradition. The bank once held the accounts of the colonial government. Next door is the former **Government Printing Office**, striking for being the only neo-Renaissance-style building in the area. It is now the **KL City Gallery**, an information centre with some historical information and a great model of Independence Square, as well as a scale model of greater KL, with screenings of video footage of important events (charge), and a souvenir shop. The building had hosted the city library until the construction

MIGRANT QUARTERS

With a several hundred thousand-strong migrant labour force in KL, sections of the city have become focal points for these new Malaysians. Near Petaling Street, along Jalan Tun Tan Siew Sin, are signboards in Urdu, Burmese and Nepali advertising shops, internet cafés and hair-stylists, as well as some good eateries. One of these, Khukri at No. 26, is a Nepali restaurant that has gained fame through food bloggers.

North of this area on Jalan Bukit Nenas, St John's Cathedral is a Sunday meeting point for Roman Catholic Filipinos. The church runs programmes for Filipino migrant workers and their families. One of the oldest buildings in KL, the cathedral has twin spires and stained-glass windows from Paris. Built in 1883 to serve expatriates and Eurasians, the church continues to draw an international parish.

Meanwhile, Chow Kit, on the northern section of Jalan Tuanku Abdul Rahman, has taken on a very Indonesian character. There are plenty of eateries, particularly from Java; this is also the unrivalled location for *nasi padang*, with its rich flavours of coconut milk and chilli. *Jamu* is readily available here, traditional Indonesian herbal remedies, among other places at the Chow Kit market, one of KL's oldest wet markets for fresh produce. At night, however, the narrow lanes and run-down buildings are taken over by drug addicts and prostitutes and it can be unsafe to wander around.

of the massive **Kuala Lumpur City Library** (Perpustakaan Kuala Lumpur) next to it.

Around the Old Railway Station

KL's neo-Saracenic architectural stretch is capped in the south by the Old Kuala Lumpur Railway Station and Bangunan KTM. En route to these from the colonial district on Jalan Sultan Hishamuddin is the **Dayabumi Complex** (Kompleks Dayabumi), the country's first steel-frame skyscraper, with its filigree-like Islamic-design arches. It is most impressive at night when it is floodlit. At its base is the **General Post Office** (Pejabat Pos Besar; tel: 03-2275 6686; Mon–Sat 8.30am–6pm).

A pedestrian tunnel south of the Kompleks Dayabumi leads to the **National Mosque ❼** (Masjid Negara; tel: 03-2693 7905; Sun–Thu 9am–noon, 3–4pm and 5.30–6.30pm, Fri closed in the morning) on Jalan Lembah Perdana, completed in 1965. This is the first local mosque to depart from the neo-Saracenic style, and is arguably a watershed in Malaysia's architectural history. The jagged 18 points of the star-shaped roof represent the 13 states of Malaysia and the five pillars of Islam. The mosque represents national unity as well, for non-Muslims donated generously towards its building fund.

Further south along Jalan Sultan Hishamuddin, the **Old Railway Station ❽** (Stesen Keretapi Kuala Lumpur) stands with magnificent turrets, spires, minarets and arches. The station was constructed in 1911 to the standards applied to Victorian public buildings all over the empire. Its construction was once held up because the roof did not meet the specification that it supported one metre of snow! Now only the intra-city KTM commuter trains and the luxurious Eastern & Oriental Express (www.belmond.com/eastern-and-oriental-express/) stop here; all interstate and city trains stop at the ultra-modern KL Sentral Station.

Opposite and connected by an underpass to the old railway station is the **KTM Building** (Bangunan KTM), headquarters of Malaysian Railways, featuring a pastiche of architectural

At the junction of Jalan Petaling and Jalan Hang Lekir, find a stall (daily 10.30am–10pm) selling air mata kucing, a sweet drink of dried longan fruit.

In the National Mosque.

Tea appreciation at Purple Cane Teahouse is best shown by tapping the table with bent index and middle fingers after your cup is filled, as a way of thanking the person serving you.

The "Gopuram" gateway into Sri Mahamariamman Temple.

elements, from Mughal-style minarets to large Gothic-style windows and ancient Greek columns.

Petaling Street

To the east of the colonial core is **Petaling Street,** both the collective name of an enclave of pre-war Chinese shophouses and predominantly Chinese businesses as well as a festive street market best known for its fake branded goods. The term "Chinatown" is often used interchangeably with "Petaling Street" as a nod to the city's Chinese beginnings. However, a 2003 rebranding exercise saw, among other things, the erection of an imaginative "oriental" gateway of the sort found in Chinatowns globally, which now clumsily bookends the area's main Jalan Petaling.

The action begins early here at the **Lee Lam Thye Market** (main entrance on Jalan Hang Lekir next to Hotel Malaya). This fresh-produce market (daily 7am–3pm) is the place to find Chinese housewives haggling for fresh chicken slaughtered on the spot, greens of all kinds and chrysanthemums for

their altars. Be warned, though – the smells are something else.

As the city wakes up, stalls begin to line both sides of the road and pedestrians zigzag from coffee shop to fruit stall and back, impervious to the heavy traffic. At midday, office executives begin to fill the eateries. Petaling Street is reputedly where the best Chinese street food can be found, from all sorts of noodles to pork ribs soup (*bak kut teh*) and roasted meat snacks. There is dim sum from 6am, mooncakes for the autumnal Mooncake Festival, and bittersweet herbal brews to cure all sorts of ailments at the roadside medicinal drinks stalls.

The **bazaar ❾**, which runs along both Jalan Petaling and Jalan Hang Lekir, is where you can find all the "genuine" copies of brand-name watches and T-shirts, as well as DVDs of movies that haven't even made it to the local cinemas yet. There are also souvenirs, precious stones, antiques and household goods for sale. Browse at leisure and shop around; when you are read to buy, remember to bargain.

Chinese temples and cafés

During the day, respite from the crowds and heat can be found in the interior of the **Chan She Shu Yuen Clan Association** ⓾ (tel: 03-2678 1461; daily 8am–5pm), at the southern end of Jalan Petaling. Serving the needs of Chinese bearing the surname Chan (as well as Chen and Tan, which are spelling variations of Chan), this clanhouse was constructed in 1906. The building is decorated with elaborate glazed ceramic tiles and ornamentation, and intricate wall paintings depicting mythological and historical tales.

Off Petaling Street behind the Traffic Police Headquarters is a little street called **Jalan Balai Polis**, which has a row of beautifully refurbished pre-war shophouses. Besides cafés and bookshops, there is the **Old China Café** (tel: 03-2072 5915; daily 11.30am–10pm), a restaurant-cum-antique shop. It was formerly the headquarters of the Selangor and Federal Territory Laundry Association, a trade guild that flourished in the pre-washing-machine days. It has a charming 1930s ambience, with elements such as the *pintu pagar* (swing doors) and pulley-drawn lights well preserved. The café serves cuisine unique to Malaysia's Straits Chinese community. Along Jalan Balai Polis and Jalan Panggung, several teahouses offer the chance to learn about the ancient Chinese art of serving and drinking tea.

Jalan Tun H.S. Lee

Head north on Jalan Panggung, turn left at Jalan Sultan and then right along Jalan Tun H.S. Lee. On the left is one of KL's most famous Hindu temples, the **Sri Maha Mariamman Temple** ⓫ (tel: 03-2078 3467; daily 6am–8.30pm, Fri until 9.30pm; free). Its tower gateway is decorated with an explosion of colourful gods entangled in an arresting design of South Indian origin. Built in 1873, it occupies an important place in Hindu religious life. This is the starting point for the annual Thaipusam pilgrimage of penance to the Batu Caves temple just outside KL (see page 146). On other days, women and children sell strings of fragrant jasmine on the pavements, and a man in a traditional dhoti sarong watches over shoes on a rack for those have entered

(see page 146)

TIP

A traditional colonial-era non-alcoholic drink found throughout the former British Empire is a "gunner", made of equal parts ginger ale and ginger beer, with a dash of Angostura bitters. It is a refreshing thirst-quencher. Order one at the Coliseum Café.

Enjoying Chinese tea and newspapers on Petaling Street.

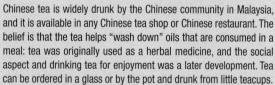

TEA TIME

Chinese tea is widely drunk by the Chinese community in Malaysia, and it is available in any Chinese tea shop or Chinese restaurant. The belief is that the tea helps "wash down" oils that are consumed in a meal: tea was originally used as a herbal medicine, and the social aspect and drinking tea for enjoyment was a later development. Tea can be ordered in a glass or by the pot and drunk from little teacups.

A wide range of teas is available in Malaysia, sourced from China and Taiwan. A visit to one of the many specialist teashops in Petaling Street is a great way to learn about the various types of teas and to sample them too. Shop assistants can give good explanations and will also normally be happy to demonstrate different methods of brewing tea to bring out the flavour of each type of tea. (Such fine distinctions are not actually well known by most city-bred KL-ites). It is all about the taste and the aroma: everything from the temperature of the water to the water quality to how the tea is poured, as well as the blend itself, is done with consideration and precision to create a superlative tea experience.

Some outlets offer courses in tea appreciation and tea culture. The teashops also sell teapots and tea sets as well as related paraphernalia. Those who cannot be bothered with the tea-brewing process can also avail themselves of convenient teabags.

the temple courtyard. Devotees emerge from prayers, their foreheads smeared with sacred white ash.

Continue on Jalan Tun H.S. Lee past the intersection with Jalan Tun Tan Cheng Lock. Almost completely hidden behind a group of pre-war shophouses is the **Sin Sze Si Ya Temple ⑫** (tel: 03-2072 9593; daily 7am– 5pm), accessed through a narrow, ornate gateway with a red sign against an image of a pair of dragons. This temple was built by Yap Ah Loy, the *kapitan* (headman) of KL's early community, in 1864 to honour the deities Sin Sze Si Ya and Si Sze Ya. The former was a *kapitan* Yap had once served under, and the latter was Yap's loyal lieutenant; both died in battle before Yap did. In keeping with the Chinese practice of ancestor worship, they were accordingly deified. After his death in 1885, Yap Ah Loy was also enshrined in the temple, on a side altar, which also holds a photograph of him.

Jalan Masjid India

North of the river confluence, and centred on the pedestrianised **Jalan**

Masjid India ⑬ and the roads leading off it, is a chaotic, crowded and noisy yet colourful district known for its very visible Indian Muslim flavour and speciality shops. This is an excellent place to shop for Indian textiles, saris and jewellery, and to observe local life. Look out for a small crowd gathered in one spot and you may find a snake charmer, or a medicine man proclaiming the miracle attributes of his wares.

Parallel to Jalan Masjid India is **Jalan Tuanku Abdul Rahman**, named after the first king, or *Yang di-Pertuan Agong*, of Malaysia. It was once KL's main shopping area, where tradesmen from the Indian subcontinent, in particular, dominated the street in the early 20th century. Today it is the city's garment district, and some family businesses here are now several generations old and still thriving, despite stiff competition from the city's mega malls. Every Saturday night, a *pasar malam* (night market) is set up along **Lorong Tuanku Abdul Rahman**, off Jalan Tuanku Abdul Rahman, with stalls offering a wide array of goods and snacks.

The underwater tunnel at Aquaria KLCC.

At 98–100 Jalan Tuanku Abdul Rahman is the **Coliseum Café and Hotel** ⑭ (tel: 03-2692 6270; daily 10am–10pm, Sat–Sun from 9am), still an institution despite its tattiness and the rude service. Its bar was once the favourite watering hole for colonial-era planters, journalists and government officials. The decor has changed little since those days and its steaks continue to attract attention for their quality and affordable prices. Next door to this establishment is one of the country's first cinemas, the **Coliseum Theatre**, a neoclassical structure built in 1920 to showcase "the highest type of films", as a 1921 daily put it, to a targeted audience of Europeans. Today, Malay, Indonesian and Tamil films are shown here.

Petronas Twin Towers

East of the historic district is the **Golden Triangle**, the city's main commercial and financial district. Its three points are roughly at the Klang–Gombak river confluence in the west, the junction of Jalan Yap Kwan Seng and Jalan Tun Razak in the northeast, and the junction of Jalan Imbi and Jalan Pudu in the southeast. Most of the high-rises here house large corporations, banks and government-linked companies.

At the heart of the Golden Triangle is the city's most eye-catching land-mark, the **Petronas Twin Towers** ⑮, on Jalan Ampang. Between 1998 and 2004, the towers held the record for the world's tallest buildings. The glass-and-steel towers remain impres-sive today, soaring 452 metres (1,480ft) to reach 88 storeys. Designed by the renowned skyscraper specialist, archi-tect Cesar Pelli, the structures combine Islamic patterns with state-of-the-art engineering techniques.

There is an immensely popular 45-minute semi-guided tour that goes up to the double-deck **skybridge** on levels 41 and 42, as well as up to Level 86, the topmost level allowed to visi-tors (tel: 03-2331 8080; Tue–Sun 9am–9pm, Fri closed 1-2.30pm; charge) for panoramic views of the city. Only 400 tickets are issued a day from 8am for walk-ins, and another 400 for advance purchases. Tickets are sold at the infor-mation desk in Tower 2.

Children can have hours of fun with the interactive exhibits at Petrosains Museum.

Shopping for fabrics in Jalan Masjid India.

Bukit Nanas has well-marked nature trails.

Tower 1 is occupied by the national petroleum company Petronas and Tower 2 is taken up by various multinational companies. The towers anchor the 40-hectare (100-acre) **Kuala Lumpur City Centre** (KLCC), a high-end condominium, hotel and commercial hub which is the heart of KL. At the base of the towers is the contemporary **Suria KLCC** mall (tel: 03-2382 2430; daily 10am–10pm), which offers a few attractions worth visiting. **Petrosains** (tel: 03-2331 8181; Tue–Fri 9.30am–5.30pm, Sat–Sun 9.30am–6.30pm; charge) on levels 4 and 5 is a terrific interactive museum for families about science and the oil and gas industry. **Galeri Petronas** on level 3 (tel: 03-2051 7770; Tue–Sun 10am–8pm; free) showcases mainly contemporary and traditional Malaysian art.

The **Petronas Philharmonic Hall** (Dewan Filharmonik Petronas; box office tel: 03-2331 7007; www.mpo. com.my; Tue–Sat 10.30am–6.30pm), located on the ground floor of Tower 2, is an intimate contemporary concert hall with superb acoustics. It is home to the Malaysian Philharmonic Orchestra and hosts a varied concert season featuring international and local performers.

The restaurant section of Suria opens up to the sprawling landscaped **KLCC Park ⑯**, where the whole family can enjoy watching synchronised fountains and frolic in the playground and the wading pool. There is more family fun at the **Aquaria KLCC** (tel: 03-2333 1888; daily 10.30am–8pm; charge), which is housed in the Kuala Lumpur Convention Centre. The aquarium has over 5,000 types of aquatic and land creatures from 150 different species.

Jalan Ampang mansions

Jalan Ampang, which runs along the front of KLCC, is the main artery through the Golden Triangle. In the late 19th and early 20th century, the road was but a trail cut through forest and swampland, leading about 5km (3 miles) to the tin mines upstream. As the city began to grow, rich Chinese miners and businessmen built their ostentatious mansions along this road. Showcasing an eclectic mix of neoclassical and local styles, many have not withstood the onslaught of city-centre redevelopment. All of the surviving ones have been converted to mainly commercial uses.

One of the best preserved of these mansions is the **Malaysia Tourism Centre ⑰** (tel: 03-9235 4800; www. matic.gov.my; Mon–Fri 7.30am–5.30pm, tourist information counter daily 8am–10pm), a one-stop visitor centre and theatre complex at the Jalan Sultan Ismail junction. Built in 1935 by a wealthy Chinese tin mogul and rubber planter, the villa served as the war office for the British army, and later, the Japanese army. Following Malaya's independence in 1957, it saw the first sitting of the new nation's Parliament. It was also the scene for installation ceremonies for Malaysia's kings. In the late 1980s, it was refurbished and commissioned for its present use.

West of the KLCC stands the **KL Tower ⑱** (Menara Kuala Lumpur; tel: 03-2020 5444; daily 9am–10pm; charge). This 421-metre (1,380ft) structure, designed with Islamic architectural features, has an observation platform with the best view of the city (the audio guide is worth getting) and the Petronas Twin Towers. From the tower, visitors should have a meander down the hill through the **Bukit Nanas Forest Recreational Park** (daily 7am–6pm; free). This 10-hectare (25-acre) lowland rainforest is surprisingly lush considering its concretised surroundings, and has well-marked trails and a children's playground.

Kampung Baru

On the other side of Jalan Ampang from KLCC is **Kampung Baru**. Literally meaning "new village", Kampung Baru came into being in 1889 in a bid by the British to encourage Malays to settle in the then burgeoning Kuala Lumpur. Even though brick houses have now replaced many of the original wooden houses here, Kampung Baru has stubbornly remained a Malay village while the city around it grew.

A prominent landmark here is the **Kampung Baru Mosque ⑲** (Masjid Jamek Kampung Baru; daily 9am–5pm except prayer times; free). An important community centre, the mosque has been completely rebuilt with faint echoes of the neo-Saracenic style of the colonial core buildings and a prominent gateway with brilliant blue mosaics. Close by is the busy Jalan Raja Muda Musa, along which are eateries selling good Malay fare; the **Pasar Minggu** (daily 7am–noon) has a huge variety of hawker food, from the ubiquitous satay and *nasi lemak* (coconut rice) to *bubur* (rice porridge) and spicy regional delights.

Nearby on Jalan Tun Razak is the **National Theatre** (Istana Budaya; tel: 03-4026 5555; www.istanabudaya. gov.my; daily 9.30am–6pm), where large-scale musicals, plays and other performances are staged. The theatre building is fashioned after a traditional *wau* (kite) in flight. The roof is inspired by the *sirih junjung*, which are betel leaves arrayed in a particular

The National Theatre is fashioned after a wau (traditional kite).

Bukit Bintang cross junction, with the Berjaya Times Square shopping mall on the left.

The indoor Cosmo's World theme park at Berjaya Times Square.

Street food in Jalan Alor.

manner for use in traditional Malay ceremonies. The **National Library** (Perpustakaan Negara; tel: 03-2687 1700; Tue–Sat 10am–7pm, Sun 10am–6pm) is down the same road. Shaped like a *tengkolok*, the Malay male headgear, it is inlaid with blue tiles to resemble the rich texture of *songket*, the gold-threaded material from which the headgear is usually made.

A sampling of local art can be found in the galleries of the **National Visual Arts Gallery** (Balai Seni Visual Negara; tel: 03-4025 4990; daily 10am–6pm) in Jalan Temerloh. This beautiful spacious building has five galleries, with the ground-floor main gallery housing the permanent collection.

Bukit Bintang

The apex of consumerism in KL is along **Jalan Bukit Bintang ⓴**, packed with large shopping malls, high-end restaurants, international hotels and swish bars. With giant billboards, blaring music and the monorail swishing overhead, the action is non-stop. This is also the venue for street concerts in conjunction with countdowns to the New Year and Independence Day.

Bukit Bintang's main draw is no doubt its shopping malls. The rabbit warren of **Sungei Wang Plaza** and the adjacent **Bukit Bintang Plaza** offer more downmarket products; **Low Yat Plaza** and **Imbi Plaza** concentrate on computers and software; **Lot 10** houses several chic boutiques and a small theatre upstairs; the upmarket **Starhill Gallery** has designer wear and fashionable eateries; likewise, the equally flash **Pavilion Kuala Lumpur** opposite. Slightly south in nearby Jalan Imbi is the **Berjaya Times Square**, which has an indoor theme park and a huge cinema in addition to retail outlets.

A large number of Arab eateries and shops can also be found in Bukit Bintang, catering to Middle Eastern tourists.

Parallel to Jalan Bukit Bintang is **Jalan Alor ㉑**, a street lined with Chinese coffee shops, which becomes KL's street-food central when temporary hawker stalls take over the road at night. Among the fare offered are

Chinese noodles, satay and grilled seafood. There is more good food along **Tengkat Tong Shin**, which runs parallel to Jalan Alor. Tengkat Tong Shin also has backpacker hotels, cafés and pubs.

Meanwhile, **Changkat Bukit Bintang,** part of the area known as Bukit Ceylon (Ceylon Hill), has long been a trendy nightlife venue with fine-dining restaurants and fashionable bars. Many of these occupy charming old-style bungalows that have been artfully renovated to attract the city's chichi crowd.

Craft complex

Away from the bustle on Jalan Conlay, off Jalan Raja Chulan, is the **Kuala Lumpur Craft Complex ㉒** (Kompleks Kraf Kuala Lumpur; tel: 03-2161 2622; daily 9am–6pm). It has good if pricey offerings of traditional and contemporary crafts, including hand-woven textiles, woodwork, batik, basketwork, pewter and pottery. There are also demonstrations of *songket* cloth weaving, batik printing, and silver and copper tooling. The

building at the back houses a small craft museum (daily 9am–5.30pm; charge) and a cafeteria. In one corner is the **Artists' Colony**, a cluster of 22 huts housing new and established artists who work and sell their art here. Visitors with a couple of hours to spare may also try their hand at making their own batik pieces.

Diagonally opposite the Craft Complex, on Jalan Stonor, is a bungalow that dates from 1925. It houses the **Heritage of Malaysia Trust ㉓** (Badan Warisan Malaysia; tel: 03-2144 9273; www.badanwarisan.org.my; Mon–Sat 10am–5pm, tours at 11am and 3pm), a non-governmental organisation advocating architectural conservation. It has an exhibition centre and a great little gift shop. Check out its website for informative suggestions on heritage trails. On its grounds is a stunning traditional Malay timber house, the **Rumah Penghulu Abu Seman**, from the northern state of Kedah (Mon–Sat 10am–5pm, tours 11am and 3pm; charge). This finely crafted structure was dismantled and relocated to KL, where it was restored as a showpiece.

A batik artist shows his skills at the Craft Complex.

In KL's Lake Gardens.

Lake Gardens

Southwest of the city centre is KL's green lung and its largest park. Fondly known as the **Lake Gardens** ㉔ (daily 7am–8pm), it is formally called the Taman Botani Perdana (Perdana Botanical Garden). The gardens comprise 104 hectares (257 acres) of lawns, trees, landscaped gardens and undulating hills, at the heart of which is the fairly unassuming lake, Tasik Perdana. In the mornings and evenings, joggers run past picnickers, senior citizens perform *t'ai chi* routines and lovers rendezvous here. It is also a great place to watch KL families at play.

Surrounding the lake are various attractions. The **Bird Park** (tel: 03-2272 1010; daily 9am–6pm; charge) and the **Butterfly Park** (tel: 03-2693 4799; daily 9am–6pm; charge) house local and foreign species in pretty, forested enclosures. Other attractions include the **Hibiscus Garden** (daily 7am–8pm), the **Orchid Garden** (daily 7am–8pm) and the excellent **Conservatory and Herbal Garden** (daily 7am–7pm; charge at weekends and during holidays). See the difficult-to-spot mousedeer, the world's smallest deer, at the **Deer Park** (daily 7am–8pm; free).

Arguably the city's best museum, the beautiful **Islamic Arts Museum** ㉕ (Muzium Kesenian Islam; tel: 03-2274 2020; daily 10am–6pm; charge), sits on Jalan Lembah Perdana. In open-plan galleries are showcased collections of spectacular exhibits from all over the Islamic world, including Korans, textiles, weapons and fine models of the world's best-known mosques. Asian and Southeast Asian Islamic art is particularly well represented here. Of note are Koranic manuscripts from the Malay Peninsula, once renowned for Islamic scholarship.

The **National Planetarium** (Planetarium Negara; tel: 03-2273 5484; Tue–Sun 9.30am–4.30pm; charge) sits close by on a hill and in a park where replicas of ancient observatories are sited. It features a 36cm (14-inch) telescope and the Arianne IV space engine used to launch Malaysia's first satellite, the Measat I, as well as a cinema where large-format documentaries are screened.

At a banana-leaf curry stall in Brickfields.

National monuments

On another hill opposite the gardens stands the **National Monument ㉖** (Tugu Peringatan Negara), which commemorates those who died in the struggle against the communist insurgency in the 1950s. The monument is modelled on Washington DC's famous Iwo Jima Monument, and the galleries at its base record the names of the units who fought, including British, Australian and Malay troops.

The **Cenotaph** nearby was erected by the British to commemorate the soldiers who died in World Wars I and II. At the base of the hill is the **ASEAN Sculpture Garden**, featuring works by artists from Southeast Asian countries. Down the road is the **Parliament House**, which is not open to the public.

At the eastern edge of the Lake Gardens is the delightful **Carcosa Seri Negara** (tel: 03-2295 0888), built in 1896. It was once the British resident Frank Swettenham's official residence, and is now a luxury hotel. Take a break here with high tea (daily 3–6pm) at the Drawing Room or on the veranda overlooking the gardens.

The **National Museum ㉗** (Muzium Negara; tel: 03-2267 1111; daily 9am–6pm; charge), accessible via a walkway from the Planetarium, has ho-hum exhibits but is worth looking at as an outstanding piece of post-independence architecture. Modelled after Kedah's Balai Besar, a 19th-century Thai-influenced audience hall for sultans, it has gorgeous gigantic batik murals depicting the country's history, culture, politics and economy.

Brickfields

Across from the building site that houses the main railway hub, KL Sentral, is **Brickfields ㉘**, a lovely old neighbourhood that was in colonial times a brick-manufacturing centre. A misguided political attempt in 2010 to recognise the local Indian population has Disney-fied the main **Jalan Tun Sambanthan** stretch, complete with gateways announcing it as "Little India".

There is an authentically strong Indian character to the area, however, and walk into the backstreets, particularly to Jalan Berhala, to discover what a multicultural and religiously diversified neighbourhood it is. So while it is the best place in KL to eat sizzling curries and buy temple paraphernalia, this is also where Buddhists come to pray at the **Maha Vihara Temple**, Christians go to the **Lutheran Cathedral**, and Hindus to the **Sri Sakti Karpaga Vinayagar Temple**.

Shoppers should head to the adjoining suburb of Mid Valley City, comprising offices, condominiums, hotels and the upsized **Mid Valley Megamall** (tel: 03-2938 3333) and **The Gardens Mall** (tel: 03-2297 0288), its luxury sister property (both daily 10am–10pm). North of Mid Valley City is **Bangsar**, which has some of the most expensive real estate in KL. Its two main entertainment areas, Bangsar Baru and the Bangsar Shopping Centre, are dense with chic bars, shops and eateries filled with the fashionable set.

Tugu Kebangsaan in the Lake Gardens is a tribute to those who died in the communist insurgency of the 1950s.

Bustling city streets.

Pilgrims marking Thaipusam at Batu Caves.

SELANGOR AND PUTRAJAYA

The state surrounding Kuala Lumpur is its industrial hub, yet offers myriad places of interest and recreational opportunities, from forests to old royal towns and traditional villages.

M uch of Selangor to the west and south of Kuala Lumpur (KL) is part of the Klang Valley conurbation, the most developed part of the country. It is an area of sprawling townships and large industrial estates linked by networks of highways. Here also are the country's main airport and port, as well as the federal territory of Putrajaya, the Malaysian administrative capital. However, man-made and natural attractions are plentiful and draw in both locals and tourists. There are great day trips to be made here from KL, whether to see a Hindu cave temple, experience a coastal forest or explore old royal towns.

Selangor's current sultanate was established in the 18th century by Bugis from Sulawesi, but there continued to exist numerous minor rulers in settlements such as Kuala Selangor, Jugra and Klang. The discovery of tin in the 19th century enriched Selangor, prompting power struggles and civil wars. This led to British interference in local affairs. In 1894, Selangor was among the first four states to become part of the British Federated Malay States, which later became Malaya and then Malaysia.

From KL to Klang

Heading southwest from KL on the **Federal Highway** towards Klang, the massive Moorish-style arches of the million-ringgit **Kota Darul Ehsan** ❶

gateway announce that you are departing the Federal Territory and entering the state of Selangor.

According to government literature, this marble *pintu gerbang* (gateway), flanked by ancient Selangor canons, was commissioned in 1974 "to mark the sacrifice" made by the sultan of Selangor in ceding KL to the Federal Government as the national capital. More than two decades later, more land was ceded, this time for the administrative capital, Putrajaya, also a Federal Territory.

Main Attractions

Museum of Asian Art
Jalan Tengku Kelana, Klang
Pulau Carey
Kuala Selangor Nature Park
Batu Caves
FRIM

The interior courtyard of Shah Alam's Blue Mosque.

Petaling Jaya

A little further on and about 20km (13 miles) from KL is **Petaling Jaya** ❷. Typified by sprawling housing estates, PJ, as it is popularly known, was built in the 1950s as a satellite town to ease KL's housing pressures. Today it is a middle-class city, and visitors here will have a chance to experience suburban Malaysia. Two of PJ's best attractions are located on the grounds of Universiti Malaya, the country's premier university.

The **Museum of Asian Art** (Muzium Seni Asia; tel: 03-7967 3805; Mon–Thu 9am–1pm and 2–5pm, Fri 9am–12.15pm and 2.45–5pm; free) is a wonderful hidden gem showcasing mainly ceramics that span 4,000 years of history in Malaysia and Asia. They include the world's largest public collection of *kendi*, a spouted water container, as well as the largest early Vietnamese pottery collection outside Vietnam.

Heritage of a different sort can be experienced about 3km (2 miles) from here at a botanical centre. En route there is the university's chancellory,

In the Sunway Lagoon Water Theme Park.

the **Dewan Tunku Canselor**, one of the best examples of 1950s Le Corbusier-influenced functional architecture. The concrete building references the architect's monumental Chandigargh High Court in Pakistan.

Rimba Ilmu (Forest of Knowledge; tel: 03-7967 4685; Mon–Thu 9am–noon and 2–4pm, Fri 9am–12pm and 2.45–4pm; charge) is a tropical botanical garden that is one of the most important biological conservatories in Malaysia. Its interpretive exhibition is an excellent introduction to Malaysia's rainforests, while its park has labelled collections of medicinal plants, palms, limes, ferns and bamboo. Do not miss the exquisite Conservatory of Rare Plants and Orchids (guided tours only).

Sunway City

Back on the Federal Highway and heading towards Klang, about 7km (4 miles) away lies **Sunway City** ❸. This former tin-mining area is today the massive, family-oriented **Sunway Lagoon** (tel: 03-5639 0000; www.sunway lagoon.com; daily 10am–6pm; charge), with five theme parks spread over 32

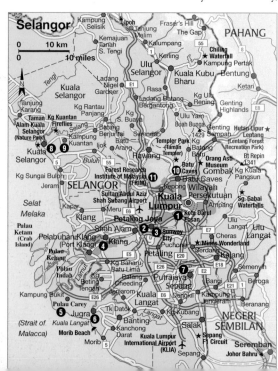

hectares (80 acres), one of which has the world's largest man-made surf beach, complete with artificial waves.

A great view of the park can be had from the adjoining **Sunway Pyramid** (tel: 03-7494 3100; daily 10am–10pm), an Egyptian-themed shopping centre anchored by a giant lion in a sphinx pose. Besides shops and eateries, there is a cinema, an ice-skating rink and a bowling alley.

Klang

Getting back on the Federal Highway, visitors will pass the state's faceless capital, Shah Alam, en route to **Klang ❹**.

Klang was established as a seat of power during the height of the tin-mining era. Given its commanding position near the mouth of the Klang river, it was obvious that whoever possessed the town controlled the lucrative tin trade. Klang became a centre of violent fighting during the Selangor Civil War of the 1870s. While its heyday is long over, and it has gone through rather haphazard development, there are pockets of the old town where time appears to have stood still. Klang is also the royal city of Selangor and home to the eclectic 19th-century **Sultan Sulaiman Mosque** (Masjid Sultan Sulaiman; daily 8–11am; free). The mosque is named after the sultan who reigned when Klang was at its peak. The British architect decided on a mixture of neoclassical and Art Deco, and even included stained-glass features. To enter, check in with the guard first and make sure you are properly attired.

Klang's biggest draw is its lively, extensive Indian quarter. Centred on **Jalan Tengku Kelana**, visitors are greeted by competing Bollywood or devotional music, the smell of South Indian spices and a sea of saris and punjabi suits, glittery jewellery and temple ornaments. Grab a banana-leaf lunch here, book a flight to India or have your fortune told. The atmosphere is electric during Deepavali, the year-end Hindu Festival of Lights. Klang is linked to KL by the KTM Komuter train system which ends in **Port Klang** (Pelabuhan Klang), best

WHERE

A good place to stay could be the Sunway Resort Hotel at Persiaran Lagoon (Bandar Sunway; tel: 03-7492 8000), the country's most successful rehabilitated mining pond, a Malaysian version of South Africa's Sun City.

A Mah Meri tribesman prepares a woodcarving in Sungai Bumbun village on Pulau Carey.

THE MAH MERI

The Mah Meri are one of two groups of Orang Asli indigenous peoples who traditionally live in Selangor, the other, larger group being the Temuan. The Mah Meri, pronounced "hma meri", once lived all along the southern coast of the peninsula, and were fisherfolk. Today, the community, numbering fewer than 3,000, lives largely on Pulau Carey, completely surrounded by oil palm plantations. There are five villages on the island, and most of the villagers now work in the plantations or in towns. Handicraft and tourism are becoming important income generators for the villagers. While the women's weaving collective has members from all villages, the remarkable woodcarvers come only from Kampung Sungai Bumbon, making it the last original indigenous woodcarvers' village in the state.

A tourist boat cruise on Putrajaya Lake, with the mosque behind.

known for its fresh seafood in the suburb of Pandamaran and the atmospheric fishing village of Bagan.

Port Klang is also the jump-off point for boats and ferries to the various islands in the Klang river delta, a favourite spot with weekend anglers. Two hours away through monotonous mangrove scenery is **Pulau Ketam** (Crab Island), probably the last Chinese fishing village on stilts in the state. Unfortunately, cleanliness is not its strong point, although it offers cheap and excellent seafood.

Pulau Carey

From Klang, head south for about 17km (11 miles) to get to **Pulau Carey** ❺, island home to the most famous of indigenous craftsmen, the Mah Meri Orang Asli traditional woodcarvers. The Kampung Sungai Bumbon Mah Meri craftsmen are best known for their dream-inspired spirit masks and unique *Moyang Tenong Jerat Harimau* tiger sculptures. Large carvings can take as long as three months to complete and cost upwards of RM300. The carvers are traditionally men, but

younger women are now picking up the trade; the women traditionally weave and their products are also sold for example at the **Mah Meri Cultural Village** (tel; 03-2282 3035; Tue–Sun 9am–6pm).

Jugra

The road south from Pulau Carey leads via Banting to yet another old Selangor power base, **Jugra** ❻. Unlike Klang, it is completely out of the development limelight and possesses a delightful small-town aura. Today, the three interesting 19th-century royal monuments here are painted yellow, the royal colour.

Follow signs to the **Makam Sultan Abdul Samad** (daily 9am–5pm; free), atop a hill on which members of the Selangor royalty and noblemen are buried. The mausoleum sports Moorish design elements and is named after the sultan who opened the doors to British interference in Selangor.

At the bottom of the hill, in a residential area, are two buildings built by the sultan's son, Sultan Sulaiman. The eclectic **Istana Bandar** palace (closed to the public unless the caretaker is

around) was built in 1905, and show-cases a real mix of styles, including Malay, Chinese, Arab and classical European. Meanwhile Middle Eastern and Indian-Muslim influences can be seen on the palace-like **Sultan Alae-ddin Shah Mosque** (Masjid Sultan Alaeddin Shah; daily 9am–5pm outside of prayer time; free) next to it. This was where the sultan used to pray.

Putrajaya

In sharp contrast to these old capitals is the newest one: **Putrajaya** ❼, the federal administrative capital. Located 30km (19 miles) from Klang and 25km (16 miles) from KL, Putrajaya was purpose-built during the boom years of the mid-1990s. As a tribute to this period of plenty, everything here is not merely big, but grandiose: government buildings, monuments, public spaces. Critics denounce this excess – its cost has never been revealed – as well as the lack of attention to local influences. Yet it remains a showcase of urban planning and postmodern architecture, and is especially pretty at night.

Precinct 1 (Presint 1) is the government quarter, crowned by the green-domed **Prime Minister's Office** (Perdana Putra), which is in the French palatial style. Next to it is the **Putra Mosque** (Masjid Putra; daily 9am–12.30pm, 2–4pm and 5.30–6pm; Fri 3–4pm and 5.30–6pm; free), a pink edifice featuring Persian influences. Walk down to the lakeside, where there is a jetty for **Cruise Tasik Putrajaya** (tel: 03-8888 5539; charge), which runs 25-minute gondola rides (daily 10am–6.30pm) and 45-minute cruise-boat sightseeing rides (daily departures 1–7.15pm) on the lake. Sunset is the best time to tour the lake.

Off the square is one of Putrajaya's ostentatious bridges, the **Putra Bridge**, inspired by the 17th-century Khaju bridge in Iran. The bridge leads to Precinct 3, part of the government quarter, where there are two noteworthy buildings: the **Putrajaya Corporation Complex** (Kompleks Perbadanan Putrajaya)

with its magnificent contemporary gateway, and the Mughal-inspired **Istana Kehakiman Palace of Justice**.

Nature-based recreation offerings in the vicinity include the **Wetland Park** (Taman Wetland) and **Botanical Gardens** (Taman Botani) (details on the official government website www.putrajaya.gov.my).

Kuala Selangor

Leave the Klang Valley to head north for the pretty, peaceful town of **Kuala Selangor** ❽ on the Sungai Selangor estuary. This is yet another former power base, and one where battles with the Dutch were conducted. The legacy from that period is in the form of an old fort, a lighthouse and a mausoleum on the historic hill of **Bukit Melawati**. The hill has wonderful, mature raintrees under whose spreading boughs it is lovely to walk around. Those who get tired can hop on to a tram (tel: 03-3289 1439; weekends and public holidays 9am–6pm; charge).

The hill overlooks the **Kuala Selangor Nature Park** (tel: 03-3289 2294; visitors' centre daily 9am–6pm;

TIP

Near Putrajaya on the old highway to Kuala Lumpur is a small town called Kajang, which claims to offer the best satay in Malaysia. And many KL-ites agree.

The Sri Subramaniar Swamy Temple inside Batu Caves.

A Dutch cannon on Bukit Melawati.

Marking the Thaipusam festival at Batu Caves.

charge). Protecting the area's coastal mangroves, and therefore its fisheries industry, the park is a joint project between the Malaysian Nature Society (MNS) and the state government. Some 170 species of birds have been recorded here, and an estimated 100,000 birds pass through during their annual migrations south. Artificial ponds that blend in beautifully with the surroundings attract the birds, surrounded by nature trails and observation hides – don't forget your binoculars. A highlight is the sight of large flocks of grey herons and purple herons, which have been breeding here for years. The park has chalet and hostel accommodation as well.

There are several interesting Chinese fishing villages around Kuala Selangor. At **Pasir Penambang**, salted fish and fishballs are prepared in seafood-processing warehouses (visitors are welcome), and there are some great seafood restaurants here with lovely river views.

Further upriver, about 9km (5.5 miles) from Kuala Selangor, is **Kampung Kuantan ❾**. When night falls, lights "come on" along the river. This is one of the few places in the world with such a large colony of synchronously flashing fireflies, or *kelip-kelip* (literally "twinkle"). Book a river cruise at the jetty on Jalan Rawang, where local boatmen in wooden paddle boats will row visitors out for this spectacular sight. A more commercial concern runs trips on motorised boats at Kampung Bukit Belimbing.

Batu Caves

One of the most amazing sights in Malaysia is Thaipusam, the Hindu festival of penance associated with Lord Murugan, which occurs in January or February. The most sacred temple for this festival is the **Sri Subramaniar Swamy Temple** (tel: 03-3289 5054; office Mon–Fri 5.30–11.30am and 4.30–9.30pm) at **Batu Caves ❿**, about 15km (9 miles) north of KL. This is the final destination for the rippling sea of devotees who follow the procession from the Sri Maha Mariamman Temple in KL.

As repentance for past sins and to demonstrate their vows, devotees carry jugs of milk to bathe the statue of Murugan at the cave temple atop 272 concrete steps. Some jugs are carried in large wooden and metal structures called *kavadi*. Some of these can weigh over 20kg (44lb). Others have their backs, chests, cheeks or tongues pierced to atone for misdeeds or as a purification ritual.

On other days, the temple is peaceful. At the base of the steps is a 43-metre (140ft) tall **statue of Murugan**, made of concrete and steel bars and painted in gold. At the top of the steps, the limestone massif's main cavern, known as the **Temple Cave** (daily 7am–9pm; free), is a huge vault pierced by stalactites that are up to 6 metres (20ft) long. Shafts of light streak down from gaps in the ceiling high above. Inside, the main shrine dedicated to Murugan is actually a *vel*, a trident which has been here since the temple was founded in 1891.

The temple grounds house other shrines, including ones devoted to

Ganesha, the elephant god, one of the most popular deities in Malaysia, and Hanuman, the monkey god, believed to ward off evil.

Adventure sports

Batu Caves is also popular with adventure sports enthusiasts. There are about another 20 caves within the massif, and one of them, the **Dark Cave** conservation site, is open to educational tours with a company appointed by the MNS (tel: 03-6189 6682; Tue–Sun 9.30am–5pm; charge, book ahead for the adventure tour). The 2km (1 mile) of passages contain ancient cave formations as well as bats and creepy crawlies.

The other side of the cliff is popular with rock-climbers and BASE jumpers (parachutists who jump from static objects), particularly at weekends. Rock-climbers also head to **Bukit Takun,** located further north along the old trunk road (Route 1). In the vicinity of Takun are several parks, offering easy treks, and pools and waterfalls for swimming. Among them is the popular **Templer Park** (Taman Templer),

and scenic **Hutan Lipur Kancing** (Kancing Forest Reserve), which has a seven-tier waterfall up which the fit can hike to get great views.

FRIM

However, a better rainforest experience is to be had at the 600-hectare (1,480-acre) **Forest Research Institute of Malaysia (FRIM) ⓫** (grounds: daily 5.30am–7pm, Sat–Sun 8.30am–7.30pm; charge). Located in Kepong, about 7km (4 miles) west of Batu Caves, FRIM sits in rainforest that is surprisingly lush considering it is not virgin forest, but merely 70 years old. Several trails let visitors soak it all in, one of which leads to the 30-metre (100ft) high Canopy Walkway (Mon–Fri 9.30am–2.30pm), which commands terrific views of the forest.

Meanwhile, as the country's top and oldest forest research facility, FRIM also has research plantations, arboreta, gardens and an excellent forestry museum. The One Stop Service Centre (tel: 03-6279 7592; 9am–5pm) can provide maps and suggestions; book a day ahead for guides.

TIP

At Batu Caves, cool down with fresh coconut juice or fill up with a vegetarian or *jaan* (no garlic or onions) meal at the eateries in the temple compound.

Braving the FRIM canopy walkway.

A tea picker at Boh tea plantation on the Sungai Palas Estate in the Cameron Highlands.

Strolling on Batu Feringghi at sunset.

THE NORTHWESTERN PENINSULA

This is an area of immense variety, spliced in the middle by a mountainous jungle-covered backbone known as the Main Range, or Banjaran Titiwangsa.

Painted chick blinds at a workshop.

Heading north out of Kuala Lumpur is like heading through the country's so-called first wave of development – this is the land of tin and rubber, and, nearer the Thai border, rice.

Perak's Kinta river valley was once the tin capital of the world. Now, a daisy-chain of huge mining ponds sit in silence amid deserts of stark, bleached sand and the odd tin dredge made of wood, but life is returning to this seeming desolation. Museums about the tin-mining days have sprouted up in the former mining towns of Gopeng and Ipoh, while the indigenous people, the Orang Asli, guide visitors deep into the forests to see the world's largest flower in bloom. In the middle of a plantation, visitors wander around a castle wondering what it would have looked like had it been completed.

Further north, the flat tin-mining lands make way for limestone hills. Large outcrops dripping with vegetation dot Perak and Perlis, and make up the entire islands of the Langkawi archipelago. Being Southeast Asia's first Geopark, Langkawi's geological formations are a sight to behold – whether it is riding a cable car to the top of a mountain, swimming in a lake or kayaking through the mangrove trees.

Swathed in mist at dawn, the limestone hills are inspiration for any number of Chinese brush paintings, while the earliest evidence of prehistoric human civilisation in the country can be found among the caves. Caves continue to fascinate modern man; at Chinese and Hindu cave temples, locals seek divine guidance for their everyday lives.

The rainforest-covered mountains of this region.

On the west coast of Perak, a unique ecosystem beckons the visitor – huge swathes of mangrove trees, the forest between land and sea, are home to hundreds of bird species, including migratory birds wintering here. Meanwhile, on the isles, it is always holiday time. The World Heritage City of George Town continues to bewitch with its plethora of colonial buildings, temples and cluttered, lively city streets, while beyond the city lie golden beaches, Malay villages and a countryside dotted with nutmeg and durian orchards. More long sandy beaches beckon at Langkawi, a hugely popular resort island, yet still sleepily wrapped in legend.

Morning light over the Boh tea plantation, in the Cameron Highlands.

HILL STATIONS

With their temperate climates and tranquil gardens, the high hill stations of central Malaysia are as popular with tourists today as they were with the British colonialists who built them.

The insufferable heat drove them to the hills. Once there, they pushed back the jungle and created little pockets of England with rose gardens and mock-Tudor bungalows; from that point on, life in the colonies assumed a more bearable aspect for the British. Today for much the same reason – cooler climes – tourists flock to the former hill stations of Bukit Larut (Maxwell Hill), Cameron Highlands and Fraser's Hill. Some of the buildings have been taken over by multinationals as hillside retreats; others are now hotels, while yet more new high-rise developments cater to city travellers looking for a short-stay respite.

Of all the hill stations, Cameron Highlands has developed the most. Forests have been cleared to make way for more vegetable, fruit and flower farms. Although the climate is not as cool as in the past, people continue to flock to Cameron for a weekend's rest and descend with a carload of fresh vegetables and strawberries as souvenirs of their stay. For the more adventurous, hiking, nature photography and bird-watching are some of the leisurely pursuits one can enjoy to experience the beauty of the highlands.

Maxwell Hill

The oldest and smallest hill station is also the one least touched by time, **Maxwell Hill ❶** (Bukit Larut) in

Perak. Rising to 1,036 metres (3,399ft) above the serene Lake Gardens of Taiping, it is largely responsible for Taiping being the wettest place in the peninsula. This is a peaceful hill resort; there are no golf courses or fancy restaurants, only gardens and jungle walks. The attraction for visitors is the cool air and the fine vistas: clouds over the Straits of Malacca, thick mist-laden jungles and the Lake Gardens (Taman Tasik) below.

From Taiping, hail a taxi to the foot of Maxwell Hill about 6km (4 miles) away. You can also walk the distance,

Main Attractions
Cameron Highlands
Mount Brinchang
Sungai Palas Tea Estate
Fraser's Hill
Resorts World Genting
Orang Asli Museum

Tea pickers loading sacks.

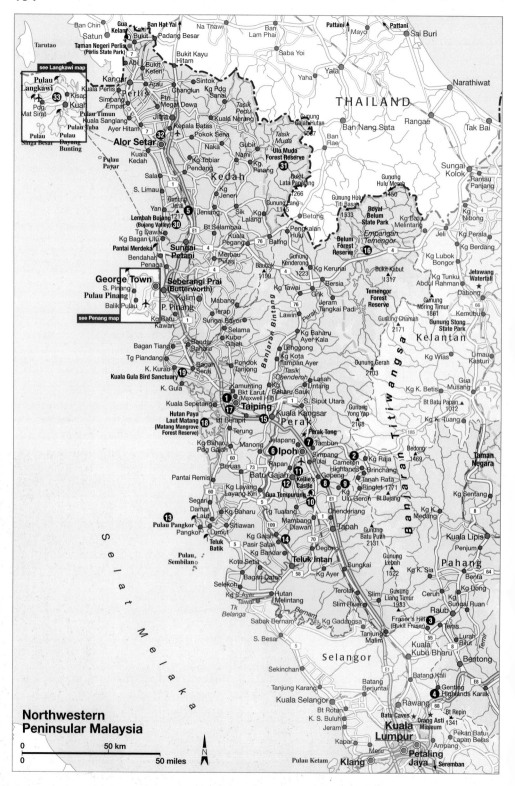

Ban Chin
Satun
Gua Kelang
Kaki Bukit
Ban Hat Yai
Na Thawi
Ban Lam Phai
Pattani
Mayo
Pattani
Sai Buri
Tarutao
Taman Negeri Perlis
(Perlis State Park)
Abi
Padang Besar
Bukit Kayu Hitam
Saba Yoi
Yaha
Yala
Narathiwat
Bukit Keteri
Kangar
Sintok
Kuala Perlis
Arau
Changlun
Kg Pdg Sanai
Yaha
Yala

see Langkawi map
Pulau Langkawi
Kisap
Kuah
Perlis
Ptn
Megat Dewa
Tasik Pedu
Gunung Gajah Hutan
1067
Ban Nang Sata
Rangae
Tak Bai
Pdg Mat Sirat
Pulau Timun
Kuala Sanglang
Jitra
Kepala Batas
Kuala Nerang
THAILAND
Pulau Tuba
Ayer Hitam
Pokok Sena
Pulau Singa Besar
Pulau Dayang Bunting
Alor Setar
Naka
Gubir
Nami
Kg Pinang
Tasik Muda
Ulu Muda Forest Reserve
Gunung Hulu Merah
1450
Sungai Kolok
Rantau Panjang
Kuala Kedah
Sala
Pendang
Kedah
Kg Jeneri
Bukit Lata Panjang
266
Gunung Hulu Titi Basah
1533
Royal Belum State Park
Kg Batu Melintang
Jeli
Kg Perala
Kg Berdang
S. Limau
Yan
Gunung Jerai
1217
Jeniang
Sik
Lalang
Gunung Lang
1145
Betong
Pengkalan Hulu
Belum Forest Reserve
Empangan Temengor
Kg Lubok Bongor

Lembah Bujang (Bujang Valley)
Tg Dawai
Kg Bagan Ulu
Bt Selambau
Kuala Pegang
Baling
Gunung Kenderong
Kg Kerunai
Bukit Kabut
1317
Kg Tunku
Abdul Rahman
Jelawang Waterfall

Pantai Merdeka
Bendahari
Penaga
Sungai Petani
Merbau Pulas
Baubak
1198
1223
Bersia
Temengor Forest Reserve
Gunung Noring Timur
1861
Dabong
Kemubu
66

George Town
Pulau Pinang
S. Pinang
Seberang Prai
(Butterworth)
Kulim
Kg Tawai
Grik
Jeram
Tangkai Padi
Gunung Chamah
2171
Gunung Stong State Park
Kelantan

P. Pinang
Balik Pulau
Mabang
Terap
Lawin
Kg Baharu Ayer Kala
Lenggong
Gunung Gerah
2703
Kg Wias
Limau Kasturi

see Penang map
Kg Batu Kawan
Sungai Bayor
Selama
Kubu Gajah
Kg Kota
Tampan Ayer
Gua Musang
Kg K. Betis
Kg K. Tuang
8

Bagan Tiang
Tg Piandang
Bandar Baharu
Pondok Tanjong
Tasik Chenderoh
Lasah
Bt Batu Papan
1012

K. Kurau
Kuala Gula Bird Sanctuary
K. Gula
Bagan Serdi
Kamunting
Bkt Larut (Maxwell Hill)
Kg Baharu Sauk
Lintang
S. Siput Utara
Gunung Yong Yap
2168
Bedong
1469

Kuala Sepetang
Hutan Paya Laut Matang
(Matang Mangrove Forest Reserve)
Bt Berapit
Taiping
Kuala Kangsar
Perak
185
Taman Negara

Kg Baharu Pdg Gajah
Terung
Manong
Jelapang
Perak Tong
Tambun
Simpang Pulai
Kg Raja
Kg Sentang
Kg K. Medang
Kuala Lipis

Pantai Remis
Beruas
73
Batu Gajah
Rapan
Ipoh
Kellie's Castle
Gopeng
Cameron Highlands
Brinchang
Tanah Rata
Ringlet 1171
Ulu Geroh
Bt Bujang
Penjum
Pahang

Segari
Damar Laut
Kg Layang Layang Kiri
Gua Tempurung
Kg Baharu
Sitiawan
Tg Tualang
Mambang Diawan
Chenderiang
Gunung Batu Putih
2131
Benta
Kg Dong
64

Pulau Pangkor
Pangkor
Teluk Batik
Pasir Salak
109
Tapah
Gunung Lebah
1522
Kg K. Sia
Raub

Lumut
Pulau Sembilan
Kg Gajah
Kg Bandar
Teluk Intan
Sungkai
Kuala Kubu Bharu
Fraser's Hill
(Bukit Fraser)
Teras
Lurah Bilut
Bentong

Kota Setia
Bagan Datoh
58
Kg Ayer
Terolak
Slim
Gunung Liang Timur
1983
Slim River
Tanjung Malim
55
Selangor

Selekoh
Kg S. Ayer Tawar
Tk Belanga
Hutan Melintang
Bernam
Kg Gadangsa
Sabak Bernam
Degong

S. Besar
Sekinchan
Batang Berjuntai
Batang Kali
Genting Highlands Karak
E8

Tanjung Karang
Kuala Selangor
Bt Rotan
K. S. Buluh
Jeram
Batu Caves
Orang Asli Museum
Rawang
68
Bt Repin
Pekan Batu Lapan Belas
1341

Northwestern Peninsular Malaysia
Kapar
Meru
Kuala Lumpur
Ampang
Petaling Jaya
Seremban

0   50 km
0   50 miles
Pulau Ketam
Klang

Selat Melaka

through the picturesque 19th-century Lake Gardens – Malaysia's largest urban parkland.

Large bungalows, complete with fireplaces, sit at different elevations of this hill (for bookings, tel: 05-807 7241). The road up the hill was constructed during World War II with the "help" of Japanese prisoners-of-war. Before that, anyone who wished to reach the top had to hike three hours or go by pony or sedan chair. At one time, the trail was used by porters carrying heavy loads of fragrant tea downhill. Now the tea plantations are no more, leaving only the **Tea Garden House**, midway up, with its view of Taiping and the Lake Gardens. A handful of labourers keep the jungle at bay and the lush gardens neatly manicured.

Access to the hill is denied to private vehicles. Instead, government-owned Land Rovers (tel: 05-807 7241) serve as mountain taxis departing every hour between 8am and 3pm daily. Land Rovers descend the hill every hour from 9am to 4pm. You can purchase your return tickets from the office at the foot of the hill. They take eight persons seated, and two standing at the back, hanging grimly on to the top bar. The one-lane road is steep and narrow; at sharp hairpin bends – 72 of them – the jungle suddenly parts to reveal the green land below divided into a pattern of roads and fields.

Depending on the confidence levels of your driver – there is one who has ferried people for more than 20 years – be prepared for either a sedate or an adrenalin-laden half-hour ride. There isn't a speed limit, so think twice about going up if you suffer from fear of heights and take precautions if you are prone to motion sickness. The 10km (6-mile) journey takes 40 minutes and you are deposited at the front step of your bungalow or accommodation.

Taiping War Cemetery

While waiting for the next available Land Rover to bring you up the hill, there are nearby attractions at the foothill to keep you occupied. Backtrack down the road and turn left towards Taiping town. On either side of the road is the beautiful, well-maintained **Taiping War Cemetery**, which

TIP

For the birdwatcher, Maxwell Hill boasts over 60 bird species. The best and only trail for birdwatching is the Mount Hijau Trail; the entrance lays 150 metres (492ft) below the telecommunication tower. The path is overgrown and it's advisable to hire a guide. Enquire at your place of accommodation.

A view of the Cameron Highlands mountains.

Cameron's trails and tours

Discover natural attractions on more than a dozen trails that bring you to mountain peaks, waterfalls, tea plantations and maybe even the world's largest flower.

In 1967, while on holiday in Cameron Highlands, the American Thai-silk entrepreneur Jim Thompson went out for an evening stroll along one of the highlands' many trails. He was never seen again.

Even today, spirit-world, wild-animal and conspiracy theories surround the disappearance of the highlands' most famous missing person. Somehow this has added weight to the otherwise standard precautions requiring visitors to tell someone which trail they are taking and to stick to the paths. Some trails are not well marked, so hikers do occasionally get lost even on some of the shorter trails. A guide is recommended, especially for longer hikes to Mount Brinchang and

A jungle trail in the Cameron Highlands.

Mount Irau. As it usually rains in the evenings, start trekking in the morning or for shorter walks, at least four hours before nightfall. Bring water, snacks, camera, raincoat and a fully charged mobile phone (most trails have coverage). Most Cameron Highlands maps include the 14 walking trails ranging from easy to very tough.

Routes

A fairly easy and popular trek at Tanah Rata is the one-hour **Robinson Descent** (Path 9), which starts at the falls and goes downhill to the power station – the last stretch is fairly steep though. The longer and flatter **Boh Road** trail (Path 9A) branches off to the left at the top of Path 9 and leads to the Fairlie Boh Tea Estate road near Habu. Another easy route is **Parit Falls** (Path 4), a flat 20-minute stroll from the New Garden Inn to Taman Sedia, known for the KHM Strawberry Farm.

All these trails join up with the circular **Mount Bereman** track (the very tough Path 8 from Robinson Falls and the moderate Path 3 from Parit Falls). The trek is steep and you need to cross some streams. It takes about 3 hours to reach the 1,800-metre (5,900ft) peak, but the sunsets and sunrises are great – bring a tent and warm clothes if you intend to camp out. Path 3 behind the Arcadia Bungalow actually ends in Brinchang at the golf course, or joins Path 2 (tough), to go past the hilltop Sam Poh Temple into town. The Bereman track splinters at various parts, so ensure you take the correct path.

There is a trail that leads north from Brinchang up to 2,031-metre (6,664ft) **Mount Brinchang** (Path 1). It is a long and tough four-hour trek, and can be wet and slippery after rain. Keep your eyes open for pitcher plants in this damp and fern-rich mossy forest. A 200-metre (656ft) long Mossy Forest boardwalk loop gives you incredible views of the misty forest.

Spotting the Rafflesia

There are several interesting tours out of Brinchang and Tanah Rata that go off the beaten track but require minimum numbers. The jewel in the crown is a Rafflesia tour, which is run only when guides encounter a patch where this rare parasite, the world's largest flower is, or is close to, blooming (see page 20). Seeing a Rafflesia is an amazing experience, more so when you know it takes a bud 10 months to flower, but it gets to live for less than a week before it rots.

commemorates over 850 Commonwealth soldiers who died in the Japanese invasion, of whom more than 500 remain unidentified. To enjoy an invigorating soak in the river or some birdwatching, turn left after the cemetery and follow the signposts to **Burmese Pool**, a naturally formed pool in the river (see page 175). Further upriver is a trail popular with bird-watchers who come here to spot as many as 114 species.

Cameron Highlands

Crew-cut tea-bush rows lend the rolling hills of **Cameron Highlands** ❷ a soft green glow in the dewy early light. Vast tea plantations distinguish this most developed of Malaysia's hill stations, which peaks at 2,031 metres (6,664ft).

Although Cameron, as it is called, is actually part of Pahang, it can be reached via Tapah or Simpang Pulai in Perak. From Tapah and Ipoh, there are regular buses to Tanah Rata, Cameron's main town, while Tapah is also on the train route. The Cameron Highlands District Council (tel: 05-491 1455; www.mdcameron.gov.my/en/home) provides information about Cameron and how to get there. If you are driving, turn off at the old trunk road just north of Tapah that leads via Chenderiang to the gorgeous **Lata Kinjang**, a towering 850-metre (2,790ft) multi-step waterfall visible from the North–South Expressway. There are picnic spots, gardens and a spray-misted suspension bridge here. Orang Asli guides who live at the foot of the falls can guide you to other cascades and to their durian fruit orchards in the forest for a fee, but you need permission from the Forestry Department in Tapah to enter the area, which is a forest reserve.

From Tapah, the Cameron road twists its way uphill for 90km (60 miles) through a dense forest of coniferous trees, thick ferns and clusters of bamboo that add the touch of a Chinese scroll painting. The hairpin bends on this road can make the journey uncomfortable. Cameron is particularly well known for its tree ferns and wild orchids. While you're travelling up, you will pass Orang Asli on motorbikes or on foot, carrying butterfly nets, on their way to their villages which dot the hills.

Lata Iskandar waterfall.

An Orang Asli house in the Cameron Highlands.

Pickers at work on the Boh tea plantation, Sungai Palas Estate.

Ringlet is the first and rather ugly little settlement at the 45km (30-mile) marker. Push on, and 4km (2.5 miles) later you will reach the **Sultan Abu Bakar Lake** (Tasik Sultan Abu Bakar), an artificial body of water formed by the damming of Sungai Bertam for Cameron's hydroelectric scheme, which is one of the country's oldest.

The road from Simpang Pulai makes for an easier climb to Cameron as it is wider and less winding. From the North–South Expressway, turn off at the Simpang Pulai exit and follow the signposts. You will pass Kampung Raja and Tringkap before reaching Brinchang, the highest town in Cameron Highlands.

Tanah Rata and Brinchang

Farmlands begin before Sultan Abu Bakar Lake, the cultivated terraces that have earned Cameron Highlands the nickname of vegetable capital of the peninsula. There are also nurseries which supply roses, carnations and chrysanthemums to domestic and overseas markets. An increasing trend among these growers is the move

The entrance to a strawberry farm.

towards organic farming, thanks to pressure against pesticide use. About 15km (9 miles) further on lies **Tanah Rata**, the principal township, a bustling tourist centre with hotels, shops and restaurants.

Discovered by William Cameron, a government surveyor on a mapping expedition in 1885, "this fine plateau with gentle slopes shut in by the mountains" was unknown even to the locals in the lowlands. After 1931, tea planters, then farmers, claimed the plateau and built a road to carry their produce to market.

Today, Tanah Rata is popular with Malaysian families, college students, retirees and diplomats alike. Boy scouts with knapsacks on their backs thumb rides up the winding hills, while Singaporean tourists lounge on colonial-style verandas, munching fresh strawberries and cream. To some, arriving from the tropical lowlands, it seems somewhat incongruous to arrive at Tanah Rata and find log fires lit every night, with Devonshire tea and English breakfast on menus. But among the Chinese hotels are several

very good Indian restaurants, serving simple snacks and meals that agree well with the climate here.

The **Yung Seng Souvenir Shop** at 29 & 30 Main Road has beautiful local crafts, including the wonderful Mah Meri masks of Selangor and Temiar fishing traps, as well as crafts from other Southeast Asian countries.

En route to Brinchang along Jalan Tanah Rata-Brinchang is one of the country's oldest golf courses, the **Sultan Ahmad Shah Golf Course** (tel: 05-491 1126; daily 7am–5pm; charge), which survived tigers, vegetable farmers and World War II to become the 18-hole public golf course it is today.

On the road to Brinchang, just after the Sri Thandayuthapani Swamy Temple, turn right into Jalan Pecah Batu, which leads to the well-kept **Sam Poh Temple**. Built in 1972 and dedicated to the Ming Dynasty Chinese Muslim eunuch Admiral Zheng He (Cheng Ho), the temple overlooks Brinchang and houses many statues including a large statue of Buddha.

The once pretty Brinchang is now populated with modern high-rise developments, a scene compounded further by tacky attractions such as Cactus Valley, the Rose Centre and Butterfly Farm. The town is also at the tail-end of the Simpang Pulai road that links to Ipoh. Just beyond Brinchang is the **Kea Farm area**, the heartland of vegetable farms and nurseries. Here farmers set up roadside stalls to sell produce ranging from wild honey and asparagus to strawberries and tomatoes.

Boh Tea estates

There are two major tea growers in the highlands – the giant Boh Tea, which operates a chain of "tea cafés" in cities as well as at both their highland tea estates and Bharat Tea, which runs three teashops in Cameron Highlands as well as a fourth in Kuala Lumpur.

The prettiest tea estate in Cameron Highlands and owned by Boh Tea is the **Sungai Palas Tea Estate**, located further north from Brinchang. It's a short but steep walk up to the estate's **Sungai Palas Tea Centre** (tel: 05-496 2096; Tue–Sun 9am–4.30pm; free), which is worth a stop. Housed in a modern architectural edifice is the **Tea'ria**

TIP

Try Boh's flavoured teas at Tea'ria. These are blended with local fruit such as lychee, and spices such as cinnamon and ginger. The teashop also has a wide range of beautifully packaged products including instant mix iced teas.

The viewing platform at Sungai Palas Estate.

souvenir and teashop, where you can savour teas and sandwiches while enjoying elevated panoramic views of the surrounding area through its high floor-to-ceiling glass windows. Seating is also available on its outdoor terrace, which protrudes out 6 metres (20ft) from the hilltop, overlooking a lush tea valley below. After savouring the fine views and tea, visitors can learn about the history of the Boh tea plantations and the tea-manufacturing process through the centre's free 10-minute tours given every 15 minutes.

The oldest tea factory belonging to Boh Tea is the one built in 1929 in the **Fairlie Tea Estate** about 8km (5 miles) from Habu, where the original processing technology is still used.

The most accessible tea estate to photograph is the **Cameron Bharat Plantation** (tel: 05-491 1133; daily 9am–6pm) between Ringlet and Tanah Rata, which has a teahouse (the first teahouse has better views than the second one) as well but no tours. The teahouse menu offers a variety of Western-style desserts and local snacks, as well as a wide selection of teas – whether

The clock tower marking the centre point of Fraser's Hill.

original, flavoured or infused.

From the Sungai Palas Tea Estate, a steep road winds 6km (4 miles) up to Mount Brinchang, which has panoramic views of the forested valley. This also makes quite a nice – if long – early morning walk that takes in vegetable farms, the bird-filled forest near the top, and the colourful periwinkles growing freely among the tea bushes.

Fraser's Hill

Much quieter is **Fraser's Hill** ❸ (Bukit Fraser) in Pahang, although its past is more colourful. The hill resort is named after Louis James Fraser, an elusive English adventurer, who had long disappeared when the hill station was built in 1922. He apparently ran a notorious gambling and opium den here for local miners and planters, as well as a mule train and, later, a transport service in the lowlands.

The 1,524-metre (5,000ft) high resort is scattered over seven hills on which sits a series of English greystone bungalows, surrounded by neat English gardens blooming with roses and hollyhocks, hence its moniker "Little England".

GETTING TO FRASER'S HILL

Driving is the best way to get to Fraser's Hill. From Kuala Lumpur, follow signposts to the quaint town of Kuala Kubu Bharu. As there are no petrol stations in Fraser's, it is advised to refuel here before heading for the hills. The winding road passes Orang Asli villages and a large lake, a result of the damming of the Sungai Selangor.

From the base of Fraser's Hill, it is a 40-minute drive up a one-way 9km (5.6-mile) road. A gateman allows vehicles to ascend every odd hour, beginning from 7am, and cars from the hilltop descend every even hour starting from 8am. After 7pm the narrow Gap road allows traffic from both directions. There is a less winding 11km (7-mile) long two-lane road, but it is more prone to landslides and can be closed to traffic. If open, travel will be up the old road and down the new road. Be sure to check on which routes are open with the Fraser's Hill Development Corporation (tel: 09-362 2195/201) prior to your trip.

After about 20 minutes, the Gap comes into view. This was once a rest stop for mule and bullock cart transporters. It was named the Gap as it quite literally occupied a gap between the boundaries of the Selangor and Pahang states.

The clock tower roundabout marks the centre of town, and here you'll find the post office, a government dispensary, a police station and small convenience stores and cafés. The prettiest and most expensive accommodation is **Ye Olde Smokehouse Hotel & Restaurant** (tel: 09-362 2226), where you can also enjoy Devonshire tea or apple pie in the lovely garden. The road to the inn leads on to **Jeriau Waterfall**, once a pretty picnic spot, but now permanently silted, the result of resort development years ago.

Because of its proximity to Kuala Lumpur, Fraser's is crowded at weekends, but there are enough walks and trails to take you away from the madding crowd. The ring road around the 9-hole golf course makes a pleasant two-hour walk, and brings you past the old bungalows and newer resorts. The picturesque course at the **Royal Fraser's Hill Golf Club** (daily 8am–7pm; charge) was carved out of an old tin mine and is one of the few public courses in the country.

There are also eight jungle trails of varying lengths, which are well marked and easy to follow. The most popular is the half-hour **Bishop's Trail**, while the scenic **Hemmant Trail** skirts the golf course. Fit trekkers will appreciate the challenging 6km (4-mile) **Pine Tree Trail**, a full-day hike which leads 1,450 metres (4,750ft) up to breathtaking views. Fraser's trails run through montane forests, where trees are generally shorter than in the lowlands, growing up to only 30 metres (100ft) tall, and are usually coated with lichens, ferns and orchids. Dominant species are oaks, laurels, tree ferns and conifers. Scientists have found over 30 species of plants that live only in these hills.

On your treks, you may encounter birdwatching groups who are drawn to the forests by more than 270 local and migratory species. June is peak season – when local and international birdwatchers armed with digital telescopes, tripods and binoculars descend on this hill station for the Fraser's Hill International Bird Race.

Genting Highlands

Newer hill resorts are popular, but lack the charm of the three "oldies". A

The Bishop's Trail on Fraser's Hill.

At the Genting Resort theme park.

definite study in contrast is **Genting Highlands** ❹, 2,000 metres (6,600ft) above sea level. Just one convenient hour from Kuala Lumpur, it is actually visible from the capital, a city of pleasure shrouded in mist, on top of **Main Range** (Banjaran Titiwangsa), the mountain range that runs down the centre of the peninsula.

Genting is the Las Vegas of Malaysia, a rambling complex of hotels, theme parks and a casino, the country's sole gambling den. This is something people either love or loathe. Amid lush surroundings, the complex is entirely artificial, giant boulders included, and it is possible not to surface for sunshine the whole time you are there. The whole development comes under **Resorts World Genting** (tel: 03-6101 1118; www.rwgenting.com), which was owned by the late businessman Lim Goh Tong, who mooted the idea for the resort, spending seven years alone on building the steep road.

Accommodation is plentiful and affordable; there are over 10,000 rooms available at four hotels, 90 food outlets and more than 40 rides at the outdoor

and indoor theme parks. There are also two theatres which feature international magic acts or cabaret dinner shows, and famous singers often make appearances.

Next to Awana Skyway's Chin Swee Station, and about a 10-minute drive down the hill is the massive **Chin Swee Caves Temple** (www.csc.org.my). When Lim was constructing the road leading to his resort, he came across this rocky slope with streams and great views, which reminded him of the Chin Swee Crag, named after a revered Chinese philanthropist in his birthplace in Fujian, China. After Lim built the first phase of his hotel and casino, he spent the next 18 years building this temple. Within the temple grounds are numerous other temples, statues, a waterfall, meditation rooms and a vegetarian restaurant. While devotees worship the Reverend Chin or pray to Buddha and Kuan-yin for better luck, visitors can explore Chinese beliefs like travel from hell to heaven in the afterlife through the use of dioramas.

Things are a little less manic 10km (6 miles) down the hill at the **Awana Golf and Country Club** (www.gentinghighlands.info/awana-resort.htm), which has an 18-hole golf course and panoramic views. Awana and Genting Highlands resorts are linked by a skyway, a cable car system covering the 3km (2-mile) journey. The **Genting Skyway** (tel: 03-6101 1118; daily 7.30am–midnight; charge) connects Gohtong Jaya town, further down the hill, to Resorts World Genting. When the Genting Skyway was under maintenance, the older **Awana Skyway** used to ferry people from Awana to Genting stopping over at the Chin Swee Caves Temple; it is now closed and due to be replaced by a new cable car system in 2016. Free shuttle bus services transport passengers from the hotels to the skyway stations.

To drive to Genting from Kuala Lumpur, head northeast to reach the Karak Highway. Drive for about half an hour before you see a multi-storey rest stop on your right, marking the turn-off to Genting Highlands. From here,

"Patung Harimau Berantai", handiwork from the Mah Meri tribe, who are famous for their artistic talent, displayed in the Orang Asli Museum.

it is a 15-minute drive up a winding road to the main resort.

Orang Asli Museum

Genting can also be accessed via the considerably more pleasant old Pahang Road through Gombak. About 24km (15 miles) down the old Pahang Road is the excellent **Orang Asli Museum** (Muzium Orang Asli; Km24, Jalan Pahang, Gombak; Sat–Thu 9am–5pm; free). Sitting on a hill at an Orang Asli settlement, it provides a fascinating insight on the Malaysian peninsula's aboriginal peoples. A good range of exhibits such as old photographs, artefacts, handicraft, and tools and implements used in daily life, make this museum well worth a visit.

Mount Jerai

Another hill station is found at **Mount Jerai** (Gunung Jerai) **⑤**, Kedah's highest peak. The 1,217-metre (3,992ft) high limestone massif has commanding views of the surrounding rice plains and the Main Range. On the other side, you can see across the Straits of Malacca into Penang, and even as far as Langkawi island. Part of the **Sungai Teroi Forest Recreation Park** (Hutan Rekreasi Sungai Teroi), which has some forest trails, the hill is also home to a forestry museum.

Jerai is accessed from Gurun from the North–South Expressway. Alternatively, from KL Sentral, you can take Malaysian Railway's Train 20 north to Gurun, and get a taxi to the peak.

Penang Hill

The 833-metre (2,733ft) **Penang Hill** resort consists of five hills and is located 7km (4 miles) from Penang's George Town and offers fantastic views – day or night – of the Unesco heritage city, the mainland and the Straits of Malacca. The official name is Bukit Bendera (Flagstaff Hill), but it was originally called Strawberry Hill during the British Settlement era when Captain Francis Light cleared the area in the hope of growing strawberries,

as it was several degrees cooler up here. There are two ways to ascend the hill – by far the most popular being the five-minute non-stop **Penang Hill Railway** ride (tel: 04-828 8880/39; www.penanghill.gov.my; Mon–Fri 6.30am–8pm (weekends and holidays to 10pm), bottom station closes an hour earlier; charge). There are five substations along the way, but these stops are exclusively for the use of the hill residents, which the railway runs on a separate schedule.

There is a 5km (3-mile) tarred road nicknamed the "Jeep Track", but again it's only open to vehicles ferrying residents to and fro. Nevertheless, hikers can use this road, which begins just off the main Jalan Kebun Bunga near the entrance to the Penang Botanic Gardens. A leisurely walk takes from three to four hours to reach the hilltop. Besides the views, there are a few restaurants and a hotel with a small aviary. To descend, hike down the Moon Gate trail near the upper railway station, finishing at the Moon Gate about 300 metres/yards before the Penang Botanical Gardens.

Looking down from Chin Swee Temple.

The interior shrine at Kek Lok Tong temple in Ipoh.

PERAK

This former tin-mining state takes pride in its built and natural heritage, encompassing colonial buildings, limestone caves, temples set inside giant caverns, prehistoric rock art, golden beaches and lush mangroves.

Perak state was once one of the world's most important sources of tin ore. In Bahasa Malaysia, *perak* actually means "silver" – it was the "silver" of the tin revolution that lined the state's coffers, making it one of the wealthiest states in the country. The accompanying feuds and power struggles prompted greater British intervention in the whole country, eventually shifting the centre of power from the old capitals along the Perak river to the tin-rich areas of Larut and Kinta.

When the bottom fell out of the industry in the 1980s, entire towns shut down. However, thanks to its well-preserved colonial buildings, many of which can be seen today in Ipoh and Taiping, and its wealth of natural attractions, including the annual and yet unexplained phenomenon of thousands of Plain-pouched Hornbills flying over one of the world's oldest rainforests, is drawing visitors back to the silver state.

One of the state's must-see highlights are the limestone hills and the many caves found within – whether it's wading through an underground cave river or gaping at astounding flowstones and stalactites from the convenience of an illuminated walkway, to being inspired by spiritual paintings in a cave temple or prehistoric rock art on a cliff face.

In Ipoh Old Town.

Ipoh city

The Kinta Valley remains Perak's leading district, and its main city, **Ipoh ❻**, the most prosperous of its settlements. Beginning as a tin-mining field in the 1870s, Ipoh developed into a hub for road, rail and river transportation. Its name comes from the *epau (antiaris toxicaria)* tree, whose poisonous sap is used for the darts of aboriginal blowpipes. When Ipoh took over as the state capital from Taiping in 1937, it was the best-planned town in the peninsula, with broad, regularly laid-out streets.

Main Attractions

Sam Poh Tong
Perak Tong
Gua Tambun
Gopeng Museum
Kampung Ulu Geroh
Kellie's Castle
Istana Kenangan
Belum-Temengor Forest Complex
Kuala Gula Bird Sanctuary

Nestled in the craggy bosom of limestone outcrops and the more distant hills of the Main Range, Ipoh is one of Malaysia's largest cities, with a population of over 700,000. Its **Old Town** on the west side is where you'll find the *Padang* (Town Green), the epitome of every Malaysian town with a colonial past. Surrounded by the Royal Ipoh Club, court houses, municipal library and the stately **St Michael's Institution**, it is the scene of important matches, school athletic meets, and parades. Near the **State Mosque** (Masjid Negeri) and the Clock Tower is the Moorish **Ipoh Railway Station** (Stesen Keretapi Ipoh), which with a silver dome, graceful arches and interminable colonnades, bears a striking resemblance to the Kuala Lumpur Railway Station.

Be sure to stop over first at the **Garden Villa**, a beautifully preserved heritage building at No. 5 Jalan Raja Dr Nazrin Shah, to obtain heritage trail maps from the Kinta Heritage Group which manages the Anglo-Malay architectural style building as a community and exhibition space.

The group, comprising locals who are concerned about preserving the city's built heritage, have produced the Ipoh Heritage Trail Map 1, which highlights the colonial buildings around the railway station. The Ipoh Heritage Trail Map 2 highlights the historical aspects of selected buildings along a different route, which starts near the playground near Sungai Kinta and concludes at the Dato' Panglima Kinta Mosque on Jalan Masjid (to arrange a guided tour, tel: 05-208 3155).

Near the Ipoh Railway Station, on Jalan Panglima Bukit Gantang Wahab, is the **Darul Ridzuan Museum** (Muzium Darul Ridzuan; tel. 05-241 0048; daily 9.30am–5pm; free). Built by Foo Choong Yit, a wealthy tin miner, in 1926, the mansion also houses an underground air shelter in preparation for World War II and a museum showcasing the state's history, Ipoh's development and the story of tin mining.

Grand mansions in huge grounds still sit along **Jalan Sultan Azlan Shah**, commonly referred to by its old name, Tiger Lane. Also along this road is the **Geological Museum** (Muzium

Heritage buildings in Ipoh.

Geologi; tel: 05-540 6000; Mon–Thu 8.30am–12.30pm and 2–5pm, Fri 8.30am–noon and 3–5pm; free). It has over 600 examples of minerals, an exhibition on tin ore, including one of the best examples of cassiterite in the world, and a fine collection of precious stones, rock specimens and minerals.

Sam Poh Tong

The naturally hollowed insides of the Kinta Valley's limestone formations, so reminiscent of southern China, have served as homes for ancient peoples as well as hideouts for bandits.

They are also spiritually significant for both Buddhists and Hindus. Devotees have built entrances to these temples that range from the simple to the ostentatious; sometimes entire buildings complete with red-tiled pagoda roofs "grow" out from the rock. Walking into the dimly lit interiors, with their altars, the smell of incense and the occasional echoes of bats and swallows, can make for a heady experience for the uninitiated. Ipoh's undisputed top attractions are its cave temples and there are more than 30 of them, with the largest concentration found in **Mount Rapat**, 5km (3 miles) south of Ipoh. The largest of the rock temples here is **Sam Poh Tong** (Cavern of Triple Gems; tel: 05-255 2772; daily 9am–6pm; free). Drive along Jalan Raja Dr Nazrin Shah (Jalan Gopeng) towards Simpang Pulai. After the Petronas petrol station, turn left and you will see three Chinese temples. Founded in 1912, Sam Poh Tong is the last temple on your left.

Statues of Buddha are dotted everywhere, even among the stalagmites and stalactites. A stiff climb up 264 steps leads to a panorama of Ipoh and its surroundings. Of renown is the temple's pond of small tortoises; visitors can buy spinach to feed them. Tortoises are Chinese symbols of longevity.

Close by is the **Kek Look Tong** (www.keklooktong.org; daily 7am–6pm; free but donations welcomed), known also as the Cave Temple of Bronze Buddhas after its gleaming statues. The cave's entrance is not naturally this large – in 1960, it was an iron-mining site, and excavators were used to enlarge the entrance so that trucks could drive in and out with the precious load of iron ore. You can walk through the cave to the back, where its dog's teeth of limestone formations frame a peaceful green valley of ponds and hills.

Another famous cave shrine is the **Perak Tong** (daily 8am–6pm; free), 6km (4 miles) north of town on Jalan Kuala Kangsar, the old trunk road. Traditional Chinese paintings adorn the walls and relate traditional folk tales and legends. Built in 1926 by a Buddhist priest from China, the temple has more than 40 statues of Buddha, the central figure being 13 metres (40ft) high.

Gua Tambun

About 15 minutes' drive east of town is **Tambun** ❼, which has the peninsula's largest rock art site at **Gua Tambun** on Mount Panjang. Don't expect to see a cave there; the star attraction is out in the open. Slightly over 600 Neolithic-period rock paintings depicting human and animal motifs

A sign painter at work in Ipoh.

The entrance to Kek Lok Tong temple.

FACT

A Hindu shrine near Kellie's Castle, erected for the plantation workers, has, among the figures of animals and gods, a man in a green suit and a pith helmet – could this be an image of the castle's architect, Kellie Smith?

are on an exposed cliff face. The main panel of paintings are found between 3–7 metres (10–23ft) off the floor. The red pigment is haematite, which is an iron oxide that is available from the surrounding hills. Although protected by the National Heritage Act, various man-made and natural threats continue to endanger the paintings including vandalism, bird's nest collection and the weather. Being high up on a rocky ledge, there are great views of Ipoh city framed by the Kledang Range. To get here, park at the Caltex Petrol Station along Jalan Tambun.

Gopeng

The old trunk road in Perak goes through mainly flat and open land, offering vistas of deserted mining pools over the bleached scars of tin tailings and glimpses of tin dredges. Just past the city as you head south on the North–South Expressway is the former tin-mining town of **Gopeng** ❽. Here you will find the **Gopeng Museum** (Muzium Gopeng; No. 28 Jalan Eu Kong; tel: 05-359 7828; Fri–Tue 9am–noon and 1–5pm; free, but donations

welcomed), privately run by four Gopeng families who pooled together their personal collection of antiques and artefacts of the famous mining town to preserve them for future generations. There are old clocks, musical instruments, cooking paraphernalia, tin-mining displays and a pictorial look of the history of Gopeng.

When they eventually ran out of space, one of the founders bought a shophouse nearby and converted it into the **Gopeng Heritage House** (No. 6 Jalan Sungai Itek; tel: 05-359 1923; Sat–Sun 9am–3pm; free). Recycled timber from demolished houses in town were used in its restoration, and today the house has more of the same offerings as those found at Gopeng Museum, including antique hardwood furniture, an old barber shop and an opium chair.

Gopeng is more than just tin-mining relics. About a 45-minute drive away is **Kampung Ulu Geroh** ❾, whose Orang Asli – the Semai – have been tasked to protect two endangered species – the world's largest flower, the Rafflesia (see page 20), and the beautiful and majestic Rajah Brooke's Birdwing butterfly. While the Birdwings can easily be seen every day, the stunning Rafflesia flowers are a rarity and are often found deeper in the jungle, anywhere from between an easy half an hour to a steeper two-hour hike.

Gua Tempurung

The prettiest view of Ipoh's limestone hills is just past the city as you head south on the North–South Expressway. Unfortunately, this gives way briefly to blasted rock, precious material for the country's development, before coming to the imposing Mount Tempurung limestone massif, which is believed to have been formed out of 200-million-year-old limestone rock. With the help of water, it took another 195 million years to carve out **Gua Tempurung** ❿ (tel: 05-318 8555; www.perak.info/kinta/Gua_Tempurung/Gua_Tempurung_Tours.htm; daily 9am–4pm except

Breakfast at a Chinese coffee shop in Ipoh's Old Town.

Fri 12.30pm–2.30pm; charge). The underground river continues to shape the cave.

From Gopeng town, head south along Route 1 and turn left after 6km (4 miles). The show cave is 2km (1 mile) down this road. Used variously by tin miners and communists on the run, it is the longest cave system in the peninsula, stretching more than 4.5km (3 miles), but only the 1.6km (1-mile) long river passageway and five caverns are accessible to visitors. An illuminated walkway lets people view the five chambers, and also passes through interesting formations such as gigantic stalagmites and flowstones. Tours run from a 40-minute basic trip to the 3.5-hour grand tour, which involves a river stint. The grand tour is available only in the mornings, with the last tour leaving at 11am. Weekends and public holidays can be crowded with tour buses and camping is allowed, but only outside the cave.

Kellie's Castle

Backtrack to Gopeng town, heading further north on Route 1. Turn left onto Jalan Gopeng, where you will find Perak's only "Scottish" mansion. **Kellie's Castle** ⓫ (tel: 05-365 1336; daily 9am–6pm; charge) was built by William Kellie-Smith, a rubber plantation owner who made his fortune in Malaya. Smith brought in Tamil workers from southern India to build the house in 1915, which was meant to remind him of home. But he died while visiting Lisbon and his widow sold the estate, halting work on the dream house in 1926. His ghost as well as his daughter's are said to haunt the mansion. At a Hindu temple just down the road, Smith is commemorated amid a cluster of rooftop statues.

Tanjung Tualang

Most of the deserted mining pools are located south of **Batu Gajah** ⓬ town. From Kellie's Castle, turn left onto Jalan Gopeng and head west towards Batu Gajah. After about 5km (3 miles), turn right onto Jalan Pejabat Pos and continue on Jalan Pusing. Currently closed, the **Tin Dredge Heritage** ship was built in 1938. Codenamed the T.T. No. 5, this massive ship was originally

Look hard enough in the countryside of Perak and you may spot abandoned wooden tin dredges, a sight from when tin was king in Perak.

Kellie's Castle.

TIP

From Lumut, ferries run to the Pangkor jetty every 15 minutes from 7am–8.30pm. The fast ferry takes about 20 minutes, while the slower ones take twice as long. Contact Tourism Jetty Centre (tel: 05-680 4000) for more information. For a Lumut map, stop over at the Lumut Tourist Information Centre (tel: 05-683 4057) on Jalan Sultan Idris Shah opposite the ferry terminal complex.

located in Teja, Gopeng, but was decommissioned 45 years later due to the collapse of the tin-mining industry in the early 1980s. It was relocated here, spruced up and reopened to the public but closed in 2014, its future uncertain.

Head southwards following signposts on Route A15 until you reach the former tin-mining town of **Tanjung Tualang**. Today, however, it is more famous for its freshwater prawns. Many of the area's mining pools have been converted to breed these tasty crustaceans, and you can try some of them at the seafood restaurants in town.

Pulau Pangkor

If you can't make it to the beaches of the peninsula's east coast, **Pulau Pangkor ⑬**, off the coast of Perak, is pleasant. If coming from Tanjung Tualang, head north on Route A15, turning left onto Route A112 until you reach the Lebuhraya Ipoh-Lumut. Turn left onto the expressway, following signposts to Lumut.

Pangkor is a smaller, less developed version of Langkawi (see page 200),

and is popular with locals and tourists. Public holidays find it packed and prices doubled, but off-peak, the taxi drivers play draughts, and the isle is enveloped in a lovely, lazy atmosphere.

Pangkor is best known for the historic treaty signed there in 1874, granting the British entry into the Malay states for the first time. The beach resort stretch is on the western side of the island, and has great sunset views. The most established of the beaches, with plenty of accommodation and eateries, **Pasir Bogak** is by no means the prettiest, but it does make a good base from which to explore the island by rented bicycle or motorcycle. Cyclists should note, though, that the island is pretty hilly.

North of Pasir Bogak is the prettier **Teluk Nipah**, packed with virtually identical backpacker accommodation. Don't be surprised to see a hornbill or two sitting on an electricity pole outside your resort. In the adjacent beach, **Coral Bay**, is a hawker centre. As with Teluk Nipah, the waters here are lovely, and great for snorkelling. Just before Teluk Nipah is **Teluk Ketapang**, where turtles sometimes come ashore to lay eggs.

Little has changed in the eastern villages of **Kampung Sungai Pinang Kecil** (better known as SPK, also a ferry stop) and **Kampung Teluk Kecil**, with their quaint tiny wooden houses on stilts over the water. Despite tourism being well established, the island's economy is dependent mainly on the sea. The villages are therefore alive with activity when the bright yellow boats leave and return from their night stints. To reach any of the jetties, just head right through the courtyard and ingeniously converted warehouses that look like someone's living room. At SPK, drop in at the famous **Hai Seng Hin satay fish factory**, where sea produce is dried, packed and sold.

South of the island, in the middle of a *kampung*, sit the remains of a Dutch fort, **Kota Belanda**, built over 300 years ago in an attempt to

The Perak river.

control Perak's tin trade and to fight the tyranny of piracy in the Straits of Melaka. Reconstructed by the National Museum in 1973, features of the original building still survive such as the Dutch East India coat-of-arms chiselled on a boulder close to the fort.

Pulau Pangkor Laut

Off the coast of Pasir Bogak is **Pulau Pangkor Laut**, a privately owned island with the exclusive patrons-only **Pangkor Laut Resort** (www.pangkorlautresort.com). Apart from beachfront and hillside villas, the resort offers villas on stilts over the sea, as well as spa treatments and a full range of amenities. The resort also has its own ferry from Lumut. The island's most famous feature is Emerald Bay, a gorgeous beach with powdery white sand and clear waters.

The gateway to Pulau Pangkor is busiest during the Pesta Laut (Sea Festival) in August or September, a popular local attraction. Pangkor can also be crowded at this time and during the Malaysian school and public holidays.

Pasir Salak

For centuries before the tin boom, Sungai Perak provided the only access to the state's interior. The river valley stretches from the royal town of Kuala Kangsar to the coastal village of Beting Beras Basah, near the town of Bagan Datoh. The main area of Malay settlement, this was also the scene of some of the most dramatic events in Perak's history. Now good roads run along either side of the banana tree-lined banks, through villages which were once the homes of the state's greatest heroes.

Some of these graves can be found in one of the country's most important sites, which saw the first local uprising against British colonialists. A well-organised historical complex, **Pasir Salak** ⑭ (tel: 05-631 8999; daily 9.30am–5pm (ticket counter closes at 4pm), closed Fri 12.15pm–2.45pm and Hari Raya; charge) was where the state's first British resident, James Birch, was assassinated in 1875 while bathing in the river. The local ringleaders, Dato' Sagar and Dato' Maharajalela, were executed. Today, there are

Huts on stilts, Pangkor Laut.

Emerald Bay in Pangkor Laut.

FACT

Perak is the only state whose royal house can claim direct descent from the sultans of Melaka. Throughout the valley, there are about 20 tombs of Perak's sultans, all carefully marked and cared for by the villagers. Some of the graves have become *keramat* (shrines), visited by humble folk in search of blessings or favours. It is also a tradition that a newly installed sultan of Perak must pay his respects at every shrine, travelling by boat, before he can truly be accepted as ruler.

memorials at the complex to both the British and local men.

The complex is a beautiful collection of original and reconstructed buildings of historic value blended into a peaceful kampung. Of particular note is the architecture, which has elements of Perak's *rumah kutai* (old houses) – two originals sit in the compound. The historical tunnel, which is also the information centre, features a diorama giving a good overview of the country's history.

To get to Pasir Salak, which is 70km (40 miles) from Ipoh, head south on the old trunk road towards Kampung Gajah through Batu Gajah. The journey there passes **Bota Kanan** at Sungai Perak, which has a breeding centre for river terrapins (tel: 05-376 2726; Mon–Fri 8am–5pm; free) and fruit orchards. There are also many delightful villages in the area, where traditional Perak-style houses are still found.

Kuala Kangsar

Perak's royal capital, **Kuala Kangsar ⑮**, is a lovely garden town about 35km (20 miles) north of Ipoh across

The Ubudiah Mosque.

the Perak river. Within walking distance of the town's attractions is the quiet Government Rest House on Jalan Istana, which overlooks the river. It also has a charming little museum.

Follow Jalan Istana past the Old Residency to reach Bukit Chandan, where the huge golden dome of the century-old **Ubudiah Mosque** (Masjid Ubudiah) gleams. Its striking and symmetrical domes and minarets make it one of the most photographed Muslim buildings in the country; if it is reminiscent of Kuala Lumpur's Moorish architecture, it is because it had the same architect.

Beyond the mosque, the road circles the sultan of Perak's palace, the Saracenic-style **Istana Iskandariah**. Next to it is the smaller but more dignified and charming **Istana Kenangan** (tel: 05-776 5500; daily 10am–5pm; free). Its name translates as the Palace of Memories and the original construction was in accordance with Malay tradition, without a single nail or architectural plans. The building, a beautiful example of Perak architecture, is now the **Perak Royal Museum** with an interesting collection of mementoes and photographs of the Perak royal family. All displays are in Bahasa Malaysia, although guided tours are sometimes available.

The **Sultan Azlan Shah Gallery** (tel: 05-777 5362; daily 10am–5pm, closed Fri 12.15pm–2.45pm; charge) is nearby on Jalan Istana. Housed in Istana Hulu, a former palace built in 1903 in Art Deco style, the gallery pays tribute to the current sultan of Perak, Sultan Azlan Shah, with an exhibition of his personal effects and achievements.

On the outskirts of Kuala Kangsar, about 20km (12 miles) along the Ipoh–Enggor road, is the pottery district of **Sayong**, also once the home of sultans. Turn off at the bridge and turn left again to get to Kampung Kepala Bendang, the original potter's village, and you will be greeted by scores of vases, ashtrays and ornaments drying in the sun all along this dirt road. The most famous of the traditional designs is the black *labu*, gourd-shaped water pitchers with broad bases and tall narrow spouts that keep cold water really cold.

Belum-Temengor Forest Complex

From the highlands of the Main Range spring the waters of Sungai Perak, the second-largest river in the peninsula. The river's flow is controlled by Perak's largest dam, 150km (95 miles) upstream from Kuala Kangsar on the Temengor river tributary. Once a "black area", where armed forces fought the communists, the region is covered by a mountainous forest, and forms the northernmost part of the wildlife corridor stretching through to two protected areas in southern Thailand. It has one of the best remaining populations of large mammals in the country, including endangered species such as the tiger, Sumatran rhino and Malayan bear.

Cutting through the area is the spectacular East–West Highway to Kota Bharu, probably the only public

place you'd see a road sign warning of elephants crossing. The road bypasses the picturesque **Temengor Dam** ⑯ (Empangan Temengor), covering 15,200 hectares (37,560 acres) and bisecting the Belum-Temengor Forest Complex.

South of the highway is the biodiversity-rich **Temengor Forest**. However, unlike the **Royal Belum State Park** north of the highway, Temengor remains unprotected and logging activity is slowly diminishing its prized trees and destroying flora and fauna habitats. Temengor is dotted with numerous beautiful towering waterfalls accessible through steep, rugged terrain across swift rivers, on ridges used by the Orang Asli to collect rattan, that follow trails left by animals such as deer or elephants. Among the area's popular sites is the seven-step thundering **Kerteh Waterfall**, where the lucky could catch sight of the giant Rafflesia bloom, and the eight-step **Kelaweh Waterfall**, with a lovely campsite at its spray-misted base.

Animals are difficult to spot, but there are plenty of fresh hoof-prints and droppings on the ground and

Gulai tempoyak at Sinar's Restaurant, Dataran Sungai Perak.

The Istana Kenangan in Kuala Kangsar.

claw-marks on trees. Trails are flanked by tall hill dipterocarp trees, medicinal plants and shrubs underfoot, and of course, the thorny rattan that grabs at sleeves and flesh. The leech-phobic would do well to stay away. The drier months are traditionally in the first half of the year, but "dry" is a relative term here.

Book tours from your place of accommodation. Tour guides arrange entry permits but the District Office might sometimes require a meeting with foreigners. All groups are guided by the Orang Asli, who comprise the friendly Temiar and Jahai peoples, and a tour usually includes a night at their thatched hut villages and a *bersewang* (traditional dance) performance.

If you come in August and September, you will see an awe-inspiring aerial spectacle, unique to this area – the large number of Plain-pouched Hornbills that move in continuous "waves" across the Belum-Temengor Forest Complex for one to two hours. The highest counted in one morning was over 3,200 birds. Malaysia's 10 species of hornbills can be found here. Access to the complex is still restricted, and a permit, which takes two weeks to process, is required from the Perak State Park Corporation (tel: 05-791 4543).

The jumping-off point to Temengor is **Grik**, one and a half hour's drive from Kuala Kangsar on a scenic and winding road. Serenely shrouded in mist in the early morning, the town has basic accommodation, including a government resthouse, and lots of eateries, though serving local food only. During the communist warfare years, Grik was the compulsory check-in point for the daytime-use only East–West Highway.

Taiping

South of Grik is **Taiping** ⑰, the former state capital. The town with the heaviest rainfall in the peninsula has one of its loveliest names: "everlasting peace" in Chinese. The name derives from the ending of the bloody struggles between rival Chinese mining factions in Larut after the Treaty of Pangkor was signed.

The beautiful 90-hectare (222-acre) **Lake Gardens** (Taman Tasik), fringed

In the Kuala Gula Bird Sanctuary.

THE PERAK MAN

The "Perak Man" is the peninsula's oldest skeleton, dating from 11,000 years ago. He was discovered buried in a cave in the Lenggong vicinity near Grik together with remnants of burial paraphernalia such as stone tools, shellfish and meat offerings. His discoverer, prominent archaeologist Dr Zuraina Majid, had also uncovered the country's oldest stone tools nearby, which are believed to date back 100,000 years. The "Perak Man" is thought to be an ancestor of the Negrito Orang Asli people, a small hunter-gatherer tribe regarded as the oldest inhabitants of the peninsula.

The Lenggong stone tools in Kota Tampan were also discovered intact. Anvils, stone hammers and tools in various stages of being fashioned – complete with residual flakes and chips – suggest that the site was a tool "factory". It was abandoned all those years ago when a volcanic eruption spewed clouds of ash that buried everything – the same eruption that created Lake Toba in Sumatra. Stone tool factories have also been excavated in Tingkayu, Sabah, and Kubang Pasu, Kedah.

The "Perak Man" skeleton and the stone implements are exhibited in the Lenggong Archaeological Museum (tel: 05-767 9700; daily 9am–5pm except Fri 9am–12.15pm and 2.45–5pm; free) in Kota Tampan.

by old raintrees, were established at an abandoned tin mine on the edge of the town in the 1880s, long before the word ecology was in use. In the grounds is a Japanese garden and the rustic 50-hectare (120-acre) **Taiping Zoo & Night Safari** (tel: 05-808 6577; www.zootaiping.gov.my; daily 8.30am–6pm and 8–11pm; charge). A road leads to Maxwell Hill, Malaysia's oldest hill station (see page 153).

The entrance to the gardens is marked by a number of architectural gems, including the colonial town hall and the government offices. The **Perak Museum** (Muzium Perak; tel: 05-807 2057; www.jmm.gov.my/en/museum/perak-museum; daily 9am–5pm, closed Fri 12.15pm–2.45pm; free), housed in a venerable Victorian building, is the oldest in the country. Its collections include excellent natural history, ceramic and ethnology displays.

It's not only historical buildings that Taiping is famous for, but also its invigorating rivers and streams. These include the **Burmese Pool**, a naturally formed pool in the river. There are no known Burmese people living in the vicinity, and no one can tell you how it became "Burmese". The water is icy cold but refreshing on a hot day. The less crowded **Austin Pool,** accessible from a nearby housing area called Taman Suria, offers more tranquillity. If you prefer modern changing-room facilities, try the freshwater **Coronation Swimming Pool** (Kolam Renang Kemahkotaan), also at the foothill. The non-chlorinated pool, which is open daily, is fed by a local spring (charge).

Kuala Gula Bird Sanctuary

Taiping was also the terminus for the country's first railway line – now disused – which ended in Kuala Sepetang (Port Weld) on the coast. The road there passes the old fort of **Kota Ngah Ibrahim**, named after the Malay territorial chief of Larut who grew rich through the tin trade, but was unable to control the turbulent Chinese factions producing the wealth.

The road also leads to the 40,000-hectare (98,900-acre) **Matang Mangrove Forest Reserve** ⑱ (Hutan Paya Laut Matang), which has a park (daily 8am–5pm; free) with a boardwalk going through a sustainably managed mangrove forest, which has been harvested for charcoal for nearly 100 years. The traditional charcoal kilns make an interesting visit, as do the fishing villages, but you need a guide, which can be arranged at the Matang District Forest Office (Jalan Muzium, Taiping; tel: 05-807 2762; charge).

A portion of the mangrove swamp further north near Bagan Serai is the 8,200-hectare (20,260-acre) **Kuala Gula Bird Sanctuary** ⑲, where many rare species feed and nest. Between August and December, migratory birds stop here en route south to Australia. The sanctuary is also home to otters, monkeys and the ridgeback dolphin. There is limited and basic accommodation here. For information and bookings, contact the Wildlife Department (tel: 05-243 6645) or the Kuala Gula Conservation Centre (tel: 05-890 2207).

Sungai Kampar waterfall.

CHICK BLINDS

Malaysian streets are always vivid and colourful, but when shopkeepers lower their chick blinds, the street fronts take on a whole new look becoming modern advertising billboards for their businesses

Made of split bamboo or thin wooden rods laced with twine, these sun blinds, known as *bidai* in Malay, serve a dual purpose.

Not only do they shade the colonnaded verandah in front of the shop, known as the "five-footway"; they also provide the shopkeeper with the perfect canvas to advertise his goods and services, giving every street a distinct and vibrant character.

With the advent of modern, Western-style shopping malls, some pundits have predicted the demise of the shophouse, and with it the chick blind. This may be true in some Malaysian cities, but in most smaller towns, rows of traditional shophouses prevail and their useful and colourful awnings are still prolific, and as popular as ever.

Names and remedies are advertised on these chick blinds in Ipoh Old Town.

A songkok (Malaysia headwear) maker in his shop.

Six centuries of history

Chick blinds have a long and colourful history. When the notorious Mongol leader Tamerlane and his "Golden Horde" sacked the Indian city of Delhi in 1398, it was noted that the tent openings of the much-feared conquerors were covered with blinds made of thin wands lined with rose-coloured silk. Indeed, the name is thought to derive from the Mongol word *tchik*.

Making chick blinds in an Ipoh workshop.

Modern examples of the chick blind style.

"FIVE-FOOT-WAY" SHOPS

The long colonnaded space, known as the "five-foot-way", or *kaki lima* in Malay, which fronts all traditional rows of shophouses is said to have originated in a directive by Sir Stamford Raffles, founder of Singapore.

Raffles decreed that all urban buildings should have "a verandah of a certain depth, open to all sides as a continuous and open passage on each side of the street", so people could walk comfortably along, sheltered from the fierce heat of an equatorial sun or a monsoon downpour. The "five-foot-way" is private property so it wasn't long before the shophouse's wares spilled over into the "five-foot-ways" and some owners, wanting more privacy, walled up either ends forcing pedestrians back onto the streets. Hawkers also began exploiting these shaded spaces, and the "five-foot-way" makeshift shop came into being.

Late in the evenings or on Sunday mornings when the shops are closed, the hawkers sell food from the roadside while their customers sit at tables set up in the "five-foot-way" sometimes stretching across three adjoining shophouses. These makeshift dining places still survive in many Malaysian towns and cities including Kuala Lumpur.

Hawkers in the "five-foot-way" area outside shops in Little India, George Town.

This jewellery salesman's chick blind in Penang is packed with information.

Medical services advertised on this Penang shop blind.

PENANG

A rich heritage and a mystic, spiritual core – as well as fine beaches and wonderful food – make the island state of Penang a perennial favourite among visitors to Malaysia.

Temples shrouded in incense smoke and palm-fringed beaches have been attracting visitors to Penang for several hundred years. One of the most famous islands in Asia, Penang is also perhaps the best-known tourist destination in Malaysia.

Throughout history, Penang has changed names like the seasons. Early Malays called it Pulau Ka Satu, or Single Island. Later it appeared on sailing charts as Pulau Pinang, or Island of the Betel Nut Palm. The British renamed it Prince of Wales Island, and finally, with Malaysia's independence, it became Pulau Pinang once again. But romance, sustained by tourist brochure copywriters, is hard to dispel: Penang is also the Pearl of the Orient, Gateway to the East, and the Isle of Temples. In 2008, Penang's George Town and Melaka in the south were designated as the Historic Cities of the Straits of Malacca, and now feature on the World Heritage List.

East of Penang island

From the mainland, the 7km (4-mile) **Penang Bridge** (Jambatan Pulau Pinang) offers exhilarating views of the harbour and the jagged skyline of condominiums and office blocks set against the hilly centre.

A very different aspect would have greeted English trader and adventurer Captain Francis Light in the 18th century, but he saw the advantages of having the island – then under Kedah – as a station for Britain's East India Company. Light saw Penang as a base to replenish company ships on their long haul to China in the flourishing tea and opium trade, and serve as a headquarters to further British interests in Southeast Asia.

Light, fluent in Thai and Malay, and a familiar figure in the Kedah court, persuaded the sultan to trade Penang for British protection against threatening Thai and Bugis enemies. But the

Penang-loving girls on Batu Feringgi beach.

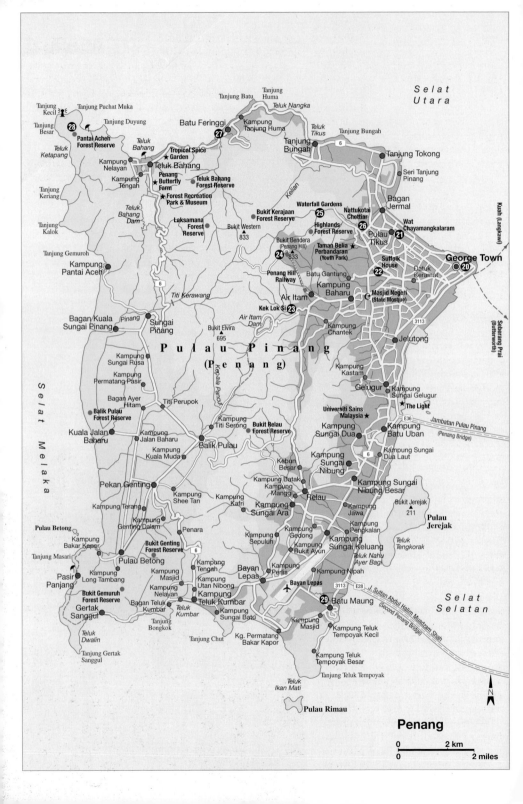

Penang

Selat Utara

Selat Melaka

Selat Selatan

Kuah (Langkawi)

Seberang Prai
(Butterworth)

Tanjung Kecil
Tanjung Puchat Muka
Tanjung Besar
Tanjung Duyung
Pantai Aceh
Forest Reserve
Teluk Ketapang
Teluk Bahang
Tanjung Batu
Tanjung Huma
Teluk Nangka
Batu Feringgi
Kampung Tanjung Huma
Teluk Tikus
Tanjung Bungah
Tanjung Tokong
Kampung Nelayan
Tropical Spice Garden
Teluk Bahang
Penang Butterfly Farm
Teluk Bahang Forest Reserve
Tanjung Bungah
Seri Tanjung Pinang
Kampung Tengah
Forest Recreation Park & Museum
Bagan Jermal
Wat Chayamangkalaram
Tanjung Keriang
Laksamana Forest Reserve
Teluk Bahang Dam
Bukit Kerajaan Forest Reserve
Waterfall Gardens
Nattukotai Chettiar
Pulau Tikus
Tanjung Kalok
Bukit Western 833
Highlands Forest Reserve
Bukit Bendera (Penang Hill) 833
Taman Belia Perbandaran (Youth Park)
Suffolk House
George Town
Tanjung Gemuroh
Kampung Pantai Aceh
Penang Hill Railway
Batu Gantung
Kampung Baharu
Masjid Negeri (State Mosque)
Datuk Keramat
Titi Kerawang
Air Itam
Kek Lok Si
Bukit Elvira 695
Air Itam Dam
Kampung Chantek
Bagan Kuala Sungai Pinang
Pinang
Sungai Pinang
Pulau Pinang (Penang)
Jelutong
Kampung Sungai Rusa
Kampung Kastam
Kampung Permatang Pasir
Kepala Pancul
Gelugur
Kampung Sungai Gelugur
The Light
Bagan Ayer Hitam
Balik Pulau Forest Reserve
Titi Perupok
Universiti Sains Malaysia
Jambatan Pulau Pinang (Penang Bridge)
Kuala Jalan Baharu
Kampung Titi Serong
Bukit Relau Forest Reserve
Kampung Sungai Dua
Kampung Batu Uban
Kampung Jalan Baharu
Balik Pulau
Kampung Sungai Dua Laut
Pekan Genting
Kampung Kuala Muda
Kebun Besar
Kampung Sungai Nibung
Kampung Terang
Kampung Shee Tan
Kampung Kafri
Kampung Batak
Kampung Manggi
Relau
Kampung Sungai Nibung Besar
Bukit Jerejak 211
Pulau Jerejak
Kampung Genting Dalam
Penara
Kampung Sungai Ara
Kampung Jawa
Kampung Pengkalan
Pulau Betong
Kampung Bakar Kapor
Kampung Sepuluh
Kampung Gedong
Kampung Bukit Ayun
Kampung Sungai Keluang
Teluk Tengkorak
Tanjung Masari
Bukit Genting Forest Reserve
Kampung Perlis
Teluk Nahu Ayer Bagi
Pasir Panjang
Kampung Long Tambang
Kampung Masjid
Kampung Tengah
Bayan Lepas
Kampung Nipah
Bukit Gemuruh Forest Reserve
Kampung Nelayan
Kampung Utan Nibong
Bayan Lepas
J. Sultan Abdul Halim Muadzam Shah (Second Penang Bridge)
Gertak Sanggul
Bagan Teluk Kumbar
Kampung Teluk Kumbar
Batu Maung
Teluk Dwalin
Tanjung Bongkok
Teluk Kumbar
Kampung Sungai Batu
Kampung Masjid
Kampung Teluk Tempoyak Kecil
Tanjung Gertak Sanggul
Tanjung Chut
Kg. Permatang Bakar Kapor
Kampung Teluk Tempoyak Besar
Teluk Ikan Mati
Tanjung Teluk Tempoyak
Pulau Rimau

0   2 km
0   2 miles

N

British did not honour the agreement, and going to war only saw Kedah lose more land to the empire – this time on the mainland, named Seberang Prai by the Malays. To encourage trade and commerce, the British made the island state a free port; no taxes were levied on either imports or exports. This strategy worked and in eight years, the population increased to 8,000, comprising many new arrivals – Chinese, Indians and Bugis, among others.

Today, the state of Pulau Pinang, or Penang, as everyone calls it, comprises Seberang Prai (or Butterworth as it was formerly known) on the mainland and Penang island, linked by both the bridge and ferry services. The ferries carry both passengers and vehicles. The ferry terminus at the Seberang Prai is linked to bus, taxi and railway stations – the transport goes all the way to Thailand.

The Second Penang Bridge is a 24-kilometer (15-mile) cable-stayed bridge linking Batu Kawan (on the mainland) with Batu Maung (south of the first bridge) on Penang island. It was officially opened to the public on 2 March 2014 and is the longest in Southeast Asia.

George Town

Like most cities of Asia that juxtapose the glass and concrete of the new with the tile and teak of the old, Penang has several dimensions. You can arrive by ferry, be transported by trishaw to a Chinese hotel on Lebuh Chulia in the heart of Chinatown, eat at the outdoor food stalls, visit the waterfront villages and, after two weeks, leave Penang having never stepped into anything built after World War II. But another visitor can have cocktails at the poolside overlooking the sea while getting a golden tan, dine in a gourmet restaurant and never brush shoulders with a Chowrasta Market butcher in town.

Vibrant **George Town** ⓴ is the heart of Penang. Named by the British after King George III, it is unmistakably Chinese, its narrow streets

congested with pedestrians, vehicles, signboards and temples. The best way to experience it is on foot, or by hiring a trishaw for the day, from which the city appears to unfurl in a kaleidoscope of changing colours. Even in the rain, the driver zips you into a plastic covering, and pedals slowly through the wet streets. At night, there is a special romance about riding in the glow of neon signs and blinking lights.

The main attractions on Penang island are divided geographically to George Town, the northern shores of Penang, west of Penang around Balik Pulau and towards the centre of the island near Penang Hill. In George Town there are a handful of clear walks that you can do, taking in distinctive aspects of the place. For an introduction to Penang, begin your tour at the **Penang Museum and Art Gallery** Ⓐ (tel: 04-261 3144; www. penang-museum.gov.my; Sat–Thu 9am–5pm; charge) on Lebuh Farquhar. Visitors can peer into a Chinese bridal chamber created in the lavish style of the 19th century, or see a bejewelled *keris*, the dagger Malays used for

Cheong Fatt Tze Mansion.

TIP

For a 2.5-hour cycling tour of western Penang's villages, paddy fields and rivers, contact **Explore Balik Pulau** (mobile tel: 016-452 2100; www.explore balikpulau.com.my). The guided tour is complimentary; you just hire the bicycles by the hour.

protection. The gallery displays work by local artists, including batik, oils, graphics and Chinese ink drawings.

Nanyang heritage buildings

West of Penang Museum on Lebuh Leith, entrepreneurs have turned a row of heritage buildings into trendy restaurants and pubs; here also stand three houses displaying late 19th-century Nanyang (South Seas) overseas Chinese architecture and decorative arts. These include the carefully restored late 19th-century **Cheong Fatt Tze Mansion** **B**, which has a unique blend of Eastern and Western architectural styles (tel: 04-262 0006; www.cheongfatttzemansion.com; guided tours daily 11am, 1.30pm and 3pm; charge). Originally built by craftsmen from China's Guangdong province, this grand courtyard house was sensitively restored and won a Unesco Asia Pacific Heritage Award for conservation in 2000. The owner also operates a boutique hotel on the premises.

Backtrack past the Penang Museum and turn right onto Jalan Masjid Kapitan Keling, and further on make a left onto Lebuh Gereja (Church Street). Narrow alleyways off the bustling roads lead to quiet rows of Chinese homes with carved lintels and elaborate doorways. At No. 29, the mansion built by millionaire Chung Keng Kwee is now the **Pinang Peranakan Museum** **C** (tel: 04-264 2929; www. pinangperanakanmansion.com.my; daily 9.30am–5pm; charge). Inside the temple is a lifelike bronze statue of Chung in the robes of a Chinese mandarin. Chung made his fortune from the tin mines in Larut, Perak, and was one of the leaders of the Chinese factions in the Larut Wars of the 1860s. North of the mansion at No. 4 Lebuh King is the **House of Yeap Chor Ee** (tel: 04-2610 190) who migrated from China and founded a local bank. Inside is The Sire, a museum restaurant, featuring furniture from the Yeap residence.

Colonial quarter

George Town is perhaps best known for its colonial quarter, and a tour of this begins at **Fort Cornwallis** **D** (Kota Cornwallis; tel: 04-226 1461; Sat–Thu 9am–5pm; charge), the place

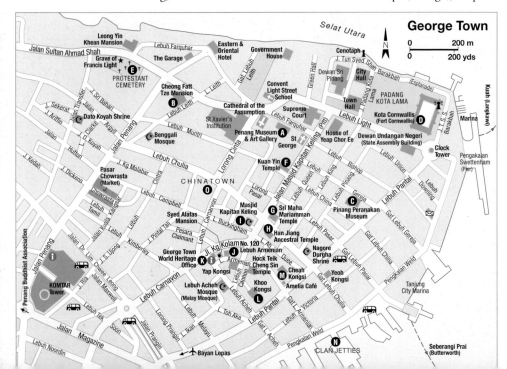

from which probably the most costly cannon ball in history was shot. When Francis Light was clearing land for his settlement, the thick undergrowth proved arduous work for the sepoys, the name given to Indians employed as soldiers by the British and other European powers. To motivate the disgruntled sepoys, Light loaded a cannon with silver dollars and fired it into the jungle – this prompted them all to work to retrieve the coins; and before long the land was cleared and the first camp established.

Originally a wooden structure, Fort Cornwallis was rebuilt with convict labour in the early 1800s. Today, the old fort's precincts have been converted into a public park and playground. Its ramparts are still guarded by old cannon, the most venerable and famous of which is Seri Rambai, presented by the Dutch to the sultan of Johor in 1606. Seven years later, it was captured by the Achehnese and taken to Acheh, where it remained for almost 200 years. The cannon was then sent to Kuala Selangor in the quest of a Bugis alliance. After the

British bombarded Kuala Selangor in 1871, the cannon was brought to Penang. Just inside past the ticket counter, you will see a statue of Francis Light.

Next to Fort Cornwallis lies the *padang* (town green) and the Esplanade (Jalan Tun Syed Sheh Barakbah). The handsome 19th-century colonial **State Assembly Building** (Dewan Undangan Negeri) stands at one end of the *padang*; at the other, near the entrance to Fort Cornwallis, traffic circles the **Clock Tower**, which was presented to Penang by a rich Chinese *towkay* (businessman), Cheah Chin Gok, in commemoration of Queen Victoria's Diamond Jubilee. Walk west to the other end of the Esplanade to view the **Cenotaph** in memory of those who had fallen in World War I. Walk down Jalan Padang Kota Lama and your left is the **City Hall** and **Town Hall**. Turn right onto Lebuh Light to see the renovated and expanded Palladian style **Supreme Court** complex built on the same site as the original courthouse. Further down the road is the **Convent Light Street**. Built in 1859, it is the oldest girls' school in Malaysia. Within

FACT

The clock tower opposite Fort Cornwallis in George Town was a gift from a Chinese millionaire to celebrate Queen Victoria's Diamond Jubilee in 1897.

The ramparts at Fort Cornwallis.

A porch detail of the Khoo Kongsi clanhouse.

The Penang State Legislative Building.

the grounds is the much older **Government House** built by Francis Light that served as governor's office and council chambers when the founder of Singapore, Stamford Raffles, worked in Penang.

South of the school at the end of Lebuh Farquhar is the dignified **St George's Church**. Built in 1818, it is the oldest Anglican church in southeast Asia. Nearby, the **Cathedral of the Assumption** was established in 1787, but the present building is from 1860. However, the original manual pipe organ is still in use. Continue onto Jalan Sultan Ahmad Shah; along this road is where Francis Light lies buried in the frangipani-shaded **Protestant Cemetery** ❸ along with other notables of old Penang, many of whom succumbed early in life to the rigours of the tropics. Across the cemetery is the **Leong Yin Khean Mansion.** Designed by Scottish architect Joseph Charles Miller in 1926 for the Cambridge-educated Leong, it is now the Thirty-Two Restaurant (tel: 04-262 2232). Further east along Lebuh Farquhar stands Georgetown's oldest hotel, the **Eastern**

& Oriental Hotel (www.eohotels.com), which once played host to luminaries such as Rita Hayworth and Somerset Maugham. Built in 1887 by the Armenian Sarkies brothers, the property is one of Asia's grandest hotels.

Nearby is an Art Deco building on Upper Penang Road. **The Garage** was originally a car showroom of Wearne Brothers Ltd, and later became a car service centre and a furniture shop. Today, it has been restored and houses speciality shops and bistros.

The "Street of Harmony"

Over a 1km (0.6-mile) stretch, places of worship for many faiths are found in peaceful coexistence. Starting at the Cathedral of the Assumption on Lebuh Farquhar, walk to the end of the road and turn right onto Jalan Masjid Kapital Keling. Along that road is Penang's oldest Buddhist temple, the **Kuan Yin Temple** ❻, which is the most humble and crowded. The temple belongs to the people in the street – the noodle hawkers, trishaw riders, and workers building cupboards, repairing bicycles or selling sundry goods. A Buddhist deity who refused to enter Nirvana so long as there was injustice on earth, Kuan Yin typically personifies mercy. She is ever-present on Chinese altars, whether Taoist, Buddhist or Confucian, and is perhaps the most beloved divinity.

Jalan Masjid Kapitan Keling leads into the tiny **Little India,** where saris, garlands and jewellery deck the stores, and the spicy scent of curry wafts through the air. Indian merchants arrived in Penang with the British, as did Indian convicts, who built the first roads and filled in the swamps on which the town now stands. Assimilated into local society, it is not surprising to find their descendants fluent in Tamil as well as in Bahasa Malaysia, English and some Hokkien.

In Lebuh Queen sits the **Sri Maha Mariamman Temple** ❼, which was built in 1883 and boasts an ornate South Indian gateway. However, many

Indians who came to Penang were Muslim, and the state has a large Indian Muslim population, whose delicious *nasi kandar* rice and scorching-hot curry dishes are relished by all Malaysians. Turn left on Lebuh Chulia where the Tamil Muslim's **Nagore Durgha Shrine** is located.

At the corner of Lebuh Queen and Lebuh Chulia is the **Han Jiang Ancestral Temple**  which was built in 1870 and later won a Unesco Asia Pacific Cultural Heritage Award in 2006 for the building's preservation efforts.

The Tamil Muslims' oldest place of worship, the state's oldest mosque, is on Jalan Masjid Kapitan Keling. The Moorish-style **Kapitan Keling Mosque** (Masjid Kapitan Keling), which dates from 1800, is named after the Indian Muslim merchant headman, or *Kapitan Keling*, Caudeer Mohudeen.

Lebuh Armenian and Lebuh Acheh

The small enclave bordered by Lebuh Armenian in the north, Lebuh Cannon in the east and Lebuh Acheh in the southwest with a small park in the middle is the meeting point of Confucian and Islamic civilisations. Start the tour at **Hock Teik Cheng Sin Temple**, the mid-19th-century Hokkien secret society headquarters. Inside there is a secret passage that leads to Lebuh Armenian. Across the road is one of the many Chinese guild halls that honour both ancestors and outstanding members. The **Yap Kongsi** was built in 1924 on land that was donated by Yeap Chor Ee, a local tycoon. Next door is the Choo Chay Keong Temple, where the altar to the Yap patron deity is located. Lebuh Armenian is flanked by early 19th-century shophouses originally belonging to Malays and Sumatrans. **No. 120 Lebuh Armenian** (tel: 04-262 0123; www.lestariheritage.net/sunyatsen/sunyatsen06.html; daily 10am–5pm; charge) was the Penang headquarters of the Tongmenghui, the political party of the Chinese leader Dr Sun Yat-Sen. It was set up in 1910, a year before the Manchu rule was toppled in China. You can walk through the ground floor; there is a guided tour available with a minimum of eight persons, but if they are not very busy, they may oblige you

Kongsi are Chinese associations, each made up of individuals from the same dialect group and from the same part of China. They look after kin in Penang, hold ancestral records and have altars for ancestral worship.

A Khoo Kongsi clanhouse roof detail.

CHINESE CLANHOUSES

Chinese immigrants arriving in Malaysia in the 19th century fell under the protection and control of clan associations, whose functions were not unlike those of medieval European guilds: to promote the interests of their members and provide help to those in distress. You'll find the ancestral halls or *kongsi* of associations such as the Khoo, Ong, Tan and Chung clans scattered all over George Town.

Many of these clanhouses are beautiful pieces of traditional Chinese architecture and house important antiques and artworks. But there is concern about their future, as well as the shophouses in their vicinity, due to the abolition of the Rent Control Act in 2000. The act limits the rent that owners can charge tenants, but it is feared that its abolition will see owners looking to maximise profits by redeveloping the land, or selling it off for money-raking highrises. The non-profit Penang Heritage Trust (www.pht.org.my) is lobbying hard to save these important buildings.

At the community level, clans are taking steps to preserve their heritage. The Khoos, for instance, owners of the Khoo Kongsi clanhouse (see page 186) have turned the buildings around their *kongsi* into a cultural and heritage village, with souvenir and retail shops and budget accommodation.

with a 15–30-minute tour regardless. Further down the street at No. 128 is the 19th-century **Syed Alatas Mansion**, which houses the Penang Islamic Museum, closed at the time of writing.

At the corner of Lebuh Acheh and Lebuh Carnarvon is the **George Town World Heritage Office** Ⓚ (tel: 04-261 6606; www.gtwhi.com.my; Mon–Fri 8am–5pm; free) which has an exhibition about the World Heritage Site, a resource library and tourist information. Walk southeast and an octagonal minaret at the end of the road marks the entrance to a Malay Mosque also known as **Lebuh Acheh Mosque**, which is a mixture of Egyptian and Javanese styles.

The most elaborate clanhouse is the **Khoo Kongsi** Ⓛ (18 Cannon Square; tel: 04-261 4609; www.khookongsi.com. my; daily 9am–5pm, closed eve of and first day of Chinese New Year; charge) at the junction of Jalan Masjid Kapitan Keling and Lebuh Acheh. Designed to capture the splendour of an imperial palace, it has a seven-tiered pavilion, "dragon" pillars and hand-painted walls engraved with the Khoo rose emblem.

The original design was so ambitious that conservative Khoo clansmen cautioned against it, lest the emperor of China be offended. After eight years, the building was completed in 1902; but on the first night after it was finished, the roof mysteriously caught fire. Clan members interpreted this as a sign that even the deities considered the Khoo Kongsi too palatial for a clanhouse. The Khoos rebuilt it on a more modest scale. Following a massive renovation by 16 Chinese artisans using traditional Chinese materials, the clanhouse has been restored to its former splendour.

At No. 8 Lebuh Armenian is **Cheah Kongsi** Ⓜ (Cheah Si Sek Tek Tong; daily 9am–5pm), another guild hall that helped its clan members from China to settle down in Penang by providing accommodation and financial help until they were settled.

Clan Jetties

At George Town's waterfront near the ferry terminus, entire villages belong to clans. These are the **Clan Jetties** Ⓝ, comprising wooden houses perched on stilts over the sea, which in the pre-condominium era were the most outstanding feature to greet visitors who travelled to the island by ferry. Each of the six villages has its own temple, and houses just one clan, except for one "mixed" village. Therefore, on Lim's Jetty, you'll find only members of the Lim family, while Tan's Jetty is the sole property of the Tan clan. Nearly all but the Chews have abandoned the fishing trade, but all the houses are occupied and no one minds if a visitor strolls along the plankwalks.

Chinatown

The hotchpotch of streets and alleys of **Chinatown** Ⓞ are home to over 8,000 examples of 19th- and early 20th-century buildings. In the coffee shops, old men exchange daily news over cups of coffee with bread and *kaya* (coconut jam). For shopaholics there are antiques and curios galore, as well

Hokkien opera preparation.

as more contemporary items such as leather goods and batik. Second-hand bookstores are treasure-troves of old tomes, as well as paperback bestsellers left behind by backpackers in Lebuh Chulia.

The tiny old Chinese hotels have held out against time, and are some of the best places to soak up Chinatown's old-world atmosphere. You may catch sight of a funeral procession through the streets, complete with drums and gongs and mourners. In the afternoon, a lion dance may be staged to bring luck to a new sundry goods shop – a noisy affair with more drums and gongs. The hotels are supported by cafés offering Western food, tours, bicycles for hire and money-changers.

Jalan Penang (better known as Penang Road), the old shopping area, ends in the towering air-conditioned KOMTAR complex above the bus station, which also houses a tourist information centre and the Tourism Malaysia office. Take a lift up its circular tower for a bird's-eye view of the city (charge). The complex houses retail units, government and other office space, performance space and a hotel.

Take a walk through **Chowrasta Market** (Pasar Chowrasta), between Jalan Chowrasta and Lebuh Tamil. A wet market with the inevitable aromas, it has a section facing Penang Road that offers the Penang specialities of local biscuits and preserved nutmeg and mango prepared in a wide variety of styles. On Lebuh Tamil is the row of *nasi kandar* (mixed curry rice) stalls whose food is reputed to be the best in the country.

Indeed, food is Penang's favourite export to the rest of the country. Here, hawker centres commandeer every corner, the most famous of which (and you pay the price for it) is on the seaside **Gurney Drive** stretch, open in the evenings. However, wander into the **Pulau Tikus** area behind Jalan Burma, and you pay far less for food that is perhaps twice as good. Pulau Tikus is also the heartland of the *Baba-Nonya*, descendants of Chinese immigrants who married into and absorbed Malay culture (see page 70). Also known as Peranakan or Straits Chinese, these

TIP

Be prepared to get soaking wet if you visit Wat Chayamangkalaram in April, during the Thai Songkran festival. Mischief-makers hurl water-filled plastic bags on passers-by on the pretext of "purifying" them.

Stocking up at Chowrasta Market.

The interior of a George Town Baba-Nonya house.

A detail of Wat Chayamangkalaram.

Northeastern Penang

The variety of Buddhist worship in Penang is so striking it makes every temple a new experience. One can enter the gigantic meditation hall at **Wat Chayamangkalaram ㉑** (Lorong Burma; mobile tel: 04-226 8503; daily 6am–5.30pm; free) and find a workman polishing the left cheek of 32-metre (100ft) long reclining Buddha. The *wat*, on Lorong Burma, is a Thai Buddhist monastery. Gigantic *naga* serpents, mystical creatures that link earth to heaven, form the balustrades at the entrance, while fierce-visaged giants tower over the doorways in the role of otherworldly bodyguards. Inside is an impressive gold-plated reclining Buddha, while the walls are covered with thousands of Buddha images.

Another form of Buddhist worship can be seen in the **Dharmmikarama Burmese Buddhist Temple** (24 Lorong Burma; tel: 04-226 9575;

communities are predominant in the British Straits Settlements states of Penang, Melaka and Singapore.

daily 7am–7pm) on the other side of the road. An 8.3-metre (27ft) tall standing Buddha with a haughty yet serene expression is worshipped here. Another shrine is surrounded with a moat over which "heavenly" bridges fly. On either side are Buddha images. Little shops in the shaded walkways sell little pink and green lotus flower-shaped candles to worshippers, who leave the lighted candles reverentially in front of the shrines.

Suffolk House

At 250 Jalan Air Itam, and next to the Malaysian-German Society, is the magnificent **Suffolk House ㉒** (tel: 04-228 3930; www.suffolkhouse.com.my; daily 10am–6pm, but call to check if closed for private function; charge, but redeemable against refreshments), Penang's first "Great House". Once dilapidated, it is now beautifully restored through public and corporate funds spanning seven years, although the campaign to save the house actually began in 1974. The conservation architects relied on paintings of Suffolk House between 1811 and 1818

CHINESE NEW YEAR

The eve of Chinese New Year at the **Penang Buddhist Association** on Jalan Anson is a more formal affair compared to the mad rush of devotees at other temples. Association members busily arrange bright flowers, fruits and coloured cakes on a large, shiny table of blackwood imported from Canton. Enthroned on the high altars are six white marble statues of Lord Buddha and his disciples. Crystal chandeliers from the former Czechoslovakia hang overhead, and the walls are decorated with paintings depicting Buddha's path to enlightenment. A teenage girl patiently leads her dignified grandfather across the wide marble floor, where a seated congregation chants praises to Lord Buddha.

As temple bells tinkle, the chanting rises to usher in the new year. Outside the front door, beggars know benevolence is a precept of the Chinese New Year and they receive it passively.

Ordinarily, the large, luminous hallway that dominates the Chinese Buddhist Association is the most serene sanctuary in Penang. The building, completed in 1929, reflects the desire of a Buddhist priest who wanted to indoctrinate his followers with orthodox rites and ceremonies. Joss-stick hawkers or paper-money burners are not found here. Prayers are considered the essence of Buddhist worship, and the association cherishes the simplicity inherent in its Buddhist faith.

and together with intensive research and in-situ evidence, their restoration efforts were rewarded with an Award of Distinction from the Unesco Asia Pacific Heritage Awards for Culture Heritage Conservation. Guided tours will introduce you to the Anglo-Indian garden house on the pepper estate once owned by Francis Light and thereafter you can adjourn to the restaurant for separate sittings of lunch, high tea or dinner (tel: 04-228 3930; daily, lunch 12–2.30pm, afternoon tea 2–6pm, dinner 7–10.30pm).

Kek Lok Si

Penang's loftiest temple sits on a hilltop at Air Itam, 6km (4 miles) from the Buddhist Association. **Kek Lok Si** ㉓ (tel: 04-828 3317; daily 9am–6pm), the largest Buddhist temple complex in Malaysia and indeed in the region, owes its existence to Beow Lean, a Chinese Buddhist priest from Fujian province in China who arrived in 1887 as the resident priest of the Kuan Yin Temple in Lebuh Pitt. Impressed by the religious fervour of Penang's Buddhists, he founded a monastery on a hilly site reminiscent of Fujian. A good time to visit is the Chinese New Year period, when the temple is beautifully adorned with hundreds of lanterns.

The main buildings were completed in 1904. The seven-tier great Pagoda of Ten Thousand Buddhas (charge), erected in 1930, is dedicated to all manifestations of the Buddha, hence its name. Its walls are decorated with 10,000 alabaster and bronze Buddha images, and it is renowned for having three architectural styles: a Chinese base, a Thai middle section and a Burmese top.

The Kek Lok Si complex is split into three sections spread over Crane Hill. The three "Halls of the Great" honour Kuan Yin, Goddess of Mercy; the Laughing Buddha, who spreads prosperity and happiness; and Gautama Buddha, founder of the faith. It is here that the monks pass their hour in prayer. The Tower of Sacred Books

on the topmost tier houses a library of Buddhist scriptures and Sutra, many of which were presented by the Qing dynasty emperor Guang Xu. An edict from the same emperor, cemented into a wall of this block, grants imperial approval to the establishment of the temple.

A 3km (2-mile) road from Kek Lok Si winds its way up to the **Air Itam Dam** (daily 6am–6pm), with an 18-hectare (45-acre) lake reflecting the lush green foliage of the surrounding jungle. The dam is popular with walkers and joggers in the early morning and late afternoon for its cool air and steep road. There are great views of George Town from here.

Penang Hill

Jalan Air Itam also leads to **Penang Hill** ㉔ (Bukit Bendara), established as a quiet getaway in 1897. This 833-metre (2,733ft) high hill station was saved about 80 years later from large-scale commercialisation by public petition, a rare people-power victory. The best part of the experience is the five-minute non-stop Penang Hill Railway

A roadside food stand.

TIP

Watch out for pesky monkeys in Penang's Waterfall Gardens, some of which can be aggressive. Feeding them is discouraged, but the notice is often disregarded.

ride. (Tel: 04-828 8880/39; www.penang hill.gov.my; Mon–Fri 6.30am–8pm; weekends and holidays 6.30am–10pm; bottom station closes an hour earlier; charge). With lower temperatures, the summit makes for a lovely respite from the tropical heat, and provides good vantage for views of Penang island and the Straits of Melaka. On the hilltop, there are also gardens, private bungalows, a food court and a British-inspired restaurant. Attractions include a 200-metre (656ft) long zigzag Canopy Walkway (charge) from which you can see the tops of trees and even chance upon small animals in the forest, together with an educational nature trail and English-style botanic garden. It is advisable, however, to call the Penang National Park (tel. 04 881 3500) to make sure the walkway is open before you visit.

Waterfall Gardens

You can also hike up Penang Hill on any one of the three trails that start from the **Waterfall Gardens ㉕**, also known as the Penang Botanic Gardens (tel: 04-228 6075; www.

Kek Lok Si Temple.

botanikapenang.org.my; daily 5am–8pm; free), on Jalan Kebun Bunga. If you aren't so keen on the idea of a hot, sweaty trek, you'll enjoy strolling through the gardens. This mature and beautifully cultivated showcase of tropical plants is about 2km (1 mile) from Pulau Tikus, with waterfalls that start over 100 metres (328ft) above the gardens and cascade through the greenery. On holidays, families round up relatives for a picnic lunch by the stream, while barefoot children romp on the rocks or play follow-the-tourist. Benches are scattered throughout the gardens and provide pleasant resting spots in the shade.

Nearby, atop a hill and reached only by a long flight of steps, is the Hindu temple of **Nattukotai Chettiar ㉖** (daily). A good time to visit is 5–5.30pm, when a simple ceremony of bathing and unveiling the main statue takes place. Every January, this becomes the centre for the Hindu festival of penance, Thaipusam. After a period of fasting, devotees carry devotional *kavadi* structures made of metal,

and pierce their flesh with skewers. Many consider the processions here more dramatic and interesting than the one in Selangor's Batu Caves. Certainly, more coconuts are smashed in George Town's streets, including by non-Hindus, who see no harm in amassing some good luck too.

Penang's northern shores

Penang's holiday beaches are in the north, from Tanjung Bungah to Batu Feringgi and Teluk Bahang. The road up from Jalan Tanjung Tokong follows the curve of the land, twisting up and around a hill, or skirting the fringe of the sea. Rocky headlands divide the shoreline into small bays and coves, each with a different character and charm. The beaches are popular for swimming, sunbathing and aquatic sports.

The northern beaches are self-contained; there is little need for visitors to venture to town. Accommodation choices range from apartments for longer-stay guests to beachside places for backpackers. At night, the naked bulbs and blaring music of a *pasar malam* (night market) add to the bustle of the shops and bus station. Car and bicycle hire is available, and most hotels have a free shuttle service to George Town.

Activities are centred around **Batu Feringgi** ㉗. This is where several famous luxury hotels are located at the start of the stretch. However, small inns and motels are plentiful too, as well as accommodation offered by villagers. Likewise, the whole range of eateries can be found here, from air-conditioned steak and seafood restaurants to hawker stalls under winking fairy lights.

Some 6km (4 miles) further down the coast is the fine **Teluk Bahang** beach. En route you'll find the **Tropical Spice Garden** (tel: 04-881 1797; www.tropicalspicegarden.com; daily 9am–6pm, last admission 5.30pm; guided tours daily 9am–5pm; charge), a quiet haven of flora and foliage set on a hill slope with a restaurant, cooking school and souvenirs galore.

On Jalan Teluk Bahang, there are souvenir shops and a batik factory. Further along at No. 830 is the **Penang Butterfly Farm** (tel: 04-885 1253; www.butterfly-insect.com; daily 9am–6pm, closed eve of Chinese New Year; charge), where large varieties of butterflies and unusual insects are bred. A couple of minutes down the road are the **Forest Recreation Park and Museum** (daily 9am–5pm, Fri closed 12–12.45pm; charge), which is good for a picnic, and the **Tropical Fruit Farm** (mobile tel: 012-497 1931; www.tropicalfruitfarm.com.my; daily 9am–5pm; charge). For more trekking and resort-free beaches, head towards the northwestern tip of the island to the Penang National Park at **Pantai Aceh Forest Reserve** ㉘ (tel: 04-881 3530; daily 8am–6pm; free; register at the office for an entry permit), where there are trails to Muka Head. The park also has a meromictic lake which has two layers of water – salty sea water and fresh river water – that will not mix. This phenomenon only

Lanterns at the Batu Feringgi night market.

A monk at the Kek Lok Si Temple.

happens during the monsoon change, usually from April to May and from October to November. The rest of the year it is grasslands.

At the fishing village at the entrance to the forest reserve, you can arrange for a boat to pick you up. The road to Balik Pulau goes down the west coast and around the island. Here, a different Penang begins: an agrarian world, quiet, peaceful and thinly populated.

Western Penang

As much as the port is Chinese, so is the countryside Malay. The winding and sometimes mountainous round-island road runs for 74km (46 miles), a journey you can cover in air-conditioned buses with guides, by Rapid Penang bus leaving Komtar, taxis, or rented chauffeured cars. Before exploring this area on your own, pick up the very informative Penang Heritage Trails brochure on "Discover Balik Pulau – the other side of the island" from Penang Heritage Trust (26 Lebuh Gereja; tel: 04-264 2631; www.pht.org.my).

The Penang Hill funicular.

The road through the rolling hills offers striking views of the island dropping to the sea far below. Dense, damp jungles are interspersed with the plantations of pepper, clove and nutmeg that lured Arab, Spanish, Portuguese and other Western traders to this part of the world long ago. When in season, nets are spread out below the durian trees in the orchards, to prevent damage to the fruit. Visitors throng the temporary roadside stalls, savouring the pungent flesh or haggling over prices.

At Titi Kerawang, there are waterfalls and a serene view of the Indian Ocean. The natural freshwater pool is filled from the waterfalls, and is suitable for bathing, although a big water pipeline mars the scenery.

Southeastern Penang

As you head south, the scenery gives way to flat land. Several small roads branch off to the coast, usually the commercial link between a fishing village and the trunk road. It was in small villages such as these that the few Malays lived when Francis Light established

the first settlement. Although updated with bricks, the *kampung* (village) houses look much the same today as they did 100 years ago.

As you head to the east coast, bustling urbanity starts to rear its head. Turn off to **Batu Maung** , about 3km (2 miles) from the Bayan Lepas Airport, and you will reach a shrine built around an 85cm (33-inch) footprint in stone, believed to be that of Admiral Cheng Ho, the Chinese Columbus. The well-kept shrine sits in a beautiful Chinese garden that overlooks the jetty and fishing boats of the village.

It is believed that Cheng Ho called at this spot on one of his seven voyages to Southeast Asia. On Pulau Langkawi, 96km (60 miles) further north, is a similar footprint. The two are believed to be a pair, and anyone who lights incense sticks and places them in the urns at the shrine will enjoy good luck and great fortune.

Penang mainland

The mainland section of Penang state is nearly twice as large as the island, a thriving industrial area built around Seberang Prai (Butterworth) that has become one of the world's leading producers of microchips, disk drives and other computer parts. Both sides of the North–South Expressway and the approach to the Penang Bridge are covered with sprawling high-tech factories. East of Seberang Prai, the **Penang Bird Park** (tel: 04-399 1899; www.penangbirdpark.com.my; daily 9am–7pm; charge), on Jalan Todak, has over 200 species of tropical birds from around the world housed in specially designed homes, including a huge walk-in aviary and geodesic domes.

Another patch of green is the 37-hectare (92-acre) **Bukit Mertajam Recreational Park**, about 18km (11 miles) from the Penang Bridge. It has numerous walking trails for trekkers and rest huts for when you tire. Near its entrance is the stark-white **St Anne's Church** (stannebm.org), a well-preserved 19th-century colonial relic. Its annual candlelight procession on the Feast of St Anne from 21 to 30 July draws some 80,000 pilgrims from as far as Europe and Australia.

FACT

The **Bayan Lepas Free Trade Zone** is the Silicon Valley of Malaysia. The huge area is the home of high-technology industries, ranging from microchip-manufacturing multinationals such as Dell and Intel to success-hungry export-orientated local giants. A highway runs the length of the east coast from here to George Town. This is built on reclaimed land, and Penangites joke about how this has changed the shape of the island; before it resembled a tortoise, whereas now it looks more like a rather pregnant one.

Strolling on Batu Feringghi beach.

KEDAH AND PERLIS

The most traditionally Malay of the northern states, Kedah and Perlis offer the modern traveller ancient Hindu settlements, lush mountain parks and the carefree resort isle of Langkawi.

The mountain beckoned, a bluish-grey mass which towered in the distance, and so civilisation took root in the land. At 1,217 metres (3,900ft), Mount Jerai in the state of Kedah served as a lodestar to early merchant voyagers; it was at its foot that one of the peninsula's first known kingdoms was established.

Kedah

Kedah's position at the crossroads of Southeast Asian trade also exposed it to constant danger. Initially controlled by the great trading empires of Funan in Vietnam, and then Sri Vijaya in Sumatra, Kedah later became part of the Melaka sultanate. Until the beginning of the 19th century, Kedah's rulers were remarkably successful in preserving their independence. However, despite having put their faith in British power (and losing Penang in the process), Kedah fell to the Thais, and Perlis had to be given up as well. Both states were transferred to British suzerainty in 1909, but the mainly Malay population somehow managed to maintain their way of life, unlike other peninsula states. Even on the resort island of Langkawi, Kedah's pride and joy, the Malay community have the best of both worlds – enjoying the simple way of life in villages that are scattered throughout the island and at the same time being exposed to a burgeoning tourism industry. Langkawi has readily embraced the international limelight – hosting high-profile sailing events and maritime and aerospace exhibitions set against a backdrop of mountains and blue-green seas.

Bujang Valley

Unlike the sailors of old from across the Bay of Bengal, modern-day travellers approach **Mount Jerai** (Gunung Jerai, see page 163) on the North–South Expressway through **Sungai**

Main Attractions

Lembah Bujang
 Archaeological Museum
Ulu Muda Forest Reserve
Setar Tower
Cave of Darkness
Dayang Bunting Marble
 Geoforest Park
Underwater World Langkawi
Temple Tree at Bon Ton
Panorama Langkawi
 (SkyCab)
Kilim Karst Geoforest Park

Paragliding on Canang beach in Langkawi.

TIP

Located about 14km (9 miles) inside the Ulu Muda forest, and only accessible by a 1.5-hour boat ride across Tasik Muda and up Sungai Muda is **Earth Lodge**, an eco-lodge and field research centre (mobile tel: 019-442 8926; www.earthlodgemalaysia. com) run by nature-lovers. They offer researchers and eco-guests an all-inclusive rainforest package to explore its biodiversity in the hope that it will raise awareness of the conservation value of the forest.

Nobat Hall.

Petani, Kedah's second-largest town and the country's fastest-growing. Close by is one of the largest archaeological sites in the country, dating back to the 5th century.

After over a century of digging, archaeological finds from the edges of villages, riverbanks and the foot of jungled hills point to many more treasures in the whole area between the **Bujang Valley** (Lembah Bujang) and **Sungai Muda**. One of the earliest Hindu settlements in Southeast Asia, it also had an earlier Buddhist phase, and possibly even a prehistoric Malay settlement before that. More than 50 ancient *candi* (temples) have been excavated and restored, the largest and best-preserved being the **Temple of the Hill of Chiselled Stone** (Candi Bukit Batu Pahat). Inscriptions in Sanskrit, porcelain pieces from China, Indian beads, and glassware from the Middle East point to the site's importance as an international entrepot.

The **Lembah Bujang Archaeological Museum** (Muzium Arkeologi; tel: 04-457 2005; www.jmm.gov.my/en/museum/lembah-bujang-archaeological-museum;

daily 9am–5pm, closed on Hari Raya; free) showcases important finds from the area and has a display of photographs and models. Guided tours must be prearranged. To get there, exit the North–South Expressway at Sungai Petani and head towards Merbok; when you reach this point, look out for signposts to the museum.

Beyond Merbok, the road winds prettily on and eventually turns south to **Tanjung Dawai**, a postcard-perfect fishing village at the mouth of Sungai Merbok. A foot ferry crosses the estuary to Pantai Merdeka, a popular beach which can also be reached 40km (25 miles) from Penang by road.

Sungai Petani is also the jumping-off point on the spectacular East–West Highway to the peninsula's east coast. The road goes via Baling, overlooked by a spectacular limestone massif, and Grik in Perak, an important post during the communist threat of the 1960s.

Northeast of Sungai Petani, about 2km (1 mile) from the town of Gubir is the **Lake Muda** jetty, the gateway to the **Ulu Muda Forest Reserve** ③

SACRED ORCHESTRA

The **Nobat Hall** (Balai Nobat) in Alor Setar houses instruments for playing in the *nobat*, the royal orchestra. The musical instruments comprise two barrel drums – *gendang ibu* and *gendang anak* – two wind instruments – the *nafiri* and *serunai* – and a gong. Only four such orchestras exist in Malaysia today, the others being in Terengganu, Perak and Selangor. Kedah's *nobat* is reputedly the oldest, a gift from Melaka's last sultan, and considered sacred and an important part of the state regalia: no Kedah sultan is considered a legitimate ruler if he has not been installed to the accompaniment of the *nobat*. The orchestra also plays on other state occasions when the sultan is present, at royal weddings and funerals, and may be heard daily during the Muslim fasting month.

where large mammals such as elephants, tigers and clouded leopards roam. If you cannot sight any of these majestic creatures, you can still content yourself with the amazing hornbills that soar above or the dexterity of kingfishers while hunting, amongst other wildlife species.

Alor Setar

To get to the state capital of Alor Setar, head north from Sungai Petani on the North–South Expressway. Here the country flattens out, and depending on the season, oceans of rippling green or gold or brown fallow ground merge with the distant cloud-flecked hills of the Main Range. This is the country's rice bowl, producing half the locally grown rice. There are biannual harvests, thanks to the massive Muda Irrigation Project, which covers 127,000 hectares (300,000 acres). This is one of the few schemes financed by the World Bank which has fulfilled the aims of its sponsors and provided adequate returns. A much older irrigation canal actually runs alongside the old main road from Mount Jerai to Alor Setar. Built in the 19th century by Wan Mat Saman, the then *menteri besar* (chief minister), the canal is perfectly straight throughout its long length, a feat achieved by aligning kerosene-fuelled flares.

For a taste of a local glutinous rice cake candy, called *dodol*, head along the main road, Lebuhraya Darul Aman. Just before the Alor Setar Art Gallery, turn right onto Jalan Tunku Ibrahim. Halfway down the street on your right is **Pekan Rabu** (Wednesday Market), a colourful double-storey market popular with the locals (daily 8am–9pm). The original marketplace used to be situated 1km (0.6 mile) away at the edge of Sungai Kedah. In 1930, it was an attap-roofed (the attap is a type of palm) farmer's market that operated every Wednesday, hence its name, but due to its popularity, it was relocated to its present site and is now a complex of over 340 shops selling everything from Malay food and spices to local handicrafts and clothes.

Alor Setar ❸❷ generally serves as a springboard to the holiday isle of Langkawi, but it does have some fine architecture along the main road. The large **Zahir Mosque** (Masjid Zahir), built in 1912, has the graceful colonnades and domes of Moorish tradition. Opposite it is the **Royal Museum** (Muzium DiRaja; daily 10am–6pm, closed Fri noon–3pm; free), a former palace interesting for its layout as well as its royal family displays, including Sultan Abdul Halim's African animal trophies.

Next to the museum is the Thai-style **Great Hall** (Balai Besar), built in 1898. Used as an audience hall by Kedah's sultans of old to receive public petitions and hear grievances, it is today the site of ceremonial and state functions. Further down Lebuhraya Darul Aman at No. 99, you can't miss the 165.5-metre (543ft) tall **Setar Tower** (Menara Alor Setar; tel: 04-720 2234; www.menaraalor star.com.my; daily 9am–10pm; charge). Located in downtown Alor Setar, the telecommunications tower is the 19th-tallest in the world and houses a

Making charcoal in a traditional factory.

Kedah is the country's rice bowl.

TIP

There are convenient ferry services (3 hours) between Kuah in Langkawi and the jetty in George Town, Penang. Alternatively, organised day tours are offered by travel agents in Penang.

revolving restaurant at the top, a souvenir shop and an observation deck which is also used to sight the crescent moon to determine the beginning of Muslim months. There are good views of the town and occasionally on clear days you can see across to Thailand.

Heading further down the road, near the stadium, is the **State Museum** (Muzium Negeri; tel: 04-733 1162; Sat–Thu 10am–6pm, Fri 9.30am–12pm and 2–6pm; free). This is another Thai-style building, with collections that include Chinese ceramics as well as exhibits from the Bujang Valley.

Outside the capital

The highway north of Alor Setar ends in **Bukit Kayu Hitam**, the exit point to Thailand. There is an uninteresting duty-free emporium there, and a market that is popular with locals. About 1.5 hours' drive east of the capital is **Pedu Lake** (Tasik Pedu), a dammed lake retreat in peaceful surroundings that attracts anglers. The road there goes through tiny wooden settlements among rolling oil palm and rubber plantations.

Malay-style seafood is best at the small fishing village of **Kuala Kedah**, 12km (7 miles) west of Alor Setar. The local *ikan panggang* (barbecued fish) and chilli crab are favourites, as is the Thai-influenced noodle dish of *laksa*.

On the other side of the river is the well-preserved **Kota Kuala Kedah Historical Complex** (Kompleks Sejarah Kota Kuala Kedah; tel: 04-731 9297; www.jmm.gov.my/en/kota-kuala-kedah-historical-complex; Sat–Thu 9am–6pm, Fri 9am–12.30pm and 2.30pm–6pm; free), whose fort was originally built in 1771 for protection against the Achehnese, Bugis and Siamese who attacked from the sea. In the midst of Kuala Kedah's wooden warehouses and fish market is a modern jetty (tel: 04-966 9439, www.langkawi-ferry.com), serving Langkawi's holiday-makers (see page 200).

Perlis

Perlis, Malaysia's smallest state, is really an extension of the Kedah plain, but the scenery is even more rustic, the peaceful atmosphere more lulling. Unlike Kedah, stark, limestone

Mangroves on Langkawi.

outcrops stand like sentinels over the flat rice fields. Spectacular and mysterious, many contain subterranean caves, with flora and fauna unique to limestone habitats. The vegetation here is also more similar to Thailand's, with the canopy turning a golden autumnal brown during the marked dry season.

About 15 minutes' drive from **Kangar**, the capital of Perlis, is **Kuala Perlis**, another jumping-off point to Langkawi. It is a busy but not particularly attractive fishing village, although there are some excellent seafood restaurants.

While the North–South Expressway ignores Perlis completely, the railway line goes through **Arau**, the royal town. The Malaysian railway system meets its Thai counterpart 50km (30 miles) north at **Padang Besar**, which has a market that comes alive at weekends. You can also cross into Thailand by road via Padang Besar, but a more spectacular drive is west through the hills to **Kaki Bukit** (literally "the foot of the hill"), a former tin-mining outpost comprising a charming wooden

Chinese village. A must-see is the **Perlis State Park** (visitor centre 04-945 7898; Tue–Sun 8am–5pm, but call ahead to check opening times and get permission to visit; charge), close to the Thai border, with good trails threading through the country's only semi-deciduous forest. The state park comprising the Mata Ayer and Wang Mu Forest Reserves is located on the 38km (24-mile) long Nakawan Range, the longest continuous range of limestone hills in Malaysia. The range is believed to be more than 500 million years old. The road from the park goes to Satun in Thailand.

Within the park is the **Cave of Darkness** (Gua Kelam; tel: 04-976 5966; Mon–Fri 9am–6pm; charge), a former mining tunnel, which has a well-lit 370-metre/yard walkway. For the physically fit and those without claustrophobia, the unique cave biodiversity and streams can be explored by crawling through narrow wet passages. This 3.5-hour adventure requires a permit and a park guide, which you must prearrange. After a half-hour hike on a former logging trail, you'll

In a Langkawi batik factory.

Cenang beach on Langkawi.

A Langkawi waterfall.

reach the cave entrance. There are two main chambers in the upper level with remarkable stalagmites and stalactites formed some 400–500 million years ago and a lower stream passage that can get flooded after heavy rain.

Langkawi

Once upon a time, **Pulau Langkawi** ③③ was a sleepy island believed to be under a spell cast by a legendary princess, Mahsuri, who lived in the 14th century and was unfairly executed for adultery. It is largely through the efforts of Kedah-born former prime minister Dr Mahathir Mohamad that it has been elevated to the status of a major tourist destination and a venue for international events and exhibitions.

A beautiful limestone cliff and forest archipelago of some 100-odd islands, some of which are mere rocks that vanish at high tide, Langkawi is today marketed as a modern-day legend. There is an international airport on the southwest part of the island and it is well serviced by ferry links from the mainland of Peninsular Malaysia and from Thailand. Langkawi has good roads, steep and windy in some places, that go round the island; a nonstop round trip takes about two hours. Island taxis are expensive, and if you plan to stay more than a day, it's more economical to hire a car or a scooter.

Kuah

Langkawi's duty-free status has succeeded in injecting life into the island.

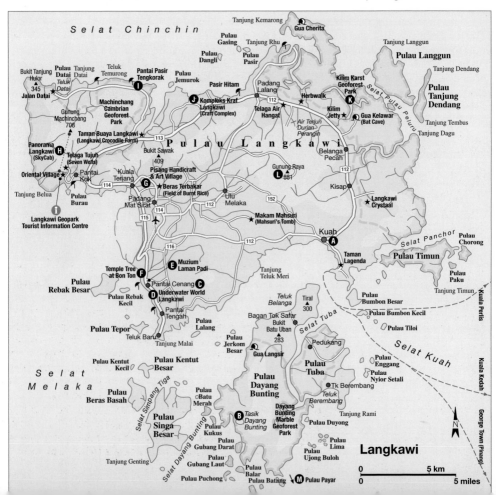

From the jetty to the main town, **Kuah** , nearly every shop is crammed with chocolates, electronic items and household goods. Yet more shops sit on the reclaimed land which starts right next to the jetty. Here you'll see an enormous statue of an eagle; among the many interpretations of its name, Langkawi is thought to derive from the word *helang*, Bahasa Malaysia for "eagle". The statue of the majestic creature about to soar is perhaps a fitting symbol for the tremendous success of the island resort.

There are hotels and good seafood restaurants in Kuah, but the more enjoyable option is to stay at one of the island's many beach resorts, only to head into town for a spot of shopping and sightseeing.

Dayang Bunting Marble Geoforest Park

Langkawi's claim to fame is not just for its duty-free shopping but also for its natural geological formations. On 1 June 2007, the Langkawi archipelago became Southeast Asia's first geopark, a status accorded by Unesco which is re-evaluated every four years. The 478 sq km (185 sq miles) of park include mountains, limestone caves, lakes and amazing biodiversity. Within the geopark, there are three parks, each with unique karstic features that can be easily accessed.

The **Dayang Bunting Marble Geoforest Park** comprises Pulau Dayang Bunting (the "Island of the Pregnant Maiden") and neighbouring Pulau Tuba and boasts beautiful 370 million-year-old marble-limestone hidden beneath the rainforest. Weather and erosion by water and waves have carved the landscape into various forms and shapes into vertical limestone cliffs, tower karsts, pinnacles, caves and sea arches. The park's biggest attraction is a unique, deep freshwater lake, **Tasik Dayang Bunting** ⓑ, situated on Pulau Dayang Bunting, the second-largest island. The lake's waters are good for swimming and believed to aid conception. However, the mounting rubbish and aggressive monkeys make this attraction a quick stopover, especially during busy periods when it's crowded.

Lake Dayang Bunting.

ISLAND OF LEGENDARY NAMES

Langkawi's legends are legion and often more interesting than the places they celebrate. The main tale concerns Mahsuri, accused of adultery by the chief's wife who was jealous of her beauty. At her execution, white blood spurted out, confirming her innocence. Before she died, Mahsuri laid a curse upon the island's next seven generations.

Immediately after, the Thais attacked Langkawi, and the villagers at **Padang Mat Sirat** burnt their rice fields rather than let them fall into Siamese hands – few grains remain at **Beras Terbakar** (Field of Burnt Rice).

A Romeo and Juliet-type legend is behind several other place names. A union between a couple was refused by the girl's parents, and in a family feud, pots and pans were thrown at **Belanga Pecah** (broken pots). The gravy jug landed at **Kuah** (gravy), while jugs of boiling water formed the **Telaga Air Hangat** hot springs. The fighting ended when the two fathers were transformed into mountains – **Mount Raya** and **Mount Machinchang**.

Lake Dayang Bunting got its name after a Kedah princess, forbidden to marry her lover, fell pregnant after drinking from the lake. The angry king banished her to the island where she was said to have drowned herself in the lake and become a rock.

TIP

Book an island-hopping tour including a visit to the freshwater lake and the beautiful beaches of **Pulau Singa Besar** and **Pulau Beras Basah**. Boats from Tanjung Rhu, Pantai Cenang and Kuah tour these islands in about four hours. Blue Water Star Sailing at the Royal Langkawi Yacht Club (mobile tel: 013-407 3166; www.blue waterstarsailing.com or 04-966 4078; www.langkawi yachtclub.com) at Kuah also organise hire private yachts.

Pantai Cenang

From Kuah town, take the Jalan Bukit Malut coastal road southwards towards **Pantai Tengah**, less than an hour from Kuah by taxi, where you will find a nice beach with upmarket accommodation and several restaurants. However, most visitors head for **Pantai Cenang C** further north. The beach here is crammed with places to stay at every budget, restaurants and souvenir shops, making this traffic-congested strip the most popular beach on the island.

At the lower end of Pantai Cenang is the **Underwater World Langkawi D** (tel: 04-955 6100; www.underwater worldlangkawi.com.my; daily 10am–6pm, public and school holidays 9.30am–6.30pm; charge), which showcases over 5,000 marine and freshwater creatures. One highlight is a 15-metre (50ft) glass tunnel within a giant salt-water tank with larger species such as sharks, stingrays and turtles.

At the upper end of Pantai Cenang is **Laman Padi Museum E** (Muzium Laman Padi; tel: 04-955 4312; daily 10am–5pm; free), displaying the

In the Temple Tree at Bon Ton.

history of rice and the various implementations used, while the surrounding fields in various stages of rice cultivation offer an opportunity to plant paddy.

Temple Tree

Just after leaving Pantai Cenang and en route to the international airport is **Temple Tree at Bon Ton F** (www. templetree.com.my). Here, you'll find an estate of stately homes – of Chinese, Malay, Indian, Arab and Eurasian origin from towns and cities around Peninsular Malaysia – which have been rescued and converted into luxurious accommodation. Many of the houses were once derelict. Each piece of wood was numbered and documented before being dismantled and brought over here to be restored to its former glory. The houses, between 70 and 110 years old, are built of aged timber with columns and elaborate wooden carvings.

Highlights include the colonial-style **Straits Club House**, the resplendent wooden red-and-green-coloured **Chinese House** and the green double-storey **Colonial House**, built by affluent Arab goldsmith traders and decorated with cornices, floor tiles and a fishscale design canopy over the porch. Also here is the **Yellow House**, a typical Malay village house from Kedah, now used as a pool house, the **Temple** around a tree that the resort has been named after and the **Plantation House**, so called because it was originally from a plantation area on Penang island. The first owner was a Malay family, which then sold it to a Chinese Hakka family who built an adjoining house in their own style. In front of it is the **Black and White House**, a charming Malay house built in the 1940s from Negeri Sembilan.

For a deeper appreciation of local art and batik culture, continue on Route 115 that skirts around the airport. Make a right onto Route 168 and at the roundabout, make a left onto Jalan Lapangan Terbang and continue along Jalan Kuala Teriang. After 1km (0.6 miles), **Pisang Handicraft & Art Village**  (tel: 04-955 7730; daily 10am–7pm; free) is on your left immediately after the road bend. Here, local artisans paint island scenes in batik. The village comprises two buildings – one is a retail shop selling local produce and home-made soap and lotions, and the other a batik workshop and gallery.

Machinchang Cambrian Geoforest Park

Head northwest on Jalan Kuala Teriang toward Jalan Pantai Kok and follow signs to Geopark Hotel – access to the hotel parking is through a small road on the left after the second parking lot. Behind, the jagged peaks of the 708-metre (2,320ft) high **Mount Machinchang** (Gunung Machinchang) provide a dramatic backdrop to the Oriental Village shopping complex (daily 10am–10pm), where you'll also find the **Langkawi Geopark Tourist Information Centre** (tel: 04-966 7186; www.langkawigeopark. com.my), which provides a general overview of Langkawi's geoforest parks. The **Geopark Hotel** (tel: 04-959 2300; www.geoparkhotel.com) offers beautiful views of the mountain from behind the hotel.

Adjacent to the Geopark Hotel is the must-do **Panorama Langkawi (SkyCab)** to the top of Mount Machinchang (tel: 04-959 4225; www. panoramalangkawi.com; Mon–Thur 10am–7pm, Wed noon–7pm, Fri–Sun, public and school holidays 9.30am–7pm; charge). The 15-minute, 2.2km (1.4-mile) cable car ride, considered to be the world's steepest, brings you first to the Middle Station where you can alight to see 360-degree views of the Andaman Sea from viewing platforms. From the Middle Station, another set of cable cars brings you to the Top Station, where you can walk onto the gravity-defying curved **SkyBridge**, which connects two smaller peaks. The 125-metre (410ft) long bridge, ranking among the world's longest curve suspension bridges, is suspended from an 82-metre (269ft) high single pylon that hangs at about 100 metres (328ft) above the forest floor. It was

A kingfisher.

The Langkawi cable car offers amazing views of the islands below.

TIP

If you're visiting the Laman Padi Museum in the months of April, May, November and December, remember that massages are available at the on-site spa overlooking the lush paddy fields for an additional fee.

no mean feat installing the bridge – a helicopter had to airlift it to the mountaintop before installation at its present site. During the dry season it can be stuffy and hot in the SkyCab, so try to ascend the mountain either in the early morning or late in the evening to catch the sunset at around 6.30pm. The last cable car down the mountain is at 7.45pm.

If you prefer to have the best of both worlds, take the SkyCab to the Middle Station, then continue on foot for a closer look at the flora and fauna to the Top Station via the **SkyTrail**, a 2-km (1-mile) trail guided by a naturalist. Pre-arrangements are required. While descending the mountain by SkyCab, you can see on your left **Telaga Tujuh** (Seven Wells), a waterfall intercepted by seven pools. Legend has it that mountain fairies come to these pools to bathe but vanish at the sight of humans, but in reality aggressive monkeys lie in wait for visitors with backpacks, thinking they are filled with food. Carrying an umbrella or a walking stick will help keep away the monkeys.

A view over the mountains from the Langkawi cable car.

Ancient Machinchang

The Machinchang formation is the oldest rock in the peninsula, and a good look at the sedimentary structure can be had at the end of the road at **Teluk Datai** in the north or further eastwards on Jalan Datai at **Pantai Pasir Tengkorak ❶**. Cars parked outside are a good indicator of the whereabouts of this beach. A second beach with rock formations is accessible via a steep concrete staircase with handrails. Avoid the weekends unless you don't mind the local crowd and the monkeys.

After enjoying the beach and rock formations, follow Jalan Datai southwards and turn left onto Jalan Teluk Yu. Follow signposts to the **Langkawi Craft Complex ❶** (Kompleks Kraf Langkawi; tel: 04-959 1913; daily 10am–6pm; free), which sells a variety of Malaysian handicraft, from batik to wooden carvings and silver work demonstrations. Within the craft complex are two museums – the **Heritage Museum** (Muzium Warisan) displays mostly Malay musical instruments and tools used in rice cultivation and fishing, while the more interesting **Custom & Wedding Museum** (Muzium Adat Istiadat & Perkahwinan) showcases a colourful overview of Malaysia's ethnic groups.

Kilim Karst Geoforest Park

Continue along the coastal road, and you'll come across white sandy beaches on Langkawi's northern cape offering scenic sunsets against a backdrop of mountainous rainforest. There are two exclusive resorts along this stretch, and additional security personnel ensure the exclusivity of the beach for resort guests. Unfortunately, to get to the Tanjung Rhu jetty where you can hire boats (it is recommended to arrive before 9.30am) across the straits to visit **Cave of Legends** (Gua Cherita), a cave attraction with ancient writings on its walls, you have to bypass a resort security checkpoint on Jalan Tanjung Rhu which is a public road. If you don't have a tour booking, you'll be advised not to wander onto the resort's beach. To avoid the inconvenience, many tour operators prefer to utilise the **Kilim Jetty** further south, the gateway to the **Kilim Karst Geoforest Park K**, where you can see beautiful limestone landscape and mangroves – a unique forest habitat between land and sea. A guided kayak tour is the best way to glide in and around mangrove trees and come up closer to vertical limestone walls that plunge into the river where regular-sized boats cannot access.

Leaving Kilim Jetty, turn right onto Jalan Ayer Hangat for a local flavour. Langkawi's predominantly Malay population of more than 40,000 live in villages all over the island. If it's a fine day, head inland to the tallest peak on the island – 881-metre (2,890ft) **Mount Raya L** (Gunung Raya) – for 360-degree views of the islands. Almost at the top, there's a resort on the right. Park there for the view, or pay a token fee to take the lift up to the eighth-floor viewing tower.

Langkawi's marine park

Langkawi's maze of islands is full of secret channels, narrows, inlets and bays. Shadowed cliffs, topped by dense virgin jungle, reach up to 600 metres (2,000ft) and drop abruptly into the sea.

Marine life is richest at **Pulau Payar M**, a marine park, one hour by boat from the main island. While underwater visibility is rarely more than 3 metres (10ft), it has lots of life, including baby black-tip reef sharks and colourful soft coral blooms on wrecks in deeper waters. Book with dive operators on the main island, or if you're interested in snorkelling and a picnic, any boat operator. There are also dive sites at the neighbouring islets of Segantang, Kaca and Lembu.

Unfortunately, fish-feeding is rife here at the marine park, an act that alters fish behaviour, making them unafraid of humans and easier for them to be caught. Fish also associate snorkellers with food, and tend to nibble at people's fingers and legs when they are in the waters.

TIP

The best time to dive in Langkawi is between November and February, the peak season for migrating whale sharks from Australia as they travel thousands of kilometres to spawn in the Seychelles.

Hopping between islands on a boat tour.

Decorative rickshaws outside Christ Church in Melaka's Town Square.

Palm-oil plantations in Johor.

THE SOUTHERN PENINSULA

Village and city, ancient and modern – the contradictions are more obvious in the south than elsewhere. Historic Melaka is to be found here, along with a thriving metropolis, fine beaches and a national park.

A detail of Sultan Abu Bakar Mosque in Johor Bahru.

Standing as it does today at the silted river mouth, it is barely conceivable that tiny Melaka (Malacca) once ruled world trade, and was responsible for the spread of Islam throughout the Malay Peninsula. Although the world still congregates at Melaka, these days it is to gaze at its ruins and relics and to ride in its riverboats, while the main trade with local merchants is in cheap souvenirs and T-shirts.

The World Heritage City of Melaka is the undisputed top tourist draw of the southern stretch of the peninsula's west coast. Walking is the best way to explore the alleyways and streets, providing many opportunities to admire resplendent mansions and quaint shophouses, to pray in centuries-old places of worship, and to observe endangered trades before they disappear. It was under the benign rule of Melaka that the people of the neighbouring Negeri Sembilan were able to remain true to the traditions and customs of their native Sumatra; this is most visible today in their architecture, notably the large sweeping roofs reminiscent of buffalo horns.

Viewing Johor, at the southern tip of Malaysia, from Singapore, across the Causeway.

The beach at Port Dickson is famous for the annual migration of thousands of birds of prey that cross the straits here. South of Negeri Sembilan is the state of Johor; its southern districts, including the capital city Johor Bahru, is collectively called Iskandar Malaysia, a growing metropolis with a logistics hub, luxury housing, a tourism-friendly waterfront city and more.

Johor's towns are relatively uninteresting, except perhaps for Muar. It was to this river-mouth port that the last sultan of Melaka fled from the Portuguese. Inland, however, is the Endau-Rompin National Park, a magnificent swathe of primeval rainforest set aside for conservation and nature-based tourism. Along Johor's eastern shores, the beaches of Desaru beckon visitors and surfers while its isles lure divers and snorkellers. On the west coast of Johor, three wetlands of international importance attract a wide range of birds, seahorses, and the endangered sea cows.

Christ Church.

MELAKA

The site of both the first settlement on the peninsula in the 1400s, and of the declaration of independence in 1957, Melaka can truly be called the birthplace of Malaysia.

History is everywhere in **Melaka** ❶ (Malacca); peeping out from odd corners, hinting truths from epitaphs, outlined in the weathered face of a fisherman. Melaka is a town with a glorious past; over five centuries ago, a Portuguese chronicler and frequent visitor said, "Whosoever is lord of Malacca has his hand on the throat of Venice." However, that golden grip lasted only 130 years; today Melaka is in a grip of another kind. Every weekend, many Singaporean vehicles jam the narrow streets. Certain traditional areas have fallen victim to urban mismanagement: in the quest for tourist dollars, traditional craftsmen have been evicted and a number of historic shophouses have been demolished or else subjected to sham restoration projects – diluting somewhat Melaka's cultural and historical environment.

In 2008, to protect whatever remained of Melaka, the city joined Penang's George Town in the north of the peninsula to become the Historic Cities of the Straits of Malacca, and is now a World Heritage Site. But with this listing, more pre-war shophouses are being converted into chic boutiques and budget-style accommodation, which do not always adhere to heritage conservation guidelines. To restore pre-war houses using original raw materials and building methods is an extremely costly affair, and short

cuts are often taken to cash in on the heritage appeal.

Historical Melaka

In the late 1300s, Melaka was a small settlement of sea gypsies, scraping a living as fishermen and farmers. Then a Malay prince, Parameswara, arrived fleeing from his own invaded domain of Palembang, Sumatra. While out hunting in the area, he encountered a tiny *kancil* (mousedeer), which managed to intimidate his dogs; he took this as a sign that this should

A trishaw driver.

TIP

Trishaw drivers actually make fine guides, as they know the sights and speak English. Not only might you learn that the Portuguese came "a much much long time ago", but also that along the seafront there is a great stall that sells some of the best fried *mee hoon* (vermicelli) in Malaysia.

be the site of his new capital. By the end of the 15th century, Melaka had become the centre of a great trading empire and held an undisputed claim over the southern Malay Peninsula, as well as east Sumatra opposite. From every seafaring nation they came – Persians, Arabs, Tamils and Bengalis from the west; Javanese, Sundanese and Sulus from the archipelago; Chinese, Thais, Burmese and Khmers – in search of profit through trade, piracy or plunder.

The West decided to assume control of the hub of this lucrative trading operation, and Melaka's golden age ended when it fell in 1511 to the Portuguese. The port was theirs for 130 years, before they were ousted by the Dutch. After 154 years, the Dutch in turn ceded Melaka to the British in 1824. Each in turn left something of their culture behind.

Small colonies of Chinese and Indian merchants and the Portuguese, Dutch and British stayed behind to found the Peranakan (Straits-born) communities, which have become the most striking and colourful

fraternities in Malaysia today. These pioneers married local women and accepted the practical realities of living in a Malay community, but upheld the social and religious norms of their forefathers. The Baba men and Nyonya women are descendants of the Chinese pioneers from Fujian, while the Melaka Chitty are descendants of the Indian traders of South India. The Portuguese-Eurasians, however, are the most complex, being descendants of Portuguese, Dutch, British and local roots.

World Heritage Site

The Unesco World Heritage Site is divided into two core zones – the St Paul's Hill Civic Zone situated east of the Melaka river and, on the west bank, a maze of ancient and narrow streets that make up the residential and commercial zones. It is easily covered on foot or by a leisurely trishaw ride through the tight streets, but when visiting attractions outside the heritage areas it is better to hire a taxi. Depending on your interests, Melaka can be seen in two or three days.

Southern Peninsular Malaysia

The best place to begin your tour is in the town centre, near the bridge built on the site where the Portuguese made their final successful assault on the town. Here you will find the helpful **Tourism Information Centre** (tel: 06-281 4803; daily 9am–6pm), where you can get the handy Melaka Street Map which includes a map of the heritage area.

The Portuguese and Dutch heritage trail

On the east river bank, at the junction of Jalan Kota and Jalan Gereja is a neat little square with a clock tower, surrounded by terracotta-red buildings and a church. They are distinctly Dutch; you almost expect to see tulips rather than tropical blooms in the flower pots.

The **Stadthuys Ⓐ** (Town Hall), constructed of incredibly thick walls and massive hardwood doors supported by studded, wrought-iron hinges, served as government offices for more than 300 years. The Stadthuys itself is an antiquity. Erected between 1641 and 1660, it is the oldest known Dutch building still standing in Asia. Today it is the **Stadthuys Museum Complex** (tel: 06-284 1934; www.perzim.gov.my; daily 9am–5.30pm, Fri closed 12.15–2.45pm; charge), and for the price of one ticket you can visit all five museums, of which the History, Ethnography and Literature Museum should not be missed. The museum tells the story of the city from the time it was an ancient Malay kingdom to the present. The collections include old coins and stamps, Portuguese costumes from the 16th century and old sepia photographs of Melaka life. Guided tours to all five museums are available 10.30am and 2.30pm at weekends.

Adjacent to the Stadthuys on Jalan Gereja is the fabled **Christ Church Ⓑ** (tel: 06-284 8804; Mon–Sat 9am–4.30pm; free), whose bricks were shipped all the way from Holland. Melaka's masons then faced them with local red laterite. The church is full of old, engraved tombstones, many telling a grim tale about the hardships the early European settlers faced. The immense rafters within the nave were each carved from a single tree, and above the altar a wooden crucifix hangs from the iron hoops fastened to the wall. Today, it is Malaysia's oldest functioning Anglican church.

St Paul's Hill

Behind the Stadthuys Complex, a path leads up to the peak of St Paul's Hill, where the only remnants of original Portuguese architecture remain.

In 1521, a chapel, later named **St Paul's Church Ⓒ**, was built by a Portuguese *fidalgo* to fulfil a vow he made on escaping death in the South China Sea. It was later taken over by the Jesuits, who completed the building and painted it white so that it could serve as a guidepost for ships out on the Straits. The famous Jesuit missionary St Francis Xavier conducted mass in the church during his several visits to Melaka.

The Dutch discontinued services in St Paul's Church when their own

The Stadthuys.

Christ Church was built. The engraved tombstones that line the inside walls are testament to its continued use as a place of burial thereafter.

As you descend the hill towards another ruin, the left path leads to the **Dutch Graveyard** established for Dutch East India Company officials and their families. In use between 1670 and 1682, only five of the 38 graves are Dutch; the rest are British. Continue down the hill to the ruins of a famous fortress.

A Famosa fortress

When the Portuguese conquered Melaka, they were determined to make it one of the mightiest strongholds in the Orient. Hundreds of slaves and captives hauled stones from demolished mosques and elaborate tombs to build **A Famosa** (The Famous) fortress.

The fortress eventually enclosed the entire hill, and withstood attacks for over 100 years, until the Dutch finally breached it in 1641 after a five-month siege. However, the Dutch did not find the rich and prosperous port of the fabulous East they had expected. The city they had struggled so hard to conquer lay in near-total ruin. The Dutch lost no time putting things in order, rebuilding the city with a Dutch flavour, and repairing the fortress and renaming the bastions. Melaka was soon a well-defended port once again.

Unfortunately, when the British occupied Melaka from 1824, they destroyed the fortifications to prevent the Dutch from reclaiming it. The

A Melaka riverside café.

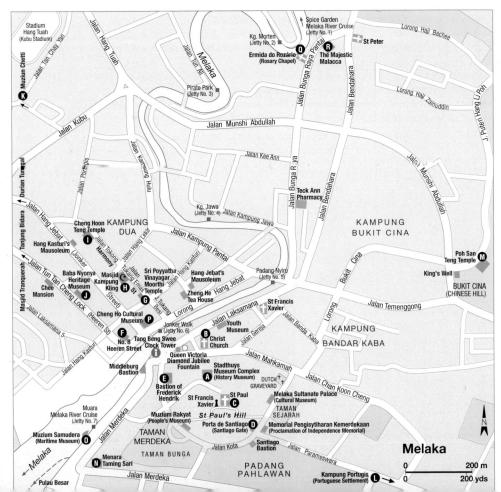

Melaka

walls and gates were badly damaged, and all that was left is what stands today: the **Porta de Santiago** ⓓ – a gate without a wall. Due to land reclamation and development, you can no longer see the shoreline from here, but you can faintly make out the mark the Dutch left on the gate; look up at the arch and you will see "Anno 1670" and above this, although no longer visible, is the VOC logo of the Dutch East India Company.

Across the Porta de Santiago, at the edge of a shopping mall, are more ruins of the fortress. Prior to Melaka's Unesco listing, modern buildings jostled for space within the historical enclave. During the construction of the Dataran Pahlawan Melaka Megamall, archaeologists discovered the site of the **Santiago Bastion**, one of the fortress's six original bastions constructed during the Portuguese era (1511–1641). Bastions were crucial to the defence of Melaka, offering soldiers a great vantage point of approaching enemies in the Straits of Malacca. After a hasty excavation that was seen as a blow to heritage

conservation, the development of the mall went ahead, and now sits atop the southeastern corner of the fort.

Wedged tightly between the Santiago Bastion and the shopping mall is a small mosaic-tiled pyramid with a large "M" in the middle inscribed with the date "31st August 1957". This is the marker that commemorates the place where, in 1956, a jubilant crowd of thousands welcomed news of Malaysia's independence from the British before it was officially declared in the nation's capital of Kuala Lumpur a year later.

Walk along Jalan Kota, heading westwards back to the Stadthuys. Before the roundabout, you will come across the foundations of the Bastion of Courassa, which, during Dutch rule, was renamed as the **Bastion of Frederick Hendrik** ⓔ in honour of King Hendrik, who ruled the Netherlands from 1642 to 1647. Archaeologists also discovered human skeletons, glass beads, cannon balls and old coins. Cross Jalan Merdeka to where, in 2006, another section of the fort's foundation

In the A Famosa fortress.

A Peranakan townhouse

The double-storey townhouses of the Straits Settlements were always longer than they were wide to reduce the amount of tax owed to the Dutch.

The front of the houses are highly decorative: including brightly coloured tiles, elaborate doors and wooden shutters. The style is distinctly oriental, but the floral plaster motifs look Western. And yet the whole is unified. This is the Peranakan townhouse.

Described as Chinese Palladian, the architectural style of these buildings of the Malaysian Straits Chinese is a unique meld of Victorian, Chinese and Malay. Lining the streets of Melaka's Old Town, they are also found in Penang's backstreets and in selected nooks of Singapore. But the Melaka buildings are among the oldest townhouses in the country, dating back to the 17th century. Those along Jalan Tun Tan Cheng Lock are particularly elaborate because they were status symbols for their affluent owners.

The houses have two sets of doors. The main wooden doors, with their intricately carved panels,

Inside a Peranakan house in Melaka.

are left open during the day to let air in. The second outer set are swinging half-doors based on the Malay *pintu pagar* (literally, fence door). On either side are large square windows with vertical bars and sometimes shutters. Above the windows are air vents, which are sometimes decorated.

A Peranakan townhouse is much longer than its entrance suggests. During the Dutch era, property owners were taxed based on the frontage width, so to reduce tax, shrewd owners built longer houses. The centrepiece of the main or reception hall is usually an altar, large and beautifully carved. More likely than not, the deity among the candles and burning joss sticks would be the white-robed Kwan Yin, goddess of mercy.

Twin arched entrances lead to the sitting room. The main furniture would usually be made of imported blackwood inlaid with mother-of-pearl and marble. These pieces were often set against the walls, from where portraits of ancestors in gilded frames peered down.

Behind the sitting room is the dining room and, right at the back, the huge kitchen. In between would be one or more courtyards or air wells to let light into the otherwise dark house. The courtyards serve as indoor gardens with potted plants, a fountain, and a well or large ornate jar filled with water, and were always lower than the rest of the ground floor, with drain holes so that the house wouldn't be flooded during a downpour.

The bedrooms sit upstairs at the top of a wooden staircase with balusters. The rooms and bathrooms are capacious and carry through the elements of carved lacquered wood, embroidery, and porcelain.

Visiting a townhouse

Many of these houses are being restored and converted into hotels, restaurants and tourist trinket shops. In the process, however, numerous traditional tradesmen have been evicted, and the quality of the restoration work compromised for a fast buck. The best preserved are probably the Chan family-owned Baba Nyonya Heritage Museum (see page 219) that straddles two adjoining townhouses and the Puri Hotel on Jalan Tun Tan Cheng Lock.

The Chan family has converted the third townhouse, once living quarters for their servants, into a café downstairs and a cosy six-bedroom guesthouse upstairs. Although not as ornately decorated as the museum next door, Café1511 (www.cafe1511.com) still retains the same architectural elements, giving guests a Peranakan living experience but with modern touches.

was unearthed during preliminary construction work for the Menara Taming Sari (Taming Sari Tower). Fortunately, the tower was re-sited further inland, and the remains of the foundation of the **Middleburg Bastion**, one of three additional bastions erected by the Dutch, were excavated. Using historical illustrations, a replica was constructed. Built in 1660 to monitor ships going in and coming out of the Melaka river, today the bastion has become yet another riverside attraction.

Heeren Street

Walk northwards towards the roundabout and, after crossing the bridge, turn left onto Jalan Tun Tan Cheng Lock – or Heeren Street as it was known to the Dutch. It was named after a leading Baba politician and architect. His family house and the palatial townhouses of several other prominent Chinese families line the street, flaunting Peranakan tiles and carved wooden doors. The street is extremely narrow, so watch out for traffic. At the top of the street is **No. 8 Heeren Street** ❺ (tel: 06-281 1507; Tue–Sat 11am–4pm, free, donations welcomed), an 18th-century Dutch-era shophouse that has been authentically restored. For a thorough understanding of typical shophouse architecture, staff will give you a 30-minute guided tour of the building's restoration process. Before you leave, be sure to pick up a copy of the Endangered Trades brochure, which describes a two-hour self-guided walking tour of Malacca's living heritage.

Jonker Street

Parallel to this road is Jalan Hang Jebat, formerly known as **Jonker Street**, Melaka's main tourist drag. This once elegant street filled with quaint Peranakan homes, Chinese clan associations, and age-old crafts and trades such as acupuncturists, herbalists and wooden clog makers, has lost some of its charm in recent years thanks to the

proliferation of tacky souvenir shops, massage lounges and restaurants.

Still, if you search hard enough, you will find what Jonker Street is most famous for – antiques. There are heavy brass irons with receptacles for hot coals, wooden bullock carts, ornate oil lamps, Peranakan-style furniture inlaid with mother of pearl, opium beds and altar stands, Victorian clocks and early gramophones, brass urns and marble statues, silver trinkets and Chinese wedding beds, as well as rare stamps and coins, and Malay *keris* (daggers). Browse carefully – as original pieces are intermingled with reproductions – and learn the art of bargaining for a price you're willing to pay.

From Friday to Sunday nights, Jalan Hang Jebat is cordoned off to traffic and becomes **Jonker Street Weekend Night Market** (6pm–midnight) – an assortment of eating stalls and souvenir shops.

Harmony Street

Parallel to Jalan Hang Jebat are three streets of interest – Jalan Tukang Besi (Blacksmith Street), Jalan Tukang

The Menara Taming Sari.

Carved stone slabs at A Famosa.

FACT

Another good example of a Melakan mosque is the 150-year-old **Tranquerah Mosque** in Jalan Tengkera, 2km (1.2 mile) away. Its cemetery encloses the tomb of Sultan Hussain of Johor, who ceded Singapore to Sir Stamford Raffles in 1819.

By the riverside in Melaka.

Emas (Goldsmith Street) and Jalan Tokong (Temple Street). During the Dutch era, the entire stretch was known as Goldsmith Street, which was then dominated by Indian goldsmiths who lived and worked here. When the British arrived, they divided the road up into three sections, but today they are locally known as Harmony Street, where three of the oldest places of worship in Malaysia are located.

The country's oldest Hindu temple, **Sri Poyyatha Vinayagar Moorthi Temple G**, is dedicated to Vinayagar or Ganesha, the elephant-headed Hindu god, one of the most popular deities among Malaysian devotees. The Chitty community built the temple in 1781 and, although most of them migrated to the Melakan suburbs in the 18th and 19th centuries, the temple remains its most important place of worship. But temple upkeep is expensive, so in 1962 they struck a maintenance deal with the Nattukottai Chettiar community of traders and moneylenders, who needed a temple at the time. But every

May, the temple's owners return for a sacred ceremony lasting several days – the Sembahyang Dato Chachar – where the Chitty, as part of an act of religious atonement, escort a wooden chariot to the Sri Maha Mariamman temple in the Chitty's Village in Gajah Berang (Rampaging Elephant) 5km (3 miles) away. In the same procession, Hindu worshippers skewer their flesh with fishhooks, sometimes tethered to harnesses held by supporters, and cheeks are impaled with long spear-like objects to thank the deity for prayers answered.

Next door is the **Kampung Kling Mosque H** (Masjid Kampung Kling), the town's oldest mosque, built in 1748 (daily 10am–7pm; closed to non-Muslims during Friday prayers noon–2pm). It sports a typical Sumatran design, with a three-tiered roof and a rather Chinese-like minaret. This style is characteristic of Melakan mosques.

Straight ahead at No. 25 Jalan Tokong is the **Cheng Hoon Teng Temple I**, or Green Cloud Temple (tel: 06-282 9343; daily 7am–7pm; free). Built in 1673, it is the oldest

Chinese temple in Malaysia. It was originally built by a fugitive from the Manchu conquest, and was later restored by local Chinese leaders. Look up and you will see the carved roof, ridges and eaves elegantly decorated with Chinese mythical figures of coloured glass and porcelain. Step through the massive hardwood gates, and you feel you are stepping back several centuries. Among the woodcarvings and lacquer work within is a stone inscription commemorating Admiral Cheng Ho's visit to Melaka in 1406. Across the street, also belonging to the temple, is a theatre compound and an opera stage where Chinese operas are occasionally staged.

Melaka's Peranakan communities

At the **Baba Nyonya Heritage Museum** ❶ (Nos. 48–50 Jalan Tun Tan Cheng Lock; tel: 06-283 1273; daily 10am–4.30pm, closed on some public holidays; guided tours 10am–1pm and 2–5pm; charge) you can explore the unique interior of a typical Peranakan house, learn about Peranakan history, culture and architecture. The house is filled with curios and furniture, including blackwood tables and chairs from China and sumptuous traditional wedding costumes.

The Baba Nyonyas are not the only Peranakans in Melaka. Take a taxi to Jalan Gajah Berang, where you will see an archway decorated with a pair of elephant-head sculptures that mark the entrance to the Chitty Village. Just past here is the **Chetti Museum** ❷ (Muzium Chetti; Tue–Sun 9.30am–5pm; charge), which offers a historical overview of the Indian traders who first came to Melaka in the 1400s and who later married the local women. Melaka's Chitty or the Peranakan Hindu also adopted certain cultural aspects of the Malays – in food, dress and language. For example, like the Nyonyas, the Chitty women also wear kebaya blouses and batik sarongs,

but of a much simpler design. You can walk around the village or pre-arrange with the Melaka Chitty Cultural Organisation for a guided tour (mobile tel: 012-601 5111).

Near the beach at Ujong Pasir, about 3km (2 miles) eastwards from Melaka's centre, is the **Portuguese Settlement** ❸ (Kampung Portugis) of about 1,200 Eurasians of Portuguese, Dutch, British and local roots, mostly fishermen.

Close to the public parking lot is a typical settlement house, which you can peer into from the outside of a white picket fence. Homes then were very basic, with wooden-plank walls, attap palm roofs and sandy floors.

The residents are friendly and will help with directions if you wander away from the **Portuguese Square** (Medan Portugis), which has several restaurants that serve spicy seafood dishes and ice-cold beer. There is little of commercial tourist value here, except for a single-room museum that is more often closed than open. In the evenings, people head to the waterfront for the seafood. Less than

Detail from an ornate wall tile of a typical Peranakan house. Antique tiles such as these are for sale at Melaka's Jonker Street.

Antiques for sale on Jonkers Street.

A cheerfully decorated Melaka rickshaw.

The ethnic Portuguese community celebrate an annual water festival.

200 metres/yards from the Portuguese Square is a row of restaurants built on reclaimed land with alfresco seating. Some stalls are pricier than others, and if the place is crowded, each stall guarantees different levels of service.

Chinese Hill

Head northwards to see a historical hill which houses more than 12,500 Chinese graves. Hills are auspicious burial grounds, according to the principles of *feng shui* (Chinese geomancy), for they block evil winds and offer the spirits of the ancestors a good view over their descendants. But while most names and dates on the tombstones on **Chinese Hill** (Bukit Cina) have been eroded, what remains eternal is the legacy of a Ming princess, Hang Li Poh (see box).

At the southern end of the hill, visit the **Poh San Teng Temple ⓜ** (tel: 06-283 6538; daily 7am–7pm; free), which was built for the benefit of the departed souls, and not for Admiral Cheng Ho, the Ming Dynasty seafarer, as originally thought. A small statue of him on the temple grounds has

led people to believe that the temple is dedicated to the admiral, but there is no historical evidence linking him to the temple. The temple is actually dedicated to the deity Tua Pek Kong. According to an ancient stone slab in the temple, Bukit Cina was the final resting place for early Chinese traders, many of whom arrived here without their families. With no one to pray for their souls, the job was left to the leaders of the Chinese community, the Chinese Kapitans. However, their tasks were always interrupted by heavy winds and torrential rainfall. In 1795, Dutch-elected Kapitan Chua Su Cheong addressed the problem immediately by building the temple so offerings could be made in peace. Outside the temple is a pathway that leads to the **King's Well** – which the sultan ordered to be dug up for the exclusive use of his wife, whose waters never dried up, even during the most severe drought.

The Melaka river

For a bird's-eye view of the Melaka river and to see how far out the original

---

PORTUGUESE FESTIVALS

The best time to come to the Portuguese Settlement to get a feel for Portuguese-Eurasian culture is during one of its many festivals. In June every year, the Portuguese-Eurasians begin a week-long celebration, starting on 23 June with the **Feast of St John the Baptist** (Festa São João), where members of the *Irmang di Greza* (Cristang for "Brethren of the Church") light their wicker torches and progressively move from house to house, lighting up little white candles on verandas and picket fences. The candles are lit in memory of St John, who led the way during the time of the pagan communities.

At the end of the week, the local fishermen decorate their boats with bunting, sacred texts and sparkling neon lights to honour their patron saint during the **Feast of St Peter** (Festa São Pedro) on 29 June.

In December, as the sun sets, part of the settlement comes alive with the Christmas spirit – streets and homes are bedecked with elaborate decorations including Santa Claus and his reindeers on roofs and popular Nativity scenes. Traffic comes to a standstill and the streets are crammed with hoards of people strolling past homes, while at the square there is singing and dancing.

river mouth has been extended due to development, head southwest to Jalan Merdeka, where you will find the revolving tower of **Menara Taming Sari** (tel: 06-288 1100; www.menaratamingsari.com; Sun–Thu 10am–10pm, Fri–Sat 10am–11pm; charge). Each ride, accommodating up to 66 passengers, rises to a lofty height of 80 metres (262ft) in a minute, then rotates for five minutes before descending to street level.

Walk westwards along Jalan Merdeka until you see a replica of the *Flor de la Mar*, a Portuguese ship that sank off the Melakan coast. Housed within it is the **Maritime Museum** (Muzium Samudera; tel: 06-283 0926; www.perzim.gov.my; daily 9am–5pm, also Fri–Sun 5.30pm–8.30pm; charge). It traces Melaka's maritime history from the 14th century to the British colonial era and features mainly artefacts gleaned from ship-wrecks in the Straits of Melaka. The only odd "ship rule" on board is that visitors have to remove their shoes before entering the museum. Your museum ticket lets you enter the Maritime Museum Complex, which also includes the nearby **Maritime Museum Phase 2** and the **Royal Malaysian Navy Museum**.

Behind the *Flor de la Mar*, walk towards the riverside, where you will find the **Melaka River Cruise** counter (tel: 06-281 4322; daily 9am–11pm; charge). Purchase a Ho-Ho Service wristband, which will allow you to hop on and off the river cruise boat at six different jetties along the Melaka river throughout the day. Alternatively, you can also purchase the regular non-stop return trip, which is a 45-minute cruise up and down the Melaka river. The river cruise with informative commentary is quite enjoyable – if you ignore its now polluted waters – as it travels past century-old townhouses and warehouses.

Until 2001, trade thrived along the historic Melaka river as it had done ever since the end of the 15th century, when traders unloaded their goods and picked up some bargains for their return journey home. In 2002, the river underwent a major facelift to boost tourism in the area and as

The view from the Menara Taming Sari.

TIP

To avoid the hour-long queues, join the Melaka river cruise in the evening or take the night cruise – when buildings along the riverfront are decorated in coloured neon lights.

a result, concrete riverside walkways have reduced the river to one-third of its original width. A series of locks also regulate the river level so cruises can operate every half-hour. After several days, the stagnant and foul-smelling river water is let out into the sea after midnight. If you have purchased the river cruise wristband, inform the driver you want to alight at the Jonker Walk (Jetty No. 6) on the west riverbank.

Cheng Ho Cultural Museum

One of Melaka's most famous sea-faring visitors was Ming Dynasty's Admiral Zheng He (Cheng Ho). In the early 15th century, he and 27,000 people embarked on seven voyages from China to Africa, stopping over in Melaka on several occasions in a fleet of up to 300 treasure ships, so called because of the treasures brought back to China. While waiting for favour-able winds to carry them home, treasures were stored in warehouses and according to an old navigational map belonging to Ma Huan (an inter-preter who accompanied the admiral

on many of his sea voyages) one of the warehouses may be on the same site as the **Cheng Ho Cultural Museum** Ⓟ (No. 51 Lorong Hang Jebat; tel: 06-283 1135; www.chengho.org/museum; daily 9am–6pm; charge). Spread out over two floors, the museum tries to encompass Melaka's history as a trad-ing port and the admiral's fascination for sailing.

Continue walking along Lorong Hang Jebat and turn left onto Jalan Kampung Kuli. On the left at No. 3 is the **Zheng He Teahouse** (mobile tel: 016-764 0588; Mon–Sat 11am–10pm, Sun 11am–6pm; charge), with no historical links to the admiral. But here you can escape from the heat and indulge in a typical Chinese tea ceremony, while learning about the many varieties of aromatic Chinese tea that have made their way from China to Melaka.

Chinatown

Return to Lorong Hang Jebat and turn left, crossing the next bridge over the Melaka river, then left onto Jalan Bunga Raya. This is the start of

A wall painting on a Jonker Street house.

A PRINCESS'S LEGACY

In the 15th century, Sultan Mansur Shah of Malacca carried on a diplo-matic war of wits with the emperor of China, which grew to be the stuff of legend, but around 1460, the Chinese emperor became so impressed by the sultan's power that he decided to send his daughter Hang Li Poh to marry him.

She arrived with no fewer than 500 ladies-in-waiting. The sultan gave them "the hill without the town" as a private residence and promised that the land they occupied would never be taken away from them.

To this day, Bukit Cina belongs to Melaka's Chinese community. Several of the graves on the hill date back to the Ming Dynasty and these are among the oldest Chinese relics in Malaysia.

the city's **Chinatown** which, in the early 1900s, was popular for its colourful nightlife and illegal opium dens. Today, however, walking northwards on this road gives you an insight into Chinese businesses – shops selling bales of cloth, rattan furniture, Chinese New Year decorations, traditional Chinese medicine and a variety of local food. Walk northwards until you reach the Melaka river and on your left, less than 100 metres/yds and beyond the hawker food centre, is a little-known attraction not on any tourist map.

The ruins of the **Rosary Chapel** ❻ (Ermida do Rozário) and the tombstone of Emerici de Souza, a Portuguese dignitary who died in 1842, are surrounded by cars and lie under grass and litter. Built around 1700, this Catholic chapel had replaced the 16th-century St Lawrence Chapel on the same site. The latter was one of several chapels built by the Portuguese outside the fortress's walls and in this case close to the docking yards along the Melaka river. When **St Peter's Church** (No. 166 Jalan Bendahara; tel: 06-282 2950; daily 7am–5pm; free) was completed in 1710 less than 150 metres/yds away and declared Melaka's main church, the functions of the Rosary Chapel declined until it was abandoned at the end of the 19th century and left to crumble to its present state.

Return to Jalan Bunga Raya, where, at No. 188, another iconic building had previously faced an uncertain future. Originally the private residence of a Chinese tycoon in the 1920s, it later changed ownership to become a hotel with a chequered past before being abandoned in 2000. Six years later, a luxury hotel chain bought the hotel and restored it to its former glory but styled to blend with the unique mix of Straits and neoclassical architecture of the mansion. Wander inside **The Majestic Malacca** (to book tel: 03-2783 1000) ❿ and note that the original fixtures such as the intricate Straits Chinese tiles in the reception, the Straits Settlement windows and the colourful stained glass at the 1920s mansion entrance have been retained. Here, the spa (reservations, tel: 06-289

The Baba Nyonya Heritage Museum.

8000; charge) offers treatments that draw on the healing heritage of the Baba Nyonya. The same ingredients used in its cuisine are also used in the spa treatments such as Malacca palm sugar, nutmeg, lemongrass, ginger, pandan leaves and limau kasturi (calamansi).

Next, cross the bridge to the Malay village enclave of Kampung Morten and flag down the **Melaka River Cruise** boat at Jetty No. 2 for its return trip to the river mouth. En route, you will pass a patch of mangroves where you may spot a basking monitor lizard, and further downriver, on the left bank, the Gothic-style twin bell towers of the **Church of St Francis Xavier** come into view. If you are feeling energetic, you can also follow a 4.5km (3-mile) boardwalk that begins after the Rosary Chapel ruins, and winds its way through the mangroves to the river mouth, concluding your exploration of Melaka's historic river.

Beyond Melaka city

Visitors heading to Melaka city from the North–South Expressway may choose to come in through **Ayer Keroh** ❷, about 12km (8 miles) from the city. Here, several good golf courses dot the area, while the **Melaka Zoo & Night Safari** (tel: 1-300 22 3000; www.melakazoo.com; daily 9am–6pm, Fri–Sat, and public and school holidays 8–11pm; charge) is home to more than 200 species of animals from Southeast Asia and Africa, including a red panda, which resembles a raccoon. For a nominal extra charge, a tram ride around the zoo with an educational commentary is available. For obvious reasons, no cameras or torchlights are allowed at the Night Zoo. Further north is Seremban, capital of Negeri Simbilan (see page 225). Thirty-four kilometres (21 miles) east of Seremban is the old royal Minangkabau capital of **Sri Menanti** ❸ (see page 225). At **The Dusun**, 15km (9 miles) northeast of Seremban, guests can experience Minangkabau meals while living in eco-friendly houses set in a fruit orchard.

About 34km (21 miles) away from Seremban is the seaside town of **Port Dickson**, popular with day-trippers and families at weekends. Nearby is the **Tanjung Tuan (Cape Rachado) Forest Reserve** ❹, in Melakan territory, where you will find Malaysia's oldest functioning lighthouse, believed to have been built by the Portuguese in the 16th century to help guide ships into the Melakan port. The lighthouse on the hilltop is closed to the public, but you can still make your way around its base for an impressive view of the Straits of Malacca. Look skywards between mid-February and mid-April from 11am to 3pm and you might see large birds of prey flying in from Sumatra. They will rest briefly in the forested area before migrating north through Malaysia to their breeding grounds in Russia, China and Japan. At the Tanjung Tuan point, the Strait of Malacca is at its narrowest, and although still 40km (25 miles) wide, it is a perilous crossing for the birds.

A Melaka trishaw driver.

The Minangkabau culture of Negeri Sembilan

The people of west Sumatra who resettled here brought with them customs that favour the women and unique architectural and cuisine styles.

The sweeping, peaked-roofed "buffalo horn" architecture is the most distinguishing feature of the Minangkabau **Negeri Sembilan**, Melaka's northern neighbour. It appears everywhere; in the National Museum in Kuala Lumpur, at luxury hotels fringed by swaying palms, even at a highway petrol station. The roofs have come to signify not just Minangkabau, but Malaysia.

It is a proud tribute to the heritage of a group of settlers from west Sumatra who made their new home in the fertile valleys and hills behind Melaka, attracted by the port's success. Their name, People of the Victorious Buffalo (from Minang (victorious) and kabau (water buffalo), is said to come from the tribe's victory in a fight between two water buffaloes.

They brought their style of architecture and, protected by the Malay sultans, continued adhering to the unique *adat pepatih* customs that follow a matrilineal system, which governs laws, political organisation, traditions and social systems. Many people consider the Minangkabau to also be a matriarchal society, where women are seen as head of the family. Most are Shafite Muslims; indeed, the Minangkabau are among Malaysia's most devout Muslims.

The more than 400,000 Minangkabau live throughout West Malaysia and speak Minangkabau, a distinct language related to that of the Malay and similar to Indonesian. Over the years, the Minangkabau have migrated to cities and towns where today, they are mainly occupied in business and trade and are one of the few ethnic groups that compete successfully with the Chinese. Those who live in villages have become highly skilled in home industries, including weaving and carving; in the countryside, they are primarily wet rice farmers.

The small principalities founded by the original settlers formed the nine *luak* or states that became the federation of Negeri Sembilan. Today, although the modern state is divided into districts, the *luak* remain. Violent clashes over tin that resulted in British intervention in the 1800s have reduced the number of *luak* to five.

State Museum Complex

Minangkabau culture and history is housed at the **State Museum** (Teratak Perpatih) within the grounds of the State Museum Complex on Jalan Sungai Ujung (tel: 06-763 1149; Sat–Thu 10am–6pm, Fri 10am–12.15pm and 2.45–6pm; free) in **Seremban** at the Seremban/Labu exit off the Kuala Lumpur–Seremban Highway. The museum showcases a fine display of ceremonial *keris* (daggers), swords, and royal ornaments. The complex's main building is the 19th-century **Ampang Tinggi Palace** from Kuala Pilah town that has been carefully reconstructed here. Next door is the **Negeri Sembilan House**, another fine piece of Minangkabau architecture and built without a single nail. Unlike the palace's attap-palm roof, the house has a cover of wooden shingles.

Green hills and landscaped gardens provide the setting for the beautiful **Diraja Sri Menanti Museum** (tel: 06-497 9653; daily 9am–5pm; free) in the royal town of **Sri Menanti.** A former palace, it was built in 1903 pieced together with hardwood dowels and rivets and no nails, the four-storey timber structure sits on 99 pillars, representing the warriors of the various *luak*. The museum showcases the regalia of the Negeri Sembilan royal family as well as ceremonial weaponry and costumes.

Negeri Sembilan architecture on the State Government Building.

JOHOR

Its proximity to Singapore makes the state's capital and resorts a favourite with visitors from the island nation, but leave the bustle behind and you will find some of the most beautiful habitats on earth.

Beware the Causeway Clog that heads daily south from Johor Bahru, the capital of Malaysia's southernmost state, into Singapore. On weekdays, the 1km (0.6-mile) road and rail link between the two countries is filled with thousands of Johoreans commuting to their jobs in the Lion City by bus, car, train, motorbike and on foot. The bottleneck is reversed at weekends, when Singaporeans flock to Johor to take advantage of the lower Malaysian ringgit to shop, party and relax in its waterfall, beach and island resorts. Thankfully, the Malaysia–Singapore Second Link to the west of Johor Bahru to Singapore has alleviated some of the weekend traffic jams at the causeway.

It is a symbiotic relationship extended to investments as well, fuelling Johor's Iskandar Malaysia development and making prices in its capital and in the Singaporeans' favourite haunts among the highest in the peninsula. Iskandar Malaysia, with its administrative capital in Kota Iskandar, is a government initiative to transform 2,217 sq km (855 sq miles) of Johor, which includes the city of Johor Bahru, into a robust economy with world-class transport facilities. Still, Johor has not lost its agricultural roots; its hinterland is covered with oil palm and pineapple plantations, fruit orchards and vegetable farms amid virgin rainforest.

Background

Johor evolved its own identity after the fall of the Melaka sultanate to the Portuguese in the 16th century. The last ruler, Sultan Mahmud, fled to Johor and turned it into a powerful trading empire. Its old capitals along the protected reaches of the Johor river were moved to the Riau archipelago, making them more accessible to trade – and attacks. Johor not only had to fend off the Portuguese and the Dutch, but also the Acehnese in Sumatra and, later, the Bugis, losing Singapore

Main Attractions
Mount Ophir
Kukup
Pulau Kukup
Tanjung Piai
Sungai Pulai
Royal Abu Bakar Museum
Layang-Layang Museum
Panti Bird Sanctuary
Desaru
Endau-Rompin National Park

Playing football on Desaru beach.

TIP

To get to Kukup island, register first at the Visitor Information Centre of the Pulau Kukup Johor National Park (tel: 07-696 9355; daily 9am–5pm) opposite the bus station in Kukup town. Then hop on a boat from the jetty. If travelling to Kukup from Singapore, avoid the traffic jam on the Causeway by taking the Malaysia–Singapore Second Link. Turn off at Gelang Patah and follow the signs to Pontian. From Pontian, head south to Kukup.

Sultan Abu Bakar Palace.

to the British in 1819. At the end of the 1800s, Johor was the fiefdom of a *temenggung*, an official of the sultan. Abu Bakar, who became *temenggung* in 1862, elevated himself to maharaja, and in 1885 was acknowledged by Britain as sultan of Johor. Sultan Abu Bakar was educated in Singapore by English clergy. He spoke fluent English and cultivated ties with influential Europeans in the business world. Under his rule, the foundations of modern Johor were laid. In 1866, he moved his capital to Johor Bahru, transforming it into a thriving new town. The sultan used western methods of policymaking and administration, introduced a modern bureaucracy and gave Johor the first constitution written for a Malay state. Johor Malays are of mainly Javanese descent, and known for *kuda kepang*, a dance set to gamelan music.

Mount Ophir

The North–South Expressway stretch from Kuala Lumpur to Singapore is a featureless, flat, ruler-straight road which encourages one to speed or doze off at the wheel. Entering the state

from Melaka on the highway, a turn-off at Tangkak towards Segamat leads to **Mount Ophir** ❺ (Gunung Ledang). While popular with hikers, the mountain is often left litter-strewn. Here, Sagil Falls tumbles off the 1,276-metre (4,186ft) peak into clear pools below. Ledang has a legend attached to it of a magical princess who finally thwarted the persistent attention of Sultan Mansur by demanding a cup of his son's blood for her hand in marriage.

Muar to Batu Pahat

The right turn-off from Tangkak goes to **Muar** ❻, a centre of furniture making and a pretty town with neoclassical government buildings, traditional Malay houses and a pleasant tree-lined walk along the river at Tanjung.

Back on the North–South Expressway, the highway leads on to **Ayer Hitam**, a popular stopover with coffee shops, pottery showrooms and rows of street stalls heavily laden with souvenirs, durian cakes, peanut nougat and other local produce as well as fresh and preserved fruits.

From Ayer Hitam the road to the coast ends at **Batu Pahat** ❼, Johor's other Malay cultural heartland and home to one of the last few genuine *kuda kepang* troupes. The town is notorious for its floods at high tide, but also known for its cheap and good Chinese food.

Southwest Johor

A more scenic way to get to Batu Pahat is via the coastal road from Muar. The road goes through little *kampung* and orchards whose goodies are heaped upon roadside stalls during the fruiting season. It ends in **Kukup** ❽, a Chinese village raised on stilts above the water and the southernmost town of the Malay Peninsula, and indeed the Asian mainland. Hordes descend on Kukup, especially from Singapore, to eat chilli crabs. The restaurants have no fancy decor – and some do not even have walls – but they do have atmosphere and great food.

Johor has three RAMSAR sites, or wetlands of international importance where visitors may see mangrove wildlife such as smooth otters, dusky leaf monkeys, mudskippers and the threatened lesser adjutant storks. Just offshore is the uninhabited mangrove island of **Pulau Kukup**, a 650-hectare (1,600-acre) national park and 800-hectare (1,980-acre) wetland sanctuary. Access to the Taman Negara Johor Pulau Kukup (tel: 07-696 9355; daily 9am–5pm; charge) is by boat from Kukup town. Nature-lovers can enjoy its unique ecosystem from its observation towers, a boardwalk and a suspension bridge.

The coastal road continues south to **Tanjung Piai**. This southernmost tip of the peninsula and mainland Asia is 75km (47 miles) from Johor Bahru and hosts good seafood restaurants and another RAMSAR site, the Taman Negara Johor Tanjung Piai (tel: 07-696 9712; daily 9am–6.30pm; charge), a 930-hectare (2,300-acre) forest. More than half of this area is a mangrove sanctuary, and visitors may chance to observe the wildlife from a raised boardwalk running through the sanctuary.

Close to the Malaysia–Singapore Second Link is an area rich in marine biodiversity and home to seahorses, pipefish and the endangered dugong. Unlike the first two RAMSAR sites, **Sungai Pulai** ❾ does not have a visitor's centre.

However, you can learn about this area from the Orang Seletar, one of the Orang Asli tribes in Johor. The Malaysian Society of Marine Sciences and Save our Seahorses (www.sosmalaysia. org/ramsar-tour.html; saveourseahorses@ yahoo.com), both non-governmental organisations, run the **RAMSAR Tour,** which engages the Orang Asli to guide four visitors at a time to see the mangroves and learn about its flora and fauna. The two-hour daytime cruise explores the Sungai Pulai mangrove estuary, while the night cruise lets you stargaze, look for nocturnal animals and listen to a couple of Seletar folklore tales and songs. If it's a full moon, you get the added bonus of seeing the river in a different light. Note that cruises are tide-dependent.

Johor's Chinese cemetery.

Kukup is a Chinese fishing village raised on stilts.

Johor, as viewed from Singapore, across the Causeway.

Just outside the protected RAMSAR site lies another hidden gem, which you can only see at low tide. At 1.8km (1 mile) long and up to 200 metres/yards at its widest, this is Malaysia's largest seagrass bed – food for the dugong and home to tiny seahorses, less than the size of your palm. A team from Save our Seahorses monitors the seahorses in this area and provides opportunities for families and individuals to help look for and tag them for research.

About 75km (47 miles) away is **Danga Bay** an up-and-coming waterfront development located along the popular Lido beach. Besides a 150-berth marina, it has a theme park and a petting zoo.

Johor Bahru

The best-known place in **Johor Bahru** ❿ is probably its immigration point leading to Singapore. Besides the Causeway, Johor also has a less crowded 2km (1-mile) second link to the island nation at Tanjung Kupang as well as ferry connections at Tanjung Belungkor near Desaru (see page 233).

Downtown JB (as the city is known) is booming with new air-conditioned shopping malls and high-rise buildings. Remnants of Old Johor can be found behind **Jalan Ibrahim** in old shophouses where Chinese and Indian traders sell everything from spices and joss sticks to tailored suits and the latest colour TVs. Scattered among the shops are cheap Chinese restaurants and Indian cafés specialising in the popular South Indian banana-leaf rice and *roti canai* (Indian bread).

The State Secretariat Building, **Bangunan Sultan Ibrahim** crowns the top of Bukit Timbalan. A huge Saracen-style building with arches, columns and enclosed stone balconies, it bears a gold seal of the State of Johor on its massive front doors.

The impressive building further down the waterfront and overlooking the Johor Straits is the **Grand Palace** (Istana Besar). Formerly the residence of Sultan Abu Bakar, the stark, white structure with sweeping lawns was commissioned in 1864. It has, over the last century, hosted royalty such as the first Duke of Edinburgh (Queen

Victoria's son), Archduke Franz Ferdinand of Austria (whose assassination sparked World War I) and King Edward VIII of England.

Although it remains in royal hands, the palace was opened to the public in 1991 as a museum dedicated to the golden age of Johor. The **Royal Abu Bakar Museum** (tel: 07-233 0555; Sat–Thu 10am–5pm; charge) is rather reminiscent of visiting the aristocratic homes of rural England, and there is no other museum in Southeast Asia quite like it.

The audience hall (*dewan*) is now a gallery detailing the history of the Johor sultanate, while the Grand Palace itself is crammed with antiques and strange knick-knacks. The four-poster teak beds in the state bedrooms have British-made Corinthian-style columns dating to the 1860s. The bedrooms are still used for the lying-in-state of deceased members of the royal family. Down the hall is the opulent Reception Room, with a Baccarat crystal table and chairs. The Throne Room, with its matching gilt thrones, is used each

year for investiture ceremonies on the sultan's birthday. The opulence of the Banqueting Room has to be seen to be believed.

The surrounding **Istana Gardens** have rolling parkland, immaculate lawns and several flower gardens, while just uphill from the Dewan is a Japanese garden and teahouse presented by Crown Prince Hirohito on his state visit to Malaysia in 1936. Within the grounds' handicraft centre sits Mawar House, a carefully restored traditional Johor Malay house.

The next landmark along the waterfront is the **Sultan Abu Bakar Mosque** (Masjid Sultan Abu Bakar; daily for Muslims only; free), completed in 1900. A bizarre blend of Italian rococo, classical Greek and traditional Muslim styles, the interior is decorated with Corinthian columns, crystal chandeliers and oriental carpets. At the front of the main hall are a fabulously ornate gilt *minbar* (pulpit) and an ancient grandfather clock. Hawkers frequent the mosque grounds selling prayer rugs, velour wall hangings and other souvenirs.

Durian farm signage.

Busy streets after dark downtown in Johor Bahru.

JOHOR BAHRU AT NIGHT

Johor Bahru nightlife draws many customers from Singapore, attracted by cheaper drinks and a relatively more liberal atmosphere, although the JB town council attempts to crack down on less salubrious spots from time to time. Still, the city has numerous nightclubs, bars and karaoke lounges. The main nightlife is at the ZON Johor Bahru, an integrated hotel, duty-free shopping, dining and ferry terminal (serving Indonesia's Batam and Bintan Islands) complex at Stulang Laut on Jalan Ibrahim Sultan. Only 10 minutes from the Singapore Causeway, Singaporean clubbers can get their fill of hip-hop, reggae, R&B, house or popular music. Most clubs have their own resident DJs, special themed nights and free cocktails for ladies, usually on a weeknight.

An Indian woman tailor in Johor Bahru.

Much further along the waterfront is **Bukit Serene Palace** (Istana Bukit Serene), home of the present ruler. The huge Art Deco-style complex is off limits to the public, but you can get a good view of the palace from Jalan Sekudai along the waterfront or Jalan Straits View. Its expansive grounds contain a private airstrip, a huge satellite dish, an orchid garden and a menagerie.

Pasir Gudang

Head east to **Pasir Gudang**  town to see the **Layang-Layang Museum** (Muzium Layang-Layang; tel: 07-251 3720; Mon and Thu 9am–5pm, Tue, Wed, Sat, Sun 8am–5pm, Fri 9am–5pm, closed for lunch Sat–Thu 1pm–2pm and Fri 12.30pm–2.45pm; charge) which showcases over 200 international and local kites, and has a workshop that teaches you how to make wau, the traditional Malay kite. If you are here during the annual World Kite Festival in February, you can see the sky above Pasir Gudang decorated with amazing-looking kites of all shapes and sizes.

Young men sport-fishing.

Kota Tinggi

Johor has the largest number of golf courses in the country. The best known include the 18-hole Royal Johor Country Club, Desaru Golf & Country Resort and Sofitel Palm Resort's Golf and Country Club, near Senai Airport.

Many of these golf and country resorts are also in the **Kota Tinggi** ⓬ area. Kota Tinggi is a small, quiet town with a loud splash. About 15km (9 miles) northeast of the town are its famous waterfalls (charge), the bottom-most section of which thunders down 36 metres (118ft) to the polished rocks below. The entire area is cemented and steps lead up to the third and highest tier. Weekends find the large natural pools and surrounding tree-rooted slopes commandeered by the locals. Chalet-type accommodation and Malay hawker food is available. North of Kota Tinggi town, about 10km (6 miles) away is the **Panti Bird Sanctuary** (off Jalan Jemaluang; tel: 07-224 3048; www.malaysiabirding.org; daily 7am–6pm; permit charge). Famous for birds (over 250 species) and wild orchids, there are several trails that lead into a variety of habitats – from lowland dipterocarp to hill and montane forests, and peat swamps. Along the popular Bunker Trail you might be able to spot babblers, pigeons, kingfishers, bulbuls, woodpeckers and hornbills. World War II bunkers on both sides of the former logging road mark the trail's entrance. Being only a two-hour drive from downtown Singapore, the sanctuary is well liked by Singaporean birdwatchers. All visitors have to register with Johor Parks.

Desaru

From Kota Tinggi, a trunk road goes south through fruit stalls and golf resorts to the golden beaches of **Desaru** ⓭, which is practically a Singapore resort. Numerous buses ply the Desaru route from the Larkin Transport Bus and Taxi Terminal Complex north of Johor Bahru city (enquire at Johor Tourism Malaysia, tel: 07-222

3590/1). Many Singaporean visitors travel via the 35-minute ferry ride between Tanjung Belungkor, 60km (37 miles) from Desaru, and Changi Ferry Terminal in Singapore. Enquire about services at Changi Ferry Terminal, (tel: 65- 6535 8696). The big hotels at Desaru provide transfers to the ferry terminal for a fee.

There is a good variety of accommodation, from hotels to golf resorts and camping grounds, all sandwiched between the beach and forest. Resorts provide the gamut of activities from water sports to mountain biking and racket games. A go-kart circuit in Desaru attracts the young, and the **Desaru Fruit Farm** (tel: 07-822 3886; www.desarufruitfarm.com; daily 8am–6pm) in Sungai Cemaran, which has 100 species of fruits and an apiary, is worth a visit.

And after the crowds disappear from December to early February, during the height of the monsoon season, local and international surfers come out to ride the high waves. The annual Monsoon Mayhem Surf Challenge takes place here every January, when angry waves 1–1.2 metres (3–4ft) high pound the beach. Look out for a surf outfit along the beach that rents boards by the hour and provides surf lessons for a fee.

Old Johor

There are also interesting side trips from Desaru. About half an hour away on the Kota Tinggi road is a turn-off that goes through an oil-palm plantation to **Johor Lama** (Old Johor) on Sungai Johor. Once a great trading centre and royal capital, Johor Lama is today a sleepy village, and its only attraction is the **Kota Johor Lama Historical Complex** (Kampung Johor Lama; www.jmm.gov.my/en/kota-johor-lama-historical-complex; daily 9am–4.30pm; free), with grassed-over massive ramparts, the remains of its old fort. About 10km (6 miles) from Desaru is **Sungai Lebam**, where visitors come for the star attraction – a nightly live show of hundreds of fireflies lighting up the *berembang* trees that they live and feed on. It's best to come when there's no full moon. Charter a boat from Bujang

On Desaru beach.

FACT

Almost every Malaysian state has its own official wau. *"Wau"* means the Malay kite. While some consider it came from the Thai word for kite, others believe it is the sound the kite makes when in flight: *"wau, wau, wau"*.

Houses raised on stilts in a fishing village.

Boat Service at tel: 019-779 6385 for a 30-minute trip downriver (charge).

Southeast Johor

Tanjung Balau, 5km (3 miles) from Desaru, has an excellent fishing museum (tel: 07-222 3590; 9am–5pm; charge), which charts the industry's history, traditions and methods, and includes displays of traditional boats. The museum fronts a white sandy beach and chalet-type accommodation. Seafood buffs should check out the excellent Chinese-style delicacies at the fishing village of **Sungai Rengit**, 25km (16 miles) south.

Endau-Rompin National Park

The road from Ayer Hitam to Mersing cuts across the state's rainforest heart, 20,000 hectares (49,000 acres) of which are the Johor section of the **Endau-Rompin National Park** (Taman Negara Endau-Rompin) **14**. Named after the Endau and Rompin rivers, the park forms the southern end of the peninsula's wildlife corridor that stretches through Taman Negara up to Belum on the Thai border.

A conservation area developed by the Johor National Park Corporation in consultation with the Malaysian Nature Society (MNS), this ancient virgin lowland forest has extensive palm species, pebbly beaches and large rivers of amazing clarity, whose headwaters plunge into waterfalls. There are four campsites within the park, and chalets and dormitories at the park headquarters. Note that the park is closed during the rainy season from November to March.

There are three entrances into the park: two from within Johor state at Kampung Peta (Kahang is the nearest town) and at Selai (nearest village is Kampung Kemidak). The third entry point is from the Pahang *side*. Enquire at the Johor National Parks Corporation office (tel: 07-266 1301) if you wish to arrange for your own entry permits, park fees, guides and boat transfers. The Malaysia Tourism Promotion Board (2 Jalan Air Molek, Johor Bahru; tel: 07-222 3591; Mon–Fri 8am–5.30pm) has comprehensive information on the park. Travel agencies in Johor Bahru, Kuantan and Kuala Lumpur run tours there as well.

The largest base camp is **Kuala Jasin**, 7km (4 miles) away, accessible on foot or by boat. Sited at the Jasin-Endau river confluence, it has great swimming areas, including an 8,000-sq metre (78,000-sq ft) pool. There are hornbills at dawn, and you can observe deer and monkeys from a hide.

The **Janing Ridge** trek can be accessed from Kuala Jasin: a steep climb to an amazing palm forest. The trail goes all the way to the park's star attraction, the Buaya Sangkut waterfalls, and is a six-hour, 8km (5-mile) trek. The first part treks through riparian (river) vegetation, with some waist-deep rope-aided river-crossings, but the later stages involve steep stretches. Most people camp at Batu Hampar, tackling Buaya Sangkut the next morning.

En route to Batu Hampar are two base camps, Kuala Marong and Upeh Guling. **Kuala Marong** overlooks the still, clear Sungai Marong, whose waters were at one time the purest of any river studied in Malaysia. A side trail goes to the **Blue Lagoon** (Tasik Air Biru), a deep, shady pool that makes for a refreshing swim.

The falls at the **Upeh Guling** base camp has remarkable "bath-tub" formations at the top of rocks, probably formed when pebbles lodged in crevices were spun round by flowing water. There is also a tiny island here, Pulau Jasin, which enjoys a remarkable diversity of plants, including wild orchids and four species of the carnivorous pitcher plant.

Batu Hampar also has playful cascades and huge sun-baked boulders. From here, a steep ascent kicks off the section to Buaya Sangkut, and the undulating trail goes through changing vegetation, including the peaty *kerangas* forest, usually found only in lowlands. The umbrella palms, whose leaves reach 4 metres (12ft) in length, just get bigger and bigger. The leaves function as roofs for the huts at Batu Hampar, fashioned using Orang Asli techniques. Incidentally, the umbrella palm leaf really does work as an umbrella in a downpour!

There is an alternative trail that climbs the final hill – this is actually part of Janing Ridge, and therefore covered by thick palm forest, mainly the indigenous *Livistona endauensis* fan palms.

Buaya Sangkut Falls

At the 40-metre (130ft) **Buaya Sangkut Falls**, seemingly static pools of water tumble down into rugged boulders, the most spectacular being the lowest of the three-step falls. The falls, first sighted on a helicopter reconnaissance of the park, has a charming Orang Asli legend to it, as do many of the sights. Translating as "stuck crocodile", the reptile in question was a mythical albino that had died in battle with a snake, and whose carcass got caught in the falls. The battle was over the hand of a lass of immense beauty, whose father made a drum of the croc's skin. Unfortunately, he hung it over his daughter's bed, and one night, it fell and killed her. Some say the rocks at a certain point at the waterfall's top-most level bear a striking resemblance to a crocodile.

FACT

Endau-Rompin National Park in Johor is home to 71 palm species, which comprises 18 percent of Malaysia's palms – all indigenous – and more than 50 percent of its rattan varieties.

An umbrella palm in Endau-Rompin National Park.

A Marang fishing boat.

Palm trees reflected in Lake Kenyir.

THE PENINSULA'S EAST COAST

A world away from its brash western brother, the rural east coast is picture-postcard Malaysia: traditional and unhurried. Those in search of holiday activity will find superb diving sites, lakes and hiking trails.

Fish at Mersing's morning wet market.

I f ever a mountain divided a land, the peninsula's Main Range (Banjaran Titiwangsa) does, isolating the east coast from the progressive west coast. As such, it has retained its rich cultural identity through the ages, despite the ravages of satellite TV. And while it remains economically less advanced, it is also relatively buffered from west coast financial and environmental woes.

Embracing the states of Kelantan, Terengganu and Pahang, and the eastern half of Johor, the east coast is the Islamic heartland of Malaysia, particularly in the staunchly Muslim north. But it is as indisputably Malay as it is proudly rural. Local dress dominates, especially among the women who are like colourful butterflies in their batik *tudung* (head-scarfs) and *baju kurung* (Malay dress). Local dialects reign, so that even west coast speakers of Bahasa Malaysia find it difficult to follow a conversation.

The coastal road.

The economy remains rooted in fishing and rice cultivation, as it has been for generations. Terengganu boat builders are famous for their handmade vessels. The fishing industry is celebrated in various museums, themselves fine examples of Malay architecture.

The coastline is a continuous broad beach. Here, turtles come ashore to lay their eggs. The most pristine beaches of tropical paradise ilk are found on the islands where shallow waters are the clearest in the peninsular. Underwater, the colourful landscapes are fascinating, and the diversity of life staggering. The east coast islands make up the majority of Malaysia's 40 marine parks, which protect fragile and important habitats.

In the rainforest interiors of the east coast, natural attractions abound at Taman Negara. Gazetted in 1932, it is the oldest national park in Malaysia, while further north, Lake Kenyir is a freshwater fish haven for anglers, and in the far south, at the freshwater wetland of Bera, the indigenous Orang Asli still maintain their lifestyles closely intertwined with the ways of the land.

MERSING AND ISLES

With long sandy beaches, unpretentious resorts, crystal-clear waters and beautiful coral reefs, these South China Sea islands achieve the difficult feat of being both popular and unspoilt.

I n the northeastern corner of Johor lies Mersing, a small fishing village whose role is clearly as a gateway for arriving holidaymakers. Well before dawn, local food stalls are already open for business around the bus terminal, beside the jetty. Customers are sleepy-eyed passengers who have just been dropped off by overnight buses from all corners of Malaysia. Further south at the Tanjung Leman jetty, the scene is not much different. Beside buses and taxis, vans pre-arranged by the resorts ferry their guests to the jetty from Johor Bahru or Singapore, and private cars unload fishing rods, tackle and cooler boxes. Several hours later after a bumpy boat or slow ferry ride, you are in an entirely different, quieter world. Idyllic beaches fringed by swaying coconut palm trees, coral reefs in a myriad of colours and, for the avid anglers, a platform shelter in the middle of the deep blue sea.

All the islands are protected marine parks, which usually means appreciating the marine life and coral reefs without touching or collecting them. Visitors are not always aware of this, and some boatmen flout regulations. But with so many islands, it's understandable that enforcement is lacking in some areas. At the Tioman Airport, dead coral has been discovered before in suitcases during baggage scans; these are confiscated and the tourists

let off with a warning, but the damage has already been done.

Of all the islands, Tioman has perhaps been the most affected by development. The plans to extend the airport runway to accommodate wider-bodied jets met with alarming opposition from nature-lovers on the island, and although it was shelved, the construction of the marina went ahead. The once beautiful house reef off the shores of Tekek is now smothered by sedimentation as a result of the marina's construction. Despite this

Main Attractions

Pulau Tioman
Pulau Aur
Pulau Pemanggil
Pulau Sibu Besar

A prize catch at Mersing's fish market.

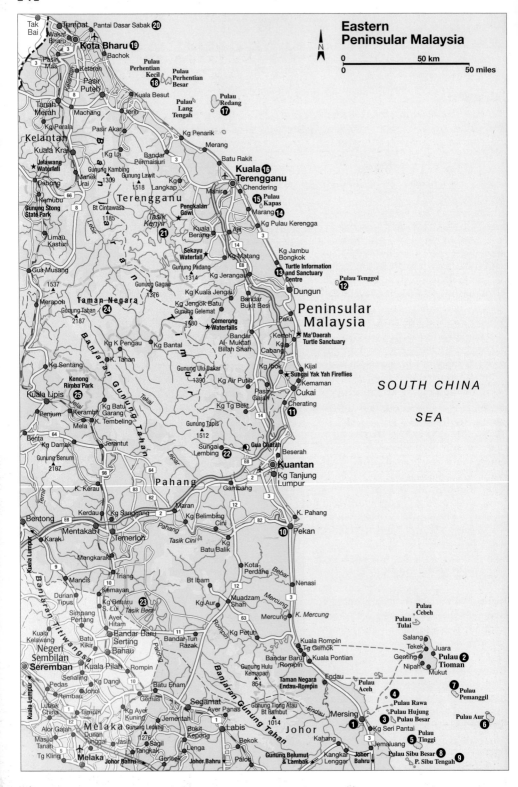

Eastern Peninsular Malaysia

0   50 km
0   50 miles

Tak Bai
Tumpat
Pantai Dasar Sabak 20
Wakaf Bharu
Kota Bharu 19
Bachok
Pasir Mas
Sri Ketereh
Pulau Perhentian Kecil 18
Pulau Perhentian Besar
Pasir Puteh
Kuala Besut
Pulau Lang Tengah
Tanah Merah
Machang
Jerih
Pulau Redang 17
Kg Perala
Pasir Akar
Merang
Kelantan
Kg Penarik
Kuala Krai
Kg La
Batu Rakit
Jelawang Waterfall
Gunung Kambing
Bandar Permaisuri
Kuala Terengganu 16
Manek Urai
Gunung Lawit
Kg Langkap
Chendering
1309
Manir
Pulau Kapas 15
Dabong
1518
Terengganu
Pengkalan Gawi
Marang 14
Kemubu
Bt Cintawasa
Kuala Berang
Kg Pulau Kerengga
66
Gunung Stong State Park
8
1185
Aji
Kuala Kenyir 21
14
Sekayu Waterfall
Kg Matang
Kg Jambu Bongkok
Limau Kasturi
Gunung Padang
Turtle Information and Sanctuary Centre 13
Gua Musang
1314
Kg Jeranga
Pulau Tenggol 12
1537
Gunung Gagau
Kg Kuala Jengai
Dungun
Merapoh
Taman Negara 24
1376
Kg Jengok Batu
Gunung Gelemat
Bandar Bukit Besi
Peninsular Malaysia
Gunung Tahan
2187
1480
Cemerong Waterfalls
Paka
Kg K Pengau
Kg Bantal
Bandar Al-Muktafi Billah Shah
Ma'Daerah Turtle Sanctuary
Kenteh
Kg Sentang
K. Tahan
Kg Cabang
Kg Ibok
Kijal
Kenong Rimba Park
Gunung Ulu Bakar
Kg Air Putih
Sungai Yak Yah Fireflies
1390
Kemaman
Kuala Lipis 25
Kg Batu Garang
Pasir Gajah
Cukai
Penjum
Kerambit
Kg Tg Belit
Cherating
Mela
K. Tembeling
Gunung Tapis
11
Benta
Kg Damak
1512
Sungai Lembing 22
Gua Charah
Beserah
Gunung Benum
2107
Jerantut
14
Kuantan
K. Kerau
98
84
E8
Kg Tanjung Lumpur
Pahang
Gambang
Kerdau
Kg Sanggang
Maran
12
K. Pahang
Bentong
62
Belimbing
82
Mentakab
Temerloh
Kg Cini
Pekan 10
Karak
Pahang
Kota Perdana
Bebar
Mengkarak
Tasik Cini
Kg Batu Balik
9
Triang
Bt Ibam
Nenasi
Mancis
Kemayan
12
Durian Tipus
Kg Baharu
Tasik Bera 23
Muadzam Shah
Mercung
Kuala Kelawang
Ayer Hitam
Kg Aur
63
K. Mercung
Simpang Pertang
Batu Kikir
Bandar Baru Serting
Kg Petuh
Pulau Tulai
Pulau Cebeh
Negeri Sembilan
Bahau
Bandar Tun Razak
Kuala Rompin
Salang
Tekek
Juara
Seremban
Kuala Pilah
Rompin
Bandar Baru Rompin
Tg Gemok
Kuala Pontian
Genting
Pulau Tioman 2
Pedas
Kg Dangi
Gunung Hulu Kemapan
854
Nipah
Mukut
Senaling
Batu Enam
Taman Negara Endau-Rompin
Endau
Pulau Aceh
Pulau Pemanggil 7
Rembau
Johol
Gemas
Segamat
Gunung Tiong Atau Bt Bambut
4
Pulau Rawa
Lubok China
Tampin
Ayer Panas
Jementah
1014
Pulau Hujung
Pulau Besar
Pulau Aur 6
Alor Gajah
Gunung Ledang
Bukit Kepong
Labis
Mersing 1
Pulau Seri Pantai 3
Masjid Tanah
Durian Tunggal
1276
Sagil
Lenga
Bekok
Kahang
Jemaluang
Pulau Tinggi 5
Melaka
Tangkak
Gerisek
Johor Bahru
Paloh
Gunung Belumut & Lambak
Kangkar Lenggor
Johor Bahru
Pulau Sibu Besar 8
Tg Kling
Johor Bahru
Johor
P. Sibu Tengah 9

SOUTH CHINA SEA

setback, there are still other coral reefs and World War II shipwrecks worth diving to see.

Mersing

Whoever planned **Mersing ❶** knew how to make the most of its views. Seen from the coast-hugging roads of this bustling fishing and jump-off port, postcard vistas of offshore island silhouettes have brought it considerable fame.

You need a car to enjoy the winding evening drives to **Kampung Sri Lalang** en route to Endau north of town (turn right just after the bridge), and through **Teluk Iskandar** on the Sekakap road (turn right at Jalan Nong Yahya opposite the hospital). There are no beaches for swimming, but lookout points and hotel rooms facing the sea almost make up for it.

Because of its proximity to the area, Mersing is becoming a reference point for tours to the Endau-Rompin National Park (see page 234). More accessible and popular with locals are the recreational forests of **Mount Belumut** and **Mount Lambak**, inland from Mersing along Route 50. The former rises up to 1,004 metres (3,290ft) and it takes about four hours along dense jungle tracks to reach the peak. At the base are some small waterfalls, which are easily accessible by families. Mount Lambak is an easier climb up to 510 metres (1,670ft) using trails of footpaths and wooden bridges. It also has pretty cascades.

However, the South China Sea islands are the prime objective of the madding crowd. Over 60 volcanic isles in crystal-clear waters make up the Johor group, six of which have tourist facilities. The Mersing jetty is also an established springboard to the popular Pahang island of Tioman. These islands are protected by their marine park status and are home to prolific and diverse marine life, much of which is endemic to the area. Some of these islands are closed during the monsoon months from November to February. The Marine Park conservation fee can be paid at the park's counter at the jetty. Boats leaving for the islands are tide dependent, so either contact your accommodation for estimated

A hornbill in Mersing.

Catching the ferry to Pulau Tioman from Mersing.

Jungle waterfalls around Mount Lambak.

A paradise beach setting on Pulau Tioman.

time schedules and arrive an hour or so earlier or the Mersing Tourist Information Centre (tel: 07-799 5212; Mon–Thu 8am–1pm and 2-4.30pm, Fri 8am–noon and 2.45-4.30pm, Sat 8am–12.45pm) for assistance.

Pulau Tioman

The largest of these islands, **Pulau Tioman ❷**, is popularly believed to be named after the *burung tiong* or mynah bird. Legend says that the island was created when a dragon, which emerged from Lake Cini inland, froze into rock while waiting interminably for its mate.

There is a mention of Tioman before AD 1000, in what was perhaps the first guide to Malaysia. Arab traders of the time noted in their "sailing directions" that Tioman offered good anchorage and freshwater springs. Much later, the island's twin southern peaks at Mukut (called "Ass's Ears") were a guide to Chinese traders between the 12th and 17th centuries, as evidenced by shards of Ming and other pottery found on the beaches and in nearby caves. It is widely believed that the waters around

this crucial trading pit stop harbour many more sunken treasures in the forgotten holds of unknown wrecks.

Beaches of Tioman

Tioman has been awarded duty-free status in an effort to attract Langkawi-like success, particularly with Singaporeans. At the moment, this translates mainly to the availability of cheap beer. Today, Tioman's beaches continue to attract tropical isle fans, and divers and snorkellers who have come to revel in the marine park's underwater life. The main beaches fringe the west coast, and all are lined with small chalet-type accommodation run by local Malay families.

The tiny town "centre" is at **Tekek**, where you'll also find the jetty, airstrip and shops. The long beach, shaded by casuarina and coconut trees, is fronted with chalets and restaurants. Further inland on the other side of the road are *kampung*-style chalets. Despite the development, during the low season Tekek feels pretty much like the *kampung* it always was. North of Tekek are the smaller beaches of **Air**

ISLAND LOGISTICS

Getting to the isles off Johor's eastern shores is possible by ferry. There are two main jetties – Mersing services Pahang's Pulau Tioman and Johor's Pulau Besar and Pulau Rawa, while south of Mersing, at Tanjung Leman, boats depart for Pulau Tinggi, Pulau Sibu, Sibu Besar and Sibu Tengah.

You can get to Pulau Tioman either by a two-hour ferry (tel: 65-900 79345; www.tiomanferry.com) or a more expensive one-hour flight from Kuala Lumpur's Subang Airport. The island is served by only one airline – Berjaya Air (www.berjaya-air.com), which also flies from Singapore's Changi Airport (Budget Terminal). There is another ferry to Tioman, but leaving from Pahang's Tanjung Gemok jetty north of Mersing.

Most, if not all, island accommodation will include travel in your package, ask which jetty and boatman when you get to the respective jetties. Try to book both accommodation and transfer beforehand.

Nine big boat operators servicing all islands belong to the Persatuan Bot-bot Sewa Pelancong Daerah Mersing, or Mersing Boat Hire Association (tel: 07-799 1222; 8am–4.30pm). Located at the jetty, they can also arrange accommodation at all the islands.

For more information, contact the Mersing Tourist Information Centre (METIC) on tel: 07-799 5212 (Mon–Thu 8am–1pm and 2–4.30pm, Fri 8am–12pm and 2.45–4.30pm, Sat 8am–12.45pm).

Batang (better known as ABC after the original chalet operation there) and **Salang**, which also have some interesting mangrove areas.

South of Tekek are **Nipah**, a quiet chalet-only stretch, and **Mukut**, way down south at the base of the Twin Peaks, whose view of the wide expanse of blue ocean is obscured by neither islands nor passing ships. Mukut also has lots of fresh springs and a couple of waterfalls, the precious water for which the ancient mariners must have been thankful. Two other stretches on the west coast are not so pretty: Genting, which sits on rocks, and Paya, which has no beach to speak of, although both have plenty of accommodation.

Juara is the sole beach on the east coast, a long white stretch with relatively little tree cover, great for sun seekers but it has no coral reefs at all. This is more of a backpackers' stretch, and can be reached from the west coast by sea bus (two-hour journey), by road from Tekek or by a jungle trail that starts at the jetty.

The two- to three-hour jungle trek across the island emerges next to the airport at Tekek, from which point you can take a sea bus back. The trail is paved in some stretches, steep in others, and climbs into thick, lush forest. Another trail goes from Tekek to Batang Air and Salang.

Tioman dive sites

Tioman has large coral reefs on the west coast, most of which are close to shore. A feature of its marine life is its giant sea fans, particularly at the top dive spot of **Pulau Tulai** or Coral Island, whose shallow waters are also popular with snorkellers. **Pulau Cebeh** provides for some fine swim-throughs, and there is cave diving just off the island, while at the cliff-like rocks of Golden Reef are pretty, submerged coral gardens. **Pulau Renggis**, opposite the airport, is an accessible site with an occasional slight drift. **Pulau Jahat** is a good site south of Mukut. It is common to spot hawksbill turtles in the waters too, as well as groups of spiny lionfish. Walk-ins and packages are available at the dive shops on the west coast beaches, as is full equipment

TIP

Kampung Mukut and Nipah are not scheduled stops on the Mersing–Tioman ferry. Notify the ferry staff in advance so they can drop you off at your destination.

Snorkelling in the crystal-clear waters.

rental. Instruction is offered too, and if you wish to explore World War II shipwrecks, technical diving is also available. The two famous wrecks – the **HMS** *Prince of Wales* and **HMS** *Repulse* – are in very deep waters at least 227 metres (745ft) below. In Tioman waters, there are also Dutch submarines, a British minesweeper, a Swedish supertanker and an unidentified tanker at Pulau Aur. The best time to wreck-dive is from late February to early June and from September until November.

The 55km (35 miles) to Tioman can be covered in an hour by scheduled ferry from Mersing (try to get there in the morning), or Tanjung Gemok near Kuala Rompin in Pahang. Boats service Genting, Tekek, ABC and Salang. All boats back to the mainland depart Tioman from 7.30am, again depending on the tides. An even quicker way to get to Tioman – with some spectacular scenery thrown in – is on board Berjaya Air (www.berjaya-air.com), which flies out from Kuala Lumpur's Subang Airport and Singapore's Changi Airport (Budget Terminal).

Pulau Tioman is one of the best diving spots in Malaysia.

Islands of Johor

Johor's islands south of Tioman are also covered in jungle and have some good reefs; the islands are particularly popular with Singaporeans. All tour agencies offer the same three-day/two-night package regardless of destination island: this comprises transfers, accommodation, tours (including snorkelling) and all meals, including a barbecue. An all-day island-hopping trip in a 10- to 12-seater boat can also be arranged. This covers a few of the nearest islands and hire of snorkelling gear, but you usually have to bring your own lunch.

The closest isle to the mainland, and the largest, is **Pulau Besar ❸**, one hour away. Pulau Besar is one of a trio of islands, including **Pulau Tengah** (a former refugee camp for Vietnamese boat people) and **Pulau Hujung**, which are popular with day-trippers. However, Pulau Besar is the only one with accommodation, which comprises mainly basic chalet operations and resorts. There is also a dive facility here. Trails from the sandy beaches lead to small plantations and wooden *kampung*.

About the same distance from Mersing is the tiny **Pulau Rawa ❹**. Rawa is privately owned by the Johor royalty and has only two resorts. It has dive facilities but no dive master. The marine life is nothing to shout about, but most visitors don't mind. They go there simply to enjoy its lovely beach (also on the island-hopping tour list) and do nothing. For the energetic, there is windsurfing, snorkelling, canoeing and fishing available.

Pulau Tinggi ❺, a 40-minute trip from the mainland, has a towering jungled peak, hence its name (*tinggi* means "high"). Like Tioman's mountains, this 650-metre (2,100ft) giant was used as a navigational marker by Chinese mariners, and is mentioned in their literature as the "general's hat island". There are lots of accommodation choices here, mainly budget chalets. Two islets nearby have some marine reefs.

Much further away are **Pulau Aur ❻** (three to four hours) and **Pulau**

Pemanggil **7** (four to five hours). Transport here is by chartered boat only, and is arranged through the respective resorts. Despite the distance, the islands are very popular, particularly for fishing and diving. Accommodation is plentiful but basic, and takes the form of longhouses and dormitories with common bathrooms. The best beach at Aur is actually on a neighbouring islet, Pulau Dayang, which has a dramatic granite rock face looming over the sole resort, **Dayang Island Resort**. Sea fans characterise its reefs, and experienced divers can explore a World War II Japanese wreck another an hour and a half east. The main island is hilly and good for trekking. Secluded Pemanggil has turquoise lagoons and offshore pools, and great shallow waters for snorkelling.

Sibu islands

Johor's southernmost pair of holiday islands is accessible from Tanjung Leman, a staging point on reclaimed land about two hours south of Mersing. The ferry takes half an hour to reach Pulau Sibu Besar and Pulau Sibu Tengah; speedboats do the journey in 20 minutes, but it's a bumpier trip. A Marine Park conservation fee is collected at the jetty before you board your boat.

Pulau Sibu Besar 8 has a longer history of tourism, and therefore has more accommodation. A large island, it also offers some good walks that weave through its small, forested hills. In the *kampung*, modern solar panels stand out among the traditional wooden houses – they are part of a government-subsidised power programme.

The smaller **Pulau Sibu Tengah 9** is being promoted as a one-island, one-resort destination, the same sales pitch as Rawa.

One option is to do an all-day island-hopping tour covering these islands from Tanjung Leman. Perched near the islands are also some *kelong*, traditional fishing huts on stilts sunk deep into the ocean floor, which are open to visitors and are popular among anglers. Food can be arranged, as well as other non-fishing activities like visiting the nearest island. Enquire at the Tanjung Leman staging point.

Pulau Aur caters primarily to scuba-divers.

Bangau boats on Bachok beach.

PAHANG, TERENGGANU AND KELANTAN

On the beaches of the peninsula's beautiful
east coast, sun-soakers and coral-lovers mingle
happily with the local folk whose families
have fished its waters for generations.

Map on page
242

The Malays say the pokok rhu or casuarina only grows near the sound of surf. So it is these trees that flourish along the peninsula's east coast, virtually one long surf-lapping beach running through four states. Between November and February, however, the rhu are lashed about mercilessly by angry winds which also whip up the seas – this is the monsoon season, where entire villages and even towns are inundated with water.

But this is the reality of life for generations of fishing folk who live on these beaches. Even the towns seem laid-back, and hold fast to age-old traditions both culturally – mainly Malay – and religiously – predominantly Islamic. Kelantan, however, being in closer proximity to Thailand, its customs, traditions, cuisine and even the spoken dialect, has Thai influences.

Life on the east coast

There is a long history of human settlement in the east coast region. Neolithic finds have been made in Sungai Pahang, while Kelantan's prehistoric finds were in interior caves. Pahang was also mentioned in Chinese texts as being a vassal of the 13th-century trading empire of Sri Vijaya, and Kelantan is thought to have been under its wing too.

Terengganu, meanwhile, was established as a cornerstone of Malay

settlement. A 14th-century Islamic inscription discovered there indicates Terengganu as one of the earliest places in the peninsula to embrace Islam, before even Melaka, whose colonisation of the east coast states only happened in the 15th century. Islam has retained its strongest hold here. The Thais, who ruled Kelantan and Terengganu before British intervention, have also left their mark in the local architecture, dialect and art forms.

The east coast is linked to the west by several main routes through the

Main Attractions

Cherating
Pulau Tenggol
Turtle Information and Sanctuary Centre
Pulau Duyong
Pulau Redang
Pulau Perhentian Kecil
Kota Bharu Central Market
Wat Photivihan
Gunung Stong State Park
Jelawang Waterfall

A craftswoman making a wau kite on Kota Bharu.

spectacular Main Range: the Karak Highway (Kuala Lumpur–Kuantan), the Gua Musang road (Kuala Lumpur–Kota Bharu) and the East–West Highway (Penang–Kota Bharu). Along the coast, Route 3 hugs the shore from Mersing all the way to Kota Bharu, a lovely drive interrupted occasionally by livestock and grinning children on bicycles. Go off the beaten track to a small fishing village, and a friendly gesture will be returned with a smile, or perhaps an invitation to tour the village, where the soothing rhythms of Malay life have endured for centuries.

Pahang

Kuala Rompin, near the Pahang-Johor state border, is a relatively untouched destination, mainly as a jumping-off point to the Pahang section of the **Endau-Rompin National Park** (see page 234; enquire at the **Pahang Tourist Information Centre**; tel: 09-516 1007), and to Pulau Tioman from the Tanjung Gemok jetty down south. Some travel agencies offer a four-wheel-drive tour to Jakun (Orang Asli) settlements inland

Bangau boats at Bachok beach.

at Iban (10km/6 miles) and Kampung Aur (25km/15 miles).

Pekan

At the mouth of the massive Sungai Pahang is the Pahang royal town of **Pekan ⑩**, the former state capital. The **Abu Bakar Palace** (Istana Abu Bakar) has an enormous polo ground which doubles as what must be the flattest golf course in the world. On 24 October each year, the town is injected with festivities for the sultan's birthday celebrations.

The **Sultan Abu Bakar Museum** (tel: 09-422 1371; Tue–Thu, Sat–Sun 9am–12.15pm and 2.45–5pm; charge) has excellent displays on old Pahang, royal family memorabilia, and ancient Chinese glassware and ceramics. Nearby are a mausoleum and two handsome, white-marble mosques with a riot of golden domes. About 5km (3 miles) from town is a silk-weaving centre at the Pulau Keladi Cultural Village (tel: 09-422 1371/8427; Mon–Sat 9am–5pm; free). Nearby in Pulau Keladi is the birthplace of one of Malaysia's famous sons – former prime minister Tun Abdul Razak, and his restored house-turned-museum can also be visited (Tue–Sun 9am–5.30pm; free).

Kuantan

Kuantan, the Pahang state capital, 44km (27 miles) north of Pekan, is not very interesting but it does have an excellent **Tourist Information Centre** (tel: 09-517 1623; www.pahang tourism.org.my; Mon–Fri 8am–5pm; closed Fri 12.15pm–2.45pm and public holidays) opposite the Kompleks Teruntum on Jalan Mahkota.

The town serves more as a springboard to inland attractions such as **Gua Charah** (30km/19 miles away), **Sungai Lembing** (45km/28 miles away) and the eight-cascade **Berkelah Waterfall** (70km/44 miles away). Most visitors prefer to stay at the pleasant **Teluk Chempedak** beach, 1km (0.6 mile) out of town, featuring the usual resort eateries, pubs, and both upmarket and budget accommodation.

An alternative is to opt for one of the many beach resorts just north of Kuantan in **Beserah**. Known for its dried salted fish, a handful of Beserah's denizens still employ tough, lumbering water buffaloes to transport fish from their boats on the beach to the processing areas.

Cherating

From the Pahang–Terengganu border, it's one long beach-resort stretch all the way up to Kota Bharu. About 35km (22 miles) from Beserah is the resort area of **Cherating** ⑪, a *kampung* (village) squeezed out of its gorgeous crescent-shaped golden beach by tourism.

Cherating was originally a backpackers' haunt, but the accommodation choices have gone upmarket. There are restaurants galore, souvenir shops (including DIY batik) and pubs; weekends can be one long party starting from Thursday, with the arrival of city folk. Somehow, though, the area has avoided the claustrophobic feel of

some other resort beaches, and maintains its friendly, relaxed air. Cherating is one of several surfing beaches in Malaysia. Although surfing is possible whenever there are strong winds, the best times are during the monsoon period where strong waves – 1–1.5-metre (3–5ft) swells – and high winds make conditions suitable for surfing. The Cherating Surf Festival takes place every December on these shores. Some resorts organise river trips and tours, and several travel agencies can also arrange transport to nearby islands as well as onward legs of your journey. Popular tours are to Gua Charah in Sungai Lembing (five-hour trip with a stopover in Kuantan). However, minimum numbers are required, so you could end up losing out playing the waiting game.

Near Club Med at Pantai Chendor, sea turtles lay their eggs at night from April through to September. The Fisheries Department runs the **Cherating Turtle Sanctuary & Information Centre** (tel: 09-581 9087; Tue–Sun 9am–noon and 3–5.30pm; free) next to the club, which is worth a visit.

TIP

If you are pressed for time, the inland Route 14 is the quicker link between Kuantan in Pahang state and Kuala Terengganu further north – but be forewarned that the drive is much less picturesque.

A Sata stall on the Kelantan coastal road.

Batik designs for sale.

Pulau Tenggol.

Terengganu

Cross into Terengganu and you hit oil country. The multimillion-ringgit oil and natural gas industry has changed the face of Terengganu's oil stretch beyond recognition. Villages now wear whitewashed brick faces, former fishermen and farmers sport imported overalls and hard hats, and grocery shops stock German beer, Edam cheese and Japanese seaweed to cater to the cosmopolitan mix of people who now calls Terengganu home. Terengganu contributes about 60 percent of Malaysia's total oil production, but 95 percent of revenues go to federal coffers. As such, fisheries remain the state's main income-earner.

The huge drilling rigs are 200km (125 miles) offshore in the South China Sea, but giant steel structures, snaking pipelines and bullying tankers dominate the scene from Kemaman to Paka. Before and after office hours, the traffic slows to a crawl in this stretch.

Sungai Yak Yah fireflies

About 25km (16 miles) north of Cherating is **Cukai**, a town famous for its seafood and coffee in Terengganu. Try the coffee at **Kedai Kopi Hai Ping** (see Eating Out, page 359). Cukai is also the base for an excursion to **Kampung Ibok**, 11km (7 miles) to the northwest, for a boat tour along the mangrove habitat of **Sungai Yak Yah** to see the largest firefly colony on the east coast (tel: 09-873 0540; daily tour from 7.45pm–midnight); enquire at the **Pahang Tourist Information Centre** (tel: 09-516 1007; Mon–Fri 8am–5pm; closed Fri 12.15–2.45pm and public holidays) or local tour operators. The best time to go is when there is no full moon.

Dungun and beyond

Terengganu is also known for its pretty beaches. A 240km (150-mile) long beach stretches from Kemaman to Besut; the beach at **Kijal** is particularly notable. At **Dungun** the messy industrial scenery falls away and dignified fishing villages and paddy fields reclaim the landscape. Dungun, a dreamy little seaside town and port, is a jumping-off point to **Pulau Tenggol** ⑫, a gazetted marine sanctuary

13km (8 miles) offshore. Actually a group of islands, this destination has clear waters for diving and 20 stunning spots that feature underwater cliffs and boulders. Its deep-dive profile attracts a good selection of pelagic (deep-water) marine life.

Inland from Kampung Pasir Raja are the majestic **Cemerong Waterfalls**, 305 metres (1,000ft) of white water thundering down a sheer rock face. To get there, you need three days through pitcher plant and palm country, across cascades and rapids. Guided tours can be arranged at Kuala Terengganu.

Turtle Sanctuary

Twenty-two kilometres (14 miles) north of Dungun is the **Turtle Information and Sanctuary Centre** ⓭ at Rantau Abang, a 13km (8-mile) stretch that used to be an important nesting ground for Malaysia's oldest marine creature – the sea turtle. Rantau Abang is one of the state's 12 protected landing sites for these lumbering reptiles. Female turtles of four species, including the 500kg (1,000lb) critically endangered leatherback, struggled ashore to lay their eggs at night between May and September every year. At the turn of the 21st century, the number of landings drastically plunged (see box). However, turtle conservation efforts by the Terengganu Fisheries Department, the private sector and non-governmental organisations have shown some results. A wealth of information on turtles, including some depressing statistics, is displayed at the Fisheries Department's small information centre (tel: 09-844 4169; Sun–Wed 8am–5pm, Thu 8am–3.30pm; free).

But all is not lost yet. South of Rantau Abang, between the towns of Kerteh and Paka, is a 1.6km (1-mile) beach where green turtles come to nest from April to September every year. Under the management of the Department of Fisheries, the **Ma' Daerah Turtle Sanctuary** (tel: 09-844 4169/830 5312) also has a hatchery, but since it is a restricted area, it is not opened to visitors except with written permission.

EAT

Cukai town in Terengganu boasts some of the best baked stuffed crab on the east coast – the restaurants are clustered on the main road facing the river.

At the Rantau Abang Turtle Sanctuary.

TURTLE WATCH

Malaysia's Fisheries Department has been collecting data on the giant leatherback since the 1960s, artificially hatching eggs and carrying out awareness programmes. Yet the largest of the four species is almost extinct: there were 1,800 landings in 1956, just 210 in 1994, and by the turn of the 21st century there were fewer than half a dozen sightings in a season. In 2011 there were no leatherback turtle landings, although there were a few the year before. The tiny olive ridley is endangered; the green and hawksbill turtles have also dwindled in numbers. Turtles are faced with many threats. Locally, the most obvious human threat is the eating of turtle eggs. Fisheries officers are fighting this by paying collectors for eggs, which they then hatch artificially. Turtle mortality due to fishing nets and propellers is also high. But the pollution that affects their habitat is the hardest to monitor – floating plastic bags resemble jellyfish, the favoured snack of turtles. Once partially consumed, the turtles slowly suffocate.

Conservation efforts by the Terengganu authorities and concerned groups have managed to reverse the trend, and there has been a gentle increase in the turtle population. In 2010, most landings comprised green turtles, followed by hawksbill, olive ridley and a small quantity of leatherbacks, bringing some hope for the survival of these graceful marine reptiles, which have existed since the age of the dinosaurs.

Marang fishermen working on their boats.

Do take note of the dos and don'ts of watching turtles. Lights and noise can scare off the females. Picking up hatchlings could tamper with the imprinting process which registers the nesting location; imprinting takes effect when they run from the beach to the sea. Shining lights at the hatchlings also distracts them – they are guided by the white breakers in the ocean. Distracting them also causes them to use up energy from the tiny yolk sack that they survive on for the three or four days it takes them to get to drift lines, out of reach of predators.

Marang and beyond

Just south of Kuala Terengganu is the district of Marang, dotted with picturesque villages. **Marang** ⓮ beach is an old favourite of backpackers, but there are also fancier establishments in the area. A cruise up the Marang river offers views of mangrove forest from whose banks peep monkeys, iguanas and sometimes otters.

From Marang, it is only 30 minutes and 15 minutes by boat respectively to **Pulau Kapas** ⓯ and **Pulau Gemia** for

Fishing boats beached in Marang harbour.

snorkelling and easy diving. En route to Kuala Terengganu, you will pass the **Tengku Tengah Zaharah Mosque** (Masjid Tengku Tengah Zaharah), also known as the floating mosque. Combining the modern and traditional, its serene white reflection gives an illusion of being afloat in the water.

Kuala Terengganu

Despite its affluence born of the state's plentiful sources of oil, enough of the old charms of **Kuala Terengganu** ⓰ remain to save it from facelessness. Possibly the east coast's oldest port, the pulse of the state capital is felt most keenly in the waterfront **Central Market** (Pasar Besar Kedai Payang) in the early morning. This is when fresh produce pours in: glistening fish by the lorry-load (the main fishing port is now in Chendering), while coconuts and *pandan* (screw pine) leaves arrive by boat from Pulau Duyong. Though less publicised than the much-photographed Central Market in Kota Bharu, this wet market is just as lively and colourful. Housed also in a concrete building, produce is sold

downstairs and in the courtyard while the handicraft shops fill the first floor. At the market's entrance, there are traditional trishaws to take you around town – still the most popular means of transport. Decide on a price before you get in.

This bustle spills out into Jalan Kampung Cina, a narrow and congested crescent-shaped street lined with Chinese shophouses. This is **Chinatown**, Kuala Terengganu's original thoroughfare, where the architecture dates back to when Terengganu was an independent state. Stroll down this street and peek into the narrow doorways – the houses seem to stretch back forever – and you might see an old lady sipping tea. The young and the trendy are moving in, though, mainly to open art and handicraft shops; this is also where many of the resort operators of **Pulau Redang** are located.

Just beyond the market in the direction of the river mouth is a broad esplanade that faces the **Maziah Palace** (Istana Maziah), the official residence of the sultan, who actually lives in another palace a few kilometres away. The Istana resembles a French country house and was built at the beginning of the century to replace an older palace destroyed by fire.

Across from the Central Market is **Pulau Duyong**, where master craftsmen once fashioned unique fishing boats with decorated fore- and main-masts, and bowsprits called *bedor*. Today, the island is famous for its handmade boats of local *cengal* wood and custom-made yachts for an international clientele, as well as for the annual Monsoon Cup match race in November. But rising raw material costs are threatening the livelihood of the remaining boat-makers. To watch the boat-builders in action, enquire with the Tourist Information Counter (tel: 09-626 2020; www.terengganutourism.com). Terengganu's beautiful traditional Malay architecture is represented in the grounds of the **Terengganu State Museum Complex** (tel: 09-622 14; daily 9am–5pm, closed Fri noon–3pm; charge). Malaysia's largest museum sits on the site of the town's first settlement,

TIP

Occasionally, the Senandung Wau (East Line) train from Sentral KL to Wakaf Bharu (the closest station to Kota Bharu) can be delayed by an hour, so allow more time if you are considering catching a flight from Kota Bharu or a boat transfer from Kuala Besut to the Perhentian islands.

Kota Bharu's Central Market.

and its main buildings are obscenely outsized replicas of the real thing, five well-preserved wooden houses with Islamic motifs and shades of Chinese and European architectural influence.

The excellent fisheries and seafaring open-air galleries showcase the gamut of boats, including two original hand-built wooden galleys used for trade in the 19th century. The museum is in Losong, which has charming kampung houses and is home to the famous Terengganu *keropok lekor*, a fishy cracker found only here and in Kelantan.

Like Kuantan, Kuala Terengganu has its own beach. **Pantai Batu Buruk** is a coconut tree-fringed sandy stretch with lots of eateries – try out the local *nasi dagang* breakfast if you can stomach rice and fish curry in the morning.

Chendering

Though village life in Terengganu has been urbanised, many of the traditional arts it fostered are as alive as ever. Seasonal fishing and farming brought village folk leisure, and from leisure came time to devote to their arts. Folk dances, shadow plays and traditional games such as kite-flying and top-spinning were celebrated during festivals after a harvest. Many processions and rituals were related to the spirit of the rice paddy, a carry-over from ancient animistic beliefs. Today, village festivals are rarer since farmers are busy planting rice twice a year instead of once, and the Islamic doctrine discourages customs connected with spirit worship.

Chendering, 8km (5 miles) south of town, houses some commercial handicraft centres, including the government-sponsored **Kraftangan Malaysia** craft centre (tel: 09-617 1033; Sun–Wed 8.30am–1pm, 2.30–5pm, Thu until 3pm), which has weaving demonstrations. Its showroom displays products from the surrounding villages.

Pulau Redang and Pulau Lang Tengah

Like jade in an ocean of clear blue, Terengganu's islands are the most beautiful in the peninsula, and worshipped by sun-soakers and coral-lovers.

Selling the day's catch at Bachok beach.

Merang, 28km (17 miles) north of Kuala Terengganu, is the jumping-off point to **Pulau Redang ⑰** and **Pulau Lang Tengah.** A range of accommodation is available on these islands, and virtually every one offers dive facilities. Visitors should book beforehand for packages with travel agents to ensure firm reservations for boat transfers, especially in the high season.

Lang Tengah is less crowded, good for easy diving and excellent snorkelling and only 30 minutes by boat from shore. Redang, two hours from shore, is famous for its great visibility and diverse dive sites, but has become very crowded. Comprising nine islands, it is also probably the peninsula's most researched island. A pleasant cross-island track through rainforest connects the pristine wide beaches of fine white sand at Pasir Panjang and Teluk Dalam. There is also a small traditional Malay fishing village on stilts where you can stop for *teh tarik* (tea) and local *kuih* (cakes).

However, diving is what has carved the island's fame. The Marine Park jetty alone has prolific marine life, including a resident moray eel. Night dives at the submerged reefs are particularly fascinating. There is also a high chance of bumping into a member or two of the large green turtle population. In situ hatching is being carried out here, as well as a research programme involving volunteers.

The Perhentian islands

Legend has it that two birds turned to stone and became the gorgeous **Pulau Perhentian Kecil ⑱** and **Pulau Perhentian Besar** isles, 21km (16 miles) from shore. *Kecil* and *besar* mean "small" and "large" respectively. The jetty is at Kuala Besut, an unspoilt fishing village where fishing boats make a dramatic show at dawn and dusk.

Accommodation at Kuala Besut is limited, but the jetty is well serviced by buses and taxis from any major town. Boats and accommodation can be booked with travel agencies at the jetty complex. Most resorts close during the monsoon season from November to February.

Perhentian Besar has a wider range of accommodation spread along the

A Malay kampung house.

Redang beach.

bay facing the smaller island. Accommodation with rock-bottom prices can still be found at Pasir Panjang on Perhentian Kecil, site of the first backpacker invasion, but don't expect much for that price. It has become really crowded here; the island's body-lined beach attests to its popularity. However, water remains a problem in the dry July/August period. To move between the two islands or to other resorts and beaches, you can board a boat taxi, which you can find in front of most resorts.

The diving here is more leisurely compared to Redang, and the shallower waters are good for snorkelling. Most of the resorts come with their own dive shop that can kit you out, each offering diving instruction. Gardens of soft coral – which grow to huge sizes – lots of shells, and large boulders make for an attractive underwater playground.

Kelantan

Coconut palms frame a house by the beach in Kelantan.

A few kilometres from the Thai border lies **Kota Bharu** ⑲, the cradle of Malay culture. Although it is ruled by the opposition fundamentalist Muslim Parti Islam, or PAS, Kelantan's capital is not corseted by the party's stringent policies but is, instead, vibrant with life and colour. Due to its close proximity to Thailand, the Kelantanese have a unique culture – a blend of Malay and Thai – very different from the Malays of Terengganu and Pahang. Intermarriages between Malay and Thais are not uncommon, and there is a small community of Thais living here.

Kota Bharu has one of the best-known wet markets in Malaysia. The **Central Market** (Pasar Besar Siti Khadijah; daily 6am–7pm) on Jalan Hulu is where traders – traditionally women – sit in their colourful headscarfs and traditional *baju kurung* on raised dais among vegetables and *keropok lekor (fish sausage)*. Upstairs is a shopping haven for east coast crafts, particularly batik and silverwork, and a good vantage point for photographers.

Just beyond the market is a cluster of museums around the old *istana*, **Balai Besar Palace**, which was

built in 1884. Next to it is the pretty **Muzium Adat Istiadat Istana Jahar** (tel: 09-748 2266; Sat–Thu 8.30am–4.45pm; charge), another palace that is now the museum of royal traditions and customs. Its displays are a good introduction to traditional Kelantan life and culture; it also has an excellent weapons section. The **Handicraft Village and Craft Museum** (Kampung Kraftangan; tel: 09-747 7554; Sat–Thu 8.30am–4.45pm; charge) on Jalan Hilir Balai is notable more for its traditional architecture than its contents, but nonetheless offers exhibits of batik, woodcarvings and other traditional Kelantanese crafts, as well as demonstrations by artisans. It is also famous for its traditional Kelantanese cuisine, which you can experience at the Restoran Nasi Ulam Cikgu beneath the craft museum. Owned by a former teacher (*cikgu*), it is open 11am–4pm daily except Friday. Nearby is the more modern **Istana Batu** or the Royal Museum (tel: 09-748 7737; Sat–Thu; 8.30am–4.45pm; charge), which houses memorabilia of Kelantan's royal family.

Kota Bharu's cultural pastimes are showcased at **Gelanggang Seni** (Jalan Mahmud; tel: 09-744 3124; Sat–Thu 10.30am–5.45pm; shadow play performances every Sat, Mon and Wed 3.30pm–5.30pm, Wed 9pm–11pm, closed during Ramadan; free), literally the "Court of Arts" but also known as the Cultural Centre. Check the latest schedules at the Tourism Malaysia office (tel: 09-747 7554; Sun–Wed 8.00am–5pm, Thu until 3.30pm) in Kampung Kraftangan. Unless you are lucky enough to chance upon festivals in Kota Bharu or its surrounding villages, this is the best place to view these art forms.

Wayang kulit siam (see box) and the Thai-influenced dance-theatre *mak yong*, two of the loveliest Malay art forms, were once banned from performance in the state because they are considered anti-Islam. Luckily, the *wayang kulit* troupes in Terengganu, Kedah and Perlis are alive and thriving. *Mak yong* and its sister art form *manohra* are now revived amid renewed interest.

Wat Photivihan

Kota Bharu is surrounded by a patchwork of villages among rice-paddy fields and orchards. What might seem surprising in a predominantly Muslim state is the number of Thai *wat* (temples) between Tumpat and Pasir Mas. Among them is the **Wat Photivihan**, which houses the country's largest statue of the reclining Buddha. Some villages even celebrate Thai festivals, like the Songkran water festival in April and Loy Krathong in November.

Tumpat is the terminus for the eastern railway line from Gemas. The line whisks travellers all the way to Bangkok. Head out of Kota Bharu on Route 3 to reach what is reputed to be the oldest surviving mosque in Kelantan. The 18th-century **Kampung Laut Mosque** (Masjid Kampung Laut) was originally on the banks of Sungai Kelantan but was moved out of flood's

Silks to buy at the Central Market in Khota Bahru.

A shadow puppeteer.

TIP

Extensive research to help turn the tide against sea turtle extinction is being conducted at the Sea Turtle Research Unit at Universiti Malaysia Terengganu. Pledge your support in cash and kind; visit their website at seatru.umt.edu.my.

harm to Kampung Nilam Puri, 10km (6 miles) south of Kota Bharu. Built of stout cengal wood and without nails, it has a pyramidal two-tiered roof, typical of a Javanese mosque.

Pantai Dasar Sabak

A great place to watch Kelantan's colourful fishing boats is at the picturesque estuary at **Pantai Dasar Sabak** ⑳ 13km (8 miles) north of the town. The boats leave at dawn and return at about 3pm, when it is all bustle with the unloading of the catch and the washing of boats. The beach also has a 20th-century claim to fame: it was here, on 8 December 1941, that the Japanese began their brutal march south to Singapore. (The attack on Pearl Harbor was not to take place until 95 minutes later – 7 December on the other side of the dateline.)

Weekenders head for the beach facing the South China Sea, which is called PCB or **Pantai Cahaya Bulan** (Moonlight Beach); the acronym actually used to stand for Pantai Cinta Berahi – The Beach of Passionate Love – in pre-PAS days. PCB is a handicraft haven. The gold-threaded *songket*, *wau* (kites), and rows of batik hanging in the sun beckon souvenir-hunters on the 5km (3-mile) road to the beach.

South of PCB, about 151km (94 miles) away is Mount Stong (Gunung Stong) in Kuala Krai, the most popular eco-adventure destination in the state. The 1,433-metre (4,701ft) tall mountain is situated in the Gunung Stong State Park, which is also home to one of the highest falls in Malaysia – the impressive seven-tier Jelawang Waterfall. As the park is linked to the Main Range, there are large mammals in the area including three endangered animals – the Malayan tiger, the Asian elephant and the Malayan tapir – and the vulnerable Malayan gaur. This area is also rich in flora, including one species of Rafflesia, and two endemic species – a fan palm and a rare bamboo – meaning it is found nowhere else but here. It's best to hike between April and June, or any time outside of the monsoon season, because of the danger of flash floods, when water levels can rise very quickly.

The coast at Bachok.

Kampung games

While the popular kampung pastimes of spinning tops and kite-flying hone the skills of agility and patience, the wit-sharpening games of *sepak takraw* and *congkak* improve concentration.

Every Malaysian is a *kampung* kid at heart; so says Lat, Malaysia's favourite cartoonist, who has a series of books contrasting the easy, down-to-earth *kampung* lifestyle with the mobile phone-punctuated life of the modern urbanite.

Despite the city-dweller's groomed image and array of gadgets, every holiday in Malaysia results in airports and highways jammed with city residents returning to their villages – *balik kampung*. Their *kampung* are their roots, and bound up in this are the traditional pastimes enjoyed there.

Tops and kites

Throughout most of the country, **top-spinning** is a teenage game, but in the Malay *kampung* of the northeast coast, a champion spinner is the village hero. Requiring great strength to spin, tops vary from a simple wooden cylinder to fantastic streamlined discs with spindles trimmed with inlaid gold; large ones can be as big as dinner plates. With the harvest completed and all the rice stored, farmers traditionally settled down to watch and bet on the top local team. Contests feature either the endurance spinners – record times for spinning are about two hours – or the strikers who spin down 7kg (15lb) fighting tops faster than a speeding bullet.

Another traditional entertainment most popular in Malaysia's northeastern states, **kite-flying** was enjoyed in the 15th century. Today, great pride is still taken in the design and the hand-crafting of each aerodynamic piece of art. Like the parts of the bird, the Kelantanese kite-maker believes that the kite also has a head, waist, wings and a base.

The paper *wau* (kite) comes in unique shapes, and bamboo pieces are often attached underneath a kite to produce a melodic humming sound (*degung*) which, according to popular belief, will ward off evil spirits. Contests are still held for serious kite-flyers, and today, international kite festivals are held in Malaysia, drawing participants from both European and Asian countries. Kite-flyers are judged on the longest time they can fly their kites at a constant height and how beautifully decorated their kites are.

Ball and board games

Sepak takraw, a traditional *kampung* game, uses a ball about the size of a large grapefruit, made of woven rattan strips, and weighing 170 grams (less than 0.5lb). The aim of the game is to keep the ball in the air as long as possible by passing it from one player to another, using all parts of the body except for the forearms and the hands. The game requires acrobatic flexibility and practised skills, and is exhilarating to watch.

Congkak is a game requiring more wits than physical skill. Comparable to backgammon, *congkak* features a wooden boat-shaped "board" and marbles or seeds. The *congkak* board has two rows of holes in which the marbles are placed, and the object of the game is to have the most marbles to finish.

The best childhood memories come from games provided by nature. The pea-sized, red saga seeds from the large saga tree, for example, are used in a game of accuracy much like marbles. The game of pick-up-sticks is played with coconut twigs or satay skewers; chicken feathers are stuck into a flat rubber disc, and this *catek*, resembling a shuttlecock, is kept in the air while being nimbly kicked using only the instep of one's foot. Even conker-like rubber seeds are the centre of numerous, imaginative kampung games, all still fresh in the minds of most Malays.

Wau kites.

THE BANGAU MARITIME FIGUREHEADS

Carved and decorated spar holders, or bangau, adorn these colourful traditional fishing boats, and are found only on the Malaysian Peninsula's east coast.

When engines began replacing sails from the 1950s onwards, it was thought that the *bangau* would become extinct. But these colourful objects have been retained, because the spars are still used as gaffs for landing fish and for poling into shore. In ancient times they were more than utilitarian objects – the *bangau* also served as a repository for the spirit of the boat, and its presence was believed to help keep the boat safe from storms and sea demons.

Bangau are found from the northern shores of Kelantan – nota2bly adorning the boats known as *perahu bauatan barat* – to Terengganu in the south, where they act as figureheads on the curved bows of *kolek* boats. *Bangau* means "cattle egret" in Malay. It is thought that originally the boat fittings resembled these birds, which, while rarely seen flying over the sea, were perhaps chosen for their symbolic value due to their well-known liking for fish.

Most *bangau*, however, bear no resemblance to this bird, although bird shapes are sometimes used. Their fanciful designs probably have something to do with the strict Islamic edicts banning the portrayal of anthropomorphic figures.

Figurehead fashions

Bangau take on various forms. Some are shaped like birds, others have the form of the *naga*, a legendary sea serpent, while a few are fashioned after figures in shadow-puppet plays. Some prows are even painted to resemble the *garuda*, a demonic birdman from Kelantanese mythology. Although the spiritual significance of the *bangau* has been long forgotten, the tradition survives of keeping them and the boats they adorn still decorated.

At Kelantan's Pantai Baru near Bachok, the colours used on a bangau are highly imaginative.

A fisherman with his boat at Bachok beach. Boat-building and tending is a traditional skill that is at risk with the decline in apprentices.

A fisherman paints his boat at Bachok beach.

A naga (legendary sea serpent) detail on a bangau boat.

THE BOAT-BUILDERS OF DUYONG

Of the several small islands located in the Kuala Terengganu's river estuary, Pulau Duyong (Mermaid Island) is the most famous. Here, amongst the villages and children playing with kites, lies an endangered industry – traditional boat-building – the east coast style. Each wooden boat is custom-made and hand-crafted to perfection.

Highly skilled craftsmen supply sturdy fishing boats for the Marang fishing fleet and the occasional international order. In the past, many traditional boat-builders were illiterate and had no use of plans. The tradition of building from memory continues today, and every part of the boat – from the keel to the hull and the *bangau* – is constructed without blueprints. Knowledge was handed down from master to son or apprentice, for example, learning how to use dowels instead of nails to fasten the boat ribs to the keel. However, a lack of apprentices is endangering this traditional craft. Coupled with rising costs for raw materials like the cengal, a slow-growing hardwood that is becoming more difficult to find in the forests near Terengganu, the boat-builders face an uncertain future.

Bailing water from a boat; fishermen often take the chance also to repair their boats in port when rough seas prevent sailing.

Intricate illustration adorns the side of this bangau boat.

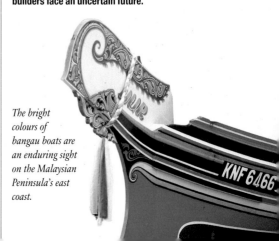

The bright colours of bangau boats are an enduring sight on the Malaysian Peninsula's east coast.

KNF 6466

EASTERN INTERIOR

Inland from the east coast lies the dark-green heart of Malaysia, a land of lakes and forest, of wild animals, ancient myths and the sublime beauty of Taman Negara.

Malaysia's eastern interior covers the state of Terengganu in the north of the peninsular down to Pahang in the south, with each state having its own highlights. Terengganu's pride is Lake Kenyir, where holiday-makers live on board houseboats, only going ashore for fishing excursions or to explore pristine waterfalls and a pre-historic cave. On fine mornings, you are greeted with a serene view of the lake, with a backdrop of mountains partially shrouded in clouds.

Pahang also has its own water catchment – Lake Bera, a wetland of international importance that lets visitors experience living with the Semai Orang Asli and exploring the lake's flora in traditional dugout canoes, and finding a myriad of pitcher plant species along the trails. Both states, along with a third – Kelantan – can lay claim to having Taman Negara in their backyard. Malaysia's first national park is rich in biodiversity, and this is where you will also find Peninsular Malaysia's tallest peak, Mount Tahan. But the arduous seven-day trek with a park guide is only for the very physically fit. You will need to carry your own camping gear and food rations, but the view from the top is your priceless reward.

Lake Kenyir

In the still of morning, before the first breath of wind, surreal sculptures of

dead wood stand perfectly reflected in the mirror of **Lake Kenyir** ㉑ (Tasik Kenyir), Southeast Asia's largest artificial lake. Nineteen hills were inundated to create the 260,000-hectare (642,460-acre) lake, whose water feeds the hydroelectric power station that supplies about 8 percent of the nation's electricity.

However, the statuesque tree trunks that used to be the lake's outstanding characteristic have been removed, except in its northern fingers. Nonetheless, Kenyir's numerous tributaries

Main Attractions
Lake Kenyir
Sungai Lembing
Lake Bera
Taman Negara
Kenong Rimba Park

Lake Kenyir, Southeast Asia's largest artificial lake.

Looking out over Lake Kenyir.

continue to be an anglers' favourite, with numerous freshwater species including the *kelah* and carnivorous *toman* (snakehead).

About 14 waterfalls dot the area's 340 thickly forested islands. The multi-tier 152-metre (500ft) **Lasir Waterfall** is 16km (10 miles) or 45 minutes south of the jetty by boat; and **Tembat Waterfall**, a series of five furious rapids and gorgeous giant sun-baked boulders, is an hour north. You will find campsites on the pebble-beached **Petuang** and **Saok** rivers, which are also popular fishing spots. Otters, eagles and amphibians are common; if you are lucky, you might even spot elephants or the elusive black panther.

The road to Kenyir

The main gateway to Kenyir is the **Pengkalan Gawi** jetty, an hour from Kuala Terengganu. Kenyir's Tourist Information Centre (tel: 09-626 7788; Sat–Wed 9am–5pm, Thu–Fri 9am–1pm) is located near the jetty, where day-trippers can hire fibreglass boats from the tour operators; these seat eight to 10 persons. The operators can also arrange

accommodation at the resorts or budget-class, double-decker houseboats that can sleep 15 people. It is, however, more convenient if you book a package or day trip with an agency in Kuala Terengganu or directly with a resort at Lake Kenyir. All resorts offer the same deal: accommodation, all meals, boat transfers, jungle-trekking, a visit to a waterfall and unlimited use of facilities.

En route to Kenyir is the picturesque seven-step **Sekayu Waterfall** (charge) in a forest reserve near Kuala Berang. A 25-minute walk up a flight of steps takes you to the top, the least slippery spot for a swim. Kuala Berang was the site of the first Malay settlement in Terengganu, but nothing remains of the original dwellings. Also discovered here was Malaysia's oldest Koranic inscription. The 14th-century *Batu Bersurat* is now in the state museum.

Towards Pahang's hinterlands

En route to Pahang's hinterlands from Kuantan, the turn-off to **Sungai Lembing** ㉒ leads to a towering limestone cliff, **Gua Charah**, whose inner cave

houses a 9-metre (30ft) long limestone statue of a reclining Buddha built by a Thai Buddhist monk. The taxing climb up to the ledge is rewarded by a great view. The cathedral-sized outer cave has thin shafts of light filtering down through cracks hundreds of metres above. There are other caves to explore, but a guide is needed. On the same road is the world's second-largest and deepest tin mine, open to tours if prior arrangements are made with Pahang Consolidated Ltd. For details, enquire at Sungai Lembing.

Lake Bera

About three hours from Sungai Lembing is **Lake Bera** ㉓ (Tasik Bera). Though the largest freshwater lake in Southeast Asia, its waters are contained in narrower "fingers" thanks to the greater abundance of screw pine.

Bera's 26,000 hectares (64,000 acres) of wetland and swamp ecosystems are protected under the Ramsar Convention as a wetland of international importance. The water rises up to 3 metres (9ft) in the wet months of September to January, blessing the rivers with fish, and making the post-monsoon months the best angling season. As the boat snakes through the narrow channels, a splash of colour – of orchids amid ferns and epiphytes – catches the eye. Less obvious are the pitcher plants among the tall reed fields. Above, a hawk wings its solitary way, keeping a keen eye out for supper.

The Orang Asli of the Semelai tribe maintain their traditional lifestyles living in bamboo and bark huts, using traditional implements to trap fish and fashioning handicrafts from forest products. They also collect *minyak keruing* resin from the *keruing* tree, used for making torches, boats and perfume.

Taman Negara

There is shuffling and grunting, but the torchlight picks out only a pair of eyes. Is it the black-and-white king of camouflage, a tapir? Or, against all odds, one of the park's remaining 40-plus Sumatran rhino? The experience afforded by the five animal hides in **Taman Negara** ㉔ is among the attractions that have made this arguably the best known of Malaysia's protected areas. This

The jungle canopy walkway in Taman Negara.

TIP

Mutiara Taman Negara
Resort runs buses
(RM100one way) daily
between Kuala Lumpur
(departing 9am from
Hotel Istana) and Kuala
Tembeling jetty
(departing 9am), which
are open to non-guests.
Book beforehand on tel:
03-2782 2222
(www.mutiarahotels.com;
9am–5.30pm) or walk in
at Mutiara's office in
Hotel Istana to pre-pay
for the ticket. Arrive at
least 30 minutes before
departure.

granddaddy, which simply translates to "National Park", sprawls over 430,000 hectares (100,000 acres) across three states, with the bulk being in Pahang. Looming over all this is the central massif of Mount Tahan, the peninsula's highest peak.

Taman Negara offers everything from a leisurely two-day birdwatching tour or a two-week jungle safari to a muddy crawl through bat-infested caves or a splashy ride through Sungai Tembeling's rapids. The park's hundreds of kilometres of trails are kept cleared and well marked, and meander through fascinating lowland dipterocarp and riverine forests, climbing to stunted montane vegetation.

Birdwatching is a delight. Kingfishers, bee-eaters, fishing eagles and osprey abound, and even if you don't see them, you will certainly hear them, in particular the hornbills' unmistakable squawk. Monitor lizards and the larger denizens such as elephant, black panther, *seladang* wild ox and tigers are virtually impossible to spot, so learn to identify their tracks. Nonetheless, sit quietly in the jungle, and you might be rewarded with the sight of long-tailed macaques in the treetops.

The aboriginal Batek communities are no longer a common sight around the headquarters, preferring a nomadic lifestyle deep in the forest. You might occasionally bump into them on a trail or see their temporary huts. The Batek have a natural dignity; don't be too quick to turn them into a tourist spectacle with the click of a camera. And don't be surprised if they demand a fee if you do insist on clicking. The Senoi and Semak Abri tribes outside the park area, however, live more contemporary lifestyles and are more open to visitors.

Permits are required to enter the park and there is a fee for cameras – arrange both at the Department of Wildlife and National Parks (DWNP) counter in Kuala Tembeling or at its office in Kuala Tahan (tel: 09-266 1122), or through your travel agent. Entrance to the park is usually by river from the Kuala Tembeling jetty, although a rough road also goes to the Kuala Tahan *kampung*. However, the covered 14-seater longboat ride is a great way to cover the 35km (20-mile) journey on Sungai Tembeling. The two-hour trip can take twice as long if the river level is low; sometimes, passengers have to disembark and wade while the boatmen negotiate the shallow waters.

At Kuala Tahan, visitors can book accommodation, arrange trips and get information and maps at either the Wildlife Department or the Tourist Information Counter at the Mutiara Taman Negara Resort. The resort and Nusa Holiday Village have good maps and guides to the park, and provide information to non-guests as well. They also rent out camping and fishing gear if you make prior arrangements.

Taman Negara's excellent interpretation centre in the resort grounds provides a great introduction to the park with information on trails and rainforests, and daily video screenings. Short trails can be walked independently, or you can hire nature interpretation guides. Guides are compulsory on

Lake Bera.

the major trails, and guided tours are included in packages.

Taman Negara trails

The most popular walk is the half-hour trek to the **canopy walkway** (Sat–Thu 11am–2.45pm, Fri 9am–noon; charge), a rope-and-ladder bridge among the tops of trees, up to 27 metres (80ft) up. The 400-metre (1,300ft) long walkway gives visitors a rare chance to experience the shoots, fruits and pollinating insects of the canopy at close quarters. This trail is part of the longer loop, which goes to **Tabing Hide** and **Teresek Hill** with its views of Mount Tahan.

Another popular trek is to **Gua Telinga**, a wet, ear-shaped cave (hence its name *telinga*) where you crawl through guano beneath bats clustered on the low ceilings. The lucky could spot a cave racer, a long white snake that feeds on the bats. Fist-sized toads and arthropods like spiders and cockroaches are plentiful too. Although they may be unnerving to many people, all the fauna in the cave are harmless to humans.

A leisurely alternative is to glide under arches of trees up the small, pretty **Sungai Tahan**, and soak in **Lata Berkoh**, a natural jungle jacuzzi formed by a bank of cascades. Lata Berkoh is popular with anglers, as is **Sungai Keniam**, which can be reached on foot or by boat. The trail to the latter, Rentis Keniam, takes in the large caves of Gua Luas, Gua Daun Menari, Gua Kepayang Kecil and Gua Kepayang Besar, which also boast prolific cave fauna. It's a good two-day trek, camping out at the caves or the popular **Kumbang Hide**.

For long-haulers, two options are the **Air Terjun Empat Tingkat** (Four-Step Waterfall) and the ultimate, the 2,187-metre (7,715ft) **Mount Tahan** (Gunung Tahan). Each involves a seven-day trip where you need to carry your own camping gear and food. Both follow the same route along Sungai Tahan until the Teku tributary fork. There are numerous river crossings and a stretch where you have to climb 27 hills – all in one day.

The waterfall is a major tributary of Sungai Tahan that plunges down

TIP

The best time to fish in Taman Negara is during the drier months from February to March, and June to August; equipment can be hired. But note that fishing is not always permitted; check with the park authorities.

A Jungle Railway train.

JUNGLE RAILWAY

There is no jungle railway line in Peninsular Malaysia per se, only a Malaysia Railway track that runs through the middle of the peninsula between two mountain ranges, Titiwangsa and Mount Tahan, passing through breathtaking scenery – from villages to primary rainforests and limestone hills, over bridges and through narrow gorges. This is the 526km (327-mile) long "Jungle Railway" between Gemas and Tumpat stations, which was completed in 1931. There is a pushcart drink and snack service on board, and you can buy food at some stations en route.

If you take the nine-hour daytime train, you must overnight in Gemas before boarding Train 14 the next morning to Wakaf Bharu, the closest station to Kota Bharu city. Alternatively, ride the night train directly from Sentral KL, which is more magical, especially on a full-moon night, when you can see villages and slivers of forest passing by your window. Book an air-conditioned first-class sleeper, which comes with a private two-berth cabin with a washbasin. Berths with only a curtain as privacy, and second- and third-class seats are also available. Moving between cars is not advisable after midnight, when the train accelerates and the violent rattling prevents any safe crossing.

Daybreak occurs somewhere after the Gua Musang station in Kelantan, which allows you to view the jungle and villages for an hour and a half before arriving at your station.

A cream-vented bulbul feeding on fruit in Taman Negara.

the eastern flanks of Mount Tahan and Mount Gedong. The undulating trek up to the Tahan peak, at 2,187 metres (7,175ft), involves an exhilarating climb through montane oak and cloud forests. There is an alternative route to the peak, which takes three days, but it starts at Merapoh town north of Jerantut.

Other trails snake around the 36 hectares (90 acres) of forest bordering the park that belong to Nusa Holiday Village. There are a couple of waterfalls, and the steep Bukit Warisan trek has great sunrise and sunset views of the rainforest canopy with its amazing diversity of trees.

Kenong Rimba Park

Southwest of Taman Negara is the lesser-known but no less interesting **Kenong Rimba Park ㉕**, whose specialities are birds and insects. From dawn, the 128,000-hectare (31,600-acre) park is alive with the sounds of birds, including the unique call of the white-rumped Shama and the thwack of the Malayan whistling-thrush smashing its breakfast of snails on a rock. You might even spot the *belalang dewa* in action, grasshoppers which display locust-like behaviour in travelling in groups, decimating vegetation in one go.

A two- to three-hour trail loops around the park, taking in Kenong Rimba's many limestone caves and types of vegetation. There's **Gua Batu Tangga**, a huge cave believed to provide shelter for elephants. **Gua Hijau** is named after its mossy green walls, while **Batu Kajang** has folkloric connections. According to legend, it is a boat carrying a king's messenger that had been turned to stone. A more challenging route is the undulating five-day trek to **Gua Batu Putih**, which has a delightful crystal-clear stream.

Kenong can be accessed from **Kuala Lipis**, the old Pahang capital. Kuala Lipis is also on the Segamat–Tumpat train route (get off at Batu Sembilan). A 20-minute longboat ride down Sungai Jelai goes to the park at Tanjung Kiara, where there are chalets and a campsite. Tours can be arranged at Kuala Lipis. For more information, contact the Kuala Lipis District Forestry Office (tel: 09-312 1273).

WATCHING WILDLIFE

A night in an animal hide is your best chance to observe wildlife, much of which is nocturnal. These huts on stilts are situated near salt licks, where animals come to drink. Arrive at the hides early, around 5pm. Cooking is definitely not allowed, so bring a packed supper, a powerful flashlight and insect repellent, and settle down to wait. Binoculars are handy. Take turns to "watch", shining the torch out every 10 minutes or so. Nosy jungle rats will help keep you awake.

The best time to spot wildlife at a salt-lick hide is at dawn and dusk. Dress in natural colours (ie. green and not red) and be sure not to wear any kind of perfume or deodorant as it may attract bees and wasps, as well as alert other wildlife to your presence. Most crucially, be as quiet as possible or else you may spook any wildlife in the vicinity.

As night falls, the forest comes alive with sounds and ghostly "spirits" that flit among the trees – fireflies and beetles with fluorescent wings and tails. Deer and tapir are the most common sightings, and you will see lots of spiders and snakes moving about in the undergrowth. An alternative to a night in the hide is to go on a night walk, where you can pick out luminous mushrooms or a slow loris, flying squirrels or civet cats.

Sekayu Waterfall.

A longhouse at the Cultural Village
in Sarawak.

Kuching's waterfront at sunset.

SARAWAK

Once, the much-feared tribes of Sarawak were after enemy heads. Nowadays, they are working as ecotourism guides and sharing their culture with visitors.

A woman strips canes for basket-weaving in an Annah Rais longhouse.

E ven today, the name Borneo evokes a sense of the exotic – of adventure and a journey into the unknown. While Sabah and Sarawak – Borneo's Malaysian states – share a common heritage, each with a history that involved the British, their developments took different paths. Sarawak's white rajahs had great respect for their Dayak subjects and their rule took Dayak predilections into account. Sabah grew as a trading post, with a more pragmatic and certainly less romantic attitude towards its native inhabitants. As a result, modern Sarawak retains its cultural integrity and pride in traditions.

This sprawling state makes a great introduction to Borneo. While the white rajahs and headhunters are long gone, their forts, towers, museums and residences remain behind in the capital city, Kuching. A visit to the Sarawak Cultural Village just outside the city, offers an insight into the many Sarawakian tribes and is also the venue for the annual Rainforest World Music Festival in July.

South and southwest of the city is a treasure-trove of riches – from abandoned gold mines to adventure caving and from national parks to wildlife centres harbouring a myriad of primates, birds, dolphins and crocodiles.

In central Sarawak, those with time to spare can travel along Malaysia's longest river, the Rajang, to visit remote towns, perhaps even witnessing a longhouse celebration or *gawai*.

Chillies for sale at Kuching's weekend market.

Adventure sports enthusiasts will find plenty to do in the northeast, including spelunking in the enigmatic caves of Niah, with their relics of cave dwellers from 40,000 years ago, or in the vast caves of the World Heritage Site of Mulu. Further afield, the cool Bario Highlands bring contact with the warm hospitality of the Kelabits and the chance to trek through pristine jungle to Ba'Kelalan, perhaps in time for their apple harvesting season.

Sarawak is sure to please visitors of all ages, whether in search of adventure sports thrills, wildlife or the experience of visiting a tribal community.

A river ferry passes the Sarawak State Assembly building on Kuching's waterfront.

KUCHING AND THE SOUTHWEST

Kuching has held on to much of its original character while new development spreads further away from the old town centre. The result is one of the most charming towns in Southeast Asia.

In 1839, when British adventurer James Brooke made his way up the winding Sarawak river in his ship, *the Royalist*, he had little idea that in a few short years he would be ruling a whole country. As the governor and rajah of the Sarawak region, he initiated the "rule of the White Rajahs", which lasted three generations and over 100 years.

Today, remnants of the Brooke legacy can still be seen in the fort and square tower that stand watch over Sungai Sarawak. Behind the Kuching waterfront lie historical buildings waiting to be explored, while beyond that in the north, scenic coastal parks protect the peculiar proboscis monkeys, dolphins, crocodiles and the endangered marine turtles. Two hours south of Kuching, and close to the Indonesian border is a Bidayuh longhouse where you can linger on for a day or two, while further inland a day's journey away, Iban longhouses offer glimpses into the fascinating world of former headhunters. But if that's not enough culture and nature to immerse yourself in, you can also explore the caves and gold mines of Sarawak's western corner.

Kuching

Winding through lowland *nipah* swamps, the Sarawak river has always been the focal point for Sarawak's capital city, **Kuching**. This delightful

old trading town is suffused with old memories, enhanced by the many colonial buildings that have withstood the march of progress. People are friendly and hospitable, with time to stop for a chat. Amid the noisy traffic, the shophouses squeezed between the bustling markets of the Main Bazaar and the stately old buildings give the capital an elegant and dignified air. History has always seemed close to the present in Kuching, and the town centre had changed little from a century ago until the early 1990s, when pressures

Main Attractions

Sarawak Museum
Jalan Satok Sunday Market
Sarawak Cultural Village
Bako National Park
Bako-Buntal Bay
Semenggoh Wildlife Centre
Bau

Longhouse inhabitants.

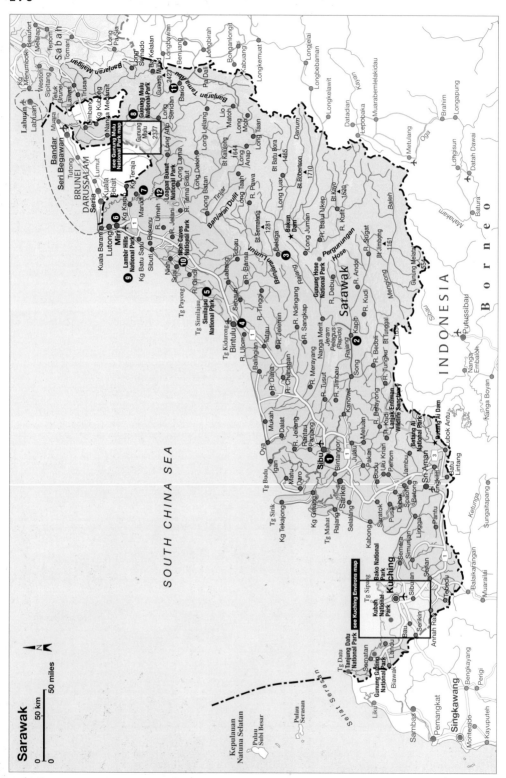

to modernise led to new roads and improvements to the riverfront.

Scattered around Kuching's colonial heart stand the buildings that played such an important part during the Brookes' rule. A Heritage Walk has been devised that covers many of these buildings. The best time to make an on-foot exploration is early morning, or break it up and continue after 4pm, when the heat of the day has begun to pall.

Take one of the gaily painted *tambang* – the small ferry boats leave as soon as they have sufficient passengers – from the various jetties or *pangkalan* along the Kuching Waterfront. First stop is the **Astana** Ⓐ. Built in 1870 for the newly married second rajah, Charles Brooke, it is now the official residence of Sarawak's head of state (and therefore closed to the public). Several renovations later, it consists of three bungalows, supported by square brick pillars, with the low, spreading roof giving shade to the interior. A little further downriver, after the Sarawak State Assembly Building, is **Fort Margherita** Ⓑ (no formal opening times, best time to catch the caretaker is early

morning from 8am; free), which holds a commanding position overlooking the town. There is little to see inside the fort apart from its bare walls. However, if you find the fort closed, you can still catch a good sunset from here. The first of a series of forts that lined Sarawak's main rivers, Fort Margherita was built in 1879, at a calm and peaceful time. The fort was never used for its intended purpose during the Brooke era; the only time it came under attack was during a Japanese air raid in World War II. No severe damage was caused, however, and since the war, the quaint fort has been used mainly as a barracks by the police force.

Back across the river is Kuching's **Square Tower** Ⓒ (daily 9am–5pm), an imaginative building dating from 1879. Its architecture harks back to the Victorian era's fascination with medieval culture. Although equipped with a real dungeon for prisoners, the tower was later used as a popular dancing hall and now houses souvenir shops.

Across the road from the Square Tower sits the **Court House** Ⓓ – a quietly impressive colonial building

Wicker fish traps at a Sarawak Cultural Village longhouse.

Travelling by water in Kuching.

TIP

At the Tanoti Weaving Gallery (tel: 082-281 0098; www.tanoticrafts. com) visitors can watch as expert weavers produce high-quality songket (silk textiles) and contemporary hand-woven fabric from start to finish.

built in 1874, standing stolidly beneath shading trees. Arguably the most beautiful colonial building in Kuching, the building has been converted into the **Sarawak Tourism Complex**, and now houses a Visitors' Information Centre (tel: 082-410 944; Mon–Fri 8am–5pm, closed public holidays) on the ground floor. The National Parks Booking Office (tel: 082-248 088; Mon–Fri 8am–5pm, closed public holidays) is also here if you want to make enquiries about visiting and/or staying at the national parks. The clock tower was added in 1883. The **Charles Brooke Memorial**, an unimposing obelisk erected in 1924, stands facing the Court House. Closer scrutiny reveals four superbly crafted copper plaques depicting, in turn, an Iban warrior, a Chinese courtier, a British soldier and a Malay warrior.

The complex also contains the Pavilion building, now home to the **Sarawak Textile Museum** (daily 9am–4.45pm, Sat–Sun and public holidays 10am–4pm; free). Next to the Court House, on Jalan Tun Abang Haji Openg, is the odd-looking **Round Tower Ⓔ**, built in 1886 to house the

town dispensary. Brooke seems to have had a predilection for fortifications; the Round Tower was intended to double up as a fort in times of attack. It is now occupied by the headquarters of the Sarawak Crafts Council (Mon–Fri 8.30am–4.30pm; free) which has a showroom displaying a wide and interesting range of crafts from Sarawak.

Kuching Waterfront

Once a collection of *godowns* and trading stores, the old waterfront was greatly transformed in 1993 to become the **Kuching Waterfront**, a kilometre-long stretch of recreational areas, gardens, walkways, stalls and restaurants. At the beginning of the Kuching Waterfront park is the **Sarawak Steamship Building**, which houses the **Kuching Waterfront Bazaar** (daily 9am–10pm, but the best time to visit is from 10am to 6pm), a collection of souvenir stalls.

Further along the waterfront is the one-time Chinese Chamber of Commerce building that has been transformed into an interesting **Chinese History Museum** (tel: 082-231 520;

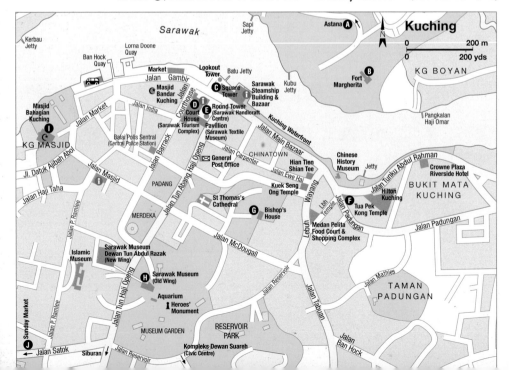

Mon–Fri 9am–4.45pm, Sat–Sun and public holidays 10am–4pm; free). This far end of the Waterfront is dominated by the impressive white edifice of the **Hilton Kuching** – the beginning of the main upmarket hotel area.

The street facing **Jalan Main Bazaar** now forms the main tourist area – a shopping mecca not just for touristy souvenirs but with pieces to interest serious collectors. Many of the old shop-houses have been taken over by travel companies, and handicraft and antique stores specialising in primitive arts.

To retrace the historical journey of Sir James Brooke amidst the modern buildings and Malay kampungs of Kuching's waterfront, you can book a cruise with dinner and dance show on board. The Sarawak River Cruise (tel: 082-240 366; charge) departs daily at 5.30pm and returns at 7pm at the pier near the police station. From the waterfront, you can also watch Kuching's legendary sunsets, when the sky over the city take on a gorgeous red-magenta hue – alternatively, hop on a river tambang to the Istana jetty or any of the jetties west of the Astana.

Chinatown

Crossing the road from the end of the Waterfront one reaches Sarawak's oldest, and possibly prettiest, Chinese temple, the **Tua Pek Kong Temple ⑥**. Its construction in the late 18th century marks the strong Chinese presence in Sarawak. The Chinese community trades not only in the main towns and cities, but also upriver, with trade boats stocked like floating supermarkets, or with boats attached to remote longhouses, supplying goods and building up a network of trade and news wherever they go.

Like many Malaysian towns, Kuching has its share of ornate Chinese temples. Built in 1895, the **Kuek Seng Ong Temple** on Lebuh Wayang is the traditional place of worship for Henghua fishermen, praying for good catches and a safe return from the sea. The temple is dedicated to the god Kuek Seng Ong, whose figure is placed on a sedan chair on the 22nd day of the second moon, and carried through the town's main thoroughfare.

On one side of the temple, Jalan Ewe Hai runs into Jalan Carpenter to form

A tiger wall carving at Kuek Seng Onn Chinese Temple.

Making offerings at the Tua Pek Kong Temple.

the most atmospheric strip in China-town, with quaint shops, great food (look for the stalls set in the courtyard of a Chinese opera stage facing a temple) and traditional tradesmen.

General Post Office

Jalan Carpenter ends at Jalan Tun Abang Haji Openg, which passes the impressively columned **General Post Office** (Mon–Sat 8am–5pm, closed first Sat of the month), built in 1931 by Vyner Brooke, the last rajah. Behind the temples and shophouses of Chinatown is one of the oldest buildings in Kuching, the sprawling **Bishop's House** . It was built in 1849 by James Brooke for the Reverend Thomas Francis McDougall and his wife. With his typical astuteness, Brooke selected McDougall as the first Anglican bishop of Kuching because he had previously been a surgeon. Nearby is **St Thomas's Cathedral**.

A cat sculpture in Kuching.

A Kenyah woodcarving of a dragon in Sarawak Museum.

Sarawak Museum

Jalan Tun Haji Openg continues past the grassy square of Padang Merdeka to the **Sarawak Museum (Old Wing)** ⓗ

(tel: 082-244 232; www.museum.sarawak. gov.my; daily 9am–4.30pm; free).

This is perhaps the most important place of interest for the visitor. Alfred Russell Wallace, the naturalist and co-founder of the theory of evolution along with Charles Darwin, spent many months in Borneo, exploring and collecting specimens. On the ground floor, you will see Wallace's painstaking efforts – in the natural history collection on Sarawak's wildlife. Upstairs, the first floor has been transformed into walk-in replicas of ethnic longhouses. Explore the Iban longhouse, with simulated fires, human skulls hanging from the rafters, as well as a warrior's elaborate headdress and weaponry resting at his bedside; you almost expect him to walk in and sound the battle cry. The Brookes insisted upon capable curators, whose Western expertise was to serve only to illuminate the ethnological richness of Borneo and the vivid expressions of the societies it nourished.

The enthusiastic influence of Cambridge graduate Tom Harrisson, one of the museum's curators and a

pioneering anthropologist, can be seen in many of the collections. There is a human dental plate on display that was found in the stomach of a 6-metre (20ft) crocodile. A rhinoceros-horn cup that can detect poison is another item. If the drink was contaminated, the liquid bubbled to the top: since princes were always trying to poison one another, rhino horn was in high demand during the days of the dynasties.

A footbridge across the busy Jalan Tun Haji Abang Openg links the museum's old wing to the new wing, the Dewan Tun Abdul Razak gallery, which was formerly the Legislative Assembly Hall. While the museum shop is located on the ground floor, the first floor exhibits material discovered during archaeological digs in Sarawak.

Jalan India Street

Continue down Jalan Barracks, past the Padang and the Central Police Station and turn right into **Jalan India Street**, a colourful jumble of shops and small businesses, little changed from 50 years ago.

Veer left into Jalan Market, the old market street that leads to the golden domes of decorative **Kuching Mosque ❶** (Masjid Bahagian Kuching), which overlooks the river. Built in 1968, it replaced the much older wooden structure built in 1852 that burnt down. Retrace your steps along Lebuh Market to Jalan Gambir, where you will find a collection of colourful shops marking what was once the main trading area. Indian Muslim traders, following the Chinese example in the 18th century, headed for Sarawak to set up textile shops and moneylending stalls; the area still exudes a faint aura of the exotic East. Tucked between these shops is the narrow facade of **Bandar Kuching Mosque** (Masjid Bandar Kuching). Built in 1834 for the Indian Muslim traders, the mosque will be replaced by a three-storey mosque and commercial space to fulfil the needs of a growing business community. The streets around the mosque are a labyrinth of small Indian shops and spicy, curry-scented restaurants. Continue the walk

Kuching Mosque.

Fish stalls at Kuching's Sunday Market.

Local fruits at Kuching's Sunday Market.

through this colourful area back to the Court House.

Jalan Satok Sunday Market

The popular **Sunday Market ❶**, which attracts Dayak tradesmen from the surrounding countryside, is situated on the outskirts of town at Jalan Satok. The stallholders arrive and set up market around midday on Saturday and continue until midday Sunday. All manner of strange foodstuffs – jungle produce, wild boar, bats, lizards, monkeys and turtles – are on sale here, alongside fruit, vegetables, pets, orchids and fish.

Sarawak's western beaches

Sun-worshippers, beach-lovers and golfers head for **Damai Beach ❷** near Santubong, just 30 minutes by road from downtown Kuching. As well as the water sports offered by the various resorts, an 18-hole golf course designed by Arnold Palmer and jungle walks on Mount Santubong increase the recreational options.

For a fine introduction to Sarawak's varied cultures, visit the state's award-winning **Sarawak Cultural Village ❸** (tel: 082-846 411; www.scv.com.my; daily 9am–5pm; charge), adjacent to Damai beach. Spread across 6 hectares (15 acres) of jungle at the foot of Santubong Mountain, the park has authentic dwellings of the seven main cultural groups, staffed by friendly helpers wearing the appropriate dress. The village offers demonstrations of traditional arts and crafts, as well as daily cultural shows, which incorporate Iban, Kayan, Kenyah, Melanau and Malay, Chinese and Bidayuh dances. The cultural village is also the site of the immensely popular **Rainforest World Music Festival** (tel. 082-423 600; www.rwmf.net) that brings together renowned world musicians from Africa, the Middle East, Europe, South America and Southeast Asia to celebrate three days of world music in July. During the day, there are also music workshops, lectures and jamming sessions.

Nearby is the seaside village of **Buntal**, which is extremely popular for seafood, especially at night. With prior permission, you may be allowed to visit the green turtle sanctuary of

Pulau Satang Besar ❹, north of Kampung Telaga Air, where precious turtle eggs are closely guarded. During the northeast monsoon season, especially December and January, the rough seas make it difficult to get there. For more information, contact the Sarawak Forestry on tel: 082-610 088; www.sarawak-forestry.com/htm/snp-np-satang.html.

Bako National Park

An abundance of nature can be enjoyed at the many national parks accessible from Kuching. Some parks can be enjoyed as day trips, although all deserve a longer visit. Gazetted in 1957, **Bako National Park** ❺ (Taman Negara Bako; tel: 082-478 011; www.sarawakforestry.com/htm/snp-np-bako.html; park headquarters Mon–Fri 8am–5pm, closed public holidays; charge), was Sarawak's first, and it offers some of the best chances to see native animals in the wild. Situated on a peninsula at the mouth of the Sarawak river, Bako's relatively small area of 2,740 hectares (6,770 acres) is uniquely rich in both flora and fauna, offering examples of almost every vegetation group to be found in the state. Primary rainforest covers one side of the peninsula, while the other side offers a picturesque coastline of steep cliffs and sandy bays with beaches for swimming. Mudflats and sandbars support a great diversity of sea birds, as well as peculiar red crabs and mudskippers.

While it is possible to visit Bako on a day trip, the rewards are greater if you stay for one night at least – a visit of two or three nights is recommended. Some people stay for a month, relaxing in the natural environment and exploring all the park has to offer. Catch the sun setting over the coloured limestone karsts of the main beach, and enjoy the unearthly experience of walking in the luminous forest at night.

The dry plateau is home to the bizarre insect-eating flowers known as *nepenthe*s, or pitcher plants; eight species exist within the park's confines. The coastal swamp forest is a favoured retreat of Borneo's endemic proboscis, or long-nosed monkey; the long-tailed macaque; bearded pig; and sambar deer, some of which

TIP

There are traditional dance performances at the Sarawak Cultural Village at 11.30am and 4pm each day. Call 082-846 411 for more information.

The carnivorous pitcher plant, found in Bako National Park.

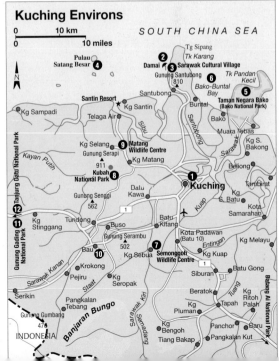

At the Sarawak Cultural Village.

find their way down to the beaches. Within the park is a good system of well-marked paths; ask for a guide map at the Park Ranger's Office. Settle down and get ready to explore the wonders of Bako.

A magnificent plank walk leads through a tidal mangrove forest that changes character throughout the day with the rise and fall of the sun, and the ebb and flow of the tide. Here in the early morning, when the water is low, lucky visitors may encounter the shy proboscis monkey or the silver leaf monkey, feasting on the young leaves. Tread quietly and keep your eyes wide open. The popular **Lintang Trail** leads through nearly all the vegetation types and up to the arid plateau, where pitcher plants can be found among the scrub.

Within the park, accommodation is available at the resthouse, dormitories and chalets at the headquarters at **Teluk Assam**. A small shop supplies basic provisions for you to cook yourself, or the canteen offers a perfectly acceptable menu. Beware the cheeky long-tailed macaques that will

A Sarawak longhouse.

try to find their way into your chalet kitchen or steal food right off the table in the main dining area. They are a basketful of trouble, providing high entertainment for onlookers. Book your accommodation with the National Park's desk (tel: 082-610 088; Mon–Fri 8am–5pm, closed public holidays) at the Visitors' Information Centre located in the old Court House in Kuching.

Bako-Buntal Bay

Between Santubong and Bako National Park lies **Bako-Buntal Bay ❻**, a birdwatcher's paradise and Malaysia's most important natural site for migratory water birds. At low tide the sea recedes, exposing inter-tidal mudflats rich in the type of food that entices 15,000 migratory birds to escape their harsh winters for. Birds like the Spotted greenshanks and the Far-eastern curlews have been flying here since the early 1900s, feeding on crustaceans and mudskippers, and sometimes a stranded fish or two.

The bay also supports at least three species of dolphin – the Indo-Pacific

LONGHOUSE TOURS FROM KUCHING

A visit to a longhouse in Sarawak – mostly found in the Skrang, Lemanak or Batang Ai regions – is a must (see page 296). You get to see an integrated community living under one roof, and the Iban people are generally great fun and very hospitable, earning a little side income from the visits.

The Iban and most of the Orang Ulu build their dwellings near rivers, which once offered their only means of access. Today, many are accessible by road and boat. Many longhouses have tourist accommodation nearby, ensuring privacy for both the longhouse-dwellers and visitors. When visiting the longhouses at Batang Ai, you can also visit the nearby national park, which is home to the endangered gibbons, orang-utans and hornbills.

Closer to Kuching and within one and a half hours' drive is the Annah Rais Longhouse, where you can easily make your own arrangements with the Bidayuhs. If you are visiting for a day, plan to arrive by 9.30am, as activities start from 10am onwards. You can also stay with the Bidayuhs and learn how to build bamboo rafts, perhaps catch your own fish or enjoy the nearby hot springs and refreshing waterfall. To arrange for a day visit including transfer or an overnight stay, contact Macheree's Homestay on mobile tel: 019-817 5229 or www.mdrlonghousehomestay.com.

humpback dolphin, the Irrawaddy dolphin and the Finless porpoise, while the estuarine crocodiles prefer to bask on the delta banks. Mangrove trees fringe the bay and along Sungai Buntal in the west and Sungai Tabo in the east, where a population of proboscis monkeys live. Local nature conservationists call the Bako-Buntal Bay the "Kinabatangan of Sarawak" after Sabah's famous Lower Kinabatangan river that also teems with wildlife. Several local tour operators provide wildlife cruises in the bay area; contact the Visitors' Information Centre in Kuching at tel: 082-410 942/944; www.sarawaktourism.com.

Semenggoh Wildlife Centre

Some 22km (14 miles) southwest of Kuching is the **Semenggoh Wildlife Centre** ❼ (tel: 082-618 324; www.sarawakforestry.com/htm/snp-nr-semenggoh.html; daily 8–12.30pm and 2pm–4pm; charge), where you'll find Sarawak's first dedicated reserve for orang-utans. From the main gate, it is a 20-minute walk to the centre. This is another must-visit excursion and a great chance for an encounter with these delightful animals. Rehabilitation for orphaned babies and adult animals which have been kept as domestic pets is an ongoing process as they are taught to climb trees, find food, make nests and otherwise survive in the wild. The Semenggoh Nature Reserve where the centre is located is also the home for hornbills, monkeys and Malayan sun bears.

Northwest of Kuching

Only 21km (13 miles) from Kuching is the 2,230-hectare (5,500-acre) **Kubah National Park** ❽ (tel: 082-845 033; www.sarawakforestry.com/htm/snp-np-kubah.html; park headquarters Mon–Fri 8am–5pm, closed public holidays; charge). Within its confines are streams, waterfalls and bathing pools. A five- to six-hour return trail leads to the park's highest peak, **Mount Serapi** (**Gunung Serapi**), while the most popular waterfall trail leads through dipterocarps with plankwalk sections in front of the waterfall. Kubah makes a good day trip from

TIP

You can stay in four of Sarawak's national parks at Bako, Kubah, Matang and Mount Gading; for latest room rates or to book, tel: 082-610 088 or request rooms online at ebooking.com.my.

A dance performance in traditional dress at the Sarawak Cultural Village.

TIP

Park staff closely monitor the beaches of Tanjung Datu. The endangered green turtle and the olive ridley turtle regularly lay their eggs here. A fenced-off turtle hatchery ensures the survival of egg clutches that are vulnerable to natural predators such as pigs, monitor lizards and snakes.

An orang-utan at Semenggoh Wildlife Centre.

the capital; chalets are available for longer stays. The **Matang Wildlife Centre 9**, some 14km (9 miles) further along, is home to a number of orang-utan and other local fauna which are contained in large enclosures found within the rainforest.

Bau

About 36km (22 miles) from Kuching are the historic gold-mining limestone hills of **Bau 10**. Gold mining began in the mid-19th century when the Chinese discovered it in the limestone walls. Although mining activities closed in 1921, illegal diggers continue to mine occasionally. Beyond the glitter, Bau has two show caves worth a visit – the Wind Cave and Fairy Cave. But there are also other caves to explore – with and without technical know-how – even a cave that is associated with burials, rock art and Neolithic stone tools. If you do not fancy caves, you can also try your luck with an old gold mine. For more information, call Kuching Offroad at tel: 012-886 2347; its tours require a minimum of two participants.

Sarawak's northwestern corner

The little-explored northwestern part of the state has more surprises for those who want to visit. The road west leads to **Lundu** and **Sematan**, where remote beaches – try Pandan Beach 12km (7.5 miles) outside Lundu town – are among the many attractions. Out from Sematan, a relaxed little fishing village, are several deserted islands, one of which, **Talang Talang**, is a turtle sanctuary.

More national parks can be visited in the northwest. The town of Lundu is the access point to **Gunung Gading National Park 11** (tel: 082-735 144/610 088; www.sarawakforestry.com/htm/snp-np-gading.html; park headquarters Mon–Fri 8am–5pm, closed public holidays; charge). Gazetted in 1983, the park covers an area of over 41,000 hectares (101,100 acres), on both sides of the Lundu river. Within the park are waterfalls and an eight-hour trail to the summit of Mount Perigi. Giant Rafflesia blooms, growing up to 1 metre (3ft), can be found in the park, and chalets are available. According

to legend, Mount Gading (Gunung Gading), or Ivory Mo untain, is named after a Javanese princess who used to bathe at one of its numerous waterfalls. The trails are steep, but it's worth hiking them to see both rafflesia blooms and the falls, especially Waterfalls Nos. 3 and 7.

Gazetted in 1994, **Tanjung Datu National Park** ⓬ (tel: 082-610 088; www.sarawakforestry.com/htm/snp-np-datu.html; park headquarters Mon–Fri 8am–5pm, closed public holidays; charge) is Sarawak's smallest park, covering an area of just 1,379 hectares (3,400 acres). Right at the westernmost tip of the state, the park has clear rivers and fine beaches with unspoilt reefs. It is accessible by boat from Sematan, and the whole journey takes around three and a half hours – but there is no park accommodation available due to the need to protect turtle nesting areas in the vicinity.

Batang Ai National Park (tel: 082-610 088; www.sarawakforestry.com/htm/snp-np-batangai.html; park headquarters Mon–Fri 8am–5pm, closed public holidays; charge) and the adjoining **Lanjak Entimau Wildlife Sanctuary** are favoured haunts of orang-utans, gibbons, barking deers, leaf monkeys and wild boar, as well as several hundred species of birds. Both areas are located in the Sri Aman Division, east of Kuching and north of the **Batang Ai Dam**. The Batang Ai river, a tributary of the Batang Lupar, was dammed to create Sarawak's first hydroelectric power plant, which became operational in 1985. A subject of great controversy at the time, the dam flooded over 10 longhouses belonging to the Iban and Orang Ulu, and also affected the flora and fauna in the area. During the drier times of the year, the dam is not a pretty sight as thousands of dead trees protrude from the water. The dam is fed by several tributaries where many longhouses are found.

Once past the Batang Ai dam – a four-hour trip from Kuching – the journey to the park takes about two hours upriver by longboat. There are no facilities in these two reserves as yet, but visitors can stay in one of the nearby Iban longhouses or at the more comfortable Hilton Batang Ai Longhouse Resort.

TIP

Sarawak Forestry takes its conservation role very seriously. You cannot overnight at the Semenggoh Wildlife Centre or the Tanjung Datu National Park because of the wildlife it seeks to protect – the orang-utan and marine turtles – and there is no accommodation nearby.

Dragonboats take to the water by Kuching.

A Borneo Anglehead lizard adopts
a defensive posture in Bintulu.

SIBU AND CENTRAL SARAWAK

Sibu is the bustling gateway to the Rajang, Malaysia's mightiest river. A trip upriver will reward you with a glimpse of the lives of the Orang Ulu and Iban peoples of the region.

Travellers to central Sarawak come here for the experience of travelling on Malaysia's longest river – the Batang Rajang – and visiting the remote towns of the interior. From Sibu, express boats, long and narrow, rather like wingless 747s, depart regularly. They head downstream to Sarikei and Kuching, and upriver (*ulu*) to Kapit, and also past the treacherous Pelagus Rapids to Belaga. Tourists mingle with an assortment of other passengers: Chinese merchants taking their wares to distant longhouses; river and inland officials (usually Iban) going about their business; the odd longhouse-dweller returning home after a visit to the big city, or schoolchildren who attend school in Sibu, but return to their family longhouses for the holidays.

But the region also has its dark side – power plant companies build hydroelectricity dams displacing thousands, and logging companies continue to pillage the forest for its prized timber.

On the river, boats, longboats and timber tugs work their way up or glide downriver on the Rajang. Sarawak's longest river is also the natural highway for the timber industry, and you may see huge rafts stacked with logs floating downstream. Should one of these hazards become waterlogged, it presents considerable danger to outboard motors; with that very danger

in mind, the express boats have their undercarriage lined with steel, and there is always a spare propeller shaft lashed to the roof.

Sibu

Beyond Kuching, cosmopolitan city life fades away, and the innumerable rivers that mark Sarawak's green interior become the highways to remote inland settlements. **Sibu ❶**, capital of Sarawak's third and largest district, is an easy-going and predominantly Chinese town, where the

Boarding the express boats at Sibu.

TIP

Although it is possible to take a bus from Kuching to Sibu, your bones will be considerably rattled by the time you arrive. It is far more pleasant to take the express boat, which heads down the Sarawak river, out to the South China Sea, and then up the Rajang river via Sarikei. Alternatively, there is a 40-minute flight, giving a wonderful view of the never-ending jungle with its milk-coffee rivers snaking their way through the low-lying *nipah* palm swamps.

fish markets overflow with gigantic freshwater species such as carp and the much-prized kolong, which finds its way to the elegant dining tables of Hong Kong. Timber money has made Sibu rich, and the sprawling town, abounding with glitzy hotels and karaoke bars, is home to some of Sarawak's wealthiest families.

The express boat port at the western end of the Rajang Esplanade is the town's busiest spot, presided over by the imposing seven-tier pagoda that is part of the **Tua Pek Kong Temple**. From the top of the pagoda is a magnificent view of dozens of express boats lined up along the wharf, with boards in front denoting their destinations and a clock showing their departure times. The busy atmosphere lends a hint of adventure and of journeys into the unknown.

Heading up the Rajang river

Visitors tend not to linger in Sibu – often just staying overnight after arriving from Kuching by boat, before leaving to travel up the **Rajang river**

Boat trip on the Rejang.

(Batang Rajang) the next morning. Because of extensive logging, express boats now run to several of the major tributaries of the Rajang – a marvellous network that enables visitors to get around at little expense and with great ease – a situation much changed from the heady and hilarious days of Redmond O'Hanlon's explorations in *Into the Heart of Borneo*. Other, much earlier travellers had to do it all the hard way, by hiring boats themselves. Although express boat prices are fixed, hire of longboats is expensive (even for locals) and heavily dependent on the water level, weather, time of day, river currents and how willing the boatman is to hurry his journey to fit your schedule. Unless you take a direct express to Kapit, the express boat stops along the way at the smaller settlements of **Kanowit** and **Song**, from where local express boats can be taken to visit longhouses up these rivers.

Kapit

The day starts early in **Kapit** ❷ as the siren call of the first express boats

sounds through the misty dawn. As the boats fire up their throbbing and powerful engines, passengers down their last cups of morning coffee, ready to start their journeys on the river.

To those who live far up the Rajang river, the bustling market town is the big city. Kapit has electricity 24 hours a day, shops (selling goods at considerably higher prices than back in Sibu), hotels equipped with luxuries like TV and air conditioning, and fast-food outlets selling fried chicken, pizza, ice cream and other modern conveniences. As a marked contrast, the daily morning market is filled with tribal women coming to town to sell their produce before heading off to the local provision shops to buy longhouse necessities.

Only two and a half hours upriver from Sibu, and in spite of all these modern improvements, the sprawling town centre still retains the atmosphere of a frontier town, bearing marks of its origins when the Brookes established it as a trading post and fort town. **Fort Sylvia** (www. tunjugahfoundation.org.my; Tue–Sun

10am–noon and 2pm–5pm, closed on public holidays), built in 1880 by Charles Brooke, was placed strategically to prevent the movement of the Orang Ulu downstream and the Ibans moving further *ulu* or upstream, to avert more full-scale wars. Constructed solidly of *belian* or ironwood, the fort has withstood generations of floods, which in some years reached halfway up the walls. Today the fort is a historical monument and under the management of the Tun Jugah Foundation. Inside, there is a museum with photographs depicting the history of the town and of the fort during the reign of the White Rajah, a collection of Iban costumes and textiles, and displays of weaving tools and raw materials used in the making of *pua kumbu* – these are Iban textiles woven in silk or cotton using the ikat weaving style. On the ground floor, there is also a craft shop and a weaving and handicraft workshop. The museum also serves as an information centre on Kapit.

Kapit lies in the heart of Iban country, Sarawak's largest indigenous

TIP

If you are sitting atop an express boat, you will be asked to venture inside before the boat tries to navigate the raging Pelagus Rapids.

Fort Sylvia.

A local flower in bloom.

An Iban village chief.

population. Ibans were once the head-hunters who gave Borneo its romantic and primitive reputation. Some understanding of their culture will help the visitor to see that they were not merely bloodthirsty in an anarchic way. To bring good fortune to the longhouse, and fame and a bride for themselves, young Iban warriors would (and some still do) set out from home to travel "the world". Status would be acquired in the form of tattoos telling of their bravery, and the heads of a few enemies brought home to imbue the longhouse with protective spirits. Only warriors of equal strength were killed, and never children, women or the old and sick. Sadly, these traditions were much misunderstood by the 19th-century writers who revelled in writing lurid stories about the head-hunters of the Iban tribes.

Belaga

Beyond Kapit is **Belaga** ❸ – the last urban centre on the Rajang, after which it is longhouse communities all the way. Reaching Belaga means coursing through the **Pelagus Rapids**, marking the natural boundary between the Iban territory below and the Orang Ulu beyond. These rapids are the most treacherous navigable waterway in the state, and possibly in the whole of Borneo. The 2.5km (1.5-mile) stretch is a series of whirlpools and waves as the river rapidly loses altitude. Many lives and boats have been lost in this maelstrom. When the water is low – from May to August – only small longboats can struggle through, although some do try to negotiate the perils in a speedboat.

The real last outpost, Belaga, at the confluence of Batang Belaga and Batang Balui, has grown larger, due to incessant logging, but visit the town, with its few small but comfortable hotels, to see just what a bazaar of the interior looks like. Some of the old wooden buildings remain, although increasingly they are replaced with ubiquitous concrete shophouses. But sit in a coffee shop, sipping on a mug of thick coffee sweetened with spoonfuls of condensed milk, and watch the passing parade of people: Kayan women wearing heavy metal decorations in their ears, which have stretched to their breasts; young warriors who devote their ferocity to football rather than collecting heads; children sent down to school to learn the ways of the other world; a collection of traders, hustlers, would-be tour guides on the make and labourers fresh from the logging camps, money burning in their pockets. It is raw and primitive, with an energy you will never find in the city.

Upstream from Belaga

From Belaga, express boats head upstream when the water is high, but it is advisable to find a guide or an invitation before venturing afar to visit an upriver longhouse. In spite of their long traditions of hospitality to travellers on the river, most long-house folk are just not interested in entertaining people they can't talk to and who have little to offer to their

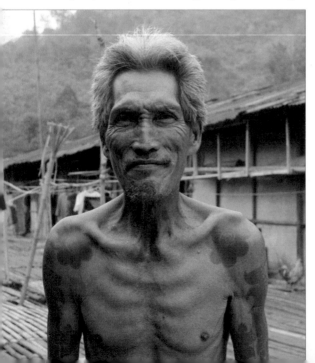

lives. Officially, foreigners wanting to head further upriver from Belaga must obtain a permit from the District Office in Kapit (9th Floor, State Government Complex, Jalan Bleteh; tel: 084-796 230; www.kapitro.sarawak. gov.my).

About 37km (23 miles) up Sungai Balui is the Bakun Hydroelectric Dam; it is 13 times the size of Singapore. During its construction, more than 10,000 locals from longhouse settlements along Sungai Balui had to make way for the dam and they were relocated to the nearby Sungai Asap Resettlement Scheme.

From Sungai Asap, enquire at your homestay for onward land transfer to **Bintulu** ❹, a four-and-a-half-hour journey by four-wheel-drive. The burgeoning oil town of **Bintulu** has developed out of all recognition in the past couple of decades. The old wooden bazaar has given way to new shops and hotels, as well as a deepwater port, chemical factories and a massive liquid petroleum gas (LPG) plant to exploit offshore reserves of natural gas.

About 20km (12 miles) away from Bintulu is the **Similajau National Park** ❺ (tel: 086-489 003, park station 086-327 284; www.sarawakforestry.com/htm/snp-np-siminajau.html). Gazetted in 1976, the 7,067-hectare (17,500-acre) national park is less visited than those closer to Kuching or Miri, but its more difficult access makes it no less attractive. Opened to visitors in 1991, the long, narrow park covers a 32km by 1.5km (20-mile by 1-mile) area and is bordered by one of Sarawak's most beautiful stretches of unspoilt beach, with jungle trails running into the forest. Small rivers and rapids on the **Sebulong river** also make for interesting exploration. Similajau is home to saltwater crocodiles, so watch your step when walking close to river inlets. Other, less spectacular, inhabitants include gibbons, banded langurs, civet cats, porcupines, wild boar and long-tailed macaques, as well as 185 species of birds, including hornbills. Green turtles come to lay their eggs on the quiet beaches between July and September.

A lorry carries away felled logs.

LOGGING IN SARAWAK

Sarawak is a major producer of tropical timber. While a handful of villages may receive donations from timber companies, losses are felt by many to far outweigh the benefits. Deforestation removes the forest's ability to hold soil together and crops and hunting grounds are diminished. Irreparable damage to the environment has affected the traditional way of life for thousands of tribal people.

In 2008, a timber company was caught illegally felling trees in steep terrain and along riverbanks. Thus, the main tributary now flows brown and is silted, making it difficult for the local people to look for potable water. In the Baram region, an entire village had to relocate to a cleaner tributary. Riverside longhouses at Long Moh were flooded not long after logging began in 2005 at the headwaters of Sungai Moh. Tribes, particularly the Penans, continue to stage blockades of timber tracks, burn logging machinery and fight loggers at the judicial courts. In 2011, a landmark decision by the Malaysian court ruled that the Penans could sue the government and a timber company for trespassing on their land.

The controversial Bakun Hydroelectric Dam is the first of several planned for the region. Chief among objectors' concerns have been environmental issues, the forced resettlement of indidinous people, corruption and questionable economics of the scheme: as of July 2014, the dam was operating at only about 50 percent of its capacity.

THE LONGHOUSES OF SARAWAK

A visit to an Iban longhouse offers a unique glimpse of an ancient way of life that – although changing fast – is still fascinating for outsiders.

Longhouse life is a microcosm of a well-run society, where a close-knit community lives together under one roof with one chief, or *Tuai Rumah*, in charge. Within the structure, a kind of horizontal high-rise, each family has its own quarters or *bilek*, where they sleep and eat. The main room is often lined with Chinese ceramic jars much prized by the Ibans. At the rear is the kitchen, where a wood fire provides the heat for cooking, adding a distinctive smoky taste to the food and a dark patina to the surroundings.

Traditional arts

Outside the *bilek* is a communal living space for meals, discussions and entertaining guests. Here, women also weave *pua kumbu*, a ritual blanket using the ikat method on backstrap looms. Decorated with Iban motifs – usually animistic in nature (animals, plants and spiritual beings), its rich, deep-burgundy colour is obtained from a ritual-filled process that uses *engkudu* and indigo plants to dye the cotton threads. On the open deck adjoining the *ruai* (covered verandah) is the *tanju* where, besides mending fishing nets and drying rice, the men lie down to have designs tapped into their skin using needles. The Iban warrior has tattoos covering the torso, arms, hands and legs to ward off evil spirits. The designs often display personal achievements such as bravery in war. The women, however, adorn themselves with tattoos on their arms, fingers, legs and feet to enhance their beauty.

Winnowing grain by hand at an Annah Rais longhouse.

A woman weaves a basket in the traditional way at an Annah Rais longhouse.

Intricately decorated longhouse supports at a Sarawak Cultural Village longhouse.

Rumah Uluyong, a traditional Iban longhouse in Kapit, Sarawak.

TRADITIONAL BELIEFS

The Ibans are traditionally animists, believing that all beings possess souls. Hence, rituals play a big role in their lives – from when to build a house to every stage of rice cultivation; from going to war to healing the sick, and in death. To heal the sick, the *manang* or shaman must recover the soul that has wandered off and join it back to the body. Their most important gods are Simpulang Gana, the god of rice cultivation and guardian deity of the soil, and Singalang Burung, the god of war and Iban welfare. Every milestone in the life of an Iban is celebrated with a *gawai* or festival, which often begins with rituals, starting with the offering of food, and then much chanting and ritual incantations. With the beating of gongs and drums, the *lemambang* or ritualist will invoke the gods to come and attend the celebrations. The ritual ceremony may last until night, including dances to welcome the spirits. To ward off evil spirits, however, natives wear oversized masks with exaggerated facial expressions.

Communal life at this longhouse on the Lemanak river.

The skulls house at a Annah Rais longhouse, a remainder from the days of headhunting.

Cockerels play an important part in Iban culture, used in cockfighting as well as in sacrificial ceremonies.

A boardwalk through tropical rainforest in Gunung Mulu National Park.

MIRI AND THE NORTHEAST

Just over the border from Brunei, the oil boomtown of Miri is the ideal spot from which to head for the magnificent Mulu caves, or make a visit to a Sarawakian longhouse.

Located on the northwest coast near the Brunei border, **Miri ⑥** became Sarawak's original "oil town" with the establishment of the state's first oil rig on Canada Hill in 1919. This oil rig finally ceased production in 1970, but remains as a landmark atop the ridge overlooking the city, with a new Petroleum Science Museum adjacent.

Today Miri serves as an overnight stop for travellers en route to Lambir Hills, Niah Caves, Gunung Mulu National Park and the Bario Highlands.

In and around Miri

Take a stroll around the heart of the old (and essentially Chinese) town close to the river. Be sure to check out the lively local market known as Taman Muhibbah located opposite the very helpful Visitors' Information Centre (tel: 085-434 181; Mon–Fri 8am–5pm, Sat–Sun and public holidays 9am–3pm) where the vendors are as colourful as their produce.

The Miri Handicraft Centre, on Jalan Raja (daily 9am–6pm; free) gives locals a chance to market their handmade goods and imports from Indonesian Borneo. Good buys here include beautifully woven rattan bags and mats.

Miri has some excellent food, especially Chinese and Muslim cuisines, plus plenty of cafés serving basic Western dishes. Don't miss the fresh and relatively inexpensive seafood, best enjoyed along the Miri river or at the coastal restaurants in Brighton beach and Luak Bay.

For a change from land-based activities, try scuba-diving around the reefs close to Miri. If you have time, however, take a live-aboard trip to the reefs.

The highway heading north towards the sultanate of Brunei crosses the Baram river at the Asean Bridge, upriver from **Kuala Baram**. From there, a ferry can take you to the duty-free island of **Labuan**. A road also heads up the

Main Attractions
Gunung Mulu National Park
Niah Caves National Park
Bario
Ba'Kelalan
Loagan Bunut National Park

A bat colony emerging from a cave at dusk in Gunung Mulu National Park.

A native hornbill.

northern side of the Baram river to the trading town of **Marudi** ❼.

While most visitors stop just long enough to catch the next express boat on their rush upriver to Mulu for a taste of outback Sarawak, Marudi is worth a day or two of exploration by itself. One of the older of the Brookes' fort posts and the main supply centre or "bazaar" for the Baram region, Marudi is a fast-spreading town which retains the atmosphere of a trading post. Upriver Iban, Kenyah, Kayan and Penan tribal folk come to sell their wares to the Chinese traders of the town. A lively daily market makes a pleasant diversion, and the provision shops stock everything an uplander could need – from chainsaws to chicken feed, plastic buckets to pullovers and even handicrafts. A day can be very pleasantly spent wandering about the town, or sitting in a local coffee shop near the express-boat jetty to watch the passing parade of people and produce as boats come and go.

A visit to Rajah Brooke's **Fort Hose** is almost mandatory. Erected in 1901 and overlooking the Baram river, the fort was built to control migrations (and wars) up- and downriver. The fort burnt down in the early 1990s, but has been faithfully reconstructed and turned into an interesting little museum.

From Marudi, there are flights to Bario, in the cool Kelabit Highlands, but book well in advance as seats are scarce.

Mulu – a World Heritage Site

A trip to **Gunung Mulu National Park** ❽ (tel: 085-792 300; www.mulupark.com; charge), together with a visit to a longhouse, are two of Sarawak's most memorable experiences. If the trip to or from Mulu follows the old **Headhunter's Trail**, using forest paths and longboats, it becomes unforgettable. With the advent of twice-daily flights to Mulu, getting to the park became much faster and more efficient, but not necessarily more pleasurable, and those with time and a love for travel still prefer to go by boat from Kuala Baram. Flying over part of the park, however, does give you a good idea of its vastness and of the variety of the terrain.

Covering 53,000 hectares (130,600 acres), Mulu is Sarawak's largest park. Gazetted in 1974, it is home to a great

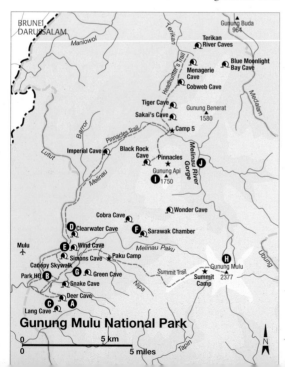

variety of flora, ranging from flowers and orchids, fungi, mosses and ferns, as well as 10 species of pitcher plants. Ten species of hornbill flourish within the vast park.

In the early evening, you can join a pre-booked 2km (1-mile) guided walk, but if it is cancelled because of inclement weather, you can wait until the rain stops and explore the park around park headquarters on your own. Move your torchlight beam up and down trees or sweep it across the foliage. If there's any wildlife, you can detect the glint of their eyes. Spotting wildlife is a hit-and-miss event, but assuredly you can find quite a lot of insects and frogs that appear out of the blue on the boardwalk.

The nearby luxurious, 5-star Mulu Marriott Resort & Spa (tel: 085-792 388; www.marriott.com/hotels/travel/myymu-mulu-marriott-resort-and-spa) has all the conveniences one may want, but for many the ideal place to stay is within the park itself, where there is a variety of accommodation options, from deluxe chalets to longhouse rooms and a dormitory. Try to book your accommodation early.

Exploring Mulu's caves

For many visitors, the centre of attraction is the magnificent cave system. While over 150km (100 miles) of caves have already been surveyed, specialists estimate that only 20 to 30 percent of this massive system has been documented. The caves are accessible by short longboat rides between the park headquarters and the various sites, and jungle plankwalks make walking easy, freeing your eyes from watching your step and giving you a chance to enjoy the surroundings.

The sheer scale of these caves will please even the most discerning statistician; within their dank confines lies the world's largest natural cave chamber, allegedly big enough to hold 16 football fields or 40 jumbo jets and to earn a place in the Guinness Book of World Records. Clearwater Cave, at 75km (47 miles), is the longest cave in Southeast Asia. Only four of the 25 caves so far explored are open to public viewing, but this is plenty to gain an idea of the immensity and complexity of this cave system. Most often visited is the **Deer Cave Ⓐ**, named after

FACT

Gunung Mulu's primary jungle contains astonishing biodiversity; every scientific expedition that has visited its forests has encountered plant and animal species previously unknown to man.

The giant caves of Gunung Mulu National Park.

TIP

Visitors who are not on a package tour (which includes a guide) are obliged to hire a park guide, which can easily be arranged at park headquarters. These independent travellers also pay a high price for transport by boat within the park, unless they join forces with others. Even though a trip to this World Heritage Site is not necessarily cheap, it is worth every penny.

Trekking in Gunung Mulu National Park.

long-vanished deer. The site is accessible by a 3km (2-mile) plankwalk from the **Park HQ** Ⓑ, passing through a peat swamp forest where orchids thrive and there is an ancient Penan burial site. This massive hall is 2,160 metres (7,090ft) long and 220 metres (720ft) deep. The plankwalk cuts a path over the mounds of guano – a tonne of which is made each day – and leads through to the **Garden of Eden**, an enclosed valley where the vegetation has existed undisturbed for millennia.

Near the entrance to Deer Cave, you can enjoy one of the most spectacular sights of Mulu – the nightly bats' exodus. Around 5.30pm, as the lowering sun turns the limestone walls to gold, the first flutterings can be seen, followed by an ever-increasing number of bats – up to 3.5 million – circling their way out of the cave, up and over the trees on their nightly forage for food. The dramatic spectacle (which unfortunately does not take place during rainy weather) lasts for a good 20 minutes. Bring a pair of binoculars for a closer look; sometimes lurking near the cave's

entrance or flying overhead are bat-hawks waiting for an easy meal.

Close by Deer Cave is **Lang Cave** Ⓒ, whose well-lit stalactites and stalag-mites make it one of the most beautiful of all the caves.

Clearwater Cave Ⓓ on the way to Camp 5 is located off the main river, a 30-minute boat ride from Park HQ. The 355-metre (1,165ft) deep cavern is very dark inside, but with a strong torch you'll be able to see the marvellous limestone formations, and creatures including scorpions, frogs and centipedes. An exquisitely clear river flows out of the cave from under a sheer rock face, providing a popular spot for bathing. Keep an eye out for beautiful butterflies, including the iridescent green and black Rajah Brooke's Birdwing.

Just a few minutes away, and accessible via a cliff-hugging walkway, is the dramatic **Wind Cave** Ⓔ, far smaller but filled with limestone stalactites and stalagmites with plankwalks passing the most spectacular examples.

Sarawak Chamber Ⓕ, reputedly the largest cave in the world, is only accessible to scientists, museum

experts and special adventure groups, much of it being extremely dangerous. Gaining access to the cavern involves a four-hour trek through the jungle from the nearest river point, to the small entrance from where you slide into the dank, inky blackness. This is an exciting excursion, but definitely not for the faint-hearted.

Mulu activities

It's a whole different world up here – from the plants and mosses that cover the tree barks to birds and insects that are airborne. The 480-metre (1,574ft) long **Canopy Skywalk** ⑥ at Mulu is between 15 and 25 metres (49 and 82ft) off the forest floor, offering good views of the surrounding forests. Group size for the return two-hour guided trip is limited to eight people, so bookings are essential (tel: 085-792 300). Tours leave daily at 7am, 8.30am, 10am, 10.30am, 1pm and 2pm.

If you prefer to sit in one spot and watch for wildlife, there is the 30-metre (98ft) tall **tower and bird hide** to consider. Just a 10-minute walk from the park's office, the tower is free to use; just book a time slot and pay a deposit for the key. For a fee, birdwatchers can also reserve the tower between the prime times of 5am–8am and from 5pm–8pm to birdwatch in solitude.

Apart from pleasant walks along jungle trails, there are two peaks to be conquered – **Mount Mulu** ⑪ (Gunung Mulu) at 2,377 metres (7,800ft) and **Mount Api** ① (Gunung Api), which at 1,750 metres (5,600ft) is Malaysia's highest limestone mountain. The stiff ascent of both these mountains is only recommended for very experienced (and very fit) climbers.

The Pinnacles

The strange limestone spikes known as **The Pinnacles**, on an alternative path on Mount Api, can be tackled by anyone of reasonable fitness in about two to three days. The razor-sharp peaks, some standing 45 metres (150ft) high, make a magnificent sight, almost worth

the effort of ascending the mountain. The journey there begins with a satisfying longboat trip upriver from the National Park HQ, and a short stop-off to visit the Clearwater Cave. A 4km (2.5-mile) walk through lowland forest brings you to the **Melinau river gorge** ① and **Camp 5** – a simple hut shelter and campsite overlooking the Melinau river, and the overnight base camp for the climb to The Pinnacles.

The steep climb, which takes three to six hours depending on fitness level, starts early morning. This allows enough time to reach the viewpoint by lunch, and to make the descent before dark. The ascent is only to be attempted with experienced guides, as the limestone pinnacles are razor-sharp. The rough trail passes through mossy forest where dwarfed trees are festooned with hanging moss and numerous pitcher plants, in an often misty environment.

Headhunter's Trail

The trip to Mulu can be combined with the **Headhunter's Trail**, either starting or finishing at **Limbang**. The trail, used by Kayan headhunters

The Pinnacles.

TIP

It is recommended that you wear gloves, long-sleeved shirts and long trousers when climbing The Pinnacles; the sharp rocks can cut easily.

in the 19th century, is a five- or six-day journey through the backwoods, either entering or exiting by Camp 5, although leaving from Mulu is the easier option. You'll need a tour company or, at the very least, a guide to arrange the boat transport and longhouse accommodation along the way from Limbang (see Travel Tips, page 386).

Lambir Hills

Back in Miri, there are a couple of side-trips which are the main attractions that draw most travellers to Sarawak. **Lambir Hills National Park** ❾ (tel: 085-434 184; www.sarawakforestry.com/htm/snp-np-lambir.html; park headquarters; tel: 085-471 609; Mon–Fri 8am–5pm, closed public holidays; charge), which is just south of Miri, is one of the world's most ecologically diverse parks. It makes a pleasant day trip, although chalets are available for longer stays. The park's highlights are waterfalls with natural swimming pools, as well as a climb up **Bukit Lambir**.

Much more famous, and with more to offer, is **Niah Caves National Park** ❿ (tel: 085-434 184; www.sarawak

forestry.com/htm/snp-np-niah.html; park headquarters Mon–Fri 8am–5pm, closed public holidays; charge), which, while less dramatic than Mulu, offers visitors freedom to explore on their own; guides are also available.

The limestone caves and their past inhabitants are the attraction here. In the 1950s the Sarawak Museum heard of the caves being an archaeologist's gold mine. Sure enough, when the curator dug down 5 metres (16ft), he found the skull of a young *Homo sapiens* who had lived here probably around 40,000 years ago. The Deep Skull, as it was known, was what remained of the earliest known community of *homo sapiens* in the east.

Other discoveries revealed that people living here worked with instruments made from bone and shell, made pottery, cut stone adzes and carved wooden coffins or burial boats. More recent objects, canoe-shaped coffins and paintings found in the cave known as the **Painted Cave**, date from only 1,000 years ago.

Then in 1400, they appear to have entered a tropical Dark Age, which

A ladder used for climbing up to collect birds' nests.

BIRDS' NEST COLLECTORS

The Penan rediscovered the Niah caves in the 19th century and found them to be unbelievably rich in the edible nests of the millions of swiftlets that live there. The glutinous saliva with which they build the nests is believed to have medicinal properties, and makes the nests the most expensive Chinese delicacy in Borneo. In the markets of Hong Kong and Singapore, the nests can fetch over US$1,000 per kg (2.2lbs).

The astronomical cost is almost understandable when you learn the way in which the nests are collected. A typical day's work might entail scurrying up 60 metres (200ft) on a slender rattan ladder, scraping the nests off rock ceilings and from within deep crevices – and keeping one's balance, as any fall could be fatal. You could say that the high cost of nests takes a man's life insurance into consideration.

Naturally, nest collectors guard their trade jealously, and pass their inherited territory on only to their sons. The hundreds of chambers, chimneys and sub-caves where the tiny swiftlets nest are divided into sectors, each privately owned. Some yield but a few hundred nests, others several thousand. The cave owners live in villages and longhouses situated in the park area, and during harvesting – normally two or three times a year, sometimes more – they bring the entire family along to help gather up the riches.

forced them to desert the caves. They then vanished from history.

To get to the Niah Caves, you must drive or take a bus or a taxi from either Miri or Bintulu, the former being much closer. From **Batu Niah** village, a short trip along the river brings you to the **Niah Caves Visitor Centre**.

Niah's caves

The plankwalk to the caves begins from **Pangkalan Lubang**, just across the river from the park accommodation. A museum is located right at the beginning of the walk – entry is free and the information available is useful. The 3km (2-mile) long path is built of the mighty *belian* or ironwood, a timber so dense that it will not float. You should get to the caves in about 45 minutes if the planks are dry. Sensible shoes are preferable to sandals both for the plankwalk and the caves. Other necessities include a strong torch (with spare batteries), some waterproof clothing and a water bottle.

It is well worth stopping during the walk to absorb the atmosphere of the forest and to listen to the jungle chorus. Down one of the forks in the plankwalk, you can visit a collectors' longhouse, although they may charge you to have a look around their home. At the end of the plankwalk you will arrive at a series of steps and the **Trader's Cave**, and a heap of forlorn bamboo scaffoldings where once the traders set up camp during the collecting season. The **Great Cave** is the main area for birds'-nest collection – and also for another interesting substance. Besides the three species of swiftlets of which there are said to be around 4 million, there are 12 species of bats, also countable in the millions. The strong-smelling guano lines the cave floor and is collected almost as avidly as the birds' nests – for it is a rich fertiliser. In fact, you may encounter guano collectors on the plankwalk up to the caves, lugging heavy sacks on their backs on their way to Pangkalan

Lubang, where it is weighed and then sent downriver to Batu Niah and to the markets beyond.

With a strong torch you will be able to pick out the creatures that inhabit the caves. Only two of the caves are open to visitors without a guide, and the second, the **Painted Cave**, can only be entered with a permit issued by the National Park Office in Kuching.

The most spectacular sight of all at Niah makes it worth taking camping equipment along. At 6pm, the swiftlets return into the caves to sleep in their nests, while the bats, being nocturnal animals, sweep past them out of the entrance of the cave into the night. While far less spectacular than the great Mulu exodus, it is quite an experience sitting at the cave mouth, surrounded by dense, green jungle, watching the show. The reverse "shift" takes place at daybreak. It is a sight that humans must have watched and wondered at even 40,000 years ago.

Kelabit Highlands

Several other interesting day or overnight trips can be arranged from

A longhouse carved pole.

Entrance to the Great Cave at Niah Caves.

FACT

Twelve species of bat live in the Niah Caves. Most common are the horseshoe and fruit bats, but other rare residents include the Bearded tomb bat and Cantor's roundleaf horseshoe bat.

Miri. **Bario**  is the sleepy "capital" of Kelabit country, in the midst of the Bario Highlands. A small airstrip, one of a series across the highlands, provides daily access – when the weather is right. Bario used to be remote and cool, but logging in the area has made Bario warmer and accessible. The 300km (186-mile) logging road from Miri into the heart of Bario is still a 13-hour journey overland. The Kelabit Highlands are the perfect place for trekking, stopping at longhouses along the way. One of the best treks is from Bario to **Ba'Kelalan**, a three- to four-day walk. If in season, be sure to try Ba'Kelalan's famous apples. This is the only place in Malaysia that grows apples – including Granny Smith, Apple Anna and Lady William varieties. Enquire at the Miri Visitors' Information Centre (tel: 085-434 181; Mon–Fri 8am–5pm, Sat–Sun and public holidays 9am–3pm).

Climbing Mount Murud

While the culture of the Kelabits has long since given way to the mores of a fundamentalist Christianity, the Kelabits are the kindest and most hospitable people you are ever likely to encounter. The Kelabit community is split across the border between Sarawak and Kalimantan, and are little troubled with the formalities of immigration checkpoints. Visitors are taken to an immigration checkpoint, and the simple formalities are generally ironed out with ease (or a few dollars). From Bario, and with the help of Kelabit guides, it is possible to climb **Mount Murud** (Gunung Murud). At 2,423 metres (7,949ft), this is the highest peak in Sarawak, and you need five clear days to ascend and descend the mountain, starting from Bario – a memorable experience. Kelabit guides and porters will also take you on a six-day walk back to **Long Lellang**, from where you can fly back to the other, hectic and more hurried world. For the fit and adventurous, one of these expeditions is definitely worth experiencing.

Lawas and **Limbang** are the two forgotten parts of Sarawak, two fingers that are interspersed with the sultanate of Brunei. Limbang is the starting point (or finishing point) for those following the Headhunter's Trail to Mulu.

Loagan Bunut National Park

Two hours' drive from Miri, on a turn-off before reaching Niah, is **Loagan Bunut National Park**  (tel: 082-248 088 or Miri Visitors' Centre tel: 085-775 118; www.sarawakforestry.com/htm/snp-np-loagan.html; park headquarters Mon–Fri 8am–5pm, close public holidays; charge). Gazetted only in 1991, it centres around a mysterious lake that rises and falls with the seasons. In the dry season, the lake disappears completely, leaving a cracked lake bed and an abundant fish population that hides in the mud. The fish are easy to catch, a fact that has not escaped the local population of 32 families who are permitted to fish here, or the vast numbers of birds that visit to capitalise on all that fish.

A Kelabit elder with distended earlobes, formed by wearing massive brass earrings for years.

Brunei

Across Sarawak's Baram river is a land of golden-domed mosques, resplendent palaces and fine Islamic architecture, and beneath it all lies Brunei's wealth – oil.

From Miri, most visitors are on tour packages heading to Brunei's capital city of Bandar Seri Begawan (BSB) 119km (74 miles) away. Brunei was built with oil, and all buses will stop at the town of Seria, where you will see rows of oil pumps In the city, the **Brunei Museum** (www.museums. gov.bn/bangunan.htm; Sun–Thu 9am–5pm, Fri 9am–11.30am and 2.30pm–5pm, Sat 9.45am–5pm, fasting month Sun–Thu 9am–3pm and Fri 9am–noon; free) on Jalan Kota Batu offers an interesting introduction to the country. For a snack, stop by the Tamu , the open-air market on the banks of the Kianggeh river (opens from 6am). To tour **Kampong Ayer**, a water village housing more than 25,000 Bruneians, ask to be dropped off first at the **Kampong Ayer Cultural & Tourism Gallery** for a historical introduction to the "Venice of the East". Next, you might get to meet Sultan Hassanal Bolkiah and his family in person at his private residence, **Istana Nurul Iman**. The largest palace in the world is closed to the public except for Hari Raya at the end of the fasting month. Thousands wait to greet the monarch, but once you are in the palace, you are feted with food and drinks until it is your turn to meet him. The palace is a wonderful fusion of modern and traditional Islamic architecture, the latter of which is also a featured on the **Sultan Omar Ali Saifuddien Mosque**. An elevator rides up to the 44-metre (144ft) minaret for a panoramic view of the city, and at sunset (around 6pm) the mosque takes on a magical quality. But it is not as grand as the golden-domed **Jame'Asr Hassanil Bolkiah Mosque** on Jalan Hassan Bolkiah, the country's largest, with exquisite interiors. When visiting mosques, non-Muslims have special visiting hours (Sat–Wed 8am–noon, and for one hour at 2pm, 5pm and 8pm; free). Southeast of the city, visitors can explore trails and wildlife at the **Ulu Temburong National Park,** where you might catch sight of that famous, long curved nose of the proboscis monkey. For more information see Brunei Tourism at www.bruneitourism.travel.

Visas and transport

Getting to Brunei's capital is easy from Miri; excluding the border crossings, it is about three hours' journey by PHLS Express Bus (tel: 673-771 1668; departs Miri Express Bus Terminal at Pujut Corner, Jalan Padang Kerbau; but call to check times). Buy your ticket on board; you will be given immigration forms to complete. From Miri, the bus will cross the Asean Bridge to the Malaysian checkpoint at Sungai Tujuh (6am–10pm) and then on to Kuala Belait for border formalities into Brunei, all in all taking about an hour. Try to avoid weekends, and public and school holidays. In BSB, the bus departs for Miri from the PGGMB Building on Jalan Sungai Kiangeh, opposite the tamu (open-air market). You can purchase your ticket on the bus or from Intrepid Tours (www.bruneibay.net/intrepidtours; tel: 673-222 1685) on the first floor of the PGGMB Building; they also sell bus tickets to Kota Kinabalu (call to check times of departures). Tickets purchased in Brunei are generally more expensive than buying the return ticket in Miri. Travel agents usually add a commission fee.

For visa requirements, check www.bruneitourism. travel/info/entry.html. If you need a visa on arrival, note that only Brunei or Singapore dollars are accepted for payment.

The Sultan Omar Ali Saifuddien Mosque at dusk.

Proboscis Monkeys.

SABAH

Stunningly beautiful, with an air of mystery, Sabah has now become a prime destination for wildlife watchers, adventure seekers and discoverers of the next new species.

A proboscis monkey in Lok Kawi Wildlife Park.

Sabah has become a serious adventure destination. It takes a visit of at least 10 days to do it any justice at all, and for most visitors, longer is better. In Sabah's west, the capital city of Kota Kinabalu is the gateway to attractions west of the Crocker Mountain Range. Borneo's only railway line, from Tanjung Aru near the city to Tenom in the south, mostly attracts eager whitewater thrill seekers, while the luxurious North Borneo Railway, the state's oldest steam train is the choice for more discerning travellers. The state also offers such star attractions as Mount Kinabalu (Gunung Kinabalu) and its via ferrata. On Sabah's eastern shores, wildlife attractions beyond Sandakan town outnumber the historical World War II sights. At Sepilok's famous Orang-Utan Rehabilitation Centre visitors can meet Borneo's "man of the forest" and, not far away, the proboscis monkeys of Labuk Bay. There are primal jungle retreats, and cruising along the Kinabatangan river to spot Borneo's pygmy elephants. Remote coral islands are the destination of green turtles, where visitors can witness these remarkable creatures laying their eggs.

Add some of the best diving in Asia off the southern shores of Sabah – the prime spot, Pulau Sipadan, is rated as one of the world's top five wall dives, while nearby Pulau Mabul is one of the world's best muck-diving sites – and it's no wonder that Sabah is becoming a favoured destination.

Sabah may lack the longhouses and distinctive tribal communities of Sarawak, but it has remarkable natural assets. Places like the untouched Danum Valley and the nearby Maliau Basin – a self-contained biodiversity lab teeming with species – are standouts. Largely unexplored, the basin is revealing new discoveries of flora and fauna rare and endemic to this area. The government has gone to great lengths to preserve this natural heritage, instilling pride in this unique environment into the hearts of the people who live here.

A meal of fried fish in Kota Kinabalu.

KOTA KINABALU AND THE WEST

Sabah's capital is dominated by stunning vistas of the towering Mount Kinabalu. Nearby, ride wild river rapids and a steam train before heading into the interior.

ompared with the rest of the state, the western part of Sabah is a mountainous region. The Crocker Mountain Range stretches from Tenom in the south to Kinabalu National Park in the north and includes the country's highest peak – Mount Kinabalu. In addition to visiting cultural villages and local markets and exploring the few nature parks here, adventurous visitors will find plenty to do – from diving off Pulau Layang Layang island to whitewater rafting on the Padas river in the south. The gateway to the region's attractions and the best introduction to Sabahans and their culture is the state capital, Kota Kinabalu.

Kota Kinabalu

Kota Kinabalu ❶, on the northwest coast, is a modern city with little old-world charm. Facing the west coast, it affords splendid sunsets over the offshore islands – sunsets which are symbolic of Kota Kinabalu's history – a litany of heated passions, fights and fires before the city reached its present, easy-going ways.

Ever since it was chosen as the site for British North Borneo's west coast base, the town has continued to encroach on the sea. Reclamation was the answer to the shortage of flat land, a process that continues as the need for this precious commodity grows. Even the "coastal highway" was pushed

inland by the reclamation of huge areas of shallow sea, and one of the few remaining water villages, which was known by the generic name of Kampung Air, was demolished in 2003.

About 3km (2 miles) north of Kota Kinabalu city is the monumental **Bandaraya Mosque ❹** (Masjid Bandaraya; for non-Muslims, Sat–Thu 8am–5pm; free), in Teluk Likas. The floating City Mosque is a fine example of contemporary Islamic architecture and shares similar features to the Nabawi Mosque in Medina. Its prayer hall can

Main Attractions

Sabah State Museum
Kota Belud's Tamu Besar
Mount Kinabalu
Mesilau Nature Resort
Poring canopy walkway
Poring Orchid Conservation Centre
Monsopiad Cultural Village
North Borneo Railway
Murut Cultural Centre
Pulau Layang Layang

In the foothills of Mount Kinabalu.

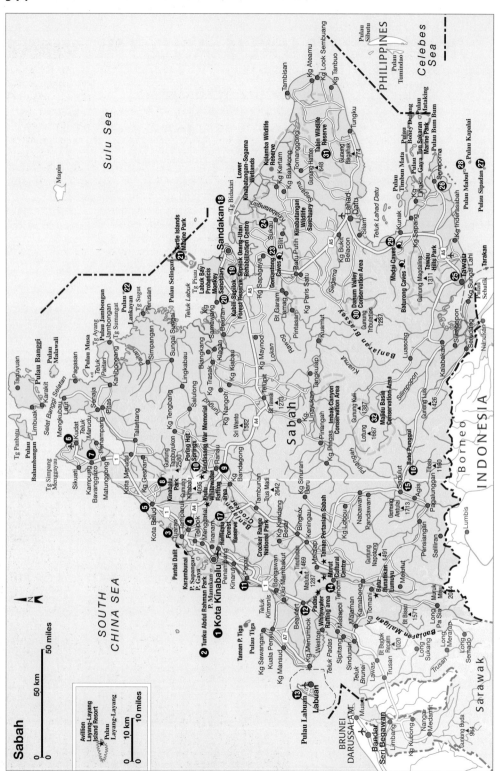

Sabah

0 ___ 50 km

0 ___ 50 miles

**Aviillon
Layang-Layang
Island Resort**
Pulau
Layang-Layang

0 ___ 10 km

0 ___ 10 miles

**SOUTH
CHINA SEA**

Sulu Sea

PHILIPPINES

**Celebes
Sea**

Pulau Sibutu

Pulau
Tumindao

Kg Look Sembuang

Kg Tanbuo

Mapin

Tg Panbatu

Tg Simpang
Mengayau

Pulau
Balambangan

Limbuak

Pulau Banggi

Karakit

Pulau
Malawali

Mengkubau
Laut

Pagasan

Tambisan

Kg Ateamu

Pulau
Tunggku
Paiting

Tg Tanjung
Bagahak

Kulamba Wildlife
Reserve

Tabin Wildlife
Reserve

Pulau
Boheg Dulang

Pulau
Mataking

Pulau Bum Bum

Tomanggong

Gunung
Bagahak
774

Pulau Kapalai

Pulau
Timbun Mata

Lahad
Datu

Pulau
Gaya

Tun Sakaran
Marine Park

Semporna

Pulau Mabul

Pulau Sipadan

INDONESIA

Borneo

Sarawak

**BRUNEI
DARUSSALAM**

**Bandar
Seri Begawan**

⓵ **Kota Kinabalu**

⓶ **Tunku Abdul Rahman Park**

⓭ **Labuan**

Sabah

also accommodate up to 12,000 people at a time. About 4km (2.5 miles) to the south of the city centre, the **Sabah State Museum & Heritage Village B** (Jalan Bukit Istana Lama; tel: 088-253 199; www.museum.sabah.gov.my; daily 9am–5pm; charge) is built in a stylised version of traditional Rungus and Murut tribal architecture. The museum has a good collection of Chinese ceramics, and the ethnological and textile sections are growing. The section on Sabah's fascinating flora and fauna helps to make sense of the bewildering variety of wildlife in the state. Also within the complex are an art gallery and a science centre with an exhibition on the oil and petroleum industry. There is also a collection of 10 life-sized traditional houses in the Heritage Village, set in the museum gardens. Each house depicts the architecture of a different ethnic group. A restaurant, a coffee house, an ethno-botanical garden with an artificial lake and a souvenir shop complete the complex.

West of the museum, off the airport road, is the famous **Tanjung Aru Beach**. The sea here is generally calm, the sand is clean and the coastal food stalls and restaurants offer delicious local cuisine.

The city itself is a blend of ultra-modern structures and old Chinese shophouses. Walk along **Jalan Gaya C** to spot the town's few remaining traditional provision shops, where a delightful jumble of groceries, canned foods and sacks of rice, displayed as artfully as a film set, invite closer inspection. On Sunday mornings, there is the very popular **Gaya Street Fair** (6.30am–1pm) – a city version of the traditional weekly *tamu*, which are markets held in venues across the state. Cheap clothes, plants, foodstuffs and, occasionally, bargain local handicrafts and antiques can be found.

The **Sabah Tourism Board D** (tel: 088-212 121; www.sabahtourism.com; Mon–Fri 8am–5pm, Sat–Sun 9am–4pm) on Jalan Gaya was once the main post office; its solid, white-stone

walls and colonial architecture make a pleasant contrast to the concrete shophouses.

Waterfront Esplanade

The **Waterfront Esplanade** stretches the entire length of Jalan Tun Fuad Stephens and is popular for locals and visitors. There are many dining and shopping options here. The bustling **Central Market E** sits midway along the Waterfront Esplanade, best seen early in the morning as fishermen unload their catch directly onto market tables. Kadazandusun women display their exotic range of fresh fruit and vegetables. One section specialises in tobacco and betel nut products, while yeast tablets for making the local rice wine, *tapai*, hang in strings like big white beads. Adjacent is the **Handicraft Market** (daily 9am–4.30pm) – a casual affair where handicrafts and souvenirs, mostly from the Philippines, are sold in rows of small stalls. Watch your wallet as you practise your bargaining skills.

At the end of the day, Kota Kinabalu's restaurants come alive, and some of the best food in the state is served

A Sabah Museum display.

Fishing boats in Kota Kinabalu.

in small coffee shops dotted around the town. As with towns in Peninsular Malaysia, night markets are ever-present, selling clothes and curios, as well as local delicacies.

Few older buildings remain in town, but take note of the **Atkinson Clock Tower ℉** at the end of the Padang. Further along Jalan Bukit Bendara, you'll reach the observatory on **Signal Hill Ⓖ**️ (daily 8am–midnight; free), which offers expansive views of the city and of the bay and islands. Situated at the eastern end of the city, the hill can be reached on foot, or by taxi or bus.

Tunku Abdul Rahman Park

Offshore from Kota Kinabalu, surrounded by azure waters, are the five islands of **Tunku Abdul Rahman Park ❷**, a popular destination whether for day trips or longer. The marine park headquarters is on Pulau Gaya, the largest of the islands. The other islands that make up the park are **Manukan**, **Mamutik**, **Sapi** and **Sulug**. Snorkelling can be enjoyed on all of these, and is best on remote Sulug. Pulau Manukan, the most

developed of the islands, has chalets, a restaurant and a swimming pool.

All the islands except Sulug have nature trails. Wildlife can be spotted on occasion, sometimes closer than you'd like; watch out for the thieving macaque monkeys on Pulau Sapi. Pied hornbills and sea eagles can sometimes be seen on Pulau Gaya, and you may even spot a turtle surfacing as you swim.

You can camp on any of the islands, but you must obtain a permit from the Sabah Parks office (tel: 088-523 500; www.sabahparks.org.my). Boats to the islands leave from the **Jesselton Point** ferry terminal, located at the end of Lorong Satu.

North of Kota Kinabalu

Sabah's long west coast stretches all the way from the Sarawak border to the northern tip at **Kudat** and **Pulau Banggi** in the Sulu Sea, almost meeting the southern Philippines boundary. This area is ideally explored by car, with the freedom to stop at will. Although some areas outside the city may require a four-wheel-drive vehicle, the trunk road linking Kota Kinabalu

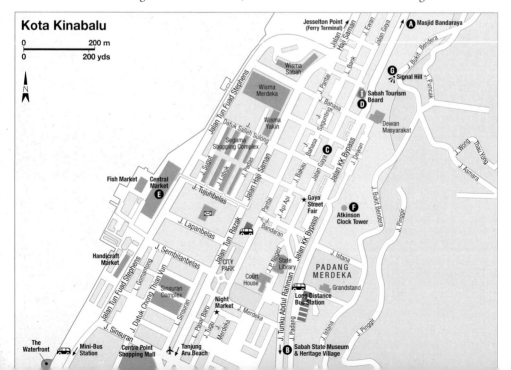

Kota Kinabalu

0 ———— 200 m
0 ———— 200 yds

N

Jesselton Point (Ferry Terminal)
Ⓐ Masjid Bandaraya
J. Ewan
Jalan Haji Saman
J. Bukit Bendera
Jalan Gaya
Bank
J. Pantai
Ⓖ Signal Hill
J. Puncak
Wisma Sabah
Jalan Tun Fuad Stephens
Wisma Merdeka
J. Bahasa
Ⓘ Sabah Tourism Board
Ⓓ
Wisma Yakin
Jalan Datuk Salleh Sulong
Segama Shopping Complex
Segunting
J. Bahasa
Dewan Masyarakat
J. Wong
Thai Yong
Ⓒ
J. Asmara
Jalan Haji Saman
Jalan Gaya
Jalan KK Bypass
J. Devan
Fish Market
Central Market Ⓔ
J. Sugut
J. Labuk
J. Padas
J. Pantai
J. Api-Api
J. Baikau
J. Tujuhbelas
Gaya Street Fair
J. Bukit Bendera
J. Pinggir
Atkinson Ⓕ Clock Tower
J. Lapanbelas
Jalan Tun Razak
Jalan Haji Saman
J. Bandaran
Handicraft Market
J. Sembilanbelas
Jalan Tun Fuad Stephens
J. Gomantong
CITY PARK
State Library
J. P. Negeri
Jalan KK Bypass
J. Istana
PADANG MERDEKA
Sinsuran Complex
Court House
Night Market
J. Pasar Baru
J. Tugu
J. Merdeka
J. Merdeka
Long Distance Bus Station
Grandstand
J. Datuk Chong Thian Vun
J. Sinsuran
Jalan Tun Fuad Stephens
Tanjung Aru Beach
Jalan Tunku Abdul Rahman
J. Padang
J. Istana
J. Pinggir
The Waterfront
Mini-Bus Station
Centre Point Shopping Mall
Ⓑ Sabah State Museum & Heritage Village

with **Sandakan** in Sarawak and the east coast is bitumen, and a cursory exploration of the state by road presents no difficulty at all.

The road north of Kota Kinabalu leads towards **Tuaran** ❸, passing en route several ceramics factories near Telipok where visitors are welcome to stop for a look and maybe make a purchase or two. At a large roundabout, you can either head north to Tuaran and a couple of beach resorts, or turn right towards **Ranau** and **Kinabalu National Park.**

Tuaran is a small town known for its colourful Sunday *tamu* (6am–2pm). Get there early morning to enjoy the market at its best. It is also noted for a local culinary speciality known as *Tuaran mee* – a delicious mixture of fried noodles, vegetables, egg, pork and pork crackling. Enjoy it in one of the shops on the main street before heading to the *tamu*. **Kampung Surusup** is about 15 minutes from Tuaran. There, negotiate a price with the boatmen at the jetty, who will take you by motorised canoe to visit **Kampung Penambawan** – a traditional Bajau fishing village, which

is slowly being deserted in favour of a nearby new village on land.

About 40 minutes north of town are a couple of beach areas. **Pantai Dalit** is a long strip of white sand backed by forested hills, while nearby is **Karambunai beach.** In the vicinity, by a road just before Tuaran, is the **Mengkabong Water Village**, a rambling Bajau sea gypsy complex of raised stilted pathways and dozens of attap-thatched stilted huts built over an estuary. Transport around the village is by canoe, although many houses are also connected to one another by precarious-looking plankwalks.

On the road leading towards Ranau, at Telibong, is a typical Sabah village house, but there is something really awkward about it. Locally known as **Rumah Terbalik**, this unusual building is Southeast Asia's first upside down house. House flipping is not new, but here it is a novelty built to demonstrate that unchecked development may affect the environment and turn the world upside down. Built on a slight incline, it comes complete with fittings and furnishings, even a car, so

TIP

For a closer look at the corals and marine life around the Tunku Abdul Rahman Park, try "sea walking" – walking on the seabed while wearing an underwater helmet – along the shores of Gaya Island. Contact Amazing Borneo Tours and Events on tel: 088-448 409.

Inspecting the day's catch on Kota Kinabalu's waterfront.

SHOP

Every major town will have a *tamu* or market where you can buy fresh local fruits and delicacies. Check with Sabah Tourism Board (tel: 088-212 121; www.sabahtourism.com) for the one closest to you.

mind your head as you explore! Further down the road is the old-world village of **Tamparuli** ❹, where the original shopping area consists of traditional wooden buildings, a sight fast fading across the country. Tamparuli is also the site of a Wednesday *tamu* (6am–2pm).

Flowing beside Tamparuli is the **Kiulu river**, a scenic area where the waters run clean. Kiulu is very popular as a scenic rafting destination, offering a more docile ride than the raging waters of the Padas river to the south.

Kota Belud

Kota Belud ❺ is less than one hour's drive north from Kota Kinabalu and has two claims to fame. Firstly, it is renowned for the Bajau "cowboys", well-known for their skills in rearing and handling horses and buffalo. Secondly, it is the scene of one of Sabah's most colourful weekly *tamu*. Bajau and Kadazandusun women, their faces crinkled by the harsh sun, squat beside their wares – tobacco wrappers, piles of fresh vegetables or sugary doughnuts – for hours on end, constantly chewing betel nuts, which stain their gums

Fishing boats docked in Kota Kinabalu.

and teeth a vivid red. There is always more on sale at the *tamu* than mundane necessities – an entire market row is devoted to the accoutrements of betel nut-chewing. These women use the *tamu* not just to sell their wares, but also as a chance to catch up on the latest news and gossip. Plan your trip to coincide with Kota Belud's Tamu Besar, which is Sabah's biggest market. Besides the best goods on sale, locals dress in colourful costumes, while the horses are bedecked in costumes of their own. The Bajau horsemen will show off their horse-riding skills, and there is buffalo racing to entertain the crowds. Contact the Sabah Tourism Board (tel: 088-212 121; www.sabahtourism.com) for more information.

Rungus country

From Kota Belud, the road heads north towards Kudat, and **Rungus** country – home to perhaps the most traditional and talented craftspeople in the state. **Kudat** ❻ was the state's first capital (albeit for a mere two years), and once an important port in the trade between China and Europe.

Today, Kudat is the centre for the northwestern administrative district, and is also an active fishing port. Although the Kudat region has escaped the attention of tourists in the past, the traditional cultures of the Rungus and the long stretches of white sandy beaches, unspoilt and unpopulated, are making it an increasingly popular destination.

The Rungus are traditional agriculturalists, and a subgroup of the Kadazandusun tribe. Known for their excellent weaving and beadwork, they live in small communities, either in longhouses or, increasingly, in single-family dwellings.

The Rungus have retained their traditional spiritualistic and animist beliefs, much longer than have the other tribes of Sabah. They are also famous for the brass coils once used by women to decorate their arms. Nowadays, this practice has been discontinued – although you might still see forearm coils on older women. While the women continue to weave shoulder sashes, other woven textiles are rare; these days, people tend to wear decorated black cloth instead.

Their excellent beadwork is quite visible in many of the *tamu* in the area.

Rungus life

It is possible to visit a Rungus longhouse, and some have been constructed especially for visitors. Built in a green valley, **Kampung Bavanggazo** ❼, not far from the road leading to Kudat, has two purpose-built tourist longhouses where visitors will get to see Rungus women at work, weaving and making handicrafts. In the evening, enjoy a performance of Rungus dance and sample the local food and rice wine. Contact Sabah Tourism Board (tel: 088-212 121; www.sabahtourism.com) in Kota Kinabalu for details. At the nearby **Kampung Sumangkap**, traditional gong-making is the major activity, and at **Kampung Gombizau**, villagers have taken up beekeeping and produce wax, honey and royal jelly.

There is also a large Hakka Chinese community living in Kudat, the first area to be inhabited by the Chinese in the 1880s; many of them are Christians and farmers by tradition. The ideal way to explore the Kudat

Planks connect the houses on stilts of Bajau Water Village.

Kota Kinabalu's city coat-of-arms.

Ratan balls.

Boys at the Bajau Water Village, Mengkabung.

region is in a four-wheel-drive vehicle, as some of the roads leading to the beaches are little more than dirt tracks. If you don't fancy staying overnight in a longhouse, then a good range of hotels is available in Kudat.

About 14km (7 miles) before Kudat, signs direct the visitor to **Simpang Menggayau**, the northernmost point of the island of Borneo. **Kalampunian beach**, just before the headland, is glorious, as are the beaches on the two bays of **Pantai Kelambu**, further south.

Mount Kinabalu

Everyone in Malaysia knows about the mysterious **Mount Kinabalu**, (Gunung Kinabalu) which, at 4,095 metres (13,435ft), is one of the highest peaks between the Himalayas and New Guinea.

The mountain is said to still be growing, at a rate of half a centimetre a year. Relatively young, its jagged crown was sculpted by the last Ice Age, about 9,000 years ago. Although Kinabalu's peak is below the snow line, it grows cold enough here in December for ice to form in the rock pool at the base of the summit. Dropping away 1,800 metres (5,900ft) straight downwards is the terrifying **Low's Gully**, its name being a typical piece of British understatement.

Well-laid trails with steps and wooden rails help today's climber ascend and descend the mountain in just two days.

Accommodation is available at the park headquarters, and high on the mountain slopes. At the former, choices range from hostels to chalets, from basic to almost grandiose. There are two restaurants (as well as a cheaper local restaurant on the main road just opposite the drive up to the park entrance), and a shop selling basic food supplies for climbers. In the administration building, on the hill to the right, just inside the park entrance, the Kinabalu Natural History Gallery (daily 9am–3pm; free) has an interesting range of exhibits. There is also a range of accommodation on the eastern side of Kinabalu National Park, at **Mesilau Nature**. On the mountain, huts at Panar Laban offer cooking facilities and sleeping bag hire, while **Laban Rata Resthouse** has a restaurant and heated rooms.

The easiest way to reach **Kinabalu National Park** ❽ (tel: 088-889 098; www.sabahparks.org.my/eng/kinabalu_park/default.asp; daily 24 hours, activities daily 8am–4pm, Sabah Parks office Mon–Fri 8am–5pm; charge) from Kota Kinabalu is by minibus. From 7am to 8pm, the bus leaves for Ranau from the long-distance bus station near the Padang. The trip to this World Heritage Site takes a little under two hours, and the driver will turn off the main road to drop travellers at the park entrance. Apart from climbing Mount Kinabalu, there is another side attraction on its northern rock face. The **Mountain Torq** (tel: 088-268 126; www.mountaintorq.com) is Asia's first via ferrata or "iron road". Located between 3,200 metres (10,499ft) and 3,800 metres (12,476ft) above sea level, it is the world's highest via ferrata, comprising two trails of iron rungs, cables and rails (Low's Peak Circuit and the shorter Walk the Torq). Every September/October, the **Mount Kinabalu International Climbathon** attracts thousands of climbers with the objective of racing to the top while covering a distance of 21km (13 miles) or an elevation of 2,250 metres (7,382ft) within four hours.

Before leaving the city, book your accommodation with **Sutera Sanctuary Lodges** (tel: 088-308 914; www.suterasanctuarylodge.com.my) at Wisma Sabah in Kota Kinabalu. Most of the year, particularly July and August and on public holidays, accommodation is tight and bookings need to be made well in advance. Alternatively, book a package tour with any of Kota Kinabalu's tour operators. Stock up on food if you want to do your own cooking, as the shop at the headquarters offers mainly noodles and chocolate. Bring a hat and gloves, as it can be extremely cold on the summit, and a waterproof garment to protect you from the frequent rainfall. If possible, leave your luggage at a hotel and take a light pack only, or use the luggage storage area at the park headquarters. A torch is also

useful for the final ascent, which usually starts long before dawn.

On the way to Kinabalu National Park, you will pass by Tamparuli, 50km (30 miles) north of Kinabalu. Less than a kilometre past this town, the road begins to ascend the foothills, through landscape that is often swathed in clouds. On the left-hand side of the road as you climb – provided the weather is clear – you can catch glimpses of tiny villages, rice fields and pineapple plantations clinging to almost impossibly steep slopes. The main centre for these villages is **Nabalu**, where a *tamu* is held every Thursday. Kadazandusun women arrive early morning, their goods carried on enormous baskets on their backs. Nabalu is also a popular stop for tour buses, as it is a good place to buy genuine native handicrafts, local fruits and wild honey. You can also get a panoramic view from the top of the wooden viewing tower.

Climbing up to Laban Rata

Although Kinabalu is an easy mountain to climb, a certain degree of fitness is required. Some regular exercise

FACT

Allied bombers used Mount Kinabalu's peak as a navigational aid to assist their raids on Japanese targets during World War II.

Transporting supplies by canoe to Bajau Water Village.

TIP

On your arrival at the park, the staff at Sutera Sanctuary Lodges will confirm your bookings, including those for the huts on the mountain. Maps, books and souvenirs are available at the souvenir store. You might choose not to climb the same day you arrive, so make yourself comfortable, acclimatise to the cool air, check out the Kinabalu Natural History Gallery and the mainly photographic display above the main restaurant, and explore the fascinating **Mountain Garden**, which houses plants from all over the park.

Sunrise from Mount Kinabalu.

is recommended before the actual climb so that you don't come down the mountain a wreck of cramps, headaches and fatigue.

After paying for a climbing permit, arrange for a local guide who will, for a fee, accompany visitors up the mountain (the guides are independent and can be found outside the registration office). Porters can also be hired at the park headquarters and will carry luggage as far as Laban Rata. Fees depend on how heavy your luggage is; anything over 10kg (22lbs) will cost more. For more information about the guide and porter fees, check the Sabah Tourism Board at www.sabahtourism.com/destination/kinabalu-park.

Just before the trail begins, there is a rather forbidding notice placed by the park authorities, recommending against climbs by those with the following conditions: hypertension, diabetes, obesity, chronic asthma, heart disease, arthritis, anaemia, ulcers, hepatitis, muscular cramps and epilepsy.

Climbing 1,500 metres (4,950ft) in one day – from the power station above the headquarters to **Laban Rata** – takes

inordinate reserves of strength and zest for those who lead sedentary lives. Although experienced and intrepid climbers have climbed to the summit and back in less than three hours in the Kinabalu Climbathon, most people have an interest not just in getting to the top, but in fully savouring the views, and the area's flora and fauna.

Passing the welcome gate at the power station (with the greeting *Selamat Mendaki* – "Happy Climbing!" written over the arch), the first steps lead down into a small, lush valley with a waterfall. After the waterfall, the climb begins, at first gently, later steeply through montane rainforest.

All around you are some of the park's 1,500 species of orchids, clinging to mossy tree trunks and surrounded by swinging vines. Steep stairs leading ever upwards are happily spaced out between gentler paths. Small rest huts and viewpoints are positioned all the way up the trail to give the out-of-breath climber an excuse to stop and admire the view. You need not bring water, as there is pure mountain water available at all rest stops. At 1,300

REVERED PLACE OF THE DEAD

The closer one journeys towards its famous jagged profile – often wreathed in feathery clouds – the better one understands the meaning Mount Kinabalu has for the local Kadazandusun people. They call it Aki Nabalu, or Revered Place of the Dead. It is believed that the spirits of the tribe's dead ancestors dwell among the forbidding peaks, and in the past no one dared climb to the top for fear of disturbing and angering them. Another legend tells of a local woman married to a Chinese prince, who went to visit his parents in China and never returned. Every night, she would climb the mountain to watch for his ship until, exhausted, she died on its slopes. The spirit of the mountain turned her to stone and the people of her village renamed the mountain "Cina Balu" or Chinese Widow in her honour.

In spite of the taboos and myths linked to the mountain, Hugh Low, a young British officer, was still keen to reach the top. In 1851, he was accompanied by a local chief and his guides. Struggling through the intense tangle of vegetation of the lower slopes, Low eventually reached the summit plateau, but never scaled the highest peak. Reportedly he claimed it was "inaccessible to any but winged animals". He made a further ascent in 1858, but the honour of reaching the summit actually ended up going to naturalist John Whitehead, who generously named it Low's Peak in honour of the earlier climber, in 1888.

metres (4,200ft), the vegetation on either side of the trail begins to change from lowland rainforest into oak and chestnut forests of more temperate flora, like ferns and flowering plants.

Proceeding up to the next level of vegetation, one has the feeling of growing larger the higher one climbs. The trail began with huge trees towering above; now the trees have shrunk and you are almost the tallest thing in the landscape. At 2,600 metres (8,500ft), you'll see small gnarled trees, twisted and wrinkled by the mountain air. The soil is poor here, and lichens cling desperately to the little trees.

The soil disappears altogether at 3,300 metres (10,800ft) and the granite body of the mountain reveals itself. Only sedges, grasses and tiny alpine flowers cling to the rocky crevices where a bit of soil might remain.

Just when you thought you'd left all civilisation far below on the trail – now a hazy ribbon in the afternoon mist – you arrive at a series of huts and the rest-house where you will spend the night.

A leisurely climb should get you here by around 2pm. At Laban, you can retreat into the cosy Laban Rata Resthouse with its magnificent balcony looking up to the peak. There is a simple restaurant, as well as dormitories and hot showers. A little further up the slope are Gunting Lagadan Hut and Panar Laban Hut, which has dormitory rooms, sleeping bags for hire, and a basic kitchen equipped with cooking utensils and electricity, but no heater.

Some climbers may find it hard to sleep on the mountain because of the thin air and the headaches caused by the altitude, so remember to bring some anti-headache tablets. Yet you will need to go to sleep extra early to be able to struggle out of bed at 2am (your guide will wake you).

From Laban Rata to the summit

On the second day, climbing from the Laban Rata Resthouse usually begins at 3am, although you can request

your guide to start at 5am to avoid the crowds at the summit. Take a hot drink before starting the climb and don't forget to stuff some chocolate into your pocket to provide instant energy for the climb and against the cold, and bring your raincoat. Other than cameras, everything else can be left at the hut for retrieval on the way down.

Soon you will be climbing rock faces of granite in the pitch black as you hold onto the rope systems that guide the way. The steepness of the incline is difficult to gauge in the dark, though, and the granite slopes can be slippery after a night's rain. With an early start, you will be labouring up the slabs of granite with the peak in sight just as the skies begin to lighten. Here the granite rock, bared to the winds, is crumbling and broken, but at last Low's Peak arises.

Venturing a look down into the depths of **Low's Gully**, the view is awe-inspiring. This does indeed seem a place for spirits, for few mortals could long endure the harsh weather that sweeps away the offerings of sacrificial chickens, eggs, tobacco, betel

TIP

Before you embark on your trek of Mount Kinabalu, get hold of the introductory leaflet, *Mount Kinabalu: A Guide to the Summit Trail*, published by Sabah Parks.

Rungus beadwork.

Sweet and sour fish at Asamanis in Kota Kinabalu.

Preparing betel nut.

nut, *sireh* leaves, limes and rice left here by the Kadazandusun.

The descent can be more leisurely, especially by climbers still glowing with the success of having reached the summit, but appearances can be deceptive. While it is easier on the lungs, the descent is hell to pay on the knees and, in the end, can be even more painful than the climb up.

After collecting your belongings from Laban Rata Resthouse, you will continue down through unique vegetation, such as pitcher plants that were probably missed on the ascent. On your arrival at the park headquarters, you can rightfully claim your certificate commemorating your ascent, only for sale to those who have made it to the top. However, there is another "best effort" certificate of a different colour for those who managed only a certain portion of the route.

Mesilau

A second 5.5km (3.5-mile) trail up the mountain begins in the eastern part of the park at **Mesilau**, a tougher, steeper climb that hardcore mountaineers will

relish. The Mesilau trail joins the main summit trail near the rest stop at Layang Layang.

Mesilau is reached by road via Kundasang (5km/3 miles from park headquarters), a densely packed market garden where some of the cool-climate vegetables and flowers grown on the hill slopes are sold at the stalls along the main road. Just down the road towards Mesilau, the Kundasang War Memorial on the right is a series of beautifully maintained courtyards and gardens honouring those who lost their lives in the infamous Death March near the end of World War II. Of 2,600 Allied prisoners held by the Japanese in Sandakan, only six survived after escaping near Ranau.

Set amid wild beauty at almost 2,000 metres (6,562ft), Mesilau Nature Resort was built almost two decades ago, and offers a range of attractive wooden chalets tucked away in the towering forest. The restaurant is set over a crystal-clear mountain stream, and the wooden deck is a great place to relax during clear weather.

Mesilau is especially noted for a hill slope where the huge *Nepenthes rajah* and other pitcher plants can always be found, along with stunning montane orchids. The guided 20-minute Nepenthes Rajah Nature Trail starting from the Crocker Range Lodge shows you a beautiful array of pitcher plants and orchids (if in bloom), and, crossing a suspension bridge over the Mesilau river, montane forest views, cascading waterfalls and the Mesilau Pinnacles can be seen. There is a self-guided half-hour trail from the Bishop's Head Hostel to the restaurant complex, which meanders through an oak-chestnut forest, with a carpet of wild gingers and a stream where the pink-blossomed Kinabalu balsam thrives.

From Mesilau, the road leads to Poring via **Ranau ❾**, the main centre for the market gardens of the Kadazandusun country around Mount Kinabalu. At the weekly tamu in Ranau, held on the riverbank just outside town, you will see rural people dressed in a mix of traditional dress (black sarong) and Western attire.

Poring Hot Springs

At **Poring** ⑩, 45km (30 miles) to the east beyond Ranau, natural hot sulphur springs (tel: 088-878 801; daily 7am–6pm; charge) will soothe those tired muscles you earned climbing the mountain.

Pleasant chalets with cooking facilities, and a couple of hostels are available, but few visitors rest long before making straight for the baths. The baths are set in park-like grounds with hibiscus bushes and frangipani trees, with the untamed jungle above and beyond. They were originally built during World War II by the Japanese, with their love of communal bathing giving them the impetus to tame the jungle, and channel in both hot and cold water – the latter to temper the heat of mineral water. If you are using the private bathtub, give yourself an hour to fill it to the brim. Your body soothed, you may like to check out the canopy walkway and the butterfly park.

Poring's 158-metre (518ft) long canopy walkway strung high above the ground between giant dipterocarp trees, which literally offers a bird's-eye view of the forest, is well worth checking out. From time to time, a Rafflesia appears in the jungle areas around Poring. Near the baths is the butterfly park, filled with beautiful local species and some other remarkable insects, while the **Poring Orchid Conservation Centre** has the largest collection of Sabah orchids.

South of Kota Kinabalu

Heading south from Kota Kinabalu, follow the signs from Putatan to the **Monsopiad Cultural Village** (Kampung Kuai Kandazon, Penampang; tel: 088-774 337; www.sabahtourism.com; daily 9am–5pm; charge), a reconstructed Kadazan village in traditional style, built on the same site where the great headhunter Monsopiad lived about 300 years ago. His collection of skulls still hangs in the rafters, and the centre is run by his direct descendants. Cultural shows featuring Kadazandusun dances to an authentic band are

> **TIP**
>
> You can also mingle with the locals by hopping on board the Sabah State Railway (tel: 088-254 611) train that leaves Tanjung Aru Kepayan station at 7.45am, arriving Beaufort station at 9.40am. Trains depart Beaufort the same day at 1.30pm, arriving at Tenom at 4pm. You return the next day, leaving Tenom (tel: 087-735 514) at 7.30am, arriving at Beaufort at 10am, before departing again at 11am and arriving back at Tanjung Aru Kepayan station at 1pm with a stop in Papar.

A gibbon in Kinabalu.

KINABALU'S BIODIVERSITY

A guide can introduce you to Kinabalu's magnificent flora and fauna, some of it unique to the region. Among the rare plants found here is the famous Rafflesia and nine species of pitcher plants. In 1858, the explorer Spencer St John chanced upon a huge specimen of the latter that contained approximately 1 gallon (4 litres) of rain-water.

The park is unique in the world of flora, containing plants from almost every area on earth: the Himalayas, China, Australia, New Zealand, alpine Europe and even America. There are 1,500 species of orchid, 26 kinds of rhododendron and 60 types of oak and chestnut, as well as 80 species of fig tree. Animals found here include orang-utan, gibbons, leaf monkeys, tarsiers, pangolin (scaly anteaters), wild pig and deer. There is also a whole host of "flying" animals, some rarely found in other parts of Malaysia, including flying squirrels, colugos, snakes and lizards. Also found here – but seldom seen – is the incredibly rare clouded leopard.

The 518 species of birds include several kinds of hornbill, the scarlet sunbird, the mountain bush warbler, the mountain blackeye, and the mountain's own Kinabalu friendly warbler. Around the area's waterfalls, look for the lovely butterflies, some as large as birds, and the less easy-to-see stick insects, well camouflaged to the human eye. You might also see squirrels, lizards, tree-shrews and bats.

TIP

It is a rare treat to see a Rafflesia bud or flower, but in Sabah chances are good, since it has the largest Rafflesia population. If in bloom, watch out for an announcement notice at the Poring Hot Spring & Nature Reserve, which has a Rafflesia flower site.

held daily (9am, 11am, 2pm and 4pm). The emphasis is on a "living museum" where Kadazandusun culture can survive and be promoted.

Western Sabah

About 50km (31 miles) south of Kota Kinabalu is **Papar** ⓫, situated on the mouth of the Papar river. Paddy fields surround the town and on the coast is a pleasant stretch of sand called **Pantai Manis**, or Sweet beach, which is popular with photographers wanting to get nice sunset shots. The Sunday *tamu* is a lively scene, as Kadazandusun traders bring their wares from the surrounding hills. The most interesting (and slowest) way to get to Papar is by local train; Borneo's only railway goes from Tanjung Aru near Kota Kotabalu to Beaufort and onwards to Tenom in the interior. The journey is even more memorable – albeit more expensive – on the restored wood-fired steam train known as the North Borneo Railway (www.suteraharbour. com). Relive the colonial days as you pass through the paddy fields on a four-hour return journey, enjoying

Hamin Do Kakadazan house in Monsopiad Cultural Village.

Continental breakfast and a curry tiffin lunch on the way. The main highway continues on to the town of **Beaufort** ⓬ and beyond to Sipitang, then to Sindumin on the Sarawak border. Beaufort is a busy highway junction, and an important stop on the railway line. It is also the staging point for whitewater rafting trips on the **Padas river** (see page 327), which is directly accessed by rail. Even if you don't participate, you can watch rafts hurtling down the rapids from the comfort of your rail carriage.

Pulau Labuan

Beaufort is on the edge of a swampy peninsula with isolated fishing villages. Just offshore is **Pulau Labuan** ⓭, an international banking centre and an island that hopes to give Bermuda, Cayman and the Channel Islands a run for their money. A British naval station was established on the island in the 1870s, and the Japanese forces in Borneo surrendered here in 1945, but other than those two events, little of significance transpired on the island.

The island is also being developed for tourism, and a number of wrecks off the coast are said to be worthwhile.

Tenom

Located right at the end of Borneo's only railway, **Tenom** ⓮ is the centre of Murut country and a rich agricultural centre. The Muruts or "Men of the Hills" are the indigenous population and though many young people of the tribe have adopted the trappings of the Western civilisation creeping in from the capital, some still prefer life in remote areas. Young warriors still take their hunting dogs out for a stroll in the jungle to catch supper, hunting with a *parang* (a large, sharp knife) and a shotgun, rather than a blowpipe. Others have turned to cultivating the countryside and growing crops.

A popular festive pastime in the few remaining longhouses is jumping on the *lansaran*, a huge trampoline-like

structure supported by a wooden platform. The largest can hold 40 people – perhaps the entire population of the longhouse – the basis for a wild party. The best longhouses can be found around Kamabong, south of Tenom.

Riding the Padas river

Tenom is also close to the starting point for the Padas river ride, run by several tour operators out of Kota Kinabalu. After arriving at **Kampung Pangi** on the train from Beaufort, having passed through the dramatic Padas Gorge, rafters disembark, and rafts are carried to the river. There is time for a brief lesson and donning of safety gear before taking the plunge. The one-and-a-half-hour ride is filled with thrills passing through some hefty waves, deep in the gorge, especially when the river is high. The ride finishes at **Kampung Rayoh,** where lunch is served before you catch the train back to Kota Kinabalu.

Tenom is also known for its **Agricultural Research Station**, 18km (11 miles) northeast of town. The station has grown from its humble beginnings as a centre for cocoa research, to include a full-scale agri-park known as **Taman Pertanian Sabah**, or **Sabah Agriculture Park** (tel: 087-737 952; www.sabah.net.my/agripark; Tue–Sun 9am–4.30pm; charge). The **Tenom Orchid Centre** is also part of the park, with numerous species of orchids. Tenom's one classy hotel, the **Perkasa**, sits on the hill overlooking the town, although hostel and camping accommodation is available within the park.

About 14km (9 miles) outside of Tenom, on the Keningau road, the **Murut Cultural Centre** (tel: 087-302 421; daily 9am–5pm; free) is remarkable for its massive timber buildings; the demonstration and sale of local crafts are available here. The centre is also the venue for the annual Murut Festival. It celebrates the culture of the group of tribes known collectively as Murut, with cultural performances, games and contests.

Some 40km (25 miles) south of Tenom at **Batu Bunatikan Lumuyu**, close to Kampung Tomani, are Sabah's only rock carvings. Strange, distorted faces and enigmatic figures are etched

Inside the Hamin Do Kakadazan house.

The canopy walkway at Poring.

onto on massive boulders. These impressive paintings are thought to have been crafted 1,000 years ago.

From Tenom, travel north through Keningau and Tambunan and from there, follow a rough road to Ranau and Mount Kinabalu or follow the road over the Sinsuron Pass to Kota Kinabalu, thus completing a round trip.

Keningau and beyond

Keningau is the centre of the interior timber industry of west Sabah, with its many sawmills and log-holding depots. The town has prospered from its timber industry, and has several hotels and a sports complex.

Driving southeast of Keningau, you come first to **Nabawan**, the last outpost of the government administration, and then to the settlement at **Sapulut** ⓯. From here, you can take a rough track to **Agis**, from where a pleasant four-hour boat ride leads to the border and a fairly easy crossing into Kalimantan at the **Pagalunggan** checkpoint (obtain a visa first) and the traditional longhouse of **Kampung Selungai**, only half an hour away. This remote area is

A Kadazan dancer demonstrates his heritage.

well worth exploring, but logging, El Niño and forest fires have taken a toll on the area in the last few years. Traditional longhouses sit along these riverbanks, where boats are built and the women engage in weaving, making intricate rattan mats and elaborate beadwork. Travellers are most welcome to stay the night, and the Muruts are renowned for their hospitality. Remember that it is polite to accept a drink when offered, as it is a host's duty to please guests with a cup of *tapai*. If you don't drink alcohol, simply touch the cup with your lips or the tips of your fingers and ask your guide to explain that you don't wish to partake of the fiery liquid. Gifts of food for the adults and toys for the children are customary, and items from your own country will be even more welcome than a product available in Kota Kinabalu.

In Sapulut, it is possible to hire a local canoe along the **Sapulut river**, for a two- to three-hour boat journey to **Batu Punggul** ⓰, a large limestone outcrop soaring 200 metres (600ft) upwards from the encircling jungle. Local guides will show you the way to the top of Batu Punggul, a rough climb, but well worth it for the spectacular view from the top. Another half-hour's walk through the forest leads to the less impressive **Batu Tinahas**, which is almost entirely obscured by the forest. Although not as high as Punggul, its cave and tunnel system is enormous and rivals the Gomantong Caves in east Sabah (see page 334).

Tambunan

The main road towards Kota Kinabalu shortly beyond **Tambunan** – a pleasant little town set in a picturesque valley – passes by a stone memorial on a grassy plain marking the site of Mat Salleh's last stand. Here, Sabah's most renowned hero built an underground fortress. He might have survived longer than 1900, had not a villager betrayed his location to the British forces, who promptly severed his water supply, and surrounded the fort. Mat

Salleh and his followers were massa-
cred when they emerged, ending the
rebellion of a native lord who refused
to pay tax to foreigners.

Crocker Range National Park

The route back to Kota Kinabalu from
Tambunan passes by the Crocker
Range National Park, with the **Rafflesia Forest Reserve** ⓱ located not
far from the summit at **Sinsuron
Pass**, which crosses the range at 1,649
metres (5,410ft). The attractive **Rafflesia Information Centre** (tel: 088-898
500; daily 8am–3pm; free) has displays
on this extraordinary parasitic flower,
and rangers can advise visitors if any
are blooming in the 50 or so identified
plots within the reserve and bring you
there for a fee.

Pulau Layang Layang

Sitting at the southern tip of the Spratly
islands, 250km (155 miles) northwest of
Kota Kinabalu, **Layang Layang** is part
of the territory that is being contested
by a number of countries in the region
– including China, Vietnam, Indonesia
and Malaysia. In the meantime, Malaysia is putting the island to good use as
a tourist destination, as well as laying a
claim that may become important in
future negotiations.

This 7km-by-5km (4-mile-by-3 mile)
coral atoll is as much a draw for migratory sea birds as it is for the big-game
fishermen, who are attracted by the
richly populated waters. Layang Layang is also the site of some of the best
diving in Malaysia. Because of the distance from the main island, the waters
are particularly clear and untainted,
and divers can enjoy spectacular coral
walls, which drop down 2,000 metres
(6,560ft) to the coral below. Sharks
and pelagic fish are common sights in
these unspoilt waters, and schools of
hammerhead sharks can often be seen
in the months of March and April.

The island has a tiny airport, and
next door is the comfortable **Avillion
Layang Layang**, which is dedicated
to divers and has a fully serviced dive
centre, a desalination plant, rooms, a
restaurant and a swimming pool. A
45-minute flight from Kota Kinabalu
covers the journey.

EAT

If you haven't yet
experienced the highly
distinctive durian fruit,
try it while in Tenom; it is
reckoned to be the best
in Sabah, smell
notwithstanding.

Klias river cruise.

SANDAKAN AND THE NORTHEAST

The lively Chinese trading town of Sandakan is the tourism focus of Sabah's east coast, and the jump-off point for Sepilok Orang-utan Rehabilitation Centre.

In the heyday of the logging industry, people called the logs bobbing in the Sulu Sea "floating money". Logs were floated down the Segama and Kinabatangan rivers from timber concession areas near and far into the hands of Chinese entrepreneurs, who shipped them to Japan. So prosperous was **Sandakan** ⑱ that at one time many investors thought the town would become another Hong Kong. But the speed of deforestation of the Sandakan region has quenched that dream. Now the logging industry is but a shadow of its former self, and the derived wealth has been moved to places far beyond. Sandakan – a medium-sized, predominantly Chinese town and the base for tourist exploration of the east – now derives most of its income from palm oil.

The capital of North Borneo from 1883, Sandakan was completely razed during the bombings of World War II; the modern town was built on these ruins. The nucleus of the original town began as a gun-running settlement.

The gun-runners were mostly Germans, although later a Scotsman called William Clarke Cowie ran guns for the sultan of Sulu, setting up a camp on Pulau Timbang which he named "Sandakan", the old Sulu name for the area. Later he became the first managing director of the North Borneo Chartered Company, whose main settlement was established here on the fine harbour of Sandakan Bay.

At one time, Sandakan was a major trading centre. Jungle products from the interior – bird's nests, beeswax, rhinoceros horn, hornbill ivory – along with marine products like sea cucumber (*trepang*) and pearls were valuable trade items which attracted a cosmopolitan collection of traders from all over the world: Europeans, Arabs, Japanese, Dusun, Javanese, Bugis, Chinese – even Africans came to engage in the wealth-generating business of trade.

Main Attractions

Agnes Keith House
Sandakan Memorial Park
Sepilok Orang-utan
   Rehabilitation Centre
Rainforest Discovery Centre
Labuk Bay Proboscis
   Monkey Sanctuary
Turtle Islands Marine Park
Pulau Lankayan
Gomantong Caves
Kinabatangan river

Gomantong Cave.

Around Sandakan town

The first Sandakan flight from Kota Kinabalu arrives in the morning, allowing time for an exploration of the town before heading out. An Asian breakfast can be enjoyed in one of the Chinese *kopi tiam*, or coffee shops, before a visit to the colourful **Sandakan Central Market**. At its busy best in the early morning, the bustling market is an important source of local vegetables and fresh seafood, which are exported across the state and over to Singapore and Hong Kong. Stop by the Tourist Information Centre (Wisma Warisan, Lebuh Empat; tel: 089-229 751) near the Sandakan Municipal Council to pick up the heritage trail brochure that highlights 15 historical attractions. Other town sights include the restored **Agnes Keith House** (tel: 089-221 140; daily 9am–5pm; charge), once the home of a famous American writer who wrote lovingly on Sabah in the 1930s and 1940s. There is a wonderful museum about her life before and during the Japanese Occupation. Nearby is the **English Teahouse**, a restaurant with a stunning view and even a croquet lawn.

A proboscis monkey.

Tourists take in the tributes at Sandakan Memorial Park.

Several Chinese temples are dotted around – the most spectacular being the huge, modern **Puu Jih Shih Buddhist Temple** on a hilltop south of town. Outside Sandakan, the **Sandakan Memorial Park** (formerly the Australian Memorial) is built on the site of a Japanese prisoner-of-war camp, and commemorates the Allied soldiers and locals who lost their lives during World War II.

Sepilok Orang-utan Rehabilitation Centre

Sandakan's main source of tourist fame is the **Sepilok Orang-utan Rehabilitation Centre** ⓳ (Mile 14, Jalan Labuk; tel: 089-531 180; daily 9am–noon and 2–4pm, ticketing counter daily 9–11am and 2–3.30pm, feeding times 10am and 3pm; charge), a 20-minute drive westwards from town. In 1964, 10,000 hectares (25,000 acres) were designated a reserve for these lovable creatures. It takes but a little interaction to fall in love with these most "human" of primates. The orang-utan reportedly shares 96 percent of its genes with a human being, while its intelligence level can reach that of a six-year-old child. The centre assists orphaned orang-utans, or those who have been forced to live in captivity, to adjust gradually to jungle life and return to the wild. Instruction to the animals includes encouraging them to climb, building nests in trees (something wild orang-utans do each night) and foraging for food in the jungle. Gradually they are weaned from the milk and provided with bananas, and taught to fend for themselves.

Those who stay longer than the obligatory hour-long feeding stop will find nature trails set around the park, where the stunning vegetation is the main feature, although you may spot birds, squirrels and macaques. Visit the nature centre and watch a video show on orang-utans in the wild. Adjacent to the centre are several lodges of various standards. Within walking distance is the informative **Rainforest Discovery**

Centre (Kabili-Sepilok Forest Reserve; tel: 089-533 780; www.forest.sabah.gov.my/rdc; daily 8am–5pm; charge), highlighting the importance of Borneo's rainforests. Join the guided walk to the Plant Discovery Garden and the Rainforest Walk, not forgetting the 300-metre (984ft) long canopy walkway that is 25 metres (82ft) high at its highest point.

Labuk Bay Proboscis Monkey Sanctuary

Northwest of the rehabilitation centre is another worthwhile visit, to see the privately owned **Labuk Bay Proboscis Monkey Sanctuary** ⓴ (Yet Hing Oil Palm Estate, off Jalan Labuk; tel: 089-672 133; www.proboscis.cc; daily; feeding times 9.30am, 11.30am, 2.30pm and 4.30pm; charge). The sanctuary is in the centre of a mangrove forest that is surrounded by oil palms. The plantation owner had learnt of the monkeys on his land, and realised that they faced certain doom if the last of the mangrove forests were developed. So he left the mangroves alone, supplemented their diet with fruits and water, and they now number 60 individuals.

Tour operators usually include a visit here after the nearby orang-utans. Otherwise, the sanctuary can provide day transfers (four and a half hours), leaving Sandakan town at 8am and 1pm.

Turtle Islands Marine Park

Pulau Selingan, Pulau Bakungan and Pulau Gulisan are the Sabah islands, which make up the trans-border **Turtle Islands Marine Park** ㉑, (www.sabah parks.org) a 1,740-hectare (4,300-acre) tropical paradise in the Sulu Sea, about 40km (25 miles) north of Sandakan. Green (*Chelonia mydas*) and hawksbill turtles (*Eretmochelys imbricata*), or *sisik* as the locals call them, come here to lay eggs nearly every night of the year, but the best time to watch is between July and September. Rangers will take you out to the beaches where you can observe female turtles after they have commenced laying their eggs. Later, the eggs are scooped into plastic buckets and reburied at a nearby turtle hatchery, where they are safe from predators. Earlier in the evening, if you are lucky and a previous batch of eggs has hatched, you can witness their

One of Borneo's defining icons.

The Kinabatangan river framed by mountain foothills.

release and watch them begin their struggle for life as they make their way down the beach to the sanctity of the sea. Only some 3 percent of these turtles will reach maturity. Permission to visit Pulau Selingan is obtained from Sabah Parks via its agency Crystal Quest located at Sabah Park Jetty on Jalan Buli Sim-Sim (tel: 089-212 711).

Pulau Lankayan

Another 40km (25 miles) due north is the exclusive and idyllic coral island known as **Pulau Lankayan ㉒**. The **Lankayan Island Dive Resort** is a tranquil place of white sand beaches that provides a wonderful escape – and utter peace. The island is particularly good for divers, with accessible wrecks to explore, and vivid marine life.

Exploring Gomantong Caves

Bats galore can be seen in Gomantong ㉓ (daily 8am–6pm; charge), where some of Sabah's largest caves are found. These caves are also home to 1 million swiftlets, whose nests are collected to furnish the tables of Cantonese restaurants both in town and abroad.

The entrance to one of the Gomantong caves.

Collectors scale the *rotan* (cane) and bamboo ladders, which hang from the cave roof up to heights of 30 metres (90ft) above the bat guano-covered ground, to collect these treasures in the vast caves. The bats are only in evidence at dusk, as they make their nightly flight out to forage for food, just as the swiftlets return home. The huge, odorous guano pile is gradually raising the cave floor level. At one time the guano was harvested for use as fertiliser, but the cave's swift population declined so quickly that the guano now stays in an ever-mounting carpet, alive with cockroaches and other tiny cave-dwellers. A wooden boardwalk makes it possible to tour the main Simud Hitam cave with ease. If visiting these caves, bring a flashlight and mosquito repellent. The fastidious might wish to bring a pair of disposable gloves. Time your visit to coincide with the bird's-nest collection, usually between February and August.

Kinabatangan river

An enjoyable excursion is a trip up the **Kinabatangan river**. Now one of Sabah's most popular tours, the river is

dominated by tour operators who shuttle guests, by bus, to **Sukau** ㉔ or **Bilit**, stopping off at the **Sepilok Orang-Utan Rehabilitation Centre** (see page 332) as well as the **Gomantong Caves** along the way. Some tour operators, however, offer a trip upriver to Sukau, beginning from **Sandakan Bay**.

After crossing Sandakan Bay, the first stage of the journey is dominated by mangrove swamps and twisting waterways of the lowland floodplain which has been recognised as of international importance by the Ramsar Convention on Wetlands and gazetted as the **Lower Kinabatangan-Segama Wetlands**. Not only is it the biggest forest-covered floodplain in Malaysia, but it also has the largest concentration of wildlife in the Southeast Asian region. The occasional Orang Sungei (river people) settlement of stilted houses can be seen along the banks. Much of the original forest along the river has been replaced by oil palm, yet pockets still remain. Beyond the Ramsar site, in the upper reaches of Kinabatangan river is the **Kinabatangan Wildlife Sanctuary**. The Kinabatangan river and its tributaries are famed for the wildlife, not least of which is the long-nosed, pot-bellied proboscis monkey. The most accessible place for close-up sightings of these unique animals is the swampy forest along the small Menanggul river, a tributary of the Kinabatangan, just upstream from Sukau. Boats leave in the afternoon (around 3.30pm to 4pm), in time to catch the monkeys as they crash through the trees, making their way to the riverside for their nightly sojourn.

Even more exciting are the wild elephants that roam the Kinabatangan area; sightings of elephants along the river are not uncommon. One of the best places to see the widest range of wildlife, including orang-utans and Borneo's pygmy elephants, is at **Danau Girang**. Upriver from here is the famous **Uncle Tan's Wildlife Camp**. The camp offers basic accommodation, boat cruises and jungle trekking.

The oxbow lakes, formed as the river has changed its slow course over the years, are exceptionally rich sources of birdlife, and you're likely to find a visit particularly rewarding. More than 100 species of bird live in these habitats.

A Borneo pygmy elephant.

PYGMY ELEPHANTS

While the mainland Asian elephants are about three metres (10ft) tall, Borneo's pygmy elephants are around half a metre (1.5ft) shorter. Pygmy elephants are found only on Borneo island, particularly in Sabah and occasionally in East Kalimantan in Indonesia. In Sabah, they are known to forage for food along the Kinabatangan river, in groups of about 100 individuals. Daily, a single adult can eat up to 150kg (330lbs) of vegetation. Pygmy elephants are much less aggressive than other Asian elephants, but single elephant bulls are known to be aggressive. Fatal attacks are rare. However, in December 2011, a tourist was killed in Tabin Wildlife Reserve where the pygmy elephants are also found.

Common lionfish amidst colourful soft corals off Sipidan island.

TAWAU AND THE SOUTHEAST

Right on the southeast tip of Sabah, near the border with Indonesia, the regional centre of Tawau is the gateway to world-class diving and some beautiful jungle habitats.

Main Attractions
Tawau Hills Park
Pulau Sipadan
Pulau Mabul
Pulau Kapalai
Madai Caves
Danum Valley Conservation
Area
Tabin Wildlife Reserve
Maliau Basin Conservation
Area

Flights from Kota Kinabalu and Sandakan arrive at an airport about 20km (12.5 miles) north of **Tawau ㉕**, Sabah's main town of the southeast. As well as being the hub of an important timber and cocoa-growing area, this busy little town has a very mixed population, where Muslim Filipinos from Mindanao and Indonesian estate workers have helped create a different atmosphere to the towns of the west coast. As well as the present timber capital of the state, Tawau is also the home of a reforestation programme situated at **Kalabakan**, where 30,000 hectares (70,000 acres) have been planted with fast-growing trees such as *Albizia facalaria*; the fastest is said to have soared 30 metres (100ft) in just five years.

However, Tawau's real pride is the cocoa plant, which thrives in the region's rich volcanic soils, making Sabah the largest cocoa-producing state in Malaysia. Oil palm is grown, too, in huge estates that stretch kilometre after kilometre across the country. Tawau also boasts several good hotels, and the **Tawau Hills Park** (tel: 089-925 719; www.sabahparks.org; daily 7am–6pm; charge), a nature reserve where hot springs and waterfalls can be found.

Semporna

Tawau's main interest to the thousands of scuba-divers who pass through each year is its proximity to **Semporna ㉖**, the gateway to Pulau Sipadan – Malaysia's only oceanic island (not attached to the continental shelf) and renowned among the international diving fraternity as one of the world's five best dive sites. An hour's drive from Tawau's airport brings visitors to the small settlement where Bajau fishermen, Suluk tribespeople and Chinese traders lend a village atmosphere and a far-flung feel. Fringing the town are numerous settlements built on stilts

Low cloud hangs over the Danum Valley.

EAT

The rich marine life around Semporna yields delicious seafood, which can be bought (often live) at the Pearl City restaurant at **Dragon Inn Floating Resort**. Prepared by Chinese chefs in any style you wish and served with fresh, locally grown vegetables, it is among the best seafood found in Malaysia.

over the water, an architectural style utilised by many of the newer resorts being built in the vicinity.

Semporna's main jetty is always a hive of activity, with locals from the nearby islands coming and going in narrow wooden boats, and sleek speedboats leaving for dive resorts. Various dive companies maintain their offices on the jetty, while a couple of hotels, a souvenir shop and an air-conditioned restaurant on the Seafest jetty opposite cater to those en route to the nearby islands.

While Pulau Sipadan is the most exceptional dive site off Sabah's east coast, the jade and sapphire seas around Semporna are dotted with countless idyllic islands, surrounded by coral reefs. Unfortunately, the illegal practice of fish bombing by fishermen causes considerable destruction to the coral reefs. Fisheries and the marine police rely on public tip-offs and attempt to arrest the problem by conducting checks on wet markets to prevent bombed fish from being sold to the public, thus reducing the motivation.

Southeastern islands of Sabah

The large islands of **Bodgaya** and **Bohey Dulang** to the northeast of Semporna, and several surrounding isles, have been gazetted as the **Tun Sakaran Marine Park or the Semporna Islands Park**. Facilities have not yet been developed, but dive operators can arrange diving in the region; divers have already seen eagle rays, barracuda, turtles and many species of nudibranchs. On Bohey Dulang, you can visit the **Tun Sakaran Marine Research Unit**, where it is spawning seven species of giant clams, two of which are near-extinct, and releasing them back into the sea after seven months. The unit also has a seaweed farming centre. To obtain a visitor's permit, contact Sabah Parks on tel: 088-523 500.

Not far from Bodgaya, **Mataking**, the last island before the international border with the Philippines, is shared by an exclusive diving resort and the Malaysian army, which – along with navy patrols – ensures security along the entire east coast. South of Semporna, **Pulau Sipadan** ㉗ is Malaysia's only oceanic island. A pinnacle of limestone and coral rising up 600 metres (2,000ft) from the floor of the Celebes Sea, it spreads out like a mushroom cap to form a 12-hectare (30-acre) island. The first divers to Sipadan in the 1980s slept in tents, disturbed at night only by nesting sea turtles burrowing in the sand before laying their eggs.

The stunning visibility and the incredible range of marine life – including large pelagic fish, brilliantly colourful hard and soft corals and underwater caverns – greatly impressed the late marine ecologist and diver, Jacques Cousteau. Tales of schooling barracuda, mating sea turtles, huge jacks, moray eels, white-tip reef sharks and shimmering schools of exquisite reef fish soon spread. In an effort to avoid environmental degradation of Sipadan and its

A Mabul island resort.

surrounding reefs, the Malaysian government closed all resorts on the island in December 2004, permitting divers to dive in the surrounding reefs but not land on the island. Most dive operators have transferred their resorts to the nearby low-lying island of **Mabul** ㉘, while **Kapalai** is occupied by a single beautiful resort perched on stilts. Both Mabul and Kapalai are renowned "muck-diving" sites, great for macro life and all kinds of unusual critters that won't be seen on Sipadan.

Madai Caves

An hour's drive from Semporna on the road to **Lahad Datu**, a turn-off leads to the **Madai Caves** ㉙, where you'll find a limestone outcrop with large caves just 2km (1 mile) off the main road. Outside the caves is a village that may be deserted except for a small nucleus of caretakers, but will be packed twice a year when harvesters come to gather the valuable edible nests built by swiftlets in the caves.

Bring along a flashlight when exploring the caves; although sunlight filters down through crevices in the limestone roof of some caves, many of the deeper caves are pitch-black. Remains found at Madai prove that people lived in the area as long as 15,000 years ago. Further evidence of ancient settlement in the region – in this case going back some 20,000 years – can be found 18km (11 miles) west of Madai. **Baturong** is another limestone outcrop, situated near what was once a lake known as Tingkayu, which drained away 16,000 years ago. With a guide from Lahad Datu or Kunak, you can visit this fascinating massif. The journey involves an hour's drive through cocoa and oil palm plantations to a mud volcano. Enquire at Kunak Regional Forestry office at tel: 089-851 863.

Beyond Lahad Datu

Lahad Datu is another of Sabah's "cowboy towns", known for its lawlessness. Situated close to the Sulu islands of the Philippines, it has been, like the Semporna area, subject to occasional pirate attacks. Visitors heading to the important **Danum Valley**

Moray eels can be vicious creatures if you reach your arm too far up their resting holes.

Boys at Bajau Water Village, Mengkabung.

SEA GYPSIES

The Bajau Laut people or "sea gypsies" live their lives on boats around the islands of Southeast Asia. Most Bajau Laut are Muslims and have settled in water villages on the islands, such as Mabul, on Bum-Bum opposite Semporna, and in Tun Sakaran Marine Park. However, there is a minority who continue to live in boats along the coastal islands off Semporna and are who still practice their traditional religion and ways. During the day, they come onto the land only to collect fresh water and firewood, and to sell their marine catch in order to buy clothing, petrol and other goods, or to bury their dead. At night, they return to fish and sleep. The kitchen is at the stern of their boats, while the bow is where the men fish and mend their nets; in between are the sleeping and living quarters. Their diet consists mainly of stewed or fried tapioca served with grilled, stewed or salted fish and seaweed.

Born without birth certificates, these stateless people are in a quandary – as one parent must be Malaysian, being born in Malaysia does not guarantee citizenship, and if they are from the Philippines or elsewhere, getting registered is not a priority. A combination of illiteracy and the travelling distance to their consulates remain obstacles.

FACT

The Regatta Lepa is held every April in Semporna to choose the best-decorated *lepa*, or single-mast boat, which is traditionally the boat of the Bajau Laut. It is also a time to showcase Bajau Laut culture – boats are gaily decorated with a multitude of coloured flags known as *sambulayang*, and on board, a female family member dances accompanied by traditional music and song.

Conservation Area ㉚ southwest of Lahad Datu usually fly into the town's small airport.

The conservation area, a 440-sq km (170-sq mile) reserve was established by the Sabah Foundation for conservation and research. The inner area is totally unlogged, and has numerous walking trails through a pristine rainforest filled with waterfalls, streams and abundant wildlife. Morning starts early with the dawn chorus, as cicadas begin the chant, followed by the calls of some of the park's 270 bird species, echoed by the cries of gibbons. Hidden within this jungle paradise are rare Sumatran rhino, gibbons, mousedeer, barking deer, sambar deer, bearded pigs, giant flying squirrels and wild elephants. The conservation area houses the highly regarded **Danum Valley Field Centre**, which is open to day visitors. Tourists are required to stay in the charming Borneo Rainforest Lodge, which has a huge open lobby with a restaurant and bar looking across the Danum river to the rainforest, and comfortable stilted chalets nestled beneath trees.

Local guides, with an intimate knowledge of their subject, can take guests on nature walks; if you are lucky, they can show you how to call the different animals, and pick out a bird hidden in the jungle at a hundred paces. Many guides grew up in the region and have turned their well-honed hunting skills to better use, tracking down animals to photograph. But you will need plenty of time and patience, standing silently, hoping to catch a glimpse. On the more remote trails, a total disregard for leeches is also an advantage during the wet months.

One of the most popular short excursions is an early morning walk to the **canopy walkway**, strung high between giant dipterocarps. It can be a rewarding experience to sit for an hour or so and watch for hornbills and honeyeaters, and possibly even the Asian paradise flycatcher – one of Danum's most exotic inhabitants. Night drives in an open jeep will often reveal deer, bearded pigs and other creatures, caught in the beam of the strong spotlight. To stay at the Borneo Rainforest Lodge and to hire guides, contact its agent Borneo Nature Tours (tel: 089-880 207; www.borneonature tours.com).

Tabin Wildlife Reserve

Forty-eight kilometres (30 miles) to the east of Lahad Datu is the **Tabin Wildlife Reserve** ㉛ (tel: 088 267 266; www.tabinwildlife.com.my). Although logging encroached on the area in the 1970s and 1980s, the re-growth has provided a home for larger mammals such as the elephant, and some orang-utans from Sepilok are now being introduced into the wild here. Comfortable chalets with fans and a restaurant are available, with nature trails for exploring the environment.

Maliau Basin Conservation Area

From the Tawau district, the north coast can be reached by road via

Viewing the dipterocarp rainforest landscape from a canopy walkway in the Danum Valley.

Keningau (over the Crocker Range) and Sapulut in the interior, travelling close to the Indonesian border along logging tracks. Nearby, the almost circular **Maliau Basin Conservation Area** ㉜ or "Sabah's Lost World" was accidentally discovered by the outside world in 1947 when a British pilot flying through a mist-shrouded jungle almost smashed into the wall of steep cliffs that rose up to 1,500 metres (4,921ft) in height. The "Lost World" was recorded in the Borneo Bulletin and forgotten until a 1988 expedition kick-started further research trips into the basin. Less than half of the basin remains unexplored, but so far the discoveries have revealed an exciting range of flora and fauna. Biodiversity-wise, it has 12 forest types, which are home to more than 30 species of mammals, 270 bird species and over 80 rare and endemic orchid species. The main highlight is the trek to the magnificent seven-tier Maliau Falls. Maliau is remote and isolated from the rest of Sabah in terms of communication and safety facilities. Like Danum Valley, Maliau also has

helipads – offering quick emergency evacuations if need be, and if you are averse to trekking and your budget allows, you can tour by air instead. Prearrange with Borneo Nature Tours (tel: 089-880 207; www.borneo naturetours.com) to gain access into the conservation area. Package includes meals, overland transfer, conservation and campsite fee, rental of VHF radio and a forest ranger who doubles as the radioman and guide.

The drive from Tawau to Keningau takes between eight and 10 hours, depending on the condition of the tracks. Four-wheel-drive vehicles, which have obtained permission to carry passengers through the logging concessions, make the trip daily. The road north to Sandakan is easy and open, passing through mile after mile of oil palm plantations on what was once rainforest. Buses – which travel north almost to Sandakan before heading west across the Crocker Range – take 12 hours to Kota Kinabalu and cost half the price of the airfare, although the flight takes just 40 minutes.

TIP

Tawau is the only non-peninsular sea-crossing point to Indonesia. Check with the Indonesian Embassy (www.kbrikuala lumpur.org) to find out if you need a visa. You can apply for a 60-day tourist visa (RM170 cash only) at the Indonesia consulate (Bangunan Yunwah, Mile 2.5, Jalan Sin On; tel: 089-752 969). Ferries depart from Tawau Ferry Terminal for Nunukan (one-hour crossing; daily at 10am and 3pm) and Tarakan (three-hour crossing; Mon, Wed and Fri at 11.30am), both in east Kalimantan.

Ginseng Falls is on a tributary of the Maliau River, at the centre of Maliau Basin – Sabah's "Lost World".

Hanging up material in Masjid India Jalan, Kuala Lumpur.

TRAVEL TIPS
MALAYSIA

TRANSPORT

GETTING THERE AND GETTING AROUND

GETTING THERE

By air

Malaysia is connected by about 57 airlines to international destinations. The **Kuala Lumpur International Airport**, or KLIA (tel: 03-8777 8888; www.klia.com.my), located in Sepang 70km (43 miles) from the city centre, is the key gateway in and out of Malaysia. The other main airports are in Penang, Langkawi, Johor Bahru, Kuching and Kota Kinabalu.

The **Penang International Airport** is linked by direct international flights from several Asian cities, including Bangkok and Singapore, while the **Langkawi, Kuching** and **Kota**

Kinabalu airports are served by direct international flights from Singapore. **Malaysia Airlines** (MAS), the national carrier (24-hour call centre tel: 03-7843 3000, toll-free within Malaysia 1300-883 000; www.malaysiaairlines.com), flies to over 100 international and domestic destinations.

Local budget airline **AirAsia** (tel: 03-2171 9222; www.airasia.com) offers cheap fares online for both domestic and Asian destinations. Another budget long-haul airline, **AirAsia X**, flies to selected international destinations in Asia Pacific, South Asia, Australia and the Middle East.

Malaysia Airlines flights depart from KLIA, while AirAsia and AirAsia X

flights depart from the new terminal KLIA2, which is located 2km (1mile) from KLIA. Billed as the world's largest purpose-built terminal for low-cost carriers, KLIA2 commenced operations and took over flights from the Low Cost Carrier Terminal in May 2014. A new Express Rail Link extension was constructed to connect KLIA to KLIA2. KLIA Express (www.klia ekspres.com) is the fastest and most convenient way of travelling from KLIA to Kuala Lumpur city centre (RM35 one way adult fare).

There is an airport tax of RM45 for international flights, which is usually built into the airfare.

Flying from the UK or US

Airlines that fly to KLIA from the UK and US include Air France, EVA Air, Emirates, Qatar Airways, Etihad Airways, Japan Airlines, KLM, Lufthansa, Malaysia Airlines and Singapore Airlines.

Passengers from the UK and EU can fly direct to KLIA in about 13 hours, though stopover flights are cheaper. Malaysia Airlines fly non-stop from London to KLIA.

A flight from the US west coast takes about 16 hours and usually involves a connection in Japan, Taiwan or Hong Kong; the east coast route via Europe takes about 19 hours. Malaysia Airlines operates flights from Los Angeles to KLIA via Taipei.

By rail

Peninsular Malaysia

Train services to and within Malaysia, operated by the Malaysia Railway, or **KTMB** (tel: 03-2267 1200; www.ktmb.com.my), are clean, cheap and

Airline offices in Kuala Lumpur

Air France/KLM
First Floor, Park Royal Hotel,
Jalan Sultan Ismail
Tel: 03-7712 4555
Berjaya Air
Skypark Terminal Building
Sultan Abdul Aziz Shah Airport
Tel: 03-7847 1338 ext.204
Cathay Pacific
Suite 22.1, Level 22
Menara IMC
Tel: 03-2035 2777
Delta Airlines
Unit A-21-5, Tower A, Menara UOA
Bangsar No.5 Jalan Bangsar Utama
Tel: 03-2282 4648
Emirates
Lot 9.03.01, Level 9
Pavilion Kuala Lumpur
Tel: 03-6207 4999
EVA Airways Corporation
Suite 1205, 12th Floor, Kenanga
International, Jalan Sultan Ismail

Tel: 03-2162 2981
Japan Airlines
Suite 20.3, Level 20 Menara
Citibank, 165 Jalan Ampang
Tel: (within Malaysia) 1800 81
3366
Lufthansa
18th Floor, Kenanga International,
Jalan Sultan Ismail
Tel: 03-2052 3428
Malaysia Airlines
Level 1 (Departure Hall), KL Sentral
Tel: 03-7843 3000, toll-free within
Malaysia 1300-883 000
Singapore Airlines
10th Floor, Menara Multi-Purpose,
Capital Square
8 Jalan Munshi Abdullah
Tel: 03-2692 3122
Thai Airways International
Suite 30.01, 30th Floor, Wisma
Goldhill, 67 Jalan Raja Chulan
Tel: 03-2034 6900

TRANSPORT

reliable. Railroads link Kuala Lumpur with Thailand in the north, Singapore in the south and the east coast of the peninsula. The rail terminal in Kuala Lumpur is **KL Sentral**.

If you are travelling from Bangkok to Kuala Lumpur, change trains in Hat Yai (southern Thailand) or Butterworth (northern Peninsular Malaysia). The express journey takes about 20 hours and costs RM150 (first class). A train from Bangkok to Butterworth costs around RM140 one way. A less travelled route is via the east coast through the Thai town of Sungai Kolok and the town of Rantau Panjang in Kelantan, from where you can take a bus to Kota Bharu, where there are other overland options to other cities.

The express journey from Singapore's Woodlands Train Checkpoint to Kuala Lumpur takes over six hours and costs about RM50.

To travel in style, opt for the elegant and charming luxury **Eastern and Oriental Express** (UK contact tel: +44 (0)1249 890205, Singapore tel: 65-6395 0678; .reservations. singapore@orient-express.com). Travelling several times a month between Singapore and Bangkok, it includes stops in Penang and Kuala Lumpur.

By road

Peninsular Malaysia
From Singapore: The peninsula is linked to Singapore by two causeways: the **Johor–Singapore Causeway** from Woodlands (Singapore) to Johor Bahru, and the **Second Link** from Tuas (Singapore) to Tanjung Kupang. From these two points, you can connect to the North–South Expressway, which runs along the west coast.

In Singapore, buses to Peninsular Malaysia depart from Beach Road (outside Golden Mile Complex), Lavender Street and Queen Street. The bus journey to Kuala Lumpur takes about five to six hours and costs RM80–100. **Pudu Sentral** is the main bus terminal for the cheaper bus services in Kuala Lumpur. Several of the pricier operators depart and terminate at various places in both cities. These include **Aeroline** (tel: 03-6258 8800, Singapore tel: 65-625 88800; www.aeroline.com. my; departs from Harbourfront Centre and terminates at Corus Hotel on Jalan Ampang and in Petaling Jaya); **First Coach** (tel: 03-2287 3311, Singapore tel: 65-6822 2111; www.firstcoach.com.my; departs from

A ferry bound for Penang.

Novena or The Plaza and terminates at Bangsar or Bandar Utama); **Nice Executive Coach** (tel: (KL) 013-220 7867/(Singapore) 65-6294 7034; www.nice-coaches.com.my; departs from The Plaza at Beach Road, Singapore and terminates at the Old Railway Station, KL); **Odyssey** (tel: 1300-888 121, Singapore 1800-639 7739; www.odysseynow.com. my; departs from Balestier Plaza and terminates at Mont Kiara); and **Transnasional** (tel: 1300-888 582, Singapore tel: 65-6333 1948; www.transnasional.com.my; departs Lavender Street and terminates at the Terminal Bersepadu Selatan, Bandar Tasik Selatan).

These companies use the more expensive VIP or Executive (24-seater) express coaches, which have comfortable reclining seats, drinks and meals on board. Cheaper non-express coaches make several stops on the way, including a 30-minute meal stop.

To get to Johor's Senai Airport from Singapore, passengers can catch the yellow **Causeway Link Express** coaches from Singapore's Kranji MRT Station to City Lounge in Johor Bahru, then transfer to the white **Causeway Link Express** coaches to Senai Airport. The total cost is about RM9. For more information, visit www.senaiairport.com.

If you opt for long-distance taxis, take SBS Transit bus 160 or 170, SMRT bus 950 or the Malaysian-operated Causeway Link buses to Johor Bahru and catch a taxi from there.
From Thailand: The North–South Expressway ends in **Bukit Kayu Hitam** (Kedah), the main border crossing between Malaysia and Thailand. Other border crossings are at **Padang Besar** (Perlis) and **Rantau Panjang** (Kelantan). Buses and taxis serve these points.

Buses from Thailand travel along the peninsula's west coast from Hat Yai. The journey to Kuala Lumpur takes about nine hours and costs RM50–65. Many buses from Hat Yai, Bangkok and Phuket also terminate in Penang, from where you can take a local express bus. The east coast route is via Sungai Kolok (Thailand) and Kota Bharu.

Sarawak
A road goes from Pontianak in Kalimantan, Indonesia, to Kuching. This route (10 hours) is serviced by regular buses. Miri is joined by a long coastal road to Brunei's capital, Bandar Seri Begawan.

By sea

Peninsular Malaysia
Malaysia has a number of official sea entry points: **Tanjung Belungkor** in Johor, with ferry links to Singapore; **Langkawi**, which is served by a regular ferry service from Satun and Ko Lipe in southern Thailand; **Penang**, which connects to Medan in Sumatra, Indonesia; **Melaka**, which links to Dumai in Sumatra; and **Port Klang** in Selangor, which has ferry services to Tanjung Balai in Sumatra.

Sarawak and Sabah
The sea entry points are: **Tawau** (Sabah), which connects to Nunukan and Tarakan in Kalimantan; **Labuan**, and **Limbang** and **Lawas** in Sarawak, which are links to Brunei. From Kota Kinabalu you can take a ferry to Labuan, from where you take a boat to Brunei. From Brunei, continue by boat to Lawas and Limbang in Sarawak. There are also boats operating between Sandakan and southern Mindanao in the Philippines.

EATING OUT

ACTIVITIES

A–Z

LANGUAGE

GETTING AROUND

On arrival

Buses and public and private taxis and limousines operate from major airports in Malaysia. Many airports, including Penang, Kuching and Kota Kinabalu, have taxi desks where you purchase a coupon; the price is fixed. Kuala Lumpur's Old Railway Station and the KL Sentral transport hub also use a coupon system. Tolls are paid by the passenger. Elsewhere, enquire about fares at the information desk. Taxi fares from airports are higher than around town.

To and from KLIA and KLIA2

Taxis: Airport Limo taxis (tel: 03-8787 3030; www.airportlimo. my) operate 24 hours and are air-conditioned. Buy coupons from the Airport Limo counters just before you exit the international arrivals gate, or just outside the domestic arrivals gate. Tickets to the city centre cost RM74.30 for budget taxis, RM102.10 for premier taxis, and RM199.80 for the luxury and family-sized ones. The journey to the city centre takes 40 to 60 minutes, depending on traffic conditions. You need not tip the driver.

To get to KLIA, you can call the Airport Limo or take any taxi. The latter's fare comprises the meter rate plus tolls, a surcharge of RM12 and that for luggage placed in the boot. The total comes up to RM100–200. **Public Cab** (tel: 03-6259 2020) also offers a limo service to the airport that seats six. You can also book a taxi the night before for an early morning flight. Note that there is a surcharge for services from midnight to 6am.
Bus: Airport Coach (tel: 03-03-8787 3894) departs from KLIA every hour from 6.30am to 12.30am for KL Sentral (RM10), and stops at major hotels in the city centre (RM18) en route.

You can request pick-up by transit vans provided by Airport Coach from major hotels in Kuala Lumpur (tel: 03-8787 3894).
Train: The **KLIA Ekspres** (tel: 03-2267 8000) takes you to the **Kuala Lumpur City Air Terminal** (KL CAT) at KL Sentral directly in 28 minutes. Trains run every 20 minutes during off-peak hours and every 15 minutes during peak hours. Trains run from 5am. Last train from KLIA is at 1am and last train out of KL Sentral is at 12.30am. Tickets cost RM35 one way and RM70 return. Check the schedule at www.kliaekspres.com.

The **KLIA Transit** service from KL Sentral to KLIA2 stops at four intermediate stations – Bandar Tasik Selatan, Putrajaya, Salak Tinggi and KLIA. The journey takes 39 minutes, with departure every 20 minutes during peak hours and every 30 minutes during off peak hours.. KLIA2 to KL Sentral runs from 5.48am to 12.59am, while KL Sentral to KLIA2 trains run from 4.33am to 12.03am. The one-way end-to-end fare is also RM35 (adult fare) or RM15 (child), but different fares apply for intermediate stops.

Tickets can be purchased online or from vending machines or ticket counters at KLIA or KLIA2 and KL CAT. To get to your hotel from KL Sentral, take a taxi or a connecting LRT, Monorail or KTM intra-city train. The monorail terminal is 200 metres/yds away.

When departing Kuala Lumpur, Malaysia Airlines, Cathay Pacific, Emirates and Royal Brunei passengers can check in at KL CAT with a valid KLIA Ekspres ticket, at least two hours before departure. A boarding pass and a claim tag for checked-in baggage will be issued.

Sarawak and Sabah

Although Sarawak and Sabah are part of Malaysia, it is necessary for both Malaysians and foreign visitors, whether coming from other parts of Malaysia or from another country, to go through immigration and customs procedures on arrival. Foreigners need to produce their passports and Malaysians their identification cards.

Kota Kinabalu International Airport is located 7km (4 miles) from the city. Taxis use a coupon system and must be paid for in advance at the airport taxi service counter; there is no bus service direct from either terminal. Budget airlines arrive at Terminal 2, near Tanjung Aru beach which is about 10 minutes by taxi from Terminal 1, where all international flights arrive.

Kuching International Airport, 12km (7 miles) from the city, also uses a coupon system. It has a taxi service counter in the arrival hall, where fares must be paid in advance. There are no public buses that run to the airport.

By air

Travelling by air is affordable and the easiest way to cover great distances in Malaysia. The country enjoys a thriving domestic airline market, which has ensured the affordability of air tickets. While Malaysia Airlines (MAS) operates out of KLIA, Air Asia operates out of KLIA2. Both airlines offer deals

Touting for business

The airport is where you are likely to meet your first tout. Unlicensed taxi operators, called *teksi sapu* or *kereta sapu*, hang around airport, train, bus and boat terminals and will charge a flat rate, usually higher than usual rates. They sometimes go round gathering a few passengers before they depart. Opt for a licensed cab if you can.

on a variety of packages, which may change from time to time. For further information, visit www.malaysiaairlines.com and www.airasia.com respectively. MASwings (www.maswings.com.my), another subsidiary of MAS, caters to travel within Sabah and Sarawak, while community airline Firefly (www.fireflyz.com.my) serves several Malaysian airports including Subang Airport (Kuala Lumpur), Johor Bahru and Penang.

Malaysia Airlines offices

Call 1300-883 000 (within Malaysia) or 603-7843 3000 (outside Malaysia) for enquiries or check www.malaysiaairlines.com.
Alor Setar, Sultan Abdul Halim Airport, Kedah
Bario, Esquire Access Sdn Bhd, MASwings BBN Agent, Bario Airport Terminal, Sarawak
Johor Bahru, Lot E4, Aeromall, Senai International Airport, Johor
Kota Bharu, Sultan Ismail Petra Airport, Kelantan
Kota Kinabalu, Level 2, Kota Kinabalu International Airport, Jalan Petagas
Kuala Lumpur, Level 1 (Departure Hall) KL Sentral
Kuala Terengganu, Level 1, Sultan Mahmud Airport, Terengganu
Kuantan, West Wing, Sultan Ahmad Shah Airport, Pahang
Kuching, Level 3, Departure Level, Kuching International Airport
Labuan, Level 2, Airport Terminal Building, PO Box 23, Sabah
Langkawi, Langkawi International Airport, Kedah
Miri, Lot 10635, Airport Commercial Centre, Airport Road, Miri
Penang, 2nd Floor, Departure Hall, Penang International Airport
Sandakan, Ground Floor, Block 31, Sabah Building, Jalan Palabunan, Sandakan
Sibu, Lapangan Terbang Sibu, Kilometer 27, Jalan Durin, Sibu
Tawau, Airport Terminal Building, ground floor, KM 33, Jalan Apas Balung, Tawau

Other airlines

Air Asia (tel: 03-2171 9222; www.airasia.com) offers low-fare, no-frills flights to most main destinations in Peninsular Malaysia such as Penang, Langkawi, Johor Bahru, Kuala Terengganu and Kota Bharu, as well as destinations in Sabah such as Kota Kinabalu, Sandakan and Tawau and to Sarawak cities such as Kuching, Miri, Sibu and Bintulu. The airline also offers a selection of holiday packages to most destinations. The airline operates out of KLIA2 from April 2013 and from Terminal 2 at Kota Kinabalu International Airport. In Sarawak, AirAsia uses the same terminal as MAS.

Berjaya Air (tel: 03-7847 1338, ext. 204; www.berjaya-air.com) is the only airline to offer flights to Tioman, Redang, Pangkor, Langkawi and Koh Samui islands. Using 48-seater Dash 7 aircrafts, Berjaya Air operates from the Sultan Abdul Aziz Airport (Subang) in Kuala Lumpur. The airline also offers flights from Singapore to Redang and Tioman.

Firefly (03-7845 4543; www.fireflyz.com.my) flies from two domestic hubs, Penang and Sultan Abdul Aziz (Subang). In addition to domestic destinations, it flies to Singapore, Koh Samui, Phuket, Medan, Batam and Bandar Aceh.

By rail

The Malaysian railway system runs from Singapore through the peninsula and into Thailand in the north. Express services stop only at major towns; the others stop everywhere. Malaysian trains are comfortable and equipped with snack cars. There are air-conditioned first- and second-class coaches and bunks on the night trains. Third-class coaches are fan cooled.

You can book seats up to 30 days ahead, and do so online. For foreign tourists (except Singaporeans), KTMB offers a **Visit Malaysia Rail Pass** for travel over a period of five, 10 or 15 days on KTMB services in Peninsular Malaysia (and Singapore). Concessions are available for children. For information, contact KTMB (tel: 03-2267 1200; www.ktmb.com.my).

Peninsular Malaysia

The west coast rail line goes through Kuala Lumpur to Butterworth (Penang) and joins Thailand at Padang Besar, Kedah. The Ekspres Rakyat departs every morning from Singapore to Butterworth and vice versa. Alternative day services are Ekspres Sinaran Utara which links Kuala Lumpur and Butterworth, and Ekspres Sinaran Selatan which links Kuala Lumpur and Singapore.

The night trains are the Senandung Malam sleepers servicing Kuala Lumpur–Singapore and Kuala Lumpur–Butterworth, and Senandung Langkawi servicing Kuala Lumpur–Hat Yai.

The east coast line branches off at Gemas in Johor, heads through the central forests and emerges at Tumpat in Kelantan, near the border with Thailand. The Ekspres Sinaran Timuran (Singapore–Tumpat), Malayan Tiger (Johor Bahru–Tumpat) and Ekspres Wau (Kuala Lumpur–Tumpat via Gemas), and night trains Senandung Timuran (Singapore–Tumpat) and Senandung Wau (Kuala Lumpur–Tumpat) run on this route.

ETS or Electric Train Services (www.ets-train.com.my) provides fast green commuting from Kuala Lumpur to Ipoh (two hours) in the north. Onboard facilities include priority seating for the elderly and disabled, a café (in coach C), LED television, and plug points for laptops. Each coach has a closed-circuit television camera system for additional security. By 2016, the double-track project will be completed, connecting Padang Besar at the border of Thailand and Malaysia to Johor Bharu, near Singapore.

There are three types of train ticket: ETS Platinum offers non-stop travel between Kuala Lumpur and Ipoh (two hours); ETS Gold stops at six stations (Kuala Lumpur's Old Railway Station, Rawang, Tanjung Malim, Slim River, Kampar and Batu Gajah) en route (two and a quarter hours) and ETS Silver stops at all stations (two and a half hours). The ETS Silver ticket also allows you to ride the Malaysia Railway Komuter and Intercity train to Seremban (one hour) stopping over at Bandar Tasek Selatan, Kajang, Bangi, and Nilai. Enquire with KTMB (in Malaysia), tel: 1300 885 862 (8.30am–9.30pm) or tel: 03-2267 1200 (7am–10pm).

Sabah

The only public train in Borneo operates daily from the Tanjung Aru Station in Kota Kinabalu via Beaufort to Tenom in the interior. **North Borneo Railway** (tel: 088-318 888) operates steam-powered tourist

Ferry to Pulau Tioman from Mersing.

services between Kota Kinabalu's Tanjung Aru Station and Papar twice a week.

By boat

Around the peninsula, boats are the chief means of travel to the islands and in parts of the interiors. Regular ferries service the islands of Pangkor (7am–8.30pm), Penang (6am–midnight) and Langkawi (7am–7pm). Ferries service Langkawi (Kuah Jetty) from Kuala Perlis between 7am and 7pm (45 minutes), tel: 04-985 2690; from Kuala Kedah between 7am and 7pm (one and a half hours), tel: 04-762 6295; and twice a day from Penang at 8.15am (three hours) via Pulau Payar and at 8.30am. During the monsoon months of July to September, seas can be choppy, and services may be cancelled.

From the Lumut Ferry Terminal, there are ferries to Pulau Pangkor, Pulau Sembilan and Pulau Jarak. There are also ferry services to Belawan, a town in Medan, Indonesia. For more information, contact Tourism Jetty Centre at tel: 05-680 4000.

Boats out to islands on the east coast generally do not follow schedules, and in the monsoon season (November to February), services may stop altogether. Note that the sea can be choppy just before and after the monsoon period and services may be cancelled.

In the northeast, services begin between 8.30 and 9am and stop between 2am and 2.30pm. Other than during public and school holidays, it is generally fine to arrive on the Perhentian islands (from Kuala Besut) and Kapas (from Marang) without having booked your accommodation, but it is safer to pre-book accommodation, and therefore boats, at Redang and Tenggol (from Merang and Kuala Dungun respectively).

In the southeast, Mersing services the bulk of the Johor islands and Tioman, while Tanjung Leman is the staging point for the Sibu isles. Scheduled boats depart from Mersing only to Tioman (arrive at Mersing as early as possible), as these trips are tide-dependent. For services to other destinations, make arrangements directly with the boat operators or through your accommodation provider. Tioman can also be accessed from Tanjong Gemok. The Tanjung Leman boats depart daily at 9am, 2pm, 6pm and 9pm.

In the interior, Taman Negara is accessible by boat from Kuala Tembeling. The ride to park headquarters at Kuala Tahan takes two to three hours.

Sarawak

There are no scheduled shipping lines to Sarawak, but within the state express boats and local river crafts are still the main forms of transport to the interior.

There is a lot of traffic on the rivers inland throughout most of the year as roads are still few and far between and are generally in poor condition.

On the Rejang river, regular boats run between Sibu and Kapit, and if the waters are high enough, they go on to Belaga to longhouse territory. Express boats travel to many of the smaller rivers, stopping at remote longhouses along the way. Chartered boats can be fearfully expensive.

Bigger boat services operate between Kuching and Sibu – currently just one daily departure – with a three- to four-hour ride. Regular ferry services also connect Kota Kinabalu with the duty-free island of Labuan and then on to Brunei and the Sarawak divisions of Lawas and Limbang.

Cruises

Short-term cruises have been popular in the peninsula with a niche market, partly because of onboard gambling in international waters. Besides casinos, ships are usually equipped with a swimming pool, cinema, disco and karaoke. There are usually live band or cabaret-style performances, ballroom-dancing classes and other activities, and packages are full-board. StarCruises (tel: 03-2302 1288; www.starcruises.com) provides cruise packages from Singapore to Melaka, Penang, Port Klang, Langkawi and Phuket. Bookings may be made through **Asian Overland Services** (tel: 03-4252 9100; www.asianoverland.com.my).

By road

Malaysia's interstate (outstation) buses and taxis are a fairly comfortable and convenient way of covering the country. Both the roads and public transport are better in the peninsula than in Sabah and Sarawak, but there are generally good networks linking capital cities and major towns.

Sarawak's road system is pleasant enough for exploring the areas surrounding Kuching and up to the Kalimantan border. The longer drive to Miri is now relatively comfortable, thanks to the completion of much of the new Trans-Borneo Highway and bridges across major rivers previously crossed by ferry.

Interstate buses

Peninsular Malaysia

Three types of interstate buses operate in Malaysia: non-air-conditioned buses plying between the states; air-conditioned express buses connecting major towns; and non-air-conditioned buses that provide services within each state. With the exception of the express buses, the others seldom adhere to the schedule, but are frequent between 9am and 6pm.

Express buses usually connect two or three major towns, and will break the journey for a stop at a restaurant or food centre along the highway for half an hour. There are several classes of buses: the VIP or business-class coaches have the most legroom, and do not cost that much more (recommended for longer journeys).

At bus stations, you will inevitably be accosted by touts selling tickets for unlicensed operators. Tickets might be cheaper but these buses do not depart until enough passengers are rounded up; they also make numerous stops and often break down.

Different operators handle different towns – information and fares are displayed at counter windows. Outside public holidays, you don't need to purchase your ticket beforehand (bookings are rarely taken).

Plusliner (tel: 03-4042 1256; www.plusliner.com) and **Transnasional** (tel: 1300-888 582; www.transnasional.com.my) operate extensive networks of coach services to different destinations in Peninsular Malaysia. Their comfortable and air-conditioned coaches depart daily from Kuala Lumpur's main bus stations (see below). Plusliner's Nice Executive Coaches service only selected destinations such as Penang, Johor Bahru, Kuantan, Kota Bahru and Singapore, with several departures daily from KL's Old Railway Station (see page 129).

In Kuala Lumpur, northbound and southbound services are found at **Pudu Sentral** on Jalan Pudu and the **Old Railway Station**; coaches to the east coast and Tasik Kenyir depart from the **Putra Bus Station** (opposite the Putra World Trade Centre); and the interior destinations such as Kuala

Lipis are serviced from **Pekeliling Bus Station** on Jalan Pekeliling. Some northbound buses leave from **Duta Bus Station** on Jalan Duta and southbound buses from Terminal Bersepadu Selatan at Bandar Tasik Selatan (tel: 03-9051 2000).

To reach Genting Highlands' cable-car complex at the foot of the hill, there are express buses daily from Kuala Lumpur's Pudu Sentral, KL Sentral Station and KLIA. The ticket price covers the cable-car ride. Go Genting Express (First Floor, Counter 27, Pudu Sentral; tel: 03-2072 6863; daily 7.30am–7pm every hour and returns to Pudu Sentral 9am–8.30pm every hour).

If travelling from Ipoh to Cameron Highlands, the Unititi Express (tel: 05-491 4181) leaves at 11.30am and 5pm (two hours) and returns at 8am and 2.30pm. From Pudu Sentral in Kuala Lumpur, buses leave at 9am, 10.30am and 1pm (four hours) and return 8.45am, 1.45pm and 3.30pm with an additional stop at KL Sentral.

In 2014, Penang opened the Second Penang Bridge between Batu Kawan (on the mainland) and Batu Maung on Penang island. This 24km (15-mile) long cable-stayed bridge is the longest in Southeast Asia, and at 80kph (50mph), it takes about 20 minutes to drive across.

Sarawak

There are small bus terminals in Kuching, and each bus company has its own operating area. From Kuching and southwest Sarawak, the Sarawak Transport Company can take you to Semonggoh and other points west. The distinctive green and yellow buses leave from Lebuh Jawa. Petra Jaya Transport buses go to Damai, Buntal, Santubong and Kampung Bako and leave from the bus area near the Open-Air Market.

Sabah

Buses and minibuses operate in Sabah. In Kota Kinabalu, the buses to Kinabalu Park and Kudat leave from the **Long-Distance Bus Station** near the *padang*. Buses to Sandakan, Lahad Datu and Tawau depart from the **City Bus Terminal** (North) in Inanam, while buses south to Beaufort and Lawas in Sarawak depart from the **Minibus Terminal** opposite Wawasan Plaza.

Interstate taxis

Share taxis go to any destination and are quicker than buses. They are mostly old Mercedes Benz vehicles

Bumper-to-bumper taxis in Kuala Lumpur.

and some are air-conditioned. However, you have to wait until there are four passengers unless you want to pay for the whole cab – but remember, you do not have to charter the whole taxi. So turn up early and be prepared to wait. If you book a cab to yourself, the driver can pick you up from your hotel for free if you are close to town.

Note that there is a quota for the number of taxis that can ply a route. During public holidays, this quota could be full, in which case you would be asked to pay extra for non-quota taxis because the driver would not be allowed to pick up passengers on the return leg. Sometimes, if the traffic is heavy, you might have to pay more, so make sure you sort all this out with your driver first. Night journeys have a surcharge. Long-distance taxi stands are usually near the interstate bus stations. In Kuala Lumpur, the stand is at **Pudu Sentral**.

City transport

Buses and taxis

All big towns have a public bus service and taxis. Buses usually charge according to distance. Timetables are a mystery, and listings of stops and routes elusive, except for the signs on the front of each vehicle. However, bus rides are great for rubbing shoulders with the locals, and the drivers are friendly towards travellers.

Taxis can be hailed at taxi stands or by the roadside. In larger cities, taxis are usually metered, but in smaller towns, bargain and agree on a price before you get in.

Trishaws

Despite slowly dying out, trishaws are still used in Kota Bharu, Kuala Terengganu, George Town and Melaka. They are a memorable way to cover a city as their slow pace allows you to see points of interest along the way. The bicycle is usually at the side of the carriage, except in Penang, where the two passengers sit in a sun-hooded carriage in front of the cyclist. Trishaw drivers will warn you to hold on to your bags firmly for fear of snatch thieves on motorcycles. Fix the price before you get on.

Kuala Lumpur city transport

Taxis

Taxis in Kuala Lumpur are required by law to use meters. Fares start at RM3 for the first kilometre, with a 10-sen increase every 115 metres/yds. From midnight to 6am, there is a surcharge of 50 percent on the metered fare, and extra passengers (more than two) are charged RM1 each. Surcharges also apply for bookings (RM2) and baggage placed in the boot (RM1 per piece). Additional charges include road tolls.

Taxis of different colours belong to different companies. All have a sign on top, which, when lit, means the taxi is available. Note that there are blue executive taxis that have a RM6 flagfall and charge 20 sen every 200 metres/yds. There are taxi stands, but you can usually wave taxis down anywhere.

Often, during peak hours, taxis will not go to places where traffic

A monorail train makes its way through Kuala Lumpur.

Touch 'N go card

If you are driving in Malaysia, this easy-to-use electronic card is handy. It can be used for toll payment at toll booths on highways, and on all major public transport in the Klang Valley, some parking sites, hotels, hospitals, theme parks and selected food outlets. Buy one for RM10. Subsequent top-up of between RM10 and RM500 can be done at selected toll booths, banks, convenience stores and petrol kiosks. Some places other than toll booths charge a small service fee to reload. Please note that as of 1 April 2015, products and services provided have been subject to GST. More information on tel: 03-2714 8888 and www.touchngo.com.my.

is horrendous and passengers are hard to come by on the return leg. In such cases, drivers either decline passengers or will charge a flat rate. If you have to bargain, note that fares around town start at RM5 and it should cost you no more than RM15 to go across the central city area.

KL Sentral and tourist places like Menara Kuala Lumpur enforce prepaid coupon systems, whose fares are higher than the meter system's but are lower than flat rates. At Suria KLCC only the blue executive taxis can pick up passengers, but you can wait just further ahead at the side of the main road to hop into any taxi for much less.

City taxis cannot legally pick passengers up at KLIA and KLIA2, where a coupon system is in use, but you can take a city taxi to the airports.

Half- and full-day taxi charters to places in the Klang Valley cost RM30–35 per hour, excluding toll charges. Reliable call taxi services can be booked with **Comfort Taxi** (tel: 03-2692 2525), **Public Cab** (tel: 03-6259 2020), **Supercab** (tel: 03-2095 3399), and **Sunlight Radio Taxi** (tel: 03-9057 1111).

Buses

Rapid KL's buses (tel: 03-7885 2585; www.myrapid.com.my) cover most major areas in the city and provide feeder services to train (mainly LRT) stations. City Shuttle buses have a red disc on their windscreens and side windows near the front door, and they ply routes 101 to 115. Fares charged depend on the zone travelled. Within the city, the fare is RM1. Have exact change

ready, especially during peak hours. You can also get the RM100 monthly pass for unlimited rides and a RM150 integrated LRT-Rapid KL-Monorail ticket.

Services run by other bus operators are more chaotic and information is lacking, but you can get buses to outlying areas in Petaling Jaya, Shah Alam and Klang from major stops in the city, such as Pudu Sentral, and the Bangkok Bank near Petaling Street.

The major inner-city bus stops are Pudu Sentral, Bangkok Bank near Petaling Street, Lebuh Ampang and the Jalan Tuanku Abdul Rahman/ Jalan Ipoh intersection in Chow Kit.

There is a double-decker city tour bus that allows you to hop on and off as you like at any of 22 attractions; RM45 for 24 hours or RM79 for 48 hours; discounts for children, students and people with disabilities (www.myhoponhopoff.com).

Trains and light rail

KL's rail system consists of three types of services – the LRT which covers most of the city and inner suburbs; the semicircular KL Monorail looping through the Golden Triangle; and the KTM Komuter for trips to the outer suburbs. The main rail terminal is **KL Sentral**, where you can get on any of these systems.

The **Light Rail Transit** (lrt; tel: 03-7885 2585; www.myrapid.com. my) has two lines which intersect at Masjid Jamek Station: the Ampang/ Sri Petaling line that runs from northern KL (Sentul Timur Station) to Ampang in the east and Sri Petaling in the south; and the Kelana Jaya line (to

be extended in the first half of 2016) that runs from Terminal Putra Station in Gombak in northeastern KL to Petaling Jaya, ending at Kelana Jaya Station in the southwest. Trains run every seven to eight minutes (every three minutes during peak hours) from 6am to 11.50pm (11.30pm on Sundays and holidays). Fares start at 70 sen. Monthly travel cards (RM100) can also be purchased (RM150 for integrated LRT-Rapid KL-Monorail travel card).

The elevated **Kuala Lumpur Monorail** (tel: 03-7885 2585; www.myrapid.com.my) covers central KL, from KL Sentral to Titiwangsa Station. Fares are RM1.20–RM2.50 and trains run every seven to 10 minutes (four to five minutes during peak hours) from 6am to midnight. RM20 and RM50 stored-value tickets are available.

The **KTM Komuter** (tel: 1300-885 862; www.ktmkomuter.com.my) is an intra-city commuter train service covering greater KL. It offers services between Port Klang–Batu Caves, Rawang–Tanjung Malim and Rawang–Seremban. Fares range from RM1 to RM8.10. Tourists below the age of 30 holding the ISIC, YIEE Card or Youth Hostel Card are entitled to unlimited travel for seven days for RM130.

Langkawi transport

If you're staying for several days, it's more economical to rent a car, motorbike or scooter than to hire a taxi whose driver charges fixed prices for different destinations and who might not be too keen to travel to out-of-the-way places. Car rental is available from Kuah jetty and the Langkawi International Airport, and from several resorts. Most of them are in the same price range. Car rental ranges from RM60 to RM160 per day for the smallest car, but motorbikes and scooters can be hired from some hotels and from Pantai Cenang for less. If you are planning to rent for a week or more, you can get a better rate. However, during the public and school holidays, cars are much more expensive and you have to book in advance if you want a car. Always check your vehicle, noting existing damages (either on a form or in photographs) in case you're blamed for them upon returning it. For cars, review the insurance coverage and understand what you're liable for in case of an accident (some cars-for-hire are unlicensed and are not insured). Although Kasina Rent-A-Car (www.kasina.com.my; tel: 04-644 1842) is more expensive than the others, it is the most reliable and comes with insurance coverage, and a 24-hour contact number is provided in case of emergency. As long as you can provide a copy of your country's driving licence, a credit card and a refundable deposit, you can have a car that comes with unlimited mileage and a full tank of petrol.

Driving

Driving is the best way to see Peninsular Malaysia, which has an excellent network of trunk roads and highways. Driving is also enjoyable in Sabah and Sarawak, but you need a sturdier vehicle or even a four-wheel-drive and lots more time.

Petronas-owned petrol stations.

An international driving licence is required except for tourists from the US, EU, Australia, New Zealand, Japan and Singapore. Car-rental firms are found in major cities and in airports.

Driving is on the left-hand side of the road. Keep to the speed limits indicated on road signs. Generally, the speed limit is 50kph (30mph) in towns, 80kph (50mph) outside towns and 90–110kph (56–68mph) on highways. Slow down when you go through a village and before a school, and keep left unless overtaking. The wearing of seat belts is compulsory.

International traffic signs apply along with local ones. If the driver in front flashes his right indicator, he is signalling to you not to overtake. This is usually because of an oncoming vehicle or a bend in the road, or he himself might be about to overtake the vehicle in front of him. If he flashes the left indicator, this means to overtake with caution. A driver flashing his headlamps at you is claiming the right of way or indicating police ahead. At roundabouts or traffic circles, the driver on the right has the right of way, although pushing in has become the norm.

Malaysian drivers can be speed maniacs. In towns, motorcyclists can shoot out from nowhere or hog the road. Don't lose your cool; take it easy. On local roads or on highways near plantations or forested areas, do watch out for cattle and wildlife crossing, especially at night. Heavy rain can be hazardous, so switch on your lights, drive slowly and be prepared for delays as entire roads are sometimes flooded. At worst, pull over until the rain eases.

Main routes

The North–South Expressway starts at the causeway connecting to Singapore and runs north along the west coast to the Thai border. The old trunk road runs roughly parallel to that through small towns.

Several main routes link the east and west coasts through the Titiwangsa Range. From Kuala Lumpur, the busy Karak Highway goes to Kuantan (three hours). A fork at Bentong heads north through Kuala Lipis to Kota Bharu on the Gua Musang road (nine hours). Kota Bharu is also linked to Penang via the East–West Highway (five hours), and Kuala Kangsar in Perak at the Grik fork.

From Johor Bahru, the Segamat Highway goes to Kuantan (four hours), but a more scenic and much longer route hugs the east coast from Desaru all the way to the Thai border.

A parallel inland road with less traffic runs from Kuantan to Kota Bharu.

In Sabah and Sarawak, the Trans-Borneo Highway links Sabah and Sarawak through Brunei. Sealed roads connect major towns. Roads leading inland are often unpaved or rough, and a four-wheel-drive is advisable. For day trips to Santubong, Damai, or west towards Lundu and beyond along the coast, a normal saloon car can be used. In Sabah, too, most of the main destinations along the coast are trouble-free, as is the road to Kinabalu Park and north to Kudat.

Breakdown services

The Automobile Association of Malaysia (AAM) has a prompt breakdown service for members (tel: 03-2161 0808). Rental cars may be covered by AAM services – check when you hire the vehicle.

Car rental

Car-rental firms have branches in the main towns throughout Malaysia and at big airports. Rentals are usually based on time rather than mileage and most allow you to pick up a car from one place and drop it off at another. Credit cards are preferred.

Kuala Lumpur
Avis Rent A Car, tel: 1800-882 847 (reservations); 1800-882 054 (24-hour breakdown service); www.avis.com.my
Hertz Rent A Car, tel: 1800-883 086; tel (within Malaysia): 03-7966 7000; www.hertz-malaysia.com
Pacific Rent A Car, tel: 03-2287 4118/9; www.iprac.com

Kota Kinabalu
Kinabalu Rent A Car, tel: 088-232 602; www.kinabalurac.com.my

Kuching
Mayflower Car Rental, tel: 082-410 110; www.mayflowercarrental.com.my
Padas Jaya Rent A Car, tel: 088-239 936
Pronto Car Rental, tel: 082-236 889

Langkawi
Kasina Rent-A-Car, tel: 04-955 5999; payment by credit card, car comes with insurance and full tank of petrol
Mahamas Travel & Tour, tel: 04-966 6562; payment by cash; car comes with insurance and RM15 petrol
Sea Hill Management & Tour, tel: 04-955 8829; payment by cash, car comes with insurance and quarter-tank of petrol

EATING OUT

RECOMMENDED RESTAURANTS

WHAT TO EAT

Malaysia offers a wide range of food choices, ranging from fine dining to street food. Breakfast is usually served 6–10.30am, lunch 11.30am–2.30pm and dinner 6.30–11pm, although some places open until 2am or even later. However, you can usually find restaurants or stalls serving food any time of the day.

Ethnic and religious influences play a role in determining ingredients used and the preparation of dishes. Restaurants holding halal certification indicate that they follow strict Muslim dietary regulations and do not serve pork or alcohol. All restaurants offer the use of table utensils, but at some eateries (especially where roti canai or rice is served) customers prefer to use their hands. If you are using your hands to eat, use your right hand, never your left. Scoop up the rice with your fingers only, not onto your palm.

Certain dishes are associated with the festive occasions celebrated in the country. Lemang (rice cooked with coconut in a hollowed bamboo stick over charcoal or wood fire) and rendang (meat curry) are associated with Hari Raya Aidil Fitri. Snacks such as laddu and muruku are favourites during Deepavali. And no Chinese New Year celebration would be complete without the tossing of yee sang, a fish salad with sweet dressing.

Vegetarian options can be found at Chinese and Indian restaurants as encouraged by Buddhist and Hindu beliefs.

For the full Malaysian experience, try the local fare, which is not only different according to where you are, but subdivides into ethnic and regional varieties too. Peranakan (or Nonya)

cuisine, which combines Chinese and Malay ingredients and cooking styles, is best enjoyed in Melaka and Penang. Popular dishes include kari kapitan (curry chicken) and otak-otak (fishcake with spices steamed in banana leaf). The east coast states of Kelantan and Terengganu offer authentic Malay cuisine, including rice and fish dishes such as nasi dagang and barbecued chicken (ayam percik). In the south, Batu Pahat, Johor, is known for its nasi briyani gam (rice cooked with spices and raisins) and Muar for its mee bandung (noodles with prawns and beef in gravy).

Sarawak has its own specialities derived from its Malay, Indian, Chinese and Dayak heritages. The spicy Sarawak laksa is a big favourite, as is umei – a Melanau dish of raw, marinated fish blended with limes, chilli and shallots. Fresh seafood, venison, wild boar, pansoh manok – an Iban chicken dish cooked in bamboo tubes with rice wine – are not to be missed. In Kuching, the old streets of Chinatown are lined with coffee shops serving fresh Chinese noodle dishes. Sabah is known for its excellent seafood, as well as its vegetable dishes. Best of all is sayur manis, a green leafy vegetable with a slightly crunchy stem and sweet green leaves. Try it in oyster sauce.

WHERE TO EAT

Fine-dining establishments are found mainly in the cities or the tourist belt, but elsewhere restaurants and food stalls are readily available. All of Malaysia's medium- and top- class hotels have decent restaurants, with some of the nation's best found in five-star hotels.

In addition to Malaysian cuisine,

restaurants serving Indonesian, Italian, Japanese, Korean, Mediterranean and Vietnamese food are easily found. The best regional food is often served in hawker stalls, sold on the streets or in coffee shops. The main shopping malls will also have a range of food choices, and an assortment of street foods can be found at pasar malams (night markets), which include restaurants, fast-food places, food courts and places for nibbles. Although you can sometimes get authentic preparations in restaurants, the atmosphere at these venues cannot be replicated.

DRINKING NOTES

Alcohol is expensive in Malaysia compared with some other Asian destinations. It is freely available in pubs, hotels, Western restaurants and Chinese eateries, as well as in supermarkets in most towns, though less so in the traditionally Islamic states of Terengganu and Kelantan.

Wine is growing in popularity and easily found at Western restaurants, wine shops and supermarkets. Imported beer is mostly served at pubs, beer bars and microbrewing outlets. Local brews include toddy and rice wines such as tuak and li hing. Toddy is made from the fermented sap of coconut palm. If trying this brew, make sure it comes from a regulated source.

Local coffee and tea pack a punch, and may be too sweet for unsuspecting drinkers as they are sometimes served with condensed milk and sugar. Ipoh white coffee has won a wide following because of its creamy smooth taste and strong flavour. Teh tarik (pulled tea) is also a Malaysian favourite. Tea is poured back and forth with outstretched arms from a mug into a glass.

KUALA LUMPUR AND ENVIRONS

Kuala Lumpur

Arab
Al-Amar
Lot 6.10, Level-6, Pavilion Kuala Lumpur, 168 Jalan Bukit Bintang
Tel: 03-2166 1011
www.al-amar.com
Lebanese lamps, shishas, plush red chairs and weekend themed entertainment set the tone for a fine Lebanese dining experience here. Of note are the delicious *manakeesh* with selections of toppings including *zaatar*, spinach and cheese, while the koftas and grills are consistently juicy and well marinated. **$$$$**

Al-Andalus
48 Jalan Damai, off Jalan Ampang
Tel: 03-2144 9414
The customers are largely Middle Eastern, which is testament to the quality of this restaurant. Dine alfresco on balmy evenings on a tasty tajine with saffron rice and a *fattoush* (pitta bread salad) and end your meal with an Arabic coffee. This is also where you get arguably the cheapest shisha in town. **$$**

Sahara Tent
41 & 43 Jalan Sultan Ismail
Tel: 03-2144 8310
www.saharatent.com
This is one of the oldest Arab eateries in Kuala Lumpur, now in a new location. Its popular buffets are as varied as ever, the notable dishes including creamy hummous and tender lamb. Vegetarian options are good, such as the chef's speciality, which features eggplant, and the vine-leaf *waraq-enab*. **$$**

Asian and Southeast Asian
Baan26
26 Changkat Bukit Bintang
Tel: 03-2142 8878
All the usual Thai favourites are cooked well in this restaurant, whose pink-and-yellow decor would not go amiss in the streets of Bangkok. The food is full-bodied and can be spicy. Drinks are reasonably priced for this area, although diners might find that the bar gets a little loud after 10pm. **$$**

Ginger Restaurant
Lot M12, Central Market, Jalan Hang Kasturi
Tel: 03-2273 7371
Tucked away on the upper level of Central Market, the eatery dishes up great Thai fare, including the creamy green curry chicken, refreshing mango *kerabu* salad and a wicked

tom yam soup. A good place to take a break from souvenir shopping. **$$**

Sao Nam
25 Tengkat Tong Shin
Tel: 03-2144 1225
Featuring a contemporary approach to traditional Vietnamese cuisine. The mangosteen salad is unique and so popular that regulars ring to pre-order. Reservations are essential. A well-priced wine list complements the superb food. **$$$**

Still Waters
Hotel Maya, 138 Jalan Ampang
Tel: 03-2711 8866
This serene, small restaurant is known for its exquisite *sosaku* (creative) cuisine, combining Japanese and Western ingredients. However, patrons can also now select from a Cantonese menu. **$$$$**

Tamarind Springs
Jalan 1, Taman Tun Abdul Razak, Ampang Jaya
Tel: 03-4256 9300
www.samadhiretreats.com/dining-experiences.html
Like its sister restaurant Tamarind Hill (19 Jalan Sultan Ismail; tel: 03-2148 3200), this atmospheric, open-concept outlet specialises in Indochinese cuisine – Thai, Laotian, Cambodian and Vietnamese. It has a complimentary shuttle bus service from major hotels in KL. **$$$**

Chinese
Esquire Kitchen
1st floor, Sungei Wang Plaza, Jalan Sultan Ismail
Tel: 03-2110 0264
www.esquirekitchen.com
Juicy Shanghainese fried dumplings and Shanghainese steamed meat dumplings are the specialities to go for in this popular chain restaurant. Other offerings include the signature Tung-Po meat, a saucy pork dish. If a snack is all you want, the Chinese pastries are delicious. **$$**

Hakka Restaurant
6 Jalan Kia Peng
Tel: 03-2143 1908
With a heritage of over 50 years of solid Hakka culinary tradition, this family-run restaurant is the best place for authentic Hakka food. Unmissable are the Hakka noodles with minced pork sauce, *mui choy kau yuk* (braised pork belly layered with preserved vegetables) and the unique stewed fish head with fermented red rice. **$$**

Li Yen
The Ritz-Carlton, 168, Jalan Imbi
Tel: 03-2142 8000

www.ritzcarlton.com/en/Properties/KualaLumpur/Dining/LiYen/Default.htm
Fine Cantonese fare in a sumptuous setting is on offer at this award-winning restaurant. Be pampered by faultless service and enjoy live classical music every evening as you dine on classics such as Peking duck, suckling piglet and pork ribs. There is also an excellent spread of dim sum at lunchtime. **$$$$**

Nam Heong
56 Jalan Sultan
Tel: 03-2078 5879
Hainanese chicken rice is a staple for many Malaysians and Nam Heong is one of the city's oldest names in chicken rice. While Nam Heong has become a brand, the food in this historic outlet is still good: a simple meal of "white" or roast chicken with rice cooked in chicken stock accompanied by garlic and chilli sauces. **$**

Purple Cane Tea Restaurant
G01-02,1 Jalan Maharajalela Shaw Parade (behind Berjaya Time Square)
Tel: 03-2145 3090
"Tea cuisine" is served in a calm ambience, food in which Chinese tea is an ingredient, yes, even in the desserts. However, besides being most visible in the rice, the tea flavour is very subtle. The Cantonese style has lots of vegetarian options in the form of green vegetables and tofu. The range of high-quality tea to have with your meal is naturally huge. **$$**

Soong Kee Beef Noodles
3 Jalan Tun Tan Siew Sin
Tel: 03-2078 1484
The best beef dumplings in the city are here at Soong Kee. Enjoy them in soup, accompanied by springy egg noodles tossed in a soy-based sauce with minced beef and garlic. These Hakka specialities are wonderful dipped in the own-made hot and sour garlic–chilli sauce. **$**

Yut Kee
1.Jalan Kamuning
Tel: 03-2698 8108
A rare traditional Hainanese coffee shop where the *roti babi* is still served, a deep-fried meat sandwich served with Worcestershire sauce.

PRICE CATEGORIES

Price per person for a three-course meal without drinks:
$ = under RM30
$$ = RM30–60
$$$ = RM60–90
$$$$ = over RM90

The shop is also famous for its *kaya* (coconut jam), good with toast for breakfast or in a Swiss roll for tea. Note that it is usually packed. **$**

European
La Bodega
Level 3, Pavilion KL, 168 Jalan Bukit Bintang
Tel: 03-2148 8018
www.bodega.com.my/labodega
The newest outlet of one of the longest-standing hangouts in Bangsar, this chic, cosy Catalan eatery serves tapas favourites such as spicy prawns Andalusia-style, grilled lamb cutlets with garlic mayonnaise, and lobster and prawn croquettes. The restaurant is accessible from the mall taxi stand. **$$$**

Ciao Ristorante
20A Jalan Kampung Pandan off Jalan Tun Razak
Tel: 03-9285 4827
www.ciao.com.my
Relocated to a gorgeous bungalow, this well-established Italian restaurant continues to use high-quality ingredients to make straightforward tasty meals. The menu ranges from fresh pasta dishes and pizzas to succulent lamb. The set lunches are good value. **$$$**

Cilantro Restaurant
MiCasa All-Suite Hotel, 368B Jalan Tun Razak
Tel: 03-2179 8082
www.micasahotel.com/dining.html
Exquisite dishes that combine French and Japanese cooking styles and ingredients. The amuse-bouche and clear soups have a devout following, while the inspiring main courses include the likes of the classic French Maine lobster in Américaine sauce and grilled Japanese wagyu. **$$$$**

Cuisine Gourmet by Nathalie
Menara Taipan, Jalan Puncak, Off Jalan P. Ramlee
Tel: 03-2072 4452
www.nathaliegourmetstudio.com
Self-taught chef and caterer Nathalie Arbefeuille has been wowing Kuala Lumpur with modern French cuisine in her fine-dining outlet. The creative menu changes monthly, and diners can select from the à la carte menu or the set menu, which includes a dégustation option. Not to be missed are her signature macaroons. **$$$$**

Racks Bar and Baby Backs
18-1 Changkat Bukit Bintang
Tel: 03-2110 1550
Undistinguishable in decor from the rest of the trendy, hip Changkat row, this eatery is however, notable for its pork offerings, which range from

pigs-in-blanket appetisers to burger variations and ribs galore. Chase the food down with test-tube shooters, which come in a rack if there are enough of you. Opens until late. **$$$**

Weissbräu
Level 3, Pavilion, 168 Jalan Bukit Bintang
Tel: 03-2142 0288
www.weissbrau.com.my
This German bistro dishes up hearty platters of pork sausages, schnitzel and a superb pork knuckle, which you can wash down with a range of German beers. For lighter meals, try the regional favourites of the flammkuchen pancake or spätzle noodles. **$$$**

Indian
Olive Tree
G6–G7 Menara Hap Seng, Jalan P. Ramlee
Tel: 03-2031 7887
www.theolivetree.com.my
This cheerful contemporary restaurant serves up good North Indian tandooris, kebabs, dhals and breads. The biryani house special is a treat featuring chicken, lamb and prawn. The lunch buffets are particularly popular. **$$**

Passage Thru India
4A Jalan Delima, off Jalan Bukit Bintang (behind the Indonesian Embassy)
Tel: 03-2145 0366
Housed in a bungalow, this restaurant has a cosy interior decorated with Indian collectables. It is best for tandoori prawns, chicken *tikka*, naan breads and delicious, creamy *lassi* (yoghurt drink). Live traditional music is played on Thu–Sun evenings. **$$$**

Sangeetha Vegetarian Restaurant
65 Lebuh Ampang
Tel: 03-2032 3333
Simple, spicy South Indian vegetarian *thali* (platter) meals are the pride of this eatery. Try the Sangeetha Special Thali for its assorted yoghurts, dhals, vegetables and spicy *rassam* soup with rice. Complete your meal with a semolina *kesari* from the *chat* North Indian dessert counter with Indian filter coffee. **$**

Saravanaa Bhavan
52, Jalan Maarof, Bangsar
Tel: 03-2287 1228
www.saravanabhavan.com
For a global chain, this Tamil Nadu, India-originating eatery consistently dishes out outstanding vegetarian food. The variety available is unique in Malaysia; try one of the numerous bread options such as a *dosa* or *uthappam* or a larger meal of pulao (rice) and various curries. Other outlets are in Bangsar and Petaling Jaya. **$$**

Sri Paandi Restaurant
254 Jalan Tun Sambanthan, Brickfields
Tel: 03-2274 0464
A favourite for hearty Tamil banana-leaf fare that you can savour virtually 24 hours a day, which suits Malaysians just fine. This is also a good place to start your morning, with tasty puri or roti canai breads and *teh tarik* or local coffee. Rice meals are served after 10.30am. There is also an outlet in Petaling Jaya. **$**

Vishalachirs Food Catering
19 Jalan Travers, Brickfields
Tel: 03-2274 6819
This simple Chettiar family-run restaurant serves excellent traditional meals that are subtle blends of sweet, sour and lightly spicy. A typical meal offers rice on banana leaf with dhal and condiments such as *puli kulambu* (tamarind curry) and *rassam* (spicy soup), ending with sweet *payasam* (pudding). There is also a branch on the other side of Brickfields on Jalan Scott. **$**

International
Alexis BSC
Lot F51a, 1st Floor, Bangsar Shopping Centre, 285 Jalan Maarof
Tel: 03-2287 1388
www.alexis.com.my/html/bangsar.html
Alexis serves fine examples from various cuisines: Italian (Napoletana and Margherita pizzas), English (fish and chips) and Malaysian (Sarawak laksa). Order the flavoursome herbed rice *nasi ulam*, with a spread of Malay-style dishes such as prawns on lemongrass skewers and jungle fern in chilli paste. **$**

Ben's General Food Store
G17 & 18 Ground Floor, Bangsar Village 1, 1 Jalan Telawi Satu, Bangsar Baru
Tel: 03-2284 8790
Salads, pies and sandwiches are the forte of this charming contemporary café in trendy Bangsar. Literally rub shoulders with locals at the canteen-style tables and cool down on hot days with a thick milkshake or frostie. Local favourites are also available. **$$**

Peter Hoe Beyond
2nd Floor, Lee Rubber Building, 145 Jalan Tun H.S. Lee
Tel: 03-2026 9788
After shopping at Peter Hoe's ambience-filled homeware store, head for his café. The staples are the quiches, salads, pastas and soups. Teatime features cupcakes and lemon pies. The café is open daily noon–6pm. **$$**

Marmalade Café
1F-18, 1st Floor, Bangsar Village II, Jalan Telawi 2

Tel: 03-2282 8301
www.ilovemarmalade.com
This kid-friendly café serves breakfast, a healthy range of salads and sandwiches, limited Asian fare but imaginative kids' choices served on BPA free plates. Leave some room for dessert. Daily 10am–10pm. **$**

RAW Café
Wisma Equity, 150 Jalan Ampang
Tel: 019-313 8978
www.rawcoffee.my
A vegetarian and vegan haven, this coffee roastery also serves up salad sandwiches, hummous wraps and vegan cakes. The ingredients are organic to boot. Serious coffee-drinkers will find their perfect latte or macchiato here. Follow the smell of roasting coffee across from the Petronas Twin Towers to this tiny café. Closes at 8pm on weekdays and 6pm on weekends. **$**

Stuff Your Face Café
Lot 4-09, Level 4, Bangsar Shopping Centre, 285 Jalan Maarof, Bukit Bandar Raya
Tel: 03-2287 3070
Serves Western and Asian cuisine with a healthy and imaginative menu for kids. For the adults, try the signature colonial-style chicken chop smothered with gravy or the Dad's lamb stew cooked with potatoes and carrots. **$$**

Top Hat
7 Jalan Kia Peng
Tel: 03-2142 8611
A gorgeous old bungalow behind the nightspots, with excellent Malay, Peranakan and Western fusion fare such as the Peranakan "top hats" (pastry cups filled with shredded yam bean) chicken and mushroom pie, and grilled rack of lamb. The set meals are good; book ahead. **$$$**

Yogi Tree
F-237B, Level 1, The Gardens, Mid Valley City
Tel: 03-2282 6163
This café serves juices, breakfast, and a Western and Asian cuisine that is tasty and healthy. Try the Hainanese chicken rice (brown rice and antibiotic- and hormone-free chicken) or the flavoursome quiche Lorraine with bacon strips. **$$**

Malaysian
Bijan
3 Jalan Ceylon
Tel: 03-2031 3575
www.bijanrestaurant.com
A cosy contemporary setting decorated with Malay artefacts, contemporary paintings and heritage textiles. Sumptuous Malay offerings include the *masak lemak udang*

tempoyak (prawns in fermented durian curry), chargrilled short beef ribs with *sambal* (chilli paste), and *kerabu pucuk paku* (jungle fern salad). Reservations recommended. **$$$**

Coliseum Café
98–100 Jalan Tuanku Abdul Rahman
Tel: 03-2692 6270
A colonial setting so real it is easy to imagine bushy-moustached white planters at the bar complaining about the heat. Try a gunner or a gin sling – then have a sizzling rib eye steak, baked crabmeat, or an English potpie from the wood-fired oven. Chinese and Malay dishes are on the menu too. **$$**

CT Rose
Jalan Datuk Abdul Razak (opposite Sekolah Kebangsaan Kampung Baru)
When the craving strikes, droves head for this biggest *nasi lemak* (coconut rice) stall in the city, complete with a stunning view of the Twin Towers. The *nasi lemak* is served with *sambal* (chilli paste) and a variety of sides, such as deep-fried anchovies, quail eggs and fried chicken. **$**

Enak
LG2 Feast Floor, Starhill Gallery, 181 Jalan Bukit Bintang
Tel: 03-2141 8973
www.enakkl.com
Time-honoured family recipes are on the menu. The food is beautifully presented and the service is notable. The signature dishes include the prawns in tamarind sauce and slow-cooked beef with spices and herbs. The young coconut custard meringue is not to be missed. **$$$**

Jalan Alor Hawker Street
Jalan Alor, off Jalan Bukit Bintang
Local street food is at its best here, down a bustling lane. Just sit down at any of the coffee shops and order away. Everything from grilled chicken wings and grilled fish (such as stingray and mackerel) to oyster omelette and chilli-fried cockles and satay. **$**

Kafe Old Market Square
2 Medan Pasar
Tel: 03-2022 2338
After 85 years, Sin Seng Nam served its last meal in February 2013. Kafe Old Market Square brings old memories back to life. The new owner wanted to retain as much of the past as possible. The old cooks prepare the same Hainanese food, including fabulous Hainanese chicken rice and chicken chops. Other must-tries include fish curry, *mee rebus* (noodles in a spicy gravy) and Indian *rojak* (salad). For breakfast, don't miss the local-style breakfast of toast with

kaya (coconut jam), soft-boiled eggs and coffee. The top of the building has been transformed into a gallery that showcases old Kuala Lumpur. **$**

Little Penang Kafe
Lot F001 & F100, Mid Valley Megamall, Lingkaran Syed Putra
Tel: 03-2282 0215
Well regarded for its Penang-style noodles, from *char kway teow* (fried flat rice noodles) to the hot and sour *asam laksa* with a spicy tamarind fish gravy, to Hokkien prawn noodles. Order the multicoloured ice *kacang*, a sweet shaved ice treat. It has another branch at Suria KLCC (tel: 03-2163 0215). **$**

O'Mulia Satay
300–301 Jalan Tun Razak (intersection of Jalan Tun Razak and Jalan Semarak)
Tel: 019-371 3639
O'Mulia's fame comes partly from the fact that the beef and chicken on the sticks are chunky when every other satay maker is paring down. The meat is tender, beautifully marinated and the peanut sauce packs a punch. No-frills but atmospheric. **$**

Old China Café
11 Jalan Balai Polis
Tel: 03-2072 5915
www.oldchina.com.my
Best time-trip café in KL, where the old-world ambience, vintage photos and memorabilia, and marble-topped tables provide the perfect location for just as memorable Nyonya cuisine. Specialities include *laksa* (noodles in spicy gravy) and fish head in tamarind sauce. Try the delicious sago dessert called *gula melaka*. **$$**

Precious Old China Restaurant & Bar
Lot 2 Mezzanine Floor, Central Market, Jalan Hang Kasturi
Tel: 03-2273 7372
The sister restaurant to Old China Café is as beautifully decked out and has super-fast service. Perennial Nyonya favourites served here include the tasty "top hats" (pastry cups) filled with shredded yam bean, and two relatively difficult-to-find concoctions: *cincaluk* (fermented shrimp) cooked in an omelette or chicken, and chicken with *buah keluak* (mangrove seed). End with the coconut durian meringue (*santan durian*). **$$**

PRICE CATEGORIES

Price per person for a three-course meal without drinks:
$ = under RM30
$$ = RM30–60
$$$ = RM60–90
$$$$ = over RM90

Selangor and Putrajaya

Batu Caves
Seafood Sin Kee
8 Jalan SG1/10, Pusat Penjaja, Taman
Industri Bolton, Batu Caves
Tel: 03-6189 7972
Order the crabs in this Chinese
eatery with a spicy-sweet sauce, best
mopped up with deep-fried bread
rolls. Try also mussels in superior
stock and wine, prawns tossed in
cheese, and belly pork in soy sauce.
Open daily for lunch and dinner. **$$**

Klang
New Colombo Restaurant
2nd Floor, Sri Murugan Building, 79B Jalan
Tengku Kelana, Klang
Tel: 03-3371 3314
Good Ceylonese food is not easy
to find in Malaysia, but this is one
place that gets the thumbs-up from
Sri Lankan Indians. The food might
take a while to arrive, but it is worth
waiting for the likes of the tomato-
based Jaffna crab curry (wait time of
20 minutes). End your meal with tasty
appa (hoppers). Closed every third
Tuesday of the month. **$**
Sri Baratha Matha Vilas Restaurant
34 Jalan Tengku Kelana, Klang
Tel: 03-3372 9657
This is *the* place to have Indian *mee
goreng*, spicy fried noodles that even
the late sultan of Selangor used to
order to bring with him to London.
S. Govindasamy has prepared this
dish for half a century. It is served on
a banana leaf, with slices of crispy
battered prawn cakes. Wash it down
with a refreshing lime juice. **$$**

Kuala Selangor
Kuan Hwa Seafood Restaurant
1A Jalan Bagan Yu, Pasir Penambang
Tel: 03-3289 6719
Enjoy views of the river and
mangroves while supping on

specialities such as stir-fried clam
vermicelli, steamed prawns with a
zingy chilly onion dip and the excellent
crab in salted egg; ask for deep-fried
bread to soak up the gravy. Service is
quick and the eatery clean. **$$**
Rahmaniah
80 Jalan Sultan Ibrahim
Tel: 03-3289 7723
Near Bukit Melawati in Kuala
Selangor, this simple food outlet has
excellent Indian breads like *roti canai*
(flaky bread), with curries. It also
serves *roti jala* (lacy pancakes) with
chicken curry, *murtabak* (flaky bread
with minced meat filling) as well as
mee goreng (fried noodles). **$**
River View Seafood Restaurant
1 Jalan Besar, Pasir Penambang
Tel: 03-3289 2238
Very popular with tourists, this family-
run eatery serves quality seafood
dishes cooked Cantonese-style. It is
breezy, and offers commanding views
of the bridge, Bukit Melawati and
the village. You won't go wrong with
dishes such as buttered prawns, and
fish in black pepper sauce. **$$**

Petaling Jaya
Avanti Ristorante
Sunway Resort Hotel & Spa, Persiaran
Lagoon, Bandar Sunway, Petaling Jaya
Tel: 03-7492 8000
www.kualalumpur.sunwayhotels.com/eat/avanti.
aspx
The cuisine is described as Italian-
American, but expect traditional
Italian favourites with a creative
twist. The tenderloin with pan-seared
goose liver and slipper lobster with
pasta are recommended. With a good
Italian and New World wine list. A live
band plays from 7pm. **$$$$**
Grand City Restaurant
No. 51 Jalan 11/4, Petaling Jaya
Tel: 03-7957 3158
A great breakfast place close to
Universiti Malaya with a nice spread

of South Indian breads. The light
and fluffy sweet *appam* (pancake)
is a must-try. At lunch and dinner,
the banana-leaf meals are superb,
while the range of sweet and savoury
teatime treats draws fans as well. **$**
Paya Serai Restaurant
Hilton Petaling Jaya, 2 Jalan Barat,
Petaling Jaya
Tel: 03-7955 9122
www.3.hilton.com
Deservedly recognised for its buffets,
this restaurant is renovated regularly
to remain beautifully contemporary.
While pricey, this is a great way to
try out well-cooked Malay dishes,
although the almost overwhelmingly
large spread includes other local and
international dishes too. **$**
Woods Macrobiotics Restaurant
AG-8 Block A, Ground floor, Happy
Mansion, 17/13 Jalan, Petaling Jaya
Tel: 03-7958 5795
www.macrobiotics-malaysia.com
This restaurant serves vegan
macrobiotic organic food cooked
without any preservatives,
monosodium glutamate, colouring
or chemical additives. Try the five-
colour salad with mayonnaise and
the popular rendang rice set, which
is rice served with coconut chutney
and a portion of sweet potato cooked
in fragrant but spicy coconut sauce.
$$

Putrajaya
Penang Village
Alamanda Putrajaya Shopping Centre,
Presint 1
Tel: 03-8888 4268
Penang favourites in this chain eatery
include the oyster omelette for lighter
fare and the Malay *tomato* (tomato
rice) with curry chicken for a bigger
meal. The desserts are great to cool
down with on a hot day – try the
cendol, melon with ice cream or sago
pudding. **$**

NORTHWESTERN PENINSULA

Cameron Highlands

Gonbei
Cameron Highlands Resort
Tel: 05-491 1100
Excellent Japanese cuisine is served
in a Zen-like setting that opens out
to the rainforest. Has a *sake* bar with
a range of traditional Japanese rice
wines and whiskies. **$$$**
Kumar's
26 Main Road, Tanah Rata
Tel: 05-491 2624
Located near Starbucks, Kumar's
serves Indian food at affordable

prices. Naan, tandoori and banana
leaf-rice are recommended dishes. **$**
Palm Leaf Garden Cafe
3 Bandar Baru Brinchang
Tel: 05-491 4208
In front of Rosa Pasadena, dishes up
good Thai, Western and local dishes
at reasonable prices. **$**
The Smokehouse Hotel
Tanah Rata
Tel: 05-491 1215
Delectable cream teas, lunch and
afternoon teas on the terrace, which
on a fine day offers a view of the

peaceful hills. English fare includes
steaks, pies, seafood; light meals all
day long in the conservatory. **$$$$**
Uncle Chow's Kopitiam
C2-G-01 Block C2 Taman Royal Lily,
Tanah Rata
Tel: 012-205 2778
As the name *kopitiam* suggests, it
serves a variety of local dishes and
dessert (including *local kuihs*) in a
café-style atmosphere. Favourites
include *nasi lemak* and *assam laksa*.
To get to the restaurant, go past
Maybank (on your right) to the end

of the road, and follow the signs to Uncle Chow's. **$**

The Smokehouse Hotel
Jalan Jeriau
Tel: 03-362 2226
Excellent high tea with scones and apple pie on the garden patio or in the cosy tearoom. Dine in an elegant candlelit room on superb English pot roast with Yorkshire pudding, beef Wellington and home-made pies. Dress code applies. **$$$**

Fu Tien Vegetarian Restaurant
34 Jalan Medan 1B, Medan Ipoh Bestari
Tel: 05-549 9098
Vegetarian fare served with a modern twist, the menu includes vegetarian and fruit sushi rolls, seaweed salad and chicken rice. **$**

Indulgence Restaurant and Living
14 Jalan Raja Dihilir
Tel: 05-255 7051
Award-winning establishment serving Modern European-fusion cuisine, it takes pride in using the freshest ingredients to create an eclectic menu. Specials include Australian Wagyu and Japanese Kobe beef. Its ambience adds to the air of indulgence. **$$$**

Lucky Seafood
266 Jalan Pasir Puteh
Tel: 05-255 7330
This is a very popular restaurant where the seafood is fresh and of excellent value. It is really popular; bookings are recommended. Most of the locals come for the steamed fish. **$$**

Ming Court
36 Jalan Leong Sin Nam
Tel: 05-255 7134
This popular and good dim sum venue near Excelsior Hotel is packed during breakfast. **$**

Pakeeza Restaurant and Catering
15–17 Jalan Dato Sri Ahmad Said, Greentown
Tel: 05-241 4243
Good Indian food in an air-conditioned setting. Popular dishes include its *nasi briyani* and fish-head curry. **$**

Restoran Yum Yum
5 Persiaran Green Hill
Tel: 05-253 7686
Eateries on Ipoh's gourmet lane, which is perpendicular to Excelsior Hotel, are more upmarket than those along Jalan Leech. Among them is this excellent outlet with great Chinese-Nyonya ambience; it serves an excellent grouper in basil, and Yum Yum fried chicken. **$$**

Sin Yoon Loong
Jalan Bandar Timah (near Jalan Silang)
Tel: 05-241 4601
This is the original Ipoh coffee shop, where a fragrant local coffee brew tastes its best. Try the excellent home-made coconut jam (*kaya*) and toast for breakfast. **$**

Thean Chun
73 Jalan Bandar Bijih Timah
Close to the market, this coffee shop has long been a favourite amongst locals and visitors. Famous for its *Ipoh Koay Teow*, *chee cheong fun*, spring rolls and satay. Be prepared for a long wait for tables at lunchtime. **$**

Cendana Hut Café
There's a limited menu but with not many eating options around, the food is still considered the best on the hill. Local favourites like *nasi lemak*, *roti canai* and fried noodles are available, as well as the staple Western fare of hot dogs, sandwiches and burgers. **$**

The Bungalow
Lone Pine Hotel, 97 Jalan Batu Feringgi
Tel: 04-886 8566
Facing the hotel pool and the casuarina-lined beach, this restaurant housed in a colonial-era building has indoor and outdoor seating. At night, the atmosphere is very romantic. The Chinese menu concentrates on Hainanese dishes, but includes dishes such as fish curry, chicken rice and *filet mignon*. **$$$**

Edelweiss Café
38 Lebuh Armenian
Tel: 04-261 8935
Set in a beautiful 1890s shophouse, this café is a hangout for local artists. The diverse menu includes sandwiches, salads, macaroni and cheese, and local dishes like fried rice and *mee soto* (noodle soup with chicken). Affordable three-course set lunch menus and bottled beer available. Closed Mondays. **$$**

Hainanese Delights
227 Burma Road (at 1926 Heritage Hotel)
Tel: 04-226-1926
Family-run restaurant serving dishes cooked in Hainanese style such as *Inche Kabin* (fried chicken), chicken rice and chicken pie. Closed Mondays. **$**

Hameediyah Restaurant
164A Lebuh Campbell
Tel: 04-261 1095
Six generations of an Indian Muslim family have run Hameediyah's. Famous for its chicken curry, *murtabak* (flat bread filled with

minced meat) and mutton *biriyani* (rice cooked with spices and ghee). **$**

Kapitan's
93 Lebuh Chulia
Tel: 04-264 1191
Open round the clock, this eatery serves up North Indian fare. The fresh naan and sweet or mint chutneys best accompany the mild tandoori chicken, marinated in the signature spice mix and cooked in ovens. An iced fruit *lassi* (yoghurt drink) is the perfect complement to the spicy food. **$**

Lily's Vegetarian Kitchen
98 Noble House, Madreas Lane
Tel: 04-226 3810
Serves oriental, Nyonya, Western and fusion-style vegetarian dishes. In addition to the variety of cooking styles, it provides two distinct dining moods – on the first floor, food is served in a restaurant atmosphere, while the ground floor fare caters to the fast-food crowd. Closed Mondays. **$**

Mama's Nyonya Cuisine
31D Abu Siti Lane
Tel: 04-229 1318
A family-owned restaurant specialising in traditional Nonya (Peranakan) cuisine. A complimentary appetiser of *ikan bilis* with onion and chillis with a *kerabu* twist is the start to a delicious meal. Mama's speciality dishes are *tau eu bak* (pork cooked in dark soya sauce) and *perut ikan* (stewed fish stomach with vegetables – tastes better than the name suggests). Closed Mondays. **$**

Sigi's Bar and Grill by the Beach
Shangri-La's Golden Sands Resort, Batu Feringgi
Tel: 04-886 1852
Guests have the option of having their meals in the air-conditioned dining hall, open-air patio or its upper-deck dining area with a view of the beach. A wide selection of prime meat, salads and Asian dishes cater to the palates of children and adults alike. Seafood dishes such as fish & chips and pan-fried cod are amongst its signature dishes. The wine list leans towards New World vintages. **$$$**

Tajuddin Hussain
49 & 51 Lebuh Queen
Tel: 04-262 5367

Price per person for a three-course meal without drinks:
$ = under RM30
$$ = RM30–60
$$$ = RM60–90
$$$$ = over RM90

Having been around for 45 years, Tajuddin Hussain has perfected its *nasi kandar* (Penang-style rice and curries). The huge dining area is simply furnished, with wooden tables and plastic chairs. While the outlet specialises in tomato rice and roast chicken, the *nasi briyani* is also worth trying. **$**

That Little Wine Bar
54 Jalan Chow Thye
Tel: 04-226 8182
www.thatlittlewinebar.com
Warm, cosy European-style wine bar and restaurant housed in renovated former government living quarters. As the name suggests, carries a fine selection of wine. Open for dinner only. Closed Sundays. **$$$**

Langkawi

Beach Garden Resort Bistro & Beergarden
Pantai Cenang
Tel: 04-955 1363
Tables on the beach offer great sunset views. Excellent steaks, buttered potatoes, herb salad, waffles and cream, and coffee, not to mention the fabulous margaritas, possibly the best on the island. The menu changes nightly. **$$$$**

The English Tea Room and Coffee Bar
Pantai Cenang (in front of Landcons Hotel)
Mobile tel: 013-491 2343/017-556 1573
Try the Devonshire cream tea set – a tall cup of tea and delicious scones served with Australian fresh double cream and home-made strawberry jam. A range of sandwiches like tuna and chicken are available, but they will also make you an eccentric sandwich using any of these fillings: Marmite, Vegemite, Nutella, or even ketchup if you so wish. This is a halal establishment, so don't expect to see ham in your sandwiches. **$**

The Loaf Bakery & Bistro
C9 Perdana Quay, Telaga Harbour Park, Pantai Kok
Tel: 04-959 4866
Co-owned by one of Malaysia's former prime ministers, this bakery churns out premium breads and pastries using traditional Japanese techniques. Its upmarket bistro serves Western fare. Try its Tuba Isle harvest grilled mixed seafood. Although it has several outlets nationwide, this is the first one. Outside seating area has a view of the marina. **$$**

Nam Restaurant
Pantai Cenang
Tel: 04-955 6787
Located at Bon Ton Resort, this restaurant has a menu featuring tantalising "West-meets-spice"

cuisine. The Nyonya platter is the house speciality – nine different types of meat and seafood cooked in a variety of spices and served with rice on a banana leaf. Leave room for dessert if you can. Also caters to animal-lovers, vegetarians and children. **$$$$**

No. 7 Sup Corner
Jalan Penarak
Even if you miss this self-service restaurant at the road bend after the surau (mosque), you will not miss the number of cars parked at the road shoulder or the locals heading to it during lunchtime. Serves an assortment of Malay dishes buffet-style and soup. First get your plate of rice, and then take whatever you would like to eat. Present your food plate to the lady at the counter and pay for it. You can also order ABC, a sweet dessert topped with ice shavings. Open Sat–Thu 10am until the food runs out, closed on Fridays and during Ramadan. **$**

Passage thru' India
8 Jalan Pandak Mayah 6, Kuah
Tel: 04-4966 7384
www.passagethruindia.com
This popular Kuala Lumpur restaurant now has a Langkawi branch in Kuah town. Serving South and North Indian, and vegetarian cuisine. Try the prawn or pomfret masala and tandoori chicken with biryani rice. **$$**

Pappadam Ria's Kitchen
No.1, Lot 1556 Jalan Pantai Cenang
Tel: 04-955 7775
Located on Penang's beach. Opened in 2013, this spot has quickly cemented its reputation as one of the area's best Indian restaurants. Try their palak paneer, dry kadai chicken and mysore rogan josh. Open 11am–11.30pm. **$$**

The Pavilion
Datai Langkawi, Jalan Teluk
Tel: 04-950 0500
www.thedatai.com/langkawi/the-pavilion/
From its elevated spot in a rainforest canopy, this upscale hotel eatery serves up amazing views and an array of gourmet Thai dishes to dazzle the senses. Open from 6.30pm **$$$$**

Privilege Restaurant & Bar
B8, 1st Floor Perdana Quay, Telaga Harbour Park, Pantai Kok
Tel: 04-956 1188
www.privilegerestaurant.com
An upmarket restaurant that serves Malaysian fusion cuisine as well as a few vegetarian and gluten-free choices. Try their Australian beef rendang with jasmine rice or the prawn sambal served with three types of rice (brown, turmeric and jasmine). **$$$**

Red Tomato Restaurant & Lounge
5 Casa Fina Avenue (opposite Underwater World), Pantai Cenang
Tel: 04-955 4055
www.redtomatolangkawi.com
Has a good selection of Continental breakfast choices so get there before 10am or it can be busy. Try their speciality Farmer's Choice, a generous serving of potatoes, mushrooms, beef bacon or turkey ham topped with egg and cheese served with home-made bread. For dinner, the pasta is a crowd favourite. Pay a little extra and you can have gluten-free penne and pizza. **$$$**

Rose Tea 2
Lot 1054, Kampung Pantai Cenang
Tel: 017-514 9986
Serves tasty Thai cuisine, and one of the cheapest along this beach. Try the green curry or the fried fish with Thai sauce, but you can't go wrong with the other choices on the menu. Vegetarians welcomed. **$$**

Scarborough Fish 'n' Chip Restaurant
Lot 1388, Jalan Tanjung Rhu, Mukim Ayer Hangat
Tel: 04-959 4667
Try the signature English-styled dory fish and chips served with vinegar and a slice of lemon. If you are not a fan of fish, they also have chicken chop and home-made chicken nuggets. The New Zealand rib eye steak is very reasonably priced. With a limited selection of beers, it's a good spot to catch the sun disappearing behind the hill. **$$**

Sun Café
8 Sunmall, Jalan Teluk Baru, Pantai Tengah
Tel: 04-955 8300
The menu features hearty sandwiches, thin-crust pizzas, vegetarian meals and spicy local fare. The *crème brûlée* and milkshakes are delightful. **$$**

Wonderland Food Store
Lot 179-181, Pusat Perniagaan Kelana Mas, Kuah
Mobile tel: 012-494 6555
This riverside eatery is popular for its good-value Cantonese seafood. Try the stir-fried fresh greens with garlic, oyster egg omelette, squid stir-fried with dried chilli, and shrimp in batter cooked in a spicy tamarind sauce. Pork-free. **$$**

Pulau Pangkor Laut

Guan Guan
Pangkor town (near jetty)
Chinese seafood eatery that is good but pricey. **$**

Pangkor Island Beach Resort
Teluk Belanga

Tel: 05-685 1091
Enjoy Western dinners at the Pacific Terrace, happy-hour cocktails at the bar, seafood barbecue on Wednesday and Saturday, and buffet with daily themes at the poolside Hornbill Terrace Restaurant. You can also dine and watch the sunset on a beautiful beach (upon request). **$$$$**

Taiping
Bismillah Restoran
(opposite the Town Market)
Enjoy fresh *roti canai* (flaky bread) with tea for breakfast. For lunch, try Indian *biryani istimewa* (rice and curries). **$**
Jalan Kota
A number of Chinese seafood restaurants line this road, with fresh

produce from the Kuala Sepetang fishing area. **$**
Jalan Panggung Wayang
There's a multi-ethnic food centre beneath Fajar Supermarket, serving local delicacies such as *popiah*, satay, *rojak sotong* (squid salad with peanut sauce) and fresh ginger tea. **$**

SOUTHERN PENINSULA

Johor Bahru
Chez Papa French Bistro
38–40 Jalan Jaya, Taman Maju Jaya
Tel: 07-333 4988
Excellent food, friendly service and welcoming decor make this a favourite. Its signature dish is its sirloin steak with pepper cream sauce. Lamb shank, *foie gras chaud* and pan-seared duck are other favourites. Open for dinner only. **$$**
New Hong Kong Restaurant
69A–C Jalan Sultan Ibrahim
Tel: 07-222 2608
Located in the Stulang Laut area, this restaurant opened its door in 1954. Signature dishes are its charcoal roasted meat, chilli crab, dim sum and mooncakes. **$$** (dim sum), **$$$** (à la carte dishes)
Restoran Singgah Selalu
36-F, Jalan Skudai, Danga Bay
Tel: 07-237 7255
Located opposite Tune Hotel, this 24-hour eatery serves local and Western dishes. Recommended dishes are its black pepper crab and steamed sea bass. **$$**
Tepian Tebrau Food Centre
Jalan Skudai, Danga Bay
Tel: 07-223 4935
A favourite among locals for its seafood steamboat, *nasi biryani* (rice with mutton or chicken) and *ikan bakar* (grilled fish). **$**

Melaka
Calanthe Art Café
11 Jalan Hang Kasturi
Tel: 06-292 2960
www.calantheartcafe.blogspot.com

Friendly staff serve a variety of local and Western cuisine with sinful desserts to finish. Their set menu is good value; try the Calanthe laksa (noodles in curry coconut milk) or coffee from any of the 13 Malaysian states. **$**
Hoe Kee Chicken Rice
4 Jalan Hang Jebat
Tel: 06-2833 4751
There are many shops selling Melaka's famous Hainanese chicken and rice balls, but this shop is by far the most popular. If you come at the height of lunchtime, you will have to wait at least half an hour or more for a seat. If you don't fancy rice balls, try the Assam fish head (served in a spicy tamarind based soup) with rice. **$**
Limau Limau Café
9 Jalan Hang Lekiu
Mobile tel: 012-698 4917
A tiny café that serves good milkshakes, sandwiches and breakfast; try the special toasted ciabatta sandwich with roasted chicken for lunch. If it is in season and you are a fan, try the durian milkshake or else the coffee. Thu–Tue 9.30am–noon. **$$**
Little Momma Fresh Fruit Juice & Café
52 Jalan Kampung Pantai
Tel: 06-286 2993
This Peranakan-run family café serves reasonably priced Malaysian and Western cuisine. They have daily specials, but the speciality here, however, is their fruit juice concoctions. Try the dragon fruit with lemon juice. **$**

Restaurante San Pedro
4 D'Aranjo Road, Portuguese Settlement, Ujong Pasir
Tel: 06-284 2170
Serves authentic Portuguese cuisine. There are various styles of cooking the seafood, chicken or vegetables, but the recommended dishes are the baked fish (sea bass or red snapper), curry *debal* chicken (can be quite spicy), fried brinjals and the black pepper crabs. Call ahead to reserve a table (and your fish), because once their stock of fish runs out, they will close for the day. Closed on Wednesdays. **$$**
Veggié Planet
41 Jalan Melaka Raya 8, Taman Melaka
Tel: 06-292 2819
www.veggieplanet.my
Serves healthy vegetarian and organic food that is free of MSG (monosodium glutamate), artificial colouring, preservatives and microwave cooking. Try the local curry handmade ramen noodles or the cheese (made from vegetable oil) sandwiches. **$**
Zheng He Teahouse
3 Jalan Kampung Kuli
Mobile tel: 016-764 0588
The owner grew up on coffee but instead opened up a teahouse in the heritage area. For a fee, you can ask for a tea ceremony that lets you taste the various grades of teas. Lunch is a set menu – of a main dish and a soup; you can request if you want vegetarian or pork-free. **$**

PENINSULA'S EAST COAST

Kota Bharu
Central Market
The bustling first floor is packed with food stalls selling local Malay rice and curries – try the *nasi kunyit*, a yellow, turmeric-flavoured glutinous rice concoction. There is also a large variety of local

kuih (cakes) that cannot be found outside Kelantan. **$**
Kedai Kopi Hai Ping
Kedai Kopi Hai Ping, No. 3735, Jalan Sulaimani, Cukai, Kemaman
Tel: 09-859 7810
Drop by for its famous coffee and kaya toast – the home-made kaya is

TRANSPORT

EATING OUT

ACTIVITIES

A – Z

LANGUAGE

a local jam made from eggs, sugar and coconut milk, while the coffee is a blend of Arabica coffee beans from Indonesia, Brazil and Colombia. **$**

Kedai Kopi White House
Jalan Sultanah Zainab
Located opposite the State Mosque, this is the best place to enjoy *nasi dagang* – long-grain rice and glutinous rice cooked with coconut milk and eaten with tuna curry and vegetables. Serves traditional charcoal-toasted bread with *kaya* for breakfast. **$**

Kow Lun
Jalan Kebun Sultan
Tel: 09-744 7839
Chinese coffee shop with a variety of dishes including piping-hot noodles, *bak kut teh* as well as beer. **$**

Ulang Corner
Jalan Wakaf Mek Zainab
A Chinese food stall specialising in Kelantanese-style cooking, it is a local favourite. The *nasi kerabu* at this restaurant is cooked with 40 different herb extracts. Nasi *dagang* is another favourite dish. **$**

Good Luck Restaurant
11Y & Z Jalan Kota Lama
Tel: 09-622 7573
Popularly known as Lucky Restaurant, it is centrally located, next to a *bak kut teh* (herbal pork ribs soup) eatery, and serves seafood specialities and Cantonese-style frog legs, as well as one-dish noodle and rice meals. Air-conditioned upstairs. **$**

Nils Restaurant
Pantai Batu Buruk
Renowned Malay seafood restaurant, famous for its *ikan bakar* (grilled fish with sambal sauce), right on the

beach. Favourite dining spot with locals, including royalty. **$–$$**

Madam Bee's Kitchen
177 Jalan Kampung Cina
Mobile tel: 012-988 7495
Located in Chinatown, Madam Bee is well known for local Peranakan dishes, which are different from those found in Melaka and Penang. Here, they are blended with Kelantanese budu sauce with an emphasis on spice and seafood. Try also the *laksa Terengganu*, noodles in a creamy coconut gravy with shredded fish meat and herbs, and its signature dish – *rojak cerenang* – a mixed fruit salad served with fish crackers in a Chinese-based gravy. **$**

Restoran Meka
66/16 Taman Seri Intan
Tel: 09-623 1831
Traditional Terengganu-style Malay cooking with mainly fish dishes in various spicy coconut concoctions, and *ulam*, traditional salads eaten with a prawn paste-based chilli condiment called *sambal belacan*. The dishes are laid out in trays. **$**

Crocodile Rock Pizza and Grill
Lot 4360B, Jalan Datuk Mahmud, off Jalan Teluk Sisek
Tel: 09-567 5757
Located in an old colonial bungalow, it serves excellent pizza and other Western dishes such as pasta and steak. Great dining place for families, with a live band on Thursday evenings. **$$**

Kampung Restaurant
Hyatt Regency Kuantan, Teluk Cempedak
Tel: 09-518 1234
A casual restaurant with teakwood chairs and tables. Enjoy good Malay and Continental food and excellent

pizzas in this restaurant built on stilts over the sea. Features an open kitchen and ravishing views of the South China Sea. **$$$**

Pak Su Seafood Restaurant
Batu 6 (6th mile), Kuantan–Beserah Road
Tel: 09-544 8025
About half an hour north of Kuantan, just before De Rhu Beach Resort, sits this breezy Chinese restaurant overlooking the sea. It is well known for its stuffed crabs, salad lobster and spicy-sour *asam* (tamarind) steamed fish. Air conditioned. **$$**

Babura Sea View Chinese Restaurant
Babura Sea View Resort, Kampung Tekek
Tel: 09-419 1139
Located at Said Bay. Breezy beachside Chinese restaurant with excellent seafood and good beers. **$**

Cabana Beach Bistro
Tekek Village
Tel: 09-419 1045
A nice beach bar with friendly atmosphere and good music. The menu is simple with freshly caught seafood BBQ and vegetarian options. Licensed. **$**

Nazri's Place II
Kampung Air Batang
Tel: 09-419 1375
Set amongst green surroundings, Nazri's serves Malaysian and Western food. **$**

Salange Dreams Restaurant
Salange Beach Resort
Tel: 07-799 2337
www.tiomansalang.com
Located in the north-west of Pulau Tioman, this no-frills restaurant specialises in Chinese and western cuisines. **$$**

SARAWAK

Benson's Seafood Centre
Jalan Chan Chin Ann, off Jalan Abell
Tel: 082 255 262
Located behind City Inn and beside the Sarawak river, Benson's is famous for its fresh seafood and relaxed atmosphere. Simply point to the vegetables and fish, crabs or prawns of your choice and say how you'd like them cooked. **$$**

The Dyak
29 Ground Floor, Panovel Commercial Complex, Jalan Simpang Tiga
Tel: 082-234 068
Learn more of the Dayak culture while enjoying Iban and Orang Ulu

cuisine. In addition to food, Dayak music, art and culture are displayed prominently within the decor. Try the *tuak* (rice wine) to accompany your meal. Vegetarian meals available too. **$$**

Jambu Restaurant and Lounge
32 Jalan Crookshank
Tel: 082-235 292
www.jamburestaurant.com
Housed in a pleasant converted colonial-era bungalow with a patio and a lounge with TV screen, this restaurant-cum-tapas bar is a firm favourite with locals and visitors alike. The tapas bar has live jazz on Friday nights, while the restaurant offers a

mix of Western and fusion Borneo cuisine. Closed on Mondays. **$$**

The Junk
80 Jalan Wayang
Tel: 082-259 450
Noted for its Western dishes including steaks and pastas, which come in generous portions. An eclectic decor adds to its attraction. It is located in Kuching's city centre. **$$**

Li Garden
1st Floor, Hock Lee Centre, Jalan Datuk Abang Abdul Rahim
Tel: 082-340 785
A local favourite for refined Cantonese cuisine, this is open for both lunch and dinner. If you yearn for a good

Peking duck, this is the place to come to, even though the restaurant's location will mean a taxi ride. Booking is essential for dinner. **$$**

Lyn's Thandoori
7 Jalan Song Thian Cheok
Tel: 082-234 934
Serves authentic North Indian tandoori dishes and naan and has over 200 items on its menu. It also has a wide selection for vegetarians. Located close to the MAS building in the city centre, it is within a 10-minute walk of most major hotels in the city. **$**

Magenta
Sarawak Tourism Complex, Old Court House, Jalan Tun Abg Hj Openg
Tel: 082-254 500
Popular for its Western dishes with an Asian twist. Fine examples are seafood bouillabaisse, and grilled salmon with salsa and potato ragout – all artfully presented and served in generous portions. **$$**

Minoru
Lot 493G, Section 10, Rubber Road
Tel: 082-251 021
Regarded by many as Sarawak's best Japanese restaurant, Minoru offers a selection of fine Japanese cuisine for both lunch and dinner set in a traditional Japanese decor, and is known for its attentive service. **$$$**

See Good Food Centre
53 Jalan Ban Hock
Tel: 082-232 609
Excellent seafood, fresh and affordable, served in a simple, open-sided eatery with some tables outside. Don't miss the curried bamboo clams if they're available, and assam steamed fish. Delicious noodle dishes are served between main meal times. **$$$**

The Steak House
Hilton Hotel, Kuching
Tel: 082-223 888
Although this place has the best steaks in town, it is even more popular for its sophisticated international cuisine served in elegant surroundings. Try the set meal for really good value. River view adds to the ambience. Dinner only (6–10.30pm). **$$$**

Ting Noodle House
117B, Lot 132, Jalan Ban Hock
Tel: 082-232 250
Located not far from the end of Jalan Soon Thian Cheok, this air-conditioned and moderately priced restaurant is packed at lunchtime. Open from 8am to 8.30pm, this is the place to come for all kinds of noodle dishes (the Taiwanese beef noodles are recommended) and interesting dumplings, as well as rice-based dishes. **$**

Toh Yuen
Hilton Kuching, Jalan Tuanku Abdul Rahman
Tel: 08-222 3888
One of the best Chinese restaurants in town with views of the river, decorated in decadent red and gold. Serves favourites from the provinces of Guangdong and Szechuan. Can seat up to 200 and features four private rooms. Open 11.30am–10.30pm. **$$$**

Top Spot Food Centre
5th Floor, Jalan Bukit Mata Kuching
An open-air seafood plaza where half a dozen eating outlets vie for business with tempting displays of fresh seafood on ice. **$**

Waterfront Café
Hilton Kuching, Jalan Tunku Abdul Rahman
Tel: 08-222 3888
Gaze out across the Kuching river in air-conditioned comfort as you enjoy excellent espresso, freshly baked bread, salads and sumptuous buffets, as well as à la carte Japanese dishes. The café features different food promotions each day. Open 6am–11pm. **$$**

Zhun San Yen Vegetarian Restaurant
Lot 165, Jalan Chan Chin Aun
Tel: 082-230 068
Vegan-friendly restaurant that serves buffet-style lunch and dinner. Some meals contain eggs. Serves a wide variety of food and juices. Closed Sundays. **$**

Al Fresco Sidewalk Café
Ground Floor, Pelita Commercial Centre, Jalan Bulan Sabit
Tel: 085-428 928
One of a cluster of casual restaurants in a popular district situated a short taxi ride from downtown. This friendly spot has fish and chips, pizzas and grilled dishes. **$$**

Apollo Seafood Centre
4, Ground Floor, Jalan South Yu Seng
085-420 813
A local favourite. Customers can choose their own fish or crabs on display. Popular dishes are butter prawns, claypot seafood, curry fish head and stewed pork leg. **$$**

Café Miri
Taman Yakin Shopping Centre, Jalan Bulan Sabit
Tel: 085-425 122
A few kilometres from the town centre, this relaxed café run by a local Chinese man and his Australian wife serves a great array of drinks and Western dishes. Closed Tuesdays. **$$**

Imperial Restaurant
Jalan Pos

Tel: 085-431 133
Located at the Imperial hotel, this dining establishment serves both Asian and Western cuisine. Peking duck is one the recommended items on the menu. **$$**

Le Ark Café
Rejang Esplanade
Tel: 084-321 813
One of the trendiest places in Sibu, situated on the waterfront. Serves up a variety of satisfying cocktails and dishes drawn from local and international cuisines. **$$**

Café Café
10, Jln Chew Geok Lin
Tel: 084-328 101
One of the best fusion restaurants in town. Dishes include fantastic Nyonya-style dishes with an excellent mix of spices, great sauces and exotic flavours. Vegetarian dishes also available. Open lunch and dinner; closed Mondays. **$$**

Hai Bing Seafood and Coffee Shop
31, Jln Maju
Tel: 60-321 491
This place has two options: choose from the café-style street side or the indoor, air-conditioned Chinese restaurant. Open for lunch and dinner. **$**

Hock Chu Leu Restaurant
30, Jalan Blacksmith
Tel: 084-316 524
A popular Chinese restaurant specialising in Foochow dishes; particularly popular for its duck, meatball soup, *siew mai* (dumplings) and fried noodle dishes. **$$**

New Capital Restaurant
46 Jalan Kampong Nyabar
Tel: 084-326 066
This Chinese restaurant, near Tanahmas Hotel, is known for its deep-fried fish and butter prawn dishes. Lunch and dinner (closes 9pm). **$$**

Pepper's Café
Tanahmas Hotel, Jalan Kampung Nyabor
Tel: 084-333 188
Casual dining in one of Sibu's top hotels. Both Western and local dishes are available à la carte or buffet-style. Good selection of desserts as well. **$$**

PRICE CATEGORIES

Price per person for a three-course meal without drinks:
$ = under RM30
$$ = RM30–60
$$$ = RM60–90
$$$$ = over RM90

SABAH

Kota Kinabalu

Borneo 1945 Museum Kopitiam
24 Jalan Dewan
Mobile tel: 019-883 3829
An atmospheric coffee shop where coffee is served in old-style cups, and charcoal-toasted bread is slathered with rich coconut jam (*kaya*). Lunchtime specials are as flavourful as they are nostalgic. Located on the site used by the Australian Armed Forces during the rebuilding of Sabah after World War II, the coffee shop displays many historic photos. Pork-free. Open 7.30am–midnight. **$**

Fatt Kee Coffee Shop
28 Jalan Bakau, Jalan Pantai
Located within Ang's Hotel Restaurant, it serves popular Chinese food. Try its oyster-sauce chicken wings and sizzling Japanese tofu or ask for the chef's recommendation. Open 11am–10pm. **$**

GRAZIE Ristorante
3-36, 3 Floor Suria Sabah Shopping Mall
Mobile tel: 019-821 6936
www.grazierestaurantkk.webs.com
Try one of their three Italian specialities – the spaghetti lobster, spaghetti vongole, or the gnocchi served with meatballs in tomato sauce and you can't go wrong. Open 11am–10pm. **$$$**

Kohinoor North Indian Restaurant
Lot 4, The Waterfront
Tel: 088-235 160
The only North Indian restaurant in the city, Kohinoor offers air-conditioned dining as well as tables on a seaside boardwalk. An extensive menu with plenty of vegetarian options, with inexpensive yet generous set lunches and lavish set dinners for four. Good food in unprepossessing surroundings. **$$**

Liew Chai Vegetarian
Lot S24 Basement, Centre Point Sabah, 1, Jalan Centre Point
Mobile tel: 012-833 7768
Located in the Wan Chai Food Corner, Liew Chai attracts a local crowd to the buffet-style spread of curried or stir-fried vegetables, tofu and mock meat (some dishes may contain eggs). **$**

Little Italy Pasta & Pizza Corner
Ground Floor, Hotel Capital, Jalan Haji Saman
Tel: 088-232 231
www.littleitaly-kk.com
Located in the heart of town, this offers Italian favourites (with emphasis on pastas and pizzas) at reasonable prices. Outdoor and air-conditioned indoor dining available. **$$**

Luyang Seafood Restaurant
Shop No. 1, Luyan Phase 1, Jalan Kolam
Tel: 088-252 431
Located some 3.5km (2 miles) from the city centre, just before the Esso petrol station on the left, is this reasonably priced restaurant. Seafood is fresh and excellent; try the stir-fried Sabah vegetables, braised grouper in claypot and spicy-sour noodles. As locals like to eat dinner early, plan to arrive before 7pm for a table. **$$**

Nagisa Japanese Restaurant
Hyatt Regency Kinabalu, Jalan Datuk Salleh Sulong
Tel: 088-221 234
Fine Japanese restaurant in the city offering Japanese favourites. It is tastefully furnished and has a separate sushi bar and teppanyaki counters. With views of the sea and Gaya island. **$$$**

Suang Tain Seafood Restaurant
No. 12 Ground Floor, Block A Sedco Complex, Kampung Air
Tel: 088-223 080
Open daily from 3pm to 1.30am, this seafood restaurant dominates a popular open-air evening eatery. A large range of fresh seafood is available, and the restaurant is known for its reasonable prices. Try the butter prawns, deep-fried clams with spring onions and the cuttlefish cooked in black sauce. **$$$$**

Supertanker
Lot 12 & 13, Grand Industrial Estate, Jalan Bundusan (off Jalan Penampang)
Tel: 088-717 889
This large and popular restaurant, located about 10 to 15 minutes by taxi from the city centre, serves some of the best Chinese food in town. **$$**

Wisma Merdeka Food Court
2nd floor, Wisma Merdeka, Phase 1, Jalan Haji Saman
Always busy, this collection of food stalls offers an amazing variety of Malaysian food, plus a few Western favourites such as pastas, pizzas and hamburgers. The large Malay stall near the exit offers some of the best Malay and Indonesian food in town. Some stalls open for breakfast; closes around 9pm. **$**

Sandakan

Balin Roof Garden Bar & Bistro
Jalan Pelabuhan Lama
Tel: 089-272 988
Located at the NAK Hotel, this Western restaurant and bar has a breathtaking view of Sandakan Harbour. Enjoy refreshing drinks and cocktails while watching the sunset. It is located at the top of the NAK Hotel. **$$**

The English Teahouse and Restaurant
Jalan Istana
Tel: 089-222 545
www.englishteahouse.org
This beautifully restored colonial-era bungalow overlooks Sandakan and the bay. English favourites, including bangers and mash, and selected Asian cuisine. You can even play croquet. **$$$**

Ocean King Seafood Restaurant
Jalan Batu Sapi (4.5 km), Pasir Putih
Tel: 089-618 111/616 048
A large open-sided restaurant built on stilts over the bay. There is a vague menu/price list written on a board on the veranda, but basically, if it swims, you can order it. Fish, crabs, prawns, lobster, squid and various shellfish are all available, and the beancurd and vegetable dishes are good. **$$**

Restoran Habeeb
There are at least eight restaurants in this chain featuring Indian and local Muslim cuisine. One of the most convenient is located directly in front of Wisma Sandakan on Lebuh Empat (4th Avenue), another one is at Jalan Preyer 5B **$**

Tawau

Azura Restoran
Jln Dunlop
Tel: 12-863 9934
Its all about tasty South Indian food: good fish curry, fish sambal, Tandoori and kurma chicken, prawn and crab masala. Open from 8am to 9pm; with another branch at the Sabinda Hawker Centre. **$**

Kam Ling Seafood
24 Sabindo Open-Air Food Stall
Tel: 089-756 457
A simple restaurant that is a Sabah legend with its wide range of live fish, crustaceans and other seafood. Despite the unprepossessing surroundings, eager diners flock here for seafood at its best – and for the very reasonable prices. Open 11am–10pm. **$$**

Rasa Sayong Restoran
Jln Haji Karim
Tel: 089-777 042
A good Chinese place for lunch or dinner. Serves specials such as prawn mango rice. **$**

PRICE CATEGORIES

Price per person for a three-course meal without drinks:
$ = under RM30
$$ = RM30–60
$$$ = RM60–90
$$$$ = over RM90

ACTIVITIES

FESTIVALS, THE ARTS, NIGHTLIFE, SHOPPING, SPORT AND SIGHTSEEING TOURS

FESTIVALS

In addition to the religious festivals Malaysians celebrate each year (see page 384), festivals celebrating the arts, music and culture are held in different parts of the country each year. These festivals honour the diversity of Malaysian culture by celebrating traditions of the past and promoting new experiences. A selection of major festivals is shown below. Before you arrive, check the respective festival websites or the Tourism Malaysia website (www. tourism.gov.my) for the exact dates, including the full festival calendar.

Pasir Gudang World Kites Festival (Feb, www.kitefestpasirgudang. com) Kites of all forms, shapes and colours fill the skies of Pasir Gudang in Johor every year as thousands of enthusiasts flock in to watch kite-flying skills on display. In addition to competitions, there are workshops on kite-making and the history of kiting.

Borneo International Jazz Festival (May, www.jazzborneo.com) Held annually in Miri, Sarawak, it is performed outdoors in an informal atmosphere. A mix of local and overseas talent performs a range of jazz genres.

Tadau Kaamatan (end May, www. sabahtourism.com) People who have been working in towns and cities return home to their longhouses in anticipation of this festival that marks the end of the rice harvest. The natives of Sabah celebrate it with ceremonies to thank the gods for a bountiful harvest, and then follow with days of merry-making, dance and music.

Gawai Dayak Festival (early June, www.sarawaktourism.com) Sarawak's version of the rice harvest celebrations. Each tribe has its own unofficial dates for its rituals, held usually after the rice harvest, to thank the gods for the bountiful harvests. The official statewide holidays are on the first two days of the month.

Rainforest World Music Festival (in 2015 in August,www.rwmf.net) Held at the base of Mount Santubong just outside Kuching, the festival celebrates the diversity of world music. It showcases global traditional music and instruments in an environment of fun. Performances, jam sessions, mini concerts and ethno-music lectures are held over three days.

Sabah International Folklore Festival (July, www.sabahtourism. com) Sabah celebrates world cultural diversity through music and dance. International and local folk dances are a highlight of the East-meets-West musical extravaganza.

1Malaysia Contemporary Arts Tourism Festival (nationwide, July–Sept) A travelling art exhibit of established and upcoming young Malaysian artists to promote Malaysian art to a wider community. There are also seminars and workshops during the three-month festival.

Malaysia International Gourmet Festival (Oct, www.migf.com) This gastronomic event promotes the country's best fine-dining venues and focuses on the artistry of resident world-class chefs in preparing gourmet food for diners. However, participating restaurants are mainly in Kuala Lumpur.

Penang Jazz Festival (Dec, www.penangjazz.com) The festival started in 2004 and is held on the first weekend in December in Penang. Activities include performances, forums, workshops and competitions amongst jazz lovers.

THE ARTS

Art galleries

Malaysia's serious art gained credence only in the 1960s after independence. The appreciation for art is rapidly growing, particularly in Kuala Lumpur and other urban areas. This interest is reflected in the increase in the number of art galleries and correspondingly, in the number of exhibitions mounted. Local galleries tend to focus on local and regional artworks. The diversity is staggering, from Chinese brush painting to abstract art, sculpture, glass and wood. However, it is hard to define what Malaysian art really is. Batik art comes closest to being a unique Malaysian visual art form, which was pioneered by the late Chuah Thean Teng. Yahong Gallery features some of his work including those by his sons.

Kuala Lumpur

Galeri Petronas
Lot 341–343, Level 3, Suria KLCC
Tel: 03-2051 7770
www.galeripetronas.com.my
Funded by the national oil company, this is the city's most accessible, located within the busy Suria KLCC shopping mall. An elegant space for traditional and contemporary art. Tue–Sun 10am–8pm.

Islamic Arts Museum
Jalan Lembah Perdana
Tel: 03-2274 2020
www.iamm.org.my
Southeast Asia's largest museum of Islamic art houses artefacts and texts from Southeast Asia, China and India as well as the heartlands of Persia and the Middle East. Daily 10am–6pm.

KL Lifestyle Art Space
Lot G.36 Ground Floor,
Tropicana City Mall, 3 Jalan
SS20/27 Petaling Jaya
Tel: 03-2093 2668
Features modern and pioneer
artworks in encouraging the growth of
the secondary market for Malaysian
art. Daily 10am–10pm.
Kuala Lumpur City Gallery
27 Jalan Raja, Dataran Merdeka
(Merdeka Square)
Tel: 03-2698 3333
Housed in a century-old building next
to Dataran Merdeka, it houses prints,
photos and miniatures highlighting
the development of Kuala Lumpur.
Daily 9am–6pm.
National Visual Art Gallery
2 Jalan Temerloh, off Jalan Tun Razak
Tel: 03-4025 4990
www.visionkl.com/directory/national-
visual-arts-gallery
A striking purpose-built gallery
housing a permanent collection
of over 2,500 works by local and
international artists, including
ceramics, textiles and sculptures.
Daily 10am–6pm.
Shalini Ganendra Fine Art
8 Lorong 16/7B, Section 16,
Petaling Jaya
Tel: 03-7932 4740
www.shaliniganendra.com
Established in 1998, this gallery
specialises in Asian contemporary art
and design, with a focus on emerging
movements and regions. Tue–Sat
11am–7pm, public holidays and
other times by appointment.
Valentine Willie Fine Art
1st Floor, 17 Jalan Telawi 3, Bangsar
Baru
Tel: 03-2284 2348
www.vwfa.net
With a busy calendar of exhibitions,
this contemporary art gallery has an
extensive selection of Malaysian and
Southeast Asian paintings, sculptures
and drawings. Mon–Fri noon–8pm,
Sat noon–6pm.
Wei-Ling Gallery
8 Jalan Scott, Brickfields
Tel: 03-2260 1106
www.weiling-gallery.com
Caters to local and international
art enthusiasts keen to support
contemporary art. Mon–Fri noon–
7pm, weekends by appointment.
Zinc Art Space
Lot 61, Jalan Maarof, Bangsar
Tel: 12-658-9988
www.kl.asia-city.com/kuala-lumpur-art-
gallery/zinc-art-space
A multi-dimensional art space with a
varied exhibition range that includes
photography, art, installation, art toy
collectables and sculpture. Mon–Sat

noon–7pm, Sunday and public
holidays by appointment.

Penang
A2 Art Gallery
27 Bangkok Lane
Tel: 04-227 4985
www.a2artgallery.com
Features local and international
artists, with the focus on young and
upcoming artists. Mainly exhibits
contemporary modern art pieces.
Daily 10am–6pm.
ChinaHouse Art Space
153–155 Lebuh Pantai
Tel: 04 263 7299
This gallery features a mixed bag
of exhibitions including drawings,
paintings and photography. Works of
local and foreign artists are presented
here. Daily 10am–10pm.
Yahong Art Gallery
58D Batu Ferringhi
Tel: 04-881 1251
Home to the works of the late Chuah
Thean Teng and his sons. Chuah
pioneered the use of traditional batik
techniques in modern works in the
1930s. Daily 9.30am–6.30pm.

Kuching
Artrageously Ramsey Ong
94 Main Bazaar
Tel: 082-424 346
www.artrageouslyasia.com
Featuring the works of flamboyant
Sarawakian artist Ramsey Ong, as
well as those of other local artists.
Prints, cards and handicrafts are also
on sale. Mon–Sat 9.30am–6.30pm,
Sun 9.30am–5.30pm.
Galleria
Suite 1–3, Wesberley House
Lot 2812, Rubber Road West
Tel: 082-246 197
www.wesberly.com.my
A short taxi ride from the heart
of Kuching, this spacious gallery
has contemporary paintings by
local artists, including those of the
talented Iban artist, Melton Kais.
Mon–Fri 8.30am–5.30pm, Sat
9am–12.30pm.

Kota Kinabalu
Borneo Trading Post
Lot 16, The Waterfront
Jalan Tun Fuad Stephens
Tel: 088-231 655
www.borneotradingpost.com
Showcases the art culture of Borneo.
The mezzanine level of this quality
souvenir store offers original artworks
from around Southeast Asia at
reasonable prices.
Sabah Art Gallery
Mile 2, Jalan Penampang
Tel: 088-268 748/825

www.sabahartgallery.com
Set adjacent to the main museum
building, the gallery houses a
collection of paintings and 3D works by
local artists. Daily 9am–5pm; charge.

Classical music

Interest in Western classical music
has grown since the establishment
of the Malaysian Philharmonic
Orchestra (MPO) in 1998. It
has helped to encourage young
Malaysians in pursuing a classical
music career abroad; a number
have since returned to perform with
the orchestra. The establishment of
the Malaysian Philharmonic Youth
Orchestra is another indication of the
MPO's commitment to encouraging
Malaysian talent. Local musicals are
still rare, but the larger productions
with established performers have
been successful.
  Traditional Chinese opera is staged
on temporary platforms set up in the
suburbs during the Hungry Ghost
(*Por Thor*) Festival held in the seventh
month of the Chinese Lunar New Year.
The Chinese believe that the gates of
the underworld are opened during this
month and spirits allowed to roam the
earth. The performances are held to
entertain these spirits and the deity
known as the King of Hades (*Tye Soo
Ya*) who is in charge of the underworld.
Traditional Chinese costumes and
heavy make-up are features of
these performances. Kuala Lumpur
Performing Arts Centre (KLPAC)
and Penang Performing Arts Centre
(PenangPAC) also hold occasional
Chinese opera performances.
  Other than the Dewan Filharmonik
Petronas, which is home to the MPO,
there are no major venues that cater
strictly for classical music. Other
classical musical acts share venues
with theatre performances (see list of
venues under "Theatre").
Dama Orchestra
M-2-10 Plaza Damas
60 Jalan Sri Hartamas 1, Sri
Hartamas
Tel: 03-6201 9108
www.damaorchestra.com
The Dama Orchestra blends Eastern
and Western harmonies in its
performance. Although it specialises
in popular Chinese music from
the first half of the 20th century,
usually featuring the sublime
talent of soprano Tan Soo Suan, its
repertoire is wide. Dama's creativity
and versatility have been displayed
through performances in Australia,
China and Singapore. Mon–Fri
9.30am–6pm.

Dewan Filharmonik Petronas
Ground Floor, Tower 2,
Petronas Twin Towers, Kuala Lumpur
Tel: 03-2331 7007
www.dfp.com.my
This purpose-built classical concert
hall has a full programme of classical
music all year round performed by
the resident MPO, as well as by guest
orchestras and soloists from all over
the world, including renowned jazz and
world music exponents. A dress code
is imposed for evening performances.
The MPO's performance calendar
is available on the website. Sunday
matinees are good value for money.
Free lunchtime and midweek
performances are occasionally
scheduled. Mon–Fri 10am–6pm.

Comedy and theatre

Comedic acts are mainly centred
in Kuala Lumpur and are a popular
form of entertainment. Well-known
Malaysian stand-up comedians
include Harith Iskandar, Jit Murad,
Joanne Kam Poh Poh and the duo
of Indi Nadaraja and Allan Perera.
Many of the jokes are aimed at the
Establishment and the social quirks
of Malaysians. The Comedy Club
brings in overseas comics from
around the world. Performances are
held at different venues including
KLPAC, PJ Life Arts Centre and Velvet
Underground at Zouk (113 Jalan
Ampang, tel: 03-2171 1997).

Like comedy, theatrical activities
are mainly centred around Kuala
Lumpur, with some productions in
Penang and Ipoh. The Actor's Studio
is a major player in putting on local
and foreign productions, while
Gardner & Wife (tickets tel: 6017-
2289 849) brings international acts to
perform in Malaysia. Popular overseas
musical theatre performances tend
to do well here. For listings, check the
www.kakiseni.com websites, or daily
newspapers.

Kuala Lumpur
The Actors Studio, Malaysia
KL Performing Arts Centre
Sentul Park, Jalan Strachan
Tel: 03-4047 9000
www.theactorsstudio.com.my
A small, contemporary performing arts
space run by the country's top theatre
company, featuring mainly local
productions; scheduled performances
are held almost every week. In
addition to putting on performances,
the Actor's Studio played a large role
in setting up and managing KLPAC
and PenangPac. It also has training
academies at both locations.

Istana Budaya (National Theatre)
Jalan Tun Razak, Kuala Lumpur
Tel: 03-4026 5555
www.istanabudaya.gov.my
In addition to hosting traditional
musical performances and dance,
the country's main theatre stages
big local and international acts,
including Broadway musicals and
symphonic orchestra performances.
It is home to the National Symphony
Orchestra, Malaysian Traditional
Orchestra and Traditional Theatre.
The building is modelled after the *sirih
junjung*, a traditional arrangement of
betel leaves used in Malay wedding
ceremonies and guest receptions.
**Kuala Lumpur Performing Arts
Centre (KLPAC)**
Sentul Park, Jalan Strachan
Tel: 03-4047 9000
www.klpac.org
A beautiful, award-winning space
managed by The Actors Studio,
with a 500-seat main theatre and
various other performing spaces. In
addition to hosting performances,
KLPAC is home to The Actors Studio
Academy, which provides training on
the performing arts, a community
orchestra and theatre for young
people. Ample parking space
available; however, it's tricky to get
there by public transport. Mon–Fri
10.30am–6.30pm, Sat 10am–2pm.
PJ Live Arts Centre
2A-3 Block K, Jaya One, 72A Jalan
Universiti, Petaling Jaya
Tel: 03-7960 0439
www.pjlivearts.my
A 300-seat performing arts theatre
that aims to encourage community
participation in the arts and to nurture
young talent. Hosts plays, comedy
acts, dances and concerts.

Penang
**Performing Arts Centre of Penang
(PenangPAC)**
Level 3A, Quay One Wing, Straits
Quay, Jalan Seri Tanjung Pinang,
Tanjung Tokong
Tel: 04-899 1722
www.penangpac.org
The first major arts centre in the
northern region, PenangPAC hosts
comedy, drama, dance and music
performances. Like KLPAC, it is also
managed by The Actors Studio and
has a speech and drama academy.

Dance

The dance scene is relatively quiet in
Malaysia. An exception is the classical
Indian art form with performances
held regularly, particularly in temples.
The most famous troupe is the Kuala

Lumpur-based Temple of Fine Arts,
known for its epic productions. It
also incorporates contemporary and
Malaysian elements in its shows.

Authentic cultural performances are
difficult to catch these days, outside
official functions. Performances
during the National Day celebrations
and Colours of Malaysia (*Citrawarna
Malaysia*) festival offer glimpses into
modified traditional dances set to
contemporary music. A handful of
hotels also stage performances, as
does Kuala Lumpur's Central Market.

For indigenous dances, the
Sarawak Cultural Village in Kuching
has regular shows, as does the
Monsopiad Cultural Village in Kota
Kinabalu. The best dances, however,
are at longhouses, the further into the
interior the better. Plan your trip to
coincide with the rice harvest festivals
at the end of May and early June to
watch these mesmerising dances.

Contemporary dancers have small
companies and some are generally
good, training and performing
internationally. Chinese dances
are performed only during official
functions, but there are many dance
groups who use traditional dance as a
base for modern works.

Classical dance

Kuala Lumpur
Istana Budaya (National Theatre)
Jalan Tun Razak
Tel: 03-4026 5555
www.istanabudaya.gov.my
A venue for all kinds of performance
including traditional dance.
Pasar Seni (Central Market)
Jalan Hang Kasturi
Tel: 03-2031 0399 or (information
counter) 1300 22 8688
www.centralmarket.com.my
Cultural performances are regularly
hosted in the main foyer area and on
the outdoor stage, while alternative
music performances are occasionally
held in its annexe. Daily 10am–10pm.
Sutra House
12 Persiaran Titiwangsa 3
Tel: 03-4021 1092
www.sutrafoundation.org.my
Owned by the Sutra Foundation, one of
the most vibrant non-government art
centres in the country. Spearheaded
by classical Indian dance guru and
odissi exponent Ramli Ibrahim, Sutra
House has a landscaped outdoor
stage where Indian dance and music
recitals are held under the stars; there
is also an indoor art gallery.
Temple of Fine Arts
116 Jalan Berhala, Brickfields
Tel: 03-2274 3709

www.tfa.org.my
Non-profit cultural organisation with centres in Malaysia, India, Singapore, Australia and Sri Lanka. It hosts classical Indian art forms. You can also learn dance and play music here.

Kota Bharu
Gelanggang Seni (Cultural Centre)
Jalan Mahmud
Tel: 09-744 3124
Kelantan's traditional pastimes such as *gasing* (top) spinning and *silat* (Malay martial arts) performances are staged here, usually from March to October, but not every day (particularly during the fasting month of Ramadan). Enquire at the Kelantan Tourist Information Centre for forthcoming events (Jalan Sultan Ibrahim, tel: 09-748 5534).

Sarawak
Sarawak Cultural Village
Pantai Damai, Santubong
Tel: 082-846 411
www.scv.com.my
Billed as a living museum, this award-winning cultural village is located in the foothills of Mount Santubong, 45 minutes' drive from Kuching and close to the resorts of Damai beach. Sarawak's ethnic diversity is highlighted in traditional homes and a cultural show at 11.30am and 4pm daily.

Sabah
Monsopiad Cultural Village
Kampung Kuai Kandazon, Penampang
Tel: 088-774 337
www.monsopiad.com
Although most famous for its House of Skulls, with trophies taken by the infamous headhunter Monsopiad, this excellent cultural village aims to highlight and preserve the indigenous Kadazan culture. Traditional games, food, a cultural show (daily 11am, 2pm and 4pm) and a guided tour are included. Daily 9am–5pm.

Films

A major source of entertainment, cinemas in major cities are air-conditioned and comfortable, with some offering thx sound system and luxury halls. Tickets are cheaper on certain days and in the mornings. Some of the larger venues and operators offer online or phone booking services. Cinemas screen mainly mainstream offerings from Hollywood, Bollywood and Hong Kong, as well as a scattering of local Malay-language films, Southeast Asian fare and art house releases. Blockbusters

often get released the same day – in order to foil DVD pirates – as in the US, UK and Hong Kong, and queues can be long. Non-Malay-language movies have subtitles in Bahasa Malaysia and Chinese. English-language films rarely make it to the small towns. For listings, check the dailies or www.cinema.com.my.

In deference to the official religion of the country – Islam – nude, semi-nude and even kissing scenes between unmarried people are diligently, but not always professionally, censored – so sometimes, vital dialogue disappears too.

There are two main cinema operators, whose multi-screen halls are located in malls in major cities and screen mostly mainstream movies. **Golden Screen Cinema** (www.gsc.com.my) theatres in Kuala Lumpur are located in the Mid Valley Megamall, Berjaya Times Square and 1 Utama, Petaling Jaya. The other operator is **Tanjung Golden Village** (www.tgv.com.my), whose Kuala Lumpur theatres are in Capital Square, Suria KLCC, the Mines and Sunway Pyramid, Petaling Jaya. Berjaya Times Square also has a 3D IMAX Theater (tel: 03-2117 3046).

Jazz

Interest in jazz is reflected in the popularity of the jazz festivals held in Miri (Sarawak), Kota Kinabalu (Sabah) and Penang each year. Outside these festivals, jazz can be enjoyed in pubs and restaurants. In Kuala Lumpur, Alexis Ampang (Ground Floor, Great Eastern Mall, tel: 03-4260 2288) has live performances on Friday and Saturdays, and No Black Tie (17 Jalan Mesui, off Jalan Nagasari, tel: 03-2142 3737) has performances most evenings. In Penang, The Canteen at ChinaHouse (153–155 Lebuh Pantai, tel: 04-263 7299) has jazz bands playing Fridays to Sundays. Live bands can be found playing at Sully's Bar (Block B, KK Times Square) in Kota Kinabalu on Tuesday, Wednesday, Friday and Saturday evenings from 9.30pm.

Museums

Traditional museums in Malaysia are still mainly government-run, but there are an increasing number of government-funded and private museums catering to specialised subjects. Some of these subjects are of historical and cultural significance, such the Islamic Arts Museum in Kuala Lumpur (see page 138), Baba

Nyonya Heritage Museum in Melaka and Gopeng Museum in Perak. Others are collections of general interest such as the National Automobile Museum (Sepang, tel: 03-8787 4759) and Penang Toy Museum, which is especially fun for children (next to Copthorne Orchid Hotel, Tanjung Bungah, mobile tel: 012-460 2096).

NIGHTLIFE

Pubs, discos and karaoke lounges are where Malaysians party at night. The best nightlife is in the capital. Elsewhere, the action concentrates in hotel lounges and discos. Other than in Kuala Lumpur, people tend not to dress up, but shorts and sandals are definite no-nos. For the most up-to-date information, check out the What's Happening section of social magazines such as *Faces*, *Juice* and *KLue*, which are available free at Dome, Starbucks and Coffee Bean & Tea Leaf outlets.

Kuala Lumpur

Nightlife in the capital tends to congregate in specific areas; the main ones are **Jalan Sultan Ismail/Jalan Ampang**, **Asian Heritage Row** around **Jalan Doraisamy**, **Bukit Bintang**, **Bangsar**, and **Sri Hartamas**.

Generally, club crowds swell after 11pm. Clubs charge an entry fee from 10pm or 11pm, which includes one drink. Wednesday is ladies' night in most places, which means free drinks for women. Happy hour is usually 5.30–9pm, when drinks are half price, which should be taken advantage of since alcohol is very expensive in Malaysia. Beers start at RM10 a glass and RM40 a jug, alcohol RM15, and wine about RM20–25 a glass and RM80 a bottle. Wines have become very popular, and a wide range is available, especially in wine and cigar bars. You can keep a tab going until you leave. Waiters generally expect a tip.

KL-ites tend to dress up to go the fancier clubs and some places enforce a dress code which for men stipulates, at the minimum, a collared T-shirt, long trousers and covered shoes, while other places have a "no jeans, shorts and sandals" rule. Most clubs adhere to the 21-year-old age limit (the legal drinking age in Malaysia), but there are cases where this is openly flouted.

Live bands are popular and almost all the larger hotels have bars featuring live music, which usually begins at around 10pm. This is usually broad-appeal, middle-of-the-road music.

Bars and pubs

Alexis The Bar Upstairs
29A Jalan Telawi 3, Bangsar Baru
Tel: 03-2284 2880
Alexis exudes chic and class with its trendy design and purple-hued bar. Acid jazz plays in the background. Go early if you want a seat at its famous balcony overlooking the Telawi street action.

Lax Club Lounge
56 & 58 Jalan Doraisamy,
Asian Heritage Row
Tel: 03-2694 8188
Club-lounge with a sophisticated air. Trendy-looking decor and DJ attracts a hip party crowd. Alternatively, you can chill out on the sofas.

The Library
Ground Floor, e@Curve, Mutiara Damansara,Petaling Jaya
Tel: 03-7726 2602
A great place to unwind while enjoying a drink on the balcony, which overlooks the mall. Good selection of beers and cocktails.

Luna Bar
Menara Panglobal, Jalan Puncak
Tel: 03-2332 7777
A rooftop, outdoor lounge bar with a pool in the middle and views to die for. An exclusive chill-out venue.

The Poppy Collection
18-1 Jalan P. Ramlee
Tel: 03-2170 6666
Several sexy bars share this boutique entertainment space with floor-to-ceiling glass windows and alfresco balconies and gardens. Upstairs is the small and sensual lounge, Passion, while Bar Mandalay and the Havanita Cigar Lounge are for serious unwinding.

Pisco Bar
29, Jalan Mesui
Tel: 03-2142 2900
Noticeable for its eclectic decor featuring industrial chic and contemporary pop culture references, and its outstanding Spanish tapas and cocktails. An unpretentious and laid back vibe combined with a diverse range of after-dark events.

Sid's Pub
M-5A The Village, Bangsar South
Tel: 03-2287 7437
www.sidspubs.com
Sid's prides itself as a community pub with happy, friendly people having a great time together. Speaking of fun, catch the "Swingers", take over a section of the pub each week for a spot of fandango dancing.

Skybar
Traders Hotel, KLCC
Tel: 03-2332 9888
Simple and sleek, its large sunken alcove and ceiling-to-floor windows allow guests to appreciate the beauty of the Kuala Lumpur skyline at night including a sublime view of the Twin Towers.

SOULed Out
20 Jalan 30/70A, Desa Sri Hartamas
Tel: 03-2300 1955
Chill out in a large airy area outside – the dance floor is upstairs. A favourite with football fans; packed at weekends.

Village Bar
Starhill Gallery
Jalan Bukit Bintang
Tel: 03-2782 3852
Glitzy-looking decor unmatched elsewhere. Glass bottles stacked up as pillars and dangling lanterns give it a unique look. Amongst its wide selection of drinks are Chinese and Japanese rice wines and international beers.

Clubs

The Beach Club Café
924 Jalan P. Ramlee
Tel: 03-2142 6666
A popular tropical-themed hotspot featuring live bands on Sunday and rave parties nightly until the wee hours. The Beach Club plays all kinds of pop music and also serves Asian food. Can be a bit of a meat market late at night.

Elixir
37 & 39 Changkat Bukit Bintang
Tel: 03-2145 8222
A club that expects its patrons to be well dressed, Elixir is a favourite with the younger crowd. The blend of hip-hop and house music keeps feet moving.

Hard Rock Cafe
Ground Floor, Wisma Concorde, Jalan Sultan Ismail
Tel: 03-2715 5555
This oldie-but-goldie international chain keeps them coming with live local and regional bands playing mainstream music. Attracts a mainly young crowd. Good American-style fare in large portions served in the café.

Qba
Westin Kuala Lumpur, Jalan Bukit Bintang
Tel: 03-2773 8338
Samba, cha cha and salsa to a live Latin band at this Havana-themed club. Cigars and boutique wines are the other attractions of this classy two-storey place. Be sure to try its rum-based mojitos and cachaca-based caipirinhas.

Rootz Dance Club
Roof Top, Lot 10, Jalan Sultan Ismail
Tel: 03-2782 3557
Inspired by Russian museums and palaces – opulence describes Rootz to a tee. High-top couches encourage lounging, but the DJs are excellent in getting the crowd back on their feet.

Zeta Bar
Hilton Kuala Lumpur, 3 Jalan Stesen Sentral
Tel: 03-2264 2596/2264
Styled after the Hilton London's namesake nightclub, this sophisticated place is patronised by the who's who of Kuala Lumpur. DJs spinning rock and 1980s tracks alternate with a live band.

Zouk
113 Jalan Ampang
Tel: 03-2171 1997
This dome-shaped, Singapore-owned club strikes all the right chords. Velvet Underground's popular Wednesday Mambo Jambo nights draw the crowds with 1980s music, while the Loft's ever-changing line-up of local and international DJs keep electronic music fans happy.

Gay and lesbian venues

Blue Boy
50 Jalan Sultan Ismail
Tel: 03-2142 1067
Malaysia's oldest gay club, which is almost 20 years old now. Packed at weekends, especially after midnight, it's friendly but smoky. Mainly Malay crowd. Good house dance tracks.

Frangipani
25 Changkat Bukit Bintang
Tel: 03-2144 3001
A seductive gay bar that attracts a stylish crowd. Offers a large selection of cocktails and shooters. DJs spin house music. Fancy couches and chairs add to its ambience.

Liquid Bar
Mezzanine, 2.04 Central Market Annex, Jalan Hang Kasturi
Tel: 03-2026 5039
Newly renovated with bead curtains, box lounges and interesting bathrooms, this sophisticated gay venue draws people especially on Wednesday, Friday and Saturday. The music is a mix of different strains of house.

Market Place
4A Lg Yap Kwan Seng
Tel: 03-2166 0750
http://mpkualalumpur.com
Gay-friendly nights on Fri and Sat and a superb view of the Petronas Towers from the pleasant roof terrace.

Shook!
Starhill Gallery, Jalan Bukit Bintang
Tel: 03-2719 8535
This classy gay-friendly hangout, which is spread over half the basement, has a circular cocktail bar where you can chill while listening to live jazz. There is an enormous array of food choices here and in the surrounding restaurants.

TRANSPORT

EATING OUT

ACTIVITIES

A – Z

LANGUAGE

Penang

Most of the action in George Town tends to centre at the Upper Penang Road area near The Garage, Gurney Drive and Batu Feringgi.

Bars and pubs

Berlin's Bier House
3E-G-3B Straits Quay, Jalan Seri Tanjung Pinang
Tanjung Tokong
Tel: 04-899 8887
The Germans guard their brewing recipes closely but share their beer with the rest of the world freely. A wide selection of German and other imported beers is available to go with traditional German pork knuckles, sausage and meatballs. The splendid coastal view is an added delight.

The Canteen at ChinaHouse
153–155 Lebuh Pantai
Tel: 04-263 7299
Fridays to Sunday evenings this is the place to go to for jazz. Enjoy its menu of tapas before the band strikes up at 10pm.

Farquhar's Bar
E&O Hotel
Farquhar Street
Tel: 04-222 2000
With its deep armchairs and long darkwood bar, Farquhar's exudes the air of an exclusive private club. Its ambience brings back memories of colonial Penang.

G Spot Live Music Bar & Lounge
G Hotel
Gurney Drive
Tel: 04-238 0000
Hip atmosphere enlivened with live jazz bands. Plush furnishing and stylish interior adds elegance while maintaining a cosy, relaxed atmosphere. It has a good selection of cocktails and Martinis.

Hard Rock Cafe
Hard Rock Hotel
Batu Feringgi
Tel: 04-881 1711
One of the hippest scenes in town, with live bands and a heavy rock 'n' roll theme.

Hong Kong Bar
371 Lebuh Chulia
Tel: 04-261 9796
Opened in 1920, this institution was a regular hangout for military personnel based in Butterworth. Today, it still attracts an assortment of prominent characters, many of whose photographs, medals and plaques plaster the walls and whose stories fill the guest book.

Lebuh Leith Pub and Wine Bar
20 Lebuh Leith
Tel: 04-261 8573

Housed in a restored mansion in the heart of George Town, guests can choose to dine at its Japanese bistro, or sit at the bar. Cosy atmosphere with friendly staff.

Slippery Senoritas
Lot B3A, The Garage
2 Penang Road
Tel: 04-263 6868
A salsa bar and Mexican restaurant where DJs spin a combination of R&B, house and current hits until 10pm when a live band takes over. Its cocktail menu offers 69 variations, which bartenders will deliver to you with an impressive stunt or two. Ladies' night is Wednesday.

Soho Free House Pub
50 Jalan Penang
Tel: 04-263 3331
A British tavern with a pool table, football on the telly and hearty pub grub, this tiny place draws local professionals as well as Britons and Australians. Generous servings at lunch and non-stop happy hours keep customers happy.

Clubs

ChillOut Club
The Gurney, Gurney Drive
Tel: 04-261 1045
This club is actually a complex of four bars and clubs, each playing a different style of music, including funk and R&B. The place is packed at weekends and on Wednesdays, when it is ladies' night. Post-partying, chill out at any of the cafés or 24-hour local eating outlets right on the doorstep of the complex.

Soju Room
B2, Entertainment City, Penang Time Square
Jalan Dato Keramat, George Town
Tel: 60-12 556 5876
One of the oldest dance clubs in George Town. Expect an eclectic music soundtrack and a menu of imported beers and alcohol.

Langkawi

The nightlife here is a little more laid-back. While there are many free-standing and resort bars, nightlife concentrates in Pantai Cenang and Pantai Tengah in restaurants such as Beach Garden and Bon Ton. These offer places for quiet drinks and good food and conversation.

Beach Garden Bistro
Pantai Cenang
Tel: 04-955 1457
One of the most popular nightspots in Langkawi. Sip margaritas under the stars after a dinner of steaks and pizzas.

Chin Chin Bar
Bon Ton Restaurant and Resort
Pantai Cenang
Tel: 04-955 1688
Enjoy cocktails or wine from an extensive wine list in this bar in a restored Chinese shophouse. Liqueur-flavoured coffee is its signature.

Rhu Bar
Four Seasons Resort
Tanjung Rhu
Tel: 04-950 8888
This Middle Eastern-themed bar with Turkish water pipes and Indian mogul hanging swings is one of the best sites on the island to appreciate the sunset. It also has an extensive wine list.

Sea Shell Beach Café
Mutiara Burau Bay Resort
Pantai Kok
Tel: 04-959 1061
Groove to live music under swaying palms. Café snacks and main courses are also served.

Kuching

Kuching's nightlife centres on a few areas, such as **Jalan Padungan** and **Jalan Bukit Mata Kuching**. There are also bars and nightlife outlets in the hotels and resorts.

Jambu Lounge Bar
32 Jalan Crookshank
Tel: 082-235 292
A popular place to hang out, especially on Friday nights when there is live jazz from 8.30pm onwards.

Mojo@Denise
Jln Chan Chin Ann
A very fashionable cocktail lounge at the back of Denise's wine shop.

Ruai
7F Jln An Hock
An Iban-owned bar with a laid-back and welcoming atmosphere. A great place to meet people. Bar offers good and affordable beverages, including the hard-to-find (in a bar) locally brewed tuak (rice wine).

Soho
64 Jalan Padungan
Tel: 082-247 069
Considered the chicest bar in Kuching, Soho is packed to the rafters at the weekend. Plays a mix of jazz, Latin and dance tunes. Serves good bar food and its restaurant caters to patrons looking for a more substantial meal as well.

The Victoria Arms
Merdeka Palace Hotel, Jalan Tun Abang Haji Openg
Tel: 082-258 000
Upmarket English pub with a restaurant and a wine bar. Friday is ladies' night, and happy hour is 4–9pm.

Kota Kinabalu

A range of bars and pubs in the downtown area known as **The Waterfront** offers drinks and entertainment both indoors and on the boardwalk.

Cock and Bull Bistro
The Waterfront
Tel: 088-250 982
Popular pub with a live band performing every night. Pool table, wide-screen TV broadcasting football, and free Wi-fi internet access. Happy hour is 4–9pm.

The Loft
Waterfront
Tel: 88-270 387
Located in the middle of the Waterfront. Features a stage for live bands and other performances. A smaller bar is surrounded by an open area for mingling with a pool table and comfortable couches.

PLUtonic
Lot G-4—1, Block G, Time Square
Tel: 19-812 0030
This bar is popular with the LGBT communities, among others. Serves dangerous cocktails to a friendly crowd.

Shenanigan's Fun Pub
Hyatt Regency Kinabalu
Jalan Datuk Saleh Sulong
Tel: 088-295 300
Irish pub Shenanigan's remains a firm favourite, especially late at night, for its creative drinks and live performances by international acts. Ladies' night on Thursday, when special door gifts and lucky draw prizes are available.

SHOPPING

From international brands to hand-crafted ethnic artworks, Malaysia offers variety and choice for shoppers of every budget.

The best times to shop are during the mid-year 1Malaysia Mega Sale Carnival and the Malaysia Year-End Sale when promotions are on offer and prices slashed. Throughout the year, large department stores also hold sales. Since April 2015, however, the bargains will never be the same again, due to the implementation of the Goods and Services Tax (GST) at a standard rate of 6 percent.

Open-air night markets (*pasar malam*) are good for soaking up local atmosphere and finding bargain-priced items, including clothes (which you try on in the open), shoes, trinkets and household items. There is also fresh produce, including fruit and

street food. The traders are itinerant, so check locations at your hotel. The *pasar malam* at Bangsar is located on a slip road running parallel between Jalan Maarof and Jalan Telawi 2 on Sundays. Stalls are open for business from 3pm to 9pm.

Fresh produce is available at supermarkets and wet markets as well as at the agricultural or wet markets (*pasar tani*), where farmers sell their produce directly to customers. The older generation prefer to shop at the wet markets in the belief that the food is fresher and cheaper. However, supermarkets now offer competitive pricing for fresh produce. You can find a *pasar tani* on Jalan Cochrane (near Sekolah Cochrane), where trading is done from 7am–noon on Sundays.

What to buy

Antiques, arts and crafts

Handicrafts can be found in stalls, but serious collectors may prefer to make their purchases at shops specialising in crafts and antiques. Bargaining is a must in most places. Pewter, which harks back to Malaysia's history as a tin-mining country, is available at Royal Selangor outlets. A stroll through Kuala Lumpur's Central Market with it numerous arts and crafts shops could take up a whole day. Note that the export of antiques and historical products is not permitted unless an export licence has been obtained from the Director General of Museums Malaysia, or unless these items were originally imported and declared to customs at that point. Make sure you check with the seller of the antique on this point.

Kuala Lumpur
Karyaneka
Kompleks Kraf Kuala Lumpur, level 8
Jalan Conlay
Tel: 03-2164 9907
Carries a wide collection of handicraft reflecting Malaysia's ethnic and cultural heritage. Batik, songket, Sarawak woodcarving and Kelatanese silvercraft can be found here.
Mon–Fri 8.45am–8pm, Sat–Sun 8.45am–7pm.

Royal Selangor Pewter
Lot 118B, 1st Floor, Suria KLCC
Tel: 03-4145 6000
One of Malaysia's best-known brands, Royal Selangor Pewter has a wide range of products including clocks, cufflinks, tableware, trinket boxes and vases. Daily 10am–10pm.

Royal Selangor Visitor Centre

4 Jalan Usahawan 6, Setapak Jaya
Tel: 03-4145 6122
visitorcentre.royalselangor.com/vc/
Drop by the visitor centre of this successful home-grown label for a fine range of stylish pewter gifts and tableware, jewellery and sterling silverware. Don't miss the interesting (and free) factory tour. Daily 9am–5pm; free, but there is a charge for the "School of Hard Knocks" – a pewter dish-making workshop; prior booking is essential.

Scent of the Orient
39-1 Jalan PJU 8/5A, Bandar Damansara Perdana
Tel: 03-7729 3628
Deals in antiques of Chinese and Tibetan origin. Located close to Mum's Place restaurant. Tue–Sun 10am–6pm.

Melaka
Abdul Antiques
93 Jalan Tun Tan Cheng Lock
Tel: 06-282 3633
www.syarikat-abdul.com
The first antique shop in Jonker Street, it specialises in lights, tiles and Nyonya-style furnishing. Daily 9am–6pm.

Malacca Antiques & Curios
25 Jalan Hang Jebat
Tel: 06-284 1860
This shop is brimming with antiques and reproductions almost right to the ceiling. The owner, Mr Low, is attentive and chatty. Thu–Tue 10am–6pm.

Malaqa House
70 Jalan Tun Tan Cheng Lock
Tel: 06-281 4770
This art gallery, housed in a heritage building, carries a good selection of wood furnishing and decorative items. A small garden within adds to its charm. Daily 10am–6pm.

Markets and bazaars

Kuala Lumpur
Central Market
Jalan Hang Kasturi
Tel: 03-2031 0399; Information counter: 1300 228 688
www.centralmarket.com.my
Probably the best place for souvenirs, with its two levels offering Malaysian and Asian artworks and handicrafts. Check out the more distinctive pieces at Pipit at its annexe.

Jalan Tuanku Abdul Rahman/Jalan Masjid India
Small, interesting shops along Jalan Tuanku Abdul Rahman sell Asian wares such as Chinese embroidery and antiques. Kamdar along this road has affordable clothes and textiles. Lorong Tuanku Abdul

Rahman is closed to traffic every Saturday 5–10pm and transformed into a pasar malam (night market) with stalls selling bargain goods. Jewellery, Indian saris and comfy cotton pyjamas are found in Jalan Masjid India.

Petaling Street Bazaar
The famous and crowded Petaling Street pasar malam comes to life from 5pm to 11pm every evening, with a variety of stalls offering clothes, leather goods and copy watches. Watch your bags and pockets, as it is usually packed.

Books

Major bookshops can be found in shopping malls and carry a wide selection of titles. Silverfish is a smaller, independent outfit, which focuses on works written in English by Malaysian authors. With the exception of Kinokuniya and Silverfish, the bookshops listed below have more than one branch in Malaysia.

Kuala Lumpur
Borders
11–13 Lower Ground Floor, Berjaya Times Square, 1, Jalan Imbi
Tel: 03-2141 0288
www.borders.com.my
Daily 10am–10pm
Kinokuniya
Lot 406–408, 429–430 Level 4, Suria KLCC
Tel: 03-2164 8133
www.kinokuniya.com.my
Daily 10am–10pm
The MNS Shop
Malaysian Nature Society, Jalan Kelantan
Tel: 03-2287 3471
Small but good collection of nature books and journals, including specialist titles about books, insects, indigenous people and national parks. Mon–Fri 10am–5pm, Sat 10am–1pm.
MPH
1 Jalan Telawi, lot F7, 1st floor, Bangsar Village Shopping Centre
Tel: 03-2283 1098
www.mphonline.com
Popular
8 Jalan 7/118B, Desa Tun Razak
Tel: 03-9179 6333
www.popular.com.my
Silverfish
28-1 Jalan Telawi, Bangsar Baru
Tel: 03-2284 4837
www.silverfishbooks.com
Mon–Fri 10.30am–8.30pm, Sat until 6.30pm, open some holidays but call first to confirm.
Times
Pavilion KL, Lot 6.49.1, Level 6

168 Jalan Bukit Bintang
Tel: 03-2148 8813
www.timesbookstores.com.my
Daily 10am–10pm.

Kuching
Borneo Books
Ground and 2nd Floors, Wisma Merdeka, Jalan Haji Saman
Tel: 088-241 050
The ground-floor shop has a range of souvenirs as well as books, while Borneo Books 2 upstairs has an unbeatable selection of books on Asia, particularly Borneo, plus a book exchange. Daily 10am–8pm, except Sun until 5pm.

Fashion and accessories

Malaysian fashion stores range from the simple to the exclusive. Well-known Malaysian designers such as Bernard Chandran and Zang Toi as well as renowned shoemaker Jimmy Choo have outlets in Kuala Lumpur to complement their international presence. If you are looking for Malaysian ethnic-designed clothing with fresh looks, check out E'tho (Mid Valley Megamall, tel: 03-2282 6168) or Mayfair Designs (Bukit Bintang Plaza, tel: 03-2145 9936). International chains such as Gap, Mango, Miss Selfridge and Topman, and local brands like British India and Salabianca are found at major shopping malls.

Melaka
Orang-Utan House
59 Jalan Hang Jebat
Run by local artist Charles Cham, whose humorous T-shirts and artworks make great souvenirs.
Wah Aik Shoemaker
56 Jalan Tokong
Tel: 06-2849 726 or 019-667 8109
This shoemaker is famous for his tiny shoes made for Chinese women with bound feet, an ancient Chinese tradition that has long since died out. However, fascination with the shoes remains and they are popular souvenirs.

Where to shop

Shopping malls are found in every city and usually comprise a supermarket, department store, and smaller stores selling clothing, shoes, watches, electrical goods, computers, mobile phones, books and more. The larger ones also have tour agencies, cineplexes and video game arcades, as well as eateries, including food courts selling hawker fare, Western fast-food chains and restaurants.

What not to buy

Despite the nationwide crackdown on pirated movie and computer software DVDs, they are still available at night markets, and at least one outlet among neighbourhood shops. Sleeves on display in the neighbourhood shop, however, are empty; the actual discs are somewhere else, and after an order comes through on the walkie-talkie, a DVD swiftly appears. Some vendors also approach individuals in coffee shops offering to sell pirated DVDs for as cheap as RM6. Please note, however, that the sale of pirated DVDs is illegal. There may also be bargains offered for luxury items such as branded watches and bags. If the price seem too good to be true, it probably is. If you are looking for the real thing, make sure you buy it from an authorised dealer. Avoid buying items made from exotic animal skin or feathers, as these may be from endangered wildlife.

In Kuala Lumpur, favourite shopping haunts in the city centre are clustered around the Bukit Bintang area and KLCC. Central Market and Petaling Street, a short walk away, provide cheaper alternatives and a different atmosphere. Suburban malls such as Mid Valley Megamall and The Gardens, The Curve/IPC, 1 Utama and Sunway Pyramid offer a good range of shopping alternatives and are well patronised.

Kuala Lumpur malls

1 Utama
1 Lebuh Bandar, Bandar Utama
Tel: 03-7710 8118
www.1utama.com.my
Situated in the suburb of Bandar Utama, one of Kuala Lumpur's largest malls not only has shops, restaurants and a cinema but also houses Asia's largest indoor rock-climbing gym wall-climbing, a lush indoor tropical rainforest and Southeast Asia's largest rooftop garden.
Bangsar Village
1 Jalan Telawi 1, Bangsar Baru
Tel: 03-2282 1808
www.bangsarvillage.com
Another upmarket shopping centre catering to the Bangsar neighbourhood with anchors like the Village Grocer, which carries international food items. Its five-storey addition, known as Bangsar Village II, has more dining, lifestyle and fashion choices.

The Curve
6 Jalan PJU 7/3
Mutiara Damansara
Tel: 03-7710 6868
www.thecurve.com.my
A family favourite adjacent to IPC and near the 1 Utama shopping mall, The Curve has many restaurants lined up along its outdoor pedestrian walkway. At weekends, stalls take over the walkway selling trinkets, clothes and other knick-knacks.

Mid Valley Megamall
Lingkaran Syed Putra
Tel: 03-2938 3333
www.midvalley.com.my
Spacious walkways link over 430 outlets, including eateries, an 18-screen cineplex and an entertainment centre for children, in a well-laid-out format. Anchor tenants are Metrojaya and Carrefour. A shuttle operates to nearby Bangsar LRT station, and a walkway connects the ktm Komuter station to the mall. Adjacent to it is the upmarket The Gardens Mall, with Robinsons and Isetan as its anchor tenants.

Pavilion
168 Jalan Bukit Bintang
Tel: 03-2118 8833
www.pavilionkl.com
Home to 450 outlets, this upmarket mall in the heart of Kuala Lumpur's Bukit Bintang entertainment district houses some of the world's premier brands. A large food court in its basement serves a variety of cuisines.

Plaza Low Yat
7 Jalan Bintang
Off Jalan Bukit Bintang
Tel: 03-2148 3651
plazalowyat.com
This IT Lifestyle Mall in the shopping district of Bukit Bintang has six shopping floors, each dedicated to a particular technological gadget, while the lower ground floor specialises in feeding the number of people who walk through its doors.

Sungei Wang Plaza
Jalan Bukit Bintang
Tel: 03-2148 6109
www.sungeiwang.com
This popular mall has 500-odd retail shops with moderately priced products and services. A good place for bargains. Check out Malaysian *haute couture* on the first floor.

Sunway Pyramid
3 Jalan PJS 11/15
Bandar Sunway, Petaling Jaya
Tel: 03-7494 3100
A slice of Egypt in Petaling Jaya, the Sphinx gives Sunway Pyramid an exterior that stands out. Inside there is an ice-skating rink, bowling alley, cinema and over 800 speciality outlets.

Suria KLCC
Lot No. 241, Level 2, Suria KLCC
Tel: 03-2382 2828
www.suriaklcc.com.my
This spacious and classy shopping venue has large department stores, including Isetan, Parkson Grand and Marks & Spencer, and over 270 speciality shops and food outlets. For ethnic goods, check out the Pucuk Rebung Museum Gallery and Aseana.

Penang

George Town's maze of little shops around Jalan Penang and Jalan Campbell are great for antiques and curios such as antique clocks, old bronze- and brassware, Dutch ceiling lamps, old phonographs, Chinese embroidery and porcelain, and Malaysian batik. Saw Joo Aun at 139 Jalan Pintai Tali has a large range of antique furniture.

Elsewhere in Penang, Little India on Lebuh King and Lebuh Queen has brightly coloured saris and kurta (men's shirts), brassware and jewellery.

Chowrasta Market specialises in all kinds of cotton, silk and other materials, as well as dried local foods such as nutmeg and preserved fruits.

More bargain-priced Chinese souvenirs are at the Kek Lok Si Temple in Ayer Itam. Batu Feringgi and Teluk Bahang offer brightly coloured, hand-painted batik sarongs and T-shirt souvenirs; the night market at the former sells fake but decent-quality designer clothes and watches.

Modern shopping malls are 1st Avenue Mall in the city centre, Gurney Plaza (on Gurney Drive) and Queensbay Mall (Bayan Baru).

Melaka

Jalan Hang Jebat, formerly known as Jonker Street and once the place to shop in Melaka, has been a victim of money-driven urbanisation in recent years. Traditional craftsmen have been evicted and several historic shophouses have been demolished or else subjected to sham restoration projects where only the facades are kept, while the interiors have been modified beyond recognition. Still, antique collectors and bargain hunters will find what they want if they search hard enough. Authentic artefacts and relics, some over 300 years old, can be found along with a host of other more recent collectables. Amid shops selling traditional crafts are trendy modern and creative handicraft shops. On Jalan Merdeka, the city's biggest shopping mall, Mahkota Parade, also has an Asian antique and handicraft centre. Other major shopping malls include Medan Samudera and Hang Tuah Mall.

There are more handicraft stalls in Taman Merdeka, and a pasar malam (night market) takes place on Sunday at Jalan Parameswara.

Terengganu

In Kuala Terengganu, the Central Market on Jalan Sultan Zainal Abidin is the place to go to for batik and local handicrafts. Outside of town, the Chendering industrial estate offers handicrafts and batik, and along the beachfront to Marang, at Rusila, are numerous batik and basketware shops, as well as vendors of the area's famous salted fish.

Noor Arfa Batek House
Chendering
Tel: 09-617 9700
www.noor-arfa.com
Out at the Chendering industrial area is the Noor Arfa Batek House, Malaysia's largest, which welcomes visitors to watch and even participate in batik production. There is an excellent showroom as well.

Teratai Arts and Craft
151 Jalan Bandar
Tel: 09-625 2157
A lovely gallery/shop owned by renowned artist Chang Fee Ming. It showcases his depictions of local life, as well as curios from all over Asia, including coconut-shell crafts and textiles.

Kelantan

Kelantan is an excellent place to purchase truly unique Malaysian gifts. The ultimate handicraft heaven is the road to PCB Beach (Pantai Cahaya Bulan), along which certain kampung (villages) are renowned for their particular handicrafts – contact Tourism Malaysia for more information.

Bazaar Buluh Kubu
Opposite the Central Market
Four floors of tiny shops display the best array of batiks in the peninsula. There's everything from hand-painted lengths of silk to hand-stamped sarongs, tablecloths and cushion covers.

Central Market
Kota Bharu
The Central Market has copious amounts of arts and crafts and batik items on the second level and produce stalls on the first.

Kuching

Many of the shopping malls in Kuching are located next to hotels. These malls include Crowne Square (Jalan Petaling), Hills Shopping Mall (Jalan Bukit Mata Interhill Place), Sarawak Plaza (Jalan Tunku Abdul Rahman) and The Spring (Jalan Simpang Tiga).

Antiques, Iban textiles, handicrafts, and quality collectables as well as pretty and interesting handcrafted souvenirs are readily available in Kuching, particularly along the Main Bazaar. Here, old trading houses and shophouses have been converted and restored into galleries and shops selling a range of goods.

Anggun Collection
157E Jalan Satok
Tel: 082-422 495
It's well worth a short taxi ride from downtown if you're looking for exclusive fabrics and ready-made garments with Sarawakian motifs. Beautiful embroidered *kebaya* (some in organza), men's silk shirts, sarong and long scarf (*selendang*) sets as well as embroidered handbags and accessories are available.

Atelier Gallery
104 Main Bazaar
Tel: 082-243 492
Lucas Goh's atelier opposite the Chinese History Museum is filled with ethnic and primitive arts including blowpipes and woven fabrics, furniture and tasteful accessories.

Edric Ong
12 Ong Kwan Hin Road
Tel: 082-420 042
www.edricong.com
Edric's designs of textiles, outfits, crafts and interior furnishing are influenced by native Sarawakian art. The designer works with traditional weavers and craftsmen of Sarawak in his designs, using raw material sourced from Sarawak's rainforest.

Fabriko
56 Main Bazaar, Kuching
Tel: 082-422 233
www.fabriko.com.my
Fabriko specialises in fabric, particularly high-end natural-dye silk and cotton. You can find custom-produced batik shirts, sarongs and T-shirts here.

Nelson Tan Gallery
84 Main Bazaar
Tel: 082-411 066
Nelson Tan's gallery is so well known, it has no shop name displayed. It offers an eclectic collection with some very fine pieces of tribal art and ceramics tucked away under reproductions from Kalimantan.

Sarawak Handicraft Centre
Round Tower, Sarawak Tourism Complex
Watch crafts being fashioned by hand and buy the results; a good range of authentic, high-quality handicrafts.

Sunday Market
Jalan Satok
Despite the name, this street market starts at noon on Saturday and runs until Sunday afternoon. The market is filled with Dayak vegetable sellers, Chinese and Malay stalls selling all manner of handicrafts, jungle products, wild honey, pets and plants, including gorgeous orchids.

Kota Kinabalu

Borneo Trading Post
Lot 16, The Waterfront
Tel: 088-232 655
For quality handicrafts, jewellery, homewares, souvenirs and paintings from Borneo and the rest of Southeast Asia, this attractive, spacious shop is unrivalled. Daily 11.30am–9pm.

Centrepoint Shopping Complex
Jalan Centrepoint
This is the largest shopping complex in town. Higher-quality branded goods are available on the 4th level in Palm Square, while food outlets can be found in the basement. Daily 10am–9pm.

Gaya Street (Sunday Market)
A favourite family hangout on Sunday mornings, you can find batik, handicraft, art prints, souvenirs and food here. Located at the central business district.

Handicraft Market
Jalan Tun Fuad Stephens
A rabbit warren of tiny stalls filled with handicrafts from the Philippines (hence its local name of Filipino Market), Indonesia, Sabah and Sarawak. Located at the waterfront, a five- to 10-minute walk from the city centre. Take care of your bag, and be sure to bargain. Daily 7.30am–7.30pm.

Wisma Merdeka
Jalan Haji Saman
Sabah's first shopping centre still offers a wide range of goods, particularly clothing (most of the cheap and cheerful variety) and shoes. Shops open at 9am or 10am and close around 9pm.

SPORT

Malaysia is generally a sport-loving country. Much like the rest of the world, Malaysians adore football (soccer). Badminton would probably come in a close second. Being one of three nations to have won the coveted Thomas Cup (World Men's Team Championships), Malaysia has had a long, proud history with badminton. Its fiercest rivals are Indonesia, China and Denmark. National Circuit matches played at different venues across the country (www.bam.org.my) feature top local professionals and up-and-coming youngsters, while international competitions are held several times each year, usually at the Putra Indoor Stadium at Bukit Jalil.

Malaysia also plays host to professional tennis and golf events on both the men's and women's circuits. Like much of Asia, interest in golf has risen over the last 20 years. This has resulted in an increasing number of golf courses built to meet local and tourist demands. The courses are designed to exploit the natural landscape and offer something for all levels of golfers, be they experienced or beginners, amateur or professional. The quality of courses here is reflected in major professional tours adding Malaysia to their golfing schedule.

Though not widely known as a surfing destination, Cherating (Terengganu) and Desaru (Johor) have hosted Asian Surfing Championship (ASC) events.

Malaysian corporations have increasingly invested in sporting teams in recent years, giving fans more reason to get behind these teams. Petronas has sponsored several Formula 1 teams since the 1990s and is the main sponsor for the Malaysian Grand Prix. AirAsia is the key partner of the Caterham team (formerly Team Lotus) as well as a sponsor of Queen's Park Rangers football club in London.

Participant sports – golf

Generally, clubs are private. However, the so-called "resort clubs" are open to anyone, especially in holiday destinations. Courses are generally of international standard and are well maintained; equal care is taken in the design and facilities of club houses. Equipment can be hired, and bought at affordable prices. Updated lists of golf clubs and resorts plus descriptions can be found in the monthly Pargolf magazine (www.pargolfmagazine.com), sold throughout the country and with listings of major golf courses. The Malaysian Golf Tourism Association (www.mgta.com.my) provides further information on golf courses and packages available to visitors.

Peninsular Malaysia

Awana Resorts World Genting, Pahang, tel: 03-6436 9000; www. rwgenting.com/hotel/awana-hotel. At a cool 1,000 metres (3,000ft) up in the Genting Highlands, this scenic 18-hole course is fairly demanding but enjoyable. Bunkers, ponds and streams add to the challenge. There is a three-tiered driving range.

Clearwater Sanctuary Golf Resort, Batu Gajah, Perak, tel: 05-366 7433; www.cwsgolf.com.my. Built on a former tin-mining site, it is set across 400 hectares (1,000 acres) of forest, jungle and lakes. Straight drives are imperative over the 18 holes of the Raintree and Lakes nines. The Wetlands nine is a unique par 3 course for those seeking to master short holes.

Glenmarie Golf & Country Club, Shah Alam, Selangor, tel: 03-7880 4630; www.glenmarie.com.my. There are two 18-hole courses here. The Garden Course meanders through a tropical garden, while the Valley Course is narrower with more water challenges.

Kuala Lumpur Golf and Country Club, off Jalan Bukit Kiara, tel: 03-2011 9188. A 36-hole course with a fully automated computerised driving range. Visitors must produce their handicap cards upon registration.

Pulai Springs Golf Resort, Johor, tel: 07-521 2121; www.pulaigroup.com. The two 18-hole USGA courses – the Melana, designed by Peter Scott, and the Pulai course by Robert Trent Jones II – both pose challenges with their varying terrain, water elements and change in elevation. Accommodation and other recreational facilities are available at the Pulai Springs Resort.

Staffield Country Resort, Negeri Sembilan, tel: 03-8766 6177. Regarded as one of the country's best, this 27-hole course sits on 136 hectares (335 acres) of transformed rubber estate, with 82 bunkers and seven lakes. The Tudor-style clubhouse offers food and a wide range of sports facilities.

Sarawak

Damai Golf Course, Santubong, tel: 082-846 088; www.damaigolf.com. An Arnold Palmer-designed course, it is popular and accessible with full facilities adjacent to Damai beach and the resort hotels.

Eastwood Valley Golf and Country Club, Jalan Miri-Pujut By-Pass, Miri, tel: 085-421 010; www.estwoodvalley.com. An 18-hole course carved from a forest setting, with a driving range, timber chalets for rent and a restaurant.

Sabah

Borneo Golf & Country Club, Km 69, Papar–Beaufort Highway, tel: 087-861 888. An 18-hole course designed by Jack Nicklaus, this is located about one hour's drive south of Kota Kinabalu. Apart from the restaurant, there are chalets for overnight accommodation.

Dalit Bay Golf and Country Club, tel: 088-791 333. Near Shangri-La's Rasa Ria Resort, about 45 minutes' drive from Kota Kinabalu. Offers smooth greens, sea views and a luxurious clubhouse.

Nexus Golf Resort Karambunai, Sabah, tel: 088-411 215; www.nexus resort.com. This award-winning 18-hole golf course, designed by Ronald Fream, is demanding yet fair. Set between the South China Sea and Bornean jungle, it has a natural feel which may challenge your golfing focus.

Sabah Golf and Country Club, Kota Kinabalu, tel: 088-247 533. A tricky 18-hole course with wide fairways and fast greens. The wind makes play even more interesting, especially during the monsoon months. Facilities include a swimming pool, gym and karaoke lounge.

Sutera Harbour Marina, Golf and Country Club, Kota Kinabalu, tel: 088-318 888; www.suteraharbour.com. Features a 27-hole Graham Marsh-designed course looking out to sweeping views of the South China Sea. Night golfing facility until 11pm.

Local sporting events

Aside from popular sports such as futsal (a variation of football played indoors on a smaller pitch), martial arts, table-tennis and sepak takraw (a local game), there are also a number of speciality sporting events that often attract international participants, and hordes of fans. Months indicated are an approximation; check websites for actual event dates.

Le Tour de Langkawi (Feb/Mar, www.ltdl.com.my) is an international cycling event that takes riders across the country covering over 1,000km (621 miles).

Sabah Adventure Challenge (April, www.sabahadventurechallenge.com) A multi-day 150km (93-mile) adventure race on foot, mountain bikes and rafts across Sabah's rugged terrain. The format of the race changes from year to year. Participants are expected to be self-sufficient in navigating their way around the jungle and mountain ranges.

KL Tower International Towerthon (May, www.menarakl.com.my) A race to the top of the tower. It's an 800-metre (0.5-mile) run from the bottom of the hill to the base of KL Tower, then a run up 2,058 steps to reach the top of KL Tower.

KL Tower International Base Jump (Sep, www.kltowerjump.com) An exhilarating 421-metre (0.3-mile) jump off KL Tower for brave-hearted souls.

The Most Beautiful Thing (Sep, www.sabahadventurechallenge.com) An ultra trail marathon with competitors running along village trails, open gravel roads and hanging bridges across Sabah's Crocker Range mountains. There are three categories: 25km (16 miles), 50km (31 miles) and 100km (62 miles).

Mount Kinabalu International Climbathon (Oct, www.climbathon.my) Deemed the "World's Toughest Mountain Race"; participants will attempt to run up and down Mount Kinabalu in under three hours. This race is part of the Sky Runners World Series.

Penang Bridge International Marathon (Nov, www.penangmarathon.gov.my) An annual run across the Penang Bridge, which connects the island to the mainland. In addition to the full marathon race, there are also half-marathon, quarter-marathon and 10km (6.2-mile) fun races.

Monsoon Cup (Nov, www.monsooncup.com.my) Held at Pulau Duyong, Terengganu each year, this competition is part of the World Match Racing tour.

Spectator sports

Football (soccer)

Support for the national football team, known as **Harimau Malaysia** (Malaysian Tiger), is strong, with tickets sold out for many of the matches played at its home turf at the Stadium Nasional, Bukit Jalil in Kuala Lumpur. In the **Malaysian Super League**, the nation's premier football league, matches are played countrywide. Results and upcoming fixtures can be found at www.malaysiansuperleague.com.

Football matches are screened daily on Astro, a subscription satellite broadcaster. At weekends, many eateries and pubs screen live English league football action. The atmosphere at some of these venues can be loud, as regular crowds turn up to cheer on their clubs in the company of fellow fans. Crowds are especially lively during the screening of the FIFA World Cup every four years, with work productivity taking a hit as fans stay up late to follow matches.

Motor sports

Malaysia hosts a number of motor-sport events each year. It is home to the **Formula 1 Malaysian Grand Prix** (Mar, www.f1-malaysia.com.) and **Malaysian Motorcycle Grand Prix** (Malaysia-motogp.com). Both races are held at the Sepang International Circuit (tel: 03-8778 2222, www.sepangcircuit.com), which is close to KLIA. In addition to these two global events, Sepang also hosts other motor-sporting events such as the Superseries races.

Outdoor activities

Aerial sports

Taking to the skies is a thrilling way to see another perspective of Malaysia. The **4B Flying Club** (tel: 06-317 6717/019-521 6905; www.4bflyingclub.wordpress.com) is the country's only DCA-authorised club for microlight instruction. Based in Melaka, they also offer joy rides over the historic city. **Oxbold** are motorised paragliding specialists based in Pulau Indah, Klang (www.oxbold.com/paramotor-malaysia.htm; general enquiry tel: 019-6638 336). They offer a minimum of 25 hours of instruction, using trikes in their training.

Birdwatching

Malaysia's location on the Australasian cross-migratory path attracts a vast number of bird species. Its rainforests can be generally divided into three distinctive habitat types, each of which attracts particular type of birds. The Common kingfisher can be found at coastal mangroves where salt and fresh water meet. Lowland rainforests are homes to Storm's stork, Green imperial pigeon and over 200 other species. The Mountain peacock-pheasant and Mountain blackeye can be found in mountain forests where elevation is 900 metres (2,952ft) above sea level.

Birdwatching can be done just about anywhere in Malaysia – in towns and cities or at local parks. You could even join a bird race like the one at Fraser's Hill in Pahang (June, www.pacdome.com/bird-watching-at-fraser-s-hill) or the Sarawak Bird Race at Padawan near Kuching (Oct, www.sarawaktourism.com). In a bird race, the team with the highest number of bird species sighted wins. If you

prefer to hide while birdwatching, you could try the Tree Top Tower in Mulu Park, Sarawak, or the Kuala Selangor Nature Park in Selangor. For more bird sites and bird routes, check www.malaysiabirding.org.

Cave exploration

Exploring the abundant limestone caves (gua) in the country makes for good adventure. Spelunking or caving enthusiasts can observe the changes in stalagmite and stalagtite formations over mere months, as well as wildlife such as fruit bats and swifts in their natural environment. Favourite caving spots include Gua Tempurung and Gua Kundu (Perak); Gua Kelam (Perlis); Gua Ikan (Kelantan); Gua Telinga, Gua Daun Menari and Gua Luas (Taman Negara), and Gua Taat and Gua Bewah at Tasik Kenyir (Terengganu). In Sarawak, Mulu Caves have some of the biggest and longest networks of caves in the world, whilst the Painted Cave in Gua Niah has wall paintings depicting early civilisation. The Malaysian Nature Society (tel: 03-2287 9422) is able to provide contact information of cavers willing to act as guides.

Fishing

Malaysia offers good fishing, but the sport is not regulated or organised. Boats range from bare basics to converted trawlers, and unless you go with a tour, you have to bring your own equipment. Shops stock the range, but do not rent. Malaysia is a manufacturer of rods and reels and is, in fact, a good and relatively cheap place to buy fishing equipment. Fishing tackle shops are found in all major towns.

Freshwater fishing

Malaysia's rivers and lakes provide rich fishing grounds. Fast-flowing rivers offer good fishing of smaller fish upstream. Many of these are found in pristine rainforest environments, usually accessible via four-wheel-drive and some walking. Good spots include upper Sungai Endau in Johor, and the higher reaches of rivers that flow into Kenyir (Terengganu) and Temenggor (Perak). Here, you get the *kelah* (Malaysia Mahseer), a good fighter with which locals usually practise catch-and-release, and *tengas*, which also make fun fishing. Bigger-sized *kelah* are found in the middle river, as are *kaloi* (giant gouramey), *belida* (giant featherback), *sebarau* (Malaysian jungle perch) and the powerful *toman* (giant

snakehead), the so-called shark of Malaysian freshwater fish.

Rivers in Sarawak and Sabah are excellent fishing grounds, particularly near the Kalimantan border, but the distances are great, and they are difficult to get to.

Lakes and reservoirs are where the other big freshwater-fishing opportunities are. Since Malaysia has few natural ponds, anglers head for dammed lakes such as Kenyir and Temengor, where the ferocious toman is the main prize, and the natural lake of Bera in Pahang, which is shallow and classified as a wetland area.

Saltwater fishing

Deep-sea bottom fishing is expensive, but compared to other countries in the region, relatively affordable. This involves going out with a rod and line with one or two hooks, using bait such as small fish and prawns, and fishing at depths of 50 to 100 metres (150 to 300ft).

There are plenty of boats for hire on the coast. Most are basic, but a handful offer reasonable facilities. Nonetheless, some anglers find this primitiveness an attraction. Minimum numbers are needed before a boat will set off.

Some locations could be up to four hours away. A two-day/one-night trip can be arranged, including boat, ice and bait. Meals can also be arranged.

Anywhere along the peninsula's west coast is good for fishing all year round, including Bagan Datoh and Pangkor (Perak), and Langkawi (Kedah). Table fish are the norm, including *kerapu* (grouper) and *ikan merah* (red snapper). Sarawakian locations include Miri and Tanjung Datu near Kuching.

The peninsula's east coast is good for blue-water game fishing. A popular centre is Mersing, the jumping-off point to the islands of Aur, Dayang and Pemanggil. Here you get black marlin, mackerel, barracuda and giant trevally. Sailfish are found in abundance near the islands off Rompin. Redang is another good location. In Sarawak, Miri is a centre; in Sabah, Labuan is good for billfish, and Semporna and Sipadan are the spots for yellow fin tuna, great fighters that go up to 100kg (220lb). The best times for this sport are March to September.

Angling operators providing full facilities include:
Cherry Bird Travel & Tours, 31A, 1st Floor, Jalan Barat, off Jalan Imbi, tel: 03-2141 1399

Fook Soon Trading Co., 39 Jalan 20/16, Petaling Jaya, Selangor, tel: 03-7874 3066
High Adventure Travel, 20 Jalan 21/19, Sea Park Shopping Centre, Petaling Jaya, Selangor, tel: 03-7876 1771
Hook, Line & Sinker, 22 Jalan SS22/3, Damansara Jaya, Petaling Jaya, Selangor, tel: 03-7725 2551; www.hook-line-sinker.net.

It's also worth checking out angling magazines. Remember to ask about group sizes and facilities.

Horse riding
Horse riding is still growing in popularity. In Langkawi, **Island Horses** (tel: 04-959 4753; www.langkawihorses.com) own a stable and stud farm. They provide rides through mountain trails, jungle track or on beaches. **Riders Lodge** in Sedenak, Johor (tel: 07-652 5330; www.riderslodge.com.my) offers overnight and day packages for rides through jungle and oil palm plantations.

Mountain-biking
Challenging trails in Kuala Lumpur are at Batu Dam, Kampung Pusu and Hulu Gombak Forest Reserve. Pahang's Sungai Dua site reaches into the Lentang Forest Reserve. The reward at the end of this 40km (25-mile) trail is the sight of the 30-metre (98-mile) high Kerau waterfall. The **Kuala Lumpur Mountain Bike Hash** (www.klmbh.org) and **Pedalholics Cycling Club** (www.PCCMalaysia.com) offer more information on biking activities in Kuala Lumpur.

In Sarawak, trails around rural areas outside Kuching, and near Damai beach, are increasingly popular with many locals. For inexpensive bicycle rental and off-road cycling, contact **WG Cycles**, 36A, 1st Floor, Nam Meng Building, Jalan Ban Hock, tel: 082-238 239.

In Sabah, popular trails include rural areas around Kota Kinabalu. A good route is to bike down from park headquarters on Gunung Kinabalu to Tamparuli, passing through magnificent verdant vistas and undiscovered villages. Contact **TYK Adventure Tours**, tel: 088-232 821; www.tykadventuretours.com.

Rock-climbing
This is fairly new activity for Malaysians has enormous untapped potential. Rock-climbing enthusiasts have a choice of indoor and outdoor sites offering varied degrees of difficulty. Indoor sites in Kuala Lumpur include Camp 5 (1 Utama Shopping Mall), PutraClimb (Putrajaya) and Shah Alam Extreme Park. Outdoor sites near Kuala Lumpur include Batu Caves, Bukit Takun and Kramat Valley. Contact Nomad Adventure, tel: 03-7958 5152; www.nomadadventure.com to arrange trips.

Water sports

Sport diving
Dive operators are divided into on-site operators and those that arrange scheduled trips. Most dive operators are licensed to offer a range of dive courses from the most basic open-water certification all the way up to becoming a dive instructor. Some also offer dive introductory lessons to older children. There are many different diving agencies – PADI is the most popular, but you can also choose to study the syllabus offered by SSI, NAUI and BSAC.

Most operations are dive shops with dive masters and instructors; a few are certified dive centres offering the full range, from retail to rental and equipment servicing. Retail outlets are usually in the city rather than on the beach. **Mythasia** (tel: 03-4149 2828; mythasia.com) is an experienced specialist dive-tour agency, offering packages in Malaysia and Southeast Asia.

Peninsular Malaysia
B&J Diving Centre, tel: 09-419 5555; www.divetioman.com. This DSAT and IANTD technical diving training facility offers technical diving education up to trimix instructor. Provides technical diving trips to the various World War II wrecks in the vicinity.
Bubbles Dive Resort, tel: 012-983 8038; www.bubblesdc.com/dive.htm. Located at Tanjung Tukas, Pulau Perhentian Besar, it specialises in macro-diving, muck-diving and diving with photographers.
East Marine, tel: 04-966 3966; www.eastmarine.com.my. Offers dive courses and trips to Pulau Payar and surrounding waters.
Pacific Dome, tel: 03-2166 9673; www.pacdome.com. Reputable company that offers tours and dive instruction anywhere in Malaysia, including Mabul, and to Manado, Indonesia.

Sarawak
Although diving is not a sport normally associated with Sarawak, there is interesting diving off the coast of Miri. **Planet Borneo Tours & Travel**, Lot 273 Brighton Centre, Jalan Temenggong, Datuk Oyong Lawai, tel: 085-414 300; www.planetborneotours.com. This tour operator has a scuba-diving division offering dives on the reefs within an hour or less of Miri; wreck dives and night dives are also available.

Sabah
Among operators for scheduled trips, including instruction, are:
Avillion Layang Layang Island Resort, tel: 03-2170 2185; www.avillionlayanglayang.com. The sole resort on an island one-hour's flight west of Kota Kinabalu. World-class diving and a luxurious resort.
Borneo Divers, tel: 088-222 226; www.borneodivers.info. Dive pioneer specialising in Sipadan, nearby Pulau Mabul and the Labuan wrecks. It maintains a training centre on Mamutik island in Kota Kinabalu, where dive courses are given.
Pulau Sipadan Resort and Tours, tel: 089-765 200; www.sipadan-resort.com. These resorts run their own excellent dive centres on Sipadan, Pulau Kalapai (close to Sipadan) and on beautiful Pulau Lankayan situated to the northwest of Sandakan.
Diverse Borneo, tel: 088-299 262; www.diverse-borneo.comA Kota Kinabalu-based operator, a PADI 5-star instructor centre that offers the very best scuba diving.

Whitewater rafting

Peninsular Malaysia
Minimum numbers are required for whitewater rafting trips. Some companies also arrange transport from the city. Good rafting sites include Sungai Sungkai in Perak and Sungai Selangor in Kuala Kubu Baru. Both are close enough to Kuala Lumpur for a day visit. Sungai Endau, Jeram Pasu, Sungai Lipis and Sungai Tembiling in Taman Negara are further away from the city. **Nomad Adventure**, tel: 03-7958 5152; www.nomadadventure.com specialises in whitewater kayaking and rafting in Sungai Sungkai and Sungai Kampar, Perak, while the **Malaysian Rafting Community** (www.raftmalaysia.com) provides rafting opportunities.

Sabah
Sabah has some of the country's best white-water with trips available to the scenic Kiulu and wild Padas rivers. Call **Riverbug**, tel: 088-260 501; www.traversetours.com to arrange.

Wildlife viewing

Malaysia's rainforests are home to a variety of wildlife, but it's not very often you can see them unless you know where to look. Ecotour operators are able to guide you to the places giving you the best chance to see the endangered orang-utans, Borneo pygmy elephants, hornbills, birds and bats. On the peninsula, Langkawi, Ulu Muda and Taman Negara are good places to begin with, but Sabah and Sarawak are better known for their wildlife and nature tours.

Peninsula

Earth Lodge, 5–11 The Reef, Jalan Low Yat, Batu Ferringhi, Penang, mobile tel: 019-442 8926; earthlodgemalaysia.com.
Junglewalla, 1C Lot, 1392 Jalan Tanjung Rhu, Langkawi, mobile tel: 019-225 2300; www.junglewalla.com.
NKS Travel, Hotel Mandarin Pacific, 2–8 Jalan Sultan, Kuala Lumpur, tel: 03-2072 0336; www.taman-negara-nks.com.

Sabah

Borneo Eco Tours, Lot 1, Pusat Perindustrian Kolombong Jaya, Mile 5.5, Jalan Kolombong, Kota Kinabalu, tel: 088-438 300; www.borneoecotours.com.
Wildlife Expeditions, Lot A 1202-1, 12th Floor, Wisma Merdeka, Phase 1, Jalan Tun Razak, Kota Kinabalu, tel: 088-246 000; www.wildlife-expeditions.com.

Sarawak

Borneo Adventure, 55 Main Bazaar, Kuching, tel: 082-245 175; www.borneoadventure.com.

SIGHTSEEING TOURS

The whole gamut is available, from city and night tours to week-long packages that cover several destinations, and any combination of fly, drive and coach choices with accommodation and sometimes transfers and food. Ask at your hotel, the tourism information centre, or check newspapers for the latest listings.

The **Eastern & Oriental Express** is the ultimate in luxury rail travel, complete with mahogany marquetry and Burmese rosewood inspired by the 1932 Marlene Dietrich film Shanghai Express. The 132-passenger train travels 2,000km (1,260 miles) from Singapore through Kuala Lumpur to Bangkok (or vice versa) and stops along the way in Penang. For reservations, tel: 65-6395 0678 (Singapore); oereservations.singapore@orient-express.com.

The naturalists from **Dev's Adventure Tours** will guide you to an up-close-and-personal experience with Langkawi's flora and wildlife without harming the environment. When exploring the mangroves of Kilim Karst Geoforest Park, try the mangrove kayak trip, which allows you to glide between the mangrove tree roots and small river channels to see the wildlife that live here and even right up to one of the limestone cliffs. Also includes a visit to the Bat Cave. To book, mobile tel: 019-494 9193; www.langkawi-nature.com.

KTM offers good-value rail packages to various destinations in Malaysia that include train tickets, transfers, accommodation, some meals and tours. Try the Langkawi, Penang, Perlis or the popular Hat Yai (Thailand) package, or book a homestay package, tel: 03-2267 1200.

Licensed nature guide **Green John Chan** provides visitors with opportunities to soak up nature, heritage and culture – from the headhunters of Batang Ai in Sarawak to rafflesia-spotting in Temengor Forest Reserve, the mystical land of Jahai, and discovering Penang's back lanes. He runs his tours a few times a year and some only once. Contact him on mobile tel: 016-356 9169; www.facebook.com/greenjohnchan for details of his next tour.

For people who are unafraid of heights, **Langkawi Canopy Adventures** provides tours of the forest canopy. Participants have to complete several obstacles – from tree-climbing to walking gingerly on a tightrope high above the trees before the final descent – a 140-metre (459ft) long Flying Fox into a very tall strangling fig tree, and then abseiling 30 metres (98 feet) down to the ground. To book, call mobile tel: 012-466 8027; www.langkawi.travel.

MAS's subsidiary, **MAS Golden Holidays**, offers a range of holiday packages including flights, transfers, accommodations, meals and guided tours. There are options of fly-drive and coach holiday packages, as well as golf, scuba-diving and adventure packages. Tel: 03-7843 3000. A professional wildlife photographer manages **North Borneo Safari** out of his Sandakan base. Together with his team of naturalists/photographers, he brings visitors out on photo safaris to capture the beauty of Sabah's wildlife and exquisite landscapes in destinations like Kinabalu National Park, Kinabatangan, and Semporna. Enquire on tel: 089-666 196; www.northborneosafari.com.

Kuala Lumpur

City Tours

The **Kuala Lumpur Hop-on and Hop-off Bus** is an excellent way to experience the city. This service offers a convenient way of visiting the city's tourist sights on a double-decker bus. With a route taking in 23 stops around the city, the buses run 9am to 8pm daily. Waiting time is roughly 30 minutes, and you can board and alight from the bus at any of the designated stops along the way. Prerecorded commentaries in eight languages are available on headsets. One-day tickets at RM45 for adults and RM24 for children and senior citizens can be purchased on board the bus, at selected hotels and travel agents or online at www.myhoponhopoff.com. For enquiries, tel: 03-9282 2713.

The **Malaysia Helicopter Tour** provides a unique look at the city from the air. Contact Shajasa Travel and Tours (tel: 03-2026 8668) for further information.

If you prefer to keep your feet firmly on the ground, try the KL Heritage Walk, which takes you on a tour of the old part of the city. This walking tour is organised by volunteers keen to share the history of the city. It is free, but you will need to call **Be Tourist** (tel: 60-17-989 1031) to book and provide information such as your arrival and departure dates, entry point, nationality and passport number, as these tours are strictly for foreign visitors only. Meet at the **Be Tourist** office in the Central Market Annexe at 10.30am. The tour lasts for one and a half hours.

Food trails

If you would like some local company in seeking out the food trail in Kuala Lumpur and Petaling Jaya, check out **Food Tour Malaysia** (www.foodtourmalaysia.com) or **FoodFoodFood** (www.kuchingculture.com). Your guide will take you to the eating spots favoured by locals and for the latter, inclusive of a visit to the produce market.

A − Z

A HANDY SUMMARY
OF PRACTICAL INFORMATION

A

Accommodation

Choosing accommodation

Malaysia offers visitors an abundance of accommodation choices: international brand hotels, home-grown chains, resort-themed and boutique establishments, serviced apartments, resthouses and backpacker hostels. Accommodation options – even high-quality ones – are remarkably affordable (see budgeting). Hotels are rated one to five stars. For details, visit the Malaysian Association of Hotels website (www.hotels.org.my).

In beach areas such as Pulau Pangkor, tour companies and taxi drivers get a commission for recommending accommodation.

Hotel chains

Hotel chains include Cititel Hotel Management Hotels (www.chm-hotels.com), Tune Hotel (tel: 03-2082 5777; www.tunehotels.com), Hotel Seri Malaysia (tel: 03-2299 7800; www.seri malaysia.com.my) and Vistana (tel: 03-4042 8000; www.vistanahotels.com).

Rates and booking

To get the best hotel rates, plan to book during the week and outside public or school holidays and major festival times. In Melaka city, room prices are lower by 30 percent on weekdays. The beach resorts at Desaru, Johor are more expensive because of its mostly Singaporean clientele and weekend rates are about 20 percent higher.

Always enquire about packages, which may include a buffet or local breakfast and sometimes tours and entrance fees. If you stay more than one night, you can try bargaining for better rates. Most hotels are fine with triple-share requests. Hotels are required to display net rates (including the 10 percent service and 6 percent government taxes). However, hotels often have special internet rates, sometimes up to 70 percent cheaper than published rates. Hotel and travel websites include www.agoda.com, www.asiarooms.com, www.booking.com, www.cuti.my, www.malaysia-hotels.net and www.wego.com. If you have a Youth Hostel Association membership card you are entitled to a discount at youth hostels in Johor Bahru, Kuala Lumpur, Melaka, Pahang, Pangkor island and Penang (www.hihostels.com).

Homestays

Staying with a local family in Malay or Orang Asli villages is growing in popularity. Visitors are able to share their host family's traditions, cooking and eating their way and participating in their hosts; and village life. In the peninsula, the Malaysian Homestay by Rail packages (www.malaysiarailexplorer.com) combine train travel with the homestay experience..In east Malaysia, a homestay at a native longhouse, especially during the rice harvest festivals (end May/early June), is a cultural feast. Longhouse visits can also be arranged through tour companies; visit www.go2homestay.com. In Sabah, contact Sabah Tourism (tel: 088-212 121; www.sabahtourism.com).

National Park stays

Most of the national and state parks allow overnight accommodation apart from a handful in east Malaysia. In Peninsular Malaysia, chalets, dormitories and campsites can be found at the staging points of the national parks of Taman Negara (tel: 03-2031 0898; www.taman-negara.com) and Endau-Rompin (tel: 07-788 2812; www.endaurompin.net). Booking is essential. Otherwise there are campsites, including Pantai Burung, Kuala Jasin, Kuala Marong and Batu Hampar. If entering via the Selai gateway, only hut accommodation and campsites are available.

Prices for accommodation at Sarawak's national park chalets range between RM100–200, while hostel accommodation costs less than RM100. For bookings and further information contact the National Park Booking Office, Visitors' Information Centre, Sarawak Tourism Complex, Old Court House, Kuching, tel: 082-410 944, or visit www.sarawaktourism.com. To stay at the World Heritage Site of Kinabalu Park is more costly even for hostel accommodation (over RM100). Contact Kinbalu Park headquarters (tel: 088-889 098; www.sabahtourism.com) for more information.

Admission charges

Charges for entry to public attractions depends mainly on whether they are run by public or private institutions. Nominal admission charges of under RM5 may apply for national and state museums. Private museums charge a higher fee of RM10–20. Entrance to most galleries is free. Zoos, bird parks and the Aquaria KLCC oceanarium have higher entry charges ranging from RM20–50.

B

Budgeting for your trip

Travelling in Malaysia is relatively cheap. If you arrive at KLIA and want to go to Kuala Lumpur's city centre, the taxi fare is around RM100. If you are travelling light, you may want to catch a bus or the train (ERL) instead (see page 346).

Accommodation prices generally start from RM40 a night in budget places to over RM700 a night in some five-star hotels, though booking ahead gives the best rates. Many hotels include breakfast with the room rate. For those who stay in three-star accommodation and are prepared to eat with the locals, expect to pay about RM300 per day for lodging, transport and meals.

National park accommodation in Sabah is more expensive than in Sarawak, where dormitory beds can cost as much as RM180.

Good food of excellent value can be found at hawker centres, coffee shops and food courts in shopping complexes, where RM7–8 can buy you a meal and a non-alcoholic drink. At the other end of the scale are fine-dining establishments where the prices reflect the setting, quality of food and service on offer. Alcoholic drinks are expensive; expect to pay at least RM6.50 for a beer in a coffee shop and up to around RM20 in luxury hotels and nightclubs. A glass of wine costs upwards of RM25 at moderately priced restaurants where a meal for two could total over RM200.

Public transport is cheap (RM1–4) and urban taxi fares are moderate (RM15). Although required by law, meters are not always used, especially during peak hours. Bargaining may be required. In such cases, make sure the price is agreed on before entering the taxi. In Kuala Lumpur, there is a 50 percent surcharge for taxi trips between midnight and 6am. Car hire is reasonably priced, but parking in city centres and five-star hotels is very expensive.

C

Children

There is plenty to keep children occupied when travelling in Malaysia. However, children might be more susceptible to heat and food-and water-related ailments. Suitable food could be a problem off the beaten track. Malaysian infrastructure is not at all baby-friendly, even in the cities. There are few mothers' rooms or nappy-changing tables in toilets, and it may be difficult to buy infant products in rural areas. Public transport and public areas are unsympathetic to pushchairs. However, a helping hand is never far away.

Children under 12 travel for half-price on buses and boats. Four- and five-star hotels and resorts offer clubs with children's activities. Bigger malls and fast-food outlets have play areas, and there are enough attractions in the cities to keep the young ones happy.

Climate

Malaysia's weather is generally hot and sunny all year round, with temperatures averaging 32°C (90°F) during the day and 24°C (75°F) at night. If it rains, it will usually be in the afternoons, which may range from a brief drizzle to up to two hours of heavy rain. Humidity is high at 80 percent. Thus, many Malaysians prefer to spend their weekends in air-conditioned malls instead of the outdoors. Temperatures in the highland areas, such as Cameron and Genting, are lower and much more tolerable.

When to visit

Malaysia experiences different weather patterns depending on which part of the country you visit. The monsoon season of April/May brings heavy rain to the west coast of Peninsular Malaysia. The east coast of the peninsula and Sabah and Sarawak experience their monsoon season between November and February. The inter-monsoon periods can also be wet. Light showers come and go, helping to relieve the heat.

Thick haze has been recurrent from July to October, especially for the Klang Valley and east Malaysia, for some years. Most of the smoke and soot is blown in by the southwest monsoon from parts of Indonesia hit by forest fires, which have been worsened by the dry weather caused by the El Niño phenomenon.

What to wear

In Malaysia's tropical climate, think cotton and natural fibres. Sunglasses, sunblock and umbrellas or raincoats are advisable. If you plan to visit the hill stations, bring along a light sweater for the cooler evenings or a raincoat if you plan to hike in the mossy forests. If planning to trek in jungle areas, you might want to consider bringing anti-leech socks.

Malaysians are fairly informal but they do dress up for dinner or a night out (especially in the cities), depending on the establishment they dine at. In fact, the fancier establishments have a dress code. For some formal occasions, men have the option of wearing a batik shirt instead of a suit.

In rural areas like in Malay villages, and when you go off the beaten tourist track, dress more conservatively, in which case, keep your legs and upper arms covered.

Crime and safety

Like anywhere else, pickpockets and snatch thieves are your biggest worry. Snatch thieves tend to be two men on a motorcycle or men leaning out of moving cars to grab your bag. If your bag is snatched, give in, because many thieves carry knives which they do not hesitate to use. On pavements, always walk in the direction of oncoming traffic and make sure your bag is on the side away from the traffic.

Unless you are in a luxury hotel, do not leave valuables in your room, except in a safe. Carry your passport and money with you at all times – even while sunbathing – or keep them in the main hotel safe. Sling your camera around your body, and make sure your backpack is firmly strapped on. If you are going diving or snorkelling or taking part in any other adventure sport, put valuables in a small backpack which you can leave with the operators. Travelling on public transport is safe – just keep an eye on the luggage that is taken out whenever your coach stops. Walking around at night is generally safe, especially in tourist areas, but keep to well-lit places.

Hitchhiking is very uncommon and hence can be frustrating and even dangerous. Public transport, while

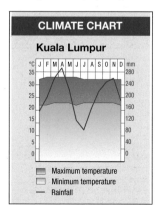

CLIMATE CHART

Kuala Lumpur

- Maximum temperature
- Minimum temperature
- Rainfall

slow and erratic in some places, is cheap and plentiful.

The **Tourist Police** (tel: 03-2149 6590) patrol tourist spots. Their uniforms feature a chequered hatband, dark-blue shirt and trousers, and a red-and-blue badge with the letter "I" (for information) on the breast pocket. They can help with the loss of passports and other documents, as well as give general advice. Otherwise, do not hesitate to head to any police station or booth when you need help (tel: 999 from fixed lines or 112 from a mobile phone).

Common scams

Although Malaysians are friendly, they rarely approach foreigners or engage them in conversation. Always be on guard and walk away if they ask you to meet a "relative" who has "always wanted to visit your country", or to partake in a gambling session with "guaranteed winnings". You may also come across beggars on the streets: while some are genuinely poor, others are not.

Be aware of people pretending to be police and demanding to see your ID. The police will not do so unless you have committed an offence or you are in a nightspot that is being raided.

Never buy anything from touts, whether bus, train or other tickets.

Customs regulations

Import duties seldom affect the average traveller, who may bring in 225 grams of tobacco, 50 cigars or 200 cigarettes, and a 1-litre bottle of liquor duty-free as well as personal cameras, watches, cosmetics, etc. The duty-free guidelines do not apply on domestic flights, or for Singaporeans.

On rare occasions, visitors may be asked to pay a deposit for temporary importation of dutiable goods (up to 30 percent of the value), which is refundable upon departure. Be sure to get an official receipt for any tax or deposit paid.

Currency restrictions apply on the amount of currency notes (which include traveller's cheques) brought in and out of Malaysia. Non-residents

Electricity

Electrical outlets are rated at 220 volts, 50 cycles, and serve three-pin, flat-pronged plugs. Most supermarkets stock adaptors for different voltages. Major hotels can supply adaptors for 110–120-volt, 60-Hz appliances.

are required to make a declaration to Customs if carrying ringgit currency of RM1,000 and above on arrival and departure. If you are carrying foreign currency of US$10,000 and above (or equivalent in other foreign currency) into the country, you will need to declare it on Customs Form 22. On departure, you may bring out foreign currency notes and traveller's cheques up to the amount you had initially declared upon your arrival. For amounts exceeding those stated above, the prior written approval of the Malaysian Central Bank is required. For more information, contact the Central Bank of Malaysia at tel: 03-2698 8044 (Mon–Fri 9am–5pm).

Pornography, firearms, ammunition and walkie-talkies are strictly prohibited. The export of antiques requires a licence from the Museum Department. Possession of narcotics and other illegal drugs carries the death sentence. For details, call Customs at tel: 03-8882 2100 (or 1300 888 500), as regulations may change over time.

D

Disabled travellers

Basic accessible facilities, like extra-wide parking bays, wheelchair ramps and toilets, can be found in major hotels, malls, theatres, fast-food chains and some government buildings in the bigger cities such as Kuala Lumpur. The Kuala Lumpur International Airport and the Light Rail Transit (LRT) system in Kuala Lumpur are also wheelchair accessible. But in general, Malaysia falls short on accommodating the disabled. Urban streets are uneven and sometimes potholed and difficult to navigate, while ramps are not that common. Taxis will usually not transport people in wheelchairs or will apply additional charges.

E

Embassies and consulates

Embassies and consulates are located in Kuala Lumpur.
Australia, 6 Jalan Yap Kwan Seng, tel: 03-2146 5555; www.malaysia.embassy.gov.au
Canada, 17th Floor, Menara Tan & Tan, 207 Jalan Tun Razak, tel: 03-2718 3333; www.canadainternational.gc.ca
China, First Floor, Plaza OSK, 25 Jalan Ampang, tel: 03-2163 6815; my.china-embassy.org

India,1 Jalan Mon't Kiara, level 28, Menara 1 Mon't Kiara, tel: 03-6205 2350; www.indianhighcommission.com.my
Indonesia, 233 Jalan Tun Razak, tel: 03-2116 4106; www.kbrikualalumpur.org
New Zealand, Level 21 Menara IMC, 8 Jalan Sultan Ismail, tel: 03-2078 2533; www.nzembassy.com
Singapore, 209 Jalan Tun Razak, tel: 03-2161 6277; www.mfa.gov.sg/kl
Thailand, 206 Jalan Ampang, tel: 03-2148 8222; www.thaiembassy.org
United Kingdom, level 27, Menara Binjai, 2 Jalan Binjai, tel: 03-2170 2200; www.ukinmalaysia.fco.gov.uk
United States, 376 Jalan Tun Razak, tel: 03-2168 5000; malaysia.usembassy.gov
Vietnam, 4 Persiaran Stonor, tel: 03-2148 4036

Malaysian embassies/consulates in other countries:

Australia, Canberra, High Commission of Malaysia, 7 Perth Avenue, Yarralumla; www.kln.gov.my/web/aus_canberra/home
Melbourne, Consulate General of Malaysia, Level 1, 432 St Kilda Road, tel: +613-9573 5400; www.kln.gov.my/web/aus_melbourne/home
Perth, Consulate General of Malaysia, 252 Adelaide Terrace, tel: +61-8-9225 7055; www.kln.gov.my/web/aus_perth/home
Canada, Ottawa, High Commission of Malaysia, Haut Commissariat de la Malaysie, 60 Boteler Street, tel: +1-613-241 5182; www.kln.gov.my/web/can_ottawa/home
Vancouver, Consulate General of Malaysia, Suite 1805, Terasen Centre, 1111 West Georgia Street, tel: +1-604-685 9550; www.kln.gov.my/web/can_vancouver/home
Ireland, Embassy of Malaysia, Level 3A–5A, Shelbourne House, Shelbourne Road, Ballsbridge, Dublin, tel: +353-1-667 7280; www.kln.gov.my/web/irl_dublin/home
New Zealand, High Commission of Malaysia, 10 Washington Avenue, Brooklyn, Wellington, tel: +64-4-385 2439; www.kln.gov.my/web/nzl_wellington/home
South Africa, High Commission of Malaysia, 1007 Francis Baard Street, Arcadia, Pretoria, tel: +27-12-342 5990; www.kln.gov.my/web/zaf_pretoria/home
Open Mon–Fri 8.30am–4.30pm.
United Kingdom, High Commission of Malaysia, 45–46 Belgrave Square, London, tel: +44-20-7235 8033 (general line); www.kln.gov.my/web/gbr_london/home

United States, Los Angeles, Consulate General of Malaysia, 550 South Hope Street, Suite 400, tel: +1-213-892 1238; www.kln.gov.my/web/usa_los-angeles/home
New York City, Consulate General of Malaysia, 313 East 43rd Street, tel: +1-212-490 2722; www.kln.gov.my/web/usa_new-york/home
Washington DC, Embassy of Malaysia, 3516 International Court, N.W., tel: +1-202-572-9700; www.kln.gov.my/web/usa_washington/home

Etiquette

Malaysians smile a lot, and are more often than not polite and helpful. They are remarkably tolerant and forgiving of foreigners' gaffes. In cities and tourist areas, they take a more liberal approach, but it helps to know a few local norms.

Greetings

Seniority is much respected. The oldest male member of a family is greeted first, often sits in the best and highest seat, and is consulted first on most matters. It is considered rude to address older people by their names. Unless you know your business associates well or you know otherwise, always use titles such as Mr (Encik), Mrs (Puan) or Miss (Cik). If you are a man, you must never offer to shake a Muslim lady's hand unless she offers it first. A simple nod or smile will suffice. Similar rules apply to women wanting to shake a Muslim man's hand. If you get what you think is a limp handshake, it is actually a Malay greeting (*salam*), which involves brushing the palm of the other person and placing the hand on one's heart. This signifies "I am pleased to meet you from the bottom of my heart".

Head and feet

The Hindu religion regards the head as the wellspring of wisdom and the feet as unclean, so it is insulting to touch another adult's head, point one's feet at anything, or step over another person. Malays consider it rude to point the index finger at something, so when indicating direction, make a fist with the right hand with the thumb folded on top and then aim at the subject. Use the right hand to pass or accept anything. The left is traditionally "dirty" because of its washroom connections.

In Malaysian homes, it is rude, especially for women, to cross your legs in front of your host. If entering a Malaysian home, remove your shoes. It is courteous to come bearing a gift, no matter how small. If you are given a gift, accept with both hands and a slight bow of the head. Never refuse drinks or snacks served to you, even if it is to take a sip or bite. In a Malay home, when passing in front of someone, bow slightly while walking and point an arm down to indicate the path to be taken.

Places of worship

Remove your shoes before entering any place of worship. At the mosque, non-Muslims are prohibited from entering certain areas; signs are clearly displayed. Conservative clothing is advisable – meaning visitors, both men and women, must have their arms and legs covered. Some mosques, like the Putra Mosque in Putrajaya, provide robes as well as scarves for covering your hair.

Certain Hindu temples are not open to non-Hindus to keep the place "pure" from people who consume beef. If you enter a Sikh temple, be sure to cover your hair. Be sensitive about photographing worshippers in prayer.

Public behaviour

While holding hands is common, displaying other forms of affection in public is considered bad form. The government is particular about upholding Islamic and Asian moral values, so such behaviour in public places is unacceptable, especially if you are with a local or look like one. Shouting and talking loudly, even outside a nightspot, is considered rude.

G

Gay and lesbian travellers

Like in many Asian societies, the gay scene in Malaysia is discreet although present. Homosexuality is illegal in Malaysia, although the society is generally tolerant. Gay visitors can travel safely and without fear of persecution in Malaysia, usually facing only minor harassment from the police if it happens at all. However, note that there are provisions in the Penal Code – and for Muslims, Islamic Shar'iah laws – that penalise same-sex sexual acts, sodomy, fellatio and cross-dressing.

Kuala Lumpur has a sizeable gay and lesbian community, unofficially estimated at 60,000. Comprehensive information and newsgroups are available on gay portal **Utopia** at www.utopia-asia.com/tipsmala.htm. For more information on the community, contact community rights and Aids/HIV outreach organisation, **PT Foundation** (tel: 03-4044 4611; www.ptfmalaysia.org). For gay-friendly establishments, see page 367.

H

Health and medical care

Visitors entering Malaysia are not required to show evidence of vaccination for smallpox or cholera, but it is a good idea to immunise yourself against cholera, hepatitis A and B and tetanus. If you are visiting remote rainforest areas, it is advisable to take protection against malaria. See your doctor before leaving home. Malaria tablets are only available on prescription in Malaysia. To keep mosquitoes at bay, use insect repellents, mosquito coils and mosquito nets at night. There are also periodic outbreaks of dengue fever for which there is no immunisation, so take preventive measures like using insect repellent. If you suffer from a very high fever while (or shortly after) visiting Malaysia, consult a doctor immediately.

Healthcare and insurance

Treat open cuts and scratches immediately, as infection in humid climates can delay healing, and at worst, cause tropical ulcers. Over-the-counter medicine is readily available in most towns and cities. It is advisable to read up on the rainforest and marine creatures to avoid.

Many first-time visitors to a tropical country take a while to adjust to the heat and humidity; make sure you drink at least 2 litres (8 to 10 glasses) of water to keep hydrated. Keep out of the sun during the hottest part of the day (11am–3pm). Tap water in the cities is potable but, to be on the safe side, drink boiled or bottled water. Avoid ice cubes at streetside stalls and small coffee shops, as they are usually made using unboiled water.

Emergencies

In case of emergencies, call 999 (or 112 from a mobile phone) for police, fire brigade/rescue services or ambulance service.

In Sabah and Sarawak, you may want to contact the hospitals directly in case of medical emergencies. Contact numbers for such hospitals are under the "Health and Medical Care" section.

Refrain from eating peeled fruit at street stalls. Otherwise, food served in restaurants and hawker centres should give you no problems.

If you are in Malaysia during the haze period, be aware that the haze affects those with respiratory illnesses, especially asthmatics. Stay indoors or wear a mask when outdoors. Thankfully, the monsoon season right after helps clear the air. It is advisable to buy your own health insurance before arrival.

Pharmacies and hospitals

Most towns, shopping centres and shopping malls have pharmacies often operated by chains like Watson's, Georgetown Caring, Vitacare and Guardian. Usually, a licensed pharmacist is on duty on weekdays from 10am to 5pm. Many medicines are dispensed without prescription, but controlled drugs require a doctor's prescription. Do check the expiry dates. Pharmacies also stock nutritional and personal care products. There are no 24-hour pharmacies, but medication can be obtained at 24-hour private clinics after consultation with the doctor-in-charge. Poliklinik Bangsar (No. 30, Jalan Telawi, Bangsar Baru, 59100 Kuala Lumpur; tel: 03-2282 3753) is open 24 hours and can perform minor surgery procedures.

In Sabah and Sarawak, 24-hour polyclinics also provide medications. Prices are very reasonable, especially for Malaysian-manufactured drugs. Malaysia has some of the best doctors in the region, both locally and overseas trained and who speak good English. Kuala Lumpur, Penang and Melaka have been heavily promoted as healthcare destinations in recent years, and private hospitals have invested in service improvements to cater to overseas demand. Advance medical care is available in both government and private hospitals, which are well equipped and have specialised clinics and good medical staff. Foreigners can seek treatment and get health screenings in Malaysia for fees much lower than in the West. Consultancy generally starts at RM20–30 for a general practitioner and RM80 for a specialist. Government hospitals charge a fraction of the price of private ones, but there is usually a longer waiting period. See the Ministry of Health website (www.moh.gov.my/v/ch_fo) for a list of treatment charges for foreign citizens at government hospitals, including dental treatment charges. For a list of government hospitals,

see www.moh.gov.my/gov_hospitals or www.moh.gov.my/gov_dentals for government dental clinics. Private hospitals are located in larger urban areas, thus rural areas tend to be underserved. For minor problems, there are smaller private medical clinics found all over the cities, with some open 24 hours. These dispense most generic medicines.

Kuala Lumpur
Gleneagles Kuala Lumpur
282 & 286 Jalan Ampang
Tel: 03-4141 3000
www.gimc.com.my
A medium-sized private hospital with top-notch medical services. Favoured by expatriates.

Hospital Kuala Lumpur
Jalan Pahang
Tel: 03-2615 5555
www.hkl.gov.my
The largest government hospital, it offers 28 clinical services, 14 support services, a large specialist team and good facilities.

Pantai Hospital Kuala Lumpur
8 Jalan Bukit Pantai
Tel: 03-2296 0888
www.pantai.com.my
This 332-bed hospital has over 160 specialists. Has Centres of Excellence in breast care, spine and joint, hand and microsurgery, cancer and heart care.

Prince Court Medical Centre
39 Jalan Kia Peng
Tel: 03-2160 0000
www.princecourt.com
Provides rooms designed for comfort and comprehensive care with hotel-like amenities and concierge services, as well as an international business lounge for international guests checking in for medical treatments.

Tung Shin Hospital
102 Jalan Pudu (near Pudu Sentral)
Tel: 03-2037 2299
www.tungshin.com.my
A good, medium-sized, private not-for-profit hospital offering Western and traditional Chinese treatments.

Penang
Adventist Hospital
465 Jalan Burma, George Town
Tel: 04-222 7200
www.pah.com.my
Not-for-profit Christian hospital with various specialisations.

Gleneagles Medical Centre
Jalan Pangkor, George Town
Tel: 04-227 6111
www.gleneagles-penang.com
This private hospital has a wide range of specialisations and health-screening packages.

Loh Guan Lye Specialist Centre
19 & 21 Logan Road
Tel: 04-238 8888
www.lohguanlye.com
Private hospital offering specialised services in over 30 areas of medicine.

Melaka
Mahkota Medical Centre
3 Mahkota Melaka, Jalan Merdeka
Tel: 06-285 2999
www.mahkotamedical.com
Various clinical specialisations are covered by Mahkota, which also offers a dental centre and a health-screening centre.
Sarawak

Kuching
Kuching Specialist Hospital
Lot 10420, Block 11
Tabuan Stutong Commercial Centre
Jalan Setia Raja
Tel: 082-365 777
www.kpj.kuching.com
Normah Medical Specialist Centre
Lot 937, Section 30 KTLD
Jalan Tun Abdul Rahman
Tel: 082-440 055
www.normah.com

Miri
Miri City Medical Centre
Lot 916-920, 1202 and 1203
Jalan Hokkien
Tel: 085-426 622
www.mcmcmiri.com

Sibu
Sibu Specialist Medical Centre
52A-G Brooke Drive
Tel: 084-329 900
www.kpjsibu.com
Sabah

Kota Kinabalu
Sabah Medical Centre
Lorong Bersatu
off Jalan Damai
Tel: 088-211 333
www.sabahmedicalcentre.com
Queen Elizabeth Hospital
Jalan Penampang
tel: 088-517 555

Sandakan
Duchess of Kent Hospital
Km3.2 Jalan Utara
Tel: 089-248 600

Tawau
Tawau Hospital
Jalan Tanjung Batu
Tel: 089-773 533

Dental clinics

Dentists are called *doctor gigi* (teeth doctors). Many dentists have trained overseas, so the services offered are of a high standard. Dental fees are substantially lower than those paid in the West.

Although major public hospitals in Sabah and Sarawak offer dental services, a higher standard of care is provided in private practice. Call first to make an appointment.

For a complete list of clinics, check the Malaysian Dental Association website at www.mda.org.my. Consultancy rates start at RM30.

Kuala Lumpur
Dentalpro Dental Specialist Centre
263 Jalan Maarof, Bangsar
Tel: 03-2094 3333
Jaya Dental Surgery
Jaya 33, Jalan Semangat, Section 13
Petaling Jaya
Selangor
Tel: 03-7957 5611
Twin Towers Medical Centre KLCC
Lot LC 402-404, Level 4, Suria KLCC
Tel: 03-2382 3500

Penang
Eng Dental Surgery
287 Burmah Road, Pulau Tikus
Tel: 04-226 2440

Kuching
Yong Dental Surgery
No. 5, 1st Floor, Jalan Song Thian Cheok
Tel: 082-246 472

Kota Kinabalu
Pantai Dental Clinic & Surgery
Lot 2, Ground Floor, Block 5
Api-Api Centre, Lorong Api-Api
Jalan Centrepoint
Tel: 088-251 663

I

Internet

Cybercafés with broadband internet can be found in all the capitals and most towns and tourist areas. Rates start from RM2 per hour. Most hotels and backpacker establishments provide internet services, although the more moderately priced hotels may only provide these in common areas such as the lobby or café. Some hotels provide access as a complimentary service either in the reception lobby or in the guestrooms; others charge for it. Wireless broadband (Wi-fi) is also becoming quite widespread. In cafés, Wi-fi is usually free with any purchase; the cashier will give you a log-in name and a password. Prepaid internet

starter packs are also available from major telecommunications providers such as Maxis, DiGi and Celcom, starting from RM100.

L

Left luggage

Hotels usually provide free left luggage services for their guests. **KLIA** (tel: 03-8776 5035) and KLIA2 (tel: 03-8775 2667) have locker rental services (RM28–38 per day) and storage services (RM18–48 a day). **KL Sentral** (tel: 03-8787 4210) has lockers on Levels 1 and 2 (RM1–1.50 per item per day). Left luggage services are also provided at Madam's Keeper (Level 1) and Matang Luggage (Level 2). Please enquire at Pudu Sentral's information counter for left luggage services at the bus terminal.

There are no storage facilities at the airports in Sabah and Sarawak. Excess luggage can be stored at your hotel or tour operator's office if you are travelling to a longhouse or a jungle lodge. Kinabalu Park Headquarters has a luggage facility for those climbing Mount Kinabalu.

Lost property

About all that can be done about lost property in Malaysia is making a police report and hoping that whoever finds it is honest. Call the **Tourist Police** at 03-2149 6590 or lodge a report at the nearest police station. A police report will be important for making an insurance claim; check your policy claim instructions carefully.

At KLIA and KLIA2, contact the relevant airline you were travelling with, or if the items were lost at the airport terminal, seek assistance at the nearest information counter. At **KL Sentral**, the Auxiliary Police will assist you. Approach the police booth or Customer Relations Officer at the information counter on Levels 1 or 2. If you have left anything in a taxi or long-distance bus, try calling the relevant company as well.

M

Maps

Basic maps are available free at most hotels, Tourism Malaysia offices and the Sabah and Sarawak Tourism Board offices. You can also purchase

decent maps from any good bookshop or newsagent. The *Insight Fleximap Kuala Lumpur* and *Insight Fleximap Penang & Langkawi* are good ones to get. Also check out www.malaysia-maps.com/kl for a basic online map of the capital.

Media

Newspapers and magazines

The main daily newspapers are in Bahasa Malaysia and English. There are also Chinese- and Tamil-language newspapers. The *New Straits Times* and *The Star* are sympathetic to government policy, while city-based *The Sun* takes a more issues-focused approach and champions more transparent government. The main business weekly is *The Edge*. Sabah and Sarawak have their own papers, including *The New Sabah Times*, *Daily Express*, *Sarawak Tribune* and *Borneo Post*.

Most of these papers have online editions; *The Star Online* (www.thestar.com.my) is one of the most popular websites for Malaysian news. There is also a large number of local magazines, from leisure to entertainment to business. Foreign newspapers and magazines can be purchased in large cities.

To find out what is happening in the cities, look at the "What's On" sections of magazines like *Juice*, *KL Lifestyle*, *KL Vision*, *KLue* and *Time Out*, which are some of the popular local lifestyle and entertainment magazines with news and listings. For food and dining information, check out Tatler *Malaysia's Best Restaurants*.

Sabah Tourism's informative monthly magazine (*Malaysian Borneo Sabah*) can be collected at its office in Kota Kinabalu. In Kuching, *The Official Kuching Guide*, updated annually, is very helpful; also informative is the quarterly *Borneo Talk*. Both are available at Kuching Airport and the Visitors' Information Centre in the city.

Radio and television

Malaysia has a wide range of radio stations in different languages (Malay, English, Chinese, Indian) and music genres (pop, rock, jazz, classical). The main national English-language radio stations include: Hitz FM, Mix FM, Light & Easy (format radio stations which play a mix of local and international music), BfM, which is business- and lifestyle-oriented, and Capital Radio, aimed at women listeners. Television is the most popular medium in Malaysia, watched in both international hotel rooms and longhouses with the same enthusiasm. Programmes are cosmopolitan and American sitcoms and documentaries are shown alongside Indonesia's hottest films, Korean serials and Koran reading competitions. Sports are given generous amounts of airtime. Pubs, restaurants and mamak (Indian Muslim) stalls are popular gathering places to watch English football matches at weekends.

The government television stations are RTM and 2, the private operators are TV3, 8TV and NTV7, while the subscription-only satellite TV broadcaster, Astro, offers over 50 channels, including ESPN, MTV, Al Jazeera, BBC World and CNN. Some hotels either have an in-house cable station as well as selected Astro satellite channels. Check the local newspapers for selected programme details.

Money

Malaysia uses ringgit and sen. RM1=100 sen. Coins come in denominations of 5, 10, 20 and 50 sen, and notes in RM1, RM2, RM5, RM10, RM50 and RM100.

Carry a combination of cash and traveller's cheques and/or a credit card. Cash is imperative in rural areas, but you can change traveller's cheques and use credit cards in urban areas and established tourist areas.

Banking hours

In all states except Kelantan and Terengganu, banking hours are Monday to Friday 9.30am to 4pm. Some open on the second and fourth Saturdays of the month, 9.30am to noon. In Kelantan and Terengganu, banks open Sunday to Thursday 9.30am to 4pm.

Changing money

Most currencies can be exchanged for ringgit, but the popular ones are US dollars, British sterling pounds, euros and Singapore dollars. Licensed money changers (open from early morning until late at night) offer better rates than banks, while hotels and shopping centres levy a service charge (usually 2–4 percent).

Local and international banks handle the gamut of transactions, and automated teller machines, from which you can use your credit card to withdraw cash, are widespread in cities, towns and transport hubs.

Credit cards

The most widely used credit cards are Visa and MasterCard. Diners Club and American Express are less welcome, but accepted. Note that some retailers add a 2–3 percent surcharge for the privilege of using plastic – so ask first before paying. As with everywhere in the world, be watchful of credit card fraud. Make sure you have enough cash before you leave a city.
American Express tel: 1800-889 559
Diners Club tel: 03-2161 1055
MasterCard tel: 1800-804 594
Visa tel: 1800-802 997

Tipping

Tipping is not obligatory, although it is appreciated and is common in the cities and major tourist spots. In large hotels, bellboys and porters usually receive tips from RM2 to RM5 depending on the service rendered. In smart restaurants you can just leave behind the loose change. Tour guides expect a tip, although a simple "thank you" (*terima kasih*) and a smile may be sufficient.

Traveller's cheques

All major brands of traveller's cheques and cash in major currencies are readily accepted in the larger cities. Some big hotels exchange traveller's cheques for cash but their rates are not as good as banks, which have better rates.

O

Opening hours

In an Islamic nation with a British colonial past, the definition of the working week varies. It runs from Monday to Friday in all states except Terengganu, Kelantan, Kedah and Perlis. These four states with a stronger Islamic tradition retain the traditional half-day on Thursday and businesses are closed on Friday, not Sunday.

The working day at government offices begins at 8am and ends at 5pm, with time off on Friday from noon to 2.30pm for Muslim prayers, although some government-run museums may close either earlier or later than the official Friday prayer time. Most private businesses stick to the 8.30am–5.30pm routine. Large supermarkets, department stores and shopping malls are open 10am to 10pm daily. Smaller shops are open 10am to 7pm and close on Sunday.

Most museums and galleries open at 10am or 11am.

In addition to clubs and bars, stalls serving Muslim food (known as "mamak stalls") open until late. Some are open 24 hours.

P

Photography

These days most photographers use digital cameras, and there is an extensive selection of all the latest cameras, accessories and memory cards for sale in Malaysia.

Most imaging shops have equipment to download images and can store them on CDs for between RM5 and RM10 per CD. It's also possible to print directly from memory cards.

Be prepared for rain, even on sunny days – always have a plastic bag handy for your equipment. Note that rainforest excursions are damaging to cameras because of the humidity. Pack a dry, non-lint cloth to wipe your camera dry and consider bringing dry-packs (to absorb moisture) and anti-fog inserts.

For rich colours, snap your shots before 10am or after 4pm. At noon, the light is too strong. Early morning or late afternoon sidelight produces softer contrasts and deeper colour density.

Most Malaysians are more than amiable about having their pictures taken. It usually takes a group of schoolchildren about 15 seconds before they merrily begin jabbing peace signs in front of your camera. Mosques and temples are rightly more reserved about photographers posing their subjects in front of altars. Whatever the situation, it's best to ask for permission. This is imperative during religious ceremonies, when you should keep a respectful distance. Likewise with tribal people, ask your tour guide.

Postal services

The **Malaysian postal service** (www.pos.com.my) is reliable, and there are post offices everywhere, generally open Monday to Friday 8am to 5.30pm. If the post office is closed but you have sufficient postal stamps to send your envelope or letter then you can deposit it into the red post boxes, available outside every post office and scattered in every town and city. A handful in large housing estates and shopping malls may stay open longer. The full range of services is available, including registered mail, parcels as well as the cashing of postal and money orders. PosLaju courier service, usually cheaper than private courier services, and overnight Pos Ekspres services are also offered.

Most large hotels provide postal services. Stamps and aerogrammes are often sold at small Indian sweet and tobacco stalls on street corners.

Courier services

International courier services include the following:

DHL
Tel: 1800-888 388 (within Malaysia)
www.dhl.com.my
Federal Express (FedEx)
Tel: 1800-886 363 (within Malaysia)
www.fedex.com
United Parcel Services (UPS)
Tel: 03-7784 2311 (Kuala Lumpur and Penang), 1800-180 088 (Penang), 05-241 4070 (Ipoh), 06-284 5440 (Melaka), 07-354 0066 (Johor); www.ups.com

Public holidays

Many of Malaysia's public holidays relate to cultural festivals, the dates of which are not fixed but follow the lunar or Muslim calendar. These include Hari Raya Puasa, the main Muslim festival, a two-day holiday celebrating the end of the Muslim fasting month of Ramadan; Hari Raya Haji, celebrating the annual Muslim pilgrimage season; Awal Muharam, the Muslim New Year; and the Birthday of Prophet Muhammad, during which prayers and Koran recitals are held at mosques.

Some festivals are observed only in certain states; for example, the birthday of the respective state sultans. If a public holiday falls on a Saturday or Sunday, the following Monday is a holiday; likewise, if a holiday falls on a Thursday or Friday in the states that follow the Muslim week, the following Saturday is a holiday. Check dates with **Tourism Malaysia** (tel: 1300-885 050 within Malaysia; www.tourism.gov.my).

January New Year's Day (1st)
January/February Chinese New Year, a two-day holiday for the main Chinese festival celebrated over a 15-day period (many hotels and shopping malls will have a lion dance performance during this period); Thaipusam, the Hindu festival of penance, celebrated colourfully in Kuala Lumpur (Batu Caves).

April Mukah Kaul, a Melanau festival celebrated in the fishing communities around Mukah on Sarawak's north coast (thanksgiving festival of this seafaring community); Good Friday (Sabah and Sarawak only).
May Labour Day (1st); Vesak Day, temple celebrations to mark Buddha's birth, death and enlightenment; Harvest Festival, a two-day holiday, the main festival for the different groups of the state of Sabah.
June Gawai, a two-day holiday that is the main official festival for the different tribal groups of Sarawak; Birthday of the Yang Di-pertuan Agung (King).
August National Day (31st), Independence Day for Malaya from British rule (peninsula only).
September Malaysia Day (16th) marks the day Sabah and Sarawak joined Malaya to form Malaysia.
October/November Deepavali, Hindu festival of lights.
December Christmas (25th), midnight mass, celebrated in churches throughout the country.

For more information on Malaysian festivals and events, see page 363.

Try to plan your trip outside of the Malaysian public-holiday and school-holiday period (March, May, June, August, mid-November to December), as during this time it is high season and will be harder to find accommodation and transportation, and you will pay additional surcharges.

R

Religious services

The main and official religion is Islam, adopted by the Malays, but religious tolerance sees the open practice of Buddhism and Taoism among the Chinese, Hinduism among the Indians and Christianity among non-Malays. Some indigenous people retain their animist beliefs.

As the majority of the population are Muslim, mosques proliferate and all public buildings have at least one *surau* (prayer room). There are also ample places of worship for Buddhists, Taoists, Hindus, Sikhs and followers of other faiths. However, churches might be difficult to locate outside urban centres and in the predominantly Muslim east coast of Peninsular Malaysia. Check with your hotel.

The following churches offer English-language services.

Kuala Lumpur
Cathedral of St John (Catholic)
5 Jalan Bukit Nanas
Tel: 03-2078 1876
Sat mass (and Novena) 6pm, Sun masses 8am, 10.30am, 6pm.
Church of the Holy Rosary (Catholic)
10 Jalan Tun Sambanthan, Brickfields
Tel: 03-2274 2747
Sat mass 5pm, Sun mass 8.30am.
Church of Our Lady of Fatima (Catholic)
Jalan Sultan Abdul Samad, Brickfields
Tel: 03-2274 1631
Sun masses 7am, 8.30am, 10.30am, Tue–Sat masses 6.30am.
St Mary's Cathedral (Anglican)
Jalan Raja
Tel: 03-2692 8672
Sun services 7am, 8.30am, 10.30am, 6pm.
Wesley Methodist Church
2 Jalan Wesley
Tel: 03-2072 0338
Sun services 9am, 11am, 5pm.

Penang
Church of the Assumption (Catholic)
3 Lebuh Farquhar
Tel: 04-261 0088
Sat mass 6pm, Sun mass 10am.
George Town Baptist Church
14 Jalan Larut, George Town
Tel: 04-229 7757
Sun services 9am, 11am.
St George's Anglican Church
1 Lebuh Farquhar
Tel: 04-261 2739
Sun services 8.30am, 10.30am.
Trinity Methodist Church
16 Jalan Masjid Negeri, George Town
Tel: 04-828 7445
Sun services 9am, 11am, 5pm.

Kuching
St Thomas Cathedral (Anglican)
Jalan Haji Openg
Tel: 082-242 625
Sun services 6.45am, 8.15am, 5.30pm.
St Joseph's Cathedral (Catholic)
Jalan Tun Haji Openg
Tel: 082-423 424
Sun masses 6.30am, 5.30pm.

Kota Kinabalu
All Saints Cathedral (Anglican)
Jalan Tunku Abdul Rahman, Karamunsing
Tel: 088-231 824
Sun services 7.30am, 10am.
Sacred Heart Cathedral (Catholic)
14B Jalan Menteri (off Jalan Mat Salleh)
Tel: 088-224 741
Sat mass 6pm, Sun mass 9am.

What to wear

As Malaysia is a Muslim and conservative country, observance of local customs is important. Smart casual wear is fine in temples, but in mosques, keep your legs and arms covered. Women travellers will also need to cover their heads when visiting some mosques, so bring along a shawl. Shoes should be removed before entering temples, so slip-ons are handy.

S

Smoking

Like other countries, Malaysia has taken steps to discourage smoking. Smoking is prohibited in government premises, public transport, hospitals, clinics, the World Heritage Site of Melaka and air-conditioned areas including offices and selected restaurants. Despite the increase in prices, there has been little impact on demand. Selling cigarettes to those under the age of 18 is illegal.

Student travellers

Several attractions and accommodations offer discounts for holders of the International Student Identity Card (ISIC) and the International Youth Travel Card (IYTC). Check www.isic.org for a list of benefits in Malaysia. Hostelling International – Malaysia (www.hihostels.com) cardholders enjoy discounts on accommodation in Kuala Lumpur, Johor Bahru, Langkawi, Melaka, Pangkor island, Penang and Taman Negara. To apply while in Malaysia, contact MSL Travel (www.msltravel. com), which is the issuing authority of these cards, at tel: 03-4047 3722.

T

Taxes

There is no general sales tax on purchases, but there is a service charge of 10 percent and a 5 percent government tax in most large establishments. Hotels and restaurants usually separate the cost and various taxes, which may be written as "++". Large restaurants charge a 10 percent service tax and 6 percent government tax.

In April 2015, the Malaysian Government introduced the Goods and Services Tax (GST) at a standard rate of 6 percent. GST is charged on all taxable supply of goods and services such as transport, accommodation, hire and drive, meals, entry to exhibitions and entertainment centres, and travel agency services, except those specifically exempted (for more information see www.mltic.my/tax).

Telephones

You can find public phones in malls, usually in corridors leading to the toilets. Phones marked "international" allow you to make overseas calls. Local calls from a public phone cost 30 sen per three minutes. Booths are either coin-operated or use phone cards. Phone cards in denominations from RM5 to RM50 are available at phone shops, newsstands and petrol stations. In cities and towns, there are also shops providing IDD (international direct dialling) services.

You can also call from major hotel guestrooms, but charges are high. To call overseas, refer to the calling instructions in your room.

Dialling codes

The **country code** for Malaysia is 60. To call a Malaysian fixed-line number eg in Kuala Lumpur (local code 03) from abroad, dial (international dialling code) + 60 + 3 + number. If in Malaysia, to call a number within the state, simply dial the number without the area code. To call another state, for example to call Penang from Melaka: 04-xxx xxxx. Note that phone numbers in Kuala Lumpur and Selangor are eight digits instead of the usual seven for those in other states.

Area codes

Johor 07
Kedah 04
Kelantan 09
Kota Kinabalu 088
Kuala Lumpur 03
Kuching 082
Labuan 087
Melaka 06
Miri 085
Negeri Sembilan 06
Pahang 09
Penang 04
Perak 05
Perlis 04
Selangor 03
Terengganu 09

International dialling codes

To dial an international number, dial 00 + country code + city area code + number
Australia 61
Canada 1
Ireland 353
New Zealand 64
South Africa 27
United Kingdom 44
United States 1

Mobile phones

To call a Malaysian mobile number from overseas, dial your international dialling code followed by the country code and the local prefix, dropping the initial zero, then the number you want; for example, dial international dialling code + 60 12-xxx xxxx. If your mobile phone has a roaming facility with your home service provider, it will automatically hook up to one of Malaysia's digital network providers (Celcom, DiGi and Maxis) that use the GSM network.

Roaming charges are often very expensive, so if you want to make and receive local and international calls, you can purchase a local SIM card with any of the mentioned providers. Starter packs cost a minimum RM8.50 and come with your own mobile phone number and limited air-time credit which you can easily top up at newsagents, convenience stores (7-Eleven) and petrol stations. Visit the nearest Hotlink (www.hotlink. com.my), DiGi (www.digi.com.my) or Celcom (www.celcom.com.my) outlet with your passport.

To call a mobile number with the same prefix as yours, for example if your number starts with 012 and the number you want to call is 012, then you just dial the number after the prefix. Things get a bit tricky when you want to call a mobile number with a different prefix than yours; you will have to dial 019 followed by the number. Same thing for any local fixed line number; you have to dial the area code 03 followed by the number, even if you are calling from within Kuala Lumpur itself.

If you want to call an overseas number, press the plus sign followed by your country code, city code and number. For example, dial +852-xxxx xxxx. As prepaid network providers may have their own methods to make calls, please check the mini booklet that comes with the starter pack.

To call Singapore from within Malaysia, simply dial the access code 02 followed by the Singapore number. Call 103 for **telephone directory assistance** if you are unable to find the telephone number of a restaurant or an attraction. For **operator-assisted** local and international calls, dial 101 (A service fee of RM1.50 per local call, RM5 per international call applies).

A much cheaper alternative to making international calls from either a Malaysian mobile number or fixed line is to buy a **prepaid IDD card** like iTalk (www.tm.com.my/ap/personal/voice/cards/Pages/About-iTalk.aspx) from any 7-Eleven convenience stores (24 hours) in denominations of RM10, RM20, RM30 and RM50. To activate the service, call the toll-free number listed on the receipt or card and punch in your 12-digit number on your receipt. iTalk is valid for three months from date of activation or until your credit runs out.

Toilets

Public restrooms can generally be found near markets, parks and transport terminals, as well as in shopping complexes and tourist areas. Many still have squat toilets which visitors may not be familiar with. Toilet paper is not always available, although you can sometimes buy tissue paper at the entrance, but it is still advisable to bring your own. Most malls charge a toilet entrance fee of 20–50 sen, but there is also a premium toilet (RM2) on Level 1 of Suria KLCC shopping centre, which is as clean as a four-star hotel washroom and provides you with hand lotion, amongst other toiletries. If you are very particular, use hotel toilets.

Tourist information

Tourism Malaysia (www.tourism.gov.my; tel: 1-300-885 050) has offices in every state. The amount of travel literature available in TM offices varies, but there are usually comprehensive brochures on each state and sometimes on local places of interest. The officers are also informed and helpful. The regional offices can also be contacted for information on reliable tour and travel operators, who have to be registered with them. In addition, both Sarawak and Sabah have their own state-run tourism offices (www.sarawaktourism.com and www.sabahtourism.com).

Tourist offices

Tourism Malaysia – Head Office, 9th Floor No. 2, Tower 1, Jalan P5/6 Precinct 5, Putrajaya, tel: 03-8891 8000
Malaysia Tourism Centre (MATIC), 109 Jalan Ampang, KL, tel: 03-9235 4800
Johor (Johor Bahru) 50C, Bangunan KPMNJ, Jalan Segget , tel: 07-222 3590

Kedah (Alor Setar) Seksyen 20, Jalan Raja, tel: 04-731 2322
Kelantan (Kota Bahru) Ground Floor, Kampung Kraftangan, Jalan Hilir Balai, 09-747 7554
Labuan tel: 087-422 622 (Ministry of Tourism)
Melaka 6,Jalan Plaza Merdeka, Jalan Merdeka, tel: 06-288 3304
Negeri Sembilan (Seremban) 1st Floor, Seremban Plaza, Jalan Dato' Muda Linggi, tel: 06-762 4488
Pahang (Kuantan) Lot G.01, Bangunan Mahkota Square, Jalan Mahkota, tel: 09-517 7111
Penang Level 56, Komtar, Penang, tel: 04-264 3494
Perak (Ipoh) 12 Medan Istana 2, Bandar Ipoh Raya, tel: 05-255 9962
Perlis (Kangar) No. 21, Jalan Satu, Taman Pertiwi Indah, Jalan Kangar-Alor Setar, tel: 04-978 1235
Sabah (Kota Kinabalu) Lot 1-0-7, Ground Floor Blok 1, Lorong Api-Api 1, Api-Api Centre, tel: 088-248 698
Sarawak (Kuching) Parcel 297-2-1, 2nd Floor, Riverbank Suites, tel: 082-246 6575
Selangor (Shah Alam) 6th Floor, Wisma PKPS, Persiaran Perbandaran Seksyen 14, tel: 03-5510 9100
Terengganu (Kuala Terengganu) 11 Ground and 1st Floor, Pusat Niaga Paya **Keladi, Jalan Kampung Daik,** tel: 09-630 9433

Tour operators and travel agents

Peninsula

Asian Overland Services, 39C & 40C Jalan Mamanda 9, Ampang Point, Kuala Lumpur, tel: 03-4252 9100; www.asianoverland.com.my. Offers nature tours incorporating sightseeing and other tour packages. Good for long-haul journeys.
Cameron Secrets Travel and Tours, c/o Father's Guest House, No. 4, Jalan Mentigi, P.O. Box 90, 39000 Tanah Rata, Cameron Highlands, Pahang, tel: 05-491 2888; www.cameronsecrets.com. Specialises in nature-inspired itineraries for people with niche interests (eg wild plants, birdwatching and nature photography).
Holiday Tours & Travel, Level 8, Block A, Menara KIP, No. 1 Jalan Seri Utara 1, Sri Utara off Jalan Ipoh, Kuala Lumpur, tel: 03-6286 6000; www.holidaytours.com.my. Offers domestic packages such as to Kuching's Rainforest World Music Festival.
Mudtrekker Adventure Travel, MTZ Shah Alam, Jalan Hijau Serindit U9/68, Syksyen U9, Cahaya SPK,

Time zone

Malaysia's standard time is eight hours ahead of Greenwich Mean Time and 16 hours ahead of US Pacific Standard Time.

Shah Alam 40150, Selangor, tel: 011 3350 1512; www.mudtrekker.com. Offers four-wheel-drive adventure tours to Negeri Sembilan and Pahang.
Nomad Adventure, tel: 03-7958 5152; www.nomadadventure.com. Specialises in whitewater rafting activities and provides Rescue 3 training. Also arranges packages for rock-climbing, mountaineering, caving with Flying Fox at Gua Kandu and waterfall abseiling.
Ping Anchorage, 77A Jalan Sultan Sulaiman, Kuala Terengganu, tel: 09-626 2020; www.pinganchorage.com.my. This is your best bet for the east coast, especially Terengganu.

Sarawak

In Sarawak, tour companies are very helpful when it comes to longhouse visits and trekking tours. Unless one speaks at least a little Malay, visiting a longhouse without a guide is not recommended.
Borneo Adventure, 55 Main Bazaar, Kuching, tel: 082-245 175; www.borneoadventure.com. Although it handles almost every type of tour, it specialises in ecotourism.
Borneo Transverse, 15 Ground Floor, Jalan Green Hill, Kuching, tel: 082-257 784; www.borneotransverse.com.my.
CPH Travel Agencies, 70 Jalan Padungan, tel: 082-243 708; www.cphtravel.com.my. One of Sarawak's oldest travel agencies, and the first to offer boat trips spotting Irrawaddy dolphins in the Damai region (May–Oct).
Planet Borneo Tours, Lot 273, Brighton Centre, Jalan Temenggong Datuk Oyong Lawai, Miri, tel: 085-414 300; www.planetborneotours.com. Miri-based adventure tour outfit offering whitewater rafting, diving, rock-climbing, tribal trekking and caving packages; specialises in Mulu Caves.

Sabah

As in Sarawak, any excursions in Sabah are difficult without the help of a tour company, or at least a guide.
Borneo Adventure, Block E-27-3A (Level 3A), Signature Office, KK Times Square, tel: 088-486 800; www.borneoadventure.com. Specialises in individually tailored

tours and lets visitors experience the people and the land.

Borneo Eco Tours, Lot 1, Pusat Perindustrian Kolombong Jaya, Mile 5.5, Jalan Kolombong, Kota Kinabalu, tel: 088-438 300; www. borneoecotours.com. Specialises in environmentally oriented tourism, with trips focusing on the flora and fauna of Sabah. The company also runs an eco-friendly lodge at Sukau on the Kinabatangan river.

Discovery Tours (Sabah), Lot G22, G/F Wisma Sabah Jalan Tun Fuad, Kota Kinabalu, tel: 088-257 368; www.discoverytours.com.my. Tours include half- and full-day packages to Lok Kawi Wildlife Park, Mantanami snorkelling, and Kinabalu National Park.

Traverse Tours, 2nd Floor, Wisma Sabah, Jalan Tun Fuad Stephens, Kota Kinabalu, tel: 088-260 501; www.traversetours.com. An adventure tourism specialist for whitewater rafting, safari river cruises, caving and trekking.

Wildlife Expeditions, Lot A 1202-1, 12th Floor, Wisma Merdeka, Phase 1, Jalan Tun Razak, Kota Kinabalu, tel: 088-246 000; and Room 903, 9th Floor, Wisma Khoo Siak Chiew, Sandakan, tel: 089-219 616; www.wildlife-expeditions.com. Tours including Mount Kinabalu, Rungus longhouses, Danum Valley and Kinabatangan.

V

Visas and passports

Passports must be valid for at least six months at the time of entry. Check the **Immigration Department** website (www.imi.gov.my) for details about formalities and visa requirements, as conditions may change from time to time.

A social single-entry visa valid for three months can be applied for at Malaysian diplomatic missions overseas (see Embassies and Consulates, page 379). Citizens of Commonwealth countries (except Bangladesh, Cameroon, Ghana, Mozambique, Nigeria, Pakistan and Sri Lanka) do not require a visa if their stay does not exceed a certain period. Citizens of the US, Singapore and Brunei do not need a visa.

Headquarters of the Department of Immigration Malaysia Level 3 (Podium), No. 15 Pesiaran Perdana, Precint 2, Putrajaya, tel: 03-8000 8000; customer service, tel: 1800 22 1777

Kuala Lumpur, Kompleks Kementrian Dalam Negeri, 69, Jalan Sri Hartamas 1, Jalan Duta, tel: 03-6205 7400

KLIA Immigration Office, Bangunan Airport Management Centre (AMC), tel: 03-8776 8001

Alor Setar, Kedah, Tingkat 1-2 Bangunan KDN, Pusat Pentadbiran Kerajaan Persekutuan, Bandar Muadzam Shah, tel: 04-733 3302

Ipoh, Aras 2–4, Kompleks Pejabat, Kementerian Dalam Negeri, Persiaran Meru Utama, Bandar Meru Raya, Jelapang, tel: 05-501 7100

Johor Bahru, Johor, Wisma Persekutuan, Jalan Air Molek, tel: 07-224 4255

Kangar, Perlis, Tingkat 1, Bangunan Persekutuan, Persiaran Jubli Emas, tel: 04-976 2636

Kota Bharu, Kelantan, Kompleks Yakim, Jalan Gajah Mati, tel: 09-748 2120

Kota Kinabalu, Sabah, Kompleks Pentadbiran Kerajaan Persekutuan, Jalan UMS, tel: 088-744 1833

Kuala Terengganu, Terengganu, Wisma Persekutuan, Jalan Sultan Ismail, tel: 09-622 1424

Kuantan, Pahang, Jabatan Imigresen Negeri Pahang, Kompleks Imigresen, Bandar Indera Mahkota, tel: 09-571 7999

Kuching, Sarawak, Bangunan Sultan Iskandar, Jalan Simpang Tiga, tel: 082-230 280

Labuan, Kompleks Ujana Kewangan, Jalan Merdeka, tel: 087-412 134

Melaka, Aras 1–3, Kompleks Kementerian Hal Enwal Dalam Negeri, Jalan Seri Negeri, Ayer Keroh, tel: 06-232 2662

Penang, Jalan Kelasah, Seberang Jaya, tel: 04-397 3011

Seremban, Negeri Sembilan, Wisma Persekutuan, Jalan Dato' Abdul Kadir, tel: 06-762 0000

Shah Alam, Selangor, Kompleks pkns, tel: 03-5519 0653

W

Websites

www.cavesofmalaysia.com Cave expert Liz Price offers a wealth of information about caves and limestone hills that also include show and temple caves, as well as cave flora and fauna.

www.friedchillies.com Honest reviews and a guide to food in Kuala Lumpur and Malaysia.

www.journeymalaysia.com Comprehensive information related to travel.

www.kakiseni.com Features Malaysia's contemporary arts scene.

www.nature-escapes-kuala-lumpur. com Has nature escapes categorised by number of hours from the city and escape itineraries to forests and islands further away.

www.sabahtourism.com A useful guide of how to plan your trip to Sabah with suggested travel itineraries.

www.sarawaktourism.com A comprehensive website of how best to spend your time in Sarawak.

www.SoutheastAsianArchaeology. com If and when archaeological digs take place in Malaysia, this site keeps visitors informed about new discoveries and where to see them, including upcoming exhibitions by the National Museum.

www.virtualmalaysia.com Highlights the country's best travel destinations.

www.waterfallsofmalaysia.com Provides a comprehensive review and images of a growing list of waterfalls in the country categorised by either state or access level of difficulty.

www.wildasia.org A website concerned about conservation and responsible tourism comes with plenty of practical travel information, articles and a photo library.

Women travellers

Travelling alone is fairly safe for women, but to avoid unwanted attention a single woman may want to give a "Yes, I'm married" reply to the inevitable query. Ignore wolf whistles and catcalls. If you are approached, be polite but firm. Mostly people are just being friendly, even if some might be hoping for something more; if you start feeling uneasy, walk away. Be careful about being over-friendly with your tour guide.

Toiletries are readily available in most towns and cities. Tampons may not be available in small towns, but other sanitary products are.

Malaysians stare – both men and women – but wearing revealing clothes in areas that are newer to tourism will invite uncalled-for attention. In Malaysia's rural societies, young women rarely approach or speak to male strangers. Topless and nude sunbathing is prohibited.

Weights and measures

Malaysia follows the metric system, but people in rural areas might still use miles (*batu*) rather than kilometres for distance.

LANGUAGE

UNDERSTANDING THE LANGUAGE

The official language is Bahasa Malaysia (Malay), but English is the language of business and technology. The Chinese also use Mandarin and various Chinese dialects, while the Indians use Tamil and other Indian languages. The indigenous people retain their own languages.

BAHASA MALAYSIA

Bahasa Malaysia is an Austronesian language also spoken in Indonesia, Singapore, Brunei, the Philippines and southern Thailand. Although there is a standard Bahasa Malaysia taught in schools and used formally, there are actually many regional Malay dialects that are not mutually intelligible. This is in addition to a simplified form of Bahasa Malaysia known as "bahasa pasar" or "bazaar Malay".

Bahasa Malaysia is also known as Bahasa Melayu and popularly abbreviated as BM. Since it is the official language, all signboards and public displays of writing are in Bahasa Malaysia, so it is useful to learn some words. It is written in the Latin alphabet, and is an easy language to learn.

The language is polysyllabic, with variations in syllables to convey changes in meaning. Words are pronounced as they are spelt. However, spelling can be tricky, for despite standardisation efforts, place and street names, for example, still follow different spellings. For instance, baru (new) is standard but also appears as bahru, bharu and baharu. Another example is cangkat (hillock), which is sometimes spelt changkat, and tingkat (lane) as tengkat.

Root words are either nouns or verbs and prefixes and/or suffixes are added to change the meaning. Therefore, while makan is "to eat", makanan is "food" and memakan is "eating". The adjective always comes after the noun, so "my husband" is suami saya. To indicate plural, you often just repeat the noun, so "many rooms" are bilik-bilik.

When constructing a sentence, the order is subject-verb-subject: Dia (he) makan (eats) nasi (rice) goreng (fried). Dia makan nasi goreng = He eats fried rice.

You will find Sanskrit, Arabic, Tamil, Portuguese, Dutch, Chinese and English words in Bahasa Malaysia. English words are also increasingly being incorporated into the language, particularly in relation to business and technology.

FORMS OF ADDRESS

When addressing someone formally, the form for men is encik (sir), which can be used on its own, or to precede a person's name, eg Encik Razak. The female equivalent for married or older women are puan (Madam) and Puan Miriam (Mrs Miriam), and for single or younger women, Cik (Miss) and Cik Ros (Miss Ros). For men and women who are the same age, you may use "comrade", as in saudara (men) and saudari (women).

The informal form for older men of your father's age is pakcik (literally "uncle") and abang (literally "older brother") for men slightly older than you. For women the equivalent is makcik (literally "aunty") and kakak (literally "older sister"). Meanwhile the gender-free informal form for younger men and women as well as children is adik ("younger brother/sister").

The terms "abang", "kakak" and "adik" are sometimes truncated when used in conversation. Thus, "abang" becomes "bang", "kakak" becomes "kak", and "adik" becomes "dik" (pronounced as "dake"). However, truncation is not used for terms used to address the elders, ie "pakcik" and "makcik".

Regardless of formal or informal use, the word for "you" (anda, etc.) is rarely used as it is considered rude. Instead replace it with the form of address or name, for example, Encik dari mana? or Encik Razak dari mana? ("Where are you from?") Note that other than for older people, the English pronoun "you" has become common, for example, "You dari mana?"

PRONUNCIATION TIPS

In general the pronunciation is the same as in English, with some exceptions. The "a" is pronounced "ar" as in "tar" when it appears in the middle of a word. But when it ends a word, it is pronounced with an "er" sound as in "observe". Therefore apa (what) is pronounced as "arper". The "e" also has an "er" sound as in "observe".

"I" is pronounced with an "ee" sound unless it ends as an "-ik" or "-ih", in which case it is pronounced like the "a" in "agent", so bilik (room) is pronounced "bee-lake". The "u" has an "oo" sound unless it ends as an "-uk", "-up", "-uh" or "-ur", in which case it has an "oh" sound. Therefore sepuluh (ten) is pronounced "sir-poo-loh". "C" is pronounced "ch" as in "chair"; "sy" is pronounced "sh";

and "ai" is pronounced "i". A tricky one involving "ai", which you are likely to use, is *air* (water) – is pronounced "i-yeah".

"G" is always hard, as in "gun"; the "h" is always pronounced, and you may come across "ny" and "ng" sounds that may not be common in your native language.

Although nearly all syllables are given equal stress, sometimes the final syllable of a word is emphasised, especially the last word in an utterance. This has led to the widespread use of the appendage *-lah* to the important word, whose purpose is purely emphatic. However, *-lah* is also liberally used in English; for instance, you could get thrown a *"Cannot-lah!"* when you are trying to bargain.

USEFUL WORDS/ PHRASES

Greetings

How do you do? *Apa khabar?*
Fine/good *Baik*
Good morning *Selamat pagi*
Good afternoon *Selamat tengah hari*
Good evening *Selamat petang*
Goodbye *Selamat tinggal*
Bon voyage *Selamat jalan*

At the hotel

sleep *tidur*
bathe *mandi*
Can I see the room first? *Boleh saya tengok bilik dulu?*
I want to change rooms *Saya hendak tukar bilik*
Does the room rate include breakfast? *Adakah kos bilik ini termasuk sarapan pagi?*
Where is the breakfast place? *Di mana tempat sarapan pagi?*
What time is breakfast? *Pukul berapa sarapan pagi?*

Shopping

shop *kedai*
How much? *Berapa harga?*
That's too expensive *Mahal sangat*
Can you reduce the price? *Boleh kurang?*
Too big *Besar sangat*
Too small *Kecil sangat*
Any other colour? *Ada warna lain?*
Don't have any left *Tak ada lagi*
money *wang, duit*
I would like to change money *Saya hendak tukar duit*
buy *beli (membeli)*
sell *jual (menjual)*

Travelling

airport *lapangan terbang*
What time does the bus leave? *Pukul berapa bas bertolak?*
Where are you going? *(Pergi) ke mana?*
I want to go to... *Saya hendak pergi ke...*
Turn right *Belok (ke) kanan*
Turn left *Belok (ke) kiri*
Go straight *Jalan terus*
Please stop here *Sila berhenti di sini*
Where is this place? *Di mana tempat ini?*
How far? *Berapa jauh?*
How long? *Berapa lama?*
How long more? *Berapa lama lagi?*
Right *kanan*
Left *kiri*
Turn *belok*
Go *pergi*
Stop *berhenti*
Follow *ikut*
Near *dekat*
Inside *dalam*
Outside *luar*
Front *hadapan* or *depan*
Behind *belakang*
Here *sini*
There *sana*

Eating out

Is there any eating place nearby? *Ada tempat makan dekat sini?*
eat *makan*
drink *minum*
coffee shop *kedai kopi*

Menu decoder

Bread *roti*
Beef *daging lembu*
Chicken *ayam* (pronounced "ah-yarm")
Lamb *daging kambing* (pronounced "da-ging come-bing")
Fish *ikan* (pronounced "ee-karn")
Vegetables *sayur*
Fried noodles *mee goreng*
Fried rice *nasi goreng*
Salt *garam*
Spicy *pedas*
Sweet *manis*
Less spicy *kurang pedas*
Delicious *sedap*
A cup of coffee (with milk) *kopi satu*
A cup of coffee (without milk) *kopi oh satu*
A cup of tea (with milk) *teh satu*
A cup of tea (without milk) *teh oh satu*
Water *air* (pronounced "i-yeah")
Less sweet *kurang manis*
Without sugar *tanpa gula*
Without milk *tanpa susu*
Without ice *tanpa ais* (pronounced "ice")

Not enough *tak cukup*
Not hot/cold enough *tak cukup panas/sejuk*
Add *tambah*
A little *sedikit [sikit]*
A lot *banyak*

On the road

Road *jalan*
Lane *lorong*
Street *lebuh*
Highway *lebuhraya*
Bridge *jambatan*
Junction *simpang*
Danger *awas* or *merbahaya*
No overtaking *dilarang memotong*
Slow down *kurangkan laju*
Speed limit *had laju*
Enter *masuk*
Exit *keluar*
Keep left/right *ikut kiri/kanan*
One-way street *jalan sehala*
North *utara*
South *selatan*
East *timur*
West *barat*

Emergencies

Emergency room *bilik kecemasan*
I want to go to the nearest hospital *Saya nak pergi ke hospital terdekat*
Where's the nearest clinic? *Di mana klinik terdekat?*

General

I *saya*
you (to someone the same age or younger) *awak, anda* or *kita* (in Borneo Malaysia only)
you (formal) *encik/puan/cik*
he, she *dia*
we *kami* (excluding the speaker), *kita* (including the speaker)
they *mereka*
what? *apa?*
who? *siapa?*
where (place)? *di mana?*
where (direction)? *ke mana?*
when? *bila?*
how? *bagaimana?*
why? *mengapa?*
which? *yang mana?*
come *datang*
road, walk *jalan*
post office *pejabat pos*
minute *minit*
hour *jam*
day *hari*
week *minggu*
What time is it? *Jam berapa sekarang?* Yes *Ya*
No *Tidak*
Thank you *Terima kasih*
You're welcome *Sama-sama*
Please *Tolong/sila*

Excuse me *Maafkan saya [Maaf]*
May I ask you a question? *Tumpang tanya?*
Can you help me? *Bolehkah cik tolong saya?*
I am sorry *Minta maaf [Maaf]*
Please come in *Sila masuk*
Please sit down *Sila duduk*
Thank you very much *Terima kasih banyak-banyak*
You're welcome *Sama-sama*
Where do you come from? *Asal dari mana?*
I come from... *Saya datang dari...*
What is your name? *Siapa nama anda?*
My name is... *Nama saya...*
Can you speak Bahasa Malaysia? *Boleh anda bercakap Bahasa Malaysia?*
Only a little *Sedikit sahaja*
Where is the toilet? *Di mana tandas?*
Wait a minute *Tunggu sekejap*
Please wait here *Sila tunggu di sini*

Days of the week

Monday *Isnin*
Tuesday *Selasa*
Wednesday *Rabu*
Thursday *Khamis*
Friday *Jumaat*
Saturday *Sabtu*
Sunday *Ahad*

Months of the year

January *Januari*
February *Februari*
March *Mac*
April *April*
May *Mei*
June *Jun*
July *Julai*
August *Ogos*
September *September*
October *Oktober*
November *November*
December *Disember*

Numbers

1 *satu*
2 *dua*
3 *tiga*
4 *empat*
5 *lima*
6 *enam*
7 *tujuh*
8 *lapan*
9 *sembilan*
10 *sepuluh*
11 *sebelas*
12 *dua belas*
13 *tiga belas*
20 *dua puluh*
21 *dua puluh satu*
22 *dua puluh dua*
30 *tiga puluh*
40 *empat puluh*
100 *seratus*
263 *dua ratus enam puluh tiga*
1,000 *seribu*

FURTHER READING

CULTURE/GENERAL

Culture Shock! Malaysia, by Heidi Munan. A witty and invaluable treatise on Malaysian customs, can-dos and absolutely-nots.

The Encyclopedia of Malaysia. A highly illustrative topic-categorised presentation of Malaysiana from early history and architecture to plants, arts, literature and economics.

Heritage Houses of Penang, by Khoo Salma Nasution and Halim Berbar. One of the finest collections of urban domestic architecture in Southeast Asia, these charming heritage houses – from Straits Eclectic mansions to bungalows and shophouses and a Chinese courtyard home – are beautifully photographed. Within these pages is a rich tapestry of stories linking history, artistry and vision.

Lat: the country's sharpest and funniest cartoonist has illustrated many comic strips, often about hilarious depictions of Malaysian life and psyche. Try *Kampung Boy*, where Lat recounts the life of Mat, a Muslim boy growing up in a rural Malay village in the 1950s and his ensuing adventures.

The Nyonya Kebaya: A Century of Straits Chinese Costume, by Datin Seri Endon Mahmood. The designs of Nyonya kebaya, an Arab-inspired top of plain-woven cotton decorated with intricate embroidery, crosses several generations and cultures. This coffee-table book also explains the type of accessories worn with this timeless classic and showcases the author's personal Nyonya kebaya collection.

Our Land Within, by Liew Suet Fun. Explores the lives of ethnic communities in Southeast Asia through music, cuisine and belief. For example, how culture transcends borders at the villages of Ba'kelalan (Sarawak) and Long Bawan (Indonesia), and the influence of Malaysia's northern neighbour are illustrated through Pondok Tanjung in Perak, once a popular stop for those travelling between the Thai-Malaysian border.

Portraits of Penang: Little India, by Gareth Richards and Himanshu Bhatt. These black-and-white fine-art photographs taken over a span of one year in 1979 but only seeing the light of day 32 years later are complemented with essays and commentaries.

Sarawak Crafts – Methods and Motifs, by Heidi Munan. Written by a Sarawak expert, this small book is filled with a wealth of information.

FICTION/BIOGRAPHY

Among the White Moon Faces: An Asian-American Memoir of Homelands, by Shirley Geok-Lin Lim. A biographical recount of a Malaysian childhood and later life in the United States; the author has also published short stories.

Send Us Your Thoughts

We do our best to ensure the information in our books is as accurate and up-to-date as possible. The books are updated on a regular basis using local contacts, who painstakingly add, amend and correct as required. However, some details (such as telephone numbers and opening times) are liable to change, and we are ultimately reliant on our readers to put us in the picture.

We welcome your feedback, especially your experience of using the book "on the road". Maybe we recommended a hotel that you liked (or another that you didn't), or you came across a great bar or new attraction we missed.

We will acknowledge all contributions, and we'll offer an Insight Guide to the best letters received.

Please write to us at:
Insight Guides
PO Box 7910
London SE1 1WE
Or email us at:
hello@insightguides.com

The Gift of Rain, by Tan Twan Eng. Set in colonial Penang, the loyalty and bond between a boy of British-Chinese parentage and his Japanese mentor is tested during the World War II Japanese invasion.

The Harmony Silk Factory, by Tash Aw. Set against the backdrop of World War II, it follows the notorious life of a poor boy of Hakka roots and his rise in stature. His life is seen through the eyes of three different narrators.

The Long Day Wanes: A Malayan Trilogy, by Anthony Burgess. A three-part novel depicting the life of a British education officer as the sun sets on the British Empire in Malaya. Humorous cast of supporting characters.

FOOD

Cuzinha Cristang: A Malacca-Portuguese Cookbook, by Celine J. Marbeck. A lovely collection of 600 years of Melaka-Portuguese Cristang cuisine.

Flavours of Malaysia: A Journey through Time, Tastes, and Traditions, by Susheela Raghavan. Not purely a recipe book, but also a detailed introduction to the cuisines of many of Malaysia's colourful ethnic communities and how food plays a role in traditional ceremonies.

Penang Passion – Food and Food Tales of Penang, by Koh Tze Yin. This is a story about how passionate people are in serving Penang cuisine, from the chef to the restaurateur to a homemakers' club.

HISTORY/POLITICAL

A Doctor in the House: The Memoirs of Tun Dr Mahathir Mohamad, by Tun Dr Mahathir Mohamad. The longest-serving former prime minister of Malaysia tells how he shaped modern Malaysian political history and the reasons behind his achievements.

The End of Empire and the Making of Malaya, by T.N. Harper. An insight into how modern Malaya was born in a time of war, revolution and social

TRANSPORT EATING OUT ACTIVITIES A – Z LANGUAGE

upheaval, and how colonisation left an enduring legacy.
Government and Society In Malaysia, by Harold Crouch. An insider's view from an outsider on Malaysian politics, founding his analysis on the fact that Malaysian politics and society operate essentially on the basis of a "moving equilibrium".
A History of Malaya, by Barbara Watson Andaya and Leonard Andaya. Non-colonial objective interpretation of the country's development.
Islamisation and Activism in Malaysia, by Julian C.H. Lee. Looks at the impact of political, legal and social Islamisation in Malaysia, and civil society's reactions.
Malaysian Maverick: Mahathir Mohamad in Turbulent Times, by Barry Wain. This book portrays the long-serving former prime minister as a man of contradictions, laying out the strengths and flaws of the man, his policies and influence.
The War of the Running Dogs, by Noel Barber. Only three years after the end of the Japanese occupation, war came again to Malaya. The Chinese-backed guerrillas called it 'the war of the running dogs' – the contemptuous term for those in Malaya who remained loyal to the British.
What Your Teacher Didn't Tell You: The Annexe Lectures (Vol. 1), by Farish A. Noor. Malaysia's most accessible and hippest academic elucidates on Malaysia's history and politics through topics such as race and heroes.

NATURAL HISTORY

A Diver's Guide to Underwater Malaysia Macrolife, by Andrea Ferrari and Antonella Ferrari. This volume is illustrated with more than 800 colour photographs and describes in full detail 600 different Indo-Pacific marine species, focusing on those found in the South China, Sulu and Sulawesi seas.
Enchanted Gardens of Kinabalu, by Susan M. Phillipps. A beautiful book of botanical paintings that include coral gardens, too.
A Field Guide to the Birds of Peninsular Malaysia and Singapore, by Allen Jeyarajasingam. A comprehensive illustrated guide to identifying all 673 species known to occur in the region.
A Guide to Bako National Park: Sarawak, Malaysian Borneo, by Hans P. Hazebroek and Abang Kashim bin Abang Morshidi. Bako may be one of the smallest parks in Borneo, but as this guide shows you, it is teeming with wildlife, and almost every type of vegetation in Borneo can be seen here.
Limestone Hills and Caves of the Kinta Valley, by S.L. Wong. This coffee-table book, through photographs that were taken over two decades, aims to raise awareness of the rich natural resources that the Kinta Valley in Perak has in its spectacular karst landscapes.
Wild Malaysia: The wildlife and landscapes of Peninsular Malaysia, Sarawak and Sabah, by Junaidi Payne. A pictorial introduction containing colour photographs of animals and habitats. The text, by a British conservation biologist based in Sabah, examines conservation and development, as well as peoples and natural history.

TRAVEL

The Golden Chersonese: the Malayan Travels of Victorian Lady, by Isabella Bird. Lyrical 19th-century impressions of the experiences of this intrepid traveller.
Into the Heart Of Borneo, by Redmond O'Hanlon. A heart-warming and laugh-aloud treatise on O'Hanlon's hilarious expedition to Borneo, told with great sympathy and style.
The Malay Archipelago, by Alfred Russel Wallace. A classic tale of a Victorian naturalist who spent several years wandering through the archipelago. He was also instrumental in assisting in the setting up of Sarawak Museum and his theories on evolution coincided with those of Darwin.
World Within: A Borneo Story, by Tom Harrisson. A classic story, by the man who later became curator of Sarawak Museum, tells of Bario's Kelabit Highlands during the Japanese occupation years of World War II.

CREDITS

Photo Credits

Alamy 9, 231B, 291, 293, 297TR, 319B, 337, 341
AWL Images 7ML, 102, 103, 297BR, 301, 302
Bon Ton Resort 202
Chien Lee/Minden Pictures/FLPA 290, 299
Chris Mattison/FLPA 298
Corbis 55, 63, 304
Dreamstime 60, 61
Fotolia 6M, 288, 292, 294B, 307, 325, 335, 339T
Genting Malaysia Berhad 161B
Getty Images 12/13, 29, 31, 32, 56, 58, 59, 143, 220B, 247, 269, 306
Hans Höfer 26/27, 33, 37, 39, 40, 169T
iStock 7BR, 240, 245, 283, 322, 338, 391L
James Tye/Apa Publications 1, 6BR, 6BL, 7TR, 7MR, 7ML, 7BL, 8B, 10/11, 14/15, 16, 17T, 18, 19, 20, 21, 22, 23R, 25, 28, 62, 64/65, 66, 67, 68L, 68R, 71, 72, 73, 74, 75, 77L, 77R, 78, 79, 80, 81, 82, 83, 84, 85, 86, 88, 89, 90, 91, 93, 95TR, 95BL, 95BR, 96, 97, 98, 99, 100, 107, 109, 110/111, 112/113, 114/115, 116, 117T, 117B, 120, 121T, 121B, 124, 125, 127T, 127B, 129B, 131, 136B, 137B, 139B, 140, 141, 146B, 147, 148/149, 150, 151T, 151B, 152, 153, 155, 156,
157T, 157B, 158T, 158B, 159, 164, 165, 166, 167T, 167B, 168, 170, 172, 173B, 173T, 176BL, 176/177T, 177TR, 178, 179, 183, 184T, 185, 188T, 190, 191B, 191T, 193, 194, 195, 197B, 201, 203B, 204, 205, 208, 209T, 209B, 210, 211, 214, 215, 216, 217T, 217B, 218, 219B, 219T, 220T, 221, 222, 224, 226, 227, 228, 229B, 229T, 230, 231T, 232T, 232B, 233, 234, 236/237, 238, 239T, 239B, 241, 243B, 243T, 248, 249, 250, 251, 252T, 253, 254T, 254B, 256, 257T, 258, 260, 261, 262/263T, 262BL, 262BR, 263BL, 263BR, 263ML, 263TR, 264, 265, 266, 267, 271, 272/273, 274, 275T, 275B, 276, 277, 279B, 279T, 281T, 281B, 282T, 282B, 284B, 284T, 286T, 286B, 287, 289, 294T, 295, 296BL, 296/297T, 296BR, 297ML, 297BL, 300, 305T, 310, 311T, 311B, 312, 313, 315, 316, 317, 318, 319T, 320B, 320T, 321, 323, 324T, 324B, 326, 327T, 328, 329, 330, 331, 332B, 332T, 333, 334B, 334T, 339B, 344, 347L, 349L, 350, 351L, 362/363, 376/377, 388
John Holmes/FLPA 270
John Ishii/Apa Publications 23L, 24, 47, 70, 92, 94BR, 95ML, 104, 106, 176BR, 177ML, 177BL, 184B, 186, 187, 188B, 189, 192, 197T,
198, 199T, 200, 203T, 345L
Jon Santa Cruz/Apa Publications 17B, 69, 76, 87, 101, 163, 177BR, 352
Jungle War in Malaya 51, 52
Mary Evans Picture Library 42
Museu Militar, Lisbon 36
Muzium Negara, Malaysia 35, 44L, 44R, 45, 48, 50, 53
National Archives, Singapore 43
Nikt Wong/Apa Publications 8T, 94BL, 126, 128B, 128T, 129T, 130T, 130B, 132, 133T, 133B, 134, 135T, 135B, 136T, 137T, 138, 144, 145, 146T, 160, 161T, 162, 342
Norbert Wu/Minden Pictures/FLPA 336
Photoshot 308/309, 340
Private Archives 54
R. Mohd. Noh 30, 38
Robert Harding Picture Library 206/207
Shutterstock 4/5, 34, 94/95T
SuperStock 7TL
The Straits Times, Singapore 49
Tourism Malaysia 41, 57, 105, 108, 139T, 142, 169B, 171B, 171T, 174, 175, 181, 196, 199B, 213, 223, 225, 235, 244T, 244B, 246, 252B, 255, 257B, 259B, 259T, 268, 285, 303, 305B, 327B
Westfries Museum, Hoorn 46

Cover Credits

Front cover: KL *Shutterstock*
Back cover: Cameron Highlands *James Tye/Apa Publications*
Front flap: (from top) FRIM canopy walkway; satay; Sarawak Mueum;
Bangau boat fisherman *all James Tye/Apa Publications*
Back flap: Rungus beadwork *James Tye/Apa Publications*

Insight Guide Credits

Distribution
UK
Dorling Kindersley Ltd
A Penguin Group company
80 Strand, London, WC2R 0RL
sales@uk.dk.com

United States
Ingram Publisher Services
1 Ingram Boulevard, PO Box 3006,
La Vergne, TN 37086-1986
ips@ingramcontent.com

Australia and New Zealand
Woodslane
10 Apollo St, Warriewood,
NSW 2102, Australia
info@woodslane.com.au

Worldwide
Apa Publications (Singapore) Pte
7030 Ang Mo Kio Avenue 5
08-65 Northstar @ AMK
Singapore 569880
apasin@singnet.com.sg

Printing
CTPS-China

First Edition 1972
Twentieth edition 2015

Every effort has been made to
provide accurate information in this
publication, but changes are
inevitable. The publisher cannot be
responsible for any resulting loss,
inconvenience or injury. We would
appreciate it if readers would call our
attention to any errors or outdated
information. We also welcome your
suggestions; please contact us at:
hello@insightguides.com

www.insightguides.com

Editor: Sarah Clark
Author: Malgorzata Anczewska,
Siew-Lyn Wong, HonYuen Leong
Head of Production: Rebeka Davies
Update Production: AM Services
Picture Editor: Tom Smyth
Cartography: original cartography
Colourmap Scanning, updated by
Carte

Legend

City maps

	Freeway/Highway/Motorway
	Divided Highway
	Main Roads
	Minor Roads
	Pedestrian Roads
	Steps
	Footpath
	Railway
	Funicular Railway
	Cable Car
	Tunnel
	City Wall
	Important Building
	Built Up Area
	Other Land
	Transport Hub
	Park
	Pedestrian Area
	Bus Station
	Tourist Information
	Main Post Office
	Cathedral/Church
	Mosque
	Synagogue
	Statue/Monument
	Beach
	Airport

Regional maps

	Freeway/Highway/Motorway (with junction)
	Freeway/Highway/Motorway (under construction)
	Divided Highway
	Main Road
	Secondary Road
	Minor Road
	Track
	Footpath
	International Boundary
	State/Province Boundary
	National Park/Reserve
	Marine Park
	Ferry Route
	Marshland/Swamp
	Glacier / Salt Lake
	Airport/Airfield
	Ancient Site
	Border Control
	Cable Car
	Castle/Castle Ruins
	Cave
	Chateau/Stately Home
	Church/Church Ruins
	Crater
	Lighthouse
	Mountain Peak
	Place of Interest
	Viewpoint

Contributors

This brand new edition of *Insight
Guide Malaysia*, the twentieth in the
book's history, was commissioned
for the second time by Senior
Commissioning Editor **Sarah Clark**
and updated by intrepid writer
Malgorzata Anczewska. It draws
upon the extensive work of the
previous edition, in which local
Malaysian writers **Siew-Lyn Wong**
and **HonYuen Leong**
comprehensively revised the book

and added new features to its
original structure.
The stunning photography in this
book is the work of photographer
James Tye. James has travelled
extensively throughout Asia for
various editorial and corporate photo
commissions. His work can be seen
at www.jamestye.com
The book was copyedited by
Naomi Peck and the index was
compiled by **Penny Phenix**.

About Insight Guides

Insight Guides have more than
40 years' experience of publishing
high-quality, visual travel guides. We
produce 400 full-colour titles, in both
print and digital form, covering more
than 200 destinations across the
globe, in a variety of formats to meet
your different needs.
Insight Guides are written by
local authors who use their on-the-
ground experience to provide the

very latest information; their local
expertise is evident in the extensive
historical and cultural background
features. All the reviews in **Insight
Guides** are independent; we strive
to maintain an impartial view. Our
reviews are carefully selected to
guide you to the best places to eat,
go out and shop, so you can be
confident that when we say a place
is special, we really mean it.

INDEX